THE ULTIMATE OXBRIDGE

INTERVIEW GUIDE: HUMANITIES

UniAdmissions

Hardback ISBN: 978-1-913683-13-9
Paperback ISBN: 978-1-915091-24-6

Published by *RAR Medical Services Limited*
www.uniadmissions.co.uk
info@uniadmissions.co.uk
Tel: +44 (0) 208 068 0438

THE ULTIMATE OXBRIDGE INTERVIEW GUIDE

HUMANITIES

DR TOBY BOWMAN

OLUWASIKEMI ADETOLA

SAM ADAMSON

MADELEINE PIGGOTT

DR. ROHAN AGARWAL

Edited by
Dr. Ranjna Garg

UniAdmissions

About the Authors

Toby is an academic researcher and publisher, who has supported students through the Oxbridge admissions process for nearly a decade. Since the completion of his DPhil in the History of Technology at Green Templeton College, Oxford, he has worked on research projects examining the impact of immersion on virtual reality technology adoption, and maintains a teaching presence at Oxford and with Oxbridge candidates. He also works as an examiner for Oxford's HAT exam, and as a civilian consultant to the NASA Ames Research Centre's Human Factors division in California. In his spare time, Toby creates digital art and music, and is an avid player of games.

Oluwasikemi is a geography student at Murray Edwards College, Cambridge. Specialising in human geography - her favourite topics are development and inequality. An aspiring solicitor, Sikemi's current research is focused on sustainability for law firms. She's an avid volunteer and recently walked a marathon for a charity that aims to end human trafficking. In her spare time, she enjoys playing netball, rugby, and lacrosse at university.

Sam is a researcher and analyst with a background in Archaeology and Anthropology. After graduating from the University of Oxford, Sam completed a master's degree in Evolutionary Anthropology, specialising in cross-cultural communication and engagement. He has a particular current interest in international problem solving and dynamic leadership solutions, and is now an Analyst for business research firm Meissa Ltd. Sam maintains an interest in Archaeology, and is an experienced interview coach.

Maddie is an expert in the history of art and literature. Having finished her undergraduate degree in English at the University of Oxford, she is now completing a masters degree in Paris on the history and philosophy of art. She's an avid musician and regularly performs in national concerts, which she does alongside her current research into creative programming. In her free time, Maddie is a keen debater and rock-climber.

Rohan is the **Director of Operations** at *UniAdmissions* and is responsible for its technical and commercial arms. He graduated from Gonville and Caius College, Cambridge and is a fully qualified doctor. Over the last five years, he has tutored hundreds of successful Oxbridge and Medical applicants. He has also authored ten books on admissions tests and interviews.

Rohan has taught physiology to undergraduates and interviewed medical school applicants for Cambridge. He has published research on bone physiology and writes education articles for the Independent and Huffington Post. In his spare time, Rohan enjoys playing the piano and table tennis.

CONTENTS

Preface

Oxbridge interviews are frequently the source of intriguing stories. You'll frequently hear tales of students who were asked seemingly obscure questions e.g. "Why do we have two nostrils but only one mouth?", or impossibly difficult ones e.g. "How many grains of sand are there in the world?"

If taken in context, both of these are very fair Oxbridge interview questions. The first would naturally lead to a discussion concerning the evolution of sensory organs and the pros/cons of having multiple mouths e.g. reduced risk of infections vs. inability to eat and speak simultaneously etc.

The latter question would test a candidate's ability to breakdown an initially very large problem into more bite-sized chunks in order to manage it e.g. surface area of the Earth, percentage of the Earth covered by land, percentage of land covered by sand, average depth of sand and so on.

Oxbridge interviews are not about testing your knowledge. Instead, they are about testing what you can do with the knowledge you already possess. Remember, once you're at university, you will rapidly assimilate a great deal of new information (so much so that you will start to wonder what all the fuss A-levels were about).

This is the main reason why it's not particularly useful for interviewers to ask purely knowledge based questions e.g. "What is the normal plasma concentration of magnesium?". Knowledge of isolated facts is neither necessary nor sufficient for a successful Oxbridge interview. Instead, it is the application of some basic facts to novel situation that is the hallmark of success.

One of the best ways to demonstrate this is to discuss my interview experiences at Cambridge when I applied to study Medicine several years ago.

Interview One:

This was my first science interview and the interviewer was delighted when he found out I studied physics at A2. His opening question was "What have you read recently?" I explained I'd been reading about the new drug Rosuvastatin – a statin that was being recommended for everyone above a certain age (regardless of their actual cholesterol levels). The follow-up questions were what you would expect e.g. "How do statins work?" (Ensure you know the basics of any topic that you voluntarily bring up), "What are the risks/benefits of giving them to everyone?"

This led to a discussion on how I would convince someone that this drug was useful for them, followed by how I would convince someone that blue light was more damaging than red. I struggled with this for a while, bouncing ideas back and forth (with each of them sequentially shot down) until I finally stumbled onto Einstein's E=hf. This led to a discussion about why the sky is blue and sunsets can be a myriad of colours. All of this culminated in the classic- "What colour is the Sun in reality?" (Hint: It's not yellow, orange or red!). This is the question that tabloids would take out of context to make the interview seem like an array of bizarre questions when in fact this was perfectly reasonable giving the preceding questions.

This interview serves as a perfect example of a non-scripted interview, i.e. one where the interviewer was happy to bounce ideas between us and forced me to think about concepts in ways I never had. I'm certain that if I had offered a different answer to the initial question about my reading, the discussion would have gone along a significantly different route.

Interview Two:

My second interview was more scripted – the interviewer had a pre-set agenda with corresponding questions that he wanted to discuss. Given that this person is known to ask the same interview questions annually, I've refrained from including specifics in order to not spoil the plot for everyone and to unfairly put future applicants at an advantage (or disadvantage!).

After going through my BMAT essay very briefly, he asked me to draw a graph on his whiteboard. This was no easy task. I spent fifteen minutes struggling with this graph due to its unusual axis. Like many candidates, I made the mistake of learning about excessively complex topics like the Complement Membrane attack complex and ignored much core A-level topics like human physiology. This meant that I wasn't completely sure about a basic fact that was required for the graph. This was a tough interview and at the end of it, I was certain I had flunked it. This was compounded by the fact that other candidates were bragging about how they had got the correct graph in only thirty seconds.

When you're in the waiting room with the other candidates, it may appear that many of them are far smarter than you and know a lot more. Again, remember that the entire point of an interview is to assess your ability to apply knowledge.

People get nervous and unconfident whilst waiting for interviews. One of the ways they try to feel more secure is by exerting their intellectual superiority. In this example (although there were some exceptions), the students who tended to arrive at the answer very quickly were unsuccessful. This is likely because they had previous knowledge of the question from their school/extra reading. Although this allowed them to get the correct answer quickly, they were unable to explain the intermediate steps that led them to it, i.e. they *knew* the topic but didn't *understand* it.

Learning Points:

As you can see, I made lots of errors in my interview preparation. Please learn from them. Good students learn from their mistakes but *great* students learn from others' mistakes.

1) **Don't be put off by what other candidates say** in the waiting room. Focus on yourself – you are all that matter. If you want to be in the zone, then I would recommend taking some headphones and your favourite music.

2) **Don't read up on multiple advanced topics in depth.** Choose one topic and know it well. Focus the rest of your time on your core A-level syllabus. You are not expected to know about the features of Transverse Myelitis, but you will be expected to be able to rattle off a list of 10 cellular organelles.

3) **Don't worry about being asked seemingly irrelevant questions** that you'll often hear in the media. These are taken out of context. Focus on being able to answer the common questions e.g. "Why this university?" etc.

4) **Don't lose heart** if your interviews appear to have gone poorly. If anything, this can actually be a good sign as it shows that the interviewer pushed you to your limits rather than giving up on you as you clearly weren't Oxbridge material.

5) **Don't give up.** When you're presented with complex scenarios, go back to the absolute basics and try to work things out using first principles. By doing this and thinking out loud, you allow the interviewer to see your logical train of thought so that they can help you when you become stuck.

Good Luck!

Dr Rohan Agarwal

THE BASICS

What is an Oxbridge Interview?

An interview is a personal 20-30 minute session with one or two members of academic staff from Oxford or Cambridge. The interviewers will ask questions and **guide the applicant to an answer**. The answers usually require a large degree of creative and critical thought, as well as a good attitude and a sound foundation of subject-specific knowledge.

Why is there an Interview?

Most of the applicants to Oxbridge will have outstanding grades, predicted exam results, sample course work and personal statements. Interviews are used to help **determine which applicants are best-suited** for Oxbridge. During the interview, each applicant has a unique chance to demonstrate their creativity and critical thinking abilities- skills that Oxford and Cambridge consider vital for successful students.

Who gets an Interview?

At Cambridge, any applicant who might have a chance at being accepted to study will be called for interview. This corresponds to approximately **90%** of applicants. At Oxford, a slightly smaller **40-80%** of applicants are interviewed (applicants are shortlisted based on their admissions test results and UCAS form). No one is offered a place to study without attending an interview.

Who are the interviewers?

The interviews are conducted by a senior member of staff for the subject you've applied to; usually this person is the **Director of Studies** for that subject. There may also be a second interviewer who takes notes on the applicant or also asks questions. Interviewers describe this experience as just as nerve-wracking for them as for the applicants, as they are responsible for choosing the right students for Oxford and Cambridge.

When is the Interview?

Interviews are held in the **beginning of December** and some applicants may be invited back in January for a second round of interviews at another college. There are usually multiple interviews on the same day, either for different subjects or at different colleges. You will normally be given 2 weeks' notice before your interview- so you should hear back by late November, but it is useful to **begin preparing for the interview before you're officially invited**.

Where is the Interview?

The interviews are held in Oxford and Cambridge **at the college you applied to**. Oxford applicants may have additional interviews at another college than the one applied to. Cambridge applicants may get 'pooled' – be required to have another set of interviews in January at a different college. If you are travelling from far away, most Oxbridge colleges will provide you free accommodation and food for the duration of your stay if you wish to arrive the night before your interview.

Very rarely, interviews can be held via Skype at an exam centre- this normally only applies to international students or for UK students in extreme circumstances. During global pandemics like COVID-19, interviews have been conducted using Microsoft Teams, and this may return in future.

How should I use this book?

The best way to gain the most from this book is to let it guide your independent learning.

1. Read through the **General Interview** section.
2. Read the **Subject Interview** chapter for your subject.
3. Read chapters on PPE & HSPS and Maths.

Finally, work your way through the past interview questions – remember, you are not expected to know the answers to them, and they have been included here so that you can start to appreciate the style of questions that you may get asked. **It is not a test of what you know – but what you can do with what you already know.**

Oxbridge Tutorials & Supervisions

Hopefully, by this point, you're familiar with the unique Oxbridge teaching system. Students on the same course will have lectures and practicals together. These are supplemented by college-based tutorials/supervisions. A tutorial/supervision is an **individual or small group session** with an academic to **discuss ideas, ask questions, and receive feedback** on your assignments. During the tutorial/supervision, you will be pushed to think critically about the material from the course in novel and innovative ways. To get the most out of Oxbridge, you need to be able to work in this setting and take criticism with a positive and constructive attitude.

The **interviews are made to be model tutorials/supervisions**, with an academic questioning an applicant and seeing if they can learn, problem-solve, demonstrate motivation for their subject. It is by considering this ultimate goal of the interview that you can start to understand how to present and prepare yourself for the Oxbridge interview process.

What Are Interviewers Looking for?

There are several qualities an interviewer is looking for the applicant to demonstrate during the interview. While an applicant may think the most 'obvious' thing interviewers are looking for is excellent factual knowledge, this is already displayed through exam results. Whilst having an excellent depth of knowledge may help you perform better during an interview, **you're unlikely to be chosen based solely on your knowledge**. The main thing an interviewer is looking for is for the applicant to demonstrate critical thought, excellent problem-solving skills and intellectual flexibility, as well as **motivation for the subject and suitability for small group teaching**. It is also important for them to see that the applicant is willing to persevere with a challenging problem even if the answer is not immediately apparent.

How to Communicate Answers

The most important thing to do when communicating your answers is to **think out loud**. This will allow the interviewer to understand your thought processes. They will then be able to help you out if you get stuck. You should never give up on a question; show that you won't be perturbed at the first sign of hardship as a student, and remain positive and **demonstrate your engagement with the material**. Interviewers enjoy teaching and working with students who are as enthusiastic about their subject as they are.

Try to **keep the flow of conversation going** between you and your interviewer so that you can engage with each other throughout the entire interview. The best way to do this is to just keep talking about what you are thinking. It is okay to take a moment when confronted with a difficult question or plan your approach, but ensure you let the interviewer know this by saying, *"I'm going to think about this for a moment"*. Don't take too long- if you are finding the problems difficult, the **interviewers will guide and prompt you** to keep you moving forward. They can only do this if they know you're stuck!

The questions that you'll be asked are designed to be difficult, so don't panic up when you don't immediately know the answer. Tell the interviewer what you do know, offer some ideas, talk about ways you've worked through a similar problem that might apply here. If you've never heard anything like the question asked before, say that to the interviewer, *"I've never seen anything like this before"* or *"We haven't covered this yet at school"*, but don't use that as an excuse to quit. This is **your chance to show that you are eager to engage with new ideas**, so finish with *"But let's see if I can figure it out!"* or *"But I'm keen to try something new!"*. There are many times at Oxbridge when students are in this situation during tutorials/supervisors and you need to show that you can persevere in the face of difficulty (and stay positive and pleasant to work with while doing so).

Types of Interviews

There are, at Cambridge and for some Oxford subjects, several different types of interview that you can be called for. **Every applicant will have at least one subject interview**. Applicants to some courses may also have a general interview, especially if they are applying for an arts subject. Either way, you will be asked questions that touch on the course you are applying to study. It may be useful to **look at your interviewers' teaching backgrounds and published work** as this could potentially shed some light on the topics they might choose to discuss in an interview. However, there is absolutely no need to know the intricacies of their research work so don't get bogged down in it. Interviews tend to open with easier and more general questions and become more detailed and complicated as you are pushed to explore topics in greater depth.

Using the Practice Questions

This book contains over 900 practice interview questions. **They are all actual questions that successful Oxbridge applicants were asked in their interview**. However, it is important you take these with a pinch of salt.

They are taken out of context and only included to give you a flavour of the style and difficulty of real Oxbridge interview questions. Don't fall into the trap of thinking that your interview will consist of a series of irrelevant and highly specific knowledge based questions.

> OXBRIDGE INTERVIEWS ARE **NOT** ABOUT YOUR KNOWLEDGE
>
> THEY ARE ABOUT WHAT YOU CAN DO
> WITH THE KNOWLEDGE YOU ALREADY POSSESS

Thus, it does little benefit to rote learn answers to all the practice questions in this book as they are unlikely to be repeated. Instead, follow our top tips, take inspiration from the worked answers and put in some hard work – you'll be sure to perform well on the day

GENERAL INTERVIEWS

A general interview is a get-to-know-you session with senior admissions tutors. This is your chance to demonstrate a passion for Oxbridge; that you have understood the Oxbridge system, have a genuine interest in being a student, and could contribute to Oxbridge if you were admitted. These are more common for arts and humanities applicants, but all applicants should nevertheless be prepared for a general interview.

- This will be less specific than the subject interview. The interviewers will focus more on your personal statement, any essays you may have submitted or have completed on the day of the interview and may discuss your SAQ form if you are applying to Cambridge.

- One of the interviewers may not be a specialist in the subject you've applied for. Don't be put off by this – you aren't expected to have any knowledge of their subject.

- Ensure that you have read your personal statement and any books/journals that you've claimed to have read in your application. You will seem unenthusiastic and dishonest if you can't answer questions regarding topics and activities that you claim to know about. Remember that it is much better to show a good understanding of a few texts than to list lots of texts that you haven't properly read.

- Read and re-read the essays you have submitted. Be prepared to expand on the ideas you have explored in them. Remember, that the interviewers may criticise what you've argued in your submitted essays. If you believe in it, then defend your view but don't be stubborn.

- You will normally be asked if you have any questions at the end of the interview. Avoid saying things like, *"How did I do?"* – Instead use this as an opportunity to show the interviewers the type of person you are e.g. *"How many books can I borrow from the library at one time?"*

What type of questions might be asked?

The three main questions that are likely to come up in an Oxbridge interview are:

- *Why Oxford/Cambridge?*
- *Why this subject?*
- *Why this college?*

You may also get asked more specific questions about the teaching system or about your future career aspirations. This will also be the time for discussing any extenuating circumstances for poor exam results and similar considerations.

To do well in a general interview, your answers should show that you understand the Oxbridge system and that you have strong reasons for applying there. Thus, it is essential that you prepare detailed answers to the common questions above so that you aren't caught off guard. In addition, you should create a list of questions that could potentially be asked based on your personal statement or any submitted work.

WORKED QUESTIONS

Below are a few examples of how to start breaking down general interview questions- complete with model answers.

Q1: How did you choose which college to apply for?

This question is a good opportunity to tell the interviewer about yourself, your hobbies, motivations, and any interesting projects you have undertaken. You can demonstrate that you have read about the College thoroughly and you know what differentiates your College from the others. The decisive factors can include a great variety of different things from history, alumni, location in the city, community, sports clubs, societies, any positive personal experiences from Open Day and notable scholars.

This is a warm up question – an ice-breaker – so just be natural and give an honest answer. You may not want to say things like, *"I like the statutes in the garden"*. The more comprehensive your answer is, the better.

Good Applicant: I chose which college to apply for based on a number of factors that were important to me. First of all, I needed to consider how many other students at my college would be studying the same subject as me; this was important to me as I want to be able to engage in conversation about my subject with my peers. Secondly, I considered the location of the college as I wanted to ensure I had easy access to the faculty library and lecture theatres. Thirdly, I am a keen tennis player and so looked for a college with a very active tennis society. Finally, I wanted to ensure that the college I chose would feel right for me and so I looked around several Cambridge colleges before coming to my conclusion.

This response is broken down into a set of logical and yet personal reasons. **There is no right answer to this question** and the factors which influence this decision are likely to be unique for each individual. However, each college is unique and therefore the interviewer wants to know what influenced your decision. Therefore, **it's essential that you know what makes your college special** and separates it from the others. Even more importantly, you should know what the significance of that will be for you. For example, if a college has a large number of mathematicians, you may want to say that by attending that college, it would allow you to discuss your subject with a greater number of people than otherwise.

A **poor applicant** may respond with a noncommittal shrug or an answer such as, *"my brother went there"*. The interviewers want to see that you have researched the university and although the reason for choosing a college won't determine whether or not you get into the university, a lack of passion and interest in the college will greatly influence how you are perceived by the interviewers.

Q2: Why have you chosen to apply to study at 'Oxbridge', rather than another Russell Group university?

This is a very broad question and one which is simply designed to draw out the motives and thinking behind your application, as well as giving you an opportunity to speak freely about yourself.

A **good applicant** would seek to address this question in two parts, the first addressing the key features of Oxbridge for their course and the second emphasising their own personality traits and interests which make them most suited to the Oxbridge system.

It is useful to start off by talking about the supervision/tutorial system and why this method of very small group teaching is beneficial for studying your subject, both for the discussion of essay work and, more crucially, for developing a comprehensive understanding of your subject. You might also like to draw upon the key features of the course at Oxford and Cambridge that distinguish it from courses at other universities.

When talking about yourself, a good answer could take almost any route, though it is always productive to talk about which parts of your subject interest you, why this is the case, and how this ties in with the course at Oxford/Cambridge. You might also mention how the Oxbridge ethos suits your personality, e.g. how hard work and high achievement are important to you and you want to study your chosen subject in real depth, rather than a more superficial course elsewhere.

A **poor applicant** would likely demonstrate little or no knowledge of their course at Oxford/Cambridge and volunteer little information about why studying at Oxbridge would be good for them or why they would be suited to it. It's important to focus on your interests and abilities rather than implying that you applied because Oxbridge is the biggest name or because your family or school had expected you to do so.

Q3: What do you think you can bring to the college experience?

This is a common question at general interviews and **you need to show that you would be a good fit for the College** and that you are also really motivated because you have researched the college's facilities, notable fellows and alumni, societies and sports clubs etc. You can mention that you have looked at the website, talked to alumni and current students.

This question also gives the interviewer an excellent opportunity to learn about your personality, hobbies and motivations. Try to avoid listing one thing after the other for 5 minutes. Instead, you should try to give a balanced answer in terms of talking about the College and yourself. You should talk about your skills and give examples when you had to work in a team, deliver on strict deadlines, show strong time-management skills etc. You should also give a few examples from your previous studies, competitions or extracurricular activities (including sports and music).

Q4: Tell me about a recent news article not related to your subject that has interested you.

This can be absolutely anything and your interviewers just want to see that **you are aware of the world in which you live** and have a life outside of your subject. You could pick an interesting topic ahead of time and cultivate an opinion which could spark a lively discussion.

Q5: Which three famous people would you most like to be stuck on a desert island with?

This is a personal question that might be used by your interviewers as an 'ice-breaker' – you can say absolutely anyone but try to have a good justification (and avoid being melodramatic). This is a really **good chance to show your personality and sense of humour**. This is also a good question to ease you into the flow of the interview and make yourself feel more comfortable.

Q6: Do you think you're 'clever'?

Don't let this one faze you! Your interviewers are not being glib but instead want to see how you cope with questions you may not have anticipated. You could discuss different forms of intelligence, e.g. emotional vs. intellectual, perhaps concluding that you are stronger in one over the other.

Q7: What experiences do you have which suggest to you that you'll cope well with the pressures of Oxbridge?

The **interviewers want to hear that you know what you're signing up to** and that you are capable of dealing with stress. If you have any experience of dealing with pressure or meeting strict deadlines, this would be a good opportunity to talk about them. Otherwise, mention your time management skills and your ability to prioritise workloads. You could also mention how you deal with stress, e.g. do you like running? Yoga? Piano? Etc.

Q8: Why are you in this room right now?

There are hundreds of potential responses to this type of question, and the interviewer will see this as a chance to get to know your personality and how you react to unusual situations.

Firstly, **take the question seriously**, even if it strikes you as funny or bizarre. A good response may begin with: "There are many reasons why I am in this room. There are lots of smaller events and causes that have led up to me being here". You might choose to discuss your desire to attend Oxbridge, the fact that you have travelled to the college to take your interview. You might choose to discuss the interviewer or college's taste and budget when it came to selecting the chair you are sitting in, as that determined why and how you have come to be sitting in that particular chair, rather than any other chair. You might then simply mention that you were invited by the interviewer to take a seat.

A weak response to this type of question would be to dismiss it as silly or irrelevant.

Q9: *Let's say you're hosting a small private party, and you have a magical invitation which will summon anyone from time and space to your dining table. Who's name do you write on the invitation?*

This is a fairly straightforward question to get in a general interview, so use it to show your personality and originality, and to talk about something you are really passionate about.

If you are asked a question like this, give an answer that is relevant to your application. This is not the time to start talking about how you are a huge fan of Beyonce and would just love to have dinner together! You should also avoid generic answers like "God".

If you would love to meet Obama and know more about him, consider what that would be like. Would he be at liberty to answer your questions? Might you not get more information from one of his aides or from a close friend, rather than the man himself? As this is a simple question, try to unpick it and answer it in a sophisticated way, rather than just stating the obvious.

Q10: *What was the most recent film you watched?*

This question seems simple and appears to require a relatively short answer. However, a good candidate will use a simple question such as this as an opportunity to speak in more depth and **raise new and interesting topics of conversation**: "What I find particularly interesting about this film was…. It reminded me of….. In relation to other works of this period/historical context, I found this particular scene very interesting as it mirrored/contrasted with my previous conceptions of this era as seen in other works, for example… I am now curious to find out more about… This film made me think about…etc."

Whilst it is extremely important to respond accurately to the questions posed by the interviewer, do not be afraid to **take the conversation in the direction led by your personal interests**. This sort of initiative will be encouraged.

Q11: *How do you think the university will evaluate whether or not you have done well at the end of your degree, do you think that this manner of assessment is fair?*

This question invites you to show your potential and how diverse your interests are. There are three aspects of this question that you should consider in order to give a complete answer: "end of your time here", "measure" and "your achievements". You may want to discuss your hobbies and interests and potential achievements regarding various aspects of university life including academia, sports, student societies, jobs, volunteering etc.

Then you may want to enter into a discussion about whether there is any appropriate measure of success. How could you possibly compare sporting excellence to volunteering? Is it better to be a specialist or a generalist? This ultimately comes down to your personal motivation and interests as you might be very focused on your studies or other activities (e.g. sports, music). Thus, multiple things would contribute to your success at university and your degree is only likely to be one way to measure this. Finally, it might be a great closing line to mention that getting your degree might not be the "end of your time here".

Q12: Tell me why you think people should go to university.

This sounds like a very general question at first but it is, in fact, about your personal motivations to go to university. You don't need to enter into a discussion about what universities are designed for or any educational policy issues as the interviewer is unlikely to drive the discussion towards this in a general interview.

The best strategy is to **discuss your motivations**- this could include a broad range of different things from interest in a certain field, inspiring and diverse environments, academic excellence, opening up of more opportunities in the future and buying time to find out more about yourself etc. As it is very easy to give an unfocused answer, you should limit yourself to a few factors. You can also comment on whether people should go to university and whether this is good for the society.

Q13: I'm going to show you a painting, imagine that you have been tasked with describing this to someone over the phone so that they can recreate it, but you only have a minute. How would you describe the painting in order to make the recreation as close to the original as possible?

This question is very common and surprisingly difficult. **You can take a number of approaches**. Ensure that you have a concrete idea of the structure you will use to describe the painting. For example, you could begin with your personal feelings about it, then the colours and atmosphere the painting creates, then the exact objects, then their respective position and size. It does not matter which approach you take but this question is designed to test your way of organising and presenting your ideas.

You could also comment on the difficulty of the task and argue that human language limits you from adequately describing smell, taste, sound, and vision. Modern language applicants may have read about Wittgenstein, in which case, they can reference his works on the limitations and functions of language here.

Q14: Which person in the past would you most like to interview, and why?

This is a personal question but try to **avoid generic and mainstream answers**. Keep in mind that you can find out much more about a particular period or era by speaking to everyday citizens or advisors for politicians or other important figures. It is much more important to identify what you want to learn about and then set criteria to narrow down the possible list of persons. This question opens the floor for developing an analytical, quasi-scientific approach to your research.

Q15: What's an interesting thing that's been happening in the news recently?

Whilst this question may be asked at a general interview, it's a good idea to come up with something that is related to your course. Instead of going into technical detail with an interviewer who may be from a completely different discipline, it is better to give a brief overview of the article and then put it into a broader context.

For example, an economics applicant may want to discuss the most recent banking scandal. A physics applicant may want to discuss a recent discovery.

A **good** candidate might say something like "That's a great question, there are lot of really interesting things which have happened recently. For me I think the most interesting one is the confirmation of increased magnetic movement in muons at the Fermi National Accelerator in America.

This is mainly interesting for two reasons, I think that it as always interesting when you have examples of the standard model perhaps not working as it should. It's seemed like there have been problems with the way we understand everything working for some time now, but actually being able to perhaps find a new force, and write new laws of physics is incredibly exciting! The other reason this in particular is interesting is because it shows some of the strengths and weaknesses of the scientific process. Even though this magnetic movement has been detected in multiple experiments for over twenty years, it is still not something which we can consider confirmed, because this movement has not been confirmed to the five-sigma level of certainty needed to announce an actual discovery. This rigour helps ensure that we don't have incidents like the Pons and Felischmann Cold Fusion scandal, but does also mean that we will have waited more than two decades to start re-writing the textbooks at the point that this can be confirmed, assuming of course that it ever is. Events like this one really show how thorough and reliable scientific work can be, but also that in areas like theoretical physics things can be very slow to change."

The answer should not be a complete analysis of the issue but an intuitive and logical description of an event, with a good explanation of why it is interesting to you, personally. They really want to see here your enthusiasm for the topic of the article in question (and hopefully the topic of your chosen course) as well as your ability to reflect in a mature way on its most general themes.

Q16: Can people be entirely apolitical? Are you political?

In general, you should avoid expressing any very extreme views at all during interviews. The answer, *"I am not political"* is not the most favourable either. This question invites you to **demonstrate academic thinking in a topic which could be part of everyday conversations**. You are not expected to present a full analysis of party politics and different ideologies. It doesn't matter if you actually have strong political views; the main point is to talk about your perception of what political ideas are present and how one differs from the other.

With such a broad question – you have the power to choose the topic- be it wealth inequality, nuclear weapons, corruption, human rights, or budget deficit etc. Firstly, you should **explain why that particular topic or political theme is important**. For example, the protection of fundamental human rights is crucial in today's society because this introduces a social sensitivity to our democratic system where theoretically 51% of the population could impose its will on the other 49%. On the other hand, it should be noted that Western liberal values may contradict with social, historical and cultural aspects of society in certain developing countries, and a different political discourse is needed in different countries about the same questions. Secondly, you should discuss whether that topic is well-represented in the political discourse of our society and what should be done to trigger a more democratic debate.

Q17: One of the unique features of the Oxbridge education is the supervision system, one-on-one tutorials every week. This means a heavy workload, one essay every week with strict deadlines. Do you think you can handle this?

By this point, you should hopefully have a sound understanding of the supervision/tutorial systems. You should also be aware of the possibility of spending long hours in the library and meeting tight deadlines so this question should not be surprising at all. It gives you an opportunity to **prove that you would fit into this educational system very well**. Firstly, you should make it clear that you understand the system and the requirements. On average, there is one essay or problem sheet every week for each paper that you are reading which requires going through the reading list/lecture notes and engaging with wider readings around certain topics or problems. Secondly, you should give some examples from your past when you had to work long hours or had strict deadlines etc. You should also tell the interviewer how you felt in these situations, what you enjoyed the most and what you learned from them. Finally, you may wish to stress that you would *"not only be able to cope with the system but also enjoy it a great deal"*.

Q18: If you had to live in the world of a book you have read, which book would it be, and whose role would you take?

This question is an ice-breaker- the interviewer is curious to find out what type of novels you read and how thoroughly you are reading them. You want to show that you are capable of thinking on your feet, talk them through why you've chosen their particular world, does it have advantages which outweigh its pitfalls. For example, if you say you like Robin Hood, it is a world in which you could carry out noble deeds in an idyllic setting, but you also have to deal with poverty, homelessness, and a brutal regime. If you would like to live here, then tell them why. As for the character, centre in on who you want, for instance Robin himself, explain his situation briefly as becoming an outlaw, resisting the authorities, and aiding the poor and his fellow men. Would you like to take his role because you would like to do the things he did, or do you feel that you could 'be' him differently, or even better? Would you be able to learn or grow from entering your chosen world, and being a certain character - think of what course you are applying to, and see if there are particular skills which you think this experience could teach you, empathy, if you're applying for medicine, or social responsibility, if you're applying for economics & management, as examples.

The main point is to be able to **give a very brief summary of the character and the world in which they live in**, (especially if you choose a less well-known work), and have a good and interesting justification for choosing them.

Q19: Do you think that we should give applicants access to a computer during their interviews?

This is a classic open question for an insightful debate. The most important thing to realise here is that **Oxbridge education is about teaching you how to think** in clear, structured and coherent ways as opposed to collecting lots of facts from the internet.

Internet access would provide each candidate with the same available information and therefore the art of using information to make sound arguments would be the sole decisive factor. On the other hand, the information overload can be rather confusing. In general, a braindump is not helpful at the interview as it does not demonstrate in-depth understanding and analysis of any problems. At the end of the day, it comes down to the individual candidate, i.e. what would you look up on the Internet during the interview? Would you want to rely on unverified knowledge? How reliable is that information on the internet? How could you verify this information?

Q20: What was your proudest moment?

This is another chance to highlight your suitability for the course, so try to **make it as subject-relevant as possible**. *"I felt proud to be awarded first place in a poetry competition with a sonnet I wrote about…"* (if you're applying for English). *"I recently won the Senior Challenge for the UK Mathematics Trust."*, *"Achieving a 100% mark in my AS-level History and English exams – an achievement I hope to emulate at A2"*.

Of course, it's not easy to pick one moment and this is not a question you might have expected. You could also argue that you can't really compare your achievements from different fields e.g. your 100% Physics AS-level and football team captaincy, but be careful. You should always try to settle on one in the end, this will show the interviewer that you are able to answer the questions you are given, even if they are very challenging, which is a vital skill. A useful tip here is to talk them through your thought process, there are several competing moment which could be your proudest, and you need to work out which one was the best. Try separating out the ones which impressed others versus those which were more personal to you, and decide on one which, overall, was the most impactful. This way, you have talked through a number of impressive things with the interviewer, but you have shown critical thinking skills and attention to detail in providing a definitive answer.

Q21: Would you ever use a coin-flip to make a choice, if so, when?

This question can be quite tricky and aims at revealing how you make decisions in your life, your understanding of abstract concepts, rationality and probabilities. You should begin with answering the question from your perspective, you can be honest about it but give a justification even if you never want to make decisions based on luck. Try to **give a few examples when tossing a coin could be a good idea**, or would cause no harm. Then you can take the discussion to a more abstract level and argue that once all yes/no decisions are made by tossing a coin in the long run, the expected value should be fifty-fifty so you might not be worse-off at all and you could avoid the stress of making decisions (although this is very simplistic).

You could also reference the stock markets where high returns may be purely luck-dependent. On the other hand, **rational decision-making is part of human nature** and analysing costs and benefits would result in better decisions in the long-run than tossing a coin. In addition, this would incentivise people to conduct research, collect information, develop and test theories, etc. As you see, the question could be interpreted to focus on the merits of rigorous scientific methodology.

Q22: If you had omnipotence for a moment, but had to use it to change only one thing, what would it be?

This question tests your sound reasoning and clear presentation of your answer and the justification for it. There is no right or wrong "one thing" to choose. It is equally valid to choose wealth inequality or the colour of a double-decker bus if you argue it well! It should be noted that if you've applied for social sciences, it is a better strategy to choose a related topic to show your sensitivity to social issues.

Firstly, you should choose something you would like to change while demonstrating clear thinking, relevant arguments. Secondly, you are expected to discuss how, and to what extent, you would and could change it. Again, a better candidate would realise that **this is not necessarily a binomial problem** – either change it or not – but there may be a spectrum between these two extremes. Once you've identified the thing you'd like to change, talk them through why. A good way to make sure you always do this is by thinking aloud, and walking the interviewer through the way you would reach this conclusion yourself.

Q23: Oxford, as you know, has access to some very advanced technology. In the next room we actually have the latest model of time machine, if we gave you the opportunity to use it later, when would you go?

This is a question where you can really use your imagination (or draw on History GCSE or A-level). **You can say absolutely any time period** in the past or the far future but you must have a good reason for it which you communicate to the interviewer. This doesn't necessarily need to be linked to your subject.

For example, *"I would love to see a time when my parents were little children and see where and how they grew up. I'd ideally like to stay for some time to gather as much information as possible. This would be really valuable to me as I'd get to see them when they were people without children, just as they themselves were developing, and could give me opportunities to better understand them. I think understanding ones parents is often a good way to help you understand yourself. The pursuit of self-understanding never stops, but this opportunity would give me a unique chance to improve that."*

Choosing something personal or creative will make you stand out and you are more likely to get interesting questions from the interviewer if you are able to involve them in an intriguing conversation. It is also fine if you choose a standard period like the Roman Empire or a time which has not yet come to pass, say the year 4000, if you have a good reason.

Q24: Should interviews be used for selection?

This question may appear slightly inflammatory on the surface, considering that you are answering it in an interview, to an interviewer who likely believes in the merit of interviewing for selection. However, remember that the interviewer is interested in your opinion, and will not take offence providing you respond in a measured way, providing examples/evidence. Another important thing to remember for any question that addresses interviews and/or selection, is that what you are currently sat in is not the only form of interview, and what you are being selected for is not the only form of selection. As a result, you could wildly disagree with interviews for selection in most situations, but agree with them in the situation you are currently sat in, or vice versa.

"One up-side to using interviews for selection, is that it forces the interviewee to think on their feet (providing the questions aren't known to them in advance), which can demonstrate their real-world knowledge of a subject and is likely to bring out more honest answers about themselves. One down-side is that an interview is quite a short and high-pressure situation, as a result, an interviewee could easily make a number of mistakes or say something inappropriate and tarnish the interviewer's opinion of them. By extension, interviews rely somewhat on the opinion of the interviewer, therefore, are prone to bias."

This would be a good answer, as it addresses one for and one against aspect, justifying each point with an explanation. However, a great answer would be one that takes this further, and considers interviews' appropriateness for different types of selection.

"In some situations, the ability for an interviewee to make a mess of the interview due to the short time they are with the interviewer, and the pressure they are under, is a bad thing. This is in the same way that an entire year's work boiling down to one exam is often criticised as a way of measuring someone's academic ability. However, if the interview is for something that requires working in that situation, such as a politician who will be subjected to questions and interviews throughout their job, then an interview is a great way to measure their suitability."

By considering the appropriateness of an interview in different scenarios, you are not only demonstrating your breadth of consideration, but also your ability to remove yourself from your own head and think outside of your current situation. This question could, however, specify a type of interview and/or a particular thing being selected for. In this case, make sure you stick to that specific concept. You may address an alternative concept for comparison, but always bring the conclusion back to the question's specific elements.

Q25: Would you ever choose to go to a party rather than write an essay for university?

At first glance, this might feel like a trick question. As an interviewer, they are likely a practicing academic at the university and could well be a subject tutor you could end up having! However, it's important to remember two things. Firstly, tutors are human too and like to have fun occasionally. Secondly, all universities have 'parties' that are sanctioned by the university or an individual faculty, therefore, it's perfectly fine to want to go to parties! There are a couple of distinctions to make when constructing an answer for a question like this, and they hinge on the importance of each element.

In isolation, you might consider it impossible to argue that a party is in any way important. However, there are lots of ways in which it could be. This could a big, once in a lifetime faculty ball, it could be a party for a close friend's birthday, it could have valuable networking opportunities, or it could simply be a party you really could do with as you're feeling a bit down at that moment. The other aspect of this question is, of course, the essay. When picking something over something else, you should be considering the importance of each thing in isolation to the current situation, rather than just the concepts in general. For example, if the essay is due tomorrow and the party is a small get-together down the hall which is going to result in you not sleeping properly and not being able to finish the essay in time, then it would be quite difficult (although not impossible in the 'right' circumstances) to argue that you would pick the party over the essay.

Under some circumstances, the party might be a well-deserved break from your work, and not directly impact your ability to submit the essay by the deadline. For example, if an essay is due at the end of the following day and the party is that night, it might initially seem sensible to finish the essay first and relax after. However, you won't be able to go to the party tomorrow afternoon once you've finished the essay, as it won't be going on then. So, in that case, it would make sense to go to the party and then finish the essay the following afternoon before the deadline (providing you have enough time to do so). This sort of decision-making is more likely to go approved by an interviewer if the party has some kind of important element (e.g., a big, one-off organised event or a birthday party), but even if not, it is important to be able to back your decisions. As long as you are completing the work to a high standard and on time, it's also important that you enjoy yourself!

Q26: Who do you think has the most power: Biden, Merkel or Adele?

Answering a question like this first rests on your knowledge of each person. You don't need to know a great deal about them, but it is important you know what their role is. If you don't know that, make sure you ask the interviewer! Once you have established who each person is, you need to address any words in the question that have multiple interpretations. In this case, that word is 'power'. In order to answer the question, you need to decide how to measure power. As with all of these types of questions, you are welcome to pick one definition and go with it, or address the fact that there are multiple definitions and briefly approach each one individually. You can always make a comparison/conclusion at the end of the latter to potentially pick the 'best' definition for that particular situation.

When defining power, there are two key starting points. The first is how many people are aware of what each person says or does. This is probably the easiest to answer.

"If you consider power to be the potential of each person's words or actions to affect others, then the most influential would probably be Adele. Her music and name are known worldwide so, while she is probably not known by as many people in the US as Biden is, her reach is more global and likely through to a younger audience. More people will have heard her, and responded in any number of different ways, even turning off the radio is affecting others. However, as Biden progresses through his presidency and makes more headlines, that could easily change!"

Due to the simplicity of this definition, in this case, it is probably best to address at least one other definition of influence. One alternative definition is how much those who hear what that person says or sees what they do, will change their thoughts or long-term actions based on it.

"If defining power as how much people will change their actions or thoughts based on the actions and words of that person, then the most influential person is probably Biden. As the Amercian president, the majority of the US population will be brought into his words and actions, even if it is to vehemently disagree with them!"

You could go on to explore whether power can be just as valid when someone disagrees with the words or actions of an influential individual, or how many more people would someone need to affect a little bit to make them more powerful than someone who influences a smaller number of people a lot. The important thing is that you explore your thought processes aloud, and see them through to a conclusion each time. The conclusion doesn't need to be right, as with a concept like this it is hard to be 'right', it just needs to be some kind of decision (even if that decision is there is a tie!).

Q27: What would you say was "your colour"?

With a question as basic and seemingly abstract as this, there are two ways you can approach it. The first is to delve into the question in-depth and explore each concept and its origin. The alternative is to answer the question succinctly and give a clear reason for your conclusion. Below is an example of the latter.

"I believe that red is a colour that represents me best as it is my favourite colour. I think it came about as my favourite colour because my parents' car when I was a child was red, as was the front door on the first house I remember living in, so I always associated red with my family and home".

That would be enough detail to give a valid answer. You have given the basis of the reason (that it is your favourite colour), and then discussed the origin of that reasoning. Alternatively, you can choose to explore the question in much more detail. The first concept to approach when doing this, is the idea of representation. Is this self-representation, how others would represent you, or perhaps how you relate to what the colour typically represents in society. Below is an example of a succinct approach to all three of those concepts, something you could state after outlining the three concepts aloud.

"For myself, the colour green represents me best because it is my favourite colour, I own lots of green clothes and decorations in my room and would love to have a green house! If other people had to choose, I'd say they would pick blue because I spent a lot of time in rivers in my parents' canoe, and enjoy spending time in the sea on holiday. If I had to be represented by a societal norm, I would day that red best represents me because I have a fiery temper."

While, in the real interview you would probably approach each of these in a bit more details, this gives a basic outline of how you would separate the three concepts. You don't have to address every concept in your answer but, as usual, it is always good to outline all the concepts in the beginning to demonstrate to the interviewer that you are thinking comprehensively. Remember, when you are addressing multiple concepts in an answer, it is all too easy to drift away from the origin of your thoughts. Bring it back each time by answering the actual question at the end of each of your thought processes, in the context that thought process has been discussed in.

Q28: What shape is man? What shape is time?

On the surface, this question seems impossible to answer because it is simply too abstract. There is no shape that fits the shape of a person, and time isn't a physical concept. However, this is a test of how you address something seemingly impossible to answer. There is no wrong way to answer this question, providing you actually answer it! The important thing to remember is to get started with answering it quickly, the longer you spend pondering the wider concept, the more difficult it will be to get started!

Addressing each question individually is important and something you need to conclude on so, as a result, it is easy for you to separate two concept discussions by addressing one per question. When considering the first question, you can start by providing the obvious answer, and follow-on by delving into the concept more deeply.

"There is no named shape that is the shape of a person, so you would refer to 'man' simply as being 'man-shaped'. We refer to things in this way all the time, so not having a named shape to represent something shouldn't limit you. One important differentiator is that 'man' is not an exact shape, as every person is different. Therefore, if your definition of shape must be precise such as a square having four equal length sides with four ninety-degree corners, then that would not be possible to apply to 'man'. However, a shape like an oval doesn't have explicit parameters, so is closer to the idea of a shape which could define 'man'."

There are clear caveats to this answer, such as an oval having the strict rule of no straight edges and being entirely symmetrical, but the consideration of two different types of existing shape definitions is a great way to start the discussion. When moving that discussion on to consider time, it becomes even more abstract. You could open the discussion with the fact that time is not considered a physical concept, thus it would be inappropriate to allocate it a shape. However, you then open the discussion around space-time, where time can be considered represented physically. An interviewer may not choose to entertain such a discussion, as it is not exactly psychology related, but making sweeping and abrupt statements like that are best avoided anyway. A better way to open the discussion might be to explain that time is often considered a circle (history repeating itself, the circle of life etc.). While it would be inappropriate to state that time is a specific shape, acknowledging these ideas demonstrates your ability to think conceptually and compare it to real societal discussion.

Q29: Do things have to have specific names?

When answering why, the first thing to consider is 'what's in it for the user'. In this case, what is gained by naming things.

"One reason why things have names is to avoid having to describe them every time we refer to them. Once you have learned what the name refers to, conversations can be had much more quickly, and more easily across different languages. Rather than having to learn all the terms that describe a thing, you would only need to learn the name of that thing in order to tell a person about it in a different language."

You can centre the entire discussion around this idea of what we gain from something, but it is important to broaden your horizons a little if you want to make the discussion as interesting and engaging as possible. You may consider a few gains we make by naming things, but the next step is to consider the origin of naming things and the reason for the concept. The first reason is that we gain something from doing it, so it justifies the effort of coming up with and learning the names, However, another example which would explain the origin of naming something is that we want to take ownership of it. By giving something a name, it can be recognised by that name and associated with one person as its 'owner'. This could be considered the origin of naming, whereby everyone would have a different name for the few things they considered to be there. Gradually, through communication, perhaps we established it would be easier to have a unified naming process, such that there were fewer names to remember. This could have led to the origin of possessive pronouns, to go with these unified names.

None of this is necessarily true, and would be almost impossible to prove either way due to how long-ago naming things came about as a concept. Discussions of this type do, however, demonstrate your ability to consider both the value and the origin of a concept or action and link them together. The importance of a question like this, is to evoke a discussion of the abstract that you can tie together into a coherent conclusion. As such, it is vital that regardless of the content of your discussion, you conclude with an actual answer. This is welcome to be a brief touch of each of the discussion points you have made, as it is often impossible to make an explicit decision on which is 'right', but it needs to be clear and concise.

"I believe things have names because it was a way of identifying them as our own, which developed into a way of communicating what they were between people who didn't know of each other's possessions. It stuck as a concept, because it enabled shorter discussions through not having to fully describe a thing each time it was mentioned."

Q30: Do you read any international publications, do you think there is a value to doing so?

This question requires honesty above all else. This doesn't mean you couldn't implicitly overstate quite to the extent that you read a particular publication, but you absolutely should not discuss something you haven't actually read. Many of the interviewers you will speak to will ask this question because they are very well read, thus could easily pull you up on a particular publication. As a result, you need to have actually read an international newspaper or publication to answer this question. It would be best if you have read at least one of each, but if you have only read one, open with that.

What the interviewer will be looking for is your critique of the publication. It would be a bonus if it is psychology-related, but don't think it to be necessary. The important thing is that you recognise and address the context under which the publication is written, and how that might influence what they write about and how they write about it. When critiquing an academic paper in an essay, these are the sorts of things a tutor will be looking to see, and it is what the interviewer wants to assess your ability on at this stage. This isn't to say that you should construct your entire discussion of the publication around this critiquing, but it is definitely something you should include.

"I read [American Newspaper] online quite regularly, and tend to focus on the 'social issues' section of the paper. It is interesting to read about American social issues because some of them are so similar to our own, whereas others are so distinctly different. One article I read in the most recent version [don't be this specific if you're not sure it was] *highlighted the ease with which someone could buy a gun as a non-American citizen, meaning that someone who's history is unknown to American authorities could enter the country and buy a weapon with bad intentions. I wonder whether gun culture contributes to xenophobia and racism, as the risk that someone coming into the country with bad intentions poses, is potentially much higher than if the same thing happened where guns weren't accessible to the public."*

While this is a very simplistic discussion of a point and you would want to delve into some more detail and evidence in the real interview, it demonstrates how you can bring a psychology them to a seemingly unrelate article. The next stage in your discussion would be to critique the paper itself. With gun culture being alien to a UK resident (if indeed you are one), you could consider your views on the topic to be biased. You could also make a suggestion to rectify that, by discussing the article with an American person or someone who is in favour of guns being legally accessible to the public. This last bit is important as it is key to consider how you can broaden your views in a practical way. If the context is right, you can link it to how you might do this during your time at university.

Q31: Can you hear silence?

There are two elements that can be considered in almost any question which touches on biology in a psychology interview. The first is the biological element, and the second is the concept that we experience/express as a result or in anticipation of that biological effect. In this case, there is the biology of hearing something, and the interpretation of that into neural signals. In this case, how you explain the biology is very much dependent on your biology knowledge. Unless it is something you have mentioned in your personal statement or in the interview, the interviewer won't expect you to have comprehensive knowledge of the biology behind hearing. However, they will expect you to have a general understanding that sound travels in waves, and those waves are interpreted into neural signals (which we 'hear') by bones in your ear.

When considering this from a biological perspective, then you can be pretty conclusive in your statement that we cannot hear silence. If there are no sound waves, then we do not 'hear' anything from our environment. However, this doesn't mean that we don't interpret the silence as something other than nothingness, from the neural signals we receive. Without making any sweeping statements about the complicated biology around neural signalling, it would make sense to assume that neurons aren't ever 'silent'. Things in biology are rarely as cut and dry as being 'off' or 'on', so you could use that train of thought in the following discussion.

"I imagine that neurons are never at a point when there is no transmission of chemical between them. It is more likely to imagine they have a 'resting rate' of transmission, which is then greatly increase when 'active'. As a result, even when there is no noise, you might assume there are still some signals being sent between neurons related to hearing. In order to create a silent environment, humans have gone to great lengths to create sound-deadening material. Therefore, one could assume that silence is not something you would come across in a natural setting. If the human hearing system has not evolved to consider true silence, when faced with it, its reaction will likely be to 'hear' the 'resting rate' of signals that would normally never be reached due to ambient noise. With that in mind, while you cannot actually hear silence because there are no sound waves to hear, the experience of true silence is likely to manifest as some kind of ambient sound."

Making one point per statement in a discussion like this enables you to create an argument that is easy to follow. This is beneficial for three reasons. Firstly, the interviewer can take note of every point you have made. Secondly, the interviewer can see you are proficient at organising your thoughts. Thirdly, the interviewer can be invited to target a new discussion (even if that is to disagree with you) at any one of your points. The more discussion the better!

Q32: You mentioned having good thinking skills in your personal statement, can you tell me how many golf balls can you fit in a Boeing 787 Dreamliner?

This question is testing a few things, all related to your thinking process, despite its seemingly pointless nature. The first thing it is testing is the comprehensiveness and commitment of your subject consideration. What the interviewer will be looking for is you to exhaust all aspects of the question, in order to work towards the answer. Part of this is considering the physical nature of the objects in mind. The two elements in this question are the plane, and the golf balls. To consider the physical size of the plane, it might be best to get some clarification from the interviewer if you don't know the size of the plane. The number will be very different between a double-decker transatlantic plane compared to a private jet! If you know the size, make sure you state it out loud, it doesn't really matter whether you are right or not, just that the interviewer knows what you are working from. When discussing the golf ball, make sure you also give the rough size you are working from.

The next step has two options. The first is to take a mathematical approach, based around volume. The other is to consider all the places you could put a golf ball on a plane (overhead storage, under seats, in cockpit etc.). Depending on your maths confidence, the choice would be yours. Don't worry if the maths you do isn't exactly right, just make sure you talk through each step out loud and ensure that the number you come out with at the end seems believable. If working through the different places a ball could go, try to attribute a number to each one (e.g., 300 golf balls in each overhead storage area, 300 passengers so 100 areas, 30000 total golf balls in overhead storage), and make sure you write it down! It's far too easy to get caught up in the line of sums, without being able to add them together to an answer at the end!

Once you reach a point of concluding, ensure that your answer appears believable and answer the question! Don't let yourself tail off at the end of your last consideration and not actual provide a number. It doesn't matter (within reason) what that number is, as long as the methods you used to get to it made sense.

Q33: How would you work out the number of flights passing over London at this moment?

This question is testing just one thing, that being the degree to which you can work through a large series of thoughts, considering all possible options. While it is vital that you give a numerical answer, the value of that answer (within reason) doesn't really matter, what matters is how you got to the answer. When beginning this question, it might be helpful for you to outline some parameters. If you know how many airports London has (6), then you can start from there. There will definitely be more than 6 planes over London as they will be coming and going from each airport. So, from your starting point you can work out a realistic maximum.

If you know anything about airport scheduling then absolutely discuss it, any colourful insights into your life will be memorable for an interviewer. However, most people won't have that kind of insight so will be starting from scratch. It would be safe to assume that there is a gap of at least two minutes between planes landing, in order that they can taxi off of the runway. At the speed planes travel, they could probably traverse London in 15 minutes or so. Considering of the 6 airports, there are maybe 10 runways, assuming planes are always nose to tail coming in and out, you could sum 7 planes per 'queue' times the 10 runways, making a total of 70 planes.

It doesn't matter if this is entirely wrong, it may be hugely more than this or hugely fewer. The important thing is the steps taken to get to that value. If you want to extend your discussion, you can go on to review the number you have reached. If you look up at the sky at any given time, you can only see a couple of planes at most, and your view extends quite a few miles in every direction. As such, you might choose to assess that 70 seems like too many, and perhaps halve your answer. If you add in the explanation that maybe there is a 4-minute gap between landings, rather than the originally assumed 2, the numbers would add up. Being comprehensive and explanatory in your thought processes is vital and will be most well received by an interviewer.

Q34: How many deliveries are made in the UK every day?

As with any numerical question, the value is your method, not the answer. However, you must give an answer to 'complete' the process. To reach any kind of answer to the scale that this will be will take some considerable calculations. If you have any prior insight (such as knowing how many they delivered last year, or how many your local post office receives), then outline and apply it aloud. Each bit of information you can bring to inform your calculation will not only likely make it more accurate, but also impress the interviewer that you have such niche knowledge and have thought to apply it.

When starting your calculations, it can be helpful to set parameters. You can assume that not every person in the UK receives something every day, so the number is likely going to be less than the total UK population (if you know it accurately, great, if not it can be generally helpful to know it's around 70 million people). Your next point of consideration is that commercial mail exists as well. While much of mail is sent via email now, businesses still account for a lot of the mail sent each day. As such, you may choose to reconsider your original 70-million limit, to account for commercial mail.

None of the assumptions and considerations you make matter in their accuracy to reality, only in their abundance and degree of thought. Within reason, in a question like this, the more times you reconsider a particular point, the greater depth of understanding it demonstrates to the interviewer. When you have made all the considerations you think are reasonable (it can be helpful to write them down to keep track), make sure you conclude with an actual value. Once you have a value, it can often be insightful to reflect upon that relative to a reasonable assumption you might pick out of the air. If this calculated value and the 'random' value are distinctly different, perhaps spend a moment discussing why that might be, relative to the calculations and considerations you have just undertaken.

Q35: Have you been to this college before?

This question is unusual, in that it is not testing anything in particular. It is far more of an exploratory question which seeks to bring out your experience of university and the college, as well as your expectations for it going forward. When answering any question based on your experiences, it is important to be honest. You can embellish the truth in part if you wish, but always ensure that the core of what you're saying is true. The interviewer will probably expect you to have visited Oxford at least once before the interview (unless you are an international student), but it is not a problem if you have not.

If you have not ever visited the college before, the interviewer will want to know what attracted you to it, and that will likely be the next question. As a result, your considerations should immediately be looking towards why you were interested in the college, as soon as this initial question is asked. The best way to approach that, is to describe in what context you have seen the college (e.g., through the university website) and what it was that you liked about what you saw/read.

If you have visited the college before, the first thing to outline is under what context. If it was a family trip to Oxford and you looked around as a tourist, it is fine to focus on the 'tourist things' that you liked about the college e.g., the architecture. If you visited quite recently (during the time you might be expected to have been thinking about university) or as a school trip, where the focus was a little more on the academic side, then make sure you address some of the 'non-tourist- aspects too. It is fine to talk about the grounds and the architecture, but having done some reading around the library, subject foci and alumni/faculty members will go a long way.

This is one of the few questions where it wouldn't really be fitting to conclude by answering the question. Answering the question should be the very first thing you do, everything that follows is simply an extension of that. One key thing to make sure is that you don't end up talking too far into the subject. It may be that the interviewer was simply asking this as a yes/no question, precursory to a more in-depth question. With that in mind, try to read the interviewer's body language to see if they were expecting you to take the reins on the discussion!

Q36: Do you think that Oxford/Cambridge will suit you?

This question is testing two main things. The first is your understanding of (and, by extension, your reading up on) the university, and your self-awareness. You want to ensure that the overriding message of this answer is 'yes', as that is the whole reason you are applying. However, don't be afraid to touch on some elements that may not be 100% positive. For example, if you feel like you don't have much in common with the stereotypical student of the university, you can say that! However, what is important is to express your realisation that the stereotype isn't the reality.

If you want to go down this route of discussion, the safest is way to is to describe your experiences once you have arrived. By the time you have gone into your first interview, you will have had quite extensive contact with some other prospective students. More than likely, you will have found some people with things in common with yourself, take that on board I your discussion. The more recent the experience and the more truth behind it, the better! If this process of meeting your fellow interviewees has squashed some doubt about whether you would fit in, that's a fantastic result and you should definitely share it!

The next part is to make sure that you have read up on the university, and to make that clear! If the university is very research heavy, match that up to your own academic interests! The same goes for if they have a particular department that is of interest to you. Don't be afraid to add a little more personality to the discussion, perhaps the location is convenient for you in some way, but make sure your answer hinges on the more impactful content.

"After my undergraduate degree, I would really enjoy pursuing a PhD in psychology. I'm not sure exactly what I would want to specialise in yet, but the opportunity to be surrounded by practicing academics to discuss that with is invaluable. In addition, I'll be able to stay on my undergraduate campus for my postgraduate studies, and have access to some incredible research facilities and equipment. In addition, the university is only 45 minutes' drive from my home town, so I'll be able to visit there easily for birthdays and other special occasions!"

Remember, this question is about why the university is the right fit for you. You could easily be asked why you are the right fit for the university, and you would have to phrase your answer slightly differently. To explain why the university is the right fit for you, you should be assessing why the features of the university fit into your life and personality. If you're answering why you're the right fit for the university, then that answer is the other way round!

Q37: *What do you think you'll be doing in a decade? How about in two decades?*

No interviewer will expect you to have an actual plan for the next 10 or 20 years of your life. Instead, what they're looking for is an understanding of how you gaining your degree might set out a path for you in life. This is far more about understanding your options than it is deciding which one you are going to pursue. It is important to distinguish the sections of your answer between the 10 and 20-year mark. Remember if you wanted to do a PhD, you wouldn't likely finish that until around 8 years from the point that you're in this interview. As such, if that was your plan, you wouldn't be far into post-doctoral research/your first 'proper' job in the first 10 years. It is important to articulate details like this, even if you haven't definitely decided you want to do a PhD. Any understanding of your options in this way demonstrates to the interviewer that you have considered these things.

If you are more concerned with the industry you want to go into than any postgraduate studies, then discuss how you might want to pursue success there. At the 10-year point, if you have spent 6 years of that in an industry, what would you like to have achieved. You have the classic milestones such as being a team leader, running your own project, owning your own home, or any other 'standard' aspirations. However, you should try and add in some things which are unique to you and your preferred industry. If you wanted to go into marketing, something that is quite common for psychology graduates, then it would be great to aspire to have one of your projects on national television, or up in the store of a 'household name' business.

It is, however, important to remember that the interviewer is likely to be an academic, and is likely to (be it potentially implicitly/subconsciously) want you to aspire to do the same thing. As a result, you should consider how you 'tune' your answer to appease those who are listening to it. I would never expect a tutor to reject an applicant on the basis that they didn't want to pursue studies beyond undergraduate, however, it is easier to engage with someone on a topic they are interested in. The more engaged you are with the interviewer, the more likely they will remember and the better a conversation they will have with their peers after you are gone. This isn't a hard and fast rule, but it is human nature to frame memorable things in a positive light (unless of course it was objectively bad!). in sum, you want to approach this question with honesty, but make sure that you consider your audience!

Q38: What is your favourite activity outside of school?

This is a question which 'assesses' your personality outside of academia. It's great if you have genuine hobbies which are subject-related, but most people don't and no interviewer will expect you to. What they are looking for is ways in which you unwind, what environments you choose to put yourself in (rather than those which are thrust upon you!), and how competitive you are. If every hobby of yours involves playing a competitive, spectator sport to a high level, then the interviewer can deduce that you are outgoing, competitive and have an interest in exhibiting your skills. This is very different (although by no means better/worse) than someone who's hobbies are all quiet activities to pass the time that you engage with alone.

As you discuss your interests, remember that the interviewer will likely be comparing their stereotypical view of someone who has these interests, alongside their experience of you in this setting. If you are describing yourself as confident and outgoing through the activities you like to do, but are aware that you have been shy in this setting, it could be a good thing to highlight that! Having a high level of self-awareness is a great sign of emotional intelligence and will only be another point in your favour!

When talking about your interests, it is always beneficial to highlight any achievements you might have made in them. This doesn't mean you should tune the entire conversation into a list of your achievements (as that wasn't the question!), but it can be useful to highlight where you have committed yourself and gained success. In addition, spend some time on the less usual hobbies. This is the perfect opportunity to inject some real personality into the interview and, you never know, the interviewer might even share an unusual hobby of yours which you can engage on!

Lastly, it can be a good idea to describe how you are going to continue pursuing those hobbies through university. The interviewers don't want someone who is going to drop everything and become a sheep when they arrive on campus, they want someone who is going to bring something new to the table! As a result, whether it's simply a hobby you'll keep up in your own time, or a club that you'd want to set up in your college, make sure you outline how you'll go about keeping these things up! Make sure these are realistic and measured against the amount of commitment you will need to bring to your academic studies, but by all means dream big!

Q39: How will your fellow college residents see you?

There are a few ways in which you can contribute to college life as a student. One, which could be easily overlooked when considering college life specifically, is simply being a friendly and approachable person. When talking in the context of college life, it's easy to forget the things that make you a contributor to a pleasant society in general. When it comes to college-specific things, it's good to open with some more general points, with some demonstration that you have read up on college-specific things as well.

What this means is first considering what makes a good contributor in any small community. You could contribute by applying your skills in a particular sport (or otherwise) to the college team, you could apply your academic ability and commitment to success to enhance the college's academic rankings. You could even include something like experience in party-planning or finances to contribute to the college ball (should there be one). The next step is to introduce some college-specific things, to demonstrate that you've done some reading around the college, and to highlight your specific suitability.

An easy (although predictable) one would be if the college has any particularly successfully (or perhaps even unsuccessful, although that would be more difficult to find out!) sports teams. You could highlight this if you have an interest/skill in any one of those, and highlight that you would be keen to join in. Some of the less predictable things would be societies outside of sport, or whether your college has a chapel and you'd like to be involved in that. There is a wealth of different things which a college could be interested in having someone contribute to, it's just a case of matching one up from your research to something you're interested in. The important thing to remember is that it doesn't have to be something you have dine already, it could be trying something totally new!

Lastly, you want to make sure you can contribute to the college after you leave. Something that many people wouldn't consider is going on to be a respectable and successful person in your industry, adding to the college's notable alumni. As with any question that requires you to speak well of the college/university, it is a fine balance between selling yourself as an admirer of the college, and seeming over the top or fake. Strike the balance well by practicing talking around these kinds of subjects, you'll soon develop a way that works for you.

Q40: Why do you think we structure the course in the way that we do?

This question doesn't try to hide what it's assessing at all. One of the big indicators of someone who is committed to the application process (and, by extension, the university) is how much preparation they have done for the interviews. The first thing you should have looked at when deciding which course to choose, is what the actual course content in. There are two sides to a course decision, the first is how it will help you get to the next stage if your education/career (if you have planned that far ahead!), and the other is whether it will interest you while you study. The latter can only be answered by exploring and reading around the course content.

When talking about the course structure, it is best to keep the objective details to a reasonable level. You don't want to sound like you're simply reciting a list of modules, nor do you want to risk getting muddled and saying something that is objectively wrong. You are much better off making a point which you have come to the opinion of through your reading, and then evidencing it in the discussion thereafter.

"I can see from reading up on the course that it focusses a lot on social psychology in the first two years. This was one of the things that attracted me to it, as I think undertaking a social science independent study in third year would be really interesting. The focus on social psychology seems to come from the disproportionately high number of modules which approach topics in the field, when compared to subjects like perception."

Above is a bit of a clunky answer, but one that demonstrates you've read around the course content and are very happy with what you have read (which is arguably the most important bit!). You could construct an answer in a more coherent manner, by opening with the number of modules on one particular subject, highlighting that it appears to be a particular focus of the course, and then finishing with why that is a good thing for you. However, when opening with the number of modules on a course, it sets up the answer to feel too over-prepared. Your preference between them is, of course, your own and either will make a good structure to answer a question like this.

As aforementioned, the most important bit is to highlight why the course content works for you. Make sure to not have that as the conclusion of your answer, because that isn't the question, but always make sure it is included.

Q41: What would you say was your single greatest weakness?

Answering this question well is very difficult. There are two ways in which you could go wrong. Neither of these ways would necessarily be terrible, but they are best avoided if possible. The first way is to give an answer that is simply a positive attributed in disguise. An example of this would be 'admitting' that you can sometimes be too much of a perfectionist or be too detail oriented. These are things which would certainly be bad traits under certain circumstances, but the combination of the fact that in a lot of cases they are good and that they have been presented as 'sometimes' being an issue, makes them far too weak as answers.

The other way in which you could answer this question in a non-ideal way is to overshare on your weaknesses. The interviewer doesn't want to hear that as soon as there's a test around the corner you have a complete meltdown and only just drag yourself through. If your weakness has something to do with an event you'll face at university, you're best-off underselling it slightly (only if it's really bad of course!). if this is the case, it would also be beneficial to explain what you're doing, and will continue to do, to work on that weakness. Self-awareness of a real weakness is a great sign of the potential for personal growth, but the growth only comes if you actually act to solve the problem!

In an ideal scenario, you will have a genuine weakness that you are working on fixing, that doesn't really have anything to do with university. That way, you can have an honest conversation with the interviewer, without it having any chance of jeopardising their view of you as a competent student. However, this isn't normally possible and you will likely have to talk around a weakness that could affect you as a student.

As a result, you want to focus on what you are doing to rectify this weakness, and the timeline over which you are acting. The latter is very important, no interviewer will expect you to start university as a perfectly formed student, but they would be very keen to see some kind of commitment from you to have worked on that weakness prior to starting your course. It might be that you know you're a slow typist, so you're going to take a touch-typing course over summer. Or it could be that your handwriting is bad quality, so you're going to spend your last few months at school comparing your handwriting every week and looking to see an improvement over time.

There's any number of things you could list as a weakness, just remember that it needs to be honest (and an actual weakness!) but something that is fixable (or at least manageable) in a sensible time-frame.

Q42: You have mentioned a number of personal strengths in your statement, which is your greatest?

Answering this question involves just as much care as answering what your biggest weakness is. It is far too easy to list a generic skill like 'essay-writing' and explaining how it will benefit you in your degree because that is something you will spend a lot of your time doing. The key to answering this question well is finding a balance between bragging and being too modest. If you undersell your strengths, it demonstrates a lack of confidence and perhaps an indication that you might not be as good as you appeared on paper. Oversell your strengths, and it suggests a lack of self-awareness and an arrogance towards your own ability.

To balance this answer properly, you want to find a couple of strengths to 'warm-up' with, that are related to your main strength. Alternatively, you can find one main strength that is backed up with 'auxiliary' strengths. Here is an example of the former, followed by the latter.

"Leading up to my GCSE's, I spent a lot of time doing creative writing in my spare time. I was able to apply those skills and experiences to my English work, as well as my longer answer questions in other subjects. Through all that, I've built up a keen interest and strong ability to write engaging texts on a wide range of topics, making me a good essay-writer. I would say this is my biggest strength in academia."

"My biggest strength in academia is essay-writing. I enjoyed writing through school and wrote lots of stories as a child. By the time I got to my GCSE's my experience and developed proficiency enabled me to excel in English, and at the longer-answer questions in other subjects. I have continued this success into my A-Levels, securing a really good grade in English."

Both of those answers highlight the same strength, but present it in a different way. The latter is for those who are more comfortable 'selling' themselves, the former for those who struggle more with that. One important thig to note is that moth answers highlighted this as being a strength in academia. If you are going to pick that, it is totally fine, but I would open with a statement that highlights it. The interviewers know that you are more than what you can do at school, so will often be looking for non-academic strengths to answer a question like this. If you highlight in the beginning that it is specifically an academic strength, then it prompts them to ask if you have considered a non-academic one too. If you have, feel free to explain that you opened with the one you did because it is your biggest strength, and then explain your other one.

If you want to go ahead and discuss a non-academic strength, of course feel free to do so! It is often easier to add personality in this way, but is sometimes harder to evidence how you have been strong. However, if you use a similar structure, you should be able to present it as a convincing strength.

Q43: How will your experiences from the Duke of Edinburgh scheme benefit you during your time at university?

This is a question that many interviewers will be keen to ask, if you have something like a Duke of Edinburgh mention on your CV/in your personal statement. It may sound a little like they are trying to belittle the achievement by asking it in a sarcastic way, or to try and trip you up. Rest assured that is not the case, they are simply interested to see how you view the skills you have acquired through the program, and how you would apply them to the entirely different environment of studying for a degree.

The key to answering this question well, while it seems obvious, is picking out genuinely applicable skills and experiences. This means valuing relevance over and above the extent of your experience/skill. If you try to shoehorn a skill to fit your university studies, just because it was a large focus of your scheme, your answer will come across ill-fitting. It is important to be prepared for a question like this because it is quite likely to come up, if it is something you have discussed in your personal statement or have on your CV, and it is something quite difficult to come up with off the cuff.

To establish will skill to select, it is best to consider what you have actually done compared to what you will be doing in your degree. If you spent time orienteering and doing crafts, that's not something that fits the bill, however big a part of the scheme it was or how much you enjoyed it. However, if you spent one of the nights up on your own, devising a plan of action and getting everything ready for the following morning, that is something that can be very easily applied to your degree.

"On the last night before our long walk, our team remained very disorganised and we still hadn't got a route fully together, or decided exactly what we needed to pack. I decided, rather than have a frantic rush in the morning, to work into the evening and night to prepare the map route and set up a packing list for each of our team. I had to do this on my own as the rest of my team were getting early nights, so had to rely on my own intuition and conviction behind my decisions. Even though I was tired the next day, I was happy that we were able to set off with a clear route and could have all of our things packed without having to think about whether anything important was missing. I think having to work late, on my own and being able to make those independent decisions has prepared me for the independent projects I will have to take on in my degree."

You could easily have continued the explanation further, regarding the applicability of skills and experience to situations in degree studies, but this demonstrates how you can apply the experience of one isolated event, better than you could trying to apply an irrelevant experience. Remember that the relevance is so much more important than the abundance. It is much easier to oversell how big a deal the event was, than oversell how applicable it is to your degree!

Q44: Why choose Oxford or Cambridge, if you know that other universities are less competitive, and may mark your work much more generously?

There are two ways to approach this question. You can answer successfully discussing one or both. The first point you could make is that you may not actually do better elsewhere. You will likely have spoken in that interview, previous interviews or your personal statement, about how the environment of your chosen university will give you the drive to push forward and excel. At a university where perhaps that drive is not present to the same degree, you may not be pushed in the same way. This is a tricky answer to phrase, as you don't want to come across like you are unable to self-motivate, but if you feel like it applies to you then convincingly portraying that self-awareness will be received well. However, if you don't feel confident discussing that, or it doesn't apply to you, then there is the bulk of the answer to approach.

When answering the main part of this question, you need to consider the value of the university beyond the grade on your degree. If you are confident in yourself that you can achieve a first class result regardless, then that's great. It wouldn't necessarily be the best structure to lead with that, as it would be easy for that to appear arrogant. However, it is a good way to round off your answer, if you are confident talking about that. Approaching the value of the university is all about understanding what it will bring you along the way. If you want to be an academic at that university, then the grade relative to any other university is not really relevant. If you want to learn about your field in the most all-encompassing way possible, then the grade you get is not really relevant to that part of the experience.

However, it is important to acknowledge that as something you have considered. Expressing that awareness will be well-received by an interviewer. The key is to balance it against the personal points you are making. You may wish to make those points after acknowledging your concern around the topic, or you may wish to save it until the end, rounding it off as something that has been weighed up and dismissed based on your conclusion. Most importantly, you should demonstrate that you have the self-confidence to know you can do well in any environment, and not feel the need to establish a different one.

Q45: Cambridge is very intense; do you think your current approach to time management will be sufficient?

There are lots of ways in which you can say you will manage your time. However, the interviewer is going to have heard them all before. The way to make your answer convincing and stand out, is to give evidence of where you have learned these techniques and where you have successfully applied them. It would be a good idea to pick a few techniques for organisation, stress management and timekeeping (although there will. Be some overlap with organisation), and prepare some examples for when these techniques have worked for you in the past. While it would likely make your answer too convoluted if you tried to do this for every technique, it can inject some personality into the answer if you talk about where you learned one of the techniques, particularly if the story is interesting!

"One challenge I am sure that I will face is having to prioritise work. In this sort of situation, it's important to manage explicit deadlines, as well as the importance of each piece of work. During sixth form, I have been a private tutor. Having to manage marking my students' work and completing my own has been very challenging at times. I have mostly chosen to prioritise my students' work, as I have already had discussions with my teachers and they are happy to be lenient with my deadlines, providing they are not exams or coursework!"

By giving a real and honest example of a difficult situation, you'll connect with the tutors a lot better than if you try to make something up on the spot. Once you have explained the situation and experience, as above, it is then important to explicitly apply this to your degree experience.

"From this experience, I am confident talking to tutors and asking them for help with my schedule. In order to stop myself getting too stuck, I would make sure I reach out to a tutor when in need, and ask them to extend my deadline. I would make sure that I am prioritising the work that leads on to future work, so that I don't fall behind on a series of pieces."

By demonstrating your understanding of how you might prioritise something, this gives the interviewer further evidence to suggest what you are saying is something you actually have had to do. In addition, you are showing the confidence to stand up for your decisions, even if that means asking for help.

Q46: What have you read in the last 24 hours?

As with any question that asks you directly about an event, honesty is the best policy. However, it is completely realistic to assume that you may not have read anything on the morning of your interview, or the night before apart from your interview preparation notes. With that in mind, consider this question to be asking more 'what have you read very recently', rather than specifically this morning. That is, unless you have the confidence to be fully honest when, by all means, be exactly that! If you are going to be entirely honest, just ensure that you're not wandering down the road of oversharing. Remember, while the interviewers are friendly and they want to have a pleasant conversation, they are still assessing you! Saying something like "I've actually not read anything in the last 24 hours, I've been a little busy, but just the other day I read some of *The Count of Monte Cristo* in my spare time" is a good way to remain honest while still giving the interviewer something to play off, and giving you something you can explore in depth.

You should make sure you discuss a text you have read recently, and ensure that your discussion is realistic. The interviewer is not going to believe that you have spent your entire morning reading the full works of a particular psychologist, or a novel from cover to cover! The best approach to picking a text is to have read something very recently in preparation for your interviews, and discuss that! If the text is relevant to your interviews, then there's no real reason to spend a lot of time highlighting its relevance. However, if the text is a little more unusual, then by all means explain its relevance to the interviews.

If you choose to discuss a text that has nothing to do with interviews, that's fine too! The interviewer will appreciate the fact that you're reading for pleasure, not just for work! However, the text you discuss should either have an element of psychology, or an element of personality to it, for maximum impact in the interview discussion. The more you can recall about what you read, the better. That's not to say you should go about reciting it verbatim, but it enables you to discuss its content with confidence. If you open with a single point about the text after a brief description of its context, the interviewer may ask you to expand or continue, in which case that gives you the starting point from which to begin your full discussion. If they don't respond in any way to your initial point, try to make you second point psychology related. It may be that they are simply interested to know what you have read recently; in which case they may not pry beyond your initial description. Don't worry either way, all interviewers are different in the way they will want to explore what you have read and how you interpret it.

Q47: What would you say was your greatest personal challenge in life? How did you handle it?

This question is supremely personal, and you should make your answer as such. In an ideal world, you will have had a challenge which comes to mind immediately and you will have no need to prepare any thought on it at all. However, in most people's lives, there are a large number of small challenges, rather than one outstanding one. In this case, the thought you should put into this question is regarding how you overcame one of those challenges. The interviewer is looking to understand a bit more about your background, and build knowledge on how you deal with difficult situations. If you have a challenge that was not quite as big as your biggest ever challenge, but you handled getting over it in a much better way, then that might be your better bet to pick!

As with any of these personal questions, depending on your confidence, you may choose to be 100% honest. It may be that the biggest challenge you have faced was one that you did not overcome well, one that may have beaten you. That is completely fine, as long as you talk about what you learned from that experience. It is no good discussing a difficult situation that wasn't handled well, and then simply going on with your life as if nothing happened! The interviewer will be looking for honesty, self-awareness, self-reflection and the ability to better yourself after a setback. It will be very common for you to come across aa seemingly impassable challenge in your degree, so the interviewer wants to know what experience you have dealing with that kind of situation.

If there is an element of independence to your overcoming of the challenge, highlight that it might be that due to not having the support you might have had in other situations, you didn't handle the challenge as effectively as you might have otherwise. That's fine, but highlight what you learned from the experience and how you would go about approaching it differently next time! It is vital that there is at least an element of self-reflection in your answer. It might be that the challenge happened very recently, and you haven't had enough tie to process it and become better at tackling situations like it. It might be that your biggest challenge was preparing for this interview! If this is the case, then make sure you reflect on that. Don't be afraid to put yourself on the spot to evoke some more honesty out of your answer.

There are three stages to a good answer in this question; situation, specific challenge (and why it was challenging) and what you did/would do next time to overcome it.

Q48: Do you think that the impact of a good teacher can stretch beyond the walls of a school? Who do you think was your best teacher?

Of course, it doesn't matter who your best teacher was, it certainly doesn't need to be the one who is teaching you the subject you're applying for! What matters is how you have assessed them to be your best teacher, and the extent to which you understand how they have influenced you. A poor answer is one that doesn't address any of these elements in any detail, as follows.

"My favourite teacher was my year9 maths teacher. She inspired me to do better in maths and got me from really struggling at the beginning of the year, to being almost top of the class by the end, and really enjoying it!"

A better answer, is one that considers each element of the question in some detail, with a degree of reflection into why you have the thoughts that you do. Below is an answer that does this.

"My favourite teacher was my yr9 maths teacher. She inspired me to do better at maths by simply letting me get on with it, my teachers in years before had always tried so hard to engage me in the lesson when working on the board, and as a shy student I just shrank away and disengaged from the lesson. As soon as I was left to my own devices, I realised I could do it when I wasn't put on the spot! Since then, my confidence grew a lot and by the end of the year I was asking to go through things on the board! I'm not sure how she knew to treat me differently than my previous teachers, but she definitely had more patience. Maybe she saw that my homework was always right but my classwork wasn't and put the pieces together to work it out!"

This answer demonstrates a real insight into why a teacher treated you how they did, and what the result of it was. It also implies that you are a good independent learner (which is always a bonus to slip into an answer!). When you are discussing why a teacher has treated you a certain way, it is important not to consider any of your own assumptions to be fact. Remember, the interviewer is likely also an educator, and they may see that your assumptions which you have made out to be fact, are likely wrong. It is, however, important that you outline what your views on how they treated you are, as even just the fact you are considering the reasons behind teachers' actions is a great way to better understand yourself and how you work best.

Q49: What are your long-term plans in life?

This question is incredibly open, and doesn't need to be answered like a 'where do you see yourself in x years' question. You can answer this question entirely unrelatedly to academia and work if you like. If your goal in life is to own your own home and have a family, say that! The important thing is to ground it around how this degree will help you get there. It could be something as simple as the degree with unlock doors in the job market that you wouldn't normally have been able to enter, or it could be that the degree will teach you how to work hard and independently, which will help you achieve things in later life. Whatever angle you approach it from, it is a great idea to include a piece about your degree studies.

However, you want to be honest with these plans as a question as open as this is a perfect opportunity for you to discuss something memorable to the interviewer. Maybe you have always wanted to be a clown, so working a job which pays well will enable you to go to clown school at the weekends and learn! It doesn't really matter what it is, as long as it's honest. If you start talking about something because you think it will be memorable, rather than because it is the truth, the interviewer will likely see right through you, so don't!

It is totally fine to have 'boring' aspirations, everyone's life is their own! If your aspirations in life are somewhat mundane, make that part of the explanation!

"I know it seems pretty mundane, but what I'd really like is to have a house, family and a stable job by the time I am thirty. This degree will teach me the skills I need to do well in the working world, unlock access to a job that I will enjoy, and enable me to earn the money I need to own my own home."

It isn't the most personality-injected answer, but if the above answer is honest then it is totally fine to go down that route! Obviously, if you have an honest ambition that is a little more whacky then discuss it, but don't feel like you have to make something up to be memorable! Honesty is the best policy, but try to make a link between whatever you're discussing and your degree studies. It doesn't have to be forced if it really doesn't work, but ideally you want your long-term plans to be tied into your degree, to some extent!

Q50: If you had to name your three greatest strengths, what would you pick?

This is a very open question. Because of this, it would be best to make at least one of these skills something to do with your degree and another something very personal to you. Beyond that, the floor is yours! When answering, for each skill you should explain what that skills is, where it originated, and how is has/will be useful to you. When talking about how it will be useful, that's where the degree studies bit comes in! Below is an example of how to outline one of these three skills.

"One of my top skills is my ability to type very fast and very accurately. I started typing pretty young because my mum worked from home and I used to use her keyboard to type fake emails while she was on her lunchbreak. I had to touch-type to a degree because I wasn't tall enough to see over her desk! When I started school, I used to get into accidents a lot so spent a few terms in various casts. Whenever that happened, I had to do all of my schoolwork on a laptop. Since starting sixth form, I've done all of my work on my laptop and have really honed my typing skills. These will definitely come in handy when writing essays, as I can much more easily and accurately write down citations!"

This answer brings some personality as it describes the origin of the skills, from an amusing childhood story to current working conditions in sixth form. If you are lucky to have a skill with such an extensive back story, then absolutely discuss it, even if perhaps you wouldn't consider it one of your top three skills! The clearest way to explore these three skills is to tell them as three individual stories, if you outline the skills first and go into the stories after, it will be too easy to get muddled and lose track of where you are. It would be great if you had skills which spread across a variety of disciplines. For example, in addition to the skill explained above, you could have one which relates to your social skills (e.g., recognising when someone is upset, even if they're trying to hide it) and one which relates to your physical ability (e.g., your proficiency at a certain sport). Of course, it would be all too convenient if that were the case, so don't try to bend the truth too much to get it to fit this model. It is better to be honest in a question like this, providing your answers have some degree of interest and relation to your subject!

Q51: How much should you charge to wash all the windows in London?

This question is not looking for an exact answer; instead the interviewer is inviting you to take them through your thought process as you make an estimate. Ultimately the tutorial experience is all about reasoning through often ambiguous or tricky problems, and this is an opportunity to demonstrate that you can do this.

A standard applicant might estimate the total surface area of windows in London, the average surface of windows washed per hour, and the hourly labour costs of window washing and use these to provide an answer. What will set a **good candidate** apart from a standard one is the quality of reasoning behind the numbers they come to. In this specific question, you would want to recognise that residential and commercial buildings, flats, and houses all have different numbers and sizes of windows. You may also want to consider other factors, such as London being a distinctly urban area, and windows potentially needing to be washed on both sides. Remember, these are just some possible considerations; there are all sorts of factors you could bring into the discussion.

For example, let us assume that there are 8 million people in London, and the average household is 2.5 people. This would mean that there are about 3.2 million households in London. You might then assume that the average number of windows across all residential and commercial buildings works out at 7.5 windows per household, and that the average surface area is 80cm by 50cm. To account for washing windows on both sides, you would multiply by 2 to give you the total surface area. Multiplying various decimals live might seem a bit daunting; feel free to round numbers where appropriate (and explain to the examiners why you are doing this). So in this example, you would calculate 3 million x 8 x 0.8 x 0.5 x 2 which would be about 19.2 million square meters of window.

From there you could discuss per hour labour costs, and the estimated surface area of windows you could wash per hour. Again, nuance is the key to making your answer stand out. Factors you might want to consider include (but are not limited to): skill required in window washing, cost of materials, cost of living in London, competition within the London window washing market, or whether the labour market is seasonal. Introducing these considerations offers you the opportunity to show not only that you are logical and rigorous, but also creative. To conclude this example, let us say you assume a wage of 10 pounds per hour, and 50 square meters of window per hour. This would give you a total cost of 3.84 million pounds.

A **weak answer** may have a very similar structure to a strong answer but lack the justification for numbers chosen. Other pitfalls to avoid include making simple calculation errors, and failing to use common sense when estimating numbers. For example by assuming that a population of 8 million people in London means that there are 8 million households. Avoid the temptation to be funny (e.g. answering "I have better things to do than wash windows"); this will not go down well.

Q52: How many piano tuners are there in Europe?

Although questions like this might seem initially daunting, the goal here is not to accurately estimate the number of piano tuners in Europe but rather to demonstrate clear, well explained reasoning.

In other words, a **good applicant** will offer sensible numbers backed up by a brief explanation as to how they chose these figures. For example, you could estimate that there are 750 million people in Europe, about 2.5 people per household, and therefore a total of 300 million households. Then by assuming that something like 1 in 50 households have a piano, you would estimate the number of pianos in Europe as around 6 million. Factors to consider when selecting these numbers could include how popular an instrument the piano is, or the cost of a piano. From there you could ascertain the number of piano tuners by dividing the average number of times people need their pianos tuned in a year by the number of pianos a piano tuner is able to tune in a year. When creating these numbers you could consider factors such as how long it takes to tune a piano, or how many days a year a piano tuner works (these are just a few examples, feel free to introduce your own ideas). For example, you could estimate that it takes a piano tuner 2 hours to tune a piano and they work about 8 hours a day, five days a week, for 50 weeks a year. This would amount to 1000 pianos per tuner per year. So, to carry out 5 million piano tunings you would need about 5000 piano tuners in Europe. Great answers could also introduce interesting considerations such as the potential impact of the increasing popularity of electric keyboards, and whether technological changes have led to an oversupply of trained piano tuners. Answers that contain deeper exploration like this help a candidate by showing nuanced, creative and forward-looking thinking.

A **poor applicant** will be thrown by the ambiguity of this kind of question and may just guess a number, or fail to use common sense or basic general knowledge; e.g. not offering even a rough idea of the population of Europe, or merely asserting the number of pianos tuned per year rather than estimating it logically. More generally, students should avoid the temptation to waffle when uncertain. What differentiates a weak from a strong answer, at least in part, is that the strong candidate will adopt a systematic and deductive approach to answering the question.

Q53: India introduces a new population control policy to address the gender imbalance. If a couple has a girl, they may have another child. If they have a boy, they can't have any more children. What would be the new ratio of boys to girls?

Obviously, the nature of this answer may vary substantially between applicants – a political scientist and a mathematician are likely to give very different answers. However, the essential thing is to be able to clarify and justify the assumptions that you are making when you answer this question.

For example, a **good quantitative candidate** might decide to discount any parental preference for one gender or the other, and assume that there is perfect compliance with the policy. From there, the candidate would note that every birth has a 50% independent probability of resulting in a girl and a 50% independent probability of resulting in a boy. This would mean that half of all families stop at one child, and the rest go on to have another child which also has a 50% chance of being a girl. Putting aside practical considerations, this process could repeat infinitely - although the probability of an unbroken chain of girls converges towards zero. The big thing to note here is that with each pregnancy the probability resets to 50/50. However, even when offering a quantitative answer the candidate should still acknowledge practical limitations (e.g. having infinite children is not possible).

By contrast, a **good humanities candidate** may choose to focus on questions of citizen preferences, and the state's ability to enforce policies. You could draw on your real-world knowledge to consider instances where similar policies have been implemented. For example, sex selective abortion is illegal in China and the number of children per household is restricted, yet there is still a gender imbalance. A weaker answer might use this evidence to simply conclude that the policy in India would be ineffective; a stronger answer would acknowledge that the policy would have some impact, but could use the example of China to argue that this may not be enough to make the gender balance 50/50.

More broadly, a **weaker answer** is likely to contain some of these elements but fail to identify key assumptions, or make implausible assumptions (e.g. parents having infinite numbers of children). Candidates who choose to use examples should also be wary of relying on anecdote rather than reasoning. For example, a weaker answer may use the example of China to discuss the effects of birth control policies on sex ratios, but simply argue that because sex ratios remain imbalanced in China they will do the same in India; it would be more useful to explore the similarities and differences between the two countries and their policy environment, rather than making a blanket correlation.

Q54: Why are manhole covers round?

As with many of the more unusual questions you may be asked, the key here is not to find the answer, but rather to demonstrate the ability to engage with ambiguous questions and reason logically. The key advice for questions such as this is to always try to tackle the question head on, engage with the hypothetical, and ask yourself why this specific question is being asked. This should hopefully help you to avoid the sort of woolly and non-committal answers that questions such as this often provoke.

A **strong candidate** would focus on the core of this question: what is distinctive about the circular shape (as opposed to, say, a square)? A good candidate will also avoid the trap of getting hung-up on the empirical question of whether all manhole covers are round – there is no need to go beyond an acknowledgement of this doubt. Focusing instead on the unique features of circles would allow the candidate time to offer a range of explanations as to why manhole might be round. Possible explanations could be that you do not need to worry about the orientation of a circle when replacing it back on to the hole, circles can be rolled which is useful since a manhole cover is usually heavy and made out of metal, or that round manhole covers are less likely to fall down the manhole. A great candidate will be able to specifically link this answer back to the purpose of a manhole. For example, the cover being easy to roll is likely to be important if you only have one person working on the manhole, or when a manhole is deep and so preventing things (people, or the cover) falling down the hole is very important.

A **weak answer** could take several forms. Candidates who attempt to debate whether manholes are all round, are unlikely to meet with much success. Although under certain circumstances disagreeing with the premise of a question can be a fruitful tactic, this rarely tends to be the case when the premise is a factual claim. Other weak approaches include offering a vague answer such as `tradition` or `culture`. Answers such as this one fail to engage with the core of the question; a good warning sign is that your answer could apply to a broad range of other questions. If this is the case, your answer is probably lacking in specificity.

Q55: How many times per day does a clock's hand overlap?

There many ways of getting the answer other than the one provided below; however, more important than the specific method is walking through the steps in your reasoning clearly and logically. This does not just demonstrate your thinking process to the interviewer, but will also help you to avoid making silly mistakes by jumping to an answer too quickly. If you find it hard to structure your thoughts in your head, consider taking a minute to write down your thought process on a piece of paper.

A **good answer:** On a 12-hour clock face the hour hand completes two full circles in a day, and the minute hand does a full rotation every hour; i.e. 24 rotations in a day. Having established these facts, one approach is to visualise the first time the two hands cross. If you start from midnight with the hands in the same position you would need to wait for at least one full rotation before they intersect. Since the hour hand is moving from midnight to 1am the intersection would be at roughly 1:05 (it would actually be a bit later since the hour hand would actually be at the 1 when the minute was at the 12). Now we know that the two hands cross at approximately 1.05 we can visualize the next overlap which would be when the hour hand is at about 2 and the minute hand is at about 10 minutes past (again the numbers are not quite exact). What you might notice here is that the overlaps happen at about 65 minutes intervals. There are 14400 minutes in a day (60 x 24), so if you divide 14400 by 65 you get a little over 22. Therefore the total number of overlaps would be 22.

As noted above, a **weak answer** may occur due to simple calculation error or trying to jump to the answer too quickly. For example: "The minute hand goes around the clock 24 times in a day, so it presumably crosses the minute hand once each time. So that would be 24." Many candidates may slip up on this question by choosing a seemingly obvious answer. The larger lesson to draw from this is that if a solution seems obvious, ask yourself whether it is likely that the interviewer would get any value from seeing you solve this problem. Not only the content, but also the brevity may be a warning sign that your answer is on the wrong track.

Q56: You are given 7 identical balls and another ball that looks the same as the others but is heavier than them. You can use a balance only two times. How would you identify which is the heavy ball?

Although questions like this may seem somewhat intimidating the best way to approach them is to start by slowly working step by step. You do not necessarily have to start with the correct method, but try to work towards it and rule out less useful approaches as you go.

A good candidate might start by noting that they do not know how much heavier the heavy ball is. From this information they can deduce that placing 3 balls on one side of the scale and 4 balls on the other may not give us precise enough information. Instead, for a more accurate approach we must start by placing an equal number of items on each side. If one places three balls on each side, then whichever side is heavier must include the heavy ball. However, if the balance is equal then the heavy ball must be the ball that was not placed on the scale. From here a candidate could deduce that either they had solved the problem, or they would need to repeat the experiment with the three balls on the heavy side of the balance. In this instance, the candidate would compare two of the balls from the heavier side and set the third ball aside. If either of the two balls on the balance was heavier we would have our answer, or if they were equal, the remaining ball that the candidate had set aside would be the heavier ball.

By contrast, **a weaker candidate** may use a process of trial and error instead of taking a step back, drawing conclusions from their thinking and using these new conclusions to inform their next move. Note that not all strong candidates will immediately come to the solution; the difference between the strong and the weak candidate is that a strong candidate will be able to course-correct as they go and spot the nature of their error, whereas a weak candidate may not be able to identify where they made a mistake.

Q57: What is your favourite number?

This question is a great opportunity for you to demonstrate enthusiasm for your chosen subject. For example, as a mathematician you may find a specific number theoretically interesting, as a historian you could pick a specific date, or as a biologist you might pick a number that represents an interesting phenomenon in the natural world (e.g. rate of bacterial reproduction). When answering the question, take care to pick something that you genuinely find interesting and can talk about at length, rather than something you think will sound impressive. Make sure the interviewer remembers you for the whole content of and justification for your answer, not just the opening line.

Although personal stories are unlikely to harm you, choosing your grandmother's birthday, a football player's jersey number or the numbers you always pick for the lottery is unlikely to strengthen your application. The important thing to remember when confronted with an unexpected question is to take a step back and think about how you can direct the conversation to something that will bolster your case for admission.

Finally, although it is important to draw in interesting content about your subject, a good candidate will also answer the question. A **weaker answer** might use the answer as a springboard to offer a prepared answer on an unrelated topic. For example, cite a historical date and then simply talk about their interest in that historical period. By contrast a **strong answer** might talk about the role numbers play in memory, or the importance of quantification in history. These answers are stronger because they focus on the core of the question and justify why the number is a relevant feature of the answer, rather than the number being an afterthought. Directly engaging with the question is important as it shows that you are responding authentically and in the moment, rather than seeming like a poor listener or an overprepared candidate.

Q58: Who am I? (Always read up on your interviewers!)

This is a good opportunity for a candidate to demonstrate they have thought about their college choice and know who the tutors in their subject area are; this is a chance to show that you are thoughtful and engaged with your chosen degree subject.

Good answer: 'You are Professor X, you work in the field of [biomedical science, economics, etc]. I think more specifically you work in the subfield of [human anatomy/microeconomics] and some of your research looks at [cerebral cortical development/auction theory]. I was really excited about applying to this college because, as I mentioned in my personal statement, I am particularly interested in [the role of cortical development in conditions such as dyslexia/the application of auction theory to public goods tenders].'

This is a good answer because it shows that the candidate has serious academic reasons for applying to a college, and has begun to develop interests within their subject area. Of course, this is contingent on these interests being real. Do not bring up research if you do not understand it; this is likely to lead to embarrassment! There are other ways to answer this question. For example, a tutor might state on their college webpage that they love working with undergraduates, or you may have seen them give an inspiring talk at an Open Day. These are also valid things to bring up about a tutor, as they have chosen to put this information in the public domain.

A **weak answer** could go in a lot of different directions. For example, the student might attempt to move in an excessively abstract direction (e.g. what is the nature of identity?) - this might be OK if you are in a philosophy interview, but less so for subjects like maths. Alternatively, the student may simply not know who the interviewer is. You will typically be interviewed by fellows at the college, so you should have the opportunity to have a look at their research. Additionally, you are normally told who your interviewers will be prior to the interview, which should give you an opportunity to look them up.

Q59: Is there any question that you wished we had asked you?

This question is a great chance to highlight an aspect of your application that you would like to talk about. For example, you may have written about a specific book on your personal statement that you think you can speak about further in an interesting manner, or you might have written an extended essay which demonstrates your interest in and understanding of a specific subject. Thanking the interviewers and expressing enthusiasm about the content can also be a nice touch. However, it is inadvisable to simply state your desire to go to Oxbridge, or launch into abstract declarations of your love for the subject. These should be demonstrated through actions not words; over the top displays of emotion are more likely to make an interviewer uncomfortable than convince them to admit you.

More commonly, however, what will differentiate a strong from a weak answer is not the topic but rather the manner in which you talk about it. For example, a **strong answer** should highlight an aspect of your application in a concise manner that directly underscores your commitment to the subject and shows intellectual maturity. However, you do need to make the case as to why you want to discuss this; it should not come across as simply a desire to introduce impressive things you have done. Ways to avoid this include explaining why a given activity demonstrates your curiosity about your subject, or perhaps an interest in the process of academic research.

A **weaker answer** could come in many different forms. Any answer that strays into boasting or flattery is unlikely to make a favourable impression. If you genuinely do not have any topics you would like to discuss it is fine to admit to this; interviewers know that the interview experience can be stressful and not all candidates (even strong ones) will relish the prospect of further interview questions!

Q60: What are you looking forward to the least at this college?

This is a question where you can be honest to a certain extent, but must remain balanced. **Poor answers** are likely to fall into one of two extremes; the 'fake problem' or the 'too blunt'. Interviewers are unlikely to believe the candidate who claims that they are least looking forward to a choice of modules because they wish they could choose everything (is that really the worst possible thing you could think of?). As a result, this attempt to avoid admitting to any negative or undesirable opinion risks coming off as insincere. However, veering too far in the opposite direction is also inadvisable. Saying you are worried about the workload before you have even arrived is likely to raise red flags and make interviewers wonder whether you will be able to cope with the pace of Oxbridge.

By contrast a **good answer** will strike a balance between sincerity and oversharing by stating a genuine concern - but ideally one that does not relate to academic concerns. For example, you could quite reasonably express concerns about financial stability, being able to find a common cultural community, or other similar considerations. If these are genuine concerns, they are things a college will be interested in knowing so that they can try to help solve them. If you are struggling to find an appropriate concern, while not ideal it is OK to say that you will miss your cat, home cooking, or that you are mostly very excited about going to university and so do not yet have anything you are very worried about.

Ultimately, this sort of question serves two functions for interviewers: it helps them to decide whether students are applying for the right reasons (academic work not college balls), but also to make sure that they are aware of applicants concerns. Colleges really do want to make themselves accessible and friendly places, so this is a time when it can be appropriate to raise a concern or question that may have been bothering you.

Q61: Who has had the largest influence on your life?

Questions such as these should be answered in a way that is first and foremost plausible, and secondly makes the case for you as a candidate. Ways you can make that case include demonstrating that your interest in your chose subject is deep and long-standing (i.e. you didn't apply on a whim and you have specific subject interests).

Weak answers may come from candidates too eager to impress interviewers with their passion for their subject. Very few people are likely to believe that Marie Curie has had more influence on your life than a family member, or caregiver. It is important to remember that seeming genuine is just as important as seeming intelligent (if not more so). Other ways candidates can provide weak answers include being too laconic, or unreflective. Failing to relate the answer to your current subject interests, while not something that is likely to be penalised, might be a bit of a missed opportunity.

Explanation is the key to a **good answer**. For example, you might quite plausibly be able to say that your mum has been the biggest influence on your life, briefly discuss non-academic ways in which she has influenced you and then discuss how she has had a role in your intellectual development. Maybe she encountered problems when finding work that made you want to become an economist to better understand the labour market. Perhaps at a certain point she stopped being able to answer your questions about the world, and as a result you wanted to become a biologist. Ultimately, the connection you make will depend on both your subject and your chosen person. Of course, sometimes a connection to your degree will not be obvious, and that is fine. It is better to have a natural seeming answer than forcing a subject matter connection where none exists, and running the risk of seeming disingenuous.

Q62: If you were me, would you let yourself in?

Although some people might feel a temptation to answer 'no' to stand out, this is not the time for being wacky. Instead, treat this as an opportunity to advocate for yourself while also addressing any perceived weaknesses you might have. Each candidate will vary in the traits that make them distinctive, so answers will differ substantially between candidates. However, a **strong candidate** should start by considering qualities that Oxbridge might look for in a candidate, and then assess themselves against this framework. Not only does this directly answer the question, but also demonstrates to the interviewer that the candidate is a structured and rigorous thinker.

For example, you might start by defining a 'good' candidate as having both a deep interest in their subject, and academic aptitude. You might then illustrate your interest in your subject by referring to your personal statement and extra-curriculars. This could include addressing any weakness (e.g. mixed GCSE results) with reference to a mitigating or balancing factor (e.g. a strong focus on science subjects, and strong predicted A-levels). Any suggestion that a weakness is either acceptable or irrelevant should be backed up by a plausible explanation; if you believe that an explanation will simply sound like an excuse, it may be better to not raise it at all.

A **poor candidate** may have woolly reasoning or be unable to explain what makes them distinctive - many candidates will have excellent marks and a good personal statement. It is also inadvisable to speak negatively about other candidates (even in broad brush terms). For example, I am X unlike all of Y who are the same. You can make points about your own distinctiveness without coming across as mean-spirited or negative. Remember that these interviewers will have to teach you; they do not just want to know you are clever, they also want to know that working together will be an enjoyable experience.

Q63: What do you think my favourite colour is? Why do you say that?

Although many questions offer the opportunity to demonstrate your interest in your subject, in certain circumstances you may have trouble doing so naturally. Again, answering the question and demonstrating good listening skills is key. In situations such as these, rather than offering a tangential and canned answer, think of critical thinking strengths you can highlight through your answer. In this instance, good deductive reasoning and clear communication can help you demonstrate to your interviewer that you are a clear and logical student who will fare well in tutorials.

A **good answer** may discuss how a favourite colour might influence someone's clothing or room decoration choices. This would not be simple reasoning, such as "people will wear their favourite colour", but would introduce nuance by considering limitations to the evidence that they are using. For example, if you really like bright pink or bright green you might not wear that colour in a professional setting, or just limit it to somewhere inconspicuous such as a tie, or a pair of socks. Importantly, although a good answer will consider limitations to reasoning it *should* come to a conclusion. A candidate who twists themselves in knots of uncertainty will come across as a messy thinker who is not able to weigh competing pieces of evidence. By all means acknowledge weaknesses in your logic or contradictory evidence, but you should offer a guess.

A **weak answer** might suffer from a lack of nuance; or conversely a candidate may be so aware of the limitations of their reasoning that they offer a long-winded reply that ultimately comes to no conclusion. Other pitfalls include coming across as combative or annoyed by a seemingly irrelevant question. Although the interview experience can be stressful, being polite and upbeat is key; these are people you will have to work with.

Q64: What is a lie? How do I know what you just said isn't a lie?

In questions that ask you to offer definitions of complex concepts, a great way to start is by using examples to explore your initial intuition. Interviewers are unlikely to expect you to have a ready-made definition; many of these concepts are the subject of intense academic debate! What *is* important, however, is showing that you are a creative thinker who can course-correct and explore their own thinking in a structured manner.

For example, a **strong candidate** might start with a definition such as "a lie is a statement that is knowingly false", and then use specific examples to test whether this definition fits across a range of contexts. For example, what does it mean to lie to oneself? What is the role of intent in the definition of lying? Are 'white lies' still lies? These are just a few examples of questions a candidate might raise, and there are no definitive right or wrong answers. Instead, the important feature of a good answer is that a candidate can navigate from the intellectually abstract definition to a concrete situation with fluency, demonstrating both strong conceptual thinking and an ability to drive their own intellectual process. The use of examples is a great way to do this because it allows you to ground your answer in everyday experience and may help you to tease out weaknesses or contradictions in your thinking. Again, coming to a conclusion (or at least a specific definition) is critical to a good answer. You can certainly acknowledge weaknesses or uncertainties, but a good candidate should be able to weigh evidence and come down on a side.

By contrast, a **weaker candidate** is likely to be less reflective about the quality of their own answer, and perhaps rush to a conclusion (or be unwilling to come to one at all). One mistake that candidates often make is thinking that an interview is a debate; that they are obliged to stick to and defend their original statements. In fact, it is often a great idea to let your position evolve if you change your mind. Tutors are looking for people who are open-minded and intellectually flexible.

Q65: If you could keep objects from the present for the future, what would they be?

Rather than taking this as a whimsical or warm up question, use this as an opportunity to highlight your passion for your subject. This will naturally vary from candidate to candidate, but the broad lesson is that even seemingly off the wall questions can be used to strengthen your case for admission.

A **good answer** from an historian might, for example, highlight their thoughts about the importance of sources to future generations of historians. A biologist may be interested in species preservation and want to keep a patch of the Amazon. In instances where material objects might be less relevant to your subject (e.g. as an economist, or a theoretical physicist), you could show creativity by suggesting an item emblematic of a phenomenon you find interesting (e.g. promotional material from the sharing economy, or the computer used to carry out complex calculations).

A **weaker answer** could take many different forms, but failing to relate your answer to your subject or poorly justifying your choice are common errors. Many weak answers use the same examples as stronger ones, but simply fail to fully explain why they selected the item. For example, a biologist simply saying "I would preserve a tree in the Amazon because I think that the biodiversity in underexplored areas of the rainforest is enormous, and I think deforestation might eradicate our chances to access this knowledge" does not fully demonstrate that the candidate understands what they are talking about. Their answer remains very general and does not specify what sort of information they are concerned about preserving. A candidate in this position could easily strengthen their answer by drawing on examples of findings they have read about, thus demonstrating that their example is not a vague concern about the environment but rooted in specific knowledge indicative of a deep curiosity about their subject.

Q66: What is more important – art or science?

As with many abstract questions, a **good answer** will offer clear reasoning, an acknowledgement of alternative positions, and an explicit conclusion. For example, you may believe that *generally speaking* science is more important than art because science is central to material improvements in people's well-being. You might then acknowledge some weaknesses in this position, e.g. that this is not true of all science (certain forms of pure mathematics have no known practical application), or that art can be critical to social or moral progress. Finally, do offer a rebuttal (e.g. physical life is the basis of all other values and so although art is important, medical advances are necessary to enjoy art). These are just a few examples of arguments that could be raised, and a compelling case could be made on either side.

A **weaker answer** may offer the same general reasoning as the strong answer, but simply fail to offer much justification. Another common trap is listing the advantages and disadvantages of both disciplines but failing to explain how you weigh these different considerations. This is a question that may arouse strong feelings in many candidates who want to demonstrate their interest in their chosen subject; however, you should be careful about coming across as brow beating, or arrogant. Even if you – as a scientist – believe that art can only exist because of scientific progress, there are ways to explain this view without seeming dismissive of something that many others value enormously. The same applies to humanities students who believe that life only has meaning due to art – beware of sounding pretentious! Once again, always remember that your interviewer may tutor you in the future, so coming across as friendly and open-minded is just as important as seeming clever. Launching into a tirade is more likely to make you seem unreflective than passionate.

Q67: If you could have one superpower, which one would it be? Why?

Seemingly random questions can often be used as an opportunity to talk about your interest in your subject. One way of answering this question would be to think of a problem that you face in your field, and select a superpower that would help you resolve it. Obviously, omniscience might do this, but probably also makes for a less interesting answer.

As with other questions of this variety, what will differentiate a good answer from a weak answer is not the topic chosen, but rather the explanation given. For example, a historian could talk about their desire to time travel; but what would distinguish a good answer from a weak or commonplace one would be the justification. For example, a **weaker candidate** might simply say "I am interested in Napoleonic history so I would love to be able to observe the Battle of Waterloo". While the candidate may talk specifically what they would like to see and demonstrate strong understanding of Napoleonic history, enthusiasm for historical facts is not the same as showing a scholarly approach.

By contrast, a **strong candidate** might discuss their desire to go to a specific period and then relate this to an interest in collecting oral history sources. In an answer such this, the student not only explains their reasoning and relates it to a specific personal interest, but they also display good knowledge of the problems scholars of their subject might face. All of this suggests a mature thinker who would do well at university.

Although a time travelling historian might seem like an obvious example, similar answers can come from a variety of disciplines. A physicist might want to be able to observe unobservable events, a biologist might want eyes with the power of microscopes. Ultimately this sort of question is very open to interpretation and the strength of the answer will lie in the justification.

Q68: Would you ever go on a one-way trip to Mars? Why/why not?

As ever, you should treat every question as an opportunity to highlight why you would be a good candidate for admission. Even questions such as this, which may appear to be utterly random, can often be related back to your chosen subject. However, it is also fine to inject human concerns into your answers; it is always important for your reply to seem natural.

For example, a **good answer** from a biologist might talk about their desire to know more about microbial life on Mars, and their interest in the findings of the Mars Curiosity Rover, but ultimately conclude that they would rather rely on earth-based study than abandon their family. The student expresses enthusiasm for their subject, but also sets out quite reasonable limits on what they are willing to sacrifice for science. This honesty may come across as more credible than the candidate who claims that they would be willing to abandon their family and friends. A word to the wise: if you do raise specific examples (e.g. microbial life) then be certain that you can talk about them in more depth if probed. For non-STEM candidates, a clear relationship to your subject may be harder to draw; but creative thinking should allow you to find one. For example, historians might draw parallels with prior explorers of the globe, and philosophers could establish an ethical framework for evaluating such a choice. However, even if you cannot think of a link to your subject, remember to offer clear reasoning and a conclusion.

A **weak answer** could fall into any of the pitfalls mentioned above. Although it is fine to answer that one would indeed take a one-way trip, making sweeping claims such as "I love physics so much I would abandon my family and live alone on Mars" may ring somewhat hollow. Other weak answers may simply fail to grasp the opportunity to relate their thinking back to their subject. While this is unlikely to actively harm the your chances, it would be a missed opportunity.

Q69: Does human nature change?

Questions which ask candidates to discuss abstract concepts are a great opportunity to demonstrate to your interviewer that you are a structured thinker, who can engage with high level concepts and not get muddled. To answer this question well, the candidate needs to explore what people mean by the term 'human nature'. The candidate may also want to explore what is meant by the term 'change', and under what circumstances their answer might vary.

A **good candidate** might, for example, discuss whether the use of the term 'nature' implies some unchanging essence. There are a variety of strategies a candidate could adopt to do this effectively, including looking at examples of when people use the term 'human nature' and what they tend to be explaining when they do this. Alternatively, the candidate may want to provide a direct definition of human nature (e.g. the basic motivations of all homo sapiens). Strong candidates will also seek to define the parameters of their answer. Rather than simply providing a yes or no conclusion to their answer the candidate may offer a qualified response, e.g. "Yes, human nature can change over time, but a single individual cannot change their nature". While this is just an example, answers such as these show to the interviewer that the candidate has thought deeply about their answer and is able to generate a rigorous conceptual framework on the fly.

Weaker answers are likely to fall into one of a few different traps. Some candidates mistake conversations such as these for a debate and try to defend their instinctive initial answer; however, this can often come across as intellectual inflexibility, or arrogance. Showing willingness to engage with new ideas and revise your own when confronted with (reasonable) criticism can be a strength. Other candidates struggle with the lack of structure provided by this question and will throw out a range of possible considerations but be unable to draw them together into any coherent answer. Taking a minute before answering the question to jot down some thoughts can be a good way to give your answer more structure.

Q70: Define 'success' in one sentence.

This question, like many of the more abstract questions asked, is an opportunity for the candidate to showcase the quality of their thinking when confronted with an unfamiliar topic. Beyond simply showing clear and logical reasoning, candidates can also excel by using this question as an opportunity to emphasise their passion for their subject through their choice of examples.

For example, **a good candidate** might start with an initial definition that is further refined as they reason out loud. One way to do this would be work through a few examples to test whether the definition of success they came up with holds true in each case. An answer would be enhanced if the examples the candidate chooses not only draw on their subject matter expertise, but are also a little unusual. For example, an art historian could, of course, discuss whether Van Gogh (who died in penury) can be considered a success; but this is an example even a non-subject specialist might come up with. By contrast, selecting an artist from a period the candidate mentioned in their personal statement would allow them to demonstrate that their interest has real depth to it.

As with many with many of these abstract questions, a **weak answer** to this question is likely to be caused by a lack of structure, or under-explanation. A good answer and a weak answer may start off with the same definition; but where the quality of the answers will diverge is in the explanation of how a candidate came to that answer. A weaker candidate may offer examples of success as evidence, whereas the good candidate will use examples to pick out specific features of what could and could not be called success. Returning to the Van Gogh example, the strong candidate might point to the tension between the lack of recognition during his lifetime and his subsequent acclaim, and then examine whether or not we would call him a success if he had been famous during his lifetime and then forgotten. By contrast, the weaker candidate's exploration may be limited to noting that 'success can happen outside of your lifetime'.

Q71: Is there such a thing as truth?

Applicants can adopt one of two strategies to answer this question well. As ever, students can draw examples from their own subject to illustrate their answer; for example, mathematicians might want to talk about proofs, and historians might want to talk about source reliability. Alternatively, students can take this as an opportunity to simply show clear reasoning, and good verbal expression. The best applicants may be able to combine these two approaches.

A **good candidate** might start with a simple answer that they explicitly state they plan to refine. An example of such an answer would be "I think there is such a thing as truth, and I will define truth as a statement that describes a situation that exists or has existed in the world". From there, the candidate might use situations which appear to be truthful but do not cohere with this definition to examine whether it is possible to come to a meaningful definition of truth. For example, they might examine whether statements which are mildly inaccurate can be called truth and whether it is possible to make truly accurate statements (e.g. can we say that 'the cat jumped on the table five minutes ago' is a lie, if the cat jumped on the table 6 minutes ago?). Good candidates will also note that certain domains might have 'truth' and others might not. For example, do moral or aesthetic statements have truth value?

A **weaker applicant** is likely to offer a less thoughtful answer. The weakest answers are likely to be characterised by brevity: "Yes, because I can say that this chair is here, and it is. That's a true statement". Although you may believe this to be true, it is always worth fleshing an answer out by exploring where you could be wrong. Less obviously weak answers are likely to suffer from a lack of structure. It is very possible for a candidate to raise a few interesting thoughts but fail to explore them comprehensively or organise them well. While intellectual promise is helpful, without clear explanation a candidate's answer may simply be interpreted as scattershot.

Q72: You are shrunk down so you're the size of a matchstick and then put into a blender with metal blades. It is about to be turned on – what do you do?

This question can be used to demonstrate all sorts of different skills, from creativity to analytical thinking, and could even show how you are able to apply subject knowledge to an unusual problem. The physicists, biologists, and engineers out there may want to ask clarifying questions about the scenario to gain more information, such as the density of the shrunken human body. If you can explain why these questions are relevant and how they influence your answer, then ask away – it is often an excellent way to engage.

For those for whom there may be no obvious subject connection, a **good candidate** could simply work through the problem by breaking it down into component pieces. As with any non-traditional question there is no single correct way of doing this. For example, certain candidates might identify that there are two solutions: break the machine or avoid the blades. They could then discuss which of these two solutions would be more likely to succeed and then select that solution. Other equally successful candidates might consider whether someone is trying to blend them intentionally - and if not, how someone so small might be able to attract the attention of the person about to turn on the blender. Candidates are, of course, also expected to show basic common sense; just because a situation is fantastical does not mean that they can posit absurd solutions. Candidates should try to consider realistic features such as the centrifugal force of the blades, or strength of the machine relative to someone the size of a matchstick.

Weaker candidates are less likely to be let down by the content of their answers, than by the lack of enthusiasm, intellectual curiosity, or flexibility that they demonstrate. Note that even the good candidate may not find a satisfying solution to this (rather strange) problem; but what they will do is explore a variety of ideas, and demonstrate the ability to evaluate their own thought process while remaining engaged with the interview.

SUBJECT INTERVIEWS

Subject interviews are where subject-specific questions are asked to test critical thinking and problem-solving skills. These interviews are very likely to follow the format of tutorials/supervisions. You will be interviewed by one or two senior academics from the college you applied to. They will be experts on the subject you've applied for and will ask academic questions around a central theme. **The questions are intended to be difficult** so as to push you and test your critical thinking abilities in a learning situation. You are not meant to know the answers, but to use your existing knowledge to offer creative and original thoughts to address the questions.

Here are some general tips to keep in mind:

- Apply the knowledge you have acquired at A-Level and from your wider reading to unfamiliar scenarios.

- **Stand your ground if you are confident in your argument**- even if your interviewers disagree with you. They may deliberately play the devil's advocate to see if you are able to defend your argument.

- However, if you are making an argument that is clearly wrong and are being told so by the interviewers - then concede your mistake and revise your viewpoint. Do not stubbornly carry on arguing a point that they are saying is wrong.

- Remember, making mistakes is no bad thing. The important point is that you address the mistake head on and adapt the statement, with their assistance where necessary.

- The **tutors know what subjects you have studied at A-Level** so don't feel pressured to read EVERY aspect of your subject.

In the chapters that follow, each humanities subject is discussed in detail – including common types of questions and model solutions to previously asked interview questions. This book is not intended to be an exhaustive list of all that you need to know for your Oxbridge interview (if that's even possible!). Instead, it is designed to guide your learning by exposing you to the style and difficulty of questions that might come up and how to best approach them.

ECONOMICS

This interview will require you to demonstrate passion and a genuine desire to study your chosen subject. You can be asked to discuss a source extract, a diagram or a mathematical problem.

In E&M interviews, business-related questions will also feature, where applicants have to tackle basic problems related to the operation and management of a firm.

An economist may be asked economics-related questions or questions from a related subject, such as mathematics, business or even politics and history. An applicant for Economics and Management will be asked questions on both economics and business/management. (The **interviewers understand applicants may not have studied economics** before – be prepared to explain why you think you want to study economics and show through extra-curricular reading or activities how you've fostered your interest). Before the interview, it should be clear which subject will be the focus of any interview.

Candidates are not expected to have studied the subject they are applying for previously at A-level. Instead, candidates should have good general knowledge and to demonstrate interest in and enthusiasm for studying economics (and business in the case of E&M applicants), to demonstrate logic and critical thinking, and to communicate clearly and effectively.

Many of the questions asked in the interview will be a larger question, with many smaller sub-questions to guide the answer from the start to a conclusion. The main question may seem difficult, impossible or random at first, but take a breath and start discussing with your interviewer different ideas you have for breaking down the question into manageable pieces. Don't panic. **The questions are designed to be difficult** to give you the chance to show your full intellectual potential. They will help guide you to the right idea if you provide ideas for them to guide.

This is your chance to show your creativity, analytical skills, intellectual flexibility, problem-solving skills, and your go-getter attitude. Don't waste it on nervousness or a fear of messing up or looking stupid.

For economics, the questions will usually take one of a few possible forms based on highlighting skills necessary to 'think like an economist'. The six main question types are:

- Critical reasoning questions ("Tell me what your view on … is").
- Normative questions ("Should the government do the following?").
- Practical questions ("How would you determine that…").
- Statistical questions ("Given this data…").
- Questions about proximate causes (mechanism; "How does…") and MultiMate causes (function; "Why does…"), usually both at once.
- Quantitative questions for example from game theory or economic principles.

The questions also have recurring themes because they are also prevalent topics for economic and management theory and research: markets, money, development economics, profit maximisation of a firm, game theory, unemployment and inflation, growth theory and international trade.

WORKED QUESTIONS

Q1: I'm going to give you £50. You have to offer some of it to another person, but you won't get to keep a penny unless they accept the offer, with that in mind, how much of your £50 would you offer to them?

This is a mathematical question that will, therefore, require a numeric answer. The most important feature of a strong candidate is the ability to answer the question directly and from an analytical point of view the interviewer set through the phrasing of the question.

Applicant: So, I'm looking for a nominal value between 0 and £50 to be offered to the other person. This seems to be a question related to the field of game theory; the area that focuses on understanding optimal strategic decisions and their modelling. Unfortunately, I'm not familiar with the tools of this discipline but I will try to tackle the question using my basic economic intuition and mathematics. I understand that economics primarily deals with incentives, and here the two participants have very different incentives. Let me consider both of them and then outline who will get their way or what kind of a compromise they will reach. Both me and the other person want to get as much money as possible, but we both can't get the £50, **there is a trade-off**.

We also have different ways of achieving our aims: I set the amount, the other person decides whether to accept or not. The other person can stop me from having any money whatsoever; this seems to be a strong tool against me. So I will have to make the other person happy otherwise we will both walk away without anything. Given this, how can I get the best outcome for myself while navigating through my dual objective: getting money, but satisfying the other one? I have to give the person something, even though I don't want to.

Anything I give should make the other happy since the alternative is 0. Therefore, mathematically, I should probably offer the least amount: £1. But would that be acceptable? At this point, I could consider other, alternative methods to understanding cooperation that can better deal with phenomena like envy, fairness, altruism, etc.

Assessment: The student immediately sets the context and frame of the question, which suggests a very strong candidate who is not trying different things but knows the direction of the answer. Identifying the relevant area in Economics for the question is a nice touch that doesn't require extensive prior knowledge of that particular field, but still shows that the student has a general understanding of what belongs to the subject. The interviewers don't expect you to be an expert in a niche field. Instead, they want you to apply your existing knowledge and experience to a new problem.

A good candidate will always **draw from multiple disciplines** and apply the seemingly most relevant knowledge they have. Structuring the answer is always key, most importantly, to make it easier for the interviewer to help with the solution. If they know what the plan of attack is, they can guide the applicant in the direction that leads to the correct answer most easily. An outstanding candidate goes beyond conventional wisdom and demonstrates real outside-the-box thinking by having the ability to challenge seemingly fundamental assumptions. In this particular example, the candidate could point out that there are many people to whom getting the highest amount of monetary gain might not be a primary goal, hence making the simple mathematical analysis problematic.

Q2: You've mentioned globalisation in your personal statement, how would you define it, and what would you say the benefits of it might be to ordinary people?

The main challenge in this question is clearly the broadness of the topic. This is a subject hundreds of academics and other pundits have written hefty books on. How does one answer this question in 2-3 minutes so the response has sufficient content but is still structured?

The important thing to keep in mind here is that sometimes the applicant's first response serves only as a discussion starter. There is no need to include everything you would want to talk about in excruciating details, the interviewers only want to hear a few points they can start from. Then they will drive the discussion in a direction they want to.

Applicant: Let me start by clarifying the concept of globalisation. It's a household concept by now, but I'm not sure we have a universal agreement on what is meant by it. To me, globalisation is the process through which national and regional borders become increasingly irrelevant, as a result of culture, business and general economic activity all become more homogeneous and are formed by actors unrelated to any single country. This definition allows me to capture the different aspects of globalisation each of which requires a different analytical perspective: sociology, economics, politics, international relations, etc.

From an economics point of view, **the average citizen gains in two main ways from globalisation**. First, the citizen benefits from the diversification of products and services available for consumption at lower prices. Second, the broadening of opportunities allows citizens to have a better match between their skills and their occupation.

I will first consider the benefits of free trade. The emergence of transnational corporations and wider political movements supporting globalisation have put increasing pressure on governments to allow for greater freedom in international trade. This has resulted in an unprecedented expansion of consumption goods and services available for all customers. Just think about all the exotic fruits, spices, and craft goods one can buy even in their local Tesco. International competition, another benefit of globalisation, has furthermore allowed all goods to be priced competitively on a global scale, leading to significant price drops. This process clearly benefits the average citizen.

My second point relates to the tendency that globalisation comes with the **expansion of cross-border mobility** too. This happens for a range of reasons: better and more easily available information about opportunities abroad, the internationalisation of communication (English as lingua franca) and the transnational HR procedures and multinational corporations. The average citizen benefits from being able to find a position more ideally suited for them than before globalisation had emerged.

Having said that, I believe it's important to note the likely negative consequences of globalisation too: the threat of dumping in developed countries, the threat of exploitation in developing countries or diminishing cultural diversity are just a few on the list.

Assessment: The interviewers most likely have already interrupted the interviewee by this time somewhere. They might be interested in a discussion on free trade, the applicant's thoughts on multinational corporations, etc. But by presenting a clearly outlined structure in the beginning, the applicant ensured that the interviewers know that a strong and well-argued presentation would follow had they not interrupted. It is also advisable with such a complex question to take some time before starting the answer, this allows any applicant to articulate any thoughts in a more organised manner. A focus on the economic arguments is also important as this is an economics and not a sociology interview, and the points, therefore, need to be chosen accordingly.

Q3: I'm going to show you a teapot. Feel free to examine it in as much detail as you'd like - once you've done that, tell me about whether you could value it.

An odd question that clearly is not interested in specific knowledge, but rather pushing the applicant way out of their comfort zone. A question like this can easily appear on both an Economics and a Management interview as it requires out-of-the-box thinking and independence to solve challenging, unfamiliar problems, crucial in both fields. Each student would answer this question differently; the only important point is to show confidence and originality in an answer.

Straight Economics Applicant:

I can certainly look for a suitable price for this teapot from my perspective. However, the valuation different individuals assign to the same product often vary significantly and also with changing circumstances too. Therefore, my monetary valuation is not going to be a universal one.

I would start by stating that the monetary value of the teapot will fundamentally be linked to the concept of a market. I am not looking for the intrinsic value (i.e. the 'usefulness' of the teapot) but the ideal monetary amount it should be exchanged for. Thus I turn to the basic knowledge I have about the market and try to understand how those will determine the optimal exchange price of the teapot. There are two key factors on a market: supply and demand. I will consider both of them in relation to our example.

I know that if goods are supplied widely, its prices or monetary value will be lower than of goods in limited supply. Consider the example of water vs. diamonds. It's not that diamonds are more 'useful' than water, but that they are only available in a very limited amount; hence their supply is constrained. Whereas, water is essential for life but is abundant in supply. Consequently, diamonds have a much larger monetary value than water. In our case, a teapot can probably be bought in any large department store, however, its cracks and tea marks on its side make it unique. Therefore, one could argue that the supply of this teapot is extremely limited, indicating a high monetary price.

Equally, demand for the teapot is also probably fairly limited. While these qualities are visually pleasing, it is probably fair to assume that there aren't many who could appreciate its artistic beauty. Modest demand suggests a low monetary value, as people would not be willing to pay much for the item. This **concept of willingness-to-pay** is a central one for our analysis, and we would have to conduct a more thorough investigation into the existing demand for an artistically cracked teapot.

The two sides (supply and demand) put together suggest that **this teapot should be valued similarly to other niche products** with both small demand and supply. Such products include pieces of art, rarities or unique luxury products (e.g. custom made sports cars or watches).

Assessment: This is an economist's take on the question who tries to analyse the problem with the tools provided by the discipline. The question provides a great opportunity to enter a discussion on markets and prices, complemented by a basic summary of the forces present on a market. With such a question, a specific, numeric answer is not necessarily required as the process of understanding the determinants of prices is much more important. A clear outline, clarification of definitions and real life examples all add to the answer and the image communicated to the interviewers. But once again, many alternative answers could be presented here. The important point is that the applicant shouldn't feel intimidated by a seemingly unrealistic and unsolvable question.

Finally, if the starting point of the question is already ridiculous, then the applicant is free to make unrealistic assumptions too, as long as those can be defended somehow (e.g. the artistic cracks on the teapot add extra monetary value to it).

Economics and Management Applicant:

From a firm's perspective, it is crucial to understand the underlying processes that determine the monetary value of a product. In our situation, the monetary value is equivalent to finding the price of the teapot. I am going to consider three methods to establish that value:

- Pricing based on competition
- Pricing based on cost
- Psychological pricing

The first method seems to be the most obvious to me as it simply builds on the competitive tendencies in a market. This would require us to look at any other seller of similar teapots and record their prices. Afterwards, we simply have to decide if we want to undercut them or simply price it according to their set monetary valuations. Online retailers and, in this particular case, used goods' resellers can both provide a starting point.

Secondly, I could simply figure out how much it costs me to produce it if I'm a decision-maker in the company involved in the creation of the product. Then I would add some profit margin on my costs and that would give me the monetary valuation of the teapot. The **production costs,** in this case, could include raw materials (porcelain, paint, etc.), labour costs, electricity, rent for the workplace and so on. A profit margin is required to make it worthwhile running the business and provide a payout to the company's owners.

Finally, I have read about behavioural economics before, for example in the book *Freakonomics* or in *Predictably Irrational*. These books showed me, how psychological factors play a crucial role in our perceptions of prices. The idea about the **relativity of prices explains the lack of a fundamental link between products and their monetary value**.

Therefore, the **prices of this teapot could be anything in a wide range**, depending on the psychological connections I create, through procedures such as *anchoring*.

Assessment: The student always has to tailor the answer to the subject of the interview. One of the most important requirements on an interview is to show that the applicant is capable of analysing problems from the perspective of the given discipline. Thus, in this case, the student had to demonstrate the ability to consider the firm's view, collecting thoughts around basic concepts that an applicant might be familiar with: costs, competition, etc. The brightest candidates shine through their ability to complement the basic materials with extra reading and real life examples.

Q4: Considering recent events, do you think that the creation of the Eurozone was a good idea?

A good response: "For me, the main objectives of the Eurozone were to improve trade between European nations and to provide more economic stability for those nations involved. I think the European Union has been successful in the first of these goals, however, when addressing the latter, it is clear that the last two decades have been rather turbulent for all Eurozone countries, especially considering the issues with the COVID-19 vaccine rollout. Proponents of the Euro may argue that weak nations such as Greece would never have survived the economic crisis of 2008 without the presence of the Eurozone, but others may argue that a lack of control over individual countries' monetary policy contributed to the severity of the recession. One interesting aspect of the Eurozone process is that it has highlighted the high geographical mobility of labour in many European nations…"

Assessment: This is an extremely open-ended question, which provides the candidate with the opportunity to talk about a multitude of topics and issues. It is easy to get side-tracked with such an unstructured question, but the applicant should make sure they answer the question. However, there is potential for them to talk about areas that interest them, and display their enthusiasm for the subject in doing so.

Candidates should, however, be wary about trying to suggest they have a substantial knowledge of areas that they don't, in reality, know much about.

This question may be followed up with further questioning by the interviewer on more specific aspects of the questions, and the least helpful thing a candidate can do when trying to impress a tutor is falsify knowledge of certain topics and then get 'caught out' doing so.

It is worth bearing in mind that not only is the tutor looking for intelligence; **they are looking for someone that they are happy to teach for the next few years**. Personality can be a factor in determining their decision: arrogance or attempting to deceive a tutor may not be looked upon fondly.

Q5: What would you say if someone used the fact that people who went through higher education get higher wages to argue that going to uni makes you rich?

This question invites the applicant to address a situation closest to what an economist is qualified for. Take a dataset and form a hypothesis. Then test the hypothesis using the dataset to form a conclusion and thus, provide policy recommendations. In an interview, a student might be asked to perform any part of the above process or to give an account of an understanding behind the approach in its entirety. In this case, an externally formed hypothesis and policy recommendation needs to be evaluated. The key, once again, is not to go into a detailed discussion about econometrics, but to demonstrate some basic aptitude for numerical analysis.

Assessment: In my answer, I am going to focus on the plausible conclusions that can be drawn from a statistical result – in this case, that individuals who go to university have a higher average salary than those who don't – while I am going to take the statistical result itself as given. We could, and ideally should discuss the methods used to arrive at that result and. of course. their validity, but this would be too time-consuming in the current circumstances.

We can illustrate the result on a graph that would look something like this. [Draws a simple x-y diagram with a 45-degree line from the origin and with scattered points around it. The axes would be labelled: earnings and education]. More education is *correlated* with higher earnings.

This is an important result; making us wonder about the likely benefits of education towards people's wages and their living standards, which is one of the government's primary objectives.

However, as we know it well, **correlation is not causation**. While the former simply means that two variables change their values similarly, the latter means the changes in one variable lead to changes in the other variable. Basic statistical methods, such as a simple graphical illustration as seen before, are only able to show us *correlation;* we don't know why education and wages are high at the same points. More advanced statistical analysis would allow us to go into further details and hopefully enable us to form statements about *causation,* too. With the information given in the question, it could well be that there is **reverse causality**; a situation where causation actually runs reversely. Those who are richer might decide to go to university as they can afford not to earn wages while studying.

Equally, it could be that there is a third, unknown variable that affects both variables. For instance, the geographic area individuals live in: urban citizens can have both higher wages and better access to higher education when compared to rural inhabitants.

In both of these cases, we would see a correlation between education and wages, but that would not mean that education causes higher wages. Therefore, I would say we need to **further investigate the data** to understand whether in this case, there is indeed a causal effect running from university education to higher earnings.

Assessment: This question allowed the applicant to demonstrate a number of vital skills. First of all, priorities needed to be set. The applicant had to understand that there is no time to address all aspects of the question, from data analysis to recommendations.

Second, the applicant could make use of graphs, the confident use of which is a fundamental skill any aspiring economist or management student should have. Third, the basic notion: **correlation is not causation** was required for the answer. This is a concept all applicants should feel comfortable about as it's the basic principle of statistics.

The interviewee could also shine by bringing in originality in trying to come up with reasons other than education → wages. In an interview situation, the interviewer would likely specifically ask about this rather than expecting the applicant to feel the need to list examples, but the importance of original thoughts is evident nonetheless. Finally, the applicant needed not to forget that the question was: "What would you say?", therefore, the answer needed to be specific. Had the applicant stopped before the last paragraph, some points would have been taken away for not directly answering the question.

Q6: Do you think the government should privatise the NHS?

This question provides an opportunity for the applicant to present their understanding of the issue, but they must be wary not to be drawn into giving a political argument. The focus should be placed on the economic impacts of privatisation, rather than personal opinions. The applicant has to formulate an argument about a topic that is both important and probably relatively unfamiliar for most A-level students. As always, it is not the factual knowledge of healthcare economics which is required, but **good structure and critical thinking**.

Applicant:

Privatisation is the act of transferring assets from public ownership (effectively state ownership) to private owners through the sale of the assets. Political parties from the left and the right have had a long-standing debate over the desirable extent of public ownership of certain strategic companies and sectors, e.g. schools, hospitals, utilities or public transportation operators. Out of these, the transfer of the healthcare provider, the NHS, has been one of the most controversial topics in UK politics, effectively since the creation of a universal health care provider shortly after WWII.

There are strong reasons for both supporting and opposing the transformation of the healthcare system into a market-driven system. However, I still believe that the arguments against it are stronger, thus I would not support the privatisation of the NHS. I have **three main reasons** to believe so: adverse effects on doctor-patient relationships, social injustice, and insecurity of continuous provision.

Firstly, I have always thought that **doctors choose their profession very differently** from what economists assume about rational agents, who only care about monetary reward. They are dedicated to helping the sick and doing everything they can to do their jobs best. If the NHS was privatised, there is a good chance business owners of hospitals would introduce measures to motivate doctors to think more business-mindedly. This would, however, endanger the personal trust patients need to feel when they see their doctor about their health.

Secondly, allowing private owners to supply healthcare services would threaten with them **seeking profits above patient care**. They could increase prices of services as demand for basic health services is inelastic (we are all willing to pay nearly anything for the health of our loved ones). While the well-off could probably still pay for their healthcare, with higher prices many would not be able to purchase even basic services.

Finally, a private owner might decide to continue the supply of profitable services and cut back on others or even shut down loss-making hospitals in less developed areas. This could mean that **healthcare is not universally available across the UK**, undermining citizens' inevitable right for equal treatment.

Of course, privatisation doesn't have to take such an extreme form and it can also be heavily regulated to improve some of the above-mentioned areas. Yet, the potential problems are so serious that **even if the NHS is not an economically viable business and costs the State a lot, it should remain in the public domain.**

Assessment: The applicant started with placing the question in a historical and political context, which is always a good idea with questions of this sort. It shows the interviewer that the applicant didn't just memorise arguments for topics but actually understands how things come together. A clear structure and a strong stance are also qualities of a strong applicant. Of course, such a question is bound to lead to a discussion where the interviewer challenges the applicant and comes up with strong counter-arguments. The applicant is expected to respond to those challenges, but not to give up their stance unless factually proven wrong.

Another good response: "There are economic benefits and costs of privatisation, which would be particularly emphasised in the case of a large institution like the NHS. The benefits of privatisation may include the potential for improved competition in the healthcare provision industry. Improved competition has benefits for an economy as it means that firms have an incentive to improve efficiency and innovate. This could mean lower costs for consumers and an improved service. However, it could be argued that this is a welfare issue and that health care would be underprovided to poorer citizens in a free market. It may also be reasoned that the high barriers to entry make healthcare provision a natural monopoly and that privatisation would lead to one firm dominating the market and exploiting its powers to overcharge. I would not support privatisation of the NHS as I do not think healthcare is a good that should be made excludable based on price."

Q7: Let's say I'm the CEO of a major company, what do you think my biggest concern will be?

The applicant has to show the ability to 'think like a manager' and to analyse questions from their perspective. With such an open-ended question, the challenge is not to find something to talk about but to be able to make a proper case out of it with valid reasons. There is no wrong answer, only insufficient reasoning.

Applicant: Chief Executive Officers are the people in charge of the overall business and with the final say on most daily issues, where the Board of Governors doesn't intervene. The pressure and responsibility on them are tremendous and finding a way to prioritise their tasks and problems is crucial. CEOs serve as the **ultimate link** between the company's employees, owners and customers. Therefore, rather than any individual task of their own, I think it's the management of opposing incentives and goals which are the biggest problem facing CEOs.

The workers in the company strain themselves to achieve better working conditions, higher wages and are often trying to minimise the work effort they exert. Shareholders seek a return on their investment. Thus, they expect the CEO to deliver growth and, most importantly, profit which is already in conflict with higher wages and less work. Customers care the most about price and quality.

The former needs to be low to attract customers, but high to have profits and pay wages. The later is costly to produce and requires stringent work effort. Finding the perfect middle ground is challenging and requires constant monitoring and re-evaluation from the CEO.

This is a big problem for CEOs because other challenges are one-dimensional, e.g. developing future growth plans, creating more equality between workers, fighting competition, etc. Whilst these are all difficult areas, the desired outcomes are obvious. In the case of managing different interest groups, it's often **unclear what outcomes CEOs need to achieve**.

Assessment: After demonstrating familiarity with the main stakeholders in a firm (CEO, Board, workers), the applicant took a clear stance and named a topic thought to be the most difficult. This was then analysed from the point of view of the CEO or any other business professional. The applicant didn't lose track of the question. And by mentioning other potentially important topics, a wider familiarity with the subject could be highlighted. After this intro, the interviewer would likely invite the applicant to further discuss those other areas and compare their relative importance.

Q8: Would you be able to tell me about the relationship between restrictive monetary policies and the bond market?

A good response: "I may be wrong but I believe that restrictive monetary policy involves raising short-term interest rates. I don't know if there is any formal relationship between interest rates and bond prices, but if I was investing in bonds at a time with high interest rates, I would expect higher returns in order to stop me investing the money in a bank instead. Therefore, I would imagine that the **price of bonds would probably fall** in order to make them more attractive to investors who might otherwise save their money in a bank."

Assessment: The main point of this question is to identify an interviewee's ability to determine relationships between two ideas and their understanding of how economic mechanisms allow policies to work. The candidate shows the interviewer that they are not completely certain on the topic, but this is perfectly acceptable – the tutor is attempting to test thinking skills and not knowledge. The logical, step-by-step approach shows that the candidate remains calm and methodical even when presented with unfamiliar information. Given the testing nature of the Oxbridge courses offered, it is important for tutors to establish the ability of potential students to work under pressure.

Q9: You've mentioned an interest in counter-factual history, what is the point of it?

- Counter-factual history is the history of *what if?* It challenges the historian to consider what would have happened had something else occurred. Common counter-factual examples include: *What if Germany had won the First World War?*

- Consider the merits and limitations of this type of history.

- The advantages are that you can consider crucial turning points – such as battles, political events or wars. An event is significant if the *What if* leads to a drastically different turn of events.

- They are an interesting and engaging way to deal with the past.

- However, some would argue that creating stories or ideas is not good history. We should be evaluating the evidence of what did happen, not following a distracting path of what might have happened.

- History is about the events, people, and changes which occurred in the past. Arguably, counter-factual history is a subversion of that.

Q10: What do you know about economic theory? Tell us about Classical economic theory, how do you think it compares to the theories of economists like Keynes?

Keynesian economists believe that the immense resources of the state should be deployed during periods of economic slowdown (recession). Classical economists, on the other hand, believe that the interference of the state distorts the working of the market to an extent that any well-intended policy will actually further hinder economic recovery and that, where possible, government spending should be limited and taxes cut.

It would be good to use a relevant example from current affairs. In 2008, Gordon Brown used a **fiscal stimulus** (Keynesian) to attempt to kick-start the economy – he brought forward capital spending and cut VAT to boost consumption. While in 2010, the Chancellor, George Osborne, began austerity to restore confidence in UK public finances and reduce the budget deficit while supporting monetary expansion through the reduction of interest rates to facilitate business lending.

Who are classical economists? Friedrich Hayek *A road to serfdom*, Milton Freeman (negative income tax), Adam Smith *The Wealth of Nations*.

Who are Keynesian economists? Paul Krugman or Nicholas Kaldor (and obviously John Maynard Keynes).

Q11: Have you ever heard of the term 'rational agent' used to describe a consumer - can you think of examples of consumers being 'irrational'?

A good response: "To answer the question, we must first understand what rationality is. In my view, a rational decision is one that makes sense based on the facts or evidence presented to the decision maker. In the case of addiction, the facts available to the addict are the feeling which their addiction gives them – which may be seen as benefits, and the associated costs of the addiction.

If the benefits to the addict outweigh these costs, then it may be argued that addiction is rational. However, it could be suggested that an addict has a distorted view of these costs and benefits, and, therefore, their ability to think rationally is compromised."

Assessment: This response is well-structured and focuses on attempting to answer the question at hand. By initially outlining a definition of rationality, the candidate displays that they fully understand the question and are engaging with it critically. The response shows a consideration of both sides to the argument without being side-tracked into an irrelevant discussion. One area for potential improvement is the conclusion where no definitive answer is given. Tutors will be looking for students who can articulate their own opinions, and the lack of a conclusive response may suggest that an interviewee does not possess these skills.

Q12: Inflation is often talked about as a bad thing, but governments don't try to prevent inflation from taking place, why do you think this is?

A good response: "0% inflation may seem like a good idea as lower prices provide consumers with the opportunity to get more for their money. Price increases are often poorly received by consumers as they have to reduce what they buy. However, there is often a **trade-off between inflation and economic growth**, and aiming for zero inflation may lead to stagnation in an economy. Inflation only forces a reduction in consumption when prices are rising faster than wages, so a government may compromise on inflation – such as the Bank of England have done with their 2% target – in order to ensure that economic is being achieved."

Assessment: The candidate effectively pre-empts, and dispels, arguments in favour of 0% inflation goals. Given that this is probably a topic that the interviewee has never had to tackle before, it is advisable to ensure they can present a structured logical argument before attempting to answer. This may involve asking for a moment to think, and a good candidate should not be discouraged from doing this as it gives themselves a moment to collect their thoughts.

This response is clearly well organised and thought through, which is clearly preferable to a rushed and illogical answer, even if it comes at the expense of a momentary pause. The candidate has the opportunity to show the extent of their understanding by referring to current policies or additional knowledge from further reading.

Q13: Economics is often thought to sit between the humanities and the sciences, do you think economics should be classed as a social science?

A good response: "I would define a social science as any academic discipline that studies human interactions using scientific methods. Economics seems to fit this definition. Firstly, it is clearly the study of a human phenomenon; the core issue at the heart of the subject is how humans allocate resources. The methodology used is what provides the science part of the description in my view. Economics is based on quantitative analysis and modelling, and much of the theory is built upon scientific methods. Some people might disagree with the description of economics as a social science. They may argue that it has no real scientific grounding given that there is often very little irrefutable evidence to prove an economic theory. However, I believe that this is inevitable in any study of humanity as **human behaviour is so unpredictable** – and that if economics is not a social science, then neither is any other field of study."

Assessment: A clear definition, even if it is one the candidate has concocted rather than one taken from a textbook, shows a real understanding of what the question is asking. This is a very difficult question to answer given the vague nature of a 'social science' and the difficulty in pigeonholing an entire subject such as economics. However, by considering how well certain criteria are met and assessing contradictory points of view, the interviewee is able to display their ability to grapple with testing problems and use logical reasoning to answer the question at hand. The answer may have been improved by suggesting alternatives to the description provided (e.g. "perhaps a better description of economics is as a series of 'fads and fashions'…")s and then assessing the credibility of those alternatives.

Q14: How much do you think CEOs should be paid?

A good response: "I do not know a lot about current CEO pay levels, but it would seem to me that any **employee should be paid based on their contribution** to the firm. If the CEO has a serious positive impact on the business, for example, if they are responsible for securing high levels of profits, then they deserve a large salary. However, if they have no greater impact than any other employee, then they should not be compensated any more generously. If the cost of paying a CEO outweighs the benefits they bring, they are being overpaid."

Assessment: The candidate is honest in their response, acknowledging the fact that this is a topic they know little about. However, by applying more general economic intuition, they are able to provide a concise argument, and more importantly, demonstrate their ability to engage with unfamiliar concepts. This is a very attractive skill to an Oxbridge tutor and is preferable to an interviewee who attempts to deceive an interviewer into believing they know a lot about the subject.

Q15: Moving away from the UK, let's take a look at OPEC - do you think that a cartel is a wise choice for running a global market?

A good response: "Am I right in the understanding that OPEC is the organisation that maintains oil prices?" [Interviewer: "*Yes, that's right.*"] "In that case, I believe that OPEC has run the oil market relatively well. However, I do not believe that the market has even been close to efficiency as many OPEC members have made large profits on the back of the cartel, and in a perfectly efficient market, these profits would not occur. Large price fluctuations, particularly the fall in oil prices, in the last 18 months suggest to me that OPEC does not have as much control over the industry as it would like…"

Assessment: Asking for clarification on a question is not something a candidate should be afraid to do. It displays a willingness to fully understand the concepts that they are dealing with, and so would not be frowned upon in most scenarios.

If the topic in question was of a very basic level, there may be some questions raised, but tutors will not expect a candidate to know about every economic issue and will be expecting some gaps in their knowledge. In this case, the student was right to establish exactly what the question was before attempting to answer. Bringing in **knowledge of current affairs** regarding oil prices also displays interest in the subject, and this enthusiasm for the subject will be taken well by interviewers.

Q16: The economy of scale is a widely acknowledged concept, where average unit costs decrease as a company's output level increases - do you think the opposite, a 'diseconomy of scale' if you will, could ever exist?

A good response: "If average costs are rising as output increases, this suggests that it would be beneficial for firms to stay small. I think we can see plenty of examples of cases where it is beneficial for a firm to stay small. If a company would have to increase its spending on marketing greatly in order to sell any additional goods produced, then the average costs of those products may rise and the company would be suffering from diseconomies of scale.

Assessment: Some applicants, particularly those who have previously studied economics, will have a good understanding of this topic whilst others will have almost none. However, the interviewer is not using this question as a test of existing knowledge, but rather will be looking at the way in which it is approached. The ability to apply theory to real life is important and this question may be designed to test that ability. The candidate excels by showing good real world knowledge.

Q17: What do you think is the difference between a floating currency and a pegged currency, what difference would switching to a pegged currency have?

A good response: "A pegged currency is when a country chooses to set its own currency as a direct proportion of that of another economy, usually when a less developed economy aligns with the exchange rate of a more established country.

This means that an economy has more stability in their exchange rate, which can lead to less volatility in the balance of payments. However, it means a government cannot use economic policies to affect its exchange rate, so they are more susceptible to shocks from external factors – particularly from the nation they are pegged to. It also means that government policy elsewhere has an impact, so the pegged country needs to ensure congruence between the two nations' objectives."

Assessment: The candidate clearly shows a great understanding of the topic, which may not have been covered in any real depth during A-Levels or equivalent. They are able to present a balanced argument even in a short answer and draw on a variety of ideas. To improve, the applicant could refer to real life examples, which shows that they have read around their subject and can be an indication of enthusiasm for the subject. However, in a situation where they don't know any examples, then considering the types of nation that might use pegged currencies – "a less developed economy" – is a good alternative which still displays good understanding.

Q18: You're the new Chancellor of the Exchequer - you've been appointed on the promise of growing the economy, would you pursue this from the demand side or supply side?

A good response: "Classical economists believe in a vertical long-run average supply curve, and thus would argue that demand side policies are useless in stimulating growth. However, I feel like the Keynesian model is more realistic and demand side policies can be effective when an economy is not at full employment. Despite this, I believe that supply side policies usually stimulate more long-term sustainable growth rather than one that boosts to economic performance. If a government is seeking growth, I think supply side policies would be preferable."

Assessment: This answer is good and comes to a solid conclusion, but seems to lack the depth to impress an Oxbridge tutor. To improve, the candidate could spend more time analysing why a government may disagree with their viewpoint, and then providing evidence to support their own argument.

Another extension to the answer may be to consider the circumstances under which one approach is more suited than another. Questioning the context surrounding the question shows an inquisitive nature and shows that the candidate is analytical of information presented to them. In this case, a conclusion along the lines of "if a government is facing *situation x*, it should pursue *policy y*…" may add some substance to the arguments presented.

Q19: Would 0% inflation be a good thing or a bad thing?

This question is looking to assess both your basic knowledge of a simple economic concept (inflation) and then your ability to use this knowledge to answer a difficult hypothetical. You should first make it clear that you can clearly and coherently explain what inflation is and why it exists. Then you have some scope to come up with some issues that might arise if there was no inflation. You can be imaginative here but to a degree, as your answers must be rooted in economic knowledge.

Good Applicant: Inflation is the sustained rise of the price level, or the average price of goods and services, in the economy over a period of time. It can also be understood as a fall in the value of money as, after a period of inflation, a fixed amount of money now has less purchasing power. Inflation therefore means that, over time, our money becomes less valuable and so it encourages consumers to spend and keep their money flowing through the economy rather than save it for long periods of time. This is known as inflation 'greasing the wheels' of the economy. If there was no inflation and purchasing power didn't change, then there is less incentive for consumers to spend and it is more likely that they will delay spending and keep their money in banks where they will make a standard interest rate return on it. This could cause the economy to become stagnant with less spending. Inflation is also a signal of a healthy, growing economy and if there was no inflation then this could signal to markets that there is no economic growth which could cause uncertainty and falling consumer confidence.

A **poor applicant** might respond with a simple view that no inflation might be considered a good thing because prices will stay the same and they prefer it when things are cheaper. They might be able to identify that most central banks aim for a small but stable level of inflation, but not go into any detail on why this is the case and what the benefits of inflation are. They may also confuse no inflation with deflation, and this is something to avoid.

Q20: A lot of economics revolves around the use of economic models, do you think these are used too much?

This question is trying to get you to explore concepts relating to the method of economics rather than pure economic concepts themselves. It is important to not let the wording of questions like this sway your answer too much. The question is clearly leading you in a negative direction (to criticise the use of models in economics) but you need to make sure that your answer carefully considers both sides of this debate. Also, you will be interviewing with an economist so you shouldn't try to dismantle the whole nature of models in economics but instead you should be trying to understand why economists use models and what the benefits are.

Good Applicant: Economists use models to simplify the complicated world so that they can understand and analyse specific impacts and effects in economic systems. Economists are attempting to explain how changes in policies or incentives will affect behaviour and the wider economy, but they are unable to use controlled experiments due to the huge amounts of other influencing factors. This is why they use models – to simplify reality and run experiments of what will happen and what the causality effects may be. The issue with these models is that their conclusions rely on lots of assumptions that are made to simplify the model, but that are extremely unlikely to hold in reality. This is why it can be argued that economists rely too heavily on models as they are unlikely to accurately predict reality. This is an issue, but it is one that economists are aware of and constantly trying to address. One way in which they do this is by testing models against empirical data to identify which models are best and most accurate. If a model is found to not represent reality well, there is still something to be learned about the economy and by explaining what is different in reality compared to the model.

A **poor applicant** would be someone who may identify the issues with models and their strict assumptions but does not explore in any detail why economists still use these models and what their benefits can be despite the assumptions. Furthermore, a poor answer would not take into account the idea that economists are aware of the limitations of models and actively seeking to improve and test them. Finally, a poor answer would be one that criticises the use of models but does not provide any alternative or guidance for solving this problem.

Q21: If economics is a social science, does it follow that sociology is a valuable tool for studying economics?

This question is looking for you to identify what sociology is and how it relates to economics. Economics is considered to be a social-science, and this question is looking for you to explore the 'social' side of this understanding and how this might benefit the study of economics. You are able to ask the interviewer to clarify what exactly they mean by 'sociology' if you are not clear of the definition.

Good Applicant: Sociology is the study of social life, change and the social causes and impacts of human behaviour. From this definition, it is clear that sociology will be useful for developing a study and understanding of economics. Economics is ultimately concerned with how scarce resources are allocated in a society with unlimited desires, and so an understanding of social structures and behaviour will help to answer this question of allocation. Much of economics, specifically microeconomics, is focused on individual behaviour and decision-making. Basic economic models use assumptions of perfect rationality, but this is clearly unrealistic, and an understanding of sociology can help us to unlock this assumption and better understand human decision-making. Economic agents and markets exist in the context of society, and thus sociology will help to understand some of the external effects that are difficult to include into traditional economic models.

You could go either way with this question, but the important thing is to make sure that your answers are well supported. You could argue that the most useful areas of economics are the purely mathematical, model-based studies and that sociology has very little to offer here as these complex models use a set of assumptions to remove the societal impacts. However, if you did argue in this way, you would still have to show some awareness for the interaction of economics and sociology but explain why this is not that important (e.g. because assumptions of models remove the sociology-based impacts).

A **poor applicant** might simply state that sociology is not useful for economics without any real explanation or detail. They might also argue that sociology is useful because economics is flawed. Better answers are those which explore the links between sociology and economics and how they interact and overlap with each other.

Q22: How do we measure GDP - do you think this is reflective of reality?

This question is looking for you to show some level of understanding of what GDP is, how we measure it, what the limitations to our measurement techniques may be, and why economists care about GDP at all. If you did not know exactly how we actually measure GDP, feel free to ask the interviewer for some specific methods as this question is more focused on evaluating the potential flaws in these methods rather than knowing them off by heart.

Good Applicant: GDP is supposed to be a measure of the total value of goods and services, known as output, in a country or economy. This method of measurement is likely to be easier in a traditional, manufacturing-based economy where we can measure the value of the physical output of all goods that are produced. This, however, is likely to be much harder in a more developed, service-based economy like the UK. This is because there is likely to be some value created, especially in innovative tech firms, that is difficult to quantify and include in the measure. GDP will also fail to include the underground economy and so the measure of production will always be an underestimate. The final point to note, is that while there are some limitations to measuring GDP, it is still an important metric as it allows for consistent, cross-country comparisons to be made which is important for economists to assess relative economic performance.

The question is phrased in such a way that it is assumed you know how we 'actually' measure GDP, and the interviewer is looking for you to assess whether this 'measurement' really makes sense/can come close to representing total output in an economy. You should still look to show how GDP is actually measured, but the bulk of this answer should be debating whether measuring GDP is actually possible/should be done.

A **poor applicant** might not fully grasp what GDP is and why economists care about trying to measure it. They might say that we just add up all of the purchases in the country and so it is actually an easy measure, showing no consideration for what 'value' might be missed from those transactions.

Q23: If you were evaluating the UK's productive potential, what would be the main influences on it which you could identify?

This question should be familiar for those who are taking the Economics A-Level course. This question is looking for you to show an understanding of a fairly basic economic concept and give the standard explanation of what might influence productive potential. From here, however, you should look to extend your answer beyond the A-level course and discuss some other factors as well as potentially questioning the definition of productive potential altogether.

Good answer: The productive potential or capacity of a country is the total potential output if all resources and factors of production are utilised to their fullest efficiency. There are a number of factors which can influence productive potential. The size and productivity of the workforce are both key factors, as a larger and more productive workforce can produce more total output and more output per worker. The size of the workforce depends on the number of economically active people which is influenced by the age structure within the country as well as levels of net migration. Labour productivity, or output per worker, depends on the education, training, and motivation of the workers. Furthermore, labour productivity depends on the interaction of labour and capital, and a change in the quantity and quality of capital stock will also impact productive potential. There are also factors outside of the quantity and quality of factors of production that influences productive potential, including the level of political stability and security within a country.

You could develop this further by questioning the method in which we would measure productive potential in an economy. With technology advancing at an increasingly rapid pace, it seems that traditional measures of productive capacity might be outdated as the potential output of a country in the long-term is likely to be constantly changing.

A **poor answer** will just recite the textbook definition of productive potential which is that productive potential depends on the quantity and quality of the factors of production.

Q24: What, if any, is the value of government debt?

For this question, you should be looking to show a clear understanding of why governments have debts and what it means for a government to be in debt. From there, you need to show a clear understanding and consideration of both sides of this argument before giving your opinion on whether countries should or should not have debts. It does not matter which side you ultimately argue for, only that you have backed up your answer and that your conclusion follows on from your explanation.

Good answer: We first need to distinguish between an annual budget deficit and national debt. The budget deficit is when, over a year, the government spends more money than it generates through taxation. This deficit is often funded by the issuance of government bonds. The national debt is the net accumulation of these annual budget deficits. The key benefit of government debt is that it allows governments to increase their spending without increasing taxation. This might even be necessary during a recession when tax revenue falls and higher government spending is required. If the question is asking whether governments should have any debt at all, then the benefits of spending without increasing taxation is a strong argument for some level of government debt/borrowing. However, there are concerns about higher levels of government debt. As it increases, the risk of defaulting gets worse and worse to a point where the government is unable to borrow more. This could lead to a fiscal crisis where the government cannot adequately raise funds through either taxation or borrowing.

Additionally, this question could involve a more moral/ethical-based answer. When a government accumulates debt, it might solve fiscal problems in the short term but in the long-term it will have to be paid back by taxpayers who may not benefit from the debt in the first place.

A **poor answer** would be one that fails to acknowledge both sides of this debate and appreciate why debt is a beneficial and sometimes necessary part of the global economy. A poor answer would also fail to acknowledge the binary wording of this question.

Q25: Should you or I be bothered by inequality?

This style of question is asking you to consider the traditional stereotype of what an 'economist' cares about. You should look to answer the question directly but also question what exactly an economist would care about and why this may or may not be different to what someone else might care about (e.g. a politician). Also, you need to be clear on what it means for something to 'matter' to anyone.

Good answer: Inequality can be referring to income or wealth inequality, and this can be within individual countries or between different countries. Economists are focused on allocating resources in the most efficient way, and this usually involves trying to maximise some sort of welfare function across the economy. In this way, inequality should matter to an economist as it should be an important part of a holistic welfare function. Inequality makes people's lives worse, and therefore economists should look to reduce inequality to some extent in order to maximise societal welfare. Furthermore, inequality has important implications for economic behaviour. Some degree of inequality should, in theory, have beneficial impacts for the economy as it encourages hard work and innovation/risk-taking. This is a key theory that underpins capitalism, but we must be careful to mediate the level of inequality. These benefits will not be felt if there is not equality of opportunities so that those with less are able to work their way up. Economists should therefore care about inequality of outcomes and opportunities.

You can argue for either side of this question, but make sure to show a consideration for both sides in your answer. You should also make it clear that you understand why an 'economist' might think differently to someone else (e.g. economists are trying to maximise welfare whereas a politician might care about inequality in order to be more popular with the electorate).

A **poor answer** is one that does not consider both sides of this question. It feels obvious that an economist should care about inequality, but a better answer needs to adequately explain why this is but also why it may not be the most important consideration.

Q26: If there's a national deficit in the balance of trade, should this trouble the government?

The balance of trade should be a familiar concept form the Economics A-level course, as should some standard arguments for why it does and does not matter. For this question, you need to prove your knowledge of this before being more creative and questioning the role of a trade deficit in modern macroeconomics.

Good answer: A trade deficit is simply when a country imports more than it exports (in monetary terms, meaning the total value of imports/exports rather than the quantity). A trade deficit is not immediately a good or bad thing and it depends on the specific macroeconomic objectives of the country. A trade deficit may be a good indicator of economic growth in the country. Generally, during a boom, the trade deficit will increase as spending in the economy grows and more is spent on imports. The reverse is also often observed as the trade deficit improves due to a fall in consumer spending. However, a trade deficit can also be caused by more damaging structural factors. It can reflect falling relative productivity and capital investment in a country. Furthermore, a larger trade deficit means that the country is more exposed to what is occurring in foreign economies and likely to be less resistant to shocks. A strong economy is one that is resilient to external shocks and a level of self-sufficiency is important – something that is not present with a persistent large trade deficit. Overall, the cause of the trade deficit matters more than the trade deficit itself.

The word 'trouble' in this question is purposefully vague, and it is up to your own interpretation somewhat. You can define 'trouble' in this context in a number of ways, but the important thing is to make it clear what you think makes something 'trouble' an economist. For example, you could argue that something is only 'troubling' if it will affect total overall welfare across the economy, which the balance of trade deficit may not directly impact.

A **poor answer** will not address the reasons behind a trade deficit and will simply debate whether the mere presence of a trade deficit matters. It also may not consider both sides of this argument before concluding.

Q27: Is the Keynesian approach to market intervention correct?

This is an example of a common question/debate in economics that has a wide range of potential answers and discussion points. You should not look to answer this question from every possible angle and cover every relevant point. Instead, you should focus on giving a concise, well-measured answer that looks at one area of this debate. Since this is an economics interview, you should focus on answering this question by using economic terminology and understanding. You can still mention this debate in the context of other disciplines (e.g. politics), but you should make sure the focus of your answer is the economics behind this.

Good answer: This is a complicated question that is difficult to distil down to a simple yes or no answer. The key point for discussion will be why the government is intervening/feels as though they need to intervene in the market, and this will shape whether this should occur or not. Economists have a general focus on promoting efficiency in markets and so governments should intervene if something is preventing a market from reaching its equilibrium. A common example that we see in reality is intervention into markets for goods/services with externalities. The government should intervene to ensure that marginal social benefit = marginal social cost as this is the desired equilibrium. This is an example of government intervention to correct market failure, which should occur. The main argument against government intervention is that they are unlikely to have the correct information about the specific market and their intervention could make the problem worse. The market is the most efficient mechanism for allocation because it does not require any external 'information' – prices automatically reflect scarcity. Government intervention may be beneficial if done correctly, but the lack of information may lead to the government making a wrong decision when they are trying to help.

A **poor answer** would fail to answer this question using the appropriate economic terminology. You need to make use of efficiency and show an understanding of why economists think that 'markets' are the most efficient allocation method.

Q28: Do you think that it would be reasonable to say that a failure of regulation caused 2008's financial crisis?

As a potential economics student, you should have at least some level of knowledge about the 2008 financial crisis and the underlying causes. If you did not know in the interview, or you didn't know how it related to regulation failure then it is better to ask for some guidance rather than stumble into an answer that you do not know. The interviewer will give you some impetus, and then you should try to use the information to come to some sort of answer. If you are unsure, then try to keep it brief rather than waffling to fill time.

Good answer: The financial crisis of 2008 has a number of contributing factors and it cannot be said that it was only caused by a failure of regulation. That being said, regulation failure and deregulation were large contributors to the scale of the financial crash. The decade prior to the crash saw steady deregulation of the financial industry as banks sought to not be regulated in a harsher fashion than emerging, non-bank institutions. By 2008, there were severely low levels of supervision and regulation in the financial system and this regulatory failure contributed to the crash. Banks were able to create riskier and riskier financial instruments, culminating in the mortgage-backed securities that collapsed when the housing bubble burst. The banks were also lending to riskier and riskier borrowers with less and less liquidity to cover themselves. All of these factors should have been better regulated and this has started to occur since the crash, but there is still some way to go. Overall, the financial crisis of 2008 was not just a failure of regulation as there are numerous other root causes of the crash, but regulation failure is a key factor.

A **poor answer** would be one that is either too vague about the causes of the financial crisis, but also one that gets too carried away with proving a wide knowledge on the area and does not focus on the specific question relating to the crash and regulation failure.

Q29: Let's suppose that due to a mainframe error, the value of the American Dollar and the Japanese Yen are exchanged instantaneously - what do you think the main outcomes would be?

This question is looking for you to use your standard economic understanding to answer a difficult 'what if' question. There is no correct answer here, so you should focus on being clear with your logic and line of reasoning for how you get to an answer. You have some freedom to be creative here, so do not be afraid to speculate a bit for questions like this. If you don't know the exact (or even rough) relative values of the dollar and the yen, then feel free to ask the interviewer.

Good answer: One US Dollar is worth around 100 Japanese Yen. If these two values swapped overnight, there would obviously be a significant level of panic and a period of adjustment in global markets. While it is difficult to say exactly what happen, we can speculate some possibilities. The US Dollar has now become 1/100th of the value that it previously was, whereas the Japanese Yen is now 100x more valuable. If this suddenly occurred, financial institutions might expect that the exchange rate market would correct these values. Therefore, you might expect that anyone in possession of the Japanese Yen would want to sell it, and investors would want to buy the US Dollar before it increased in value again. This process would speed up the correction process as the difference in value is arbitraged away.

Even if this currency swap was corrected fairly quickly, there would likely be long-term damaging impacts for global markets. The key impact might be a severe loss of faith in the US Dollar. If it instantly dropped to 1/100th of its value once, there is nothing to say that this might not happen again and so the value might drop forever as it is seen as a far riskier currency to hold. Furthermore, this extreme event might undermine confidence in global FX markets generally and we could see investors move their money into other areas.

A **poor answer** would be one that gets too bogged down by the technical details of this question and fails to show any creativity of speculation in the answer. A poor answer would also be one that does not think about the difference in short and potential long-term impacts.

Q30: Sadly we aren't allowed to just sit down with you and play a game of Monopoly, but if we did, how would you try to win? Would your strategy also work in the real world?

This sounds like a slightly less serious question, but it is still clearly grounded in economic theory and, as such, so should your answer. If you are not familiar with monopoly or are not clear on what the best way to win is, then you should ask for clarification on this. The interviewer will be interested in how you apply the method to reality and the subsequent discussion of whether this is possible.

Good answer: In general, the best way to win monopoly is to play it as aggressive as possible. This means buying up every single property that you land on or that becomes available to buy in some way. Your ultimate aim is to acquire sets and owning as much as possible gives you a much larger degree of bargaining power over other players. You should not save any money as it is easy to instantly mortgage and unmortgage properties to pay anything that you owe. To apply this to real life, we need to consider what the overall goal of monopoly is. In order to win, you need to bankrupt every other player and by doing this you accumulate all of the available money and assets. For the sake of discussion, we will assume that the goal of real life is to achieve economic success through accumulation of wealth. The monopoly strategy does have some real-life application. It makes sense to accumulate as many safe assets as possible (property in this case) and then accumulate a steady flow of income in the form of rent. Bargaining power is also important in reality, and a strong set of assets is a useful bargaining tool. The crucial difference in monopoly, however, is that resources (properties) are so scarce and you are one of a small number of people trying to acquire them. In reality, both the pool of assets and potential buyers is much greater. This means that accumulating one extra property has a far smaller impact on your bargaining power. Furthermore, it is useful in real life to have some savings and liquidity to fall back on. You cannot instantly mortgage and unmortgage assets in the same way as you can in the game, and as such having no savings as coverage will increase your chances of going bankrupt.

A **poor answer** will be one that does not take this question seriously and treats it as more of a joke. While the question is not serious in tone, you need to make sure that you are still treating it with care and using it as an opportunity to show your economic knowledge and relate concepts to the specific question.

Q31: There are a wide range of materials which we go to considerable effort to extract from the Earth, one of the most expensive is diamond, while one of the cheapest is steel - why do they have their respective values?

This question asks about two raw materials. While you need to show some level of understanding about each good individually, the question is clearly framed in this way to encourage you to discuss these goods in comparison to each other. They have been chosen as they are both raw materials with a similarly expensive extraction method, and so a comparison of these two goods and the differences in their markets will allow you to form a much better answer.

Good answer: The prices of these goods depend on the relative supply and demand in their respective markets. There are both supply and demand explanations for why diamonds are so expensive. In terms of demand, diamonds are the most commonly sought-after precious gemstone. They are associated with wealth and prosperity, and there have been several successful marketing campaigns that have increased demand for diamonds by making them seem essential for expensive jewellery and engagement rings. The biggest factor, however, is the supply of diamonds. While diamonds themselves are not that naturally scarce, they have an extremely limited supply which has forced up their price. This occurred as the De Beers corporation has maintained tight control (essentially a monopoly) over diamond supply since the 19th century. This limitation in supply means that diamonds are a highly demanded but highly scarce good which makes them expensive.

In contrast, steel is a much more abundant good. It is mainly made with iron, which is a fairly plentiful ore that can be found and extracted. The demand for steel may be equally high, but the supply is so plentiful that demand is outmatched, and the price naturally falls much lower than that of diamonds.

A **poor answer** will not explain the relative prices of these goods, and it will not explain the prices of these goods in terms of the supply and demand forces within the individual markets. It is not enough to just say 'diamonds are rare, steel is more abundant'.

Q32: You are the CEO of new airline, which only flies directly between London and Tokyo - this is a route which no one else in the world currently provides, so how would you work out how much to charge in order to maximise your profits?

This question is not expecting you to give an answer with a specific, detailed knowledge of how airlines exactly set their prices. Instead, it is looking for you to identify some general factors that influence price-setting and how general firms assess costs and seek to maximise profits. You should then give your best effort to apply these general factors to the specific case of airlines. It is fine if your examples are not precisely accurate, you just have to ensure that you have sound, reasoned logic behind your answer.

Good answer: There are several influencing factors for setting the price of this ticket. The first is the general market demand for this type of ticket. The airline needs to consider how many people will be demanding this ticket from London to Tokyo, and what their individual willingness-to-pay will be. Since it is a unique route, the number of people who want to buy this ticket is likely to be low but the few people who want to buy it will likely have a high willingness-to-pay. Another influencing factor would be the price of similar airline tickets for similar routes. We could look at what other airlines are offering for flights to other locations in Japan or the surrounding area in Asia, and either look to match these prices or potentially undercut them (although this could result in a price war). Our costs will also influence this decision, as we have to ensure that the price of the ticket is high enough to cover the cost of fuel/staff involved in the flight. Finally, to ensure maximal profit we need to try and identify the level where marginal revenue of a ticket will be equal to marginal cost. This is a difficult equation to calculate in reality, but it is useful as a baseline to aim towards and be as profit maximising as we can even if we cannot be at the exact point.

A **poor answer** would be one that does not mention multiple factors influencing this pricing decision. Pricing is not a simple calculation (despite that A-Level course often making it appear to be) and so better answers will be ones that recognise the real-life challenges of pricing decisions.

Q33: Tell me about the golden ratio - why do people at banks and investment companies care about it?

This is a very specific question, and it relies on a fair amount of background knowledge. If you have not heard of the golden ratio then you should feel free to ask the interviewer to give you a definition. This is better than trying to waffle your way around it. Secondly, once you have been told what the golden ratio is, you should try to give a potential way that banks/firms may be interested in it. Even if you do not get this correct, you will still be credited for giving a plausible sounding answer that you can back up with some logic.

Good answer: The golden ratio is a unique ratio (about 1.618). It is derived from the Fibonacci sequence and the natural balance of this ratio is abundant in much of nature (e.g. the number of female bees divided by male bees in any hive). This is useful to bankers/investors as we have been able to derive some technical analysis tools from the idea that there is a unique balance to this ratio. The best example for financial markets is the use of the ratio to assess whether a chart is showing significant recovery or resistance. For example, if a stock falls from 20 to 10, we can check whether the stock reaches 38.2% recovery (up to 13.82), then 50% recovery and then 61.8%. If it passes these boundaries, then the recovery is usually very strong.

This answer is very specific, and it relies on a lot of background information about investment strategies. If you didn't have this knowledge, however, you can still give a well-reasoned answer to this question. If you asked what the golden ratio was and the interviewer told you that it was the ratio 1.618 that provides balance and solidity in nature, you could still relate this to banking and investment. One response could be that this ratio may be how banks/investors split their investments between their top two best-performing funds. It could also be how they split investments between less risky and more risky investments. The idea is to come up with some way in which a specific ratio could apply and be used in financial markets.

A **poor answer** would be one that fails to correctly describe the golden ratio and does not ask for any clarification. A poor answer would also try to argue that the golden ratio is not used in banking (to their knowledge). Even if this was the case, the question has asked you to come up with some way that the ratio can be used and so you must do this rather than question its use in general.

Q34: How would you try to predict economic changes, if you could, do you think this would help you avoid depressions?

This question is looking for you to illustrate a clear economic understanding of what a recession/depression is, why economists care about them and what the potential warning signs for one may be. It is important to clarify that recessions are fairly inevitable in the boom/bust cycle, and the question specifically wants to focus on avoiding depressions as this is the more severe version of a recession (lasting for at least a year rather than months).

Good answer: Predicting recessions is extremely difficult, with economic forecasts often being compared to weather forecasts in that there is an element of unpredictability that we cannot control for. Even with all the economic information and signals in the world, some recessions are not able to be predicted – such as the recession caused by the global pandemic. This does not mean that we should give up on predicting economic recessions entirely, and there are some warning signs. A key signal that we can use is the financial yield curve. An inverted yield curve (when the long-term yield is lower) has been an accurate predictor of every US recession since 1970. However, there is a small sample size of this and the reasons behind this prediction are still only theories. I would argue that the prevention of periods of depression is more reliant on accurately identifying when a recession is beginning rather than trying to predict it long into the future. If we can identify the beginning of a recession, then governments and central banks can start implementing policy earlier to counter the negative output effects.

The best answers to this question will be those that not only identify practical ways/metrics that can be used as early warning signs for recessions and depressions, but also go further to identify what could be done to prevent/mitigate the depression once it has been identified.

A **poor answer** would fail to appreciate the unpredictability of recessions/depressions. Furthermore, there is a certain inevitably to economic recessions and they are not necessarily an absolutely bad thing for the economy – this is something that a poor answer would not appreciate and instead give a simplistic view on why recessions are bad and how we can prevent them.

Q35: Do you think that a country which can fund its own space programme should receive international aid from countries like the UK?

This question combines some economic discussion with some ethical discussion, and it is important that you can answer from both of these angles. You should try to give a nuanced answer that appreciates both sides of this discussion while also understanding the perspective of a country that relies on aid.

Good answer: There are two fundamental reasons why countries give foreign aid (either humanitarian or developmental) to other countries. The first is for a moral reason – the protection of life and support for the most vulnerable global populations. The second is for economic reasons as developmental aid given to countries will generally be in the form of an investment which will bring benefits to the donor country in the future. The question is implying that countries with international space programs should not be recipients of aid as they should have enough funding of their own (since they can set up a space program). This view is extremely binary and simplistic. From a moral perspective, we should still look to support the most vulnerable even if their own government has prioritised something else (e.g. space travel). Secondly, countries with space programmes may still have large amounts of inequality between sectors/regions and require developmental aid to bridge these gaps. If the country already has the space program, these are significant sunk costs, and they would not be able to reverse this decision and spend the money on developmental support instead. The funding of the space program could be considered as government failure, and government failure is not a significant reason to stop providing aid in any form.

This answer phrases the decision as purely binary with only two options (to give aid or not). You should show that, in reality, this will not be the case and there might be other approaches that we would want to take. For example, you could argue that the foreign aid that we give should be correlated with the GDP per capita of the recipient countries. This would mean that countries who were previously reliant on aid, but then rapidly developed and developed space programmes should have their aid reduced to a more appropriate amount, and more aid could be allocated to countries who need it more.

A **poor answer** would fail to explain why exactly any country gives aid. Furthermore, a poor answer would not be explicit about the nuances involved or show an appreciation for who would suffer most if the aid was stopped.

Q36: *How would you assess the scale of the divide between communist and capitalist ideologies?*

If you are applying for an economics degree, then you are expected to have some familiarity with these two forms of an economy. You should explain these differences clearly and precisely. You can then be more creative for the second half of the question and come up with some ways in which they are similar (or their outcomes in the real world are similar).

Good answer: Capitalism and communism are both economic and political systems. Capitalism is when trade and industry is controlled by private owners who operate for profit, whereas communism is when all property and factors of production is public (owned by the community) and each person contributes and is compensated equally. The key difference between the two, aside from the private vs public ownership of the factors of production, is the market mechanism (or lack thereof). In a capitalistic society, the level of production and resource allocation is determined by the free market forces of supply and demand. These factors determine the price and quantity of each good. In a communist society, these decisions are made by the government who sets each of these. In theory, the capitalist society requires no government intervention in the markets as they should operate 'perfectly' and lead to the most efficient and overall beneficial outcome.

However, in reality, we often observe market failure that needs to be corrected (e.g. in the case of climate change which is a large-scale externality market failure). In these cases, the government needs to intervene to influence prices and output in the market (in the same fashion to communism). If the government had perfect information, then they would be able to intervene to bring us to the true free market equilibrium. However, since governments do not have full information, their decision becomes similar to the communist government as they both (somewhat arbitrarily) have to choose what prices/output will be.

A **poor answer** would be one that correctly identifies the similarities between these two ideologies but fails to develop the answer and come up with some ways in which the ideologies are similar (either in terms of the underlying economic/political theory or the observed outcomes).

Q37: What do you think are the main factors driving the increasing privatisation of once-public large services like the Royal Mail or NHS?

This question is essentially asking for the pros of privatising large, previously nationalised industries. You should be careful to focus on the specific question at hand and not be distracted by turning this into a full-scale debate about privatisation. Even if you do not agree with privatising these services, you need to be able to understand and appreciate the other side of the debate.

Good answer: The main reason for privatising these large services is to improve efficiency and remove political interference. Large companies are extremely difficult to manage, and this task becomes even harder when the company is not driven by a profit motive as there is less incentive at every stage to be the most efficient and productive. Private industries are motivated by their profit margins and shareholders, and so they have a more direct incentive to be efficient and run smoothy at a low average cost. Privatisation may also occur alongside significant deregulation to promote competition in these markets. Large monopoly power reduces the incentive to innovate and improve and so privatisation alongside deregulation (to encourage new entrants) may solve this. Finally, there is the benefit of raising government revenue through the sales of these services, and this may be spent elsewhere to improve the overall economy/welfare.

You should focus on the specific case of 'large services' and the effects of privatisation in these industries. The two examples given are both large-scale, traditional UK services and so you should also ensure that you answer has something that is specific to this context. For example, you could argue that the NHS is an old service and so there may be more opportunity for dynamic improvements from privatisation.

A **poor answer** is one that simply reels off the basic pros and cons of the privatisation debate, without focusing on the reasons why this may be happening as well as not focusing on the specific nature of 'large' services (e.g. likely to previously be monopolies and so deregulation may be beneficial).

Q38: On Oxford high street there are three coffee shops belonging to the same brand on a single street - why do you think this happens in populous cities?

This question is looking for you to understand a specific market and the actions of one type of firm. Even if you do not know this answer beforehand, you should be able to come up with some economic reasons as to why this would make sense for the firm and their ability to maximise profits.

Good answer: This answer comes down to understanding which areas are most popular for coffee shops, and then understanding how firms will exploit this. Crowded cities are clearly the best location for selling coffee for a number of obvious reasons (high population density, high population of working people who drink coffee regularly, high footfall etc.). In a city, there are certain areas that shoppers will naturally congregate towards when they want coffee. These areas will be in squares, near retail outlets and near other restaurants as opposed to in residential areas. This means that the coffee shop owners want to take full advantage of this demand and, since there are multiple coffee shops, the demand is greater than just one shop. Since the demand exceeds one shop, there is a decision on where to build the second and it makes much more sense to put this shop in the same area with high demand/density of coffee drinkers rather than in another location. This is why we end up with lots of coffee shops next to each other in certain areas of crowded cities, as these are the optimal locations to take advantage of the excess demand for coffee.

The key with this question is understanding why it might make economic sense to have two identical coffee shops so close to each other. We have already mentioned that there is likely to be excess demand, so you then need to explain why multiple shops makes more sense than one big coffee shop (since this seems to go against our standard theory of economies of scale). One major factor in this could be that queueing is a major drawback of getting a coffee and having two coffee shops in a similar but not identical location may split queues enough to increase the amount of customers that they could serve compared to if there was one larger coffee shop.

A **poor answer** would not take into account the supply and demand factors, as well as the myriad other factors as to why certain areas in crowded cities are the most optimal for coffee shop locations.

Q39: You have been tasked with getting rid of the UK's national debt - howt?

The aim of this question is to think step by step about the processes – what debt is, how to eliminate it and whether this is a good thing to do. It does not matter whether you are answering correctly – the interviewer will just want to see that you can think logically.

A bad answer: Would focus solely on listing ways of eliminating the debt – without thinking about their plausibility and potential negative effects. Furthermore, a bad answer would perhaps not think about what national debt actually is, and not attempt to define what it is and who the debt is owed to. **A good answer:** First would think about what national debt is – perhaps an answer would include that it is money that the government owes, and think about who it owes this money to, like other governments.

In the simplest terms, the way to eliminate such debt, would be to pay back those the government owes. The candidate would then need to think about what would have to be done to achieve this. The country would either have to reallocate current spending in order to pay the debt off or think about ways to increase the GDP of the country (through industry for example) to then have the funds to pay off the debt. Other good suggestions from candidates could include raising taxes – then discussing the pros and cons of this such as reducing household assets and consumption, which could have negative economic effects. Lastly, an excellent answer would perhaps question whether the debt needs to be eliminated at all. Thinking about the coronavirus crisis, countries have all increased their national debt hugely.

- Candidates could either argue that yes, the debt needs paying off so that the state can be seen as credible for further investment.
- Or could argue that if the country is in a financially good position, the proportion of debt would be getting proportionally smaller, and so would be less of a pressing issue and perhaps there would be a weaker need to eliminate it. The negatives of raising taxes and increasing inequality may not be worth eliminating the debt

Q40: Why do we use public money to provide healthcare to the elderly?

This kind of question is designed to get the candidate to think quite creatively and see whether it is possible to weigh up quite conflicting arguments.

A bad answer: Would go down strongly on one side of the argument without considering the alternative side at all. The lack of consideration for alternative points of view would demonstrate inflexible thinking.

A good answer: Would discuss what 'NHS money' is – the NHS is funded by the taxpayer. In this way therefore, the taxpayers are paying to keep other taxpayers, the old people alive. Old people themselves are taxpayers, so they are also funding a service that they are using.

The answer would then discuss the pros and cons of doing this.

Pros:

Society is more than the economic value of its members - almost everyone who is funding care for the elderly via tax 'NHS money' will have elderly friends and relatives that they care about. Therefore, it is likely to be a societal preference of this use of NHS money. If this is the outcome that society prefers, surely this provides a argument for using this money to keep elderly people alive.

Could perhaps discuss the fact that children are not contributors to the economy – but huge resources are used to fund their education. Although children will contribute in the future, the elderly have contributed in the past and therefore should not be excluded on this basis.

The elderly pay tax and have been paying tax throughout their lifetime so are just as much entitled to public services.

The NHS keeps many people alive – not just those that are elderly. The elderly are no more at risk of falling victim to a car crash for example – and in some cases their lower level of activity could actually reduce their likelihood of being victim to a random accident.

Cons:

Would argue that the elderly are non-productive members of society, and therefore the money would be better spent on public resources that would benefit those who contribute to the economy.

With the proportion of the population of the elderly growing, this is going to be an increasing drain in resources, if this trend continues.

A good answer would then weigh up these suggested pros and cons (and any creative ones the candidate can think of) and decide on what should be valued more. It is important to note that this kind of question does not have a right answer - being able to think of arguments and weigh up their strengths is the aim.

Q41: What do you think are the main push and pull factors behind human migration?

This question wants the candidate to think both big and small – or in economic terms, the microeconomic factors and the macroeconomic factors. A good answer will think about both the decisions of individuals to immigrate or emigrate – and the larger structural factors that drive such decisions.

A good answer: Individual decision-making towards emigration or immigration will usually be some form of cost-benefit analysis. If the decision is taken to emigrate or immigrate, the benefits from this huge move are seen to be greater than the potential costs. Such individual drivers of immigration and emigration can include financial issues such as a redundancy – the move could be to a new area with job sectors suited to the individual. Emigration or immigration may also be driven by emotional or family ties, such as marriage or moving to elderly relatives. Another reason why individuals choose to immigrate or emigration could be due to a threat of discrimination in the country of origin, for example by a religious or political authority.

The macro factors that drive immigration and emigration can be demonstrated when they cause large-scale immigration and emigration – as therefore these factors are drivers of not just an individual's decision. Whether or not the move will be immigration or emigration, such drivers suggest that the final destination will be preferential to the place of origin. Such drivers can include civil war and unfavourable economic conditions, that could make immigration or emigration an attractive option for large groups. Furthermore, policies of nations to make immigration or emigration cheaper or easier can also provide a macroeconomically favourable environment for immigration or emigration.

An excellent answer would question the scale of the immigration and emigration – as it could be a regional, national or international move. All of these different scales will have varying motivations and varying costs. For example, an international move will be significantly more costly to fund than a national one.

Q42: Here in the UK - we have a fairly well-established system of taxation which is used to fund a range of programmes. How do you think that places like Dubai, which don't use taxation at all, are able to grow at all, let alone so quickly?

This question wants you to think about other ways of development and expansion, apart from tax-generated income. The correct reason for the expansion of Dubai is not necessary, and instead the focus should be on possible routes for funding expansion without taxes.

A bad answer: would just state that Dubai is popular and therefore there is an incentive to invest and therefore expand the city.

A good answer: would think about the reasons Dubai may be a favourable place for investment. Ideas can be creative!

For example, the weather and climate of Dubai makes it an ideal holiday destination, which means that expansion of hotels and the commercial sector is very lucrative. The climate also means that the travel sector can thrive all year round, as opposed to ski resorts that often have quite a limited season. Furthermore, the increase of globalisation and reduction of air travel costs, means that Dubai is more accessible than ever and for global markets.

Geopolitics also provides an answer to this question. Dubai and the UAE are hugely rich in oil, and therefore expansion can be funded through oil revenues as opposed to tax-generated income. This reliance on oil revenues has let Dubai thrive during the age of increased industrialisation and innovation. However, this poses a question about whether the future of Dubai is secure. Global efforts to fight climate change and reduce emissions could reduce the profitability of the oil sector, and perhaps require taxation in order to fund further expansion.

An excellent answer would think about what tax generated income often provides, such as public services and schools. Such services can be privatised, and as such there can be expansion without tax-generated income. The candidate could then go on to think about whether this could apply to other states, and whether tax-generated income is a necessary feature of statecraft.

Q43: You are the infamous pirate captain "Dread {YOUR SURNAME}" and you have a standing rule where if more than half of the crew publicly disapprove of your tactics, they can execute you. You've just seized a large haul of gold, and have to divide it up. How would you distribute the wealth in such a way that you maintain the favour of your crew and get the largest possible share of the booty?

Here, they want the candidate to think of a logical answer, and then question whether the rest of the actors will act in the way that you would expect.

To divide the share to get the maximum and survive – divide the entire share equally between one more than half of the pirates – they will therefore agree and even if others get none, your share will be maximised.

However, you cannot guarantee that even the pirates who get some of the share will be happy with this - for example, one of the other pirates may want the entire share, and therefore will not agree unless they get this. Furthermore, we do not know that you will not die even if more than half of the pirates agree with you – the question does not specify this.

Lastly, a good answer would think of other ways of dividing the treasure – and what would happen on these occasions.

Examples:

Dividing it equally

This would not maximise the individuals share, but would have the highest likelihood of agreement, as there would be no inequality that could be questioned. However, pirates may not be satisfied with this amount, especially if there are many to share the treasure between

Keeping it all

You could potentially therefore use this to bargain with the pirates that are more capable of killing, so avoiding death and maximising the share of the treasure. However, this would be very reliant on perceiving which pirates have the willingness or capability to kill.

Q44: Why do people decide to change careers? If they are moving from a career which relies on extensive higher education to one which requires extensive vocational training, where do you think responsibility for funding their re-education lies?

This question is designed to make candidates think of reasons for changes in employment, and what drives such decisions. The second part of the question, in regard to who should pay for their training is designed for candidates to think about who benefits from such training, and thus who should have the responsibility of investing in it.

Reasons for teachers to become plumbers could be personal – such as the idea that they no longer enjoy teaching and would just like to try something different. Or, it could be a financial choice – such as a reduction in the wages of teachers requiring a change of employment in order to maintain a particular lifestyle.

A move in residence for the teacher could also lead to them becoming plumbers. For example, they could move to an area in which there are no vacancies as teachers, but a great shortage of plumbers. This would mean that they would be unable to continue their previous occupation.

Financially, the idea is that those who benefit the most from their training should be the ones that pay for it. As the benefits of the training will outweigh its costs. Therefore, if the teacher is likely to financially gain significantly from retraining as a plumber, they should be the one to bear the cost. However, if there is a shortage of plumbers, and they are in dire need around the country, perhaps the government should incentivise training. This would provide an incentive for teachers to retrain. Also, in this situation the country would be the one to benefit from the plumbers, and so the teachers should not bear the cost of their training.

An excellent answer would go on to think about whether the person that should pay for the training is the one that actually does pay. This very much depends on the political system – in some countries education and training is subsidised considerably more than in others.

Q45: Do you think that you could ever build an economy which was based entirely on service industries?

Firstly, an answer needs to think about what the service sector actually is. An answer to this would include the aspects of the economy that are not productive, and so do not produce an end product. Examples of this can include the hairdressing industry.

If the economy was to be based purely on the services sector, all other sectors – such as raw materials and industry – would have to be purely imported. Furthermore, as services are very difficult to export – as you cannot really send a haircut across the world, the economy would have a very small export business. This would mean that there would be a huge imbalance between exports and imports.

The next question, now we have determined what it means for an economy to be entirely based on the service sector, is whether this is feasible. This would only be feasible, if the country could afford all the imports necessary for a thriving society, such as food and fuel. These goods would be significantly more expensive than they would be if they were domestically produced, as the cost of importation would have also to be considered.

Furthermore, the inputs of the service industry, such as the food made in restaurants, would have to be imported. This would make the service industry significantly less profitable than in a situation in which the economy was not entirely based on the service sector. As businesses would have to pay higher prices for the inputs that they need, their margins would either be severely cut, or they would have to raise prices. If prices were raised, consumption would decrease as services would become less affordable.

This suggests that an economy entirely based on the service sector may be physically possible, but such an economy will be existing on a significant loss, as factor inputs of the service industry will be at inflated prices.

Q.46: Is global overpopulation a problem?

This questioned is designed to get the candidate thinking about an argument and come up with a conclusion based on their own ideas. Like many Oxbridge interview questions, there is not a set answer – the though process is the most important part, so think aloud!

A bad answer: would not fully think about both sides of the argument or would take a very strong stance on one side and not provide the evidence to back up their argument.

A good answer:

Would think about both sides if the argument. For example, arguments against there being too many people in the world could focus on the fact that some nations have larger populations due to higher levels of development. Therefore, there are not too many people in the world as not all states have had the opportunity to develop, urbanise and expand to the same extent. Another reason for there not being too many people in the world could perhaps focus on needing more people to fight problems, such as produce more food or innovate more.

The other side of the argument, that there are too many people in the world focuses on the strain on resources that more people bring. This could be in relation to the climate crisis or food production, and how more people may make current availabilities of resources need to be spread more thinly. There may be an upper limit to a population that the planet can support well – and this limit may have already been hit, which can be demonstrated by rises in extreme weather and the deforestation of the Amazon for resources.

The answer would then weigh up these sides of the argument and reach a conclusion by choosing which the candidate deems to be a stronger argument.

An excellent answer would go even further and could think of policies that could either reduce the population – such as policies designed to limit fertility. Or policies that could mitigate the effects of an increasing population on the environment, such as emissions caps on urbanised areas.

Q47: Do you think that the buying and selling of sports players by teams and managers around the world is similar to the buying and selling of people as slaves? Explain why.

This question is asking the candidate to bring more than the object in to question when thinking about sales – the context and meaning of the sale also differentiates it. If the candidate is not clear about the process of buying either option – it is a good idea to ask the interviewer before starting to answer the question. The candidate will not be penalised and it will make their answer better.

The buying and selling of a footballer, while on the surface perhaps sounding similar to the buying and selling of slaves, is hugely different. Firstly, the football player is able to not sign a contract for a sale, if they do not agree with it. For example if they do not want to move because of family commitments or they do not agree with the salary that they will be provided. In contrast to this, slaves are often taken from their homes forcibly, and sold with no freedom of choice in the matter.

Furthermore, the footballer has chosen that career. Whereas a slave would never have chosen to be an unpaid worker. Again, demonstrating that hugely different levels of choice are involved. A sale of a footballer is also often for a set amount of time, whereas the sale of a slave is indefinite – and the bad conditions they can be forced to live in often mean a sale is for the lifetime.

The surface level similarities are that they are both sales involving a human, and both provide the buyer with an employee. However, in the case of a footballer this employee is paid (often extortionately) whereas slaves provide unpaid labour.

An excellent answer may go on to think about perhaps what maintains these differences. For example, if footballers had fewer rights when signing contracts, their choice could be reduced and as such the processes could be more similar.

Q48: Why is a film actor wealthier than a theatre actor?

We can talk about the differences between the actors, the medium, and whether these assumptions will still hold true in the days of streaming.

Good Applicant: It is worthwhile noting that this is a quite dramatic generalisation. The average film actor is wealthier than the average theatre actor, but not dramatically so. However the gap between the wealthiest film actor and the wealthiest film actor is much larger, which is where the assumption comes from.

First of all, the question comes from supply. The live nature of theatre is such that a certain cast can only be at one performance, in one place, at a time. This is not so for pre-recorded film – it can be shown across the world in many cinemas and streaming at home simultaneously. It has the elements of supply over time and space that theatre lacks. This means that the average profit for a film will be much higher, despite requiring only one time commitment. Even if theatre actors acted multiple times a day for years, the issue of space will still be a practical concern.

Secondly, there is the matter of imperfect nature. Considering the nature of a theatre performance as something audiences view once but actors play for weeks, it is clear that no long-running role will be able to keep the same actors indefinitely. Theatre runs also do not always have finite limits since it is dependent on the performance popularity. Thus, except in exceptional cases, we would not expect for audiences to be attending to see specific actors. Instead, performances advertise by location, theme and story. This is exemplified by the fact that the Playbill for a musical would not have its actors names but a movie poster would.

It is important to note that many experts expect these discrepancies to begin closing. Theatre, and all the practicalities involved in it, has long since been criticised for its exclusive nature. Its high entry costs and seating arrangements make it inaccessible to the less fortunate in terms of wealth and disability. In accordance, musicals, an important form of theatre, are expected to be filmed professionally due to the success of the Hamilton recording by Disney. It is difficult to argue that what is posted is not a film, however, considering it is a still capture of – at most – a few performances out of hundreds. It can be concluded, therefore, that the inherently immersive live experience has a different value to society, and will therefore continue to exist, constrained by its nature.

A **poor applicant** may try to attribute this to non-economic reasons, such as difference in quality of acting. Not only is this untrue, it is unlikely to be the basis of the reasoning in an Economics interview.

Q49: Why is deflation a scare to the UK?

This question has three parts – what deflation is, why it is a problem in general, and why it is a problem specific to the UK.

Good Applicant: Deflation is an increase in the purchasing power of an economy's currency that comes from a fall in its overall prices. It can be viewed in contrast to inflation which is widely known as a problem to any who hold cash as inflation erodes its value. Historically, especially in wartime, inflation has been the key problem and deflation, its parallel, has not been seen as such. This has been changing recently.

Firstly, it's important to see why deflation is now considered a problem in general. An increase in purchasing power can be good in moderation when it affects certain staple products, since it increases spending and consumption. It can also reinforce the value of money and encourage saving. However, if it occurs rapidly, economic activity may contract. It may prompt a reduction in consumption since consumers hold out for lower prices, and it has increased the real value of debt. This is especially the case in debt deflation, when continued reduction in consumption hampers circulation of currency and economic growth. This can cause financial crises and recession. Interest rates can tighten, and real-wage unemployment can increase. As with inflation – it often becomes a spiral which is impossible to escape without intervention.

Now we can see why deflation in the UK is a scare. Here is important to note that deflation is thought of as a long-term occurrence. Negative inflation, if it is quickly remedied and does not spiral, is not typically thought of as a scare. However, with deflation the UK faces real issues. Discretionary goods, inessential goods with elastic demand, will not be purchased. In the UK, which has relatively low rates of poverty, purchase of discretionary goods comprises about 70% of all economic activity. If such a significant portion of the economy slowed, it could very well lead to a recession. Essentially, if the initial fall in prices comes from weak demand and not external factors, it poses an issue.

A **poor applicant** may state that since inflation is the real problem, and deflation is the opposite, it isn't one with certain constraints.

Q50: You run a sweet shop next-door to a rival sweet shop - you've both been able to drum up considerable loyalty in your customers who will flat-out refuse to shop anywhere else, provided you keep your prices below a tenner per sweet. You each have 10 such loyal customers - but there are 100 potential customers on the street who don't care as much and will buy from whoever is cheapest. With this in mind, at what price point would you have to reach for it to be more valuable to sell everything for ten pounds?

A logical way to go about this is to calculate from the bottom up. This would mean getting a piece of paper and calculating while explaining your process to your interviewer.

Good Applicant: At £10, I would be assured £100 from the loyal customers. Otherwise, I would have 90 customers who I can keep by keeping a price lower than £10. The price at which I would stop undercutting comes from dividing the baseline £100 by the 90 customers. This will give me the amount at which I would be indifferent – just over £1.10. Therefore, at any price lower than this, it would be more economically logical, and more profitable, to sell at £10.

That logic assumes that it will not be a constant bid for lower prices. Realistically, the question allows for the possibility of imperfect information - you cannot always know what your competititor will be selling for, even in the short-term, as they may see your prices and lower theirs once more. This means what we are calculating is an estimation assuming that the price was sufficiently low, and the customers know this, so as to assume that if the price was slightly lower all customers would come there.

All of this imprecision reflects one of the core tenets of microeconomic modelling. Models are not expected or required to be exact to have statistical relevance. They made broad generalisations about rational consumers and perfect information in order to accurately define trends, rather than to elucidate on specific examples. That is to say – the price calculated may not be the case in reality but on average, it will occur. In reality, we may find that the price we choose to switch over at is higher since there is imperfect information, and customers may find that the inconvenience of finding out small changes in price and moving in accordance with them is not worth the time consumed.

A **poor applicant** would make an assumption without attempting a calculation, which would suggest a lack of precision.

Q51: Why are the Chancellor of the Exchequer and the Governor of the Bank of England different jobs? What are the differences between them?

These are two distinct positions in the financial system of England, both of which are relevant to an understanding of it.

Good Applicant: The Chancellor of the Exchequer is a Minister, part of the UK government. They are also the head of Her Majesty's Treasury. It is one of the Great Offices of State and a senior member of the British cabinet. It is nominally what we could consider the finance minister. This position is currently held by Rishi Sunak. Moreover, one of their roles is appointing the Governor of the Bank of England, its most senior position. They are also the Chairman of the Monetary Policy Committee. This is currently held by Andrew Bailey. Both are positions with major economic consequence, but in different ways.

The positioning of these roles within their respective hierarchy is their most crucial difference. The chancellor works within the government. On the other hand, the Governor works within the Bank of England. These are two distinct economic institutions, as outlined in their Memorandum of Understanding. The Bank of England is the UK's central bank. It has been nationalised for over 50 years. Since 1998, the Bank has been an independent public organisation, owned by the Treasury Solicitor on the government's behalf. One key factor where the Bank's autonomy from the government is evident in the monetary policy. They decide the interest rate of the UK officially, as well as other aspects of the monetary policy framework. It works to meet certain targets given by the government, such as the Consumer Price Index measure of inflation, though how it gets there is primarily at its discretion.

This is a summarised depiction of how the Bank of England and the financial sector of the government work independently but towards many of the same goals. Thus, while the roles of their heads are different. For example, the chancellor may have a large role in setting a target inflation rate, whereas the Governor would decide and implement measures to pursue said target. The scope of roles is different, and their positioning reflect that.

Furthermore, the salary and commitments are different. The Chancellor's is around £71,000, though this does not include their salary gained as a member of parliament. By contrast the Governor's is £495,000. This larger salary makes sense with the context of being a less direct servant to the public.

A **poor applicant** would say they have the same job and position and that one may be irrelevant.

Q52: What would be the economic consequences of Scotland gaining independence from the UK? What about Wales?

This question has dramatic relevance now, given that Brexit occurred after Scotland voted to remain in the UK. It has been argued by many that this vote occurred the way it did since the UK was a member of the EU at the time.

Good Applicant: This question is increasingly relevant since the failure of Scotland's last independence referendum was heavily based around the idea that the UK would be remaining in the EU. George Galloway had some interesting points suggesting that Scotland leaving the UK would likely have much more severe ramifications for Scotland than it would for the UK, considering its size of economy.

According to Nicola Sturgeon, Scotland's first minister, Scotland would join the European Union as an independent member. Since they complied with EU law as part of the UK, this process would likely be fast-tracked if they were willing to cede to the EU's demands. Galloway outlined how Scotland in such a large union would lose much of their say. This would also imply a loss of free movement between Scotland and a post-Brexit England, and either electronic or manual checkpoints on the border between them. It is likely this would be a hard border. If Scotland became part of the Schengen Agreement, or generally decreased their immigration control with the EU, passports would be needed to cross this border. Scotland would also be losing some access to the British market. The only alternative to this would be coming to a bespoke agreement with the EU rather than joining it. Considering the priority the SNP – Scotland's primary pro-independence party – has placed on cooperation with the EU, this is unlikely. Economically it provides access to a market eight times the UK's. This is helpful for jobs and living standards. Investments may be affected in the general flux of such an unprecedented change.

With regards to the currency, some advocate for different approaches. Scotland may choose to take on the Euro, which some argue operates only in the interest of the central currencies. It would also need to fulfil certain criteria. The questions arise of separating financial systems and dividing debts and assets. Some economic agents still believe there would be a currency union in place, with strong checks and balances. However, political parties in the UK, as well as the Treasury and Bank of England are fairly unanimous in their worry of an independent Scotland using the pound: the risk two political systems with the same currency is demonstrated by the eurozone. Plausibly, Scotland could develop a new floating currency. It would risk loss of stability of the economy, but allows more flexibility.

Politically, Scotland renounced its sovereignty in the 1707 Act of Union. Since then they have had a separate devolved parliament with a large degree of autonomy except on issues where they have been mandated to defer to the UK parliament. As an independent nation, this parliament will be forced to rethink their reliance on their oil and gas reserves, the prices of which are in constant flux. This would also involve changes and greater control over their military – possibly in appealing to NATO – and health services. To some degree, they have been gradually increasing their autonomy here already and we could expect a smoother transition for it.

Wales, by contrast, would struggle more significantly than Scotland as an independent state. Both would suffer from similar issues, but the issue of poverty in Wales means that the economy does not have the strength for this. It depends heavily on public sector expenditure and infusion of funds, and would need to create new alliances immediately to replace this. It is similar to the event of leaving the EU and its funding, but on a more dramatic scale. Potentially, however, Wales could focus on their positive trade balance on manufactured goods and become more trade-oriented to sustain itself.

A **poor applicant** may try to focus too heavily on Wales, considering that is based on speculation. Avoid this by explaining Scotland's situation and then extrapolating where relevant and explaining key differences.

Q53: How do you predict oil prices will change in the next decade? How about the next century?

It is possible to use the established speculation for oil prices in the next 10 years, as well as global trends, to extrapolate its future more broadly.

Good Applicant: According to experts, the key factors determining oil prices – such as geopolitical turmoil, economic growth, shale production, and OPEC policies – will remain the same. This means that it is possible to predict with reasonable accuracy what oil price trends will occur.

Oil demands have begun to change and will do so in the next decade, but will still peak in the 2030s. This means that oil prices will gradually increase due to its use in shipping, petrochemicals and aviation. Some elements of use will begin to decrease, such as passenger cars. This means demand will continually increase, though likely at a decreasing rate. Moreover, due to limited price variations, growth in US shale production is slowing but will continue to occur for at least the first half the decade. In general, fossil fuels are non-renewable resources that are beginning to face depletion. This means that supply will continue to fall. Both these factors mean that prices will likely increase, though not substantially.

In the long term century view, we will see prices begin to fall. Supply will continue to decrease though at a much slower rate, as less will be mined. Moreover, due to global alarm over climate change, and carbon laws being implemented all over the world, renewable energy will begin to impact the energy scene. It may gradually replace oil use in transport and power, and provided governments align their policy to it, oil demand will decrease. Hydrogen use in particular will limit the demand on oil substantially. As demand falls, we will see oil prices dropping substantially and a corresponding increase in prices of renewable sources of energy.

A **poor applicant** would state that constant market forces of demand and supply would ensure that prices would remain the same.

Q54: What makes the US economy so strong?

There are a few key distinctive features of the American economy that should be explored to describe why America's economy, as opposed to other similarly structured ones, excels in the world market.

Good Applicant: The American economy is known for certain crucial features, notably: competition, consumption, resilience, flexibility, and innovation.

Competition, as in any capitalist country, can provide the fuel of economic growth. It motivates efficiency: businesses produce only those goods that are in demand and have direct incentive to reduce waste and have low prices. Citizens also seek the best jobs and work hard in order to consume the items they most want.

American consumption – while critiqued by many due to its scale – is unparalleled. In every field, including food, clothing and more, the US is expected to spend and consume to excess. This means there is heavy circulation of income and this boosts the economy from the ground up.

Resilience is the feature that ensures that in times of crisis, the other features are maintained. The US has faced some of the largest crises in the world in the last century – natural disasters, wars and the Great Recession. The economy has the durability to withstand such financial setbacks.

Flexibility is inherent in the capitalistic nature of the US system. Bureacratic red tape is minimised, maximising the amount of production and innovation. The government has sufficient regulation to ensure safety and legality, but allows business autonomy for the most part. Only key areas come under government regulation.

Innovation has been inbuilt in the idea of the American dream. Much of the culture of ambition rewards entrepreneurial spirit, meaning the US leads the world in producing new and better products.

A **poor applicant** may focus on one specific time or feature while missing the bigger picture.

Q55: Could you explain to a layman the perceived value of the G8? How would you distinguish it from the G20?

This is a question of contrast. First, give a brief description of what the G8 is. Then explain why the G8 was founded and what they meet to do. Finally, contrast the G20 by explaining what qualifies a country for the G20 but not for the G8, and why the G8 has continued relevance – if it does.

Good Applicant: The G8 is, quite literally, a group of eight countries whose representatives meet frequently to discuss issues of concern. These can be mutual, global and dependent. Most relevantly, socioeconomic development is one of the topics for ministerial meetings. The idea of the specific choice of the G8 is that its major industrialised countries, and between the eight they make up about half of the world's GDP. However, critics suggested that its use is in decline considering the situations of economies has dramatically shifted since the last change to the country line-up. For example, China's economy is currently stronger than that of seven of the eight countries, and yet it is not a member.

The G20 is a similar style of forum, but it has 19 countries and the European Union. They have replaced the G8 as the main economic council of wealthy nations. This means most economic issues and financial crises are discussed there, though political issues may still be solved within the G8. It is said that they are more useful as a means to financial stability given that the world has undergone rapid globalisation since the creation of the G8. Both use arbitrary cut-off lines of wealth, but the G20 increases the representation of countries.

David Cameron said in 2012 that the continued relevance of the G8 in this circumstance is their collective belief in free enterprise to promote economic growth. This explains the G8's roster: all Western countries, excluding Japan, which has been modelled around the US economy since World War II. One could argue that these are countries represent a traditionally Western idea of the model economy.

A **poor applicant** could oversimplify this question. It would be logical to assume that the G20 is simply a larger group of similar-minded countries. It is worth discussing, therefore, the ideological differences between the groups. The interviewer asking about both of the forums in direct succession is a sign that the important parts of the answer will come from their contrast.

Q56: What are the main similarities and differences between the Chinese and Indian economies?

As the two Eastern countries with large and booming economies, comparison and contrast of these economies is incredibly relevant.

Good Applicant: There are a number of historical and socio-political factors that play into the similarities – and differences – we see between these economies today. China is a far larger economy, with a GDP per capita of over $10,000 in 2019. By contrast, India's was around $2000 at the same point. This difference is likely to continue increasing for the time being, with China's GDP growth rate at 6.1% and India's at 4.2%. These numbers not only reflect modernising economies, they represent the wealth of human resource available in the two most populous countries. They also reflect similar unemployment rates.

China has been a closed, centrally planned economy for a long time, and it is only since the 1970s that significant reforms to this have been conducted. This has increased their efficiency dramatically. Price liberalisation, financial decentralisation, autonomy for state enterprises and more have been at the heart of this rapid transformation. One of the key statistics of note here is that shortly before China became the world's economy, it became the largest exporter and trading nation. However, China faces problems such as localised efficiency, an ageing population and low household consumption. There has always been attempts to undermine market-oriented reforms to reaffirm the power of the state, and it has proved one of their inefficiencies in the long-term.

India, on the other hand, has been an economy of varied methods and inputs. It is known for its diversity of economy – while the workforce is based around agriculture, it does not provide as much output as the growing service industry. India is gradually transforming into an open-market economy through economic liberalisation, deregulation and privatisation since the 1990s. Shocks of demonetisation and GST have recently slowed the economy, and demonstrate to a large degree why the Indian economy growth has not been as rapid as China's.

It is of note here that China is a one-party state and India a multi-party state. Further governmental reforms sought in India could not go through since the ruling party lacks a majority in their upper house of Parliament. On the other hand, the Chinese Communist Party can implement rapid development on a large scale with far fewer barriers. The authoritarian versus democracy debate is complicated by this – the inefficiencies inherent in cooperation. While it may be argued that the inclusivity provided is worth this, it is clear that the political system has a large part in creating such differences.

Another notable difference is the population. The population of China has a higher productivity of labour, producing more output with help from advanced infrastructure. Moreover, they are more urbanised. The urbanisation rate is approximately 58% in China and 37% in India for historical and cultural reasons. This adds to productivity in China, and increases economic growth.

A **poor applicant** would simply point out the difference in timeframes for reform and imply that both countries are on the same path but with different starting points. This would ignore the systemic differences between them.

Q57: Take a look at this graph. It shows the price of salt since 1800. You'll notice that it follows a recurring pattern. How can this have been sustained in the face of events like the Great War, the Great Depression, and The Second World War?

The answer to this is heavily dependent on what type of salt is being shown on the graph. Accurate graph analysis is therefore incredibly crucial.

Good Applicant: The demand for salt is split up into industrial, gritting, chemical and more. I will specifically talk about salt for consumption, an essential good. It is a nutrient, a preservative and a flavouring, and has been for many years.

Essentially, since salt is an essential good in terms of food consumption, it continually returns to its baseline through cyclical patterns. The demand for it continually increases as the population of the world increases dramatically. To match this, supply is able to continually increase. This is because salt is a very common commodity, found in abundance across the world. It is also renewable over relatively short period of time and therefore not at heavy risk of depletion.

Moreover, due to the heavy and cheap nature of salt, as well as its abundance, it is usually a regional good and not imported. This means inter-country conflits such as wars are less likely to affect it. Depressions only affect demand and supply as far as economic growth is affected, and since it is forced to bounce back through monetary and economic policy, so too does the demand and supply of salt. Therefore, the market forces governing the prices of salt always return to a baseline, promoting a cyclical pattern.

A **poor applicant** may suggest that the cyclical pattern is coincidental.

Q58: How does the job of a manager differ from that of a director, executive, or leader?

Here, the question is going to rely on an intuitive understanding of how we use these words differently.

Good Applicant: I find that there's a Peter Drucker quote that explains this well: "Leadership is doing the right things; management is doing things right." Both are ways of organising groups with a common purpose – the difference comes, therefore, in what methods they use to do it.

It is worth pointing out that a leader and a manager have fundamentally different tasks. We expect leaders to build and define their group's objectives, values and methods from the ground up. Managers, on the other hand, are expected to be one link in a larger chain and may not be the ultimate deciding factor. Their role is more akin to successfully delegating workers and resources to achieve their objective efficiently. They may be the head of their group but more often, they have higher ups to report to. If so, they may manage their team but still have no personal influence over the team's overall objectives and methods.

A good example of this would be regional and local managers of a national company. If they are inventive, unique and perform with autonomy, they may well be leaders too, but they will most likely otherwise be managers only. Similarly, leaders can be unofficially chosen if they lead through example – in this case they will not have the official position of manager. They also need not be acting with the intention of others following: that can be an indirect effect of their charisma and force of personality.

Poor applicants may try to suggest there is no meaningful difference between them without thinking critically about the question. They may also begin with a statement about their differences but end up not directly comparing them.

Q59: How might we begin to work out the ROI from Christopher Columbus's expeditions?

Return on investment is a measurement of the profitability of an investment. It is the ratio of return relative to cost, used to evaluate stand-alone investments or compare them to other potential investments. Columbus' voyages can be evaluated individually to compare them and see their overall contribution to the economy.

Good Applicant: The first step in calculating return on investment, or ROI, is usually finding the net return on investment. This is done by subtracting the initial value of investment from the final value of investment. Then the resultant value will be divided by the total cost of investment and multiplied by 100 to produce a percentage ROI.

Hence, to calculate the ROI from Christopher Columbus' voyages we would need to consider first the different voyages. He made four voyages – their ROI can be calculated collectively or individually. To calculate the collective ROI, we ought to calculate the net return on investment. This would be the value of the goods and services imported from the countries they discovered, considering the cost that would have been incurred to get them from elsewhere. It would also include imputed costs of new slave ownership and other such economic conquests. Then the resultant value will be divided by the cost of investment, easily found in the size of donation from his funders such as the Catholic Monarchs of Spain. This value will then be multiplied by 100.

It is worth noting that cost here does not include the imputed cost to the destination countries, or environmental destruction, suggesting a flaw in the use of ROI.

A **poor applicant** would say that since the statistical values of some of the inputs and outputs may not be known, the process of calculation cannot be shown.

Q60: Is it possible to calculate ROI for exploratory organisations, like NASA?

Return on investment is a measurement of the profitability of an investment. It is the ratio of return relative to cost, used to evaluate stand-alone investments or compare them to other potential investments. NASA would use it to evaluate their different operations – and potentially to see whether terrestrial or extra-terrestrial investments are more profitable.

Good Applicant: The first step in calculating return on investment, or ROI, is usually finding the net return on investment. This is done by subtracting the initial value of investment from the final value of investment. Then the resultant value will be divided by the total cost of investment and multiplied by 100 to produce a percentage.

To calculate the ROI of a NASA operations, we begin by finding its tangible and non-tangible as well as fiscal and non-fiscal net gain. Then we divide this by the cost of production, debugging, testing and verification. This will usually be given as the development cost. This resultant value will then be multiplied by 100 to produce the ROI of the operation.

There are opportunity costs to NASA's operations that are not measured in the ROI, showing how it is not a perfect measure.

A **poor applicant** would say that since the statistical values of some of the inputs and outputs may not be known, the process of calculation cannot be shown.

Q61: A dramatic election leads to the formation of a new country in Central Africa, which promptly develops and introduces a new currency. How is this currency then valued on the international market?

The implication of letting the international market decide the value of a currency is that it is a 'free' floating currency. This can be shown diagrammatically with a demand and supply diagram of the currency.

Good Applicant: As with all goods and services, the value of a currency — here we can call it Currency X - is measured by its demand. In a floating currency, this will occur due to the market forces of demand and supply. The estimated value will be the value at which the demand and supply is equal.

This leads us on to the theory of value of currency. Historically, the amount of currency in circulation in a country was dependent on that country's reserves of valuable commodities. Now, the dollar is seen as fiat money — it is instead dependent on government policy indicating how much currency ought to be printed. That would be set by their monetary policy. Due to inflation and deflation, the stability of currency value is dependent on a set amount of money being printed — usually enough to trigger a small rate of inflation. This part of the process is internal and based on mechanics internal to the country.

Then comes the question of how value is determined between countries with different currencies. There are three ways this could be done. Firstly, it could be the measure of how much Currency X would buy in foreign currency. This is done by the exchange rate, determined by forex traders on the foreign exchange market. It takes into account supply and demand, as well as expectations.

The second method is the value of the country's Treasury notes. Through the secondary market for Treasurys, they can be converted into Currency X. When the demand for Treasurys is high, the value of the Currency X rises. This is dependent on a functional, independent monetary system within the country.

The third — and most realistic — way would be through foreign exchange reserves, or the amount of Currency X held by foreign governments. The more that is held, the lower the supply, and the more valuable the currency is — until none is left. In essence, this is forming a demand and supply equilibrium based on the amount of foreign exchange passing to and from the country.

A **poor applicant** may suggest a fixed exchange rate and unchanging exchange rate, though this is not what the question implies.

Q62: Why didn't the UK adopt the Euro?

For this question, there is a number of possible factors, most of which are interlinked. Make sure you acknowledge that and then try to do it justice.

Good Applicant: 19 of the 27 member states of the European Union use Euros as their primary currency and are therefore part of the Eurozone. This eases difficulty in exchange rates during trade. However, even before leaving the EU, the UK did not use the Euro, instead using the pound sterling. Though the UK is within the EU's trading bloc, this move was strategic. The UK is also not in the EU's Schengen area, showing their commitment to individual progress and pragmatism.

The euro was proposed as a single currency system for the EU in 1997. Gordon Brown, the England's Chancellor of the Exchequer at the time, proposed five economic tests for England to use the euro. The first of these tests is that business cycles and economic structures must be compatible such that the UK could manage with Eurozone interest rates. Secondly, the monetary system must have economic flexibility to solve local and aggregate issues. Thirdly, it must create a situation conducive to investment in the UK. Fourthly, it must allow England's financial services industry to be internationally competitive. Lastly, it must promote growth, stability and an increase in job opportunities. These benchmarks have been considered too high to ever feasibly pass, so many believe that standing by them means the UK will never adopt the euro.

There are also further practical reasons for this. It is considered by many a political move – many believe it would be crossing the rubicon of EU integration. Initial popular support of Brexit is the perfect indicator of why that would have been politically unpopular. Similar opinion polls in the UK have suggested that the majority of the British were against adopting the euro.

Finally and arguably most importantly, adopting the euro would force the UK to meet 'euro convergence criteria'. This includes a debt-to-GDP ratio which would limit their fiscal policy. It also includes controlled interest rates, limiting their monetary policy. Setting interest rates is currently a task by the Bank of England, and it is set to meet the UK economy's aims. This means that though the movement of the UK and EU's interest rates may align somewhat, they will not be the same because of differing priorities. Other losses of autonomy would include not being able to issue debt in the UK's own currency and losing the shock absorber having your own currency provides. Examples such as that of Greece can prove that.

Poor Applicant: A poor applicant may consider starting with an evaluative on whether we should be using Euros. This is not what the question is asking, though you might find that the answer fits well into what you've already said once you've given a clear answer.

PPE & HSPS

A politics applicant may be asked a question relating to politics or questions from a related subject, such as sociology. Despite stating a previous knowledge in one particular area of HSPS or PPE on your application, you may be asked a question on any of these subject areas. However, you will not be expected to demonstrate specific detailed knowledge in an area not studied previously, you will simply be expected to apply your own point of view and understanding to the topics.

HSPS & PPE interviews generally consist of a large question with many smaller sub-questions to guide the answer from the start to a conclusion. The main question may seem difficult, impossible, or random at first, but take a breath and start discussing with your interviewer different ideas you have for breaking down the question into manageable pieces. Don't panic.

The questions are designed to be difficult to give you the chance to show your full intellectual potential. They will help guide you to the right idea if you provide ideas for them to guide. This is your chance to show your creativity, analytical skills, intellectual flexibility, problem-solving skills and your go-getter attitude. Don't waste it on nervousness or a fear of messing up or looking stupid.

The interviewer wants to see what you know and what you are capable of, not what you don't know – "positive interview".

When answering a question, you should be responsive to the interviewer and take on board their prompts and suggestions. If you are making an argument that is clearly wrong, then concede your mistake and try to revise your viewpoint – it is ok to say 'I didn't think of that' when taking on board a different viewpoint. Do not stubbornly carry on arguing a point that they are saying is wrong. **Making mistakes is not a bad thing** – if you can show that you have addressed a mistake and attempted to revise your argument upon the realisation of more information, you are showing a skill crucial to getting through essays and supervisions at an Oxbridge university.

Due to the amount of subjects available under the HSPS and PPE courses, **there are no set patterns to the questions you can get asked**. Most questions, however, will focus on a topic for which it is possible for any individual to have an opinion without previous knowledge of the area. This is to test the way you think about a topic and to test whether you are able to apply your own experiences and knowledge to an unknown subject area. These skills are important when studying HSPS/PPE as the courses are essay-based and rely strongly upon the ability to construct an argument based on the information provided. Many questions are related to society today and may require the individual to be familiar with current affairs and big events in the news.

A sociologist may be asked sociology questions or questions from a related subject, such as politics. An archaeologist will likely be asked questions on archaeology, history, and anthropology. Given the very broad nature of the course, candidates are required to have a general interest in all aspects of the course, but which subject will be the main focus of any interview should be clear beforehand.

The questions will usually take one of a few possible forms based on highlighting skills necessary to 'think like a social scientist.' **Five main questions types** are:

- Why do we need... (borders, welfare state, international institutions, museums etc.)?
- Compare X to Y... (normally based on your essay or personal statement, so something you are familiar with)
- Distinguish between... (state and nation, race and ethnicity, liberalism and libertarianism etc.)
- What do you think about... (the current British school system, nature vs. nurture debate etc.)?
- Why is there... (gender inequality in the workplace, poverty etc.)? How would you solve it?

Questions also have recurring themes that appear because they are important for social sciences: legitimacy and role of government, human rights, poverty, feminism, international institutions, the purpose of education and different educational systems, voting systems, inequality and social classes.

WORKED QUESTIONS

Below are a few examples of how to start breaking down an interview question, complete with model answers.

Q1: Can a violent protest ever be justified?

[Extremely clear-headed] **Applicant**: Well, I know that the law states that violence against other people or property is not acceptable, and yet I also know that violent protests still occur and this makes me wonder why. There must be a reason that people feel the need to turn to violence. This might be because of their personality or it may be something deeper such as the feeling of having no choice. If a point is important and the protest is for a serious reason, such as fighting for human rights, and all other forms of protest have been avoided, then maybe the only way to be heard is through violence. However, I don't think a violent protest can ever be justified. For example, take the 2011 UK Riots – violence didn't solve anything – it is a way of being seen and heard, but a horrific one. I don't think being heard for doing something that is wrong is the right way to be recognised.

This shows that **the question can be broken down into smaller-parts**, which can be dealt with in turn. At this point, the interviewer can give feedback if this seems like a good start and help make any necessary modifications. In this particular case, the applicant might be asked to expand on the reasons a person might resort to violence in protests and to give an example if possible. They may also be asked to provide a suggestion as to a better way to be heard than a violent protest. The details are unimportant, but the general idea of breaking down the question into manageable parts is important. The interviewer is not looking for an expert, but someone who can problem-solve in the face of new ideas.

A **poor applicant** may take a number of approaches unlikely to impress the interviewer. The first and most obvious of these is to simply answer 'yes' or 'no' with little justification or reference to an alternative point of view and with no attempt made to move forward. The applicants who have done this only make it worse for themselves by resisting prodding as the interviewer attempts to pull an answer from them, saying "fine, but I'm not going to be able to expand because I don't know anything about this", or equally unenthusiastic and uncooperative responses.

Another approach which is unhelpful in the interview is the **'brain dump'**, where instead of engaging with the question, the applicant attempts to impress or distract with an assortment of related facts or events: In this case, reeling off the law on violence or a list of historical riots and their outcomes. Having gotten off to this start isn't as impressive as a more reasoned response, but the interview can be salvaged by taking feedback from the interviewer.

Many of these facts could start a productive discussion which leads to the answer if the applicant listens and takes hints and suggestions from the interviewer.

Q2: How do you know the moon isn't made out of cheese?

[Extremely clear-headed] **Applicant**: What I am first going to think about is what needs to be considered when deciding whether or not something is true. This raises questions like "Is it patently absurd?", "Is it backed up by evidence?", and "What types of evidence do we require?". Next, I consider whether it is reasonably possible that this statement fits with other associated and established pieces of knowledge, e.g. the formation of the planets, stars, and satellites. If the claim is at odds with established knowledge, then I may be more inclined to believe it untrue. However, this does not necessarily prove anything. For example, in this case, what is meant by cheese? If we are talking poetically, or aesthetically then it may be considered reasonable to make the above claim.

Moreover, whose reality are we talking about, and indeed does the result vary depending on this? I mean, is it really possible to 'know' anything, or are we just making educated guesses based on a set of assumptions married with some data – and does this count as 'real'? Essentially, when I first looked at the statement I thought it was completely absurd and previously proven otherwise. However, after consideration of perspective, definition, reality, and knowledge, I am now not so convinced.

Just like the previous example questions, this is a step by step answer. The applicant has broken down their thoughts and provided the interviewer with a stream of their own workings of their mind. This allows the interviewer to understand how the individual is breaking down the question and gives an opportunity for the interviewer to intervene with further questions if required.

A **poor applicant** may state something like "Well because it obviously isn't" – without any further justification. The point of a question like this is to consider the many different ways in which we experience reality and develop our understanding therein. If the applicant fails to address more than the superficial, then they are unlikely to show an understanding for the point of the question.

Q3: Despite knowing the health implications of smoking, why does it remain legal in the UK?

Good **Applicant**: I'd like to think about what other areas are considered by the **legislators of the UK** when they allocate legal status to things, as it can't just be health implications. With regards to smoking, there are a number of vested parties including tobacco companies and smokers themselves. Tobacco companies rely on smoking being legal in the UK for their income. If smoking were made illegal, then these companies would lose 100% of their UK revenue, which in turn, may impact the economy as a whole (these sales are far from insubstantial). Secondly, when thinking about smokers who are 20% of the UK's adult population (equating to around 10 million people), they represent a large fraction of the potential electorate.

Therefore, banning smoking would have significant implications for political intervention due to unpopularity, loss of freedom, etc.

As another point, smokers may claim that they have an addiction which is difficult to stop. They may also argue that smoking was legal when they first started to smoke. Thus, the government may face a legal battle if they were to suddenly make the product illegal. This may make a total ban on smoking impractical and a breach of an individual's right to choose. However, banning smoker on a more gradual basis may be feasible and is happening today; for example, it is now against the law to smoke in cars, in the workplace, and in public areas. Maybe **phasing out smoking** is more realistic, and is therefore what is being attempted in the UK. This would imply that it is not the case that legislators are unaware or uncaring of the health implications of smoking, but that they are attempting to reduce smoking in a less disruptive manner.

A **poor applicant** might fail to address the reasons why smoking has not been made illegal. It is not simply a case of saying "smoking is bad, therefore the government should ban it". The question of whether it should be banned impacts many people and showing an understanding of different perspectives and potential arguments is important for answering this question sufficiently.

Q4: Politicians often claim that a 'nuclear deterrent' is vital in averting war, if every country had nuclear weapons, does it follow that there would be no war?

A **Good Applicant**: We all have learnt how dangerous nuclear weapons can be when **Hiroshima and Nagasaki** were destroyed at the end of World War 2. The threat to the environment, human lives, and even future generations is known, and the risk is too high. Nuclear weapons should not be used at all. On the other hand, it is true that there was no direct war between the USA and USSR during the Cold War and both had nuclear weapons. It seems possible that countries with nuclear weapons do not engage in war with one another as the high risk of a catastrophe deters them from using nuclear weapons, and hence the proliferation of nuclear weapons may prevent wars.

This shows that the candidate understands the question and is able to draw on some examples from A-level History. A **better candidate** would then engage in a discussion with the interviewer about the moral aspect of the topic or may choose to draw on a broader range of examples and realise that although proliferation of nuclear weapons may deter another world war, it could lead to more frequent small-scale wars. Examples of wars in Iraq, Vietnam, Afghanistan, and Korea during the Cold War demonstrate that there were, in fact, "real wars", and the USSR and USA backed smaller countries in war. So, the proliferation of nuclear weapons may have led to small-scale wars, yet prevented another world war. Making a moral case against any use of nuclear weapons, for instance, referring to the experience from Hiroshima and Nagasaki shows sensitivity about the topic.

A **poor applicant** may make a moral argument against the use of nuclear weapons before providing any insightful analysis and attempting an answer to the question. Another approach which is unhelpful is focusing too much on providing a yes/no answer to the question, and hence missing the point that the proliferation of nuclear weapons is a gradual process with various political, moral, and economic difficulties, and it is not plausible that all countries could get nuclear weapons overnight. The question is very broad and raises many interesting arguments for discussion, but 'brain dump' is not helpful here.

Q5: When we make contact with an extra-terrestrial civilisation, what should we tell them is humanity's greatest achievement?

[Extremely clear-headed] Applicant: The concept of humanity's greatest achievement is very subjective. It can either be measured in terms of effort needed to accomplish it, or in terms of impact. In the first case, humanity's greatest achievement could be the pyramids, since they required a tremendous amount of work with little technology, and are still standing today after thousands of years. In terms of impact, humanity's greatest achievement could be the discovery of penicillin for example. I think that it makes more sense to focus on a ground-breaking achievement from the past, rather than the most recent accomplishments of humanity.

If I were to tell an extra-terrestrial civilisation about penicillin, however, I would also have to provide an explanation on humanity's problems which it solved. Finally, I would have to take into account the aim of my message: am I trying to impress, intimidate, or simply inform?

A good applicant will understand the true aim of the question: creating an abstract situation in which he is encouraged to problematise the subjective concept of 'greatest achievement' and make an argument.

A poor applicant could misinterpret the question, and focus on the extra-terrestrial civilisation, talking about space technology and means of communication. Alternatively, he could choose an accomplishment and fail to justify his answer, or provide a lot of facts on the subject without problematising the concept of 'greatest achievement'.

Q6: In a democracy, can the majority impose its will on the minority?

[Extremely clear-headed] Applicant: First, I am going to think from the practical point of view: if by 'minority' we mean 'the ruling elites', does the majority have the actual ability to impose its will? The population only gets to make decisions on rare occasions: elections and referenda. Most of the time, decisions are made by a small group of people: the government. In 2002-2003, there were mass protests against the war in Iraq, but this did not stop Tony Blair from sending troops. It seems that once a government is in power, there is little that the majority of the population can do before the next elections. Secondly, we could think about the question from a normative point of view: should the majority be able to make most decisions in a democratic system? There is a difference between democracy and populism, where power is held by the masses. The latter could be problematic. If by minority we understand things such as small ethnic or religious groups, in a populist system they would have no say and could end up being oppressed. In a democratic system, minorities are protected by laws. However, we can see that the system is sometimes flawed. For example, in the US, there are only two major political parties: people with different agendas than Republicans or Democrats are pushed away from power.

This question can be answered in a number of ways, but a good candidate will show his capacity to deconstruct it, and think for a moment before replying. He will support his points with examples.

A poor applicant will rush into an answer without thinking and might end up getting confused between the different aspects of the question. He will either make generalisations without giving examples, or focus exclusively on a single real-life case, giving a lot of facts but without any argument or acknowledgment of a different point of view.

Q7: Why is there social inequality in the world? How would you resolve this issue?

[Extremely clear-headed] Applicant: I do not think that there is a single reason for social inequality in the world. Of course, it is not normal that 1% of the population controls almost 50% of its wealth. Greed and self-centeredness seem to be inherent flaws of humanity. However, I also think that there are other underlying factors behind social inequality. I cannot imagine a society in which everybody would have the same proportion of wealth and the same professional opportunities. People live in different places, speak different languages, and simply have different talents and skills. Thus, I do not think that social inequality can ever be fully resolved. Experiments such as communism in the USSR have attempted to artificially suppress inequality. This has not only entailed terrible crimes such as the extermination of entire groups in the society, but has also proved economically unsustainable in the long-term, with the Soviet economy eventually collapsing. Nevertheless, perhaps some form of **efficient taxation and governments granting more funds** to international organisations and NGOs could help reduce inequality.

A good applicant can have a different opinion on the subject, but will take into account other points of view, and will identify the difficulties associated with resolving such a complex problem, supporting his argument with solid A-level type factual knowledge.

A poor applicant could focus on only one of the two questions. He might give a 'trendy' answer such as "It's all because of the rich" or "Humans are bad so there is nothing you can do", without giving any real explanation or evidence, and refuse to engage fully with the questions.

Q8: To what extent is taxing the rich likely to lead to greater equality in society?

[Extremely clear-headed] Applicant: There is a big disproportion in terms of wealth between a small group of the 'rich' and the 'poor' majority. Therefore, it would seem logical to find a way of redistributing that wealth. As we can see, altruism does not suffice, since the problem persists despite a few notable examples of rich people giving big proportions of their fortune to charity, for instance, Bill Gates. Taxation does seem like a good solution. However, it needs to be designed efficiently. For instance, we must make sure that such a tax does not affect the economy negatively, for example, by dissuading the wealthy from opening new businesses and sources of income. Secondly, there have been cases where large funds were not used efficiently, but rather usurped by local warlords and criminal organisations, for instance in Somalia in the 1990s. It might be necessary to establish an international body of experts to design and monitor the implementation of projects funded by this tax.

A good applicant will be able to **identify both the positive and the negative sides of such a policy**. Regardless of whether he has any knowledge on the subject, he will provide a well-structured, logical answer.

A poor applicant might be intimidated by the question and refuse to answer by saying something like "I don't know anything about taxes". Alternatively, he might provide an answer which focuses only on one side of the coin, making it very vulnerable to counterarguments.

Q9: Is alcohol addiction always a result of the social environment, peer pressure, and negative role models?

[Extremely clear-headed] **Applicant:** Alcohol addiction is more widespread in certain social environments or countries: for instance, it is a much bigger problem in Russia than in the UK. I don't think that it would be appropriate to argue that nationality or ethnicity inherently determines the likelihood of alcohol addiction.

This is why explanations such as **peer pressure and negative role models** are very useful. Indeed, peer pressure can become integrated into culture. For example, drinking alcohol in large quantities on a teenage trip abroad or on an American Spring Break has become almost a ritual. In some cultures, drinking vast amounts of alcohol can be considered as a mark of virility, or politeness, which is conducive to alcohol addiction. However, we should not generalise. It is possible for someone to develop an alcohol addiction in an environment where drinking is frowned upon or rare, just as it is possible to remain abstinent while being surrounded by alcoholics. If an individual's parents and friends do not drink, and yet he becomes an alcohol addict citing a musician with questionable habits as his role model, it seems reasonable to assume that other factors, perhaps psychological, were at play. Thus, while the social environment is a very potent explanation for alcohol addiction, ignoring the possibility of other factors could have negative consequences, such as failing to properly address the issue.

A good applicant will **note the use of the word 'always'**, and attempt to come up with a counter-example.

A poor candidate might fall into the trap of agreeing with the statement without thinking of other points of view. He could refuse to reply stating his lack of knowledge on the topic, or give anecdotal evidence from his experience or environment without constructing an argument.

Q10: Imagine you are a historian a hundred years in the future, looking back on today. What aspects of society would you focus on?

[Extremely clear-headed] **Applicant:** I do not think that any aspect of history should be discarded as unimportant. However, I am most interested by politics and geopolitics. It is basically impossible to predict the future, and very hard to fully understand the present and its implications. A hundred years from now, we will have a much better understanding of some of today's unanswered questions. For instance, how successful are international organisations in fostering cooperation and preventing conflict? After all, the UN and the EU are relatively recent constructs, and did not fully exploit their potential until the end of the Cold War.

Determining whether international institutions have any real influence or whether they are just tools in the hands of self-centered states is one of the big debates in the study of international relations. Secondly, it would be interesting to see whether in the **age of mass information** and communication, humanity is able to learn from its previous mistakes. Parties of the extreme right are currently gaining a lot of votes in Europe, due partly to economic hardship. Will the fate of the Weimar Republic become relevant again?

A good candidate will demonstrate a certain degree of knowledge on the current topic of his choice, and will be able to identify the way in which it might be perceived by a historian.

A poor candidate might avoid the question by saying something like "I think that humanity will destroy itself within a hundred years so there will be no historians left". He could also lose track of his argument by trying to impress the interviewer with his factual knowledge on a current topic, or attempt to make unjustified predictions of future developments.

Q11: What are the main reasons for persistent unemployment in the UK?

Extremely clear-headed] **Applicant:** I think that people are often tempted to look for simple explanations behind complicated issues. This is why extreme political parties are so successful: they provide the population with easily identifiable scapegoats such as 'the current government', 'immigrants', or 'the EU', and blame them for every economic and social problem. In reality, issues such as unemployment have many reasons. One of them could be the discrepancy between supply and demand: what type of jobs people are prepared for at schools and universities, and what type of jobs are offered on the market. For instance, in Scandinavian countries, when an unemployed individual cannot find work for a certain period of time, he is offered courses which allow him to perform a different type of work, with more demand.

Another reason could indeed be **globalisation**, with the **international economic crisis**, and many companies moving abroad to reduce costs. However, this does not justify oversimplifying the issue by blaming solely external factors such as foreigners or international organisations. Instead, efforts should be made to better adapt the national system to the realities of the globalised world.

A good candidate will try to provide a balanced and well-argued answer, regardless of his political or moral stance. He will stay away from generalisations and normative statements based on little or no evidence.

A poor applicant might refuse to engage with a question on which he has little previous knowledge. Alternatively, he may make sweeping generalisations or provide an exhaustive list of factors without really explaining any of them.

Q12: Should prisoners have the right to vote?

[Extremely clear-headed] Applicant: I think that in a democracy, voting is one of the **citizen's basic rights**. The question is: should prisoners still be considered as citizens? It could be said that when they break the social contract of norms governing the society, their rights are also revoked. However, if a prisoner is deprived of all his rights, his eventual reintegration into society will be even harder. In my opinion, the right to vote should be granted to those prisoners who have not committed the gravest of crimes, such as murder or rape.

Moreover, in some countries, the issue of 'political prisoners' is still prominent, for instance, in China or Ukraine. If someone is imprisoned for disagreeing with the regime and has no right to vote for a different party or candidate, then there is little chance of change and the system moves one step further towards authoritarianism.

A poor applicant could focus too much on providing a yes/no answer based on personal beliefs or anecdotal evidence, without trying to engage with alternative perspectives on the question.

Q13: Is there such a thing as national identity in the world of globalisation?

[Extremely clear-headed] Applicant: In my opinion, while borders are becoming more and more permeable and people can communicate and travel from one part of the world to the other, national identity is not necessarily losing its potency. According to the Marxist theory, national identity was supposed to disappear, giving way to an international movement of workers. This was not really accomplished, and the communist countries which survived the longest such as the Soviet and Chinese systems, were those which mixed communism with nationalism. While from our 'Western' perspective it might seem that national identity is dying, this might be related to the fact that we live in relatively peaceful times: there has been no war on the current territory of the EU for decades.

However, in times of conflict, national identity becomes very powerful. We can see this on current examples such as Ukraine and Russia, but also in post 9/11 USA. I think that in times of external threat, people tend to unite under a symbol which differentiates them from the 'other'. Since the nation state remains the main actor in international relations, most conflicts are likely to oppose one nation against another, thus reinforcing the sense of national identity.

A good candidate can argue either way, but should be able to acknowledge both sides of the coin. He should be able to support his ideas with some factual A-level type knowledge.

A poor applicant might fail to engage properly with the question, instead of trying to impress the interviewer by dumping facts. Alternatively, he could make broad generalisations without supporting his argument with any real evidence.

Q14: What areas of Philosophy are you interested in?

[Extremely clear-headed] Applicant: I am interested in theories of the state. Many thinkers have attempted to tackle this issue throughout history, ranging from Plato, through Hobbes and Rousseau, to Marx. They all have very different visions of what an efficient political system should look like, whether the human being is inherently good or bad, and who should have the right to rule. What is interesting in this area of Philosophy is that the thinkers have often actually affected the reality.

The writings of Marx are the best example of this phenomenon since they have been used and abused by activists in many countries, leading to the October Revolution in 1917 and the establishment of the USSR, one of two systems dominating the international system for decades. I think that there are many interesting questions in this area of Philosophy. Is it possible to design a system which would be applicable to any setting and society? Do philosophers have a responsibility over how their writings are understood and used?

A good candidate will show both a certain degree of knowledge and of genuine interest in the topic of his choice. He will identify some of the big questions related to the field.

A poor candidate might give an exhaustive list of areas of Philosophy without going into depth on any of them. Alternatively, he could try to demonstrate his extensive factual knowledge of the writings of a single author, without engaging with the wider question on the area of Philosophy.

Q15: Tell me about some political texts that you have read.

[Extremely clear-headed] **Applicant:** I have looked at some political theory texts, such as Plato's Republic. In this text, the author is describing a perfect political system, an ideal city led by a philosopher-king. He also talks about other flawed political systems, such as tyranny or democracy. I think that this text is very interesting and useful for understanding political systems from the past, and has also inspired other, more recent authors. However, it is important to note that Plato writes from the perspective of Ancient Greece, and many of his concepts are outdated. I think that the term 'political text' could also apply to other types of documents, for example, party programmes, but even literary fiction. I recently read Bulgakov's Master and Margarita, a novel with fantasy themes such as the devil and witchcraft, written in the Soviet Union. Its focus on religion and the occult was also a hidden critique of the atheistic Soviet society. Similar things could be said about the Animal Farm or 1984.

A **good candidate** will try to go beyond simply giving factual knowledge on a text studied in class. He will try to come up with a critical approach towards the text showing a certain degree of independent thought, or problematize the term 'political texts'.

A poor candidate might panic if he has not studied texts of political theory in school, instead of making the best of it by trying to come up with different types of political texts. Alternatively, he might opt for dumping a lot of factual information on a text, instead of showing his understanding of it or demonstrating a critical perspective.

PPE INTERVIEW QUESTIONS

Q1: You've been presented with an unknown symbol - how might you go about trying to decipher its meaning?

This is a question which looks at assessing how you reason in logical tasks. This is the kind of question which may throw a candidate in an interview, so it is important to have a few moments to gather your thoughts and think about how you would logically approach the question. It is also worth noting that the question does not just want you to discuss how you decipher symbols, but what you <u>first look for</u> when deciphering symbols. This means that it is unnecessary to give a full explanation of the full process you might go through to decipher a symbol.

Bad answer: I look to see if it looks like anything I am familiar with and then we can assume that the symbol will likely be this.

This is a bad answer because the candidate assumes that a symbol will be alike something you are familiar with. Just because a symbol might look like the letter d, does not mean it represents the letter d. The interviewer will also be unimpressed by the lack of creative thinking from this candidate, and the fact that they do not consider whether the symbol will be seeking to describe words, letters, or concepts.

Good answer: The main thing I first look for when deciphering a symbol is any contextual clue which may lead us in the direction of deciphering the symbol. For example, the date or location might help us. If the date that the symbol was written is from before writing as we know it existed, then it is unlikely to represent individual letters, but may instead represent concepts or words. As well as this, the location can help us to have an idea of what language it may be written in, which can be particularly useful if, for example, it is a symbol is a part of a broader sentence. This is because we can tell that, if it is written in English, single letter words will probably be either I or A, and a similar approach can be applied towards other languages. Another thing we should initially look for, which can be helped with this context, or by looking at other symbols around it, is whether the symbol does in fact seem to represent a letter, word, concept, or any other thing. This will significantly help us to decipher it.

This is a good answer because the candidate gives a very logical approach to how this question can be tackled. They also show that they can think creatively by considering how context will help to decipher a symbol.

Q2: What makes you human?

This is a very broad question which tests the candidate's ability to think about concepts that are often taken for granted. The candidate is not expected to reach a full definition of a human being, but should instead engage in a critical discussion about the difficulty of defining what it is that makes us human.

Bad answer: What makes us human is having an opposable thumb. *Or* What makes us human is the fact that we have a conscience.

These are both bad answers because they do not go into enough detail, as could easily be done by explaining why it is that these things make people human. Furthermore, they do not engage critically with those counterpoints which may be made against their definition of what makes us human. The first answer is bad because, though it is true that humans are unique in having opposable thumbs, it does not follow that this is the specific thing which makes us human. It seems that there is a lot more to being human than this. The second answer is bad because it does not address the fact that some people may argue that other animals have a conscience too.

Good answer: I'm not sure there can be one single thing that makes us human. Instead, I think it is probably a combination of a few things. The main one, I think, is our ability to reason. We seem to be unique as animals in our ability to reason. It is likely that other animals can reason to a degree, but nowhere near as much as humans can. Secondly, another thing that makes us human is the way we interact with other humans, and form societies. Humans are sociable animals, and therefore naturally form these communities. We would not be human if we lived in highly individualistic ways.

This is a good answer because the candidate goes into a lot more detail about some of the things which makes us human. Furthermore, they develop on this, explaining why it is that each of these things makes us human. They also consider arguments against their point, such as when they claim why reasoning makes us human despite the fact that other animals may be able to reason.

Q3: How would you go about assessing the number of people in here?

This is a philosophy question on the concept of personhood and identity. It is the type of question which might throw you so make sure that before you tackle it, you take a moment to sit back, and think about what it is the interviewer is really asking you. This type of question is one which you will not be able to give a definite answer for. Given this, it is important that you explain your thinking out loud, as you try to reach some kind of answer.

For the sake of the mock answers, I will assume that there are three people in the room: two interviewers and the interviewee.

Bad answer: There are three people. There cannot be more than 3 people, as I can only see three. There cannot be less than three, because I can see three. Anyone who thinks overwise is wrong.

This is bad because it fails to consider any other potential approach to the idea of personhood. It assumes that the way we tend to count people is inherently true, without questioning this at all. It also becomes argumentative in a way which can be tempting if faced with a difficult question like this, but is unhelpful in a philosophy interview. You should show that you are willing to be persuaded to consider other potential solutions to this question, rather than immediately shutting yourself off from different ideas.

Good answer: We would usually say that there are three people in this room. However, that assumes that the other people in this room are in fact people. We do not really know this. For example, you may both be philosophical zombies [*i.e. someone who looks and acts like a person, but doesn't really have a conscience or soul*]. I don't know that you have a conscience, so, assuming that being a person is in some ways defined by the existence of a conscience, I don't know whether either of you really are "people". If we think about what defines what it is to be a "person", we will find it hard to prove, in fact, that any of us have the features which make us by definition a person. For example, we might instead claim that a person is an entity that has free will. However, we don't really know that we have free will. We may be controlled by a God or something else to perform the actions we do, and be programmed to think that this is our own freewill. Therefore, we cannot truly know how many people are in this room.

This answer is good because it considers a range of approaches to the question of what it is to be a person. This candidate does not close themselves up to considering different philosophical arguments, as the weaker one does, and instead embraces a philosophical debate. They also demonstrate that they have a basic understanding of core philosophical ideas, such as free will, and the idea of philosophical zombies.

Q4: Do you think you know anything?

This is a philosophy question on epistemology, which is the branch of philosophy concerned with knowledge. It is fairly likely that you will get a question similar to this one, or which touches on some of the ideas you will consider for this question. There are a lot of ways you may consider answering this question. One thing which is important is to know that they will not be expecting you to have an in-depth knowledge of epistemology. They are just looking to see how you go about approaching questions like these.

Bad answer: No, it is not possible to know anything because, even though I think I know something, how do I know that I know it?

This answer is bad because, whilst the candidate begins to consider an interesting point in philosophy, they do not explain what they mean by "how do I know that I know it?". This is a commonly heard expression which has little meaning if you do not go onto explain what you actually mean. This makes their answer superficial.

Good answer: I'm sure we 'know' some things, but the problem comes in trying to prove that we know anything, and in trying to define what knowledge actually is. For example, I know that this is a chair, because I see it, and it looks like a chair. However, how do I know that chair-like things which are perceive are really chairs? Just because I see it, doesn't mean that it is really there, or that it is really a chair. I have no proof that what I perceive is knowledge. We might, instead, consider non-perceptual forms of knowledge, to see if we can 'know' anything. We can use deductive reasoning to argue that 2+2=4. I know that 2+2=4. However, these numbers are purely abstract, and are only assigned by humans. I therefore don't really have any proof that 2+2=4, beyond the fact that I have been taught that this is the case, and other people assume it to be so. However, this cannot be a satisfactory account of what it is to know something. Therefore, whilst I want to say that we do 'know' some things, I think it takes a lot to prove that we do.

This is a good answer because it really considers what the question asks. It is significantly less superficial than the bad answer, and considers different approaches to the problem of knowledge, especially how it can be possible to define knowledge. Although the candidate does not know overly-technical terms, this is not expected of them. They have noticed a difference between knowledge of things which we perceive (a kind of inductive knowledge) and deductive knowledge, which shows that they are thinking deeply about the problem.

Q5: You run a sweet shop next-door to a rival sweet shop - you've both been able to drum up considerable loyalty in your customers who will flat-out refuse to shop anywhere else, provided you keep your prices below a tenner per sweet. You each have 10 such loyal customers - but there are 100 potential customers on the street who don't care as much and will buy from whoever is cheapest. With this in mind, at what price point would you have to reach for it to be more valuable to sell everything for ten pounds?

This is an economics question which relies on you being able to do relatively simple maths. However, it uses a lot of words, which may throw you in the interview. However, for these kinds of wordy questions it is best to take a breath, and think about what you need to infer from the question in order to get the equation you need.

For the sake of this question, you should assume that there is 0 marginal cost associated with every additional unit sold. A **bad candidate** will assume this without stating, as it is always important to state your assumptions and first principles when answering a question. Whereas, a **good candidate** will state this assumption, and may discuss afterword how the answer would differ if marginal cost were greater than zero.

A **bad candidate** will state the answer without showing workings. You will be given paper to write on, so make sure you use this to show the interviewer.

Answer: You will need to consider which numbers are useful from the question for working out your answer. Sometimes interviewers will throw some numbers in which are not useful. In this case, however, all numbers given are necessary to reach the solution. Note that the loyal customers will not buy **above** £10, but they will but at £10. As the business is seeking to maximise profits, if it opts for the price of the loyal customers, they should charge £10.

You should also discuss whether the non-loyal customers will also buy at £10. However, as you are in competition, once you reach the price at which it is no-longer profitable to undercut your competitor, if you raise your prices to £10, then the non-loyal customers will always go to your competitor.

Firstly, you want to show that it will be more profitable when 80 times the price is less than 10 times £10:

$$80p < 100$$

Next, solve for p:

$$p < \frac{100}{80}$$

Simplify this, and you will get the price:

$$p < £1.25$$

Remember, that you should use the less than sign, rather than the less than or equal to sign. This is because the question asks you to show when it will be more profitable to sell at £10, not when it will be more or equally profitable. This is an easy mistake to make. It is worth also mentioning that £1.25 is a game theory equilibrium. Therefore, it is likely that both competitors, in the long run, will sell at this price.

Q6: You mentioned that you read [a philosophy book], tell me about it!

This is a broad philosophy question. You are likely to be asked a question along these lines, or asking you about a specific philosophical work you may have mentioned in your personal statement. The best way to tackle this question is to talk in as much detail as you can about the work. It is worth preparing some thoughts you have on a specific work beforehand, especially if you write about any philosophical texts in your personal statement.

The most important thing is to pick a work which isn't too easy, but also isn't too hard that you can't understand enough to engage in the argumentation. Be honest, and say when you didn't understand parts of the work. The interviewer isn't expecting you to have a perfect understanding of complicated philosophical works yet.

Bad answer: I read *An Introduction to Philosophy*, and I learnt that we cannot really know that we exist, or that we have free will. I enjoyed the book because it gave me a simple overview.

This is a bad answer, firstly, because it is short. The candidate gives some examples of philosophical issues, but does not expand upon them. It's not particularly necessary to say whether you enjoyed the book or not – the interviewer is more looking for you to engage in the particular arguments of the text. Finally, the main problem with this answer is that, whilst it is perfectly fine to read introductory philosophy books, these will not be the most impressive for interviewers. Furthermore, they do not provide philosophical argumentation to engage in.

Good answer: I read Plato's *Republic*, which I think gave a unique perspective on justice and political philosophy. I found particularly interesting his discussion in the first book about whether justice goes against your own interest. I think that this is an issue Plato preoccupies the rest of his work discussing, but I'm not sure if he ever really found a satisfactory answer. I struggled to understand some of the middle parts of the text, but I think he shows that justice is the same in a city and in an individual persona, and just as it is good for a city, so too is it good for a person. However, it seems like he doesn't fully explain why this means that justice doesn't go against your own interest as an individual.

This is a good answer because it shows that the candidate is aware of the arguments within the text, and they try to engage in them. It is an honest answer which does not try to be over-smart, or pretend to understand things that they don't know, and would not be expected to know.

Q7: What do you think would happen if inflation was impossible?

This is quite a tricky economics question which asks you to apply your basic concepts within economics towards an impossible theoretical situation. This question can be interpreted two different ways. Firstly, we can take this as 'inflation equals zero'; secondly, we can take it as 'inflation as a concept doesn't exist'. It is worth mentioning both of these potential interpretations, or asking the interviewer to clarify if they mean one in particular.

A **bad candidate** will not be able to see the difference between these two, or may conflate the two when answering the question.

A **good candidate** will consider both potential approaches.

Answer:

You will be given paper, make sure to show your workings, and to draw graphs to help you to explain.

If we consider that inflation is zero, we can potentially have, for example, both demand-side deflation, and supply-side inflation in a way which will lead to zero inflation, as shown on my graph:

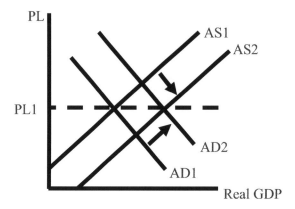

However, if inflation does not exist at all, as a concept, it will be impossible for these shifts to happen. This is because, if demand and supply shift non-simultaneously, then there will be inflation or deflation (which is a form negative of inflation). It is also theoretically impossible for both curves to shift simultaneously, due to the affect one curve shifting has on another.

Therefore, if inflation doesn't exist, it will be impossible for the aggregate demand or aggregate supply to shift at all. This means that it will not be possible for real GDP to be able to change in the short run. The same can be said of the long run, as any shift of the LRAS or SRAS curve will lead to inflation, unless done in a way, similar to our short run example, such that the price level does not change.

You can also, if we have time, consider the Phillips curve. This is probably not as important to discuss as the basic AD/AS graphs, but could give some useful insights.

Plotting the Phillips curve, which shows unemployment rate against inflation rate in the short run, you can show that it does not give a result for when inflation is zero – instead, as inflation tends towards zero, unemployment tends towards infinite. Practically, this does not make sense for an economy to have infinite unemployment. However, it may show us that, if inflation either does not exist or is zero, then, at least in the short run, unemployment will be very high.

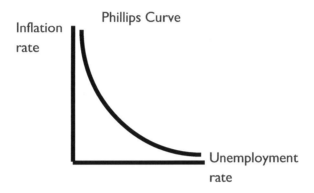

Q8: Do you feel that economists trust models too much?

This is a fairly broad economic question which will ask you to consider the merits of the way we usually approach economics, and to discuss behavioural economics, and the fairly recent academic move by behavioural economists away from relying on models.

Bad answer: No because economic models allow us to measure the economy, and therefore it is good that we have economic models.

This is a bad answer because the question does not ask the candidate to say whether economic models are good, but whether economists can rely too heavily on them. It is easy to argue that there are a huge amount of merit to economic models, and still discuss whether there are some cases in which economists rely too heavily on these models. Instead, this candidate fails to engage properly in the question.

Good answer: Models serve an important role in economics, both for helping us to try to measure the economy, and for predicting what may happen in the future. It helps to guide policy in order to aim towards good economic consequences, such as seeking high employment and economic growth. However, there are situations in which economic models will fail to properly predict what will happen in the economy, and thus, what policy makers should do. This usually happens, either because humans act in unexpected, irrational ways, or because some other thing happens which is unexpected. For example, even our most basic demand/supply models predict that the economy will follow certain rules to set the price and quantity of goods in an economic system.

However, just because there is an increase in supply, which, as the models would posit, means that there should be a decrease in the price of a good, doesn't mean that humans will automatically adhere to the new price. There may be delays in shifting to the price, or they may not change at all, due to consumer habit or other behavioural reasons. As well as this, surprise events may occur for which economists are unable to use models to prepare and plan policy. This happened with the coronavirus pandemic. Economic predictions which followed from models became invalidated by the sudden escalation of the coronavirus situation. Economists, in situations such as these, must be prepared to move away from the models and to adapt to new situations, as well as shifting focus towards examining the behaviour of how humans interact in new economic situations such as this.

This answer is good because it engages with the question. In doing so, the candidate doesn't jump to say that economic models are always either good or bad, but instead gives some examples of when they cannot be relied upon so heavily. This adds nuance to the argument, as well as showing knowledge of current affairs, and how recent events may affect the economy.

Q9: Do you think that sociology would make a valuable background for an Economist?

This question is a fairly general economics question which invites the candidate to consider economics in a cross-disciplinary way. Sociology is the study of human societies and how humans act in groups. It may be possible to link this discussion to the field of behavioural economics, but sociology specifically looks at how humans act together in society, rather than examining the behaviour of individual humans. The candidate should discuss how this can be used to enhance the study of economics.

Bad answer: Sociology is not useful for the study of economics because it studies different parts of society – sociology studies how people act in society, and economics studies money.

This is a bad answer because it is very simplistic and does not delph into the ways in which sociology may be useful for economics. Most good candidates will argue that there is at least some way in which sociology is useful, and there is a tendency in recent academia towards favouring cross-disciplinary approaches. Therefore, it is best to answer that yes, sociology is useful for studying economics. Furthermore, the definition the candidate gives is inaccurate, as economics is not only concerned with money.

Good answer: Sociology is useful for economics because there are ways in which the two disciplines can enhance one another. Economics looks into the production and consumption of goods as well as the allocation of resources, and sociology is concerned with the way in which humans interact with one another in society. Sociology can help us to study economics because no individual economic agent acts without influence from other individuals within society. For example, a study of culture can help economists to predict fashion trends which may affect the demand in an economic system for a specific type of good. On a more macro level, using sociology to look into issues such as race or gender discrimination in society can help us to find the courses of economic inequality, and to find ways to address this. This will enhance the study of economics because solving economic issues such as inequality – which may have a greater impact on the economy more broadly – relies on us being able to understand the courses, as sociology helps us to do.

This is a good answer because it explores the ways in which economics may be enhanced with the study of sociology, by using a clear discussion of the way in which the subjects interacts. Furthermore, it uses good definitions of the two subjects. It also considers the impact sociology can have on both micro and macroeconomics, which shows that the candidate is thinking about the question from multiple different angles.

Q10: What is GDP really? Do you think it can ever truly be measured?

This is an economics question which seeks for the candidate to be familiar with the concept of GDP, and how it is measured, and asks them to engage critically with this. This type of question is best tackled firstly by giving a definition for GDP is defined, then explaining how it is measured, before moving onto critiquing this. One of the most important aspect to consider will be goods that are sold in shadow markets, and therefore which aren't counted for in the calculation of GDP.

Bad answer: We can measure GDP by either working out the expenditure in an economy, by adding up the income in the economy, or by adding up the value added from output in the economy. All of these should add up to the same thing.

This candidate begins in a way which shows they have potential for a good answer. However, they miss the point of the question by only explaining how GDP is measured, and not engaging critically with this. The answer they give is also clearly knowledge that comes straight from an economic textbook, and the interviewer will not be impressed by the regurgitation of these facts without any unique analysis.

Good answer: GDP is the gross domestic product in an economy, that is, the total value of goods and services produced in a country in a year. The easiest way to measure this is by working out the expenditure in an economy by adding consumption, investment, government spending, exports minus imports. It can also be worked out by the sum of the incomes in the economy, or the sum of the value added from output in the economy.

However, these methods fail to capture every element of economic activity. This is because, some economic activity occurs in the form of shadow markets. These are underground and unregulated markets which are not recorded by the government owing to their nature. These include drug markets, which may make up some of the goods produced in the economy in a year, but which, for obvious reasons, will not be included in the government's sum for GDP. Therefore, the existence of shadow markets means that we cannot really measure GDP.

This is a good answer because the candidate explains what GDP is and how it is measured, and then engages with this critically. The candidate demonstrates good knowledge of GDP, but also good analysis skills in describing the issue which shadow markets cause for measuring GDP. They reach a clear and persuasive answer, which is stated clearly throughout.

Q11: What would you say are the major influence on the productive potential of a country?

This is an economics question which tests the candidate's knowledge of core economic theory. It requires knowledge of the productive possibility frontier (PPF), and the components which makes it shift. You will be given paper, which you may be able to draw a PPF on. However, this is not essential for the question. This is not a trick question so the best approach is to try not to overthink it.

Bad answer: If we increase investment through government spending then there will be an increase in the country's productive potential.

This is a bad answer because, whilst it is true that an increase in investment leads to an increase in productive potential, the candidate does not really engage in the question. They only give one way in which a country's productive potential can be influenced, which demonstrates a lack of knowledge on core economic principles. The candidate also does not go into detail or use real world, which would greatly enhance their answer.

Good answer: The productive potential in an economy can be modelled with a productive possibility frontier. This shows the potential output in an economy, which is also known as the productive potential. The PPF can shift either inwards or outwards by a change in a range of factors. These are the size of the workforce, the productivity of the workforce, the capital stock, the amount of raw materials, changes in innovation, political stability, and government spending or taxation. For example, the impact of coronavirus has meant that people have had to work from home. This is likely to have resulted in a decrease in productivity. If this is the case, then there will have been an inwards shift in the PPF in the UK.

This is a good answer because the candidate shows good awareness of core economic principles, and uses a current real life example to demonstrate their understanding of these on a deeper level. They also explain multiple ways in which productive potential can be influenced, making their argument significantly better than if they were to name just one.

Q12: Is there any particular value to the national debt?

This is an economic question which touches upon the core macroeconomic principle of government debt. This question asks the candidates to analyse the costs and benefits of having government debt, as well as to consider whether it is even possible not to.

Bad answer: A good thing about government debt is that the government can borrow to spend. This causes an increase in aggregate supply, which leads to economic growth. A bad thing about government debt is that the government has to pay interest on the debt which can be a waste of government resources. Therefore, whether it is good or bad to have debt depends.

This is a bad answer because the candidate does not choose one side of the argument to argue. They could also go into a lot more detail on both why it can be good to increase aggregate supply, and on why it can be bad to have interest to pay. Finally, the conclusion that the answer depends does not really seem to follow from the arguments which the candidate gives. This would need to be expanded upon to really make sense.

Good answer: I think that governments should have debt. This is because, even beyond the fact that most governments in the world at the moment have debts, and the fact that it is therefore questionable whether it is even possible not to have government debt, the overall benefits of debt outweigh the negatives, provided that the government uses the debt to fund things which will lead to economic growth. For example, the government may borrow to spend on investment. This can be used to increase productivity within the economy, which will lead to an outwards shift in aggregate supply. This causes an increase in the output of the economy, which causes an increase in real GDP. This will also have a multiplier effect. It is true that there are some disadvantages to having government debt, such as the fact that the government will have to pay back interest on their loans, and that having large debts may decrease confidence in the government. However, the fact that many countries have large amounts of government debts, and have a track record of being able to cope with these, means that, as long as debt doesn't get too large, there is unlikely to be a decrease in confidence. Furthermore, the multiplier effect is likely to cancel out some of the costs to the government associated with paying interest. And, those whom the government pay interest to, through government bonds, are likely to spend this money they gain, causing further economic growth. Thus, governments should have debts.

This is a good answer because the candidate goes into a lot of detail, showing knowledge of core economic principles, and an ability to apply them to more complicated problems. They go beyond the basic pros and cons which the bad candidate gives, to examine the affects of government debt in more detail.

Q13: Should you or I care about inequality?

This is an economic question which asks the candidate to think more about the good and bad effects of inequality. Often economics is concerned with things such as profit maximising, and being economically efficient, and in the process, forgets about inequality. This question therefore invites the candidate to discuss this in more detail, and to make the case for or against inequality. The candidate, however, does not need to focus purely on the economic effects of inequality, and can also bring in moral arguments to make their case.

Bad answer: Inequality is bad because it is unfair for some people to have less than others when it is through no fault of their own.

Or

Inequality is good because it is the result of the market deciding where to allocate resources, which benefits the economy overall.

Both of these answers are bad because they do not consider the other side of the argument. This is a very contentious debate which will lead candidates to have a strong conviction in favour of one side of the argument, but a good candidate will still consider the other side, and give reasons for why the other argument is wrong. Furthermore, the first answer fails to consider economic arguments, and the second answer fails to consider moral arguments. Both could be strengthened by exploring equality in a greater depth.

Good answer: I strongly believe that inequality should matter to economists. This is on two grounds. Firstly, inequality is morally wrong. Inequality means that a huge amount of people are born in situations where they are unable to improve their lives, due to being unable to access the same resources as those who are lucky enough to be born comparatively better off. If people were more equal, then everyone would be on a more equal level when it came to accessing opportunities, such as being able to study at Oxford. It is unfair that some humans are predestined not to have these opportunities due to the situation which they are born into. There is no way we can morally justify this, and those who argue that inequality is fine tend to overlook the moral arguments to make this case. However, there is also an economic argument in favour of reducing inequality. A small amount of inequality may be both economically and morally justifiable, however, at the moment, inequality is so large that many of the millionaires and billionaires hoard a lot of their wealth. Poorer people have a significantly higher marginal propensity to spend, and, therefore it is more economically sensible for this money to be distributed to less well off people. This would lead to an increase in aggregate demand, with a multiplier effect as more money circulates in the economy. This would lead to an increase in real GDP, and therefore economic growth. This therefore makes more economic sense than allowing the market to allocate resources, which turns out in this case to be less efficient. Therefore, inequality should matter to economists.

This is a good answer because the candidate goes into a lot of details to explain why their answer, both on an economic justification, and a deeper, moral one. They demonstrate a good knowledge of the concept of marginal propensity to spend, which is important for this question.

Q14: You're a politician in charge of the country, and you've accumulated a considerable deficit in the national balance of trade - is this an issue?

This is an economics question which asks you to analyse one of the core concepts in macroeconomics. It expects you to have a familiarity with the idea of the balance of trade, and to critically engage with the assumption that it is bad to have a trade deficit.

Bad answer: Trade deficits are bad because it leads to a devaluing of the pound and that makes the economy weak. Also, it means that people become unemployed as jobs go to those who create goods in foreign markets instead.

This is a bad answer because, whilst the candidate shows some awareness of some of the consequences of a trade deficit, they do not discuss why these consequences happen. Furthermore, it is not true that the pound being devalued makes the economy weak. A weak pound may be a sign of a weak economy, but the candidate is confusing cause and effect. It is likely that the economy was weak first, and that this caused a trade deficit, which caused the pound to devalue, rather than the other way round. Thus, the candidate shows a lack of economic understanding.

Good answer: A trade deficit isn't inherently a bad thing. It may be a sign that there is a problem with the economy, and in such a case, we shouldn't view the trade deficit as the problem, but the underlying causes of this. For example, if the economy is suffering from a lack of productivity, there may be a trade deficit as the UK will be unable to provide all the goods and services in home markets to satisfy demand, and thus may import more goods than they export. This causes a trade deficit.

However, it is not the trade deficit which is inherently bad, but the productivity. In fact, a trade deficit can be thought of as good because it naturally fixes itself. For example, when there is a trade deficit, the pound gets devalued as there is less demand for the pound owing to the fact that consumers are not buying goods from the UK. However, when the pound is devalued, it is lower in price compared to other currencies, and therefore, it becomes comparatively cheaper to buy UK goods using pounds. This means that there becomes an increase in demand for the pound. Therefore, the trade deficit should in some way fix itself, and the value of the pound should return to normal. This means the trade deficit doesn't matter as much as some might argue.

This is a good answer because the candidate demonstrates clear knowledge of the ways in which the balance of trade works. They give a clear and detailed explanation of the consequence of a trade deficit, as well as persuasively argument.

Q15: Do you believe that the market should be completely free, or should government intervene?

This is an economics question which seeks for you to discuss the problem of market failure in macroeconomics. The interviewer will be looking for the candidate to demonstrate knowledge of the ways in which the market can fail, and governments can intervene to solve this. With this type of question, it is impossible to talk about every possible way in which the government should intervene, and so a stronger candidate will try to stick to one or two examples, and go into significant detail on this.

Bad answer: The government should not intervene because the market allocates resources much more efficiently than governments will ever be able to.

This is a bad answer because, whilst the candidate is right to discuss the allocative efficient which markets may have over the government, they assume that allocative efficiency in markets is <u>always</u> higher, and in doing so, they do not consider cases when there is market failure. It is unlikely that a candidate will perform well by claiming that there is never any way a government needs to intervene, even if they are in favour of less governmental intervention more generally. They should instead opt to explain cases of market failure and how the government can fix this.

Good answer: Yes, there are cases when the government should intervene in the market. This should happen when there is market failure, as is the case with public goods and merit or demerit goods. For example, public goods are goods which are non-rivalrous and non-excludible. This means that there is no profit to be gained by providing the good, and thus the market is not incentivised to provide it. This occurs in street lighting, which local governments fund, to make up for the failure of markets to provide it. If the government did not intervene in this case no street lighting will be provided. Merit goods can also benefit from government intervention because, in the case of merit goods, the market fails to provide the good at the level which is socially desirable. These goods, such as education, have positive externalities. The government should therefore subsidise merit goods to increase the production and consumption of the merit good to the socially desirable level. Therefore, there are some cases when the government should intervene in the market.

This is a good answer because the candidate focuses on a few cases of market failure, and explains why the government should intervene in these cases. The candidate demonstrates good understanding of market failure, and gives a very good answer, especially, of why public goods need to be provided by the government.

Q16: Was the financial crisis of 2008 a failure of regulation?

This is an economics question which expects the candidate to have an awareness of current affairs, and of economics in the real world. The interviewer will be looking for the candidate to apply core economic ideas to this real life situation, and to show a strong ability for critical analysis. These kind of questions are very common, and so candidates should prepare themselves by researching some of the largest events in current affairs and the economic impact these will have, prior to the interview.

Bad answer: Yes, it was a failure of regulation because if the government told banks to stop lending to those who couldn't pay it back, there wouldn't have been a crash.

This is a bad answer because, whilst it shows that the candidate is broadly aware of the reason for the financial crisis, they clearly do not show a deep understanding of it. They also do not explain how regulation could have helped the situation. In general, this answer is far too brief, which will give the interviewer the impression that the candidate cannot think of anything to say.

Good answer: Yes, it was a failure of regulation. This is because the financial crisis happened when banks lent out large high-risk loans for mortgages in America to people who would be unable to pay them. This led to a housing market bubble which then crashed when people found themselves unable to pay back the loans with interest, and therefore had to default on the loans. This meant that many financial institutions failed in America. As a consequence, banks around the world, including in the UK, found themselves in crisis, as there became a shortage in funds to cover day to day costs, causing a liquidity crisis.

There are two ways in which financial regulation may have helped. Firstly, if the markets had been more regulated in America, then American banks would not have been able to lend out such high risk loans, which were very likely to be defaulted on. Secondly, If the financial market in the UK had been more regulated, UK banks may not have been so reliant on American banks for their own stability, and thus, they would have been more resistant to the spread of the financial crisis from America. Therefore, the financial crisis of 2008 was a failure of regulation.

This is a good answer because the candidate demonstrates an in depth knowledge of the financial crisis, and its causes. They discuss how regulation may have prevented the crisis, and therefore persuasively argue that the financial crisis was a from a failure of regulation.

Q17: Let's say that the value of the Yen and the Dollar exchange places overnight, what do you think the impacts of this would be on the global market?

This is an economics question which expects the candidate to have a good grasp of the way that currencies work. This is a very hard question, so make it is important to take a few minutes to think about it, and not to become too stuck on the question. Work through the question bit by bit to make it more manageable.

Bad answer: The Japanese Yen in America would eventually become equivalent to what the US Dollar is currently, as the currency adapts itself to the economy. The same thing will happen the other way round, with the US Dollar in Japan becoming equivalent to how what the Japanese Yen currently is. The two will therefore swap value.

This is a bad answer because, whilst it shows that the candidate shows an awareness of the fact that currencies reflect the economy they belong to, and therefore should in the long run settle down to the usual rate that the relative countries would expect their currency to be at, the candidate shows no understanding of the short run consequences. It is not enough to say that the two will simply swap value, which may well happen in the long term, but after a very tumultuous short term in which the respective countries will see huge changes in their balance of trade. Furthermore, the explanation which the candidate does give is confusing.

Good answer: If the values of the US Dollar and Japanese Yen were swapped overnight, there would be a huge swing in the economy of both America and Japan, as well as of other countries. In America, the US Dollar would very suddenly be worth considerably less. This would mean that there would be a surge to buy the US Dollar, as it becomes a comparatively more price-competitive option on the global financial market. This will cause it to suddenly increase in price. In contrast, Japan will have the opposite effect, where people will rush to sell their Yens, due to them being worth a lot of money. This will lead to a devaluation of the Yen. In the process, in America, as US Dollars are so cheap, there will be a huge increase in demand for US goods from foreign markets, leading to an increase in exports from America. This means that there will be a sudden trade surplus. The opposite will happen in Japan, where Japanese goods will become comparatively expensive, and foreign goods comparatively cheaper, and so there will be an increase in imports for Japan. This means there will be a sudden trade deficit. In the long term, the currencies will therefore return to normal. However, not without economic chaos which will result in the short term from such sudden and drastic changes. As well as this, so many other currencies linked to US Dollars, and so many countries' reserves are held in US dollars, as the currency usually considered the strongest in the world. Therefore, these countries would lose a lot of money overnight as the US Dollar suddenly became worth less. This would cause these countries to suffer from further economic problems, including the potential to enter a recession as a result.

This is a good answer because the candidate demonstrates an awareness of exchange rates, the trade balance, and the ways in which foreign markets interact. They also do well to bring in how it would affect other countries than America and Japan.

Q18: Do you think that property tycoons should pay more attention to how you win in monopoly? Why?

This is an economics question which is the type of unusual and unexpected interview question that is typical of an Oxbridge interview. The interviewer will be looking for the candidate to demonstrate that they can think creatively, and to apply some of the tactics they would use in monopoly in real life. The question also requires for the candidate to have an awareness of the problems economists face with applying economic principles to reality.

Bad answer: In monopoly I buy the properties which are most likely to be landed on. In real life, you should also produce goods and services which are most likely to be demanded by consumers.

This is a bad answer because the candidate fails to discuss the difficulties involved in applying monopoly tactics to real life. They also do not give that creative a discussion of their monopoly tactics, and only discuss demand and supply in a very simplistic way.

Good answer: In monopoly, the best way to win is to buy up properties which are most likely to be landed on, of the same colour, and then develop these as quickly as possible. In real life, there obviously doesn't exist the same colour scheme which incentivises buying one colour property in monopoly, but we can compare this to buying similar businesses in real life, which would give a company greater market share. Therefore, this it is a good tactic to purchase more businesses in the same market in order to increase your market share as much as possible, so that you have more power over price setting in order to profit maximise.

As well as this, you should, just as in monopoly, develop the business as quickly as possible in order to become more efficient, as happens with business expansion, and therefore to be more able to cover costs and profit maximise. This happens because the marginal cost per additional unit produced is often diminishing, and, thus, the business will make marginally increasing amounts of profit through expansion, until they reach economies of scale. However, such expansion is not always possible in real life, due to limited resources, other competitors who may make it significantly harder to expand than is the case in monopoly, and market regulations which prevent monopolisation and strong concentration of markets.

This is a good answer because the candidate considers creatively the ways in which monopoly tactics can be applied to microeconomics. They demonstrate a good knowledge of core business principles. They also go on to show an awareness of the difficulties that businesses face in expanding, and trying to increase market share.

Q19: What makes diamonds so much more valuable than raw steel?

This is an economics question which looks for the candidate to assess their knowledge of how goods end up having their particular level of demand, and why demand doesn't always match usefulness of the good. It also invites the candidate to discuss how supply affects price of goods.

Bad answer: Diamonds are expensive because there are less diamonds and so there is small level of supply. This means that the place on a demand/supply diagram at which the two lines cross is at a very high price. Because there are so few, there are a small amount of people who will be willing to pay lots for diamonds. In contrast, there is a large supply of steel, and so the supply curve crosses the demand curve at a significantly lower level. Therefore, steel is cheap.

This is a bad answer because, although the candidate does explain the supply side reasons for the price, they do not discuss any demand side reasons at all. This misses the point of the question, as interviewers will be looking for candidates to explain why there is such demand for diamonds, which have significantly less functionality than steel, which has a large amount of uses.

Good answer: Diamonds are so expensive for two reasons. Firstly, because the supply is very limited of diamonds in comparison to steel, the market price for diamond is very high, as the market allocates the few diamonds to those who are willing and able to pay for them. In contrast, the high quantity of steel that can be supplied means that the market price for steel is significantly lower. However, this does not really explain why demand for diamonds is so high, given the limited function we have for diamond in comparison to steel. This can only be explained by the fact that fashion has caused demand to be higher for diamond than the amount of uses we have for them would suggest. This is an irrational human behaviour which has made the relatively useless good desirable because it acts as a symbol for wealth – the lack of availability of diamond is therefore what makes them fashionable, which drives them to have such high demand.

This is a good answer because the candidate explains both the supply side reasons and the demand side reasons for why diamonds are so expensive and steel is so cheap. The candidate does well in seeing that the lack of supply for diamonds is what may actually drive demand for them.

Q20: Many industries are outsourcing less and less as it is disincentivised by government policy, do you think this is a bad thing?

This is an economics question which allows the candidate to talk about outsourcing, both from the point of view of businesses and of governments. This is a fairly simple question, so you should make sure not to overcomplicate your answer

Bad answer: Outsourcing is a bad thing because outsourced companies only look for their own profits, and therefore do not offer the best service to consumers, which the government can do better.

This is a bad answer because the candidate seems to think that the only type of outsourcing is governmental outsourcing. The candidate is right to explain that outsourcing business tasks from the government to the business introduces a profit motive which was previously not there, and therefore may mean they don't act in the interest of the consumer. However, this candidate does not realise that private companies may outsource business processes to other companies. Therefore, it cannot be the case that in <u>every</u> example of outsourcing, a profit motive is introduced which was not previously there.

Good answer: Outsourcing can be good in some situations, and bad in others. Many private companies outsource business processes to other private companies in quite simple ways which help to create efficiency. This can happen when, for example, a café outsources a painting business to decorate their café. This is quite a simple example of outsourcing and one which is non-controversial. In this case, no new profit motive is introduced where there wasn't one before. However, when the government outsources business processes to private companies, this becomes more controversial.

 In these cases, I believe that outsourcing is a bad thing. This is because, the government has the responsibility and the electoral motive to act in the interest of the public. When they outsource business processes to private companies, they do so under the argument that they are more efficient due to the fact that they have a profit motive which the government didn't. However, quite often the reason they are more efficient is because they strip the costs of the businesses down in order to increase profit margins. In the process, the consumer or the general public who they are paid to provide for, are likely to lose out on some of the services the government would have provided. Private companies will seek to act for the sake of profit, instead of in the interest of the people they are supplying the good or service to.

This is a good answer because the candidate does not simply talk about government outsourcing, but considers outsourcing more generally. They also provide a clear and persuasive justification for their argument, and consider the argument from the other side.

Q21: Imagine you have just opened up a new airline that flies a unique route (London and Tokyo). How would you determine what price to set tickets at to ensure maximal profit?

This is an economics question which expects the candidate to demonstrate knowledge of microeconomic principles, and specifically with how a company should profit maximise. The interviewer will expect the candidate to demonstrate knowledge of market concentration and monopolisation, as well as being able to work out how costs effect profits.

Bad answer: You should look around to see what other airlines are charging. Then you should charge less than them to undercut those airlines.

This is a bad answer because, whilst the candidate demonstrates some knowledge of competition theory, they do not consider other important factors such as cost of flying and the fact that , as the new airline flies a unique route, there are some ways in which the new airline is a monopoly. Therefore, the airline does not need to undercut other airlines.

Good answer: The first thing which should be considered is the cost involved in flying from point to point. Tickets must at least cover costs. The second thing to consider is the competition for pricing. If the company is a monopoly, then they will have complete market power to set prices as they please. The new company does fly a unique route, and for this reason it is in some ways a monopoly. However, it does not truly have 100% of the market share due to the fact that there will be some indirect ways to get between these two places.

Nevertheless, the company will be able to charge a very high price as their large amount of market power means they have a lot of freedom to set their own prices. The next thing to consider is at which specific price they should pick for maximum profit. It usually will be the profit maximising solution to charge the highest price that enough people will be willing and able to pay to completely fill the plane. However, if some are willing to pay such a high price that they make up for some people being priced out of plane tickets, then it may not be profit maximising. This is unlikely is unlikely as it would require for these people to be willing and able to pay a significantly higher amount. Therefore, the price the airline should set is that which is the maximum that enough people are willing and able to pay in order to sell a ticket for every seat.

This is a good answer because the candidate discusses core economic concepts in a good amount of detail. They especially do well in analysing what kind of market share the business has, and therefore what kind of freedom they will have to set their own prices. They do not make the mistake that the bad candidate does in presuming that the company will have to act very competitively.

Q22: Why do you think financiers and financial institutions are so preoccupied with the golden ratio?

This is an economics question which requires the candidate to have some knowledge of banks and investment, as well as how the stock market works specifically. Don't worry if you struggle to get the answer to this in an interview. It is a very difficult question. Start by thinking about what the golden ratio is in maths, and seeing if you can apply this to banks and investment firms.

Bad answer: The golden ratio is considered the mathematically perfect number, and therefore markets stock markets will naturally increase or decrease in proportion to the golden ratio.

This is a bad answer because, whilst the candidate demonstrates that they have some knowledge of the way in which the golden ration comes into the stock market, they do not really explain this in a non-confusing and clear way. Furthermore, they don't really explain what the golden ratio is.

Good answer: The golden ratio is a special number in mathematics, symbolised by the Greek letter phi, which is the ratio between consecutive Fibonacci numbers that the Fibonacci sequence tends towards. This is considered in many ways the mathematically perfect number, as it is a number which occurs frequently in nature. The number also occurs, so the theory holds, in the stock market. For example, when an individual stock market sees an increase in stock price, the amount it increases and then the amount it retrospectively decreases, is propionate to the golden ratio. Therefore, banks and investment firms obsess over this number because it allows them to help predict how much stock prices will rise and fall, and therefore, at which points they should sell stocks, and at which points this should buy stock. This helps them to maximise profit.

This is a good answer because the candidate shows knowledge on a complex theory. The candidate will not be expected to have perfect knowledge of this, but it is good to show knowledge of the ways in which banks and investment firms seek to predict the rise and fall of stock markets. This candidate also does well in explaining the benefit of predicting this.

Q23: How would you go about trying to identify the warning signs of an economic recession - if you could spot it soon enough, can you think of a way to avoid depressions?

This is an economics question which requires the candidate to explain some of their core macroeconomic concepts in order to show how they might predict recessions and depressions. However, the candidate must also show awareness of how economic shocks may unexpectedly happen.

Bad answer: We can predict an economic recession by seeing if GDP is about to slow down. A depression can be avoided by the government investing in the economy to encourage spending, and therefore to encourage growth.

This is a bad answer because the candidate does not really show how an economic recession can be predicted. A recession does happen following a slow down of growth in GDP, which is followed by a decrease in the rate of growth of GDP, but in waiting for the economy to slow down, we are not really predicting a recession, but seeing it happen in real time. The candidate does not acknowledge that it is actually very difficult to predict a recession. As well as this, the candidate fails to fully explain why their solution for preventing a depression would in fact prevent it.

Good answer: A recession occurs when the rate of growth of GDP is negative for two consecutive quarters. A depression occurs when there is a decrease in real GDP over a significant period of time. It is quite difficult to predict a recession as it is hard to know when the upturn of the business cycle will change (ie how long a boom will last).

However, there are some warning signs which may show that we are leading towards a recession. These may be things like a decrease in consumer confidence, which leads to decreased expenditure, or an increase in unemployment. However, often, when these things are significant enough to be noticeable, it is too late to avoid a recession. There may be earlier sign that the economy may later suffer a recession, such as the existence of market bubbles, which may crash and cause a recession. However, it is very difficult, again, to see which markets are bubbles, and when they will crash. Once there is a recession, there are some things which the government can do to prevent it being prolonged, and becoming a depression. These include investment to create jobs. This helps to tackle unemployment, and therefore to increase the disposable income available to economic agents. This mean they will increase expenditure, leading to an increase in growth of GDP, thus helping to prevent a depression. This will serve as an injection into the economy, will would also have a multiplier effect, leading to even more economic growth.

This is a good answer because the candidate shows awareness of the causes of recessions and depressions, as well as how to prevent a depression. They also demonstrate a good level of understanding of how difficult it can be to predict an economic recession.

Q24: Do you think that India, which has a substantial space programme, should still be getting aid payments from other countries?

This is an economics question which requires the candidate to discuss the controversial topic of aid, and to critically analyse whether aid should be given to countries who choose to allocate their own resources to things such as international space programmes, which do not help those in poverty. The candidates which perform best will be prepared to pick one side of the argument, rather than remaining on the fence. They must also, however, consider the arguments against their viewpoint

Bad answer: Aid should not go to countries that have international space programmes because they have enough resources to allocate to space programmes, and, therefore, they should allocate these resources instead to helping to fight poverty in the country.

This answer shows potential insofar as they begin to make a compelling argument for why aid should be given to countries that have international space programmes. However, the candidate fails to use much of an economic justification for this, and therefore gives a fairly superficial answer.

Good answer: I can see why we would want to avoid giving aid to countries which have international space programmes, on the grounds that these countries should allocate their resources to higher priority areas, such as tackling poverty. However, the fact that the countries have international space programmes does not mean that they would reallocate these funds towards helping to solve poverty in the country if aid is removed. It is true that it should be the government of India's responsibility to tackle these problems in their country if they are able to.

However, this doesn't mean that we shouldn't give aid if they do not opt to do so, as this would mean taking away financial support in the form of aid for those who may not get the support from the government instead. Furthermore, there are reasons beyond helping these people which make aid a good thing to do, such as maintaining good relations with other countries. Giving aid which is well targeted may help lift these people out of poverty, which means that they have more disposable income, and so can increasing spending, which will lead to economic growth. However, at a certain point, once the country is developed enough, the UK may be able to stop giving aid and instead increase trade with these countries, which has economic benefits for both countries involved. This is, however, most efficient once countries have a large enough level of development that consumers have disposable income to be able to increase spending. Therefore, we should not look towards whether a country has a space programme to see whether we should continue to give aid, but whether the poorest are at a level in which they will be able to survive, and the economy is strong enough to be able to benefit more from trade instead.

This is a good answer because the candidate shows a clear knowledge of the benefit of aid, ad the reasons why aid might be stopped in a country. The candidate evaluates the arguments against their position, and arrives at a nuanced answer.

Q25: How would you judge the extent of the differences between a capitalist and a communist system?

This is a question which could be asked for both economics and politics. It invites the candidate to demonstrate their understanding of the different political and economic systems, as well as to critically analyse the difference between the two. The candidate should seek to utilise real world examples where possible.

Bad answer: Capitalism is an economic system in which goods, property, and businesses are owned privately, whereas communism is an economic system in which they are owned by the state. Therefore, the two are different.

This is a bad answer because the candidate demonstrates a lack of critical analysis about the difference between the two economic systems. It is perfectly fine to argue that they are different, but the candidate fails to engage in the alternate argument. They could also benefit from stating more clearly why the two are different.

Good answer: Capitalism, it is standardly claimed, is an economic system in which goods, property, and businesses are privately owned, and resources are therefore distributed through market mechanisms. Communism is an economic system in which these are owned by the state instead, and so resources are distributed by the government. The main difference between these, therefore, is the fact that, in communism, private property doesn't exist, and so the allocation of resources does not depend upon the free market.

However, this picture is complicated by the existence of mixed economies. These exist when some things are owned and distributed by the government, and some by the free market. Most countries which have a mixed economy are considered capitalist countries, on account of the fact that they have private markets. The standard definition is in fact not that suitable for capitalism because it is impossible for nothing to be owned and distributed by the government, if a country has a government. Therefore, there is at least some way in which all capitalist countries allocate resources through the government, unless they are an anarchist country, which is an oxymoron. Therefore, a line must be drawn in order to determine at which point a mixed economy is a capitalist country, and at which point it is communist. This is what causes people to argue that they are not so different. However, I believe that the existence of any private market at all makes a country capitalist, and, therefore, capitalism does maintain a fundamental difference to communism.

This is a good answer because the candidate is able to engage with the arguments on the other side of their argument, because reaching a persuasive conclusion. They also engage critically with the standard definitions of capitalism and communism, in a way which enhances their argument.

Q26: Your friend is running a struggling corner shop, she knows you've done some work on economics and asks for your advice - they have £25 they'd like to spend on developing their sales, what three things would you recommend that they do, with or without that money?

This is an economics question in which the candidate needs to show their knowledge of core microeconomic concepts, as well as their understanding of businesses. With this kind of question, it is important that the candidate does not over think the answer.

Bad answer: The business should spend money on expanding, on marketing, and on innovation to create new and unique products.

This is a bad answer because, whilst the candidate demonstrates awareness on the ways in which businesses can increase their sales, they are overoptimistic with how far the £25 will go. As well as this, the candidate fails to explain why these things will increase sales, or give any kind of discussion on how much each measure will cost them. Furthermore, the answer is far too brief and vague.

Good answer: One thing to consider is that £25 is not that much money, and will only stretch so far. Therefore, businesses should be smart with how they utilise this money. The best way to increase sales would probably be to spend the majority of the money on advertising. Facebook provides a useful and free platform to promote the business. Some of their advertisement may come at no cost, such as by posting about the business in local Facebook pages. They can also use Facebook to target ads at people who will most likely use the goods and services they produce, and who are local to the business. Some money may also be used on making the front of the business, such as the store if it is a shop, appealing for customers.

Some cleaning products and a bit of paint can go a long way in encouraging customers to visit their store, without involving a large expenditure. Finally, the business owner can spend time teaching employees how to be approachable, and to cultivate an atmosphere of good customer relations. This again can help make the business appealing to customers, and encourage local people to see the business in a good light. These collectively will increase the number of customers and therefore increase sales.

This is a good answer because the candidate explains their three recommendations, and explains in detail why these will help increase sales. They also give a vague idea of how much each of their recommendations would cost, which helps to show the interviewer that they know what they're talking about.

Q27: Do you think the separator between a global company and a failed company is innovation, or are there other factors at play?

This is an economics question in which the candidate needs to show their knowledge of core microeconomic concepts, as well as their understanding of businesses. It also requires the candidate to have some knowledge of the difference between international markets and home markets.

Bad answer: Some brands go global because they sell highly desirable goods or services at a good price, whereas others fail because people in different countries do not want to buy their goods or services.

This is a bad answer because the candidate shows a lack of awareness about the reasons some brands are able to go global. They do not explain specifically what it is which may make a product desirable in a global market, and why some brands will fail to appeal them. This answer could also benefit from a discussion of the ways in which exchange rate mays affect which brands go global, and the ways in which marketing of a brand may affect this.

Good answer: Some brands may go global because they have a good understanding of the new markets which they are entering. As demand for a good or service may be affected by the culture of the country they look to trade in, it is important for the brand to have properly researched this, in order to cater their product towards this market. It is also important, for the same reason to cater their advertising and marketing towards the new market they seek to enter.

One of the most common reason that a brand may fail to break into a global market is because they fail to understand the cultural differences which affect demand for certain products. As well as this a brand which is based in one country may have an advantage over another, when it comes to breaking into a foreign market, on the grounds that the goods are cheaper to produce in that country, and the exchange rate is favourable to them exporting the good. This means that government policy on trade may affect whether a brand is able to go global.

This is a good answer because the candidate shows an understanding of both the microeconomic and the macroeconomic reasons why a brand may be able to go global. The candidate gives an insightful analysis on the ways in which culture affects demand in a country, and therefore shows that business should cater their goods and marketing towards the markets they wish to enter into.

Q28: What do you think were the main factors driving the American Great Depression - do you think that understanding its causes could teach us valuable lessons?

This is an economics question which invites the candidate to discuss the history of economics, and the kind of real life consequences which economics can have. It is very important that candidates should have an awareness of the cause of the great depression before the interview, as a question on this kind of topic, or related to it, has a high chance of coming up.

Bad answer: The great depression happened in America as a result of the Wall Street crash which led to millions of Americans becoming unemployed. We should avoid this in order to ensure that unemployment doesn't increase as it did them.

This is a bad answer because, whilst everything the candidate explains is true, they fail to really explain what caused the great depression, the reasons for the Wall Street crash, and how this effected markets other than the financial market. Furthermore, they do not explain why this led to unemployment, and they do not go into much detail on what we can learn from it.

Good answer: The great depression happened in America because, following a large expansion in the stock market in the 1920s, there was a sudden crash. This became known as the Wall Street crash. This led to a panic, with investors pulling out of the stock market, leading to many investment businesses going bankrupt. It sent shockwaves through the economy, and drastically reduced consumer and producer confidence, which led to a decrease in expenditure on consumption and investment, and therefore, a decrease in productive output. This meant that there was a drastic decrease in growth. One of the most significant consequences of this was that individuals got laid off, and unemployment reached a record high. As unemployment became so high, people were unable to spend, and the depression therefore continued to worsen. One lesson that can be learnt from this is for the government to regulate the financial sector to help avoid crashes in the stock market, and to temper the damages when these crashes do happen. As well as this, we can learn that, when a crisis begins to unfold, an increase in unemployment can make matters worse, and allow the crisis to dig itself even deeper. The government should therefor act early to save as many jobs as possible, by investing to create new jobs.

This is a good answer because the candidate shows a good awareness of what happened in the great depression. Furthermore, they very effectively apply their knowledge of economics to this event, and come up with some good and detailed recommendations for what can be learnt from this event in history.

Q29. What attracted you to the PPE course?

Good Answer: What excites me most about PPE is the academic breadth of the course, and the opportunity it provides to engage deeply with subjects that are both academically challenging and have real-world applications. I first became interested in studying PPE through my philosophy A level. I was excited to apply the critical thinking skills that I developed during those studies to other real-world examples and became deeply interested in the way that politics and economics interact to influence our current systems. I'd really like to look at these subjects through an academic lens during my time at university. I'm keen to continue to develop these skills during my time at university and see PPE as the perfect course through which to do so.

This answer shows that the candidate has really thought about why they want to study the course and have demonstrated both their academic interest and aptitude. They demonstrate that they have taken a wider interest in their studies at A Level and are keen to challenge themselves further through engaging with the PPE course. They also show that they are excited to tackle the challenging content of the PPE course and will approach it with enthusiasm and dedication. This is the type of candidate that an interviewer will want to have on their course.

Bad Answer: A candidate might suggest that they are applying to the course for the career opportunities it might offer them, or because they have a family member who took PPE.

While there is no "wrong" answer to this question, the answers above demonstrate that the candidate is applying to the course for a reason that wouldn't be attractive to the interviewers. Remember, you want to be showing the interviewer that you are excited to engage with the academic content of the PPE course – this is the type of student that they will be excited to teach.

Q30. Is there an area of politics that you are most interested in?

Good Answer: Yes, I'm particularly interested in how international relations and domestic government policy influence aid decisions. When I read about the cuts to the government's aid budget, I was struck by how much difference a small percentage cut can make to the total amount of aid that the UK government sends overseas. I'm really interested in learning about the mechanisms behind these decisions, and how they are influenced by wider government policies, and hope that I can engage with this through the PPE course.

This candidate is demonstrating that they engage with politics in their everyday life, through reading about government decisions (which also indicates that they try to keep up with current affairs), and that they are interested in pursuing this further through their academic studies. The candidate does not need to show that they are already an expert in this field, just that they have given some thought to what they are particularly interested in when it comes to the subject and that they are keen to learn more through the PPE course. Showing this type of enthusiasm will show the interviewer that you want to engage with their subject and will put in effort during your time on their course.

Bad Answer: A candidate might shrug or say something along the lines of "nothing in particular, just the whole subject".

A bad answer to this question is one that indicates to the interviewer that the candidate has not really taken an interest in the subject. This demonstrates that the candidate isn't really interested in studying the subject or that they haven't really thought about why they are applying. The interviewer isn't expecting the candidate to be an expert in politics already, or to be able to recite in great detail a niche area of the course. They will be expecting, however, that the candidate has taken an interest in the subject and taken the time to look into different areas of the course at least a little before applying.

Q31. What have you seen on the news recently that has interested you?

Good Answer: I've been keeping up to date with the news around the conflict between Palestine and Israel, and the social media movement that has united behind the Palestinian cause. This isn't an issue that I was aware of until recently and, given the extensive history behind the conflict, this really surprised me. I wanted to know more about the history of Israel and didn't want to rely solely on social media for my news so I dug into past news pieces on the region and was really fascinated by what I found. I was particularly interested in the role of the West in the formation of Israel and how that potentially has influenced the governmental reaction to the conflict today.

This answer demonstrates firstly that the candidate has been keeping up with relevant current affairs by watching the news/reading a newspaper regularly. This is a bonus for a PPE candidate. Secondly, the candidate is demonstrating that they are not satisfied by taking the news at face value and have decided to read more widely to fully understand the topic that they are hearing about through the news. This demonstrates an intellectual curiosity which will resonate well with the interviewer.

Bad Answer: I don't really watch the news; I'm too busy studying for my A Levels.

Interviewers will appreciate that you are busy studying and aren't expecting you to be keeping on top of everything that happens around the world all the time. They are, however, expecting you to take an interest in current affairs or at least have some engagement with the news.

Even if you can't think of anything relevant that you've seen on the news (or your mind goes blank — it happens), a strong candidate will find something of interest to say in response to this question. For example, they might try talking about an opinion piece they've read, or a documentary that they've watched recently. They will demonstrate to the interviewer that they are taking a wider interest in their subject, even if they cannot think of a news article or specific event to talk about.

Q32. Why do you think some countries are rich and some countries are poor?

Good Answer: I think it must be rooted in a number of factors. The first that I can think of is how many resources a country has. For example, if a country is rich in a valuable resource such as oil or diamonds then they have the natural capacity to be much richer than a country that doesn't have anything that it can trade. I don't think that this is enough to make a country rich or poor, however. Nigeria has a lot of oil but it isn't rich compared to the US, for example. The second factor that needs to be present is the ability to trade with other countries; it is no good simply having a lot of oil if you can't get anything in return! Therefore, I think you need to have good international relations and a secure trade route in order to be able to participate in the global market. Another factor that I can think of would be good governance and a transparent leadership system so that no money is lost through corruption. If you have all of these factors then you are more likely to be rich, as you have access to natural resources that give you a trading advantage, a secure system in which to trade your good, and a leadership structure that doesn't steal money from the country.

This answer shows that the candidate is thinking critically about the question. They indicate a number of different factors that go into making a country rich or poor, highlighting that they are taking a nuanced approach to the issue and trying to come up with a well-rounded solution rather than seizing on the first thing that comes into their head. They also use examples to back up their points which is very valuable and demonstrates to the interviewer that they have read into the subject which indicates their wider interest in studying PPE.

Bad Answer: It's just to do with how the country grew and how much money they have.

This answer really doesn't answer the question. It's not considering *why* one country might be richer than another. Instead it is simply stating a very vague response "how the country grew" and reiterating the fact that being rich/poor is to do with how much money one has. This isn't providing any sort of academic or critical thinking insight into the issue.

Q33. What makes a nation "successful"?

Good Answer: I imagine that different people would have different criteria for what makes a nation successful, depending on what they value most. From my perspective, there are a couple of factors that are most important in judging the success of a nation. The first factor would be the ability of the government to protect the rights of its citizens. For example, the nation needs to have strong governmental systems in place to protect people against crime, ensure that people have access to work, and that there is accountability in government. The ability to protect these areas means that the government would be safeguarding some of its citizens' most basic human rights and ensuring that they have access to systems that protect them. The second factor would be the nations' ability to make money, whether that is through successful trade with other nations or a strong tax system that gives the government the capacity to collect funds and resources from its citizens. A more successful nation will be able to do both, as that will give it increased capacity to generate income which can then be implemented for the good of the nation.

The candidate could now go on to give a number of other factors that can be used to judge the success of a nation, but through highlighting these two components they had demonstrated a number of things. They have demonstrated that they understand that this is a nuanced question that can be taken from a number of angles by any number of people. They have also demonstrated that they are able to think critically about which factors are most important and they have shown the interviewer that they can back up their points when they are giving them. Overall, this answer shows critical engagement with the question and uses examples and analysis to present a strong case.

Bad Answer: A successful nation is one that makes lots of money and has a lot of international friends.

This answer might have picked up on a couple of key criteria that makes a nation "successful" but is bad because it fails to explain why these are factors. To make this answer better, the candidate should consider backing up these points, for example explaining why having lots of money makes a nation more successful than another nation. Is this because they have managed to create strong institutions that keep its money safe? Is it because they have successfully managed their available resources and created strong trade networks with other nations? This candidate should elaborate more on their response and show the interviewer that they are thinking critically and responding with justified answers.

Q34. Do you think it's important to represent minorities in democracies?

Good Answer: Yes, I do think it's important to represent minorities in democracies. This is because a democratic state is one in which all citizens are represented. As citizens who are part of minorities are still citizens, it is therefore essential to represent them for democracies to truly be democratic.

This answer is short and to the point, directly answering the question that the candidate has been posed. They explain what a democracy is and why representing minorities in democracy is essential to the nature of a democracy. They then make a strong conclusion based on the reasoning they have just set out.

Bad Answer: It might be important to represent minorities in democracy but I don't think it's possible. This is because the party that the majority of citizens wants is the one that is elected, so that minority will never get representation in Parliament, unless they are able to swing more people to support them, and then they are no longer the minority.

This answer contains some good reasoning and provides an answer but unfortunately doesn't answer the question. It just assumes that it is important to represent minorities in democracies without actually explaining why that is the case. It then goes on to answer a different question to the one that the interviewer has posed – this alternative question might be "Do you think it is possible to represent minorities in democracy". It also takes a very British-centric approach to the question, implying that there are no other acceptable examples of democracy across the world.

Q35. How can we achieve minority representation in a democracy?

Good Answer: I think this is a really difficult question and one that no current political system has adequately figured out yet. I think the problem is that a system like proportional representation which represents all of the votes cast – and therefore the votes of minority groups – is quite unstable and ineffective, as there are too many parties all trying to be heard and in the end the largest or most powerful party will probably end up taking control anyway. This was shown through Weimar Germany's attempt at proportional representation. More stable political systems, like the Westminster system, only has one or sometimes two parties ruling so the votes of minorities are not represented within the actual ruling body. Therefore, I think we might need to look outside of the formal political system for representation for minorities. For example, pressure groups and protests are a means through which the voices of minorities can be heard in democratic systems, while maintaining a strong and fairly stable ruling body.

This is a carefully considered and well-rounded answer. It considers why representing minorities in democracies might be a difficult task and then presents a solution to the problem. It directly answers the question and shows that the candidate is critically engaging with the topic.

Bad Answer: The way that Parliament is structured means that we just can't represent minorities in democracy. The ruling party has the political power and that party won't get into power unless they have the support of the majority.

Again, the answer approaches the question from a British perspective, without considering the idea of "democracy" in theory – it is possible to have a proportionally representative democratic system rather than simply the Westminster system that is practiced in the UK. Furthermore, this answer doesn't even try to come up with creative solutions to the problem of representing minorities in democracy. To improve their answer, this candidate would need to suggest what could be a solution to the problem of representing minorities in democracy and then show that this wouldn't work in practice. This would be a way of coming to the same conclusion (that minorities cannot be represented in democracy) but through far more persuasive means).

Q36. Do you think that democracy is the only acceptable form of government?

Good Answer: To answer this question I think we need to decide what constitutes an "acceptable" form of government. I'm going to assume that an acceptable form of government is one that protects its citizens and their rights, and creates an environment in which they can pursue their own lives and desires. This means that any form government which by nature exploits it citizens cannot be an acceptable form of government. However, I don't think that we necessarily have to have a democracy for citizens' rights to be protected and for them to be able to pursue their own desires. I think that in some kind of dictatorship where the dictator protects her citizens, ensures that they have everything they need, and would never interfere in the lives of her citizens would also be an acceptable form of government. In practice, however, I think that this would be very difficult to achieve because people are easily corrupted and anyone with the power of the dictator is likely to act at least a little in their own interests, rather than just protecting their citizens. Therefore, I do not think that democracy is the only acceptable form of government in theory, but in practice it might be the only plausible form of acceptable government.

This answer is good because the candidate has given a reasoned, justified response to the question and has provided a conclusion that directly addresses what the question is asking them to address. They have thought about the subject in a creative way and one that pushes beyond what one might typically feel comfortable asserting.

Bad Answer: All developed nations have a form of democracy and therefore democracy must be the only acceptable form of government.

This response is bad because it assumes that just because something is currently done, it must be the only way of doing things. It fails to consider an alternative to democracy and therefore fails to address the question. The reason that it gives for democracy being the only acceptable form of government is flimsy and does not show personal academic engagement with the question, which is what the interviewer will be looking for. To improve this answer, the candidate should consider why democracy is practised in developed nations (and in developing nations) and whether this reasoning gives adequate justification for democracy being considered the only acceptable form of government.

Q37. Why do you think some countries go to war?

Good Answer: I think it's very difficult to define exactly why countries go to war but I believe there are a number of factors that contribute to that decision. One factor might be humanitarian. For example, a country might declare war on another country when they believe there has been a significant human rights violation by that country and all other methods of punishment have failed. A country might have already imposed economic and political sanctions against the other nation but this hasn't stopped the perceived abuse of their citizens. This might lead to a country invading another as a last resort. Another reason might be material gain. A country might invade another country in order to acquire their resources (oil, for example) and this leads to war breaking out between these countries. In this case, the country that is being invaded might declare war as an act of self-defence and hope that, in doing so, they gain support from the international community against their invaders. This also makes me think that another factor might be political alliances. For example, in WWI most of Europe ended up going to war because of the interlinking network of political alliances that had been drawn between all the countries. Country A might declare war on Country B because B has threatened A's political ally, Country C, and their alliance decrees that A must defend C against attack. All these factors might contribute to different extents and it might be very difficult to actually determine which one is the main reason that a country went to war, but I believe that these are some of the factors that might contribute to that decision.

This answer is very extensive but shows a nuanced and critical approach to answering the question. The candidate demonstrates that they are aware that this is a delicate subject matter and that there might not be just one acceptable response, but that they are willing to dive into the content and try to come to their own conclusion on the issue. They consider a number of different factors and even show how some might be interlinked. To make this answer even better, the candidate might try to explain which factor they think might be most important, and why, to show that they are critically assessing each of the options that they have been presented with.

Bad Answer: Countries only go to war to get something out of another country. They might want their money or resources and they go to war to fight them for it.

While this answer might identify one possible reason that a country goes to war, it fails to recognise that this is a nuanced problem. There might be a number of factors that lead to a war starting and it is rarely as simplistic as just wanting something from someone else (otherwise countries would be going to war far more often than they really do!) By saying that countries "only" go to war for this reason, the candidate is closing themselves off to being proven wrong or to considering another perspective which indicates to the interviewer that they don't have an open mind when it comes to academic problems.

Q38. How far do you think governments should interfere in the lives of their citizens?

Good Answer: I think there are some instances in which a government is legitimate in interfering in the lives of its citizens. For example, if someone has committed a crime, the government, or the systems that they enforce, should be able to prosecute the criminal and punish them appropriately. This is in order to protect the lives of the other citizens. Therefore, I think that the government should be able to interfere in the lives of its citizens to the extent that it upholds laws necessary to keep the peace and protect the rights and lives of its other citizens. However, the government should be strictly limited in the extent to which it can interfere without consequence; otherwise the government can get too powerful and use its position to exploit the nation for its own gain. For example, the government should not be able to interfere in the lives of its citizens just because it doesn't like something that they are doing (but that thing doesn't harm anyone else). One instance of this might be in the case of gay marriage. I don't think that the government should be able to stop people getting married just because they don't necessarily approve. Overall, therefore, I think that governments should be able to interfere in the lives of their citizens to the extent that they are acting to protect them and their rights, but they should not be able to interfere where no harm is posed and they simply don't like what the citizens are doing.

This is a good answer because it gives a nuanced, balanced response to the question. It considers critically when it might be the role (or duty) of the government to interfere in people's lives, but highlights that there might be limitations on this interference. It should be noted that there is no "correct" response to this question, but the candidate needs to show that they have a reasoned response and that they can adequately justify their response. It wouldn't have been enough for this candidate to just say "the government can interfere in some cases, like prosecuting criminals, and not in other, like gay marriage" without fully justifying their response.

Bad Answer: A good government never interferes in the lives of its citizens, otherwise that's just paternalism.

This candidate might have a valid answer, but they haven't given any form of justification for their response. If they do truly believe that there is no instance in which it would be acceptable for the government to interfere in the lives of their citizens then that's a perfectly fine response to give. However, just asserting that interference is "paternalism" isn't enough to support this claim. The candidate should give an explanation of what they mean by paternalism and explain why this is a bad thing when exercised by the government.

Q39. What do you think are the key differences between the UK and US forms of government?

Good Answer: The first difference that springs to mind is that in the US they have a President who is elected separately from the other representatives. There is an independence Presidential vote and the President is directly elected. In the UK, on the other hand, the Prime Minister is appointed because they are the leader of the party that has the majority of representatives in the House of Commons, in almost all cases anyway. This means that the power of the leader is separate from the other representatives in the US, while in the UK the power of the Prime Minister is more directly tied to the House of Commons. Also, the UK has the House of Lords which is a body of unelected individuals who have some power over the House of Commons. As far as I'm aware, the US doesn't have an equivalent to the House of Lords, as all of their representatives are elected. Therefore, the two key differences that I'm aware of between the UK and the US styles of government are the fact that the President is independently elected in the USA and has powers separate from the Senate, and the fact that the UK has an unelected body that oversees political decisions.

This answer directly answers the question that has been asked and has identified two key differences between the two systems of government. It is important to stress here that the interviewer isn't expecting the candidate to know everything about the two systems of government and be able to highlight all of the key differences between the two. What is more important is that the candidate is able to draw on the knowledge they do have to give an accurate comparison of the two styles of government. They haven't been thrown by the fact that they do not have a complete understanding of the subject matter, but have used the information they have available to give a comparative response.

Bad Answer: At the moment I think the key differences are that the US has a left-wing political party in power – the Democrats with Joe Biden as President – and the UK has a right-wing political party in power – the Conservatives with Boris Johnson as Prime Minister. This means that the governments will have different focuses, with right-wing governments more typically focused on security and lowering taxes, and with left-wing governments more often focused on social welfare and raising taxes on businesses and the rich.

This answer might appropriately answer a question, but it is not answering this question. The candidate has misinterpreted the question to be asking them to show that they know who is in power in the UK and US currently, and to demonstrate that they can name the difference between some of their key policies. However, the question is actually asking about the different *styles* of government employed in the UK vs the US. When answering a question, make sure to fully understand what the interviewer is asking you to do before you respond. If you don't think that you have fully understood the question, be sure to ask for clarification from the interviewer – they won't mind and it's much better that you give an answer to the question they have actually asked, rather than the one you think they've asked.

Q40. What do you think causes a rise in populism?

A candidate should not be afraid to ask for clarification on any terms in the question that they do not understand. In this case, for example, a candidate should be willing to ask for a definition of populism if they do not understand precisely what that terms means. It is much better to ask for clarification and ensure you are answering the question that has been asked, than guess what it means and end up answering an entirely different question.

Good Answer: I think that there are a number of factors that might cause populism to rise in any given society and it is likely that a combination of any of these factors might be needed to create a strong populist movement. One factor might be disillusionment with the current political status quo. For example, citizens might feel as though the main political parties do not adequately represent their political interests and so look to other actors to be their voices on the political stage. This might be particularly prevalent where members of society are particularly isolated, both socially and politically. Some groups might feel as though things are changing in society too quickly and they are being left behind. For example, in the UK, UKIP voters may have voted that way because they did not like the fact that there were a number of immigrants entering the UK. They may have felt as though their views were not being represented on the political stage and so looked to the more populist group UKIP for support and representation.

This answer is good because it directly answers the question, identifying that it is a nuanced issue. They provide a couple of different factors that might combine to cause a rise in populism and have backed up their points by using a real-life example. This demonstrates that they are paying attention to current affairs and are able to apply their real-world knowledge to a more theoretical question. To improve this answer, the candidate might want to point to unifying factors of those individuals who are feeling disillusioned or isolated. For example, they might need a charismatic leader to unite behind.

Bad Answer: UKIP was a prominent populist party in the UK, although they have recently faded from the political limelight. A Eurosceptic party, they stand for tighter border controls and appeal to rising fears of immigration and unemployment in Britain.

Using an example is a great way of supporting your answer. In this case, however, the candidate doesn't directly answer the question that is being asked. They need to give a more theory-based answer and then support this response by appealing to the UKIP case study. They need to consider a more general response to the question, supported by relevant examples, in order to fully answer it.

Q41. Why do you think political parties might have increasingly similar policies, most of which sit at the centre of the political spectrum?

Good Answer: I'm not entirely sure but let me try to work through this question. The main aim of political parties is to get into power by best representing the views of the population. In order to do this, they need to appeal to a majority of voters. If you think about the political spectrum, I think it's unlikely that everyone will be evenly spaced along it, as most people tend not to have radically right-wing or left-wing views, but tend to fall somewhat towards the centre of the political spectrum. Therefore, I think we can say that the political spectrum will look a little like a Normal Distribution curve. For a political party to gain a majority of the vote, they will want to appeal to the largest number of voters possible. It would make sense for them to do so by aligning their policies somewhat with the centre of the political spectrum, as the majority of people sit here. All parties will have the same idea so they will cluster their policies towards the centre of the spectrum in order to try to gain the majority of votes in the population.

This answer begins by admitting that the candidate is not entirely sure how to answer the question – this is absolutely fine! What is good about this answer is that the candidate then proceeds to reason through the question. They clearly set out their logical process for the interviewer so that they are able to fully understand how the candidate comes to their conclusion. After this reasoning process, the candidate clearly identifies their conclusion and responds directly to the question that the interviewer has posed.

Bad Answer: That can't be right, because in the UK the Conservatives are right-wing and Labour is left-wing. This must mean they have different policies.

This answer doesn't even attempt to address the question. The candidate might be able to come to the conclusion that it wouldn't make sense for political parties to have closely aligned policies because they sit on different sides of the political spectrum. In this case, however, the candidate has drawn on their (seemingly limited) knowledge of UK politics and made an assumption about political alignment in general. To make this a good answer, the candidate would need to try to work through the question logically, setting out why in the general case it might not make sense for political parties to align themselves at the centre.

Q42. Do you think that countries should interfere in the running of other countries when human rights are at risk?

Good Answer: I think there cannot be a black-and-white answer to this question. It depends highly on the case that we're talking about and the type of interference that is involved. For example, I think that interference such as economic or political sanctions can be a powerful force to protect human rights in other countries. If a group of countries, for example through the UN or the EU, all impose sanctions on a country where there are perceived human rights abuses, it might encourage the offending country to change their policies and act to protect the rights of their citizens. However, I do not think interference in the form of war or violence is an acceptable form of interference, unless used as an absolute last resort and done in such a way as to protect the lives of innocent citizens. This is because war itself can threaten human rights and the lives of citizens, rather than simply target the offending government.

This answer deals with a delicate topic in a nuanced manner. The candidate uses examples to justify their response and highlights why interference might be a problem, particularly in cases where we are talking about protecting human rights. Another angle that the answer might take is to consider whether the external country has the right to interfere in the running of another country. Some people might argue that nations should not interfere in the affairs of other nations, as their concern should solely be what happens within their borders. A good answer to this question does not depend entirely on the content of the answer, but on the candidate's ability to justify their response and defend their opinion using examples and reasoning.

Bad Answer: In all cases of human rights abuses I think we should deploy military sanctions against the offending country.

While the candidate might be able to come to this conclusion, this answer is problematic because it asserts a very strong viewpoint without any substantial justification. The candidate would need to explain why they think that deploying military sanctions is the answer to any violation of human rights. The answer would also benefit from the use of examples. Overall, this answer needs significantly more justification and explanation before the candidate can assert such a strong viewpoint.

Q43. Do you have a particular philosopher whose work interests you?

Good Answer: I'm not too sure about which philosopher I'm particularly interested in, but I'm very keen to study free will and determinism. I think considering whether what we do is done freely, and what impact this has on social and personal responsibility and punishment, is absolutely fascinating. I completed a MOOC recently on Free Will and Responsibility which I thought was so interesting and, while I can't remember specifically any of the philosophers that I was most struck by during the course, I am very keen to understand the topic better and look at it through a more academic lens.

While in this situation a candidate would ideally be able to name a philosopher and why they are interested in their work, this response shows that the candidate is interested in the subject and has engaged more widely in a particular area of philosophy, even if they are unable to remember a philosopher's name in that particular instance.

Bad Answer: I've read quite a lot of Mill's work on Utilitarianism because I had to for school so probably would have to say I'm most interested in him.

While this answer can name a philosopher who they've read, they do not give a compelling answer to this question. Firstly, they are only able to name Mill because they "had to" read his work for school. This suggests to the interviewer that they haven't engaged with the subject more widely which does not show any particular academic interest. Secondly, they don't give any details about what this work consists of (other than simply naming the title of one of Mill's most famous works) so don't even show that they fully understood Mill when they read him for school. A much better approach would be to say that you came across Mill's work while studying, but then wanted to take this interest further by reading more of his work and other material on the same subject to further increase your understanding.

Q44. How do you think we can know that something is right or wrong?

Good Answer: I think that we can never really *know* when something is right or wrong, but we can have an instinct about whether what we have just done was a morally acceptable thing to do. For example, when I give money to charity, I instinctively feel as though this was a morally acceptable thing to do, suggesting to me that it was a good thing to do. I think this feeling stems from the fact that giving money to charity helps someone other than myself, who is less fortunate than myself. On the other hand, if I were to steal money from someone, I would instinctively feel as though this was a bad thing to do, because it is taking something that isn't mine, therefore depriving someone else of something that belongs to them. I think that our moral instincts are quite strong and that we should listen to them when they respond to an action.

This answer recognises that it is very difficult to absolutely know whether an action is truly right or wrong. Instead, it provides a method through which we can generally judge our actions: reflecting on them using our moral instincts. Many philosophers take moral instincts to be a fairly good criteria against which to judge any moral theory and so appealing to this solution would accord with a lot of thinking in the field of moral philosophy.

Candidates should note here that the interviewer is not asking them to simply regurgitate an ethical theory that they have read about. Instead, they are asking them what *they* think about the question. A candidate might appeal to a theory that they've read about, but they should be prepared to justify why they agree/disagree with that theory. This shows the interviewer that they've actively thought about and engaged with what they've read, rather than simply taking it at face value (unlike the example of a bad answer).

Bad Answer: A utilitarian would argue that you can tell whether something is right or wrong by whether or not it brings about the greatest good for the greatest number of people. For example, when you are choosing an action, you should choose that action which brings about the greatest happiness in general society for you to have chosen the right thing to do.

This answer explains how someone else might determine whether an action is right or wrong, but it does not tell the interviewer what the candidate thinks. The interviewer isn't asking you to prove that you've read something about ethics – you might not have done! Instead, what they are asking you to do is to show that you can engage critically with a philosophical question, even if you haven't studied it before. It's much better to show that you have your own opinions and can support them with reason than to show that you've just read and remembered someone else's theory.

Q45. Consider the following case:

There is a train running down a track. There is a fork in the track a short way from where the train currently is. On the right-hand track at the fork there is tied one person. On the left-hand track at the fork there are tied five people. Currently the train will go to the left-hand fork. Whichever track the train runs down, anyone on that track will be killed by the train.

Should the train driver switch tracks so that the train kills one person rather than five people?

Good Answer: When we're talking about what the train driver "should" do, I'm going to assume that we're looking at what the right thing to do would be. The right thing in this situation will depend on whether you think that it's okay for the driver to actively choose to kill one person rather than choosing not to interfere with the current path of the train and allow five people to die. I'm going to assume that all of the six people who could die are identical so that their personalities or moralities don't need to factor into the decision. In my opinion, I think that the driver should choose to switch tracks and kill one person rather than five. This is because it is better to kill fewer people; this will result in the least pain caused by the action. This is also instinctively what I feel would be the best choice for the driver to make, even though it would be quite a difficult decision.

This answer clearly identifies what the problem is that they're being asked to solve and then reasons through their own personal response to the question. They give a justified answer and even bring in a control factor (making all the people who could die identical) so that they are just focusing on the particular moral decision that they are being asked to consider.

Bad Answer: Oh, I know this problem – it's a Trolley Problem Case. From what I've read, most people say that the driver should change tracks and kill the one instead of the five so that must be the right thing to do in this situation.

This candidate is demonstrating that they have done some further reading which is a good thing. However, they fail to provide a reasoned, personal response to the question that they are being asked. They could identify that this is a Trolley Problem Case (which it is) but then go on to work through their own personal response to the case. This would be a much better way of approaching the question, as it shows the examiner that the candidate is able to form their own opinions of things and approach questions with a critical eye, rather than just being happy to uncritically accept what they've read.

Q46. Consider the following case:

You are a Doctor with 5 patients who need immediate organ transplants; they have conditions which have been brought on by entirely natural causes. All patients have a very rare blood type, so they have been unable to find organ donors. A patient comes in to see you for a routine check-up. This patient has the same rare blood type as your other 5 patients but is otherwise entirely healthy.

The doctor could kill the healthy patient in order to donate her organs to the 5 patients. If the doctor did this, all 5 patients would live.

Do you think the case is different in any significant way to the Trolley Problem?

Good Answer: Yes I do think this case is significantly different from the Trolley problem. While we are dealing with the same numbers in both cases, here the doctor would have to actively kill the healthy patient in order to kill the 5. I think what is different here is that in the Trolley case, the train is the thing that would be killing the individuals in either case. That means that either the train kills one person or the train kills five people: it is simply a matter of which outcome would cause less pain and choosing that. In the case of the doctor, however, the doctor would need to choose to kill the healthy patient herself rather than letting the other 5 patients die from natural causes. It is interfering in the life of the healthy patient in a way that switching the train doesn't do in the Trolley case. Therefore, I think that this case is different from the Trolley case and that here the Doctor would not be justified in killing the healthy patient in order to save the other 5.

This answer is good because it demonstrates what the candidate thinks is different between the two cases and how this makes a moral difference to the case. They then come to a moral conclusion based on their response. The candidate has identified that we are dealing with the same number of individuals in both cases, but then shows why they believe that there is a difference between the cases in spite of this similarity.

Bad Answer: Why would this be any different – it's just about numbers and the numbers are the same.

This answer also identifies the key similarity between the two cases (and why the case of the doctor might be so morally difficult when considered in conjunction with the Trolley Problem) but fails to even consider why there might be differences between the two cases, which is the key focus of the question. In order to improve here, the candidate would need to then consider why there might be differences between the cases but show that these are not relevant to come to the conclusion that the differences that exist between the two cases are not significant.

Q47. Do you think that you freely chose to apply to this PPE course?

Good Answer: I think at the time I made my application I would have assumed that I made the choice freely because that's how I tend to think about all of my choices – I think automatically I assume that I had free will in the situation unless I am being obviously coerced. However, I wonder whether something like my upbringing and school situation might have influenced my decision to choose to study PPE. For example, my parents have always encouraged me to take an interest in current affairs and politics, and the economics department was really good at my school which I why I decided to take it at A Level. If these things hadn't been the case then I might not have chosen to study politics and economics at A Level, so I might not have chosen to study PPE at university. I don't think, however, that this makes the choice unfree; I just think it means that there was a certain chain of events that led me to the moment of decision, but in that deciding moment I was the one who freely chose to study PPE. Therefore, I think that while the decision in which I made the choice to study PPE was influenced by my upbringing and surroundings, at the end of the day I am the one who made the choice to take that set of circumstances and study PPE as a result of that situation. So, yes, I do think that I freely chose to apply to this PPE course.

This is a nuanced and considered answer and directly responds to the question that the interviewer is asking. The candidate takes their initial assumption and critically considers it, looking at why their assumption might not have been right. They give examples to show that they have fully understand the case that they are considering. Then they logically work through the issue at hand and come to a justified conclusion. Finally, they round their answer off by giving a direct response at the end to signal to the examiner that they have understood and answered their question.

Bad Answer: I submitted my application form and no one else made me apply so I must have applied freely.

Here, the candidate has given a conclusion without giving any kind of justification for the conclusion. They haven't demonstrated that they have in any way considered why that choice might not have been free and have simply chosen the conclusion that comes most naturally to mind when we tend to think about whether we have free will or not. To make this answer better, the candidate needs to show that they have considered at least one reason why they might not have made the choice freely rather than simply assuming that they did. Furthermore, they need to justify why this is the right conclusion in the face of that other reason.

Q48. If humans don't have free will and knew that they didn't, do you think that would make any difference to how society functions?

Good Answer: Yes, I think it would make a lot of difference. If someone knows that everything they do is determined, then that suggests that they are not responsible for what they do. If someone isn't responsible for what they do, then they cannot be blamed or praised for their behaviour. As the people in this scenario know that they don't have free will, they would know that they cannot be justifiably blamed or praised for their actions. This means that people would stop thinking about what is the society acceptable action and instead do whatever they like, knowing that they can't be blamed for any of their actions. I think that people would start to act a lot more recklessly and society would become somewhat anarchistic.

The important thing to stress here is that the interviewer probably isn't concerned about what you say in response to this type of question. What they are looking at instead is how you argue for the conclusion you come to. This candidate has taken a clear position in response to the question and have given a reasoned explanation for how they come to that conclusion. The interviewer might disagree with them and try to find a flaw in their reasoning, but the candidate at this stage has done a good job of setting out their chain of reasoning and coming to a clear and definitive conclusion.

Bad Answer: I'm not really sure. I think maybe if people knew that they had free will it might make them think differently about themselves but I don't know what that would mean for society.

This candidate needs to be more confident in their reasoning and in coming to a conclusion. They have the beginnings of a good answer, identifying that if people know they don't have free will it might make them think differently about themselves and how they act. To turn this into a good answer they need to work through this chain of logic, thinking about what impact this would have on an individual's behaviour in society. They also need to remember that this type of question is really testing how you think and how you approach difficult concepts that you might not be familiar with. The interviewer wants to see that you can think on your feet and work through difficult problems, even if you aren't automatically sure what the answer should be.

Q49. Do you think that you can trust what your eyes are telling you?

Good Answer: Let me think about this. I wouldn't be able to trust what my eyes are telling me if sometimes what I think I see isn't actually what I see. In other words, I can't trust my senses if my senses sometimes deceive me. Sometimes when it's dark in my room I think that the pile of clothes on my chair looks like the outline of a person and I get worried that there's another person in my room. That tends to only happen when it's dark though. In this case, the dark can be classed as something that is interfering with my senses. Therefore, I think that I can trust what my eyes are telling me so long as there isn't something interfering with my senses.

This answer follows the structure of a premise and conclusion argument. It sets up what would be needed for the candidate to not be able to trust their senses and then considers whether this is possible. They give an example of when they can't trust their senses but conclude that this is an exceptional case. What makes this answer a good answer is that the candidate has clearly reasoned through the logic behind their conclusion, showing the interviewer exactly how they are approaching this difficult question. Their answer is justified and well-reasoned and they have come to a distinct conclusion, rather than giving a vague answer to try to get out of thinking the case through properly.

Bad Answer: Of course I can trust what my eyes are telling me – why wouldn't I be able to?

This candidate has themselves identified why this is a bad answer: they haven't thought about why they might not be able to trust what their eyes are telling them. It is okay to come to the conclusion that you can trust what you see, so long as this conclusion is reasoned and well thought-through. And the candidate needs to show the interviewer that they have actually thought it through, rather than just asserting their conclusion without trying to explain how they reach that point. To improve this answer, the candidate needs to explain their reasoning and justify why they can trust what their eyes are telling them, rather than simply taking this as a given.

Q50. Consider the following case:

Smith and Jones have both applied for the same job. The hiring manager for the job has told Smith that Jones will get the job. Smith has also counted the coins in Jones's pocket and has found there are 10 coins there. Based on this evidence, Smith makes the following assertion:

(1) The person who will get the job has 10 coins in his pocket.

As it turns out, Smith actually gets the job and has 10 coins in his pocket, although he didn't count these coins before he got the job. This means that (1) is true.

Do you think that we can say that Smith knew that (1) was true? (Gettier Case)

Good Answer: No, I do not think that we can say that Smith knew that (1) was true. This is because the evidence that Smith uses to support his claim of (1) isn't actually why (1) is true in the end. He has based his claim on false evidence – the fact that the hiring manager told him that Jones would get the job – and evidence which doesn't contribute to the truth of (1) – the fact that Jones had 10 coins in his pocket. Smith doesn't have evidence that he will get the job and he also hasn't counted the numbers of coins he has in his pocket at the time that he makes the assertion. In this case, he is just lucky that he happens to be right in asserting (1) so I do not think that we can say that Smith knew that (1) was true.

This answer identifies the problem in this case – that the evidence Smith bases his claim on does not contribute to the truth of (1) – and clearly relates it to the question of whether or not Smith knew that (1) was true. The candidate clearly sets out their chain of reasoning for the interviewer and comes to a justified and reasoned answer. The candidate doesn't rely on any additional reading that they may have done, although if relevant they could have brought in some wider reasoning if it would have helped them, but show that they are able to critically engage with challenging philosophical problems in a logical way.

Bad Answer: Yes, Smith must have known that (1) was true because he said it before it happened.

This answer has completely missed the point of the example and doesn't even try to reason through why Smith might not have known that (1) was true before he said it. A candidate might conclude this, but they would need to give strong and clear reasoning for this conclusion for it to be a good answer.

Q51. What do you think makes a strong philosophical argument?

Good Answer: A strong philosophical argument is one in which the conclusion is fully supported by the premises. There need to be no contradictions in the chain of reasoning and the chain of reasoning needs to lead clearly and securing to the conclusion that the argument is trying to come to. An example of this might be: I am an A Level student; I am a girl; therefore, I am a female A Level student. This is a very straightforward example but the conclusion is fully supported by the premises and there are no contradictions in the chain of argument.

This clearly sets out what criteria are required for a philosophical argument to be considered "strong". While a candidate might not know the term "Premises" they could still set out the second half of this response which shows the content of a strong philosophical argument and gives a clear and concise example to show the interviewer that they have fully understood what they are talking about. If possible, the candidate should then be able to give further examples of a strong philosophical argument if questioned further by the examiner.

Bad Answer: An argument that concludes in favour of a particularly important philosophical theory.

The candidate has here misunderstood what the interviewer is asking them for. In general, these types of defining questions will be asking about the methodology behind philosophy. It will be asking the candidate what they think is important in building a strong and important argument, rather than asking them to suggest what might support pre-existing philosophical theories. Here, the candidate could instead reverse the sentiments in their answer, replying instead that philosophical theories need strong philosophical arguments in order to support them and to make them convincing. From here, the candidate could then walk through the methodology that would make a philosophical argument convincing, such as the methodology given in the "Good Answer" to this question.

Q52. Can you see any problems with the following argument?

1: Samantha can't get a job where she's currently living.

2: Samantha got a job in London.

Conclusion: Samantha will move to London.

This question is testing skills similar to those tested in some of the verbal reasoning questions in the TSA. It is asking you to look at the answer and check whether or not the conclusion follows from the stated premises. The argument might be problematic if any of the following are true: (i) the premises contradict each other or the conclusion, (ii) the argument is relying on a premise that isn't explicitly stated, (iii) the conclusion doesn't follow from the premises. There is a problem with this argument, as the "Good Answer" below will set out.

Good Answer: Yes, I can see a problem with the argument. The conclusion doesn't follow directly from the premises, as there is nothing contained within the premises that states that Samantha will move for her job. A better argument would be as follows:

1: Samantha can't get a job where she's currently living.

2: Samantha got a job in London.

Conclusion: Samantha isn't currently living in London.

An alternative argument would be:

1: Samantha can't get a job where she's currently living.

2: Samantha will move to wherever she can get a job.

3: Samantha got a job in London.

Conclusion: Samantha will move to London.

Bad Answer: I can't see any problem with this argument.

Q53. Can you see any problems with the following argument?

1: All men are mortal.

2: Socrates is a man.

Conclusion: Socrates is mortal.

As above, this question is testing skills similar to those tested in some of the verbal reasoning questions in the TSA. It is asking you to look at the answer and check whether or not the conclusion follows from the stated premises. The argument might be problematic if any of the following are true: (i) the premises contradict each other or the conclusion, (ii) the argument is relying on a premise that isn't explicitly stated, (iii) the conclusion doesn't follow from the premises. This argument is valid as it does not fulfil any of these criteria, as the "Good Answer" below will set out.

Good Answer: To me, this argument looks strong. The conclusion seems to follow directly from the premises and I cannot see any flaw in the chain of reasoning. I also can't see that the argument relies on an assertion that is not explicitly identified. Therefore, I think that there is no problem with this argument.

Bad Answer: A bad answer here would be unable to identify that this is a strong argument. It might highlight a problem that doesn't exist, for example.

HSPS INTERVIEW QUESTIONS

Q1: How would you discretise the concepts of ethnicity and race?

Race and ethnicity are both highly complex topics. Your interviewer is not expecting you to be able dissect these or necessarily give a 'correct' answer. In society, definitions of 'race' and 'ethnicity' are not specifically discussed, because they are relatively nebulous concepts that are highly political. Therefore, the interview is interested in seeing how you think critically about this question, what experiences and knowledge that you draw upon, and how you can synthesise this into a coherent answer.

Because this question is highly political, you must be incredibly careful about the kind of language you are using. Interviewers will accept minor slip-ups in terms of terminology, but do not use racial stereotypes or discriminative language.

Good Applicant: Well, I'd like to first acknowledge that race and ethnicity are interrelated, and that I don't think it is possible for us talk about one without being aware of the other, because they are both so prevalent in discussions of identity. But, broadly speaking, I think the difference between race and ethnicity, is that race is mostly situated in physical aspects of who a person is, such as their skin colour, but also other biological aspects. In contrast, ethnicity is more closely tied to socio-cultural aspects of a person, where they were brought up, their language, nationality, and regional identities. I think there's also a difference in the histories of the two concepts. Whilst race has a deep past originating from colonial times and was often used to categorise, and thereby dehumanise, different people, as a concept, ethnicity is a more recent creation that is used to better understand the complexity of identity in the post-colonial and global era. I think ultimately both concepts are difficult to clearly define, and the boundaries between the differences are often blurred.

This response is structured well, it starts by stating the relationship that ethnicity and race, and how they both relate to identity. It then clearly cites two points contrasting how race and ethnicity are different, using broad examples to back up the points, without delving into potential slippery slopes that specific examples in talking about these topics might lead to. Finally, the answer makes it clear at the end that you don't have a firm opinion on what race and ethnicity are; it has critically engaged with the question whilst making it clear that you are open to further discussion.

A **poor applicant** could go one of two ways. Firstly, you might not be willing to engage in critical examination of the two concepts because you don't want to say something inappropriate, or you are unaware of exactly what the concepts might mean. Being cautious around these topics is important, but not answering the question asked at all also doesn't help. Secondly, a poor answer might rely upon stereotypes, or even use crude terms to discuss these two highly sensitive topics.

Q2: Would you argue that the society and the state are inseparable? If not, what separates them?

This question is a good opportunity to demonstrate your understanding of definitions of state, and how society fits into it, but also how a state is reliant upon society; they are different but often interconnected. As with many concepts in anthropology and political science, concepts and definitions are important for creating benchmarks for discussion, but are still nebulous and require open thinking combined with critical engagement.

Good Applicant: Fundamentally, I think that the difference between state and society relates to the way in which they are structured. The state is typically made up of formal structures and institutions to be maintained, and is reliant upon four key aspects: population, territory, government, and sovereignty. Now, each of these four aspects are themselves debatable in their definitions and parameters, but the key thing is they form the pillars upon which the state is established. In contrast, society is typically made of informal structures, and interpersonal and intergroup relationships. They are established and maintained through human behaviours, such as exchange of goods and ideas, and are typically highly flexible. With this in mind, state and society are also highly influential upon each other. The formal structures of the state can influence the way in which people in a society interact and their relationships, whilst the state is inherently dependent on the stability of society and the ability of people to cooperate and communicate.

This answer is structured well, making it clear that the applicant understands the question being asked, and that they are able to back up their argument with evidence and examples. Bearing in mind that these are difficult concepts to discuss in a single response, the answer does not go down a rabbit hole trying to wrestle with these ideas, but shows that they are able to engage with both concepts in the question, and draw contrasts between the two. The synthesis at the end also demonstrates that respondent is able to think beyond the basic question, challenge the assumption in the question, and demonstrate the relationships between the two concepts.

A **Poor Applicant** would become tied down with trying to define the two concepts and would run out of time before actually answering the question. Whilst it is important to demonstrate your understanding of the concepts, it is important to demonstrate that you are able to see the bigger picture and critically engage.

Q3: A Roman magistrate appears on your doorstep, and asks you to tell him about the United Nations – how would you compare it to his Empire?

This question is testing your ability to draw comparisons between two seemingly unrelated organisations. In order to answer this question, you need to be able to think creatively and accept that sometimes unconventional comparisons can sometimes change your perspective and are useful heuristics.

Good Response: Well, this is certainly interesting. I think one of the first points that I would compare is that both intentionally or unintentionally acted as peacekeeping bodies. In the case of the UN, this is through mediation, forums, and small peace-keeping forces, in the Roman empire, which I would argue did maintain a decent level of relative peace for 200 years at the outset of the empire (Romana Pax), 'peace' was achieved mostly through prosperity of the empire, fairly decent governance, and the violent crushing of any rebellions. Another point of similarity is the fact that power in the both the Roman empire and UN is actually held by a small number of stakeholders. In the empire this meant the emperor and a few others, and whilst the senate existed, their power was negligible. One could argue that a similar reality occurs in the UN; power is held by the Director General and the Security Council, much of the discourse carried out in the main house of the UN by its members do not carry with it much power, similarly to the senate. I think a third point of similarity are the UN's and the empire's goals around development. Both have or had missions of developing those areas under their influence, in the formers case through sustainable economic development and the latter through its building of grandiose architecture. A final point of similarity that I would draw would be between the multi-state nature of the two organisations; although the UN does not directly govern those states that make it up, unlike the empire, both had to deal with the complexities of multiple states.

At first glance, this is a challenging question, and indeed, as outlined in this answer, the similarities are not going to be perfect. One could argue that there are far more differences between the UN and the RE. Hence, this answer has done well here because it has found ways of drawing similarities between four different points of the UN and the RE through some creative thinking, which your interviewers will be impressed by.

A **Poor Answer** could very easily struggle to find similarities, and become bogged down by the fact that any similarities you can see aren't perfect. Equally, it would be very easy to begin by talking about the differences between the two as these are much easier to identify, and never really identify any points of similarity.

Q4: Some of us think that the poor live in poverty because they don't try hard enough – what would you say to people like that?

As with many Oxbridge interview questions, this question is intentionally challenging or jarring. Whilst it may be tempting to form a strong and subjective opinion one way or the other, you must endeavour to remain balanced, whilst still reaching a conclusion. Thus, you should present your arguments, and then conclude by making your opinion clear on the matter.

Good Answer: Well, to begin with, I can understand why this point of view may be so prevalent among neoliberals. I think that it is derived primarily from those in power and those who control big media outlets influencing the general public's thought. For instance, the fact that the Murdoch empire controls multiple media outlets allows it to hold great sway among the populace in the UK and other countries. Now, media moguls such as Murdoch have two primary objectives: manipulating people to agree with their way of thinking, and making money for themselves and those whose interests align with their own. One of the easiest ways for this money to be made is to push a neoliberal agenda, both in lobbying governments and convincing people through their outlets that this is good for them and their families.

In essence, this means creating the idea that people must be productive within the capitalist system, and that the amount you work will equate directly to your income. In reality, the neoliberal agenda is to deregulate markets and state involvement so that workers' rights and pay can be cut without repercussions. Alongside the propaganda that your worth is equal to how much you work, this creates an environment where the wealthy are able to monopolise the working and middle classes by making them believe that they can be successful, whilst using this as a front to extract wealth from them. In the end, the system crushes many people, especially when state safety nets have been removed, and become poor. Thus, the system is manipulated by neoliberals to make it seem like poor people are only poor because they don't work hard enough. In reality, I think that most of the time, poor people have been exploited by a system created by neoliberals who have simultaneously convinced people through media propaganda that it is the poor's fault for not working hard enough.

This is not an easy question to answer, and in part centres around unpacking what it means to be neoliberal. This answer is strong because it puts pressure from the start on the falsehood underpinning everyday neoliberals; that they are different from poor people. In fact, most neoliberals have been manipulated into their beliefs by moguls and the super rich, and their neoliberal belief system is actually perpetuating those falsehoods that are manipulating them. As well as demonstrating this issue, the answer logically works through the relationship between the political belief system of neoliberalism, the media, and the state. In the end, the answer draws together these lines of argument to answer the question and demonstrate that poverty is not a result of laziness, but instead a failure of state as result of the influence of money within politics.

A **Poor Candidate** could react one of two ways. Someone who tacitly agrees with the notion of the question might argue positively, and agree with the question, whilst failing to challenge their own belief system, which would likely be picked up on the interviewer. On the other hand, it would be very easy to become personally offended by the question, as it is undoubtedly an insulting notion. Thus it is important to take the question apart and show that you are able to remain objective whilst still creating a forthright answer that takes a balanced approach.

Q5: What do you think lies behind the recent resurgence of Nationalism in Europe?

This question is testing several different aspects of your knowledge: your recent and deep historic understanding of nationalism within Europe, as well as how this plays out throughout the geography of Europe. In order to answer the question, it is important to highlight that nationalism is a broad idea that fluctuates over time and can mean different things to different people.

A **Good Answer:** I think first it is important to point a bit of an assumption within the question of whether nationalism ever really weakened in Europe. If we look at the history of Europe, really going back to the Roman conquests of Europe, when tribes of the different territories fought back to "protect their lands", we could argue that this is a kind of nationalism, or a kind of cultural or ethnic identity tied to the landscape. From there, throughout the history of Europe, I think that nationalism has always been bubbling under the surface in one form or another. Even when it may seem like nationalistic sentiment has diminished, there are always those factions within a state that advocate for nationalistic policies, and occasionally those with these sentiments achieve power and drive forward with those nationalistic attitudes.

With this in mind, it seems that we are in a time where people with nationalistic sentiments are gaining traction politically. I think there are a number of reasons for this. Firstly, nationalism in Europe is not isolated from the rest of the world, in the same way that nationalism within individual European countries is not isolated from other countries. To this extent, the election of Donald Trump, as well as other fascist leaders such as Jair Bolsanero, and Duterte to name just a couple, always have a knock-on effect elsewhere by emboldening other nationalists directly and indirectly (e.g., Trump's endorsement of Nigel Farage). Beyond just this, the migrant crisis, caused by the ongoing conflicts in the Middle East and North Africa, and exponentially exacerbated by Western and Russian interventions, has undoubtedly increased nationalistic sentiments in Europe as Europeans feel threatened by a sudden influx of people alongside some pretty incompetent policies and leaders unable to deal with this crisis. Finally, both of these issues are ultimately enflamed by the press, which is controlled by a small number of people who directly profit from the controversy that they drive especially around nationalistic sentiments in order to sell papers.

In summary, I think nationalism is an ever-present element of European sociopolitics, but that there are clearly events in the recent past and ongoing that continue to fuel nationalistic sentiments in areas of Europe.

This is a good answer because it shows that you are able to critically engage with the question, deconstruct and offer a foundational starting point by addressing the key assumption within the question. The answer is then structured well, outlining three key points that you feel has driven the strengthening of nationalism within Europe. Finally, it has provided a neat summary that synthesises everything you have tried to outline in your answer.

A **Poor Answer** might try to inherently question whether nationalism has strengthened at all in Europe. Whilst it is possible to play this as devil's advocate, it may inadvertently show that you have a poor grasp of current or recent historical events. Alternatively, it would be easy to become tied up in the deep history of nationalism in Europe, which whilst a useful point of comparison and grounding to your answer, would not address the idea of a recent development.

Q6. You're redesigning a map of the world, how would you go about deciding on national borders?

Whilst seemingly simple, in fact this question is seeking to have you draw upon your ability to synthesise several different disciplines, in reflection of the complexity of drawing of national borders, to answer the question. There is not necessarily a straightforward answer to this, thus you must instead draw upon your different subject knowledges, including history, geography, and politics, to demonstrate that you are able to bring together several different ways of thinking.

A **Good Answer**: At a basic level, national borders are drawn by the political or social bodies that control each side. However, the reality of the drawing of national borders is that there are often complex historical and geographical factors at play, alongside the political ones. For instance, geographical features such as mountain ranges or rivers, serve as physical boundaries that are used as straightforward and often practical borders, such as the Pyrenees separating France and Spain, or the Akagera river separating Rwanda and Tanzania. However, physical boundaries are not always a limiting factor to national borders and can even make the drawing of national borders more, not less complex. In the latter instance, take for example the occasionally conflicted border of India and China, which because of its size and location among the Himalayas, makes defining the border incredibly complicated.

Moreover, in historic terms, physical features have not always been a defining factor for drawing national borders. The invasion and colonisation of other countries, such as by the British or Mongolian empires, entirely betrayed the limitations of the English Channel and the Central Asian Steppe. Conveniently, this leads to consideration of the impact that historical events have on the drawing of national borders. In the post-colonial era, many of the national borders that still exist today are a direct result of colonial powers. Whilst these borders were still defined politically during their time between the colonial powers, it is interesting to examine how infrequently these borders are actually challenged by the modern nations that they affect. Overall, what I'm trying to elucidate, is that national borders are in fact incredibly complex and dynamic, and are affected by a whole array of factors on a case by case basis; almost no two borders are drawn in exactly the same way, and this is reflected in the way that they are drawn.

It would be very easy to write an entire thesis on this subject, as there are so many case studies that you could draw upon to provide examples and counter examples. Ultimately, this answer is strong because it is able to demonstrate that you have a wide understanding of the realities of the complexities of drawing national borders, and that it is perfectly fine, once you have outlined decent and varied evidence, as has been done here, to conclude that there is no finite answer to this question.

A **Poor Answer** would only rely upon examples that fit the narrative you create about how national borders are drawn. For example, it would be easy to argue that national borders are drawn as a result of conflict and upheaval, and then only illustrate this with one type of example, without considering the multitude of different realities involved.

Q7. Do you think that you have free will? Does free will as a concept relate to the notion of the state of nature?

This question is attempting to get you to think about what might normally be two unrelated concepts and understand how one can inform the other. This is a particularly pertinent question as it is a reflection of the kind of question that you might be asked to write an essay about during your time at the university. It should be noted that this question assumes your pre-understanding of the state of nature. If this is an unfamiliar concept to you, because you haven't studied a subject that considers it before, it is perfectly fine to say this to your interviewer, you will not be penalised. In many ways, it is better to acknowledge that you do not know everything, and ask for clarification, before attempting to answer it; interviewers are more interested in how you think than what you know.

A **Good Answer**: Well, thank you for clarifying for me what exactly the state of nature is. I think that the crux of this question centres around the idea that when the hypothetical state of nature existed, before the existence of societies, people would not have been constrained by social norms or rules, and whether or not this could potentially be defined as a time when we had true free will. In this context, I believe therefore, it is important to define free will as the ability to make decisions about your behaviour and life, unhindered by the actions of others or the rules of society. I think that this is a logical assumption to make, as so much of our modern behaviour is tied up in social contracts between people, and therefore free will in a true sense can rarely exist.

If this is case, then the issue becomes when do we consider that society actually started? If, for example, we look at other species that live in groups, such as chimpanzees, they still have social rules, ways of behaving in a group that are enforced by other members. Thus, in a sense, they cannot have complete 'free' will, because their behaviour doesn't exist in a vacuum; the things that they do have consequences for those around them. From this perspective, we could then analogously consider whether humans could achieve complete free will in a state where no groups, and therefore no social behaviours (i.e., societies) existed. However, there is an inherent problem in this assumption, and that is that the vast majority of humans do not exist in complete in isolation, nor would it be logical to assume that they ever have done, as we would have died out as a species. In reality, there will always be moments where people must interact - to have offspring etc. - and therefore, there will be moments where their free will is given up to the needs of the group.

Thus, to reiterate my original definition of free will, it is the ability to make decisions without anyone else's agency affecting or inhibiting those decisions. As I believe I've demonstrated, this kind of free-will can only exist in a hypothetical vacuum, because we as a species are never 100% isolated from the actions of others or from the effect of our actions on others. Based upon the reference I made to chimpanzees, even if there was a time before society when human behaviour was entirely 'natural', the reality is that living in any kind of group comes with implicit rules as a direct result of the agency of others. The relationship therefore between free will and the state of nature is only hypothetical, and whilst it might be easy to conclude that the state of nature was the only time when free will could have existed, as I have demonstrated here, I don't believe that even that would be possible due to our interdependent, group nature as a species.

This is by no means a straightforward question as it is dealing with two huge philosophical ideas. However, this answer is strong because whilst it would be impossible to fully elucidate the two ideas separately in an answer, it has achieved what the question is asking: for you to speculate about the relationship between the two concepts. As well as outlining generally the two ideas, it has used examples from primatology and made logical conclusions based upon your understanding of the two ideas. Ultimately, it synthesises the two ideas into a conclusion in order to answer the question.

A **Poor Answer** could become overwhelmed by the enormity of the two concepts that you are being asked to answer and get too caught up in trying to consider all the different interpretations of these ideas, without actually trying to draw a conclusion about their relationship. Equally, a poor answer might entirely focus on one or the other of these concepts, without paying heed to the other. In order to answer the question well, it is important to try to remain logical and bring each of your points back to how free will and the state of nature are related.

Q8. Do you think that primates, like chimpanzees, should be given the same rights as people?

This question hinges around two key points: how do we define 'human', and do chimpanzees sufficiently fulfil this definition. The easier option in this question is definitely to argue that chimpanzees are not human and therefore do not deserve human rights, however, there is definitely scope to make the argument that they do deserve rights. In some ways, the question can be considered: are humans unique in comparison to our closest relations, and how does this relate to rights?

A **Good Response**: Well, I think at a broad level, it is clear that whilst chimpanzees have a high level of intelligence, both social and emotional, that can be used to draw parallels with humans, that ultimately there is enough of a biological and cultural difference between humans and chimpanzees, that they probably shouldn't be afforded human rights. This being said, there is growing evidence that the 'uniqueness' of humans in comparison to chimpanzees and other animals is not as distinct as we first thought. For instance, in the Great Ape family, humans are often touted as unique due to our bipedality, but there is plenty of evidence now that whilst chimps are not habitually bipedal, they certainly have the ability to do so for extended periods. Equally, the argument that humans in general are the only species to have cumulative culture (behaviours and technologies that are passed down through generations with increasing complexity) is also being challenged by evidence from chimpanzees, with suggestions that complex behaviours, such as termite fishing, are passed between generations. I think these two examples are excellent challenges to the notion of human uniqueness, and thereby a challenge to whether human rights should be exclusively human. Based upon this kind of evidence, maybe we need to re-evaluate how binary human : animal rights are, and consider whether animals that display higher levels of culture should have different levels of rights. This is of course a slippery slope, but as more and more evidence comes in to play about the complexity of animal (and especially chimpanzee and bonobo) behaviour, these are going to become more complex debates.

Whilst this question may at first seem like a straightforward question to answer, as outlined here, once you start dealing with *why* humans are considered unique and how this plays into our ideas of human rights, the answer becomes complicated very quickly. Thus, this is a good response because it tries to take a balanced approach, suggesting at the beginning that there are obvious differences between humans and chimpanzees, before going onto elaborate how this discussion is not as binary as it may at first appear, outlining the growing evidence for the complexity of chimp behaviour. Finally, it acknowledges that there is not necessarily an easy answer to this question, and that evidence in the future may cause us to re-evaluate our position.

A **Poor Response** could quite easily dismiss this question out of hand, stating that chimps clearly don't deserve human rights. Even if one was unaware of the evidence around chimp behaviour, a basic awareness of chimps will tell you that they are clearly highly intelligent and that it is worth considering how what you know about their biology or behaviour may play into arguments for giving chimps human rights.

Q9. What do you think is one of the most fascinating facts about where you come from, what makes that so interesting?

This question is an opportunity for you to be reflexive and demonstrate to your interviewers your interest in the world around you. In anthropology, the ability to be self-reflective, to understand how your background - including your culture, personal upbringing, and the environment in which these occurred - influences your study of other cultures and societies is fundamental to acknowledging that we all have our own set biases, or constructed lenses, through which we see the world. Here, you could discuss aspects of material culture, architecture, behaviour, or pretty much anything that you feel confident talking about. Be creative!

A **Good Applicant**: Something that has always interested me about teenagers and young people in Great Britain are attitudes and behaviours towards alcohol. It has always amazed me how willing people are to get inebriated to the point of passing out in the street, or causing themselves bodily harm, and then repeating this behaviour the following week. It is this self-destructive aspect that particularly fascinates me; people are aware of how much damage that level of alcohol can cause (both directly and indirectly) to their bodies, but they do it anyway. I suppose that ultimately it comes down to a combination of cultural acceptance - both tacitly through people accepting that this behaviour is the 'norm' and pragmatically through young people's ability to access alcohol.

It is particularly interesting when you compare these kinds of behaviours to other young people in other cultures. For instance, I know that in America, alcohol is very difficult to access as a young person, but marijuana isn't, and therefore the latter is far more prevalent. In France, people are often introduced to alcohol at a younger age, and the culture around drinking has less of a tendency towards binge drinking, but then, a huge majority of French young people smoke which is in contrast to young people in Britain. I think that these comparisons and experiences of other cultures can be incredibly interesting as points of comparison. This is because they both allow us draw way markers in other cultures to help our understanding as well as give us an alternative lens through which to reflect on our own culture.

This is a good answer because it has chosen an aspect of your culture that has interested you. It doesn't necessarily have to be a positive thing, indeed, often some of the most interesting behaviours are those that seem in some way counter-intuitive or deviant. Hence, not only does this answer outline why you're interested in this particular thing, but it also demonstrates how you've thought about this issue or thing in other cultural contexts. Moreover, it has shown how one cultural understanding can inform another.

A **Poor Answer** could choose something that you find interesting, but then fail to explain why you find it interesting. Whilst this question seems open ended, in the context of which interview you are in, it is important to demonstrate that you understand that this question is about society and/or culture, and show that your interested is derived from that context.

Q10. Take a look at these cave paintings, how might you analyse them for meaning?

This question will be accompanied by pictures of cave paintings (you may be given one or more to look at). There are a whole range of cave paintings that we now know about from across the world and across a whole range of time periods. The most famous cave paintings come from Europe (mostly France and Spain), but archaeologists are discovering new cave art globally all the time. Equally, this is the kind of question where an interviewer might throw a curve ball, and for instance, show you modern "cave art" in the form of graffiti inside an urban building, for instance. Regardless, you could cover a number of topics when deciphering them: content (is it a clear shape(s) or is it abstract), colours used, medium (e.g., paint, ochre, blood), location (e.g. ceiling, floor), and finally what is it symbolic or representative of; does it have a purpose? For the sake of this question, the following answer is in response to the image in this article, from Lascaux https://medium.com/@stevechatterton/what-the-lascaux-cave-paintings-tell-us-about-the-nature-of-human-desire-4c8d06deef83:

Good Answer: In this picture, there are a number of different animals clearly depicted. There are three distinct kinds of image, a bull-like animal with horns, what appear to be two brown and black horses, and two entirely black horses. The parsimonious explanation is simply that the artists here were depicting the animals around them. If this was the case, we could speculate about whether they simply drew these animals as a kind of appreciation of their beauty or whether they represented the animals that they were hunting. If this is a literal portrayal of the animals, it is also interesting to note that they appear to be demonstrating a level of depth perception that might imply a multitude of animals such that they overlap in the image.

Alternatively, we could interpret these animals in a symbolic way, with the animals being metaphorical for different groups in a society. Perhaps the horned bull represents a leader and the horses their followers. If this was the case, then the blurring of the animals may in some way represent levels of relationships, such that the brown and black horses have a closer relationship with the bull, than the black horses do. Perhaps the physical blurring of the animals here even represents a psychological blurring of people that is similarly observed in some contemporary cultures, with boundary between self and other being indistinct, with each person's identity and personhood melting into one another.

There is no correct answer here, the interviewers are more interested in your thought process and ability to make inferences rather than finding the 'right answer' (debates about what cave art actually 'means' are infinite). Thus, this answer shows your ability to think about the cave art from different perspectives, and offers different interpretations from these. It considers both a literal and a metaphorical interpretation and tries to link our understanding of these ancient people to modern cultures.

A **poor answer** might simply describe what is you see before you, without considering its wider implications or potential inferences. Whilst there is nothing inherently wrong with using a literal interpretation as a starting point, a literal interpretation must still be used to draw inferences about the people who created these artworks and suggest potential conclusions about these people from studying them.

Q11. What is love?

This question is an opportunity for you to demonstrate your ability to synthesise the scientific and the quantitative, with the qualitative and phenomenological. That is, what science has to say about love, versus what we find first- and second- hand through the human experience. As is so often the case, there is no right answer here, instead it is more important for you to construct a clear answer and try to draw a conclusion.

Good Response: I think that this question can be approached from two different perspectives. On the one hand, we have what science tell us, that is, that love is a particular set of chemicals, hormones, and impulses throughout your brain and body that lead you to be profoundly connected to another person. This makes sense from an evolutionary perspective because evidence shows that primate groups with stronger social bonds - including what we call 'love' - provide more support to one another, protect each other more, and in general work together better. Building upon this, in reproduction, love also makes sense as it draws people powerfully together, leading to copulation, and more often than not in heterosexual couples, offspring. Logically, it may also then play a role in keeping parents around. That is, love between the mother and the father may mean that offspring are raised together, reducing the workload for both parents. Even where love between the mother and the father doesn't occur long-term, the love between parent and child is, in the vast majority of cases, incredibly powerful, such that the parents are often willing to lay down their lives in order to protect their offspring. Thus, from this perspective what constitutes love is a set of evolutionary biological functions that serve a sociobiological function.

On the other hand, I think that there is a completely phenomenological element to love. That is, love is so much about the personal experience. To reduce love to a set of biological and evolutionary processes seems to do it an injustice. Indeed, when we look at all the things done in the name of love, whether it is war, poetry, sacrifice, or the construction of monumental architecture, there definitely is more to love than just chemicals. On that last point of monumental architecture, if you think about the construction of the Taj Mahal by Mughal emperor Shah Jahan as a tomb for his wife, then this is not something constitutes a biological or evolutionary process. That is, there was no way for him to produce offspring with his wife after her death. Yet, he still had built one of the most revered buildings in the world for love of her.

Hence, I think that there are definitely elements and viewpoints from biology that we can use to consider what constitutes love, but without an understanding of that qualitative, phenomenological, almost intangible element of the human experience that we call love, we would have only a small piece of all that constitutes love.

This is a strong answer because it is very structured. It first lays out the scientific evidence that is often quoted to comprise love, demonstrating your understanding of the different biological and evolutionary functions that love may comprise. The answer then goes on to demonstrate the sociological or social anthropological perspective, including an example that directly contradicts some of the reductionist arguments made from the scientific perspective. Ultimately, it concludes by synthesising these two perspectives and providing a clear answer to the question.

Q12. On the course we are introducing a new paper this year in which we can teach you about any part of the world you like — which part of the world do you think you will pick?

This is a question that allows you to show your wider interests in the world beyond your own nation and culture. This really is an opportunity for you to show a passion for studying other cultures, political structures, and people.

A **Good Response**: I would love to learn more about Central Asia, especially the steppe, including the history, archaeology, and culture of, for instance, Mongolia. I think part of the reason that I would want to learn more about this area of the world is first and foremost is because so little is known or taught about its history or culture outside of the area. Studying history at school, even though my IB course was pretty international, we focussed on Europe, East Asia, and America. And then in discussions of international support for other countries outside of Europe, there is a lot of research done in Africa, South East Asia, and South America, but so often it seems to me that Central Asia is not nearly as talked about. In fact, I think the only time Western media covers the area is of 'flashy' aspects of the culture, such as eagle hunting. This has always somewhat surprised me as the Mongolian empire was the second largest in history stretching almost the entirety of Eurasia, Genghis Khan has 16 million direct male descendants, and in some ways it was the greatest overall influence on the world certainly in the first half of the 2nd millennium AD, with arguable influence throughout the entirety of the millennium. Beyond this, I'm aware that there is a deep past behind the Mongol empire, and the nomadic nature of those people really intrigues me, especially as so much of that behaviour continues to this day. And then finally, looking at the recent past of Central Asia and the culture there, I still know relatively little about it other than that China and Russia both have strong influence there, but I simply would love to learn more about the culture and people, and where they have come from.

This answer is particularly strong because it not only shows a passion for learning about the archaeology, anthropology, and political science of the area, but it also outlines specific examples that you would be interested in knowing about. It shows that you have an awareness of many of the potential areas and ways that areas of the world could be studied, and it provides a clear justification and answer to the question.

A **Poor Answer** might fail to elucidate exactly why you're interested in a particular area effectively. In reality, you could choose almost any area of the world, but it is important to show (especially in the context of applying for HSPS or Arch. and Anth.) how relevant disciplines might approach these areas of the world. Equally, a poor answer might inadvertently exotically describe another culture, almost fetishising it rather than offering a more objective and intrigue-based approach.

Q13. Can you think of anything happening in the news at the moment which you feel is a particularly good example of a larger significant issue?

This is an opportunity to show your broader understanding of political events in the world. This question allows you to show your ability to draw connections between micro and macro events, and is asking you to demonstrate your ability to inform a broad understanding from a focussed perspective.

Good Response: With the inauguration of US President Joe Biden, we have seen the almost immediate reversal of the damaging climate change denial and policies of the Trump administration of the last four years. Whilst it is seems true that Trump did not have a clear understanding of climate change, it does not entirely explain his actions. Indeed, some of his ulterior motivation was clear; America has been incredibly reliant upon fossil fuels both in terms of directly powering its economy and indirectly providing jobs. This latter fact is still true, and whilst Biden's policies could create a shift away from a reliance on fossil fuels whilst providing many jobs in the long term through renewable energy projects, there are plenty of Americans who will feel pain in the short term as a result of job losses. This friction between a need for a radical change in policy and practice, whilst protecting people's livelihoods is particularly indicative of a world issue.

In America, fossil fuel companies who have wielded significant wealth and influence in the last 150 years in America, as elsewhere, constantly lobby governments to allow them to continue exploiting the planet and accruing wealth. The reason that this current affair is particularly indicative of a world issue is because almost every country on earth is wrestling with these same issues. They know that change is needed and needed now, but they are under pressure on two fronts, both from those large companies that want to continue making money and their own people who are either reliant directly or indirectly on jobs and income from fossil fuels, and for finding and building alternative sources of energy. This current affair is even more indicative of many countries' situations as it is indicative of how a change in democratic power can lead to rapid changes in policy one way or the other.

This is a good answer because it has identified a well-reported current affair that is an ongoing issue. Moreover, it is an issue that affects every person in the world and every country. Not only is the complexity of dealing with climate change a world issue, but the situation in America is particularly indicative of the balance that many governments are attempting to strike between multiple issues.

A **Poor Answer** might choose a current affair that does not relate to a world issue. That is, it might be particular to specific context and wouldn't be easy to draw parallels with a world issue, or alternatively it might be irrelevant at the world level e.g., dog kidnapping in the UK.

Q14. You are an archaeologist in the year 2500, excavating Oxford – what material culture might you expect to find from my present?

Material culture includes everything in human reality that does not relate to behaviours. Thus, this question is an excellent opportunity to be creative and really show your thought process in your answer, which is ultimately what your interviewers are most interested in. For ideas you could talk about: clothing, food, furniture, architecture, computers, cutlery, or lightbulbs.

Good Answer: Well, I think Smartphones are an interesting piece of material culture in contemporary society. In some ways, smartphones represent the pinnacle of modern technology. What once required an entire room of computer hardware, can now be carried around in our pockets. Moreover, it is remarkable to think about how far the technology in smartphones has come since their inception in the 2000s. I think this is the result of two key aspects of contemporary society: a thirst for connectivity and convenience that smartphones facilitate at an unprecedented scale, and the competition between large companies to create the best product. Particularly, if you think that one of the unique aspects of being human is our cumulative culture over time, then the smartphone is an excellent example of how this operates in contemporary society. Beyond just the developments of smartphones themselves, smartphones represent the accumulation of our communication and language abilities as a species. From when we first starting writing language, to postal and messenger services, to telegrams, to telephones, to emails, and now mobile phones. Not only this, but mobile phones in general and smartphones in particular are becoming more and more ubiquitous. Even in areas of the world where very little other technology exists, smartphones can be found, and they are more and more frequently being used in transformative ways for health and education purposes in contemporary society.

This is a strong answer because the object chosen is something that is highly indicative of contemporary society. Not only that, as illustrated in the answer, they have a clearly delineated history that is representative of how material culture changes over time and how it affects society. Moreover, it is a particularly nice example, because as demonstrated, not only are they a piece of material culture that are growing in prevalence throughout many societies, but they are also having a remarkable impact in peoples' lives.

A **Poor Answer** might choose an object that whilst a piece of material culture, fails to connect with the idea of contemporary society. For instance, if the answer had chosen a printing press, whilst this is undoubtedly a piece of material culture, it has almost no role in contemporary society other than as a historical object with very rare usage. It is important to be able to situate the object within that modern context.

Q15. Do you think that one's culture can shape one's perceptions? Is the way we see colour the same as someone from a different culture would?

The key to this question relies on understanding the difference between human perception and human categorisation. In order to answer this question appropriately, you need to first have a fundamental understanding that biologically and neurologically, humans are almost identical, and any differences occur within a relatively small standard deviation. This is particularly important, as any claims about the biological differences in humans, have in the past been used to oppress, dehumanise, enslave, and destroy other humans.

Good Answer: I think that the answer to this questions by how we define perception. Essentially, perception in relation to colour is the process by which light hits a surface, and different lengths of the colour spectrum are reflected into our eyes, which then pass information to the brain and are processed neurologically to identify certain colours. Now, irrespective of cultural influences, apart from people with conditions such as colour blindness, all humans process these colours in the same way. That is to say, that perception of colours is not culturally specific. That being said, what is culturally specific are the ways in which humans categorise colours. For instance, some languages have more than one word for slightly different shades of blue - in Russian, the word 'goluboy' is used to differentiate from the slightly darker 'siniy' - but if you showed these same colours to an English speaker, they would only use the word 'blue'. So in this instance, categorisations of colour are culturally specific, and the language that we use to talk about colours varies, whilst our actual perception is the same.

This is answer has a good structure, starting by breaking down the question to get to the heart of what is being asked, and demonstrating a clear understanding of this, before answering the question. This answer is particularly strong, because it then extends the response by showing how colour is categorised differently, whilst being perceptually the same, using a well-known example to back this up. It finally ties the extended part of the answer back to the original question.

A **Poor Answer** might fail to have understood the difference between perception and categorisation, and how these relate to one another.

ENGLISH

The English interview will require you to demonstrate passion and a genuine desire to study English. Make sure you have thought, at least vaguely, about your answer to a wide question like: "Why English?", or "Why English at Cambridge?"

You will usually be asked to discuss an unseen extract from a play, poem, or piece of prose; this will enable the interviewer to see whether you can think on your feet, both in terms of subject-related knowledge (of literary forms, techniques, and genres) and forming your own critical opinions on the spot ("Is this a good poem? Why?").

Apply the knowledge you have acquired at A-Level and from wider reading to unfamiliar scenarios. You may not recognise the text you have been asked to read, but that is probably deliberate: **embrace this chance to experiment**, make mistakes, and show off your imaginative readings of new texts. Indeed, the Cambridge English course places a strong emphasis upon Practical Criticism, which encourages you to explore unseen texts in isolation from their context (by erasing the writer's name or the date written) in order to understand how the form of a text influences themes and meanings.

If you are making an argument that is clearly wrong or the interviewers are telling you it is clearly wrong, try to revise your viewpoint and expand your argument in light of this information. Remember, **making mistakes is no bad thing**; in fact, it can be very constructive to be wrong, since changing your argument shows real intellectual flexibility. The important point is that you address the mistake head on and attempt to revise your thinking with the assistance of the tutors where necessary. For instance, perhaps a tutor has asked you to try and place a poem in its literary context – say, a sonnet by John Donne from the Renaissance – and you have given it the wrong date – perhaps thinking that it could be a Romantic sonnet instead.

This guesswork can be used as an exciting springboard for a fresh discussion. How did knowing the real date of this poem change the way you viewed the themes and message? You might find it interesting that enduring features of the sonnet form existed both in the Renaissance and in the eighteenth century –what subtle changes in genre might you notice, and are these conventions ever subverted? Try and think creatively and use this correction as the basis for a wider conversation about how the sonnet form has evolved over the centuries.

The tutors know what subjects you have studied at A-Level. They will try to theme your interview around the texts and periods that you have studied. However, they may ask you about certain literary periods that you have not studied in depth or detail. If so, be open-minded and respond to the information that you are given. If you are given Wilfred Owen's 'Anthem for Doomed Youth' and you have not studied any war poets before, you can still apply techniques and ideas you have learned. While you should discuss the poem with fresh eyes, analysing the form, the metre, and imagery as you would do with any unseen poem, feel free to make connections with other texts.

For example, you may have studied Tennyson's 'The Charge of the Light Brigade'; what can this earlier poem, which uses powerful rhetoric to valorise patriotism and male honour, illuminate about Owen's more nihilistic sonnet? Such **connections show that you are thinking actively** and enjoying the challenge of approaching new texts.

WHAT QUESTIONS MIGHT BE ASKED?

Most of the questions asked in the interview will disguise a larger question within a network of smaller sub-questions to guide the answer from the start to a conclusion. The main question may seem difficult, weird, or random at first, but take a breath and start discussing with your interviewer different ideas you have for breaking down the question into manageable pieces. Don't panic.

The questions are designed to be difficult to give you the chance to show your full intellectual potential. They will help guide you to the right idea if you provide ideas for them to guide. This is your chance to show your creativity, analytical skills, intellectual flexibility, problem-solving skills, and your go-getter attitude. Don't waste it on nervousness or a fear of messing up or looking stupid: think aloud and work together with the interviewer.

An interviewer may question any decision you come to in response to a question, and it is possible that in the course of the ensuing conversation your original views will alter as your thinking becomes more nuanced. Do not panic! This is perfectly okay and shows an ability to adapt to new information and ideas and respond to them. Similarly, you should not feel the need to quickly agree with anything coming from an interviewer's mouth in order to appease them. An interview is a discussion and a chance to show the interviewer how you think and respond to the thoughts of others.

To quote Robinson College's English admissions advice, you should show:

"A readiness to respond to challenges to your opinion, holding firm and arguing your case where appropriate, but also modifying your opinion in the light of contradictory evidence."

WORKED QUESTIONS

Below are a few examples of how to start breaking down an interview question along with model answers.

Q1: Take a look at these extracts from a piece of literature, do you think they were written by someone identifying as a man, or as a woman? On what basis could you determine this, and once you have done, does it matter?

This seemingly complex question can be broken down first into a critical exercise in analysing an unseen text, followed by a wider discussion of whether biographical information is important in literary criticism: is the author 'dead'?

Your starting point for this question might be your initial gut-reaction to the two contrasting texts: **do they seem more 'masculine' or 'feminine' to you**, and how would you define these adjectives? Since the interviewer is asking you to guess this information without expecting you to know details about the authentic author, you might realise that they are interested in the assumptions that literary critics bring to bear upon texts seen out of context: *why* does this seem like a male writer wrote it?

For example, let's say you were given an extract from Ernest Hemingway's *The Old Man and the Sea*. Most obviously, the themes focus upon the traditional male pursuit of fishing, or hunting, and centre upon nature in the vein of Romantic poets like Byron or Coleridge. You might describe the main stylistic features as abrupt punctuation and short, factual statements that seem almost scientific in their logical structuring. Perhaps you notice the lack of flowery conceits or poetic set-pieces, the minimalist description and simplistic texture. Hemmingway tells it like it is, using efficient and controlled prose without stylistic excess or hyperbole. This realism and lack of explicit emotion might strike you as 'masculine', reminding you of stereotypically reticent male discourse. Then, maybe the second extract is a piece from Virginia Woolf's *Mrs Dalloway*.

Initially, it may be clear that the text is centred around a female character, her emotions and feelings. Moving deeper, you might describe the prose as smooth and fluid, linked by flowing connectives, perhaps recognising this to be an experiment in stream of consciousness. Maybe you feel that Woolf prioritises chaotic human psychology and internal thoughts rather than linear events. The way she moves by association through clusters of images, impressions, and sensations in a way that reminds you of lyrical poetry more than realist prose, striking you as a more 'feminine' way of writing.

However, you may argue none of the above and analyse these two texts in a completely opposite way, arguing for the femininity of the Hemingway piece and showing the masculinity of Woolf's prose (which is even more interesting). In a way, it doesn't matter: the interviewers just want to see you **argue your case for the author's gender with a detailed, analytical piece of prose analysis**.

Once this starting point is established, they might ask you to reassess your answers, pushing you to define these gendered observations and defend your argument. Is there – as Woolf discusses – a specifically 'feminine' or feminist, style? Can a text ever have a neutral or androgynous style, mixing both genders?

Finally, the interviews are likely to steer this discussion towards a final twist: **does the gender of the author matter?** (See question 8). Should we celebrate anonymity? Does biographical information restrict or generate meaning? The interviewers are inviting you to think broadly about texts and contexts. You might have come across theories like Roland Barthes' *Death of the Author* or be aware of *New Criticism*, which argues for texts as self-contained units of meaning liberated from biographical constraints. Maybe you have touched upon the 'intentional fallacy', a phrase coined by critics Wimsatt and Beardsley, and recognise the difficulties involved in interpreting a text solely in terms of what the author meant. Even if you have not formally studied any of these theories, it is likely you will voice some of these central ideas as you debate, aloud, whether biographical knowledge in literary criticism is useful, limiting or both. As you can see, from these two short extracts, you have covered an enormous amount of ground, both technical, in terms of analysing prose, and theoretical, asking huge questions about the author and the text.

A **poor applicant** may take a number of approaches unlikely to impress the interviewer. The first and most obvious of these is to say "I don't know who wrote these texts", or similarly uncooperative responses. In fact, the whole task assumes you won't know who wrote the texts, but rather invites you to speculate about unseen extracts in order to investigate your assumptions about the relevance of gender or biographical information when studying literature. Another approach which is unhelpful in this interview situation is the 'brain dump', where instead of engaging with the question, the applicant attempts to impress or distract with an assortment of related facts. For instance, you might offer a fantastic standalone stylistic analysis of these prose extracts, listing the different ways in which Hemingway uses punctuation, or how Woolf uses connectives in her languid sentences.

However, unless this is used to strengthen your final argument about the gender of each author and why you think that, then this is irrelevant information. Instead, listen and respond to your interviewers as they prompt you further, continually asking you to extend and defend your analysis by asking: "why?", or "so why do these connectives make the prose seem feminine to you?" These **observations should be pieces of evidence in a reasoned argument for authorial gender**, which will provide a basis for productive discussion of whether this biographical information is important or irrelevant in the task of literary criticism.

Q2: Is Fifty Shades of Grey literature? Why?

This question invites you to think about the sets of criteria used to evaluate what is 'literature', what is a 'classic' or the 'canon'. Does popularity diminish the cultural prestige of art? Does the audience matter? Can *EastEnders* ever be 'literature' in the same way as works by Samuel Beckett or James Joyce? Begin to criticise and re-evaluate these throwaway terms that you use every day, imagining how a dictionary might define them: what do we really mean when we categorise texts as 'canonical' or 'literature' and what (or whose) criteria are we using? Can a contemporary novel ever be a classic? Think about the rise of English Literature as a respected academic pursuit and your own A-Level syllabus, and the influence of criticism like F.R. Leavis's *The Great Tradition*: what has been included, and, more significantly, what is excluded, marginal, and devalued? Ask questions and probe your own answers in what will become a lively discussion.

This is a playful, provocative question which introduces the theme of popular culture, of 'high' and 'low' art, asking you to analyse shifting or enduring artistic standards and tastes of 'art' or 'entertainment'. What about the way in which Shakespeare meshes 'high' tragic art and 'low' comedic clowns? You might want to approach this in terms of obscene or taboo subject matter across the ages. Why do institutions study John Donne's – 'To His Mistress Going to Bed' – or obscene Elizabethan pamphlets, but neglect this exceedingly popular novel?

You could explore the idea of censorship by linking *Fifty Shades* to D.H. Lawrence's *Lady Chatterley's Lover*: perhaps the book deserves to be seen as a historically-interesting celebration of artistic freedom and liberated female sexuality?

Q3: What makes a tragedy?

The interviewers are pushing you to explore one of the **most famous literary genres in an imaginative fashion**.

Perhaps you might start with the classical formulation of 'Tragedy' that you might have come across in your A-Level studies, including Aristotle's tragic precepts (hamartia, hubris, *peripeteia*, anagnorisis, catharsis etc.). However, use Aristotle's definitions as a starting point, a springboard, not the answer. What does it really mean to have a tragic 'catharsis'? Can you think about of modern examples that reinforce or subvert these ideas – what about Arthur Miller's *The Crucible*, or *Death of a Salesman*? Think about plays you have studied that illustrate or undermine this term in practice. You could then move on to how these precepts manifested themselves in later literary movements, discussing Shakespearean tragedy and the moments that you think illuminate these aspects.

There is no 'correct' answer: this is an exercise in probing the boundaries of a 'genre'. What about women? Does Shakespearean tragedy prioritise the aristocratic male at the expense of the poor or female characters? What about class? What about other media – can cinema, comic books, paintings, television soap operas, news programmes, or Twitter statuses ever be tragic? Your interviewer might ask similar questions, maybe discussing iconoclastic critics like Raymond Williams who argued for a more egalitarian view of the tragic. Perhaps you might agree with George Steiner who famously argued for the 'death of tragedy' – is tragedy dead, or is it still alive and kicking? You don't have to recognise or have read these critics, but respond and be interested when their ideas are mentioned – do you agree, or not? If not, why? Use examples that spring to mind from your reading and be as varied as you like.

Q4: Do you think the ending of [Novel] is poor?

This question invites an explanation of your verdict and a consideration of what makes a 'good ending'. **What is the point of a conclusion?** Is it to provide a final commentary on the preceding themes to tie up any loose ends of the plot, to introduce a parting thought for the reader to mull over? Do different genres demand different things of their endings? Should endings have certain qualities to help the overall structure of a novel?

For example, if you were asked to comment on the conclusion of 'Mill on the Floss', you may answer that it *is* a poor ending as the sudden destruction of two characters both jars and frustrates the reader. The flooding incident was unprecedented and random, and in a way gimmicky. The preceding novel focused so much on character development and the effect of human actions, that the sudden 'act of God' disrupted the style of the book. Moreover, having invested time and energy into the heroine's struggles, the reader may well feel frustrated and betrayed at receiving such an unsatisfactory resolution for Maggie. One could argue that the ending felt lazy and that the final note that follows the drowning is sentimental. George Eliot could stand accused of having not provided a proper conclusion to her work, and opting for an easy way out of dealing with the mess Maggie's life was now in. The sudden flood could be compared to the often mocked "and it was all a dream" ending.

Alternatively, one could argue "no", as the unexpected flood was a representation of the cruelty of the world, of the ultimate futility of human struggle. Our frustrated expectations and shock could be argued as a testimony to the strength of the ending: the power it has to compel the audience to react makes it not 'poor', but great. One may argue that **an ending does not have to satisfy** if it is able to teach us something new. Or perhaps the horror of this incident justifies the work as something tragic, and in its way is true to its genre.

There is also room to discuss **what constitutes an ending.** The discussion includes the flood in understanding George Eliot's conclusion, but another person may argue the final epilogue is the ending, or demands more attention than the deadly incident. Moreover, one can explore the idea of endings and link it with the idea of literature itself: if literature is meant to please, provoke, or has different purposes in different situations, what does this mean for endings?

Q5: What do you think differentiates a short story from a novel?

This question asks you to consider the nature of form and the impact it has on a piece of literature. A weaker answer will state the obvious: "a short story is shorter than a novel". A stronger answer will take this into account and then consider how length will affect the treatment of a story's content. For example, one may consider if the significance of individual words is affected by the total word count within a work. Or they may discuss how characterization is affected by having fewer words to explore a person within a narrative and argue that short stories must establish protagonists and antagonists in ways novels are not necessarily constricted by. The answer could contrast the characters of Edgar Allen Poe to those of Jane Austen and note the differences in the way they present individuals in the plot.

One may also talk about how **structure differs between a longer and a shorter work** and how the latter needs a clearer, more concise plot, whereas the former has more space to meander and add multiple episodes within the narrative. Again, this idea could then be corroborated through examples provided by the candidate's reading. A candidate could also consider the difference between a novel and a collection of short stories, and consider how the overarching theme of a novel is explicit, whereas a theme across the group of stories is more implicit.

Q6: Tell me about a novel you've read recently.

A **weaker candidate** will simply summarise a text, whereas a stronger one will analyse it. For example, if a candidate has recently read 'Oliver Twist', they could discuss it within a context: for example, how does this book differ to other Dickensian novels or Victorian novels, or even modern novels the candidate has read? What do they think of the story's use of comedy or perhaps the characterization of Nancy or Oliver himself? Why do they think this is considered a 'classic'? How do they think the structure affects the story and does a consideration of the novel's roots – as a serial printed in instalments in a magazine – affect the way the candidate reads the novel as a whole? Does the movement from segments to a single volume improve the work or do they think something has been lost in the translation?

A candidate is invited here to show the **thoughts that have arisen through their reading** and to make a judgment. They can explain what they find interesting or enjoyable, or why they disliked a work or found it uncomfortable. Beyond simply having a reaction to the text, a stronger candidate will also explore their reaction to the text: if they felt frustrated with a certain character, why do they think this was? Was it the author's intention or a limitation in their skill? Does the context of a work affect its reception – do Dickens' idealised characters charm a certain audience and not another, and is this due to different time periods or social, economic or religious contexts?

Whatever time or location a text originates from, consider it on its own in comparison with other things you've read within its context, and consider why and how it elicits a reaction from you as a reader.

The answer does not necessarily have to mention all these different aspects, but it should mention the title and then an analysis of the text, showing what the interviewee finds interesting about the piece of literature, whether he or she likes it or not.

Q7: How would you begin to define the difference between poetry and prose, in English literature?

An applicant may wish to begin with the difference between the two by thinking about their **respective formal qualities**: poetry and its use of metre, for example. They may then wish to think if this alone is a simple distinction, prompting them to discuss prose-poetry and explain whether they believe it belongs either to prose or poetry, or is a separate category in itself, and crucially *why* this is so. One may also want to discuss other elements associated with either poetry or prose specifically and see if these elements define them (or why they do not).

For example, 'poetic devices' such as metaphor and alliteration can be found in prose. In any given subject matter, one may go on to explain that this can be explored through both: love can be discussed in *Tess of the d'Urbervilles* or in Robert Burns' *My Love is like a Red, Red Rose*. If they then dismiss other possible differences, they could again reaffirm their original thoughts on the definition that separates poetry from prose. If in the process they then wish to add to their original statement, they can do this. The movement from the original idea to a discussion of it, backed with examples and a consideration of the answers other people may provide to this question, will lead to a nuanced response to the interviewer.

Q8: Do you think that the gender of a lead character in any piece of media is meaningful?

An applicant may first wish to **define gender** – e.g. "A range of identities aligned broadly along social notions of the masculine and feminine, but not tied to biological difference."

An applicant may then say "yes" and describe the manifest ways gender affects a text: either by informing character or influencing the plot. They may go on to use many examples to explain this: for example, Jane Eyre would have been less likely to have held a romantic attachment with Rochester if she was a man at the time the novel was written, and so all the events relating to their relationship may have happened very differently, drastically changing the plot. If she was a man, and she and Rochester shared a homosexual love, it would be an entirely different book.

Moreover, one's relationship to the world can be seen as partially defined by their gender. Cathy (the elder) in *Wuthering Heights* believes her way of achieving a greater rank is through marriage to a wealthy man, whereas if she were herself a male, she might have gone the way of Heathcliff who found his fortune through mysterious enterprises. One cannot simply dismiss her gender as irrelevant: her identity is bound in the societal expectations and legal status of women of her time and this limits her expectations of what she could achieve and forces her to retreat into the status of desired marital object in order to pursue her worldly ambitions.

The treatment of women/men in different periods and places will be read in a work as it will inform the *writer's* viewpoint and so inform the book. As there is still a perceived difference between men and women, **gender identity is still important to recognise** and modern books still see the importance of gender in defining a character's history, relationship to others, and awareness of their place in the world. One may then go on to question how different *Harry Potter* would have been if Harry were a girl.

Of course, one may argue that men and women are equally capable of feeling and acting and that a female protagonist for a novel like *Harry Potter* is entirely possible. It could be argued that believing in the equal rights of men and women, gender should cease to be a definitive aspect of the character. However, "should" is very different than "is", and though feminism has come a long way in changing attitudes towards women's rights, society is not ignorant of the individual's gender. There remain preconceptions and arguments relating to notions of a female or male identity. If a girl was fighting Voldemort, different associations would arise in the reader's mind than they would when reading a boy battling the Dark Lord.

One may also argue that **certain characters within plays are considered quite gender neutral**, and can be performed by either male or female cast (for example, though Ariel is a man in *The Tempest*, he is often played by a woman). The counter-argument to this is that, though this ambiguity exists, once the neutral body is gendered through the performer, it again elicits a reaction specific to that gender.

One could argue that, on the page, a character could be considered gender-neutral, but then **this absence of gender may be of importance**, the "neutrality" becoming a third gender to consider, and eliciting a different reaction than the other two.

The answer could also go on to discuss the idea of a transgender protagonist.

Q9: Is there a book you think you should not have studied?

The question invites an exploration of what the purpose of literary study is. An applicant will look at the books they have read for schoolwork and consider and answer truthfully if they think they were all valid choices, or if one was not. Having clarified this, the candidate may then explain what he or she thinks is a requirement for a book to be worthy of 'study' – what merits does a text require to validate its place in education?

Having clarified what these qualities are – or indeed if there *are* any requirements for a book to be worth studying – they can then compare the works he or she has read for class against these requirements. If they decided that everything is worth study, the applicant can then discuss the idea of this further and explain **the value of any text within a classroom**, providing examples to corroborate their argument. This discussion may then lead to a greater analysis of the purpose of literature: is what makes a text worth studying what makes it worth reading, or is there a difference between books that should be pursued in leisure time as opposed to academic time?

Q10: Is literature inherently moral?

If the applicant answered "no", he or she may go on to explain that though literature *can* be a source of moral edification, it should not be unified by an ethical cause because there are a variety of purposes that can inform a text. It could be written simply to be beautiful (and the candidate may then talk about aesthetic criticism of literature) or perhaps to hold "a mirror up to nature" and capture something of reality or the human condition – whether this is through naturalism or through another expression of an emotional state.

One may argue, for example, that *Waiting for Godot* would be rendered absurd if a moral was added: its purpose is not to provide ethical education, and the complexity of the piece would be crudely simplified. It would be turned from a challenging work to a didactic one; simple to understand but with all its original intention and meaning deleted. One could question if literature should ever *be* or do anything.

One may, however, question whether literature that can be considered immoral can also be considered harmful. The relationship depicted in the *50 Shades* series is often considered abusive and one may wonder if this sets a bad example for impressionable readers who will go on to idealise this couple.

The candidate may then argue that **responsibility lies in the reader** and the censoring of work is in itself troubling. He or she could go on to name any number of banned books and then demonstrate their value as opposed to their potential to damage.

Q11: How would you define the words lie, deceive, and mislead? What do these words tell you about the English language?

An applicant should begin with explaining one of these on their own: for example, to "lie" is to deliberately say something the speaker knows to be contrary to the truth, such as "trees are made of purple cheese". To "deceive" is not, however, necessarily to lie: it is to lead someone to believe in something that is not true. The word is **more to do with intent**; the desire to make another believe in something false than the action of simply stating something that is not true. There are also other uses of the word – one can "deceive oneself" or an object may give a mistaken impression – which gives it different meanings, and one may wish to consider these. However, one should ensure the differentiation between "deceive" and "lie" is clearly stated. To "lie" describes an action; to "deceive" describes an action coupled with intent.

Having established the meanings of these two words, the candidate may then compare these to the definition of "mislead".

Often "mislead" is treated as a synonym of "deceive", with dictionaries using one to define the other. However, the subtle difference may be that **one can "mislead" unknowingly**. If we take "mislead" to "cause someone to have the wrong idea or impression" or to "lead astray", we can see that someone might "mislead" *without* intent, but purely by error. For example, if one believes he or she knows the quickest way to a location but is mistaken, that person may have misled a group of friends without meaning to at all. One *can* definitely mislead with intent, but one does not *necessarily* have to.

This is a question that **demands careful attention to the nuances of words**, so it is good to constantly compare the differences between these three terms. For example, one can say you might "mislead" without lying. One may even deceive without lying, by refraining from revealing crucial information that would lead to a fuller understanding of the scene. For example, if someone wanted to make you believe Mr X killed Mrs Y, he or she might say "Mr X went to Mrs Y's house an hour before the crime", and then neglect to mention that he left the same house two minutes later and went across town. One might then discuss whether one can "lie by omission" and how this would again affect the relationship between "to lie" and "to deceive."

Q12: Why do critics exist? Is there a value to criticism?

If one was to answer "yes", they could argue there is a dual purpose to criticism. Firstly, it can introduce new ideas to the reader, ones they may not have considered alone. Perhaps the critic has a **novel interpretation** of the words that inspires a new train of thought.

For example, WH Auden's description of *Twelfth Night* as a "nasty" play may encourage his reader to reconsider the nature of the comedy within the drama and potentially find darkness where previously they saw only light humour. The second purpose of criticism could be seen as *confirming* the reader's thoughts.

If the critic offers an idea that reaffirms their previous views, or that the candidate is annoyed by / disagrees with, it helps them to **solidify their own views on literature**. For example, Oscar Wilde's comment that "All art is quite useless" may be so infuriating that it provokes a strong reaction, and this reaction allows the reader to clarify his or her own understanding of the purpose of a text.

One may argue that **analysis does not necessarily require a critic**. For example, a look at the historical context of a work can inspire thought. One may also refer to the use of Practical Criticism, which asks the reader to simply respond to an unseen text and discuss the potential merit of this exercise. It is useful to respond to a text without your mind being coloured by another's critique. However, once one has gained this perspective, it can be argued that considering another interpretation can further deepen his or her analysis. Using several approaches to a text ensures a more nuanced understanding of it.

Q13: You mentioned that Hamlet was your favourite Shakespeare play. In it, Hamlet speaks to the Ghost; what significance does this have?

Firstly, you should explore "speaks to the Ghost". Another character has attempted to engage the Ghost in conversation but significantly, the spectre did not respond. Should we make a distinction between being "spoken to" and "spoken at"? Are we looking at the fact that Hamlet is speaking or at that there is communication between the two figures?

If we are looking at the fact that they have a conversation, there are several ways to look at this significance depending on how one interprets the figure of the Ghost. Hamlet himself is unsure at first whether this is truly the spirit of his father or some demonic being tempting him to sin. If the latter, this conversation means potential damnation and implies peril for Hamlet's soul. If the former, we may see this dialogue as an insight into the familial relationship between father and son.

As Shakespeare shows the father calling on the living for revenge, he portrays a character who foists the burden of vendetta onto his offspring, potentially risking Hamlet's chance of reaching Heaven, potentially dooming Hamlet to Hell. This conversation can be used to define the characters via their relationship with one another.

One may look at this conversation as a manifestation of madness: though others spot the ghost at first, he is crucially neither seen nor heard by Gertrude in the bedroom scene. Perhaps we can then dismiss the earlier sightings as a sort of group hysteria by a bunch of men on watch, not really there at all. Or maybe we can divide the Ghost into two: one which can be seen by others and one that solely haunts the guilty, addled mind of Hamlet. Again, the fact that only Hamlet can communicate with the spectre of his father may suggest madness, a reality which is solely his and inaccessible to any other.

How 'real' the ghost is can be debated because of these two very different impressions - a spectre that is seen by some, but utterly invisible to the dead man's wife. One may then go on to say that the Ghost does not wish to be seen by Gertrude, only by his son, and this in itself is significant. One may also wish to speak about how the audience can see the ghost and wonder if this implies Gertrude alone is in the dark about his presence, or whether we are being granted access to Hamlet's vision, and so his mind; something other characters cannot access.

If we decide that the phrase "speaks to" is simply the action of Hamlet trying to initiate contact, one might say the significance here is of a son who desperately wants contact with his father, who overcomes his fear of the potentially dangerous spectre due to his great need to speak to his dad. Hamlet remarks that he does not set his life at a "pin's fee", so does his conversation with the deathly spirit also suggest a desire to join it in death, a rejection of the living? As Hamlet speaks to the Ghost alone on stage, we see a living man forming a relationship with a dead one. This image is worth analysing.

Renaissance ideas on ghosts, damnation, and superstition differ to the predominant beliefs in 21st Century London (superstition is now mocked by many, though some may cling to their beliefs in spirits), and this may also be taken into context and used to describe how a Shakespearian audience's understanding of ghosts would affect how one would witness a scene.

Q14: What is the point of studying English?

This question gives you the chance to demonstrate your understanding of the subject, its beneficial long-term applications, and express your personal interest and engagement with particular aspects of studying English Literature. For example, you could discuss how studying English Literature allows students to learn literary history, theory, and criticism. Through this subject, students are also able to explore differing methods of expression and communication across an incredibly extensive range of topics and time periods. This exposes students to many new viewpoints, which enhances their understanding of differing cultures and intellectual traditions, and often enables students to practise their skills in philosophical and diplomatic debating. Studying English Literature also provides transferable skills which are highly sought after by employers, such as creative, critical and analytical thinking skills and a high command of written language.

Good Applicant: I believe that studying English assists young people in gaining critical and analytical skills which are essential for questioning the world around us. Studying texts from around the world not only broadens our own understanding of different cultures, beliefs, and ways of life, but by experiencing different writing styles and thought processes in both contemporary and historical texts we are also gaining observational skills and an important knowledge about how humans perceive their surroundings. I personally am excited to study this subject as no other subject offers such a large and varied body of material to explore. I look forward to continuing to discover how literature helps us make sense of the world, and also use my studies as an opportunity to sharpen my own ability to write, read, analyse and persuade.

This response is broken down into a set of logical responses with an additional element of the personal. There is no right answer to this question, and the possibly answers that could be given are inexhaustible. When responding to this question you should highlight what attributes of the subject you particularly enjoy or are interested in and demonstrate the valuable impact of studying this subject on your future.

A poor applicant: might only respond with a vague 'it's an interesting and/or useful subject' or only with what they like about the subject but fail to recognise the important life skills and qualities that are instilled in English Literature students, which make them high calibre employees in many different fields. Such a response only answers a fraction of the question, and will leave your interviewer feeling unsatisfied, and questioning of your understanding of what studying English Literature at a university level entails.

Q15: What do you think you'll get out of an English degree?

Firstly, this question is your opportunity to demonstrate that you have read about the specific course details for your chosen university or college at Oxford/Cambridge. What is included in an English Literature degree varies greatly from course to course. Each university will have compulsory core modules and a selection of chosen modules. The focus of these supplementary modules often makes one course more attractive than another one, so you should show that you have done your research and come to a logical decision based on both your personal and academic interests. Secondly, this question allows you to discuss the tangible skills that your wish to gain whilst studying, such as improved analytical thinking, creative writing skills, or a wider understanding of literary history and criticism.

Good Applicant: I have applied for this specific course because I am excited by the breadth of the core modules. I feel that studying English Literature from Medieval to Modern will benefit my understanding of literary history and expose me to a wide variety of writing styles and thought processes, which will aid the depth of my analytical skills. I have also read that in the third year of the course there is an opportunity to take a module on feminist writers in the 20th century, which is a particular interest of mine, having explored this topic during my A levels when we studied the short stories of Angela Carter. I would love to continue exploring this topic both by taking that module, but also by bringing feminist discussion points into every period of literature that this course covers.

This response shows that the applicant has thoroughly research and considered the implications of the course material. They understand what is on offer and have reflected on whether this aligns with their own interests and academic pursuits. This is also a personal question, so including more information about your interests is important. For example, this applicant has named the works of Angela Carter to demonstrate how their current interests will be furthered by this specific course. Remember, you are also picking the university, even though interviews feel like they are picking you, so make sure to considerer your options fully.

A Poor Applicant might simply refer to the core modules on offer, having not researched the full extent of what the course has to offer. This shows that their academic interest might not be the primary motivation for applying to this university or college. Your interviewers might possibly be your professors, so remember that they are looking for engaged and passionate students with whom they can share their insights and knowledge.

Q16: How would you define 'Literature'?

This is a question with inexhaustible answers. It is designed to test your ability to think philosophically and an opportunity for your interviewers to witness and understand your thought process. You should be prepared to explain and defend your reasoning, but also be malleable in your definition, as this is a discursive question, to be debated. Your definition could consider different types of writing, the author's intention, the merit or longevity of the writing, a dictionary definition, and how definitions might be changing.

A Good Applicant: Typically, 'Literature' is defined as written works with artistic merit, such as novels, poems, and plays, meaning that the works have more than a basic informational use, such as a pamphlet describing the effects of the MMR vaccine. Whilst I generally agree with this definition, I do think that it is a little reductive, especially when the question of what is 'art', which encompasses literature, is still hotly debated. For example, I recently came across an essay discussing the literary merit of cookery recipes, which made me both question and appreciate how broadly the term 'literature' can be applied. Another consideration when defining something as 'literature' is the authors intent behind their work, but even this is a fallible method, as often there is a discrepancy between the author's intention and the audience's perception of art. Perhaps the best approach is defining works on a case-by-case basis.

This response shows a multi-pronged approach to answering the question, covering traditional and non-traditional definitions, and an opinionated response to these variations. The student has also taken this opportunity to highlight their wider reading and engagement with this question by given a specific example – the analysis of cookery recipes. The response is logical whilst also showing an understanding of the complications in answering philosophical questions, which must be handled with a certain acceptance that there is no final, absolute answer.

A Poor Applicant: might only respond to this question with one approach, such as whether a piece of writing is 'good' or 'bad', revealing a lack of awareness of the many nuances within this type of debate. The interviewer wants to see how you compare the many different methods of definition, and observe how these affect your own opinion on the subject.

Q17: What is prose? How does this differ from poetry?

For this question you need to demonstrate your knowledge and comprehension of different literary forms and styles. To answer this question, you need to compare and contrast the different formal characteristics of poetry and prose and their literary purposes.

A Good Applicant: Prose is a form of writing which contains sentences and paragraphs, and does not have any metrical structure, as seen in novels, whereas poetry is a genre of literature which has many different forms, such as the sonnet, and often contains rhyme and line scansion, for example, iambic pentameter. They can also be differentiated by defining prose as a more lucid form of writing versus the highly structured and often ornate writing style of seen in poetry. However, prose poems do exist, where the sentiments of a poem are written in verse, meaning that it does not include the typical formal indications of poetry.

This response addresses not only the stylistic differences between poetry and prose, but the additional difference between a genre and form. Examples are given to demonstrate an in-depth knowledge of the specific features of both types of literature, and the applicant has gone above and beyond in their explanation by referencing a form of literature where poetry and prose overlap: the prose poem.

A Poor Applicant: might only say that prose is found in books whilst poetry is a different type of literature, giving a few, but non-specific details of the stylistic differences between the two. This type of response shows a basic understanding, but does not exemplify your knowledge and understanding of the difference between a genre and a form, how different forms of literature are composed, and how they might intersect.

Q18: What was the last thing you read?

This question gives you the opportunity to discuss your reading outside of the prescribed books that you are studying at school. In this question you can inform your interviewers of your wider interests and demonstrate your ability to explore and critique literature without the direction of a teacher. It is also helpful to pick a book that you are able to connect to your studies (both present and future), to demonstrate your dedication and interest in the subject.

A Good Applicant: I have recently been reading Ernest Hemmingway's *A Moveable Feast* and F. Scott Fitzgerald's *The Beautiful and the Damned*. After studying *The Great Gatsby* at school, I have become interested in the 'Lost Generation' writers, and so I wanted to experience more of Fitzgerald's writing. I chose to read Hemmingway too as I always find it interesting to compare contemporary writers. I was surprised to find that their styles are so different! Personally, I prefer the dream-like quality of Fitzgerald's novels rather than Hemmingway's realistic writing style, although both explore the themes of nostalgia which I find particularly interesting. I am looking forward to being exposed to other 20th century writers during the Modernism module to discover whether this is a particularly pertinent theme of the era.

More than just telling the interviewer what they have been reading, this applicant shows how their academic studies have influenced their extra-curricular reading and how they have developed an area of interest which they can continue to develop at university. They have given insights and analysed the differing styles of their chosen texts, from which they have based an opinion. This is a type of question that might turn into a longer discussion, so be sure to have some more detailed analysis to discuss regarding your chosen text.

A Poor Applicant: might choose a text that is completely unrelated to their academic studies and be unable to connect their chosen text to their future studies. This does not present the applicant as a thoughtful and well-rounded English Literature student. Your interviewer is genuinely interested to find out what your interests are, so be sure to pick a text through which you can demonstrate your passion for the subject – it can be as unconventional as you want, as long as it can prove you are an engaged and engaging student.

Q19: Do you think leaders would benefit from studying English?

This question is a good opportunity to explore the skill set that is gained by English Literature. The real question is, are politicians in need of improved analytical thinking, the ability to critique language, the ability to persuade, or practise in viewing the world from other people's perspectives. It is your job to analyse the role of a politician and pinpoint whether or not there is any overlap with the skills offered by this course.

A Good Applicant: I believe that it would be beneficial for politicians to study English Literature as I think it is easy to prioritise policy over humanity within this role. I feel that studying literature gives you an understanding and compassion towards people different from yourself as you are always looking at life from someone else's perspective, which would benefit politicians, whose job it is to ensure social justice and welfare. The transferable skills from an English Literature degree would also be highly useful to a politician, such as debating, critical thinking, and learning how to manipulate language to persuade.

This answer shows that the applicant is aware of the practical skills instilled by study English Literature, and also the subject's effect on personal outlook. They have then compared these skills with those required of politicians, finding the points of similarity and logical explaining why these skills would be enhanced by studying English Literature.

A Poor Applicant: might simply give a 'yes' or 'no' response without sharing their thought process, or they might fail to understand the difference between content and skill learning, arguing that being widely read is not relevant to a career as a politician.

Q20: Why do you think literature dating from before living memory is still studied, does it hold value?

This is a question designed to test your ability to think philosophically and debate a subject. There are no right or wrong answers, but you should be able to justify your reasoning with logical and detailed arguments. Amongst consideration should be the implications of studying English Literature, how we measure worth, the pros and cons of studying older texts, and even the wording of the question.

A Good Applicant: Why do we 'bother' studying any of the arts? Bother implies that studying older texts is a waste of time, perhaps because it is working under the assumption that doing so has no real-world application or use. However, the arts are designed to be enjoyed – we read and study older texts because they are enjoyable, and offer a sense of perspective into the past. In studying them too, we expand our knowledge on the human condition. Analysing writing style, plotting themes, and scrutinizing language choice and development allow us insight into humanity's ever developing thought processes and shifting concerns, which, if you so desired, can be translated into applicable data on human trends and progression. I personally love studying older texts as it gives me a new perspective through which to see the modern world.

This response shows an analytical approach to the question, first addressing the terminology used and how it attempts to influence our sense of value. They then debate whether or not it is more important that English Literature derives its worth from its practical usage or its enjoyable and educational nature. Their conclusion is multifaceted, detailing how both sides of this debate can be met simultaneously.

A Poor Applicant: might either straightforwardly agree or disagree with the statement without justifying their response. Whilst it is perfectly fine to have a strong stance, be prepared to explain why you have come to your conclusion. If rhetorical questions are used (as above), be sure to answer them and address the concerns you raise with logical or personal opinions.

Q21: How much importance would you attach to the gender of a protagonist?

To answer this question you must interrogate what is meant by 'important', and choosing a definition with which you will debate this question. You could consider if the protagonist's gender is important to the plot, important contextually/ historically, or important socially. When faced with a broad question, try not to give a broad answer, but include examples and close analysis to show that you have thoroughly contemplated the implications of the question.

A Good Candidate: I think that what is represented in literature is incredibly important, socially speaking, as literature both reflects society and can also shape it. Therefore, a protagonist's gender is significant if we are looking at texts from a feminist perspective to ensure that there is equal representation. Gender is also important when we consider the roles that characters assume in literature. Continually representing genders in the same way creates stereotypes which affect public thought about what is considered male or female behaviour. Therefore, not only is evenly depicting both genders important in literature, but presenting all characters in roles that are not defined by their gender is as important in terms of accurate representation and gender equality.

This question decides to explore the importance of gender through the foil of social significance. It addresses gender representation in literature quantitatively and qualitatively, arguing that the gender of the role and the type of role each gender plays are equally important when considering accurate social representation.

A Poor Applicant: might discuss gender theory (e.g., feminism) broadly without addressing the impact a character's gender has either socially, contextually, or historically. Make sure to consider both the impact both within a specific text and with the wider audience, and its consequences in both the short and long term.

Q22: Let's say that you are a director, and you are preparing a modern performance of Shakespeare's Hamlet, *a play you've mentioned. You have recently learned that modern audiences often prefer shorter plays, so how would you abridge it?*

For this question applicants must consider the content of the play, the concerns of its staging, and the logistical and artistic effects of cutting the play, (such as entrances and exits, and character development).

A Good Applicant: It is certainly true that Hamlet is a very long play! Whilst I think that there should still be full-length runs of the play, as the run time is typically over 4 hours long, there are many modern-day difficulties that have to be faced when staging it in this form, such as additional interval times, theatre/space scheduling, and the time commitment made by the audience, for example whether it is feasible to schedule the performance during the working week. This means that Hamlet is too long to produce easily. If I had to shorten it I would remove the Rosencrantz & Guidenstern storyline, cut down the grave-digging scene and the players and Mousetrap, and ensure that there are minimal set changes to reduce the time between different scenes. I feel that these choices do not affect the overall tone or artistic merit of the play.

This answer debates the pros and cons of a complete production versus cutting the play, prioritising the logistical difficulties of staging a longer play. They come to the conclusion that the play would benefit from being cut, and offer specific examples of where and why. They also offer a method of shortening the play without cutting lines, by ensuring that stage changes and scene changes take up as little time as possible.

A Poor Applicant: might simply agree or disagree with the question and give basic ideas of how to shorten the play, for example 'cut some lines', without offering specific examples from the play or showing a wider understanding of the artistic and logistical sensitivity required to shorten a play.

Q23: Do you think we should ever draw comparisons between literary characters and real people? Can the story of Christ's birth be used to evaluate the current prime minister, for example?

This question is an opportunity to explore how we can use storytelling and allegory to improve our understanding of another event. You will need to weigh the pros and cons of using allegory as a tool of comprehension, and debate whether or not using a religious allegory is appropriate or justifiable.

A Good Applicant: Allegory is a very useful tool when wanting to highlight certain similarities between two stories or events. Whether or not the story being used for allegorical purposes has religious sentiments does not affect whether we 'should' draw upon its elements for a different purpose, as in this instance the story of Christ' birth does not belong to anyone, but exists, certainly in the UK, where it is being used to comment upon political affairs, within common knowledge. I think that using such a well-known story to comment upon Boris Johnson's views on immigration, for example, is extremely useful as it helps audiences to engage with the subject of politics on new, familiar terms, allowing them a better comprehension of, and ability to critique, political policy. Nevertheless, it should also be noted that when using religious material for a secondary purpose, I think that we must be remain respectful.

This is a thoughtful response that shows an in-depth knowledge of the literary technique of allegory. The student has logically explored the idea of a 'right' to repurposes existing stories for allegorical purposes in respects of respecting religion, ownership of ideas, and public knowledge, concluding that using well-known stories is a useful technique when attempting to gain wider engagement with a certain topic.

A Poor Applicant: might only address whether the allegory is apt or not, but fail to address the question of whether we 'should' use the story of Christ. Many interview questions have different parts to them, all of which need to be addressed to impress your interviewer.

Q24: You mentioned King Lear, would you agree that it is a tragedy?

This question is a chance for you to show your understanding of different themes in drama, and also demonstrate your knowledge and analysis of a specific play. You should offer a continual comparison of the plot of King Lear and the tropes of tragedy plays.

A Good Applicant: Tragedy as a genre is defined by the downfall of its hero, whose hubris is often their fatal flaw, which instigates their tragic suffering. King Lear, the title protagonist of the play is undoubtably a tragic hero, and the plot of the play is driven by the power and consequence of his losses, starting with the banishment of his favourite child, Cordelia, who refuses to flatter him to receive a share of his kingdom. From this point onwards, Lear continues to fall because of his flaws of pride and his inability to distinguish between false regard and true loyalty. He loses his authority as a king, his identity as a father, and his sanity as a man. In fact, one could argue that King Lear is the ultimate tragedy as in this play there is no chance of redemption. Unlike other tragedies, there is no salvation for the tragic hero or any sign of optimism in the conclusion, with both Cordelia, a symbol of truth and familial love and duty throughout the play, and Lear himself dying.

This answer shows the student's knowledge of King Lear and their ability to connect the events of the play to traits of tragedy plays. They have also shown where and why some events do not follow the classic examples of tragedy plays, such as the ending of King Lear, and analysed its effect on whether this alteration affects the King Lear's classification as a tragedy.

A Poor Applicant: Might not have read King Lear, and failed to offer an alternative tragedy play to discuss in light of the question, or simply state that King Lear is a tragedy without explaining why or using specific examples from the plot of King Lear to justify their response.

Q25: Our course is structured by period, we start with very early works of English literature, and move towards the present. Why do you think we do this?

This question is an opportunity for you to show that you have researched and understood the particular structure of this university's course. Your interviewer is asking your opinion on this structure, so be willing to discuss the benefits or issues faced by chronological modules, as well as exploring other methods of learning. However, be careful not to critique their method too much, as you are they one that has chosen to apply to this course!

A Good Applicant: I certainly think that the order of studying literature has an effect on our understanding and interrogation of a subject. Studying chronologically can help us better track changes in thematic content, societal concerns and taste, writing and language style and the evolution of form. However, I also think that there is a benefit to a more unsystematic approach to studying period papers, such as studying modern and medieval literature simultaneously as it allows students to see connections between different eras of literature that might be unexpected or unusual, which changes our perceptions of those texts.

This is a diplomatic answer that shows the benefits of both a chronological and non-chronological approach to studying English Literature. They have taken into consideration the course structure, and addressed why it is structured the way that it is, but have also shown wider thinking, discussing what benefits there might be from a holistic approach to the subject.

A Poor Applicant: might give a non-committal 'I don't know' or simply agree with the course structure without critique. Remember, the way a course is structured is not accidental, try to analyse why this course is being structured in this way, its pros and cons, and also the pros and cons of a different approaches. You need not come to a conclusion but accept that each teaching method is worthwhile and will highlight different discussion points during the degree.

Q26: Some texts are highly spatial, they focus on a particular place. Have you ever been to a place which is heavily referred to in a text you have read? Do you think that visiting somewhere like that would have an effect on the way you read the text, and should more people do it?

This question is asking you to consider the role of context on interpretation and understanding. Literary history is a large part of any English Literature course, so demonstrate to your interviewer that you are aware of the status and usages of contextual knowledge. This question can be answered from an objective or personal viewpoint, and the inclusion of appropriate and explicated examples is advised.

A Good Applicant: Yes, I've visited Shakespeare's house in Stratford Upon-Avon. However, whilst interesting, I don't necessarily think that seeing an author's birthplace is of great significance. In my opinion, more likely to affect the reading of their works is seeing where, specifically, they were written, where the author spent the majority of the working life, or seeing where the text is set. These opportunities allow for an improved contextual basis from which to analyse and explore that author's texts, which can impact our interpretations and understanding, or even just imagination of a text, which can make the reading experience more enjoyable. For example, I have also visited Oxford where Phillip Pullman's *His Dark Materials* are set, which aided my envisioning of the young Lyra growing up in Jordan College, and improved my understanding of her character.

This answer addresses the nuance of each suggested place of visitation. They come to their balanced conclusion by weighing their own experience against their understanding and appreciation of contextual knowledge.

A Poor Applicant: might simply state yes or no, and give a personal example two, but not realise that this question is more widely addressing the significance of contextual knowledge in literature. Their examples might also not shows how visiting a place has specifically changed their opinions or interpretations of a text.

Q27: Who do you think wrote Shakespeare's plays?

There are many ways and concerns to address when answering this question. You could consider whether or not it is important to know who the author of a text is, whether knowledge about the author affects our reading of a text, legacy, the debate over the potential shared authorship of Shakespeare's plays, matters of evidence (signatures, records, folio and quarto editions of the plays), or any other reason why knowing for certain that Shakespeare did or did not write his plays affects their worth or application.

A Good Applicant: I think that it is highly likely Shakespeare wrote the majority of his plays, as there currently seems to be only unsubstantial evidence to the contrary. When considering whether any of his plays were co-authored, we have to remember that this was a common practise of the time, so we have to remove any modern-day sensationalism regarding plagiarism or a false legacy that might be associated with this idea. I personally don't think that knowing for certain whether or not Shakespeare wrote all of his plays affects their worth (either as studied texts or produced plays), or our interpretation of their content.

This response shows that the applicant has considered the question both empirically and individually, offering a balanced set of thoughts on common authorial practises, modern day perception, issues of interpretation and the evidential weight of the argument.

A Poor Applicant: might just say 'I assume so' since Shakespeare is credited inherently for his plays, or they might imply that the question is unfounded/pointless since it is unlikely that we will ever fully know the answer. Remember to never dismiss or undervalue the nature of the questions posed by your interviewer – each one is chosen to explore a different skill expected of English Literature students, and your answers to each question are extremely significant to the outcome of your application.

Q28: What poems have you read by [insert poet here]?

The poet chosen for this question will almost certainly either be one you have mentioned in your application, or mentioned in the interview. Your interviewer wants to explore your knowledge of a certain poet. Try not to simply list the poems you have read, but give some initial analysis and commentary upon to show that you have engaged fully with their body of works.

A Good Applicant: I have read quite a few of Emily Dickinson's poems, but I especially enjoyed reading the poems in which she explores the themes of mental health or where her feminist theories are exhibited, such as 'Because I Could Not Stop for Death', 'My Life Had Stood a Loaded Gun', 'It Was Not Death for I Stood Up', and 'I Felt a Funeral in my Brain'. However, I find the breadth of subject matter and emotion in Dickinson's works equally as intriguing, especially the unusually heighten sense of excitement and eroticism in 'Going to Him Happy Letter'.

In this answer the student has given a range of specific examples, linking their chosen poems through theme. They have also given an overview of the whole works of Dickinson, commenting upon their breadth of tone, offering another poem that exemplifies this opinion.

A Poor Applicant: would only list some poems, if they were able to do so, without commenting upon why they have named these specific poems, why they enjoyed these specific poems, or how these specific poems are connected to the poet's work as a whole.

Q29: How would you explain the differences between a Sonnet and a Haiku to someone who hasn't studied English?

This question is asking you to demonstrate your knowledge of different forms of poetry. Your answer should delineate the specific traits of each poem and suggest a reason for why different forms of poetry and their structures have evolved.

A Good Applicant: A Haiku is a Japanese poem written across three lines, consisting of 17 syllables, split into 5-7-5, whereas a sonnet originated from Sicily, but is commonly used across Europe. It is a love poem which traditionally consists of 14 lines of poetry, with internal rules that differ depending on whether the sonnet follows the Petrarchan or Shakespearean model. The structure of Haiku is relatively simple compared to a sonnet as its form is intended to embody the elegance of simplicity and tranquillity. Sonnets, however, have many intricate rules, such as the use of a volta, a set rhyme scheme, and ending with a rhyming couplet, which are used to show a poet's skill. Haiku and sonnets therefore differ in terms of structure not only as they are coming out of different literary practises, but because their aims are distinct, each attempting to conjure a different tone.

This answer clearly defines the characteristic of each form of poetry, offering a reason for their different structures based upon their cultural and geographical differences and the differences of their intentions and traditional uses.

A Poor Applicant: Might not fully explore the rules governing structure in each poem, or be able to reflect upon how the structure of a poem is integral to its meaning and tone, and affects the poem's content.

Q30: Every year we have applicants who mention that the structure of our course is flawed in one way, or another. Given the chance, what would you change about this course?

This question is made for you to show that you have thoroughly researched this specific course. Your answer can rely upon personal learning styles or preferences, or upon more general information. Either is fine, as long as you justify your changes in a logical and considered manner.

A Good Applicant: There is not much that I would change about the Oxford English Course, as one of the reason's I applied here is because I like the breadth of time periods studied here. However, if I could change the course in any way, I would change the distribution of coursework. The course currently consists of all coursework for finals taking place in 3rd year, when the dissertation and exams also take place. I think it would benefit all students if the coursework was spread across years 2 and 3, allowing students to prove their continued dedication to their subject after their prelim exams in 1st year, and remove some of the pressure from the final year of the undergraduate program.

This response demonstrates that the student clearly knows the layout and content of the course well. They have voiced what they like about the course, implying that they do not think much alteration is required, and the minor changes they have suggested have logical reasoning and could theoretically implemented.

A Poor Student: Would answer that they would change the course completely or not at all. Remember, by suggesting too many changes might imply that you do not like the course structure which might hinder your interviewer's impression of you. Whilst your interviewer does want to hear your honest opinion, it is important to be diplomatic, and even comment upon what you do enjoy about the course existing contents or structure.

Q31: What do you think makes a tragedy different from another genre?

This question is a chance for you to show your in-depth knowledge of the dramatic theme of tragedy. You should answer as specifically as possible, naming the tropes of the genre/ literary techniques, and possibly a textual example. This is a simpler question that might lead to a longer and more focused discussion, so be prepared to discuss in detail any examples you give for an extended period.

A Good Applicant: Tragedy as a genre of play which is defined by the downfall of its hero, whose hubris (pride) is often their fatal flaw, also known as hamartia, which instigates their tragic suffering. Sometimes there is a chance for redemption in tragedy plays, which creates a sense of catharsis in the audience, but that is not always the case. For example, in Webster's *The White Devil*, due to their greed, lust, and murdering ways nearly all of the characters are dead by the end of the play, only leaving the young Giovanni as an emblem of hope.

This answer shows an understating of the use of the word tragedy in literary contexts. They have thoroughly demonstrated their knowledge of characteristics of tragedy play by discussing the trajectory of the play and the key tropes of the genre. They have also named an example, and explained why it can be defined as a tragedy play.

A Poor Applicant: might give an answer along the lines of 'a tragedy play is where something bad happens', not giving detail to whom in the play this occurs, or why. If in doubt, give an example of a tragedy play and discuss why this play might be considered tragic, using details from its content and style.

Q32: How would you go about classifying the genre of the Holy Bible? Would you class it as a work of fiction?

This question is designed to see how you handle a controversial topic. Make sure you reflect upon the contentious variabilities of this question, such as literal vs symbolic interpretation and the significance of evidential material, and the implication of literary labels.

A Good Answer: Even though, as an atheist, I don't believe that that the bible always depicts true or real events, such as the miracles, people talking God, or faith healing, I don't think we can call it a work of fiction. This is because of the literary intention behind the text. If the person writing a text that is now included in the bible truly believed in what they were writing, then from their perspective it is non-fiction, and even if I do not agree, this does not lead to a classification of fiction. Nevertheless, there are elements of the fictive in the bible, such as heavy use of allegory and parable, and that is also how I perceive parts of the bible that I do not believe represent reality, as another allegorical learning opportunity.

This student is aware that answering this question is a highly personal affair. Their response is informed both by their own religious leanings, as well as their definition of different literary genres, discussing the issues of literary intention and the nebulous identity of primarily nonfiction texts that rely heavily on allegorical story telling.

A Poor Student: Would not take into account the delicacy of this debate. It is a contentious issue, with many different contributing arguments. No matter what religious beliefs a student has, they should be able to demonstrate that they can understand and respect different perspectives, as this trait is essential whilst studying English Literature.

Q33: Do you think that fiction should always include a lesson on morality?

This question is designed to test your ideas about literature's purpose. You should question the nature, purpose, and use of moral literature and explore forms or examples of literature that do not have a moral.

A Good Applicant: I don't think that every piece of literature should have a moral, as I find that moralistic stories can be quite simplistic, implying that there is only one, unarguable lesson, that can be learned from that piece of writing. I certainly do believe that lessons can be learned from literature, but I think these should be defined by the reader, based on their interpretation of the text, and how it affects their thoughts and life. When considering this question, we must also discuss the purpose of literature – if every piece of literature had a moral, its primary purpose becomes instructional, which I do not think is, or should be the case. Not everyone works from the same set of morals, or ethics, and it is the beauty of literature that each person has a unique connection with what they have read, enjoys literature for different reasons, and learns different lessons.

This answer takes a firm position in the debate which they are able to justify using their personal opinions and logical arguments. They discuss their perceived pitfalls of moralistic literature and compare their purpose to the wider purpose of literature in general, exploring the different ways that people interact with the activity of reading.

A Poor Applicant: might argue for or against moral literature basing their opinions solely on whether or not they like this genre, not taking into consideration he wider implications of the style on readers of the subject in general. Remember, having your own opinions is important, but you should also show your interviewer that you can also consider questions from an objective or large-scale perspective.

Q34: What do you mean when you say [X] about [X – poet/author] in your personal statement?

For example, what do you mean when you say the perverse permeates the writing of Joyce Carol Oates in your personal statement?

This question is a chance to elucidate more fully on the opinions or analysis voiced in your personal statement. What is included in your personal statement should be of great interest to you, and your interviewer will expect you to know these texts extremely well, and to have studied them, and read around their themes and analysed their style, structure, use of language etc. in sufficient detail to hold a sustained conversation on the topic.

A Good Applicant: What struck me as a continual theme across the body of Oates' works is her interest in unusual and often imbalanced sexual power dynamics. For example, a common trope of hers is having her stories explore the relationship between young female characters and older male romantic partners, which is the case in her short story 'The Evil Eye', her novel 'A Fair Maiden', and another of her short story's 'So Help Me God'. Whilst in many of her texts, these relationships commence in a seemingly innocent fashion, much like in Nabokov's *Lolita,* Oates' word choices or teasing bits of information increasingly begin to make the reader more uncomfortable and aware of the male character's perverse desires or intentions. This instils in her works a sense of morbid curiosity that includes the reader in the sordidness of the story.

In this response the student is making their in-depth knowledge of several of Oates' works clear, connecting them through their common themes and use of language. They also include a cross comparison, including into their argument a text where they same stylistic features and theme content can be found. Overall, they do not simply explain what they meant in their personal statement, but add to their argument by including any details about the effect on the audience of reading Oates' works.

A Poor Applicant: might reiterate the point made in the personal statement without broadening the discussion or bringing in new analysis or critiques. Remember, the interviewer has read your personal statement, they do not want to hear the information again, but are interest in hearing your new reflections on the topics mentioned.

Q35: Do you feel that the best way to express and communicate ambiguities or questions about the nature of particular words is through poetry?

To answer this question, you should consider how the structure, usage, and methods of communication and other characteristics of poetry might allow poetry to be able to paradoxically present a doubt over words more effectively than another form.

A Good Applicant: Poetry's most effective characteristic is that it is a unique language. In no other form does the way the words sound affect meaning and communication as much as the meaning of the words themselves. Therefore, in poetry there are several layers of meaning, a secondary, or tertiary conversation occurring within the poem. I therefore think it is a form particularly well adapted to expressing doubts over words because the words themselves are not the only vehicle for communication. Grammar, punctuation, syntax, structure, and even words themselves can disintegrate in a poem and yet meaning can still be effectively communicated. In no other form is there the ability to be so creative with the fundamentals of language, so it is the perfect form in which to encapsulate doubts over its own building blocks, words.

This answer starts by discussing how poetry communicates its ideas. Their argument focuses on the premise that poetry is more adept and communicating multiple ideas to the reader than any other literary form. They logically follow their expressed opinion by surveying poetry's key characteristics and conclude that poetry's ability to heavily manipulate language whilst still retaining meaning renders it a particularly effective form for expressing a doubt over words.

A Poor Applicant: might answer this question without addressing what makes poetry different to other literary forms, or how poetry implements its traits in a way that will affect its ability to communicate complex ideas. Remember, it is always best to be as precise as possible by giving examples which demonstrate your understanding and knowledge.

Q36: What do you think about this writer [X's] reference to [X], that you have mentioned in your personal statement?

For example, what do you think about Phillip Pullman's references to John Milton's *Paradise Lost* in his series *His Dark Materials*?

This question is asking you to consider the effect of intertextuality. Being able to recognise and understand intertextuality leads to a much richer reading experience which invites new interpretations as it brings another context, idea, story into the text at hand. In your answer you should address both the wider importance of intertextuality and discuss in detail what effect the intertextual moment has in the example text given.

A Good Applicant: Pullman's references to Milton's *Paradise Lost* are interesting as the poem clearly inspired the story arc of *His Dark Materials* greatly, particular the last book of the trilogy where the war between heaven and earth comes to fruition. By including fragments of Milton's poem in his texts, new layers of meaning are introduced, there is a certain pleasure in the sense of connection and the continuity of these texts and controversial religious topics. For example, Satan and Azrael take on a very similar role in each respective text, undermining God's authority in an extremely charismatic manner. However, these direct references also allow the reader to notice where Pullman's story differs to Milton's, as in *His Dark Materials,* there is a refusal to lament the loss of innocence.

This answer observes how intertextuality creates connections that allow the reader to engage with a broader literary heritage not just one text. They include how Pullman's intertextuality allows for cross comparisons to be made, and the effect of these references on the reader's interpretation of the text.

A Poor Applicant: Might be unable to see how intertextuality affects the interpretations of the text or how intertextuality weaves one text into a wider literary discussion. You can also consider ideas of influence and originality in your discussion.

Q37: What would you say were the most significant similarities and differences between The Lord of the Rings trilogy, and the Harry Potter series?

In this question you are being asked to compare two novels from the same genre. You should disuses how each novel does or does not comply with the characteristics of the genre, giving examples from the texts. Your answer can also reflect on language choice, readership and reception, or any other relevant contextual information.

A Good Applicant: because *Harry Potter* and *Lord of the Rings* are both fantasy series, you might expect them to have more similarities than are in fact present. The wonderful thing about the fantasy genre is that whole new worlds can be created, which is the case with these two series, and each of their respective worlds differ greatly. Even when there is overlapping material, such as the inclusion of magical creatures, their representations differ vastly. For example, in *Lord of the Rings* elves are conceptualised as an ancient and wise people, whereas their mythical counterpart in *Harry Potter* are the whimsical and subservient house elves, who do have an ancient power, but do not hold as high a position of rank or regard as the elves in *Lord of the Rings*. These differences are in part due to the expected readership. Especially at the beginning of the *Harry Potter* series, the books are aimed at children, whilst *The Lord of the Rings* series is definitely YA (Young Adult) literature.

This answer focuses on the shared genre of the two series and how that affects their contents. They give a specific example to compare their different handling of ideas, and present a reason for why these differenced occur.

A Poor Applicant: might solely the plots of the two texts, not showing an analytical ability to compare and contrast stylistic or linguistic features, or understand the respective contexts of the two series.

Q38: It looks like you had to study Romeo and Juliet *in GCSE English, did you think that Romeo was a rebel? Would you say that Romeo shared much in common with Shakespeare?*

A question like this is asking you to consider and argue both sides of an argument. You should delineate the ways that Romeo is a rebel, but also offer a counter argument, why might there a doubt over his position as a rebel?

A Good Applicant: Romeo rebels against his family but consorting with the daughter of his parent's and whole house's sworn enemies, the Capulets, and in so doing his rebellion aggrandises, as he breaks laws and rules, starting with breaking into private property and escalating to murder. Romeo will do anything to be with Juliet, but when we analyse this behaviour, we must ask what is purely angst and what is true rebellion. Nothing is expected from Romeo, we know little about his life, his familial relationships, or goals. Whilst his actions do, to some extent, show a rebellion against his family's prejudice, this only occurs to serves his own desire to be with Juliet. He seemingly didn't have problem with their family feud beforehand. On the other hand, I think that Juliet is more of a rebel because she not only rebels against her family's prejudice but against her predetermined life, full of high expectations. Engaged to Paris, she also has far more to lose than Romeo, making the stakes of her Rebellion much higher.

This applicant argues that Romeo is a rebel to the extent that he rebels against certain factors which limit his access to Juliet. However, they question whether or not this is a true rebellion, as his actions are highly in his own interest, and until his banishment, do not incur much personal loss. They posit instead that Juliet is the more rebellious of the two as there are far greater consequences for her actions than for his.

A Poor Applicant: Might fully argue that Romeo is a rebel without including any counterargument. They may include narrative details from the text, but their explications will be simplistic or vague. Remember, if a question is asking you to consider both sides of an argument, you must make valid and thoughtful made for each idea, it is this skill that is being tested more than your knowledge of the text.

Q39: Do you read other people criticisms of works you have read? Why?

This question might be used to gauge your practise of wider reading, specifically reading critical works that offer their opinions and analysis of primary or secondary texts. Remember in your answer that engaging with other people's critical discussion is a key part of any English course.

A Good Applicant: I not only think that critical reading is necessary but is an enjoyable activity. Reading other people's analysis and criticism helps to challenge your own conceptions of a text, broadening your understanding and provoking new ways of thinking about or reading of the text. For example, I often use the Cambridge companion texts when writing essays, which allows me to position my argument in a wider context and in a pre-existing literary tradition which allows for a more nuanced interpretation and analysis of the text. I also recently read Marion Turner's essay 'Discursive Turbulence: Slander, the House of Fame, and the Mercers' Petition' in preparation for writing an essay on Chaucer, which was informed me about the Medieval political tensions in Chaucer's works.

This answer argues clearly and concisely why critical reading is beneficial to one's studies as an English Literature student. They also add into the argument their personal option that is an enjoyable activity as well as academically rewarding, giving an example of critical material that they use themselves.

A Poor Applicant: might be unable to articulate why critical reading is an important part of any English literature course, simply arguing that it is something that is always done. Critical reading is more than just reading other people's opinions, it is an incredibly helpful too that can sophisticate your critical, analytical, and even writing skills.

Q40: Who is your favourite character?

For this question you should analyse your favourite character, delineating why you find them appealing. The decisive factors can include a great variety of different criteria, such as what impact they have had in your life, interesting character traits, or any other relevant topics of interest.

A Good Applicant: my favourite character is Hermione from Harry Potter as growing up she was my proto-feminist role model. We had a shared love of learning and investment in our education and from her character I learnt not to compromise my beliefs and interests for others and to never to accept less than what I deserved - lessons which I think are vital to learn, especially from a female character as to this day women are still often portrayed as accommodating figures in literature. She is also a character whose flaws, whether they be her vengefulness, irritability, or close mindedness, both lead to moments of interesting character development, but are also highly relatable, and surprisingly grounded for fantasy.

This student has been able to analyse what it is about the character of Hermione that they particularly like and admire. They have positioned their argument in the wider context of feminist role models, whilst also highlighting the literary techniques used to make her an intriguing character.

A Poor Applicant: might have a favourite character but will never have reflected on why they are drawn to this figure, or they might not have a favourite character at all. There is no right or wrong answer, but demonstrating a lack of passion will negatively impact your interviewer's impression of you. Also, don't forget that self-questioning your reaction to literature is essential for studying English Literature, as only then can you find the literary techniques used by writers to manipulate their readers.

Q41: *If we were to hand you a carrot, and ask you to use it in a prop in an impromptu performance of one of Hamlet's soliloquies would that vegetable become 'theatrical'?*

Sometimes you might encounter an odd question, designed to test your ability to think on the spot. Such questions might enter the realms of either the comic or the controversial, but in either case just be natural, give an honest response, and enjoy the thought process and ensuing discussion of a completely new and unexpected topic.

A Good Applicant: Fruits and vegetables have a long and highly symbolic history of being used as props in the theatrical world, so I would argue that yes, if a carrot is being used as a prop, it can be considered a theatrical vegetable, because it is being imbued with the same symbolic meaning as any of the characters; it is playing a role in the play.

This answer considers what it means for something to be theatrical, and explores the history of edible props in the theatre. Their answer though brief shows logical reasoning being applied to a difficult and slightly absurd question.

A Poor Applicant: would be unable to objectively think about this unusual hypothetical question. In these types of questions, what your answer does not matter as much as your ability to demonstrate the thought process that led to your conclusion. Other considerations for your argument are: what is the benefit of categorisation, is there something more theatrical about a carrot than any other fruit or vegetable, or more broadly, the importance or status of props in theatre.

Q42: Do you think the ending of [X] is poor?

For example, do you think that the ending of *A Suitable Boy* by Vikram Seth is poor?

This question wants you to consider the importance of a novel or other piece of literature's ending. You should consider ideas such as expectation vs reality, and the effect of endings, whilst also taking into account your won response to the text's ending.

A Good Applicant: Whilst I found the ending to *A Suitable Boy* unexpected, I do not think it is a poor ending. From my perspective, Lata's choice to marry Haresh felt jarring as I felt that throughout the book, she had not shown enough interest in to justify her choice. To me the two seem to have very different personalities and life ambitions, Haresh solely interested in the shoe business and his career progression, and Lata invested in her academic life and modern aspirations. Moreover, much more of the text is focused upon her relationship with Kabir, who as a fellow student with an interest in acting, seems to be to more natural choice for Lata. However, as the whole novel deeply interrogates family bonds, it is perhaps unsurprising that Lata chooses Haresh, an uncomplicated decision, but it saddens me that in so doing she seemingly gives up her desire for a different kind of life that she voices at the beginning of the novel.

This answer discusses why the ending might be considered 'poor' and expresses their personal feelings about the ending, using examples from the text to explain why they have come to that conclusion.

A Poor Applicant: might agree or disagree whilst not taking into consideration that this, or the reverse, is a possible interpretation of the ending. They may not explore how the text has or has not led to this ending, or might not use examples from the text to explain how they interpret the ending.

Q43: What is your all-time favourite novel?

This question requires you to take a firm stance on a matter and defend your viewpoint. Your answer should be personal yet informed by your critical thinking and analytical abilities. There is no right or wrong answer, you only need to answer honestly. Your passion about a book will be much more impressive to your interviewer than talking dispassionately about a book you think they would want you to pick.

A Good Applicant: I don't actually have a favourite book of all time, as I think books serve different emotional needs. I also don't tend to reread books very often as the draw of experiencing a new book is too great. However, I turn to different authors to fill my emotional cravings. For example, when I'm feeling nostalgic, I read F. Scott Fitzgerald, when I want to be inspired, I read Audre Lorde, when I want to be critically engaged I read Gertrude Stein, when I want suspense, I read Joyce Carol Oates. Even though the content of their works may differ greatly, I find that each writer's style greatly affects how I perceive the tone of their works. Therefore, I do not have a favourite book of all time, but favourite books of the moment.

This response answers the question in an atypical fashion. Rather than answering directly, this student unconventionally argues that they do not have a favourite book. Such an answer is completely permissible, as long as it is justifiable. This student logically explains why they do not have a favourite book, but a collection of favourite authors, whom they name, to suit all of their literary needs.

A Poor Applicant: might give an example book but be unable to objectively discuss why they enjoy it above any other texts. They will demonstrate little to no critical or analytical engagement with the text or author, and be unable to define what it is they enjoy about the text. Remember, questioning is an integral part of studying English Literature, you should always be asking yourself how you respond to a text and why.

Q44: Do you think the ending of [Novel] is poor?

This is a good question to open up a discussion on what is a 'good ending.' Are there any specific qualities or characteristics you feel a good ending should have? Considers the role of the ending in a novel and the purpose of it.

For example, if asked to comment on the ending of Ian McEwan's novel Atonement a **good candidate** may say: Critics and readers alike dislike the ending of Atonement because it is so ambiguous and the book itself, in a metafictional way, acknowledges that. I can see how this could be disappointing and ambiguous as it withholds a 'happy ever after' ending but also a complete understanding of what happened in the ending. I personally love the ambiguity and meta nature of the ending. To me it feels as though, as a reader, you have been tricked into the same misreading as Briony, which drew me into reading all the critical essay on the ending and suggested interpretations of it.

This is a strong response as it considers critical interpretations of the text and shows an understanding of what people are looking for in the ending of a novel. The candidate gives a clear judgement and answers the question fully with evidence.

A **poor candidate** may say " the novel has a poor ending because there's no happy ever after finish." Even if this is frustrating to the reader, consider why the author has written it this way and what greater purpose it serves. What does a poor ending teach us? More often than not these books are still taught on the syllabus, despite not having popular endings. Consider why some might like this non-fairy-tale ending but don't limit yourself to just one point of view.

Q45: Do you have a favourite book? What is it?

This question is a great opportunity to talk about a novel that you know a lot about but is not necessarily a text you've studied at A-level, but it can be related to it. This question allows you to show you have read widely and allows you to talk about a particular aspect of Literature that you find interesting, or a text that you read to support other texts you were studying. It doesn't have to be a super long or extremely complex novel but something that you have lots to say about.

Good Applicant: My favourite book of all time is *Nutshell* by Ian McEwan. It is a modern rework of Hamlet and I found it so interesting to read alongside my study of Hamlet at A-level. McEwan presents the story of Hamlet from the perspective of an unborn child in the womb which is an intriguing concept to begin with. I think what struck me most was the title which is taken from one of Hamlet's soliloquy's where he says, "I could be bounded in a nutshell and count myself king of infinite space". I found it really helped me understand the concept of Hamlet being trapped in his circumstances, like the child is restricted in the womb, Hamlet is held back by his status and the life set out for him. The novel pushed me to consider the dynamics of the play in terms of the geographical locations and how it is not until Hamlet leaves Elsinore that he is able to see and understand the corruption of the court. I found that my reading of the play helped inform my reading of the novel and vice versa.

The response shows an enthusiasm about the texts they are learning and the willingness to read further. The answer is backed up by links to other texts and even if you couldn't remember an exact quote in an interview, it still shows how you can make connections between texts you are reading. It is good to link back to what the reading of that text did for you in terms of whether it furthered your knowledge of a book you were studying, had an application to a real life situation or made you approach something in a way you hadn't thought of or considered before.

A **poor applicant** may suggest something like a childhood book that made them "love reading" or talking about a text they've studied at A-level or GCSE. Although the love of reading/literature is important for an English degree, this answer may seem a little childish. It is better to show how much you love reading by talking in depth about a book you enjoyed. The interviewer won't necessarily know the texts you've studied at GCSE or A-level, but it is more interesting to pick a book that isn't on the syllabus to show a sense of wider reading and will help you stand out more too.

Q46: What was your coursework about?

This is a good question to get onto a topic that interests you and that you know a lot about, as you will have researched the coursework yourself. Consider both the topic you spoke about in your coursework as well as the process of writing it. This can show you are prepared to take on university style essay and prove you can work independently on research and essays. It is also giving you the opportunity to talk about literary criticism and what criticism you came across in writing your coursework.

Good applicant : I wrote my coursework on Naomi Alderman's novel *The Power* and centred my argument on why I felt the text was deserving of a canonical status. This led me to have two veins of debate running through my essay: one that considered the text in terms of the suggested characteristics of 'canonical texts' whilst simultaneously questioning the validity and importance of the canon as a concept on its own. I enjoyed researching and using critical works in my coursework as I felt it allowed me to develop my own opinion on the canon and help me develop my essay writing skills. To me, *The Power,* met all the criteria of a canonical text and also challenged the stereotypical authorial profile as Naomi Alderman is, firstly, a woman, is LGBTQ+ and is an ex-orthodox Jew. I found in much of my research into the canon, there is much criticism over the elitism of what is considered to be canonical with it largely being dominated by Older, White Men. Not only is the text exceptionally well written, it is exciting and pertinent to the modern day.

This is a strong answer as it brings in different elements into the conversation. The interviewer has room to ask more questions about the specific topic of writing, as well as the process of essay writing and the possibility of talking about literary criticism. There is also room for development on your own topic of interest and gives you the ability to ask the interviewer if you would have the opportunity to continue your research in the degree such as, 'Is there room for debate around the existence of the canon in the degree course?' or 'would I be able to look at Queer writers in my three years of study?'

A **poor applicant** may say: "I wrote my coursework on what everyone in my class wrote on as it was what my teacher suggested." This is a limited answer and doesn't demonstrate their own independent research or thought that would show they are passionate about the subject. It would also avoid just explaining an argument, for example " I spoke about whether the canon is good or bad and whether the book I chose should be in it." This doesn't explain how you came across this particular argument or much enthusiasm for the subject.

Q47: You mentioned that Hamlet was your favourite play before, what would you say was the importance of family in Hamlet's plot?

These kinds of questions come up fairly often and they are designed to test that you can talk about something you are familiar with on their level. It is also often used to check that you have done the work you said you did in your personal statement or earlier in the interview. In this particular case the candidate had mentioned loving Shakespeare's *Hamlet,* but it could be anything that you've said you have read, or even something you have done in school, so be careful with what you mention! It would be easy to just focus on Hamlet in this question, but it is important to consider the other subplots in the play and the familial dynamics that are unfolding in those too. This will demonstrate a deeper knowledge and understanding of the play.

For example, a **good applicant** may say: The different subplots across the play represent different familial bonds and structures. The three main revenge plots in the play are motivated by familial action. However, Fortinbras serves to represent a man of action coming from a stable family, who is able to carry out the action that is required of him to avenge his late father. This juxtaposes Hamlet's familial relations, especially since his own uncle killed his brother (Hamlet's father) and usurped him. The plot of Polonius is also interesting when considering familial relations in the play as he mistreats both his son, Laertes and his daughter, Ophelia but is still motivated to take revenge. It is an interesting representation of familial bonds at the time . Especially if you consider Hamlet and Gertrude's relationship, particularly in a Freudian reading of the play. It is interesting to consider Hamlet's relationship with his mother and how that shapes his view on women and particularly his treatment of Ophelia.

This is a good answer as it shows a wide knowledge of the play. It is good to show an understanding of the contextual history of the play as well and possibly to ponder what Shakespeare intended when writing in these familial dynamics. Bringing in potential criticism may be helpful here to bring the answer some texture and demonstrate wider reading, such as applying a Freudian lens. Alternatively focusing on one particular family dynamic could be interesting if in more depth, such as talking about Hamlet's relationship with his mother and how that causes him to view women as well as treat Ophelia. There's potential to talk about the nunnery scene and feminist readings of the play.

A **poor applicant** might say: "Hamlet is close with his dad and that's why is he so upset when his uncle kills him, and this makes him want to kill his uncle. It is all the more tragic because they're all family and related." Avoid explaining the family trees in the play with this question, that's not what the questioning is asking. This answer doesn't show a developed understanding of the text and lacks links to wider reading or details. There is potential to talk about motivations for revenge, however this answer doesn't consider Shakespeare's intentions. Although it is impossible for us to know exactly what Shakespeare wanted to present, it is important to show, unlike in this answer, different reasoning and interpretations for this. It could be interesting instead to develop this point by talking about the role of father figures and how the loss of his father 'haunts' Hamlet.

Q48: Considering what you know about Hamlet, what do you think the Ghost has to do with madness?

This is a good question to demonstrate you know about the conventions of tragedy as well as show historical context about how madness was viewed at the time. It may also support your answer if you allude to other texts with ghosts and madness written at a similar time or in a similar genre such as Thomas' Kyd's The Spanish Tragedy or in other Shakespeare plays, such as Macbeth.

 Good Applicant: The Ghost is a really interesting character and plays into both the supernatural and madness elements that are key components of tragedy, such as in other plays like Macbeth. Shakespeare toys with the idea that Hamlet is possibly driven mad by the death of his father and makes it ambiguous as to who can see the ghost. For example, where Gertrude can't see the ghost, but Hamlet can. For me a key thing that Shakespeare does is have Horatio see the Ghost in Act 1, as Horatio is depicted as a learned and trustworthy man. But I think that ambiguity is intentional as Shakespeare wants to present the potential that Hamlet is actually mad rather than just feigning madness.

This is a good answer as it shows reasoning for the answer and considers Shakespeare's intentions. By referring specifically to acts the candidate is able to show a firm grasp of the text and the unfolding of events. It considered the typical tropes of Tragedy and that indicates wider reading of similar texts.

A **poor applicant** may say something along the lines of: "The Ghost drives Hamlet mad because he is haunted by the Ghost of his dad," or suggests that "The Ghost doesn't have anything to do with madness." This is a poor response as it doesn't show a logical chain of reasoning. It does consider the contextual relevance of the supernatural and Religious beliefs about the afterlife at the time.

Q49: You mentioned being familiar with Hamlet, when he speaks to the Ghost do you feel that there is some kind of deeper meaning that we can glean from the interaction?

This is a good question to explore the significance of specific events and their effect on the wider text. Make sure you give yourself room to consider alternative views or avenues to explore further such as by talking about context. It would be a good question to also compare the ghost in Hamlet to other ghosts in plays, either by Shakespeare or different playwrights.

A **good applicant** may suggest that although Hamlet is not the only character to see the ghost, he is the only one to engage with it in dialogue. The significance that this discourse has is however dependent on how you interpret the ghost. It's important to note that Hamlet himself is unsure whether the ghost is really the spirit of his father or a demonic being tempting him to sin. If we consider the latter, in the context in which the play was being performed, there would be a belief that this conversation would have damned Hamlet's soul to hell. Or we could view it as a significant insight into Hamlet's relationship with his late father. What is most striking to me about this interaction is how it motivates Hamlet to revenge, but he is also hesitant in his action as a result of it. This scene thus becomes a powerful and significant turning point in the play and acts to drive along the plot.

This is a strong answer as it is considered and detailed. Offering your own insight shows you have an opinion and can develop your own thoughts on a text. It also demonstrates an understanding on the religious context of the play that could be further developed.

A **poor applicant** may say: "this is significant because he's able to talk to his dad after he's dead." Arguably this statement isn't untrue, however it's a basic point and would need to be developed. It doesn't show a close reading of the play or a developed understanding of the deeper meanings or intentions of the playwright. The answer also restricts the possibility to expand or explore alternative meanings.

Q50: When Hamlet gives his famous soliloquy 'to be, or not to be' who do you think the audiences are?

It would be good in this question to talk about the different reasoning Hamlet has, as well as show that you have a deep understanding on the play's most famous soliloquy. Considering the different reasonings Shakespeare would have for presenting it this way and this would be a good time to talk about any adaptations of the play you've seen and how the scene is presented differently in these.

A good applicant: When considering whether Hamlet knows he's being listened to when delivering that famous soliloquy, I think what struck me most is that he delivers it in Iambic Pentameter, whereas usually in front of Claudius and Polonius he is trying to feign his madness. I think to consider this point of view, Shakespeare presents a candid outpouring of Hamlet's emotions that is sombre and sad, rather than Hamlet acting in order to put on a front. I found this when watching the Ethan Hawke version as he performs as if Hamlet doesn't realise, he is being listened to, until he and Ophelia are getting more intimate and he realises she is wired up with microphones. Although that is a modern depiction, I've also read that in some performances Polonius would sneeze to indicate that they are hiding.

This is a strong answer as by alluding to different performances of the play it shows you have a good knowledge of the play being performed rather than just reading it. Although it is important to note that you don't have to have watched many different live versions of the play, it is good to have seen the play performed, even just on You Tube for example, to give you a sense of how the play shapes the meaning of the text.

A **poor applicant** may suggest: " Hamlet definitely doesn't know he is being listened to as he asks Ophelia where her father is." Although this is an argument for why Hamlet may have not known he was being watched, the answer doesn't show a considered opinion. Even if you truly believe this is the answer, it is good to show an understanding of alternative options and explore those as well as having strong reasoning for your main argument.

Q51: Take a moment to read this poem – and tell us your thoughts.

It is likely that in your interview there will be some unseen poetry for example, and you will be expected to discuss what you think about. This question is designed to focus on close reading of the text rather than the author and how the authorial experience shapes the poem.

A **good applicant** may respond to an unseen poem by saying: I love the use of compound words in this poem. It gives it a sense of dividedness that I feel is further reflected by the fact there are only two stanzas. It reminds me of [another poet] who similarly uses the structure of the poem to help reinforce the underlying meanings of the poem. To me, the poet conveys a sense of duality by dividing and conjoining the words and stanzas, particularly by the use of enjambement.

This is a good response as it makes a judgement on the poem showing decisiveness. If the interviewer disagrees with you or adds something that makes you change your mind, there is ultimately no right or wrong answer here. The interviewer will probably ask to follow up questions to your initial response such as "what do you think the poet is trying to convey through the dividedness?" They will want to test your reasoning and evidence. This response is good as it also shows the candidate's knowledge of poetic terms, which don't need to be extremely complex, but should show you can recognise techniques and analyse them. Also, by comparing to a similar poem, you are able to show wider reading and interest in the subject. Don't get too distracted with the poem you are comparing the given poem to, but it may help you to feel more confident in answering unseen texts.

A **poor applicant** may simply list all the techniques they can see: 'I like it because it's got enjambement, and anaphora and metaphors and similes and it rhymes and there's iambic pentameter.' These may all be true, but the interviewer is not looking for who knows the most poetic terms, they want to see how you deal with unseen texts and analyse them, not just name-dropping techniques. Although it's not necessary to say you "love this poem", it is also okay if you 'hate it', you just need to give reasoning for this and be prepared to defend your opinion.

Q52: How would you explain the difference between a novel and a short story?

This question is asking you to consider the nature of form and the impact it has on a piece of literature. It is also a great way to 'show off' your wider reading and demonstrate your interest in different forms of literature. You can show your understanding of form and how that can be manipulated to create different meanings or different kinds of texts.

A **good applicant** may consider: Building on the obvious fact that novels are longer than short stories, it is important to consider, when differentiating the two, the impact that length would have on treatment of the stories content. A short story has less words to explore a character and establish, say, a protagonist in a different way to a novel. I found in my readings of shorts stories, such as The Bloody Chamber by Angela Carter, that in comparison to the average novel, The Bloody Chamber didn't have as developed characters, but this did not infringe upon the quality or purpose of the text, there was just a clearer more concise plot.

This response is good because it develops the idea by using references to texts demonstrating wider reading as well as a good understanding of form. It may also be god to consider the difference thus in a collection of short stories and a novel as well. A candidate may also consider the difference between the overarching themes of short stories and novels, as often in novels this is explicit whereas short stories more often have implied meaning.

A **poor applicant** may just comment on the fact that "short stories are shorter than novels." This is not developed, not does it consider thus the impact that the length has on style and structure.

Q53: Do you think that poets make their work hard to understand on purpose?

This is a great question to draw on your own favourite poets and poems and discuss the nature and purpose of literature. You can also explore authorial intentions and what we can gain from understanding poetry.

A **good applicant** may say: I don't think that the sole reason of poetry as a concept is for it to be difficult to understand, I feel that depends on the authorial intention. It also largely depends on what is meant by 'difficult to understand', I would take that to suggest whether the meanings and intentions behind the poem are implicit or explicit. Those factors being considered, it is what you want to gain from poetry, if you want a difficult poem which doesn't have any obvious meanings or is even difficult to read. I am a big fan of the poetic works of Keats for example, but I also really love the poetry of Simon Armitage. I find Keats harder to understand and interpret more often than I do Armitage's poetry, but I still feel they have value in their own right.

This is a good answer because it considers an example of two poets the candidate finds interesting. There is potential then to expand this answer to talk about specific poems and what makes them difficult to read but how that is important to the meaning of the individual poem. The answer considers authorial intent and the reason we read poetry and its uses.

A **poor applicant** may say: " Poetry must be difficult to understand in order for it to be good." This candidate does not consider the use of poetry and readership. There is no reasoning or commiseration of an alternative view point. Evaluation is needed, some poetry is intended to be difficult to understand in order to convey a deeper or clandestine meaning, whereas some poetry may be written for solely aesthetic uses.

Q54: Do you think the way we use English in writing is different to how we'd speak it?

This is a great question to explore the different forms of literature and how this differentiates from language whilst also comparing ways in which they are similar. It is asking you to explore your own knowledge of the characteristics of literature and speech.

A **good applicant** may say: in day to day usage, language and literature may be viewed as synonyms however there are fundamental differences to the terms. You could argue that language focuses solely on expression, through speech and writing. Whereas Literature focuses on written aspects of expression and communication. It is important to note however that Language came into existence before literature was, and it was the existence of language that literature developed from. Language becomes the medium of expression. Literature is a collection of expressions via language. The two are highly co-dependent and help in the development of each other.

This is a good answer because it seeks to define both terms but shows an understanding of the two terms together. In a question like this it is a test of eloquences and formulating and argument as not just something a candidate would need to know. This answer is developed and sophisticated as it considers the co-dependence of language and literature.

A **poor applicant** may say " literature and speech are the same if they're in the same language" The candidate here is not grasping at what the question is asking. There is no differentiation or comparison between the two concepts. Even if the candidate does not fully understand the question, they should demonstrate their logic and reasoning by applying it to come to an answer or understanding.

Q55: From the perspective of an English student, what do you think is the significance of Coronation Street being on air for five decades?

This is a great question to explore the relationship between literature and media. What makes something enjoyable and have a long-lasting impact.

A **good applicant** may say: I have seen some episodes but to my understanding the show is not outstanding writing or complicated plots, although somewhat caricatured and dramatized. I think what brings people back to tune in each week is how they are able to identify with the characters. From an English perspective this is interesting as for example in terms of tragedy, Aristotle argues the subject should be to do with Kings and those of Noble birth, whereas Arthur Miller suggested in his essay ,tragedy and the common man, that he felt the common man was "an apt a subject for tragedy in the highest sense that kings were.' Which is interesting to consider in terms of the development of characters and whether the success of say a play or novel depends on how much as readers, or an audience, we identify with the characters.

This is an interesting and strong answer as the candidate uses the question to make a wider comment on literature. But comparing two suggestions about the characterisation in tragedies the candidate is able to demonstrate their understanding of both tragedy as well as what makes a good character. The reference to the Arthur Miller essay shows a level of wider reading around A-level texts (as the candidate studies the plays of Arthur Miller at A-level, whilst also demonstrating key knowledge about tragedy. This answer also opens up the conversation to go on to talk about relatable characters and could facilitate a development by talking about a specific character such as Hamlet and whether an audience would be able to identify with him.

A **poor applicant** may say: " it's just good trashy tv" The candidate is not considering the wider cultural impact or linking it back to the subject of English. Or a weaker candidate might just say " I don't know I've never seen it" Although it is not required you have seen Coronation Street this then tests your ability to adapt the question to either a popular series you have seen, such as Emmerdale, Casualty etc.

Q56: Why do we study English Literature?

This is a great question to get across your enthusiasm for the subject as well as considering its wider and practical uses.

A **good applicant** may say: I think English Literature is a multifaceted subject. For me I find the way that literature can typify a genre, mood or time period fascinating. It gives you the ability to understand and consider different viewpoints , such as by reading novels like the Colour Purple or watching plays by Arthur Miller like Death of a Salesman or All my Sons. Taking the Colour Purple for an example, the reader is able to engage in a life that may be radically different from their own. They are being given insight into the life of someone who is LGBTQ+ or someone who is black, or even insight into life as a woman. Something that may be far from their personal reality and experience. There are also key skills that develop from it such as inference and analysis skills, essay writing with evidence and close reading of texts and perspective.

This is a good answer because it shows enthusiasm for the subject and demonstrates wider reading. There is also a consideration of practical skills that the subject offers that shows that the candidate understands what is required of an English undergraduate and also how that learning can then be transferred. By picking a specific novel to explore and example it shows that the candidate's answer is thoughtful and considered. This allows the interviewer to see the candidate's engagement in the course rather than just seeing it simply as something that might lead them to a specific job in the future.

A **poor applicant** may say " because it is compulsory on the syllabus and most jobs require good English." Although these things are true, there is no passion for the subject conveyed. Why is it compulsory? Why is the subject so highly valued in the job market?

Q57: Would you be able to link poetry to music and other forms of media?

This question is asking you to consider poetry and media side by side and gives you the opportunity to make some interesting links between the topics as well as space to talk about the poetry/music/media that you like and are interested in. It is a great question to demonstrate your knowledge of poetry and specific features and functions of it.

A good candidate may say: Historically music and poetry have been linked particularly because of the lyrical nature of poetry and vice versa with the poetic nature of lyrics. For example, looking at the way I am by Eminem using anapaestic verse for example shows you how closely interlinked poetry and music is. Something else that I find really interesting is how poetry has become quite 'trendy; in recent years with the likes of Rupi Kaur's poetry. I was reading an article the other day about how her poetry anthology Milk and Honey outsold Homer's Odyssey. Having read both it is easy to see one may be considered more accessible and Aesthetic than the other. Kaur's poems can be considered "more instagrammable" and before we condemn this generation for not liking the odyssey, I think what struck me most about this too is how poetry has become art and an expression in an accessible way to people which is fascinating.

This is a good answer because it shows consideration of specific examples such as Eminem, where there is potential to go into more detail about scansion and Eminem's use of it whether it is intentional or accidental. By referring to an article you've read this demonstrates an enthusiasm for the subject it may be beneficial to read a literary journal for example to widen your own scope of reading and understanding. The candidate also considers the modern reader and what they want to gain from a poem and comments on the modern reader's want of aesthetics in poetry.

A **poor applicant** may say: "poetry and music link because they both rhyme. And the media also links in as it is all to do with writing and expression." This is a weaker answer as it is simplistic in its approach. The answer would be stronger if it considered in depth the characteristics that poetry and music share such as rhythm and rhyme. It would be of value to make a comment on the uses of those techniques and effect and whether the two forms have links there or further differences.

Q58: What do you think about ambiguity?

This is a great question to bring in different texts you've read and ambiguities in them. It is also good to talk about authorial intent and whether you feel ambiguity is a necessary part of literature.

A **good applicant** may say: I guess it would depends on the context, if we are referring to ambiguity in literature then my opinion would be that sometimes ambiguity is necessary. I feel that ambiguity leaves room for more debate and discussion. Take for example the ending of Ian McEwan's novel Atonement, the ending is ambiguous, and it becomes the role of the reader to make their own decision on what happened. This can be frustrating sometimes but ultimately, that is what the author will have intended. Again, taking the example of Atonement, I felt that the ambiguous ending was McEwan's way of tricking the reader into misreading as the protagonist does, and having to form a judgement on unclear endings. So sometimes it is necessary but frustrating. Whereas say for example most Jane Austen novels have that happy ending like in *Northanger Abbey* or *Pride and Prejudice*. Both Ian McEwan and Jane Austen are considered classic writers, but Jane Austen has that 'happy ending' that sometimes people are looking for.

This is a good answer because it draws on two contrasting examples and compares them in order to evidence the point. By considering authorial intent the candidate is able to bring in to question people's motivations for reading and takes that into consideration. This answer would be able to springboard the interview in to conversations about either of the texts or a more general conversation about why we read and whether ambiguity is necessary for specific genres.

A **poor applicant** may say: "I hate it when literature is ambiguous, I just want to know what it means and what happens at the end." This answer doesn't not consider the purpose ambiguity may hold in a novel or play for example. There is no consideration of authorial intention. `Why has the Author written it this way? What wider point does the ambiguity make light of? A good way to answer this question is by comparing two texts that are on either side in order to evaluate why ambiguity is used.

Q59: Can literature be bad for you?

This is a great question to discuss the different types of literature and demonstrate your wider reading. There is a lot of potential to talk about novels/plays/poems you've read as well as consider the purpose and uses of literature. It is possibly a good idea to outline the word 'bad' and evaluate what the interviewer means when they ask this- it is perfectly reasonable to ask them what they mean with the use of the word bad in the context of this question. You could also outline how you are interpreting 'bad'.

A **good applicant** may say: It depends on how we interpret the word 'bad'. Ultimately, I don't think the consuming of literature can be inherently bad even if the literature isn't 'good'. For example, the books of the Fifty Shades of Grey series have been read by millions, but I read a review that said it was terrible writing, but to me, any books that get people to read are good. I think we should avoid the elitist notion that there are good and bad texts when it is subjective. Just because we assign value to a piece of literature based on how 'good' we think it is doesn't mean that another piece of literature is therefore "bad". I guess it depends on what we are looking to gain from literature in the first place.

This is a good answer because it considers the nature of literature and why we read for example. The candidate offers an interesting take on the modern and highly popular book Fifty Shades of Grey and there is potential here to draw comparisons to novels such as Lady Chatterley's Lover which contains smut for example. The candidate fully answers the question and gives their opinion and offers interpretation of the word 'bad' from the question. This is a good technique as it allows the candidate to manipulate the question in order to talk about subjects that they feel more confident in speaking about.

A **poor applicant** may say: " bad literature is bad for you." The candidate needs to take into consideration that literature is subjective, what one person considers bad may be praised by another. Even within the realms of the canon, some classic novels aren't liked. The candidate may also need to take into consideration why we read literature and what we hope to gain from it.

Q60: What makes a classic a 'classic'?

This is a great question to discuss features of novels and the canon and bring into the discussion both texts that you have read in your studies, as well as in your wider reading. It would be good to draw on your knowledge of the canon and what the key features of novels that are included in it after.

A **good applicant** may say: From my understanding a classic or canonical text is generally regarded to meet high standards of quality of writing, appeal, longevity and influence. It is these high standards that also generally make the novel acceptable to study. But this has pitfalls in how long it takes for a novel thus to be of value. I would argue that in some cases a modern novel can be more pertinent than an older novel because it is more relevant to the modern day. I agree that a 'classic' novel should be eloquently written and deal with pertinent and philosophical content and still have longevity. For example, Margaret Atwood's novel, The Handmaid's Tale has had much cultural success and is taught in schools and gets the label a "modern classic' as it should. I feel there is more space for female and BAME authors in the canon which has historically be dominated by white males.

This is a good answer because the candidate outlines their knowledge of canonical literature and draws on wider reading. The answers shows an in-depth understanding of the qualities that make a book classic as well as passing their own opinions on the question. By questioning the exclusivity of the canon, the candidate gives themselves a spring board to talk about different authors of different genders, race and ethnicity.

A **poor applicant** may say: "a classic novel is a really old book that we are taught in schools and are very well liked." This argument doesn't characterise what it means for a novel to be classic. It is important to draw on the subjectivity of literature and question who gets to choose what is good or classic and what isn't as no one is able to consider all the books in the world and thus which is the most value.

Q61: Is an aptitude for rhythm valuable when writing poetry or prose?

This is a great question to explore the role and effect of scansion in poetry. It is important to understand what ,both, scansion and rhythm are and how they can be differentiated. Rhythm can be defined as the pattern of stressed and unstressed syllables in a line. Whereas scansion is the words we use to describe the pattern of rhythm by dividing the lines into feet, then differentiating the stressed and unstressed syllables by marking them and counting the syllables in the lines. Then to speculate how this can be applied to prose. If you enjoy writing poetry you could also mention that in this question and refer to your own approach to rhythm when writing poetry.

A **good applicant** may say: I think an understanding of rhythm is important when writing poetry and these techniques can add to the meaning of the poem. Such as in Tennyson's famous use of dactylic diameter in 'Charge of the Light Brigade' and how it mirrors the sounds of horses in the charge. But ultimately it would depend on the style of poetry you were trying to write and the message that you were trying to convey. Even then, an irregular use of rhythm requires a good knowledge of rhythm. But the absence of a strong sense of rhythm can equally be manipulated to create tone in a poem. Free verse poems such as a personal favourite Daddy by Sylvia Plath, don't have a strong strength of rhythm but arguably this is not because the poets are unaware of it. In terms of prose, although the rigid sense of rhythm found in poetry doesn't really apply, novels have techniques that can be used to either speed up or slow down the reader and I feel like that impacts the rhythm of prose, such as polysndetic listing or lots of dashes, can affect the speed at which we read and that is often done purposefully to create a specific tone for the piece of prose.

This is a good answer because it shows a solid grasp of scansion and the effect it can have on the rhythm of poetry. By comparing two examples, the candidate is able to demonstrate their wider reading as well as a strong understanding of poetic techniques. The candidate also speculates on how the rhythm of poetry can transfer to prose and do so confidently. This answer draws specific parallels to rhythm in poetry and how this is reflected in prose by comparing specific techniques that create similar effects.

A **poor applicant** may say: "Rhythm isn't important to writing poetry, I never take it in to consideration when I write my poetry and its really good" This is a poor answer as it doesn't consider the role rhythm can potentially play in poetry. Even if the candidate feels it is unimportant, they could draw on poems that don't use a strong sense of rhythm to evidence their point, such as free verse poems, and deliberate on whether it would still require a certain understanding of rhythm to even write a poem that lacks it.

Q62: Do you think that English students should learn about the life of an author when evaluating their work?

This is a great question to explore the concept of formalist critics and draw on your wider reading to evaluate this question. A good essay to refer to in this question is Roland Barthes essay *Death of the Author*.

A **good applicant** may say: To a certain extent, the context of an author can often play a large role in their work, such as T.S Eliot writing war poetry, because he was writing at the time of war. But I understand the argument that sometimes we can get lost in what the authorial intention is by assuming based on their life. Sometimes there needs to be space to consider the work in its own right, to allow for a deeper understanding of the texts its self not the history of the author. By adding historical context or authorial context we can often view say a poem in a completely different light. Ultimately I would argue that an author's life is important when looking at a. text to a certain extent but it shouldn't be the only reading of the text we take into account, it should be considered valuable in its own right, so I wouldn't completely agree with what Roland Barthes argues in his essay Death of the Author.

A **poor applicant** may say " yes because it is only by looking at the author's life we can understand and shape meaning of the text." This is a poor answer because it doesn't consider the pitfalls of only considering the author's life when shaping meaning of a text. There is potential for analysis to be carried away with what evidence we get from the history or context and the personal meanings of the texts can get lost. It is also impossible for us to confirm that even by looking at the author's life, that this specific life event shaped this text it could be completely different unless the author has explicit stated this fact.

Q63: If you had to choose between a novel and a poem, which would you rather be?

This is a great question to discuss the nature and form of poetry or novels. It would also be a great question to demonstrate your own passions and wider reading. Particularly if you have spoken a lot about novels in the rest of your interview, this question could give you the opportunity to talk about poetry (or vice versa) to show a range of wider reading.

A **good applicant** may say: I would rather be a poem because I feel like there is so much variation in poetry. Novels are generally one length, but poems can be epic poem, and be as long as a novel, or there are haikus. Poetry gives spaces for more manipulation of linguistics and form. I particularly love modernist poetry, especially Mina Loy and I think her manipulation of form and semiotics is so interesting. Her poem parturition is such beautiful and complex to read and understand, quite like humans in a sense. She uses the form to mirror contractions and like a general ebb and flow and I think it is fascinating she is able to do that within the bounds of a poem.

This is a strong answer as the candidate demonstrates a knowledge of the characteristics of poetry. By drawing on their own favourite genre of poetry, the candidate demonstrates wider reading and enthusiasm for the subject, particularly if the poetry is not taught on a school syllabus. The candidate shows a deep understanding g of the different genres' and forms of poetry as well as the connotations and uses.

A **poor applicant** may say "I'd rather be a poem because they're shorter and quicker to read" this is a poor answer as it is not necessarily true. The candidate shows a weak grasp on the difference even in poems, for example epic poems , haikus all come under the bracket of poems but are drastically different lengths. The candidate could explore the different connotations of different poems.

Q64: Can stories be intrinsically immoral?

This is a good question to compare texts and their reception over time in order to show an understanding or the question as well a demonstrates a wide range of reading outside your A-level studies.

A **good applicant** may say: there's a famous quote by Oscar Wilde from his book The Picture of Dorian Gray that says that there's no such thing as a moral or immoral book. He says that books are basically either badly or well written. I think this is reference to the fact that The Picture of Dorian Gray was considered immoral because it was homoerotic and suggestive. So personally, in today's climate, there is no space for this label I mean especially with the wide spread popularity of say Fifty Shades of Grey maybe more similar to the Picture of Dorian Gray there's the Call Me by Your Name book that is critically acclaimed and focuses on the gay relationship between the two main characters. I would say there can be immoral themes in books, but the story itself is not immoral, just the contents. But even then, what is immoral is completely subjective.

This is a good answer because the candidate is able to draw on their knowledge of other texts and quotes to support their answer. What the candidate is able to do is draw on their knowledge of modern texts as well in order to make a comment on how what is considered moral has changed over time. It also shows a breadth of reading if you are able to compare texts over time.

A **poor applicant** may say " yes, erotic novels are complete immoral". This is a poor answer as it shows a potential intolerance to some literature without reason. It is probably best to not come across as intolerant in your interview. An interviewer is looking for someone who has opinions but is able to understand and explore other opinions as well.

Q65: Do you have a favourite word?

There is no right or wrong answer to this question. It doesn't even have to be the longest or most complicated word you know. It is a good idea to have something to say past the fact you like it. Talk about its uses, maybe how its use has changed or how it can have different meanings. You could also talk about how you use it and how often or maybe where you first heard/ read it.

A **good applicant** may say: My favourite word is probably iridescence because of just the way it sounds but also the beauty of what it can be describing. I like the link to Iris, the Greek goddess of the rainbow, who basically took messages from Mount Olympus to earth, and from gods to mortals or other gods, using the rainbow as her stairway. And that is where the word stems from, the glowing, shifting, colourful quality of a rainbow, also seen in an opal, a light oil slick, a butterfly wing, or the mother-of-pearl that lines an oyster shell.

This is a good answer because the candidate is able to give both a definition and extra information to their answer. The historical background shows a level of enthusiasm to learning as the candidate has clearly searched and remembered the etymology of the word.

A **poor applicant** may say "I don't have a favourite word there's too many" or suggest a swear word. It would be a bold move to suggest a swear word when asked this question, but it is difficult to judge how this would be received by an interviewer. It is also a good idea to answer the question even if you don't have a favourite word, it shows decisiveness. It would be possible for the student to deliberate and consider a few words.

Q66: How would you define poetry, and can you think of any 'poems' which don't fit your definition?

This is a great question to bring your wider reading into the conversation as well as showing your deeper understanding of what characteristics and forms poetry can take. It may be helpful to draw on several different examples to compare on contrast your point.

A **good applicant** may say: I once read a quote from Edgar Allen Poe, where he said that 'Poetry is the revelation of a feeling that the poet believes to be interior and personal which the reader recognizes as his own,' and he said he would define the Poetry of words as the 'Rhythmical Creation of Beauty.' I would definitely agree that poems can be rhythmical creations of beauty, but I don't think rhythm is integral to poetry. If we took what Poe says as the definition free verse poems such as Tulips by sylvia Plath wouldn't count as a poetry. I really enjoy free verse poetry such as some of the works of H.D and Mina Loy and I feel that a lack of rhythm is as inherent in poetry as rhyme. I don't think there is a particular definition for poetry, other than the work of a poet or someone who writes poetry. You could probably narrow the definition down to a piece of text or writing that express a thought, feeling or emotion that pays a particular attention to how the message is conveyed possible using a combination of techniques such as (but not limited to) Rhyme, rhythm and imagery. There's such a vast difference between Milton's Epic poem Paradise Lost and No Man Is an Island by John Donne in terms of techniques and style, but both are still considered poetry. So, it would be difficult to name any poems that wouldn't fit my definition. I have found the emerging popularity of the poet Rupi Kaur fascinating, particularly as her anthology *Milk and Honey* outsold the Odyssey and those two poems are so vastly different but still are under the umbrella term of poetry. I have had this debate before as to whether Kaur's poems can actually be considered poetry as they seem more like fragmentary lines and words pushed together. However, once you understand that Kaur draws influence for her work from a mix of ancient and eastern poets as well imagist poets such as Ezra Pound and Amy Lowell, it becomes clearer that she just has a different style of poetry.

This is a strong answer as the candidate draws on lots of examples that demonstrate lots of wide reading and a keen interest in poetry. They show a developed understanding of the characteristics of poetry and offer commentary on this. The quote by Edgar Allen Poe is an excellent touch, although it is not required to know quotes off by heart, they can be para-phrased but what they do is show that candidate has stretched themselves further than readings their required texts but to also consider literary criticism. The balance between older and more contemporary poets is also a good way of demonstrating a diverse range of wider reading.

A **weaker candidate** may say: 'Poems usually rhyme and have a strong sense of rhythm. Poems that don't have these key characteristics are probably not poetry.' This is a poor answer as the poet only identifies some features of poetry and doesn't consider free verse poetry. It would also be beneficial for this candidate to draw on some examples to back up their argument.

Q67: Do you think that language can change the way that people think? Would exclusively speaking English make us in any way different from people who speak another language?

This would be a great question to talk about how language influences us, the way we speak and interact with others. It may be beneficial to bring the subject of literature into this and consider how language affects the subject, drawing on texts possibly from different languages you have come across or literature that has been translated.

A **strong candidate** may say: I listened to an interesting podcast about this and linguistic relativity the other day. I definitely think language can changed the way the way we think for example, some languages may have more or better words for expression, such as how Innuits have around 50 words for snow whereas we just have a couple. Although it might be easier in some aspect if everyone just spoke the same language, in terms of ease of communication, but it would just water down some cultures in my opinion. Particularly in the modern day it is possible that technology facilitates inter-language communication more easily. A book I read recently by Sayaka Murata is translated from its original language Japanese, but it is still a widely popular book. As with any translation some humour may be lost in the process of translation, but I would say that is part of the experience of reading, it gives an insight in to a completely different culture that may have been out of reach before.

This is a good answer as the candidate shows a real developed understanding of use of language and the effects it can have. By bringing in a podcast or documentary for example, this demonstrates the candidate thirst for knowledge and readiness to go out and learn independently. The references to translated texts is a really interesting element to the answer and shows a breadth of wider reading and this is he furthered by the evidence of research and interest in that text.

A **poor candidate** may say: 'It would be so much better if everyone just spoke the same language then it would be easier when I go on holiday!' This is a poor answer as it does not show a developed understanding or consideration of the use or value of language. It important to also try and link questions back to the topic of English to show an awareness of the subject and why the interviewer may be asking you that specific question. What do they want to learn about you and the way you think from asking this question?

Q68: How do you think not having a written language would change the way that English is used?

Humans have only been known to have formally had written language for the past 5000 or so years so it is key in this question to consider the past and present as well as show an understanding of the impact and change that has occurred because of written language had over time.

A **good applicant** may say: written language is a massive part of English, especially the subject of English literature- it's completely based on written language. There are more aspects to written language than just books say for example letters, emails, posters even recipes. The written language is everywhere and makes up such a vital part of society and communication. Without written language, I think life would generally be less developed and information would take longer to spread. Take for example the way Religious texts and stories were first circulated by the oral tradition, this was advantageous at the tome as it was suitable for even members of society who were illiterate but it does mean that there are some inconsistency within stories as the Narrator has complete control over the final narrative. For example, the bible was written 40 years after the death of Christ, so circulated orally for all that time, so some people use that to account for potential inconsistencies.

This is a good answer as the candidate draws on historical and religious examples of texts. He answer is considered and the candidate clearly establishes examples of written language and its current uses. The student makes a decisive approach to the question as well as linking their answer to the subject of English-How would the subject exist without formal written language?

A **poor candidate** may say: 'we wouldn't be able to write things down so everyone would have to speak everything. English wouldn't be formally written.' This is a poor answer as the candidate doesn't offer any examples to back up their argument nor do they consider the difference between written and oral language and the affect that has on society.

TESTS, ESSAYS & PERSONAL STATEMENTS

Written Tests

It is crucial to have a tool-kit or checklist of techniques at your fingertips for analysing poetry, prose, and drama effectively in order to compare, contrast, and comment upon different extracts. You should always be thinking about how to explore form and structure (syntax, metre, versification, scansion) as well as language (imagery, motifs, similes, metaphors). **Try and practice your timed essay technique** and find ways to use your observations as evidence for a powerful argument, noticing what links are apparent rather than just a list of random feature-spotting. Remember, these selected texts will be set because the examiners want you to notice distinctive features, make connections and interesting arguments: look for overlapping themes or juxtaposing techniques, keeping an eye out for examples of the traditional and the subversive. You could pick up an anthology of poetry, prose or drama and pick interlinked texts at random to practice: what is similar or different about them?

Essay + Personal Statement Discussions

Read and reread your personal statement and make sure you have interesting things to say about your ideas and chosen texts. Try to pre-empt off-kilter interview questions, which will be designed to steer you away from pre-packaged speeches learned before the day itself. **Make sure you have a deep awareness of different periods** and prepare by using anthologies to gain a rough sweep of chronological developments. For instance, if you mention liking T.S. Eliot's poetry, you might be asked which other modernist poets you have read and how these have deepened your understanding of what it really means to be a 'modernist poet'. Is this a useful categorisation or not?

Expect the interviewers to undermine your arguments and to push you into defending or adapting your beliefs. Go back over texts you might not have studied for a long time and try and develop, or argue against, your ideas, which might have changed over time if you have read more widely.

Be Inventive

The interviewers may have heard forty interviewees discuss revenge in *Hamlet* or the radicalness of Jack Kerouac's *On the Road*. Why not talk about *Pericles* or *Timon of Athens* or Shakespeare's poetry – *The Rape of Lucrece* is an excellent accompaniment to *Titus Andronicus* – instead? If you are fascinated by the Beat Generation, look further than the obvious texts: make an effort to explore the writing of other ground-breaking writers like Hunter S. Thompson or William Burroughs, comparing and contrasting how their formal techniques can be used to investigate similar themes. Follow your natural interests to the furthest extreme and you will be surprised at how enjoyable the interview can be.

Branch out from your set texts and you will show off your own drive to read and study. Talk about different mediums if you feel they illuminate your discussion from films to plays, to song lyrics. For example, you could talk about how a certain set design or production aesthetic changed your understanding of a play, such as the recent all-female *Julius Caesar* at the Donmar Warehouse.

GEOGRAPHY & EARTH SCIENCES

If you're applying to Geography, it is important that you prepare for both human and physical geography questions since you could be asked questions on either sub-field. If you're applying for Natural Sciences at Cambridge (with the aim of studying Earth Sciences) or Earth Sciences at Oxford, you are also likely to have a course-work related interview.

- This interview will require you to demonstrate passion and a genuine desire to study your chosen subject. You will be asked to discuss a source extract, a diagram, or even an object depending on the subject you are applying for. You may not recognise the text you have been asked to read, but that is probably deliberate.

- The tutors know what subjects you have studied at A-Level. They will not ask you for detailed knowledge about areas of your subject that you are not familiar with. Nobody knows every aspect of their subject.

- **Apply the knowledge you have acquired at A-Level** and from your wider reading to unfamiliar scenarios. Feel confident to make references to academics whose works you have read, this shows that not only did you read widely, but you can also pinpoint specific researchers and apply this to questions they ask.

- If you begin by answering and you realise that you actually want to take a different direction, ask to start again. It's ok to change your mind. In order to help you avoid making any unnecessary comments, always take a few seconds to think about your response before saying it out loud. This will give you time to formulate your thoughts and arrange them in a logical order that you can then present before the interviewers.

- Remember, **making mistakes is no bad thing**. The important point is that you address the mistake head on and attempt to revise the statement, perhaps with the assistance of the tutors where necessary.

- The interviewers want to see students are willing and able to elaborate on their answers, so if you have something crucial to add when responding to a question, make sure to include it. At the same time, make sure not to keep on rambling when you have noted all the crucial points that directly address the question asked.

Being accepted into Oxbridge is not determined by how much you know, but by how well you think and how analytical your thought-processes and responses are.

WHAT QUESTIONS MIGHT BE ASKED?

Most of the questions asked in the interview will begin with a larger question, followed by many smaller sub-questions to guide the answer from start to end. The main question may seem difficult, impossible or random at first, but take a breath and start discussing with your interviewer different ideas you have for breaking down the question into manageable pieces. Don't panic. **The questions are designed to be difficult** to give you the chance to show your full intellectual potential. They will help guide you to the right idea if you provide ideas for them to guide.

This is your chance to show your creativity, analytical skills, intellectual flexibility, problem-solving skills, and your go-getter attitude. Don't waste it on nervousness or a fear of messing up or looking stupid. It is also important to remember that especially for a subject like Geography, **answers are often more complex and multifaceted than a simple yes or no**. This should give you some reassurance during the interview process that your responses can take one direction but also refer to anomalies or include instances where the response would be different. If this is the case, make sure to elaborate on why a response could be both yes and no, and under which circumstances.

GEOGRAPHY

For Geography, at some point in the interview, **questions will likely draw on data** (for example graphs, diagrams or photographs). These types of questions are used to test whether you are able to analyse trends, make sense of the information and therefore apply it to a real-world context. It is worthwhile using a two-step process to answer data-related questions which will give you time to think of a response if you are unsure of what to say, as well as allowing you to provide a clear and well-formulated answer. The first part of your response should describe what you see, for example; 'this graph demonstrates an X trend with a greater clustering of points towards a certain axis'. The second part of your response should comment on why the graph looks that way; for example, why does one trend rise as the other falls?

For geography, in particular, **questions have recurring themes** because they pose critical issues for both geographical research and policy makers: climate change, glacial melt, and also questions exploring the overlap between human and physical geography, for example, conservation and ecosystem loss. The interviewers want to see that you can think analytically (meaning how well you can unpack a given question and how you think of varying possibilities and topics relevant to the response), and how you can think critically (meaning whether you can identify the flaws in certain arguments or data sets and what reasons could be provided for these).

EARTH SCIENCES

No previous subject knowledge is necessary, although you'll be expected to be comfortable with the core sciences i.e. have studied at least 2 of Physics, Chemistry and Biology to A2 level.

It is important to keep in mind that the aim is to understand **how the earth functions in the manner that it does**, what led to its processes, how different processes can be interlinked, and what their influences are on the physical formations and natural landscapes we see around us. The subject also touches on pressing concerns including the urgent problem of climate change, as well as sourcing water, coal, oil, and minerals.

COURSEWORK INTERVIEWS

When applying to do Geography or Earth Sciences/Natural Sciences at Cambridge, an applicant may be asked to submit coursework and be called for a coursework interview. Usually, in the morning on the day of the interview, this work is submitted and read by the interviewer. The work is used as a basis for discussion of research and experimental methods and analysis.

The interviewer may open by asking for a summary of the piece of work, they might open a discussion about certain ideas that you mention, or they might want to understand how you reached your conclusions.

They may then ask some follow-up questions related to the work or the subject matter. This part of the interview will be very individual and depends on the nature and subject of the work submitted.

After the discussion of the work, the interviewer will probably guide the conversation toward some questions about a related topic to test the applicant's ability to think like a Geographer/Earth Scientist.

WORKED QUESTIONS

Below are a few examples of how to start breaking down an interview question, complete with model answers.

Q1: This map displays a distribution relating to a natural hazard event. What do you think the natural hazard is and what do you think the map is showing in relation to it?

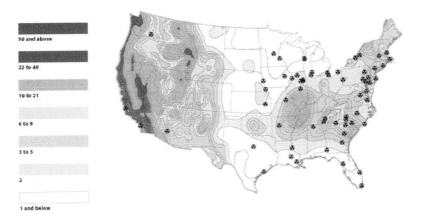

[Extremely clear-headed] **Applicant**: Well, I can tell that this is a map of North America. At a purely descriptive level, it is evident from the map that there is a higher concentration of the natural event on the west coast than on the east coast. There is also a notable hotspot located on the continent's south-western region. It could be that **darker shades represent a higher incidence of events** in particular areas like the California region. On the other hand, darker colours could also refer to places in which the effects of the hazard are more pronounced.

Before suggesting what the natural hazard could be, I want to first provide a definition of the term. The definition of natural hazards on the World Meteorological Organisation website is useful for an overall definition, refers to 'events that occur naturally in all parts of the world, with some regions being more vulnerable to certain hazards than others'.

From my knowledge of common natural hazards in California, I would say this map shows the **distribution of earthquake events**. Darker zones probably point to areas where earthquakes are more common. A different distribution which the colours may represent could be the regions most affected by ground shaking following an earthquake, and those that are less affected.

The details are unimportant, but the general idea of breaking down the question into manageable parts is important. Notice how a better applicant begins by describing what he sees in order to provide directions for his upcoming explanation and to guide his interviewer through his thought process. The interviewer is not looking for a natural hazard expert, but someone who can problem-solve in the face of new ideas. Note that even though the question begins with 'What', it is actually expecting you to consider '**Why**' certain distributions look the way they do. The point of these questions is to suggest different ideas and to show an ability to use data usefully.

A **poor applicant** may take a number of approaches unlikely to impress the interviewer. The first and most obvious of these is to say "We were not taught about natural hazards in America at school" and make no attempt to move forward anyway. It is worth providing some sort of logical response rather than giving up completely. The **interviewer is likely to help you by asking follow-up questions**, especially if they see you showing a genuine interest and if you make an obvious attempt at some sort of response that is headed in the right direction (for example, even just providing a description of what you see will be better than giving up altogether).

Another approach which is unhelpful in the interview is the 'brain dump', where instead of engaging with the question, the applicant attempts to impress or distract with an assortment of related facts: "Natural hazards are geographical events that occur naturally across the world. These become natural disasters when there is a chance for populations to be affected/at risk". This isn't as impressive as a more reasoned response.

Nevertheless, the interview could be salvaged by taking feedback from the interviewer. This would depend on the applicant's attentiveness and ability to take hints and suggestions from the interviewer.

Q2: How do human and physical geography overlap?

A question such as this is a classic way of integrating the two main streams found in Geography, and to test whether you can provide a concise response to a very broad question.

You could begin by speaking about how **each stream is integral to the other**, resulting in them both being inherently intertwined.

While human geography strives to understand how societies organise and why they organise in certain ways, physical geography strives to understand how natural systems operate and why they function in certain ways. To understand topics more cohesively, such as conservation and climate change, you need an appreciation of how physical and environmental systems function, as well as how these understandings can be applied to societies in social, political, and economic terms.

At the same time, it is important to consider the manner in which human societies affect their environments and what the short, medium, and long-term implications are of these social activities.

It would be useful to note the real-life instances in which these two streams overlap, for example, when policy makers use scientific information to implement policies that affect our lives (i.e. encouraging the use of public transport rather than personal vehicles to reduce CO_2 emissions).

A more advanced response may touch on the gap that exists between both streams, as social and natural scientists often fail to communicate effectively with one another. One example of this may be evident in the plethora of research on **climate change** existing today, and the lack of ability to communicate this to much of the population in ways that makes them understand the implications of their actions. You could then briefly discuss what other implications this gap may pose for societies.

Q3: Why is the concept of 'space' important in Geography?

This is an example of a more theoretical/philosophical question that could be asked in an interview situation, and certainly during your undergraduate career. Start with more simple and basic concepts and build from there.

First, address the concept of space. The more obvious notion of the term implies a **physical or rooted place/location**. This is important in Geography in terms of pinpointing certain locations and analysing their physical facets.

At a closer look, we can say that the concept of space in Geography is important for understanding how humans interact with the physical features of the land. For example, one place can be used differently by different people and for various purposes. Therefore, understanding space is vital in order to understand the meaning of why certain relations arise between people, arise in specific locales, and how they impact on economic and political institutions.

Q4: Why is it that in some developing countries, slum settlements have sprung up near wealthier neighbourhoods?

Before answering this question, it is useful to consider **what the term 'developing countries' refers to**. Today, many developing countries are those located in the Global South which are typically less economically and socially advanced than Western countries. However, it is also important to keep in mind that the development trajectory of each region and nation varies significantly.

That said, there are certain patterns evident across most developing countries. The emergence of slums in these countries largely refers to informal settlements in urban areas characterised by substandard housing and squalor, including unreliable sanitation services and electricity. Often, the people living in slums have arrived from rural regions of the country in search of better employment and other opportunities. The only places they can afford to live in are the ones they create themselves.

By positioning themselves near wealthy hubs, poorer settlements are able to benefit from access to various established services such as electricity and water, which they could even tap into illegally. They also have **easier access** to employment, healthcare, and educational opportunities than they would if they were in poorer neighbourhoods.

Q5: Estimate the mass of the oceans.

You can state at the beginning that calculating this accurately depends on the data you have to work with. Since this is an estimation question, you don't need to worry about being precise – rounding numbers is perfectly acceptable. An interviewer wants to see what your thought process is - they are less concerned with receiving a specific number. **It's the journey- not the destination that matters.**

The key part to providing a coherent response is knowing which key factors you need to identify for the calculation to be made. Start by breaking down the question:

Firstly, recall that Mass = Density x Volume
You should know that the density of water is 1,000 kg/m³.
The Volume of the oceans is trickier. The easiest way is to make a series of assumptions:
The Surface Area of a sphere $= 4\pi r^2$
You could then ask the interviewer for the Earth's radius (6,000 km) or use a sensible estimate.
Approximate $\pi = 3$ to give:

$$Area \ = \ 4 \times 3 \times (6 \times 10^6)^2$$
$$Area \ = \ 12 \times 36 \times 10^{12}$$
$$= 432 \times 10^{12} \approx 4 \times 10^{14} \ m^2$$

Approximately 75% of the Earth's Surface Area is covered by the Oceans, so the surface area of the oceans $= \ 4 \times 10^{14} \times 75\% = 3 \times 10^{14} \ m^2$
Finally, you need to convert the area into a volume by multiplying it via an average depth of the oceans. Again, any sensible estimate would be fine here (100 m – 10,000m).

Volume of Oceans $= 3 \times 10^{14} \times 1,000 = 3 \times 10^{17} m^3$
Thus, Mass of Oceans $= 3 \times 10^{17} \times 1,000 = 3 \times 10^{20} kg$
Real Answer: 1.4×10^{21} kg

Q6: How do mountains originate?

Geography Applicant: It is important to note at the outset that mountain formation is a phenomenon unique to the specific geography and previous conditions of a given location. That said, there are specific processes that, in general, lead to the formation of mountains.

One example is mountains originating from **fault-line movements**. For example, if a fault exists where both sections push against each other and one rock mass is moving up while the other is moving down, then the upward moving rock mass may form a mountain as it gets pushed up.
Mountains can also originate from volcanic eruptions. This can occur as rock builds up from an explosion, as magma solidifies, and thirdly, as the earth's crust heaves upwards (due to the pressure of the explosion), eventually forming a mountain. Triggers for fault line movements and volcanic eruptions are often unknown and may be the result of several processes occurring within deeper layers of the earth's structure.

In all cases, it is important to note that for mountains to form there needs to be an external trigger that allows for sufficient matter and mass to mobilise in order to create such a phenomenon. Also, while in most cases the process is rather gradual (fault-mountains), in some, the process can be more sudden (volcanic eruptions).

Q7: How do mountains originate? (Earth Sciences)

Earth Sciences Applicant: Answering this question would involve suggesting possible scenarios and important parameters. For example, a candidate could begin by explaining that mountain formation is associated with large-scale movements of the earth's crust (making a distinction at the onset between the layers of the earth which could result in such formations). Then one could discuss the various factors that lead to mountain formation, for example, volcanic eruptions and tectonic movements, perhaps providing a brief description/example of how these processes result in mountain formation.

It would then be useful to comment on the timescale and explain how mountains tend to organise over a very long timescale (e.g. due to gradual tectonic movements) or can be formed more suddenly (e.g. during volcanic eruptions). The point of these questions is to **suggest different ideas**, and to show an understanding of their strengths and weaknesses, as well as an ability to use data usefully.

Crucially, the point of these types of questions is for you to address the key terms (notably volcanoes, **global** climate), first by defining and describing them, and later by explaining their influences in a logical manner.

Q8: What is the point of conservation?

Before considering the aim of conservation, it is important to first understand that it is a loaded term. As such, it could be argued that a loose definition is most appropriate to explain the term. Many definitions include a normative judgment about how the world should be, in other words, what nature should be like given human relations to natural environments. Perhaps one of the most all-encompassing definitions is the one provided by Adams in his 2013 publication. This definition refers to conservation as a "social practice that reflects choices about relations between people and nature".

Given this preliminary understanding, we can see that **the 'point' of conservation is very context specific**. Therefore, its aim very much depends on the people carrying out conservationist activities and the ecosystem in question. Given this, conservation aims will include various parameters such as the economic betterment of involved actors, or the environmental preservation of local species, or perhaps the social inclusiveness of local people in environmental programmes.

To summarise, I would say that the point of conservation encompasses the enhancement of relations between nature and people, and the maintenance of this interaction. That said, this heavily depends on the motives of players involved in conservationist activities and the environment in question.

Q9: What effect does an increase in sea level have on coastal morphology, and why does this impact vary geographically?

The area that will see the greatest **morphological impact from sea level** rise is the shore and beach area since it is subject to wave action. Sea level rise is caused to the greatest extent by ocean thermal expansion and glacial melt. Since characteristics of coastal zones vary considerably worldwide, due to: a) the rate of relative sea level rise, b) the type of coastline, and c) human stresses, the geographical impact of sea level rise on coastal morphology varies.

Coastal landforms are extremely sensitive to changes in sea level. The likely outcome of increased sea level rise will be that submerging coastlines will become more extensive and erosion rates will increase along most coastal areas. However, other coastlines, mainly around previously glaciated regions, may see a fall in sea level and as a result, may see coastlines growing rather than retreating. In turn, we see that **different types of coastlines respond differently** to increasing sea level rise, depending on the sensitivity and resilience of the coastline, as well as the human interference implemented. Furthermore, since sea level rise is not uniform across the globe, the response of coastal areas will change depending on the region in question.

It is also essential to consider that existing models of coastal morphology are inadequate in determining responses to sea level rise as they do not take into account the variety of responses and interconnectedness of different processes. Thus, fully determining the extent of geographical variation in coastal geomorphology as a result of sea level rise remains difficult, making it subject to continuing research.

Q10: Define risk.

The field of risk is influenced by two major streams: **positivist and normative**. The former stream sees risks as real events or dangers that can be approached objectively and calculated using probabilities. Meanwhile, the second stream sees risks as being socially constructed. In this sense, the notion of risk becomes a way of dealing with hazards and insecurities. Such variation in opinions makes it difficult to define what a general 'understanding' of risk really is.

Today, in particular among policy makers, the emphasis within risk still relies on it being something calculable, with science remaining at the basis of attempts to reduce the vulnerability of certain populations in the face of hazards. However, this idea that science can provide an understanding of future risk through mathematical predictions is being increasingly challenged, particularly by academics of the social sciences and within the geographic discipline. This is especially because quantitative analysis tends to overlook the short and long term influence of communities likely to be affected by various risks.

According to one of the most prominent risk theorists, known as Beck, risk can be defined as '**the anticipation of catastrophe**'. Alongside other social scientists, Beck has played a key role in advancing a social understanding of risk so that the term can be easily understood by the societies it influences. Therefore, it is becoming increasingly clear that with time, the definition of risk is changing at its core to incorporate the social aspects of the term.

Q11: What is sustainable development?

The definition which I think best encompasses the idea of sustainable development is the one provided by the Brundtland Commission in 1987. It refers to the term as "development which meets the needs of current generations without compromising the ability of future generations to meet their own needs". This definition foregrounds **careful management of resources** in order to facilitate a high quality of life for current and future generations as well.

It is important to remember that sustainable development does not oppose the idea of humans' use of resources and manipulation of natural environments. Sustainable development, in fact, supports such activities, though in a manner which ensures that the integrity of nature's processes is preserved. The preservation of such processes is important since it allows the reproduction of key biological resources and cycles on which humans depend for sustenance.

Furthermore, it is necessary to consider that sustainable development can be divided into separate, yet intricately connected, subdivisions. For example, development may be economically sustainable, though socially unsustainable. Therefore, for development to be considered truly sustainable, it must encompass the following pillars; social, economic, political, and environmental.

Q12: How do cities act as sources of resilience in an era of heightened risk?

Before providing a response, you need to address two key aspects of the question: the **definition of resilience** and an understanding of what an 'era of heightened risk' refers to. Martin and Sunley (2006) define resilience as the capacity to bounce back to some previous state following a disruption to the system. Resilience is also about a system being able to withstand total collapse, during which some parts will inevitably become damaged and others will remain intact. Resilience is not just about the ability to recover to a previous state, it is also about reaching a new state that is arguably more robust than the previous by learning from previous catastrophes and incorporating solutions into the urban environment through infrastructures and by educating citizens. Crucially, redundancy and slack are a key aspect of resilience, referring to the idea of leaving space for the unexpected, having spare capacity. Furthermore, questions of resilience have gained new prominence in our era of heightened risk. This new era of global risks is largely the product of human activities and is worsened by the nature of the interconnected global economy in which we live.

I think the main way in which cities act as sources of resilience in today's world is by combining three central factors: resilient communities, smart infrastructures, and intelligent governance. The first makes references to societies that are characterised by solidarity and altruism in the face of a crisis. The second refers to the hardware, and software, that underpins the functioning of our cities, for example, sewage systems and electricity grids. Intelligent governance is the factor that brings the first two characteristics together, including city leaders, academic communities, and researchers. Resilience then becomes the product of a combination of sophisticated modelling, information based governance, and strong, clear and intelligent urban leadership that creates a sense of community.

In conclusion, we can see that **resilience is the product of humans and non-humans coming together**. Though the relative balance of each factor varies from city to city, and in turn, creates different forms of resilience in each urban community.

Q13: What are the limitations of hazard mapping?

Hazard mapping displays the distribution of hazards according to their geographical location. Such maps are typically created for natural hazards such as earthquakes, volcanoes, landslides, flooding, and tsunamis.

Even so, hazard mapping has several limitations. I will discuss two specific issues. Firstly, and perhaps most importantly, these maps often make no reference to hazards' **potential social impact**; either in terms of human life or economic loss.

At times, this renders hazard maps less useful or understandable for local communities. Another issue is attributable to the uncertainty inherent within natural hazards themselves, in turn, compromising the accuracy of hazard maps. For example, we are still **unable to predict the timescale** of certain hazards, such as volcanic eruptions, given that we cannot always identify which forces trigger their manifestation. Furthermore, inaccuracies in modelling tools create uncertainties in mapping, again, limiting the applicability of such maps for use in warning communities.

Q14: Does cost-benefit analysis (CBA) helps us make difficult decisions with regards to the environment?

This isn't a simple yes/no question – it requires that you address both sides of the argument.

A cost-benefit analysis is a useful tool for making difficult decisions with regards to the environment since it breaks down issues into separate factors. These can then be quantified with the numerical values of each benefit and cost being used to consider the overall soundness of the project in question. This type of analysis is also good for identifying which players are involved in decision-making and who will win or lose from the proposed project. While this type of analysis is helpful for making difficult decisions, it has its downfalls which must be considered if such a tool is adopted for decision-making. Perhaps the core issue of CBA is that some issues with regards to the environment cannot be quantified. For example, it may be difficult to quantify the aesthetic and spiritual value of environments to their indigenous populations. Furthermore, the outcome of the CBA will largely depend on the player that is carrying out such analysis, with an economic developer likely to place greater positive weighting on the economic benefits of a project, rather than the need for environmental preservation.

Overall, we can see that **CBA is a useful tool for helping us make difficult decisions** with regards to the environment. Even so, it may be necessary to adopt supplementary tools for analysing environmental questions in order to make up for CBA's shortfalls.

Q15: Do you think that access to education lies at the heart of development?

Development loosely refers to processes of social change or class that aim to transform national economies, particularly in formerly colonised countries or countries situated in the global south. Access to education is an important part of a country's development, though, given the complexity of the subject, **it's not possible to isolate one factor** that will on its own assist a country to improve economically, politically, and socially. Furthermore, since each country begins at a different stage of development, its educational needs will vary. For example, in certain countries, the state of healthcare may be so dire that economic productivity may suffer significantly. In this case, healthcare would be a more urgent factor for targeting development. Therefore, education doesn't lie alone at the core of development because the process itself is multifaceted and because it is dependent on the country.

That said, and as also stated by the Campaign for Global Education in 2010, **education remains a focal point for development initiatives** since it is an important catalyst for national economic and social growth. For example, national expenditure on education can be seen to promote development if the investment results in improvements in the quality of labour, which in turn raises GDP over the long term. The importance of education is reiterated by its status as a millennium development goal and it being one of the dimensions for measuring the Human Development Index (HDI). Furthermore, access to education has the capability of acting as an important force for social change and even political transformation (you may wish to reference specific case studies here).

In summary, since development cannot be distilled to one factor alone, it may be more useful to consider in what ways access to education can be used to propel development rather than trying to weigh its relative importance within the development field.

Q16: When it comes to climate change, does the past help us predict the future?

If we look at current publications regarding climate change, there is no doubt that the data collected about past climate trends has been instrumental in making future projections. This is because **paleo-climactic evidence** from the past sheds light onto the emergence and functioning of the Earth's climate system, and what changes it has experienced. This, in turn, suggests what path it might follow in future. In his writings on Paleoclimatology, Bruckner states that past climate reconstructions can then be 'integrated with observations of the Earth's current climate and placed into a computer model to deduce the past and predict future climate'. Additionally, in a social context, using past records is important for identifying what exposes certain physical and human vulnerabilities; which is crucial for climate change forecasting.

While the past is useful in predicting the future, it is important to keep in mind that reasons for changes in climate can be attributable to various sources. In the case of climate change, we must very **carefully analyse the impacts of humans in creating new, unusual climatic patterns**, and the potential consequences of these for society. Following from this, it is important that we are aware that the past will not provide a precise analogue of the future given inherent uncertainties in nature and inaccuracies in our modelling tools. Thus, uncertainties in measurements and forecasting must be acknowledged to ensure that inappropriate actions aren't taken by policy makers.

In sum, while the past is crucial in helping us to understand the potential future trajectory of climate change, various social factors and discrepancies in data need to be accounted for to ensure that projections about climate change's trajectory are more accurate and relevant to today's societies.

Q17: How can volcanic eruptions change global climate?

Answering this question can begin with recognition of the meaning of global climate. Since our planet's climate is comprised of a complex mixture of processes and elements, any significant influence to this system has the potential to change the climate.

You should then address how volcanic eruptions, given their nature and force, are able to influence global climate. First, you must note the **types of elements ejected** by volcanoes during an eruption, including the release of vast amounts of ash and gases into the atmosphere, as well as flows of lava and ash covering the ground. You could suggest that lava cover on the ground can have some effect on regional (though perhaps not global) climate, and how the most important influence on climate comes from volcanic gases released into the atmosphere, e.g. sulphur dioxide. The cloud formed by the gases and ash can **reduce the amount of solar radiation** reaching the earth. This can result in the Earth's surface temperature decreasing significantly.

Changes in one region's climate can result in climate changes in other regions. You can also launch a discussion of how the deep earth and biosphere are linked through the carbon cycle. For example, erupting magma releases CO_2 into the atmosphere. Years of weathering remove most of this gas – causing it to end up in the oceans as calcium carbonate sediment. Therefore, an excess of this from eruptions can offset the balance of CO_2 in the system.

The idea of **timescale is also important** here. Ash cover created by volcanic eruptions can have an immediate impact on a region's climate. Contrastingly, changes in the carbon cycle can result in long-term impacts.

Q18: Are humans ethically obligated to stop global warming and environmental change?

This is a question about Ethics. To answer a question like this, the important thing is not to have a strong opinion that you defend to the death, but to be able to discuss the different viewpoints based on different understandings of right and wrong, and always with a sound understanding of the underlying issues- both scientific and humanitarian.

One way to break down this question would be to **consider whether an ethical obligation extends only to other humans or to other organisms** as well, and whether it applies in any situation or only when contributing to a situation that wouldn't occur naturally. Similarly, one could also discuss whether humans as a whole are obliged to halt global warming or just a select few members of the human race. Showing an ability to think flexibly about abstract concepts is always good, but don't forget to then argue for the different cases using knowledge of past and present climate and environment, as this is the subject-relevant part of the question.

For instance, don't waste time discussing whether climate change is a reality – the scientific community has already reached a consensus. However, if you would like to argue against an ethical obligation instead, discuss the natural climate variations which have occurred on Earth in the past. Use probable climate-change driven events, like the Permo-Triassic extinction when 96% of species died out 250 million years ago, to argue that humans have no ethical obligation to save other species from anthropogenic extinction, because **even without human presence there are climate-driven extinctions**. Or argue the opposite, that despite past extreme environmental change being a reality, humanity is pushing the Earth further than it has ever sustained humans, and that we are obligated to do our part to leave a habitable Earth for people in other parts of the world and the future.

Alternatively, you could argue the complete opposite - that there can be no ethical obligation because everyone **contributes to the problem in their own way**, and everyone will face the consequences. Or that only those who contribute more than they suffer are in the wrong for dumping their consequences onto others. Whichever argument you put forward, be sure to include scientific examples so that your discussion doesn't veer away from the question.

Remember that climate change is not the same as global warming, and your discussion could include pollution (trash, toxins, chemicals, light and sound pollution, etc.), agriculture and monoculture, invasive species, hunting and fishing, deforestation and habitat fragmentation, or any of the other issues beyond the Greenhouse Effect which affect the environment.

Similarly, global warming is not just about fossil fuel use and carbon dioxide, but a range of gases and their effects on weather, ocean acidity, desertification, pathogen spread, etc. Show that you have a deeper understanding of these issues than you could get from skimming the headlines of the Daily Mail.

Q19: Why do you think that temperatures rise more quickly at the poles than near the equator?

This question is a good opportunity for the interviewers to test your knowledge of basic geographical concepts. Whilst you might not have been taught the specific answer to this question, the interviewers will expect you to draw on any knowledge that you might have regarding climate change and global warming in order to come up with an answer. Here you can demonstrate your ability to think out of the box. You will be expected to talk through your answer step-by-step, to explain how you got to your conclusion.

Good Applicant: Rising global temperatures are a key indicator of human-caused climate change. Temperatures are rising more in polar regions than in tropical regions due to the ice albedo effect. Ice is very reflective, meaning that some of the incoming solar radiation from the Sun is reflected back into space once it reaches the surface. However, global warming means that more sea ice is melting, leaving the underlying ocean exposed to the incoming solar radiation. This decreases the albedo, meaning that more solar radiation is absorbed by the surface, rather than being reflected off the ice. This in turn leads to more surface warming, and an increase in temperatures. Therefore, temperatures are rising more in polar regions than in tropical regions due to the ice albedo effect, which means that polar amplification occurs, and the effects of climate change are felt more greatly in these regions than elsewhere.

This response starts by introducing the context of the question: climate change. This highlights to the interviewers that you are aware of the wider relevance of the topic. The response is then broken down and explained in full detail. The interviewer wants to know that you are able to answer questions clearly, whilst still maintaining the levels of detail required for a good answer. Finally, the response is linked back to the question in the last sentence. This ensures that you are answering the question that has been asked of you, and not going off on a tangent.

A **poor applicant** may respond by saying that they are not sure, with no attempt to draw in any general knowledge when answering the question. The interviewers want to see that you are at least trying to come up with a response, even if it is not entirely correct, as this is what will be expected of you during supervisions if you were to be offered a place at the university.

Q20: How would you define 'Culture'?

This question is a great opportunity to show off to the interviewer, as it is a very broad topic where they are not looking for a specific answer. Therefore, as long as you come up with a relevant response and back it up with evidence, you cannot go wrong. You can discuss language, religion, music or even cuisine in your answer. It is important to recognise that the word culture has different meanings to different people, before you explain give your answer.

Good Applicant: Culture is a term that is often difficult to define, as it has many different meanings to different people around the world. However, to me, culture is the shared characteristics or knowledge of a particular group of people. It encompasses their religion, music, customs, cuisine, language and a number of other factors. Culture can determine how people act in certain situations, or even the way that people dress for example. Culture can be used to group people together. For example, the term 'Western culture' often refers to influences that originate from European countries or the United States, whereas African culture refers to societal ideas or norms from Africa. One key aspect to note about culture is that it is constantly changing due to globalisation which allows different customs, cuisines and other factors to be shared across the globe.

This is a good response because it identifies the fact that culture has different meanings to everyone, before giving detail about what culture means to you. It gives examples of the ways that culture can be interpreted as well as linking the term to a key geographical concept: globalisation. It is essential to try and make links to concepts such as these in your answers, as this will demonstrate to the interviewers that you are able to make connections between different topics.

A **poor applicant** might be unable to answer the question due to the broad spectrum of responses that can be given. The interviewers want to see that you are able to apply your breadth of knowledge and opinions into responses and shying away from answering questions such as these will influence how you are perceived by them.

Q21: Do you have any ideas about why the rate of glacial melt isn't linear?

This question is looking to see whether you can apply your geographical knowledge to come up with a valid reason as to why glacier melting rates are non-linear. Even if you have not studied glaciers as a topic at A-Level, you should be able to apply logic when answering a question such as this.

Good Applicant: Glaciers have been melting at an alarmingly fast rate, and at even faster rates that were originally predicted by scientists. The non-linear melting rate is due to the cleaving of glaciers when they meet the sea. The meltwater from glaciers due to heat allows the glacier to travel 'downstream' towards the sea or ocean. As they meet the sea, the glaciers become top heavy and are therefore more likely to calve. As more of the glacier calves, there is less friction between the ice and the bed, making it easier for the glacier to continue breaking apart into the sea. This cycle continues, meaning that the glacier melts at a faster rate than it originally did, explaining the non-linear pattern.

This response breaks down the answer into simple steps to ensure that it is clear, whilst not leaving out any key details. The response directly answers the question and uses geographical vocabulary which demonstrates knowledge about the topic. For example, by mentioning subject specific words such as calving, you can show the interviewer that you are aware of key terminology for the topic and the subject as a whole.

A **poor applicant** will perhaps avoid answering the question if they are unsure. Do not forget that you are encouraged to ask the interviewer to rephrase the question slightly if you are confused about what they are asking. The interviewers want to see that you have done wider reading into topics that you might not have necessarily studied as a part of your syllabus. A topic such as the melting of glaciers is very important within Geography and for general knowledge, and therefore it is important that you are able to answer questions on it with some level of detail.

Q22: Can you describe the relationship between population and carbon dioxide in the atmosphere?

This question aims to test your knowledge and ability to link human and physical geography together. The key to answering this is to start off by explaining the general relationship between global population and atmospheric CO_2 before going into detail about the points that you want to make. You need to structure your answer carefully to avoid not fully developing your arguments.

Good Applicant: There is a positive correlation between global population and atmospheric CO_2. This means that as global populations increase, so does atmospheric CO_2. The main reason for this is that every additional person that is born increases global carbon emissions. This might be through activities such as driving, which increases carbon emissions as the exhaust from vehicles emits carbon dioxide into the atmosphere, or even through the use of central heating in buildings. Generally, speaking, the countries with the largest populations tend to be the countries producing the highest levels of atmospheric CO_2. However, the burden of this tends to lie with more affluent people rather than those who are poorer. Richer people tend to drive high CO_2 emitting cars, and to take more flights amongst other things. This means that they tend to emit more CO_2 into the atmosphere than less affluent individuals. Evidence has shown that the world's richest 1% cause double the CO_2 emissions of the poorest 50%. Therefore, the relationship between global population and atmospheric CO_2 is that when one increases, so does the other but not in a linear manner.

This response is good because it starts off by giving a general response to the question by outlining that the relationship between global population and atmospheric CO_2 is that when one increases, so does the other. The answer then goes into more detail about the question, giving examples as well as some facts and figures. This shows the interviewers that you have engaged with some wider reading around the syllabus. Additionally, this response makes sure to fully develop the point that is being made and shows a critical analysis of the question by adding detail about rich people vs. poorer people and their relative CO_2 emissions.

A **poor applicant** will give a short and simple answer, only answering the question but without giving any detail. They will mention the fact that when global population increases, so does atmospheric CO_2, but they will not explain why or give any supporting detail. Although you are not directly asked to explain why the relationship between the two factors is the way that it is, the interviewers expect you to use initiative to fully develop your points.

Q23: *Please Plot a graph of CO_2 emissions over time, from 900AD onwards.*

This question tests your ability to draw together your knowledge of how CO_2 emissions have changed over time, the main causes of these changes/what might have led to an increase or decrease in CO_2 emissions since the 10th century and when each change occurred in order to create a plot of emissions. The interviewers do not expect your answer to be perfect, but they will expect you to be able to explain the reasoning behind what you have drawn and back it up with relevant facts.

Good Applicant: From my knowledge, I know that CO_2 emissions were very low, if not negligible during the 10th century. This is because at the time, the main causes of CO_2 emissions today had not yet been discovered or were not widely used. Fossil fuels were not used on a large scale, there was no industrial production and people did not own cars, electrical appliances or leisure facilities such as outdoors pools, all of which are major contributors to CO_2 emissions. Following on from this period in time, CO_2 emissions were relatively stable, with any differences in emissions being the result of events such as the Little Ice Age. Glacial events would lead to a decrease in CO_2 emissions as organic carbon is buried beneath ice sheets in the form of vegetation or soil carbon, leading to lower levels of CO_2 in the atmosphere. The main spike in CO_2 emissions came during the Industrial Revolution, where fossils fuels were burnt on large scales for energy. Between 1760 and the present day, the use of fossil fuels to run vehicles (petrol, diesel and kerosene), heat homes and businesses and power factories has continued to increase, meaning that CO_2 emissions have increased over this period. However, the burden of this falls more on the Northern Hemisphere than the Southern Hemisphere due to the fact that countries in the global North tended to industrialise before countries in the global South. Overall, the general trend of CO_2 emissions vs. time is that emissions have increased over time.

This response not only plots the graph of CO_2 emissions vs. time starting from the 10th century, but also describes the reasons behind the changes. The response also goes into detail, giving examples of why CO_2 emissions have changed over time. An interesting point is made regarding the Little Ice Age and the general effect of Ice Ages or glacial periods on emissions. This is something that many applicants will not pick up on, and it is vital that you include varied points in order to stand out to interviewers. Additionally, this response uses key geographical terminology such as 'global North/South', highlighting their knowledge of important phrases.

A **poor applicant** will simply draw the graph without explaining their thought process behind it. They will include minimal detail, or not listen to the question properly and therefore, not cover the full timeframe. It is important that you cover all aspects of the question that is asked of you and pay attention to detail. You must also fully back up all of the points that you make with valid and relevant evidence or facts and not make sweeping statements.

Q24: Why did India progress more quickly through the DTM than the countries it was based on originally?

This question seeks to test your knowledge of geographical concepts. The interviewers will want to see whether you are able to identify what the DTM is, and if not, if you hazard a guess regardless. They also want to test your logic and reasoning, as there might not be one specific answer.

Good Applicant: From my knowledge, I know that the DTM is the Demographic Transition Model. This is a model that shows population change and the historical shift from high birth and high infant death rates in societies where there is a lack of education, technology and economic development to low birth and death rates in societies where there are high levels of education, advanced technologies and economic development. There are also stages between both of these scenarios. There are five stages in the Demographic Transition Model, with Stage One being where there are high death and birth rates which typically occurs in Less Economically Developed Countries, or LEDCs, and Stage Five having low birth and death rates as is seen in advanced countries. In answer to your question, there are many potential reasons to explain why India has progressed more quickly through the DTM that the countries it was based on originally. However, one key reason is that there has been rapid social and economic change in India. For example, the rise in foreign direct investment in India due to offshoring as it is often cheaper to set up part of a company's manufacturing process in countries such as India, means that economic change occurs. The offshoring will create more jobs for people in India as well as bringing cultural influences to certain areas, especially if the business that is locating in India is from a Western country. These influences might mean that cultural norms in India change, such as the idea that women are not meant to work but that their role is in the home. Therefore, this might have led to a drop in birth rates in India, as more women are working rather than staying at home and raising children. Furthermore, death rates might have fallen as more people are working and have an income which can be used to make them less prone to illness or improving their safety. For this reason, India has progressed so quickly through the DTM due to the social and economic impacts that offshoring had on the country.

This response is good as it firstly defines the key term of the question: the DTM. It outlines the main points about the DTM before relating it back to the question and to India specifically. The response gives detail and a valid and fleshed out argument to explain why India has progressed more quickly up the DTM than the countries it was based on originally. It also identifies the fact that there might be alternative reasons for this progression, highlighting awareness of the fact that the question is complex.

A **poor applicant** would not define the DTM but instead jump straight into their answer. The interviewers will expect you to talk through every aspect of your thinking when answering the question. Therefore, by not giving this key definition you would have missed an important aspect of the explanation that would be expected. A poor applicant might also forget to answer the question, instead going on a tangent about the DTM and its relevance to Geography and not referring back to India.

Q25: Where does the Venn diagram of human geography and physical geography overlay?

This question is a great opportunity to show off and demonstrate the different ways in which human and physical geography overlap. There are a multitude of answers to this question, but the interviewer will look for a unique and well thought out response which points out a couple of overlaps between the two areas of geography.

Good Applicant: Human and physical geography overlap as they are both concerned with space and where and why things occur. However, this is a very broad link and there are other, more specific ways that the two branches of geography overlap. The link between the two has become more apparent in recent times due to the issue of climate change and the supposed age of the Anthropocene. Humans are having a grave impact on the natural environment, potentially causing irreversible climate change in the future and also leading to the extinction of certain species, amongst other negative impacts. Therefore, human and physical geography overlap when it comes to discussing the effects of humans on nature, and the ways in which they have altered it in predominantly negative ways.

This is a good answer as it goes into detail about one of the key ways that human and physical geography overlap, whilst identifying the fact that there are several other links between the two. The answer mentions the concept of the Anthropocene, which is a term that many applicants might not have come across and therefore, suggests that the applicant has done wider reading. Additionally, this answer gives examples to ensure that the response is detailed but also succinct.

A **poor applicant** might give a generic answer with no examples to back up their points. They will not refer to the fact that there are multiple ways in which the two areas link or they might oversimplify it, perhaps giving an answer such as 'human and physical geography overlaps because they both discuss the world and its inhabitants' without further explaining their idea.

Q26: How would you define a natural hazard?

This question is a great opportunity to draw on specific knowledge that you have been taught during your A-Level course. Hazards is a topic that most students are taught at this level, therefore, in order to make your answer stand out you need to be able to offer a unique perspective or discuss something interesting in relation to natural hazards.

Good Applicant: A natural hazard is an extreme phenomenon that can result in a loss of life, damage to property and disruption to human activities, amongst many other negative effects. Natural hazards can be classified into three broad categories which are geological, biological or climate. Geological natural hazards are related to the Earth and include events such as earthquakes, volcanic eruptions and flooding. Climate hazards are to do with the weather, and include droughts, tornados and wildfires. Flooding might also fit into this category, depending on what caused it. Finally, biological natural hazards are often directly related to humans, the most obvious being disease.

This is a good answer because it not only explains what a natural hazard is but also offers a unique perspective to natural hazards. By categorising natural hazards into three sections, this answer demonstrates to the interviewers that the candidate is well versed on this topic and has done extra reading around it. This will stand out to an interviewer.

A **poor applicant** will give no detail or examples in their answer, simply stating the basic definition of a natural hazard. They will not give any alternative or unique insight into hazards. It is important to show off to the interviewers, and the best way to do so is by doing extra reading around your subject and individual topic areas.

Q27: In the modern world of smartphones, what is the value of a map?

This question is designed for you to apply your knowledge of maps and their functions and to relate it to modern day society. Maps are not frequently used in their original formats (physical copies printed on paper or other materials). Nowadays, maps are mostly digitalized, and this is something that the interviewer will expect you to pick up on when answering this question.

Good Applicant: The format of maps has changed over time, with modern day maps being mostly digitalized and accessible through phones or other electronic devices. However, their role has not changed. The role of maps both in the past and in modern day society is to direct people to their destinations. What makes modern day maps different to maps from the past is that modern day maps tend to be more advanced. Nowadays, maps are interactive and not only show you where specific services can be found, but also give information such as opening and closing times for shops and restaurants, along with many other factors. Additionally, modern day maps are used to present geographical data in a simple, visual way. They are key components of geographical research as they can be further analysed in order to come to conclusions when conducting research.

This is a good answer because it gives several different roles of maps in modern day society. It discusses how maps differ now from in the past, adding a new dimension to the question. Additionally, this answer gives the role of maps in a geographical sense, when used for research projects and experiments.

A **poor applicant** will give a simple answer, offering one role of maps in modern day society and without giving much detail. The interviewers will expect you to fully explore the question in your answer, picking up on any interesting aspects to do with maps that you might identify. They will expect you to discuss multiple roles of maps in modern day society, and to relate this to the study of Geography.

Q28: How can slums form close to wealthy urban environments?

This question aims to test your knowledge of urban environments and the issues surrounding them. There are multiple ways to answer this question, and the interviewers are looking to see if you are able to give a detailed and thoughtful answer, whilst ensuring that you bring in any key geographical concepts.

Good Applicant: The reason for slum settlements springing up near high rise buildings/wealthier neighbourhoods in some developing countries is rapid population growth and rapid urbanisation. People are attracted to urban areas in hope of new jobs, better standards of living or improved quality of life for example. What they are not prepared for is the lack of available housing in these urban areas, and the high costs of living. This means that many people migrating into these urban areas are forced to set up shelter in squatter or slum settlements. The reason that these are found near high rise buildings or wealthier neighbourhoods is because these areas tend to be better situated. For example, they tend to be on higher ground, meaning that when there are extreme rainfall events these areas are not affected as badly by flooding than settlements that are at lower altitudes. Therefore, where possible, people will tend to situate around high rise buildings or wealthier neighbourhoods.

This response starts by mentioning a key geographical concept: urbanisation. The interviewers will be looking for applicants to be able to pick up on these terms and concepts without being asked explicitly. The answer then gives a detailed response to the question, mentioning the in-migration of people from rural to urban areas and giving a valid reason for this occurring. It is also possible to mention inequality as a reason for slum settlements springing up near high-rise buildings/wealthier neighbourhoods, amongst other things as long as you are able to explain them in detail. A **poor applicant** will not mention urbanisation or any other key geographical concepts. It is vital that you pick up on these when answering questions. A poor applicant might also give a statement to explain why slum settlements are springing up near high-rise buildings/wealthier neighbourhoods, but not back this up with relevant detail.

Q29: Why do we bother with conservation?

This questions seeks to determine whether you are aware of what conservation is and can identify one or two key reasons behind it. Conservation is a term that the interviewers will expect you to be aware of, whether that be through your curriculum or general knowledge. You will be expected to define the term in order to demonstrate your full understanding.

Good Applicant: Conservation is the process of caring for and protecting Earth's natural resources such as air, plants, soil, water and wildlife. This can be through the maintenance of diversity of species, genes and ecosystems amongst other things. Therefore, the point of conservation is to firstly protect wildlife and promote biodiversity. This needs to be preserved for future generations in order to maintain a functional ecosystem. Destroying the natural habitats of some species might lead to extinction. Secondly, conservation is necessary to protect the Earth. Climate change is a huge problem at the moment that is having a negative effect on communities worldwide. Therefore, conservation is necessary to reduce this impact. This is because climate change can lead to irreversible harm to Earth's life support systems, but also because the emission of fossil fuels, which are natural resources, might lead to them running out. There are several others reasons that conservation is needed that have not been picked up on, but those are two that I believe hold the most importance.

This response is good because it firstly defines conservation, indicating awareness of the term to interviewers. It also gives examples to back up points that are made. The answer is structured in a clear and simple way, making it obvious to the interviewers when another point is being made. This is vital to ensure that you are fully credited for your points. Additionally, this response identifies the fact that there are alternative points that can be made, signalling that they are aware of the wider implications that a lack of conservation can have.

A **poor applicant** will not define conservation. This is important as it gives a foundation to the answer and the way that you are going to approach it. You should always answer questions as if you are responding to someone with no prior knowledge on the topic, making sure to define any key terms. Additionally, a poor applicant might only give one, generalised answer to the question, without any detail or explanation.

Q30: Why do climate change deniers exist?

This question is a great way for the interviewers to gather your opinions on global warming and why some people might not take it seriously. There are multiple responses that you can give for this, so as long as your answer gives a valid, succinct and backed up answer with relevant evidence, this question should be relatively simple to respond to.

Good Applicant: I think that some people don't take global warming seriously due to a lack of awareness of the urgency of the issue, and the grave impacts that it might have on our planet and on us as human beings. Whilst I am sure that a majority of the population is aware of what global warming is, and the general impacts that it is having, I believe that much fewer people are aware of what this actually means for our day to day lives and at what timescales. A 1.5°C rise in the Earth's temperature probably doesn't sound like a lot to someone who doesn't know a lot about the topic of global warming. However, 1.5°C of warming can affect the air that we breathe. Therefore, I believe that the main reason why some people don't take global warming seriously is that they are unaware of the direct impact that it might have on our lives.

This is a great answer because it offers an opinion but in a convincing way, through detailed explanations and the use of a relevant and valid example. The answer uses key facts and figures, demonstrating awareness of global warming which is important for a student wishing to study Geography. This is not the only way to answer this question, but it is important to remember that whatever reason you give must be supported.

A **poor applicant** might give their opinion but without any supporting evidence. They will not use any vital facts or figures. It is vital that you do this in order to show your deeper understanding of the topic. Another common mistake might be to misinterpret the question. A poor applicant might discuss climate change instead of global warming. Although the answers might be similar, the interviewers will want to see that you pay attention to detail and by answering the wrong question, you are not demonstrating this.

Q31: Can you think of examples of how computer technologies can help us understand geographical processes, or natural hazards?

Through this question, the interviewers aim to draw on your knowledge of hazards and the ways in which ICT is used to better understand these physical processes. You can answer this question in multiple ways, touching on the use of ICT to map natural hazard events or perhaps to monitor them. The key here is to make sure that you relate it back to the understanding of physical processes.

Good Applicant: ICT can help geographers to understand physical processes and natural hazard events through hazard monitoring. Organisations such as the United States Geological Survey (USGS) can use ICT equipment to monitor tectonic activity. This helps geographers to understand these hazards as the equipment allows them to better predict or identify events. Furthermore, ICT can help geographers to map physical processes such as earthquakes or volcanic eruptions. By noting the location of these individual events, geographers can increase their understanding of where and why natural hazards occur, especially when comparing the maps of hazards to the maps of plate boundaries.

This answer directly answers the question, giving a clear example of how ICT can help geographers understand physical processes and natural hazards. It mentions a key organisation that is involved with hazard monitoring, the United State Geological Survey, highlighting an awareness of the important figures and authorities in this field. Additionally, the answer gives two different suggestions in response to the question. It is often a good idea to give alternative responses to questions as this demonstrates critical thinking, a skill that is examined in university exams.

A **poor applicant** will give a brief answer which lacks detail. As this question requires some element of thinking out of the box, many applicants might get stuck and be unable to respond well. It is important to remember that even if you are not sure, the best thing to do is to talk the interviewers through your thought process and throw out any ideas that you might have, regardless of whether you think this is the answer that they are looking for.

Q32: Is nature still 'natural'?

Interviewers ask questions such as this in order to identify any applicants who are able to give unique and well thought out answers to broad topics. The idea of nature is probably not something that you are taught about in great detail during your A-Levels. However, nature is a topic that comes up in several different Geography modules at university level, and the interviewers will want to see if you can draw on any prior knowledge.

Good Applicant: Nature is a term that is difficult to define and has different meanings to different people. In a broad sense, nature is the inherent, unmediated environment. For this reason, I believe that it is not possible to consider nature as natural in today's world due to the fact that the natural environment has been altered and adversely impacted by human beings. Nature is now used for mass production, to generate electricity and to build with, amongst several other things. Therefore, I believe that nature is natural in today's world, as it is no longer unmediated.

This is a good response as it starts by defining what nature is, in their own opinion. It is vital that you define broad terms such as this, firstly because it makes it clear to the interviewers that you are talking about it from a particular aspect, and secondly because it sets your answer up nicely and lays the foundation for what you are about to say. The response is clear and succinct, giving examples to back up the answer and it refers back to the question at the end. This gives a cyclical structure and demonstrates the fact that you have understood the question fully. Please note that it is not necessary to take this opinion and the opposite opinion or a balance of both would be just as valid if you could back it up with evidence/examples.

A **poor applicant** will not define nature, meaning that their answer might be misinterpreted by the interviewers and based off their own understanding of nature. It is important to answer questions as if you are speaking to someone with no prior knowledge of the subject or topic, and therefore, a definition is vital here as nature is such as broad term. A poor applicant might also answer the question incorrectly. The interviewers asks about nature in today's world. Therefore, talking about any other period in time is irrelevant, although this is an easy trap to fall into.

Q33: What's the impact of a volcanic eruption on the global climate – how much time does it take for this impact to be felt?

This question is split into two parts, and the interviewers will expect you to be able to answer both. They are looking for an explanation of the way in which volcanic eruptions change global climate, but they also want you to discuss the timescales over which this occurs. Most people would have been taught about the influence of volcanoes on climate and will be able to answer this question. Therefore, it is important to make sure that you answer includes all of the key points, as well as anything that you believe will help you stand out.

Good Applicant: Volcanic eruptions can lead to global climate decreases on short timescales. Volcanic eruptions release gases and dust particles into the atmosphere. These particles cool the planet because they act as a shade to incoming solar radiation. Only the smaller particles have much effect as the larger particles are too heavy to remain suspended in the troposphere. The timescale of this is mostly a few hours or days after an eruption. However, the smallest particles of dust are able to reach the stratosphere, and these particles are able to travel vast distances. These can stay in the stratosphere for months and therefore, have a longer impact on cooling.

This response is good because it uses a lot of key geographical vocabulary such as troposphere and stratosphere. These are terms that are used more at a university level, so having knowledge of them will demonstrate your wider reading. Additionally, this response answers both parts of the question, highlighting to the interviewers that you have listened to and understood the question. Finally, this is a good response as it discusses the relative sizes of particles and the impacts that each of these have on global climate. This is something that most students might not pick up on.

A **poor applicant** will only answer part of the question (e.g., how volcanic eruptions can change global climate but without mentioning the timescales over which this occurs). The interviewers will be looking to see whether applicants are listening to the whole question and it is important that both aspects are covered.

Q34: Can you think of some obstacles to disease transmission?

This is a relatively simple question that can be interpreted in many different ways. For this reason, it is important to clearly state how you have interpreted the question before you begin your explanation. You can discuss the physical barriers to the spread of disease such as landscape features, or even smaller scale barriers such as masks.

Good Applicant: Barriers to the spread of disease can be found on various scales. However, I will discuss large scale barriers in the form of landscape features. These large scale barriers can be features such as hills, mountains or even oceans. These are barriers to the spread of disease because the viruses or bacteria in diseases will often not survive across these barriers. For example, some diseases cannot survive in extremely cold environments, such as high altitudes. Additionally, some diseases cannot survive over long distances, such as across oceans. However, it is important to note that these are only barriers to communicable diseases, as non-communicable diseases are not stopped by these large landscape features.

This is a good answer because it outlines which type of barriers to disease it will cover. It is important to acknowledge that this question can be interpreted in different ways, and therefore it is important that you state your own interpretation of the question before you begin. Additionally, this response uses key geographical terminology such as communicable and non-communicable diseases which will show wider knowledge and the ability to transfer your teaching into conservations.

A **poor applicant** will not specify their interpretation of the question before explaining. They will also get flustered by the wide scope of the question and give an unclear or unstructured answer. It is important that your answer is clear and structured as this will make it easier for the interviewers to understand the points that you are making.

Q35: What do you know about Malthus's ideas regarding population?

This question aims to test your knowledge of a theory that is often discussed in Geography. It might be difficult to answer this question if you haven't come across this theory before. However, it should have come up in any extra reading that you have done around the topic of disease or any other topic that discusses population growth. It is important to remember that even if you are not sure about the correct answer, it is best to attempt to respond.

Good Applicant: Malthus's 'principle of population' is a key economic and geographical theory that was created by Thomas Malthus in 1798. It theorised that populations would continue to grow and expand until affected by disease, famine, war or calamity, all of which might reverse or stop population growth. The theory was created in the 18th and 19th centuries, as philosophers believed that humanity would not stop growing. Malthus countered this through his principle of population, demonstrating that there are several reasons that populations would not continue to grow.

This is a good response as it gives some background detail to the principle of population. Many applicants might be able to state what the Malthus's theory is, but not be able to give any background information on it. Therefore, this will make you stand out as a candidate. Additionally, the response gives a clear and direct answer to the question, showing the interviewer that you are aware of the topic and its importance in Geography.

A **poor applicant** will not attempt to answer the question or to gain an understanding of what it means. It is vital that you at least give a suggestion of what you think the theory might mean, even if it is not 100% correct.

Q36: Why do levels of biodiversity vary around the globe?

This question aims to test your knowledge of a key geographical concept: biodiversity. However, you are required to discuss biodiversity on a global scale, rather than a local or regional scale that you are probably used to. Therefore, the question requires you to apply knowledge that you might have to a larger scale.

Good Applicant: Biodiversity is unevenly distributed across the planet due to a variety of factors, including climate and the current and historical distribution of land masses and geographical barriers. Terrestrial biodiversity is usually greater near the equator due to warmer climates and therefore, higher rates of primary productivity. The tropics also tend to experience greater biodiversity, covering less than 10% of the surface of the Earth but containing around 90% of the world's species. In marine environments, biodiversity tends to be higher along the coasts of the Western Pacific where sea temperatures are highest.

This is a good response as it mentions some key facts and figures as well as geographically locating areas where biodiversity is greatest. This makes a great response as it shows the interviewers that you are well versed in this topic and that you are able to speak about it confidently and accurately.

A **poor applicant** will not have any prior knowledge of biodiversity and therefore, be unable to answer the question. Biodiversity is a concept that most students should be aware of, and interviewers will expect you to be able to respond to this question. Even if you have not been taught this topic, you should use your general knowledge of the effect of climate on species and populations and apply that to this question.

Q37: Is it important to quantify the diversity of living species?

This question is designed to see whether you can think out of the box. There is not one set answer to this question, and you might not have been taught how to respond. However, you should be able to draw on your knowledge from your syllabus to come up with a response. You are expected to discuss issues such as biodiversity and extinction.

Good Applicant: It is important to know the number of living species on Earth in order to track the biodiversity of different regions. Biodiversity is vital to ecosystems as it allows them to supply oxygen, plant pollination and pest control for example. Additionally, it is important to know the number of living species on Earth in order to avoid extinction. If we are unaware of species that might be endangered, we will not be able to attempt to protect them, potentially leading to extinction. Extinction is a problem because each species has a unique function within its ecosystem. Therefore, its extinction might prompt cascading effect through a food chain.

This is a good answer because it touches on two key points: biodiversity and extinction. These are not the only things that you can discuss in response to this question, but it is important to acknowledge that you are aware of them. The answer is detailed and concise, covering all of the main points and constantly referring back to the question to demonstrate understanding.

A **poor applicant** will not mention any geographical terms such as biodiversity. It is vital that you tie your answer back to the subject as the interviewer will be looking to see if you can make links between general questions and geographical concepts. Additionally, a poor applicant will fail to refer back to the question, perhaps going off on a tangent and losing focus.

Q38: Draw the carbon and water cycles, how do they connect?

This question aims to test your knowledge of your A-Level content. Most students would have been taught about the water and carbon cycles during their course. However, this question asks about the linkages between the two, which is something that many students might not be aware of. Therefore, this will require you to think on your feet in order to come up with a detailed yet succinct answer.

Good Applicant: The water and carbon cycles are interlinked in many ways. However, one of the key ways in which they are interlinked is that they are both affected by changes in climate. Energy from the sun sets the carbon and water cycles into motion. Additionally, increased temperatures as a result of global warming can lead to the acceleration of both cycles. Greater levels of carbon in our atmosphere has meant that the water cycle has been altered, with some areas experiencing heavy rainfall and others experiencing severe drought. These are some ways that the water and carbon cycle are interlinked.

This is a good answer because it gives a clear response to the question. It mentions several ways that the water and carbon cycles are interlinked, backing them up with detailed explanations. It is possible to just focus on one way in which the two are interlinked, but it is important to then make sure that you include sufficient detail and any evidence to support this.

A **poor applicant** will give just one way in which the water and carbon cycles are interlinked without any explanation. It is vital that your answers are detailed and contain enough information to demonstrate your awareness of the topic and your knowledge of general subject areas. Additionally, the interviewers will expect you to be able to think on your feet.

Q39: What's the significance of the concept of place?

Place is an important concept in Geography that is mentioned throughout most modules at university. It is quite an abstract concept and the interviewers will be looking to see if you are able to define it in a clear way and also relate it to the study of both human and physical geography. You would have probably been taught about place in relation to human geography, but not physical, so this might be more difficult.

Good Applicant: Place is an abstract concept which can be used to describe the physical and human characteristics of any location on Earth. It is important in both human and physical geography. In human geography, place can be used to understand the relationships between people and different locations. Place often has a meaning attached to it based on someone's emotions or emotional attachment to different areas. Additionally, place is important in physical geography. Place can be used to describe the location of geographical features such as mountains or volcanoes. This is a simpler definition of place, whereas place in human geography is constantly changing due to globalisation which has led to the spreading of different cultures and people.

This is a good answer because it discusses place in relation to human and physical geography. It is important to touch on both sides of geography since the interviewers do not specify which one they want you to discuss in your answer. This answer is also good because it includes geographical terminology such as globalisation. This shows a wider understanding of the topic and where place might come into your studies. The answer also attempts to define place which is important due to the broad meanings of the term.

A **poor applicant** will only discuss the importance of place in human geography, and not mention physical geography. It is vital that both come into your answer for reasons mentioned above, but also to show that you truly understand the concept as it becomes even more important at university.

Q40: Can you identify the impacts of economic policy on social inequality?

This question seeks to gather your understanding of social inequality which is a key topic in human geography. The interviewers will want to see that you are able to draw conclusions from what you have been taught about social inequality and what impacts it. It is important to include the terms that were used in the question (economy/policy/social inequality) as this will show that you have understood the question properly.

Good Applicant: The economy or policy can impact social inequality in many ways. However, one important way that both factors can impact social inequality is through taxation. Government policies can increase or decrease social inequality. It can be decreased if governments choose to raise income tax, as the burden will be felt more by more affluent individuals as a larger proportion of their income is being taken. The economy can increase social inequality through indirect taxes. Although richer individuals pay more in indirect taxes which can include VAT or service tax, they are paying less as a proportion of their income on these taxes. Therefore, income inequality increases. A way to tackle this might be to increase income tax for the most affluent individuals and to decrease income tax for the least affluent individuals.

This is a good answer because it discusses the impact that policy has on social inequality in depth. It chooses one impact and covers several different points to the argument. This demonstrates critical thinking and the ability to create a balanced argument. This response only covers the impact that policy has on social inequality, but it is possible to cover the impacts of both economy and policy, but this would be in less detail.

A **poor applicant** will only discuss the impact of either policy or the economy on social inequality but with very little detail and no counter-arguments. If you decide to only focus on one aspect of the question, it is important to include a high level of detail to demonstrate your understanding.

Q41: What would you say is the central component of development, education?

This question asks for your opinion on the topic of development and the role of education in it. The interviewers will be looking to see if you are able to generate a unique argument in response to this question whilst also tying it back to the general subject area. It is important to use key terminology in this answer as it will help you to stand out.

Good Applicant: In my opinion, access to education does lie at the heart of development. This is because of the cycle of poverty. The cycle of poverty is the idea that there are a range of self-reinforcing mechanisms that cause poverty, and that once you are within the cycle it is impossible to escape without outside intervention. The cycle explains how a lack of education might lead to getting a bad job and a low income, which will then mean that you can only afford poor housing leading to deteriorating health and the same outcome for your children, in brief terms. Therefore, I believe that education is at the centre of development as a good education might allow people to escape this cycle. However, the term 'cycle' suggests that poverty can begin or end at any stage. For this reason, some might argue that education does not lie at the heart of development, but instead another factor such as your housing situation does instead. This is also a valid argument and depends on individual opinions.

This is a great answer as it mentions the cycle of poverty which is vital to ensure that the response is related back to geography. The answer is framed in a way that it allows for critical thinking and a balanced argument, demonstrating to the interviewers that you are able to do both of these things. The answer shows knowledge and understanding of the cycle of poverty and relates this back to development, therefore answering the question in a detailed manner.

A **poor applicant** would not mention the cycle of poverty. This concept is very important in this answer as otherwise, you might run the risk of responding to the question in a generalised and non-specific manner. The interviewers will expect you to tie your answer back to Geography, even if this is not explicitly stated.

Q42: Are there limits to the benefits of hazard mapping?

This question requires you to draw on your knowledge of the natural hazards topic which you will likely been taught about during your A-Level course. However, even if you have not been taught this topic you should be able to answer based on your knowledge of natural hazards and their unpredictable nature.

Good Applicant: Hazard mapping is used to highlight areas that are affected by or vulnerable to particular hazards, such as earthquakes or volcanic eruptions. They are useful to gain a generic understanding of where hazards occur. However, hazard mapping has limitations because of the unpredictable nature of natural hazards. Whilst hazard mapping can be used to prevent damage or death as it highlights areas that are prone to physical events, this does not mean that hazards cannot occur in other areas. Therefore, hazard mapping is limited in its usefulness because it is not possible to predict exactly where or when a hazard will occur.

This is a good answer because it explains one of the main limitations if hazard mapping. However, it also discusses the general use of hazard mapping which is important as interviewers will be looking to see if you can define key terms. It is vital that you define any words or concepts that are not generally understood, as if you were speaking to someone who has never studied Geography before. To further develop your answer, it might be useful to use a named example of where hazard mapping has failed, such as in the Tohoku Earthquake in Japan.

A **poor applicant** will not be able to define hazard mapping. Even if you have not been taught a specific definition for the term, you should be able to come up with one by using your general knowledge. Additionally, you should be able to come up with limitations of the method by drawing on your wider knowledge of the topic of hazards and use this to support your answer.

Q43: What proportion of all the water in the world can be found in a watermelon?

Interviewers will ask questions such as this to test your logical thinking. Whilst they will not expect you to know the exact answer to this question, they will want you to talk through your thoughts step by step so that they can see how you would go about answering a question using logic.

Good Applicant: In order to measure what percentage of the world's water is contained in one watermelon, I will need to estimate how many litres of water are in a watermelon as well as how many litres of water are in the world's seas, oceans and other sources. From my general knowledge, I know that one watermelon is around 92% water. I would assume that an average watermelon would weigh around 10kg. Therefore, around 9.2kg of that would be water. You can convert that 9.2kg into 9.2L as 1L of water is almost exactly equal to 1kg. In order to measure how much water is on Earth, I will need to calculate the depth and width of the seas and oceans, as these are the main stores of water on Earth. I will also need to consider other water stores such as groundwater, ice and glaciers. The depth of the oceans is around 3.7km and the average surface area of oceans is around 350,000,000km squared. Therefore, by multiplying these figures I can assume that the average volume of an ocean is around 1,332,000,000km cubed, or 1,332,000,000L³. Therefore, using approximation I believe that less that 6.907e-7 (where e is a mathematical constant approximately equal to 2.7) of the world's water is contained in one watermelon.

This is a good answer because although it doesn't give an exact figure as an answer, it talks through the logic that an applicant should go through when answering a question like this. It is unlikely that you will know how much water can be found on Earth, but it is important to guess using prior knowledge. If you are still unsure, you should still describe the logic that you would go through to obtain an answer as the interviewers will be expecting to at least hear this.

A **poor applicant** will not attempt to respond but instead tell the interviewers that they have no idea or that it is impossible to figure out. Even if you believe that this is the case, you must at least try to answer questions such as these. The interviewers will not expect an exact answer, but they will expect you to explain your thinking.

Q44: If atmospheric pressure is 10,000 Pa., what is the total mass of Earth's atmosphere.

This question aims to test your knowledge of mathematical equations, and your ability to apply this knowledge in a geographical sense. Unless you have been given a calculator, pen and paper it is unlikely that the interviewers will expect an exact answer to this question, and therefore, you are required to use your logic to come up with an answer as close to the true figure as possible.

Good Applicant: In order to come up with an answer to this question, it is necessary to know the equation that is used to calculate the mass of the Earth's atmosphere. To calculate this, I will need to divide the atmospheric pressure of 10,000 Pa by the gravity of Earth, which is $9.8m/s^2$. This will give the mass of air per unit area, which in this case will be kg/m^2. Therefore, if we round this up to $10m/s^2$ for the purposes of the calculation, this will suggest that the mass of the Earth's atmosphere is around $1000kg/m^2$.

This is a good answer because it uses logic to try and reach an answer to this question. Although the answer that you give might not necessarily be correct, the interviewers are not looking to see how good your mathematical ability is (although they will expect it to be at a certain level), but rather they are looking to see if you are able to draw on some key equations and figures in order to answer the question.

A **poor applicant** will not attempt to answer this question due to the fact that they are perhaps not given enough information. The interviewers will expect you to know some important equations, such as how to calculate the mass of the Earth's atmosphere in order to answer this question. However, if you are not sure it is vital that you at least talk through how you would calculate it if you did know the equation.

Q45: What separates a volcano from a mountain?

In theory, this question is relatively simple and easy to answer. Therefore, the interviewers will expect you to be accurate in your answer and use key terminology when explaining the difference between the two landforms. Your answer can be supported with named examples to show your wider knowledge of the topic.

Good Applicant: Volcanoes and mountains are two very similar landforms. However, they are formed in different ways. Mountains, such as the Himalayas, form due to geological processes such as the movement and collision of tectonic plates, whereas volcanoes often form due to the build-up of lava following several eruptions. In mountain formation, two tectonic plates collide with each other leading to the thickening and deformation of the Earth's crust. Mountain peaks and valleys form due to the collision pressure. Volcano formation results from the accumulation of lava after several eruptions. The magma has high viscosity when it erupts and therefore, cools quickly and does not spread far from the vent. This results in volcano formation, such as Yellowstone.

This is a good answer because it offers one key difference between a volcano and a mountain, backing up the point by describing the formation of both landforms in detail. It also uses examples to demonstrate situated knowledge of the features. This will stand out to an interviewer as it is important to use place-specific examples in your answers not only at A-Level but university level too.

A **poor applicant** will not fully develop their explanation and will not use named examples to back up their point. It is vital that you do both of these things in order to have a detailed and fully explained argument in response to the question. The interviewers will want you to develop your points.

Q46: Can you predict the fallout from an asteroid impact in the Pacific? Let's say the asteroid is ten kilometres across.

This is a broad and abstract question that offers you the opportunity to use your imagination and come up with a unique response. Your answer should relate to Geography, perhaps discussing the impact that a 10km wide asteroid would have on the landscape. You should mention both the human and physical impacts of the asteroid landing in the ocean.

Good Applicant: If a 10km wide asteroid smashed into the Pacific Ocean, there would most likely be a large tsunami. The asteroid would displace large volumes of water which would then be transported onto land. This would have large impacts on humans and on the physical landscape. The tsunami might destroy buildings and infrastructure, flood farmlands and lead to catastrophic consequences in terms of deaths and injury. These are just a few of the impacts that a 10km wide asteroid smashing into the Pacific Ocean would have.

This is a good answer because it mentions a natural hazard that might occur if an asteroid were to smash into the ocean, making links to Geography. Additionally, this answer shows an understanding of how tsunamis are formed due to the displacement of water in the oceans. There are many other creative ways to answer this question. For example, you could discuss the impact that this might have on species living in the Pacific. The interviewers will be looking to see if anyone can come up with a unique but accurate response.

A **poor applicant** will state that they do not know or that it is impossible to say as it has not happened before. It is vital that you use your imagination when answering questions like this. The interviewers do not expect you to know exactly what will happen if a 10km wide asteroid smashed into the Pacific Ocean, but they will expect you to be able to assume what would happen based on your geographical knowledge.

Q47: If you could only save one, which of the Antarctic or the Amazon would you choose?

This question does not have a right of wrong answer. You are allowed to pick either option, but the interviewers will be looking to see if you can back up your choice with valid and convincing reasoning. It is vital to include facts and evidence to support your answer.

Good Applicant: Although both are vital ecosystems, I would rather conserve the Amazon than Antarctica. This is because the Amazon provides us with countless benefits. Not only is the Amazon a home to many people, but it is also an extremely biodiverse area and reduces worldwide pollution. The trees in the Amazon absorb billions of tonnes of CO_2 and it is home to around 10% of the world's biodiversity. In addition, it is believed that only 0.5% of the plant species in the Amazon have been studied for medicinal properties, suggesting that the cures for many diseases might be found here. Therefore, I would rather conserve the Amazon than Antarctica because I believe that the loss of the Amazon will have greater impacts on society than the loss of Antarctica.

This is a good answer because it makes comparisons between the Amazon and Antarctica before giving a detailed explanation as to why they would choose the Amazon over Antarctica. As previously mentioned, there is no right or wrong answer to this question. Therefore, as long as you are able to justify your reasoning with facts and evidence, you cannot go wrong. The interviewers will be looking for applicants who can give unique reasons for choosing one over another, such as the fact that the Amazon offers medicinal properties.

A **poor applicant** will be indecisive and not pick between conserving the Amazon or Antarctica. If you are unsure, it is important to pick one rather than sitting on the fence. The interviewers will want to see whether you are able to make a judgement on the spot based off your prior knowledge, and not answering will not resonate well with them.

Q48: How do we know what the Earth's core consists of?

This question might feel very knowledge-specific, don't worry if you haven't studied this before – everyone's academic background is different and the interviewers know this. If you have studied this before then refer to your past knowledge, if you haven't don't be afraid to mention this but you can also use this question to show your interviewer that you can tackle a problem headfirst and can use other knowledge to inform this.

Good applicant with prior knowledge: *Despite having only been able to dig down to a fraction of the Earth's radius, we are still able to understand the breakdown of the Earth's core. This is due to a range of different factors, mainly seismology. After an earthquake, seismic waves travel through the Earth and change their form and direction depending on the materials they pass through. Geophysicists have used this information to work out what is at the Earth's core. There are two different waves that travel through the Earth following an Earthquake, these are P waves and S waves. P waves travel rapidly and can travel through liquid, S waves, on the other hand, are slower and can't travel through liquid.*

This applicant obviously demonstrates a good knowledge of both the theory and the science behind the question, if the applicant had a deeper interest/knowledge of the topic they may go into even more depth on the science surrounding the topic or maybe the history/latest developments.

Good applicant without prior knowledge: *Although this is not something I have studied before, I think that using some other areas of knowledge I might be able to suggest some reasons. I am aware that the core of the Earth is extremely deep and therefore it would be impossible to dig down to find out what it consists of – therefore other methods must have been used. There are two things to be found out, one is the size/number of layers within the Earth's core and the other is what material they are made out of. The question of layers would be quite tricky to find out but may be possible using something to do with waves. In terms of what material they are made out of – this might be revealed to us by looking at the chemical present in different types of rock/lava.*

Although this applicant had no prior knowledge, they did their best to work through the question and gave reasons for their suggestions throughout.

Poor applicant: If the applicant has not studied this topic before, then a poor applicant may be unable to answer the question in any capacity, possible saying *I don't know*, and leaving it there. This applicant would be unable to show the interviewer that they are willing to tackle tricky questions. On top of this a poor candidate might also just answer with a one-line, wrong, answer such as: *they drill down.* Giving a wrong answer is not the end of the world but if you have nothing to explain it or back it up then it will look like you are just guessing.

Q49: How do you think our ancestors determined that the earth wasn't flat?

Although there is a correct answer to this, it is unlikely that the interviewer will be expecting you to know this, therefore this is a chance to prove that you can work your way around the problem and come up with some interesting suggestions.

Good candidate with prior knowledge: *The ancient Greeks knew that the earth wasn't flat due to the work done by Aristotle. He worked out that the earth wasn't flat as depending on where you are standing, the sky will look different, especially at night. If the earth was flat you would expect to see all the same stars and we don't. The ancient Greeks also managed to calculate the circumference of the earth by calculating the difference in how high the sun rose in two cities and the distance between those cities.*

This candidate showed a prior knowledge of the topic and answered in a clear and succinct way.

Good candidate without prior knowledge: There are a number of ways that the Greeks could have known that the earth wasn't flat. The Greek's were known as keen astrologers and therefore they could have predicted that the Earth was not flat due to the variations seen in the starts, Sun and moon, depending on where on Earth you are standing. Another way that the ancient Greeks might have known that the Earth wasn't flat was due to the high amounts of global trade that were happening at that time. Despite travel and transport between various parts of the world, there was no reports of an 'end of the world' or ledge, and therefore this may have informed their knowledge of the earth.

Despite having no prior knowledge, this candidate was able to form a comprehensive and well thought out answer using pieces of information they did already know. They phrased each as possibilities with accompanying explanations.

Poor candidate: A poor candidate may not see this as an opportunity to show off their problem-solving skills and other knowledge. They would likely just state that they don't know the answer without giving answering it a chance.

Q50: Suggest methods by which we could work out how old things are.

With this question if you have prior knowledge then definitely pull it out and use it. Specifically, a good method to talk about would be carbon dating if you have studied this. However, don't worry if you haven't as there are other possible methods you could talk about. It might be worth having a short discussion at the beginning as to why working out how old objects are is important. For example, it might be helpful in the realm of archaeology to date certain artifacts. For geographers we can use fossils of plants and animals to try and work out what type of environment a place used to have.

Good candidate with prior knowledge: If you have studied radiocarbon dating then it would be good to discuss it. *Radiocarbon dating is a method that provides age estimates for carbon-based materials that originated from living organisms. An age could be estimated by measuring the amount of carbon-14 present in the sample and comparing this against an internationally used reference standard.*

You could go into more depth if you have that knowledge. On top of this, it would be good to include some possible other methods mentioned below.

Good candidate without prior knowledge. If you haven't studied carbon dating before then don't worry, use your imagination to think of other methods to try and work out how old things are. *One possible method of dating objects, specifically trees, is dendrochronology. Dendrochronology is the study of tree rings, and is used to work out how old trees are. Another method that might be used is using historic records and databases to date objects. For example, if we found a type of cooking tool or implement, we might be able to use old writings to date to when they might have used this. One issue with this is that it is not a very accurate way of dating the objects but also it doesn't go very far back in time. It might work well alongside carbon dating as it would be possible to date non-living organisms.*

Another method would be dating the component of the object. For example if you had a knife covered in mammoth skin, then it's possible to work out that the object was from a certain period of time. You could also think about big events that happened around the world. For example the eruption of Pompeii left volcanic ash over the country and you could date items that are covered in it to that era.

There are many more possible ways of dating objects/things so just be imaginative and make sure you give explanations and examples to back up your point.

Poor candidate: A poor candidate might suggest possible methods but not add in any explanation, examples or criticism. For example: *You could use old books or photos to find out when items were used in the past.*

Q51: Imagine that Earth had a second moon, identical to Luna – what would this change?

This is another question to test your ability to think creatively. Think about how our moon impacts life at the moment – it provides light at night; it impacts the tides and it impacts our measurement of time. The best answer would be to work through these three roles and think about the impact that two moons would have on them and those that rely on them.

Good Candidate: *The moon has three large impacts on life on Earth, these include providing light at night, impacting the tides and also influencing our measurement of time. All three of these will be impacted:*

Light at night. Unsurprisingly if we had two moons it would mean more light at night, and fewer fully dark nights. This could influence nocturnal beings which rely on light at night. Nocturnal predators could potentially more easily see their prey. This could lead their prey to develop an adaption to have better camouflage to counteract this. Which in turn could lead to the predators becoming more intelligent.

The tides. The moon creates tides, with two moons these tides would be even stronger and higher. Thinking about who this would affect – it would be almost all of the human population. Higher and stronger tides would make living by the sea almost impossible, and many of our key ports and cities are by the sea. Stronger tides would also lead to stronger erosion and therefore it would be dangerous to live anywhere near the coast and it could have a huge impact on the coastline. The human race relies on the ocean and the coastline for a number of things and therefore our whole way of living would have to change.

Measurement of time. The light from the moon impacts how we measure months. With two moons we would have to alter our measurement to account for full and partial months with the movement of the two moons.

Poor Candidate: A poor candidate would see this question as asking a question on a topic that they don't know about and won't think around the question. A poor candidate might just focus on one of these impacts or they might mention something about the impact of having two moons on space – even though the question has asked the candidate to focus on impacts on Earth.

Q52: Do you think you'd survive for longer in the arctic or Sahara desert?

This is a fun question to answer and definitely tests your imagination and ability to problem solve. The first step would be to think of the geographies of both locations. This includes the topography, biodiversity, availability of light and water and the temperature. You could then think about which elements of these are key to human existence. Another important part of this task would be to take into account the humans that already live in these locations.

Good candidate: *I believe that you would survive longer in the Arctic, for a number of reasons. Firstly, although both locations have extreme temperatures, there is much easier access to water in the Arctic than in the Sahara. Water is key to human survival and therefore this is really important. Secondly upon looking at the mammals that exist in the Arctic (polar bears, Arctic foxes, reindeer) compared to those in the Sahara, you can see that they have certain biological characteristics such as high fat levels and fur. Although as humans we don't possess these, it would be easier to replicate fur by dressing appropriately than replicating the biological characteristics of mammals in the Sahara, such as very small body size and burrowing behaviour. Thirdly people do live in the Sahara but in relatively small numbers and they tend to congregate wherever there is vegetation that can support grazing animals or reliable water sources. The Arctic, on the other hand, is home to numerous indigenous inhabitants who are spread all across the different land regions of the arctic. They are well known and tend to survive through hunting, trapping or pastoralism. One reason for this is a climactic variation you find in the Arctic due to its large area, therefore you could more easily survive in some of the less harsh climates in the Arctic. It is important to bear in mind that indigenous groups in the Arctic find the environment to be familiar and generous, however largely this is due to their longstanding history and connection with the environment. Their lifestyle has adapted over years and they hold valuable information about surviving this environment which an ordinary person would not have. For example, Inuit groups move seasonally between the sea and inland tundra. Therefore, although you would likely survive longer in the Arctic, it would still be a challenge to live and survive there.*

Poor candidate: *You wouldn't be able to survive in either because they are harsh climates. Or You would be able to survive in the Arctic longer because there is water.* The second answer might be correct but the candidate hasn't gone into nearly enough depth and hasn't shown any more reasons or critiques of this answer.

Q53: What would happen if pandas became extinct?

This question is looking mainly at the topic of ecosystems; however, you could bring in some other areas of geography if you have some appropriate knowledge.

Good Candidate: *The main impact of pandas becoming extinct would be on their ecosystem and the food webs/networks within it. Every organism is part of a food web (it eats other organisms and then is eaten by other organisms) and then this food web is part of a wider food network. I would predict that a Panda largely eats bamboo and maybe they are eaten by larger predators. But even if they are at the top of their food chain and only eat bamboo there will still be an impact if they become extinct. Firstly, it would impact the amount of bamboo that is grown in their ecosystem, which could have knock on effects if the bamboo growing takes away nutrients or space from other species, this could then reduce the amount of food for other animals. There might also be micro-organisms that rely on the by-products produced by pandas which could play a vital role in the ecosystem without us really realising.*

Another area to think about would be how important the panda is for us as humans. For example, pandas are a big export from China, especially in zoos, and in the past have been given as a sort of geo-political statement. They are also the face of the logo of the WWF and have an emotional role in our society. Them becoming extinct would likely be big news and could spark an emotional response from a lot of people but could also impact Chinas role in the animal welfare world. Therefore, for a variety of reasons it would matter if pandas became extinct – both for the environment but also for the human population.

Poor candidate: A poor candidate might just answer this question with 'yes' or 'no', with no explanation or reasoning given. Another poor answer would be if the candidate assumed things about a panda and its ecosystem which would be widely unlikely. For example, it is common knowledge that pandas aren't big predators and therefore the following answer would be incorrect: *Pandas becoming extinct would have a big impact on their food web. If pandas became extinct then the populations of mammals they eat would grow in size and this would have knock on effect on the ecosystem.*

Q54: How could we measure sea levels, what would be some issues with this?

This is another question which if you have prior knowledge about the measuring of sea levels then definitely use this. If you do not then don't worry.

Candidate with prior knowledge. *The standard method of measuring sea level is using tide gauges at ports and harbours around the world. These measure the rising and falling tide against a benchmark on the land nearby. These measurements are also recorded with the time so that they can work out the periods of high and low tides. Some issues with this method are that, firstly, it is measured at ports and harbours across the world so it won't always be measured in the same way or accuracy in every location. Similarly, sea levels tend to rise and fall in different locations with different seasonality – such as El Nino, and therefore these have to be taken into account when looking at the sea level changes year on year. A more accurate measurement for sea level is the NASA radar beamed from satellites. This can measure sea level to a few millimetres and therefore is more accurate and will take into account climactic variations. Issues with this are likely to be more operational. They are expensive to use and also require high skill level to fix if things so wrong.*

Candidate without prior knowledge. If you have not studied this before then you could come up with a range of answers but make sure you are answering the question. Firstly suggest a way to measure sea levels and explain how it might work. Next it is important to answer the second part of the question. This requires you to critique your answer, think about some of the challenges or issues that might occur with what you suggest.

One way that we could possibly measure sea levels is by using a measurement device attached to a port or harbour, which is regularly read and the data tracked over time. There would be many issues with this, however. It would require a significant about of man power as the device would have to be regularly read. The readings would also have to be looked at alongside the tide times, as the changes in sea level will vary on a day-to-day basis. This method will also have to be carried out at ports across the world as global sea level changes will have regional and local variations.

Poor candidate: A poor candidate might only answer one part of the question. They might give a good answer to 'how could we measure sea levels'; they might even give a lot of background knowledge on tide gauges and NASA radars. However, the question is also asking for issues with these methods and if a candidate does not critique the methods that they have discussed then they will not be answering the question correctly.

Q55: How would you go about proving man-made global warming?

This is a good question to show off your knowledge on a topic that you will have been expected to have learnt about or studied. The best away to approach this is to first talk about how global warming is man-made and then look at how to prove it. For a more complex answer you could explore some of the possible natural causes of global warming and how you would prove that these are not important.

Good Candidate: *Global warming is the long-term heating of the Earth's climate which has been observed since the pre-industrial period. This is a form of climate change, but one that is human led. The human activities that have caused global warming include the burning of fossil fuels. This causes global warming as it releases greenhouse gases into the atmosphere which cause a 'greenhouse effect' by which more of the solar radiation from the sun is trapped within the Earth's atmosphere, therefore leading to a warming effect. The reasons for the increased burning of fossil fuels over the last 150 years is multifaceted, and largely derives from the industrial revolution. Since the industrial revolution we have started burning more and more fossil fuels (coal, oil, natural gas) in order to produce more energy. We have also started using more and more technology that not only requires energy but in some cases are big fossil fuel burners themselves (cars and airplanes). Another reason for the increased uptake in fossil fuels is the massive population boom that we have seen over the last 150 years and also the recent development of countries such as China and India. In order to prove that global warming is man-made we can use data to show that these increases in fossil fuel usage coincide with the recent global warming. Using the 'hockey stick graph' we can see that the changes in temperature started to occur around the mid-1800s. This is the beginning of the industrial revolution. We can look at this graph alongside the graphs of greenhouse gas emissions over the last 150 years and see that there has been a definite relationship between the rising temperatures and the rising greenhouse gas emissions. On top of this we could graph the changes in population and energy consumption which would also correlate to the recent rise in temperature.*

A global-warming sceptic may argue that this recent period of warming has been caused by natural factors, such as solar flares or axial tilt. However these processes have happened throughout history and a rapid change of temperature at this scale has not been seen before.

Poor Candidate: There are a number of ways to answer this question poorly. For starters the candidate may just discuss what global warming is, or what are the factors that have led to global warming. This does not answer the question as they want to know how you would prove this. Another key mistake would be to use 'climate change' and 'global warming' interchangeably, and not show that you have an awareness that 'global warming' is specifically the recent warming that has occurred over the last 150 years, whereas climate change is just changes to the Earth's climate, which have occurred throughout the history of the Earth. A candidate would be missing out if they did not use this as an opportunity to mention key concepts in the study of global warming, such as fossil fuels and the greenhouse effect.

Q56: What are the geographic impacts of globalisation and multi-national corporations?

This is a very classic human geography question. You will probably have been expected to have studied globalisation in some form or another, or at least be knowledgeable about what it is. Although I would not suggest going into a long explanation about what globalisation is, it might be worth giving a short definition (if you know one) and then thinking about the different areas that it impacts, it would definitely be worth mentioning how wide-ranging the impacts are. With this in mind, it would be best to pick out the areas to discuss that you are most comfortable/knowledgeable in. For example, you could discuss economic impact, environmental impact, social impacts, political impacts, cultural impacts (the list goes on). Once you've decided which impacts you are going to talk about, it is important to explain the relationships between globalisation and the impact. It would also be important to think critically about this question and maybe discuss some of the ways that certain aspects of society have rebelled against globalisation.

Good Candidate: *Globalisation is the process of interaction and integration among people, companies, and governments worldwide. The impacts of globalisation and multi-national corporations (MNCs) are multi-faceted, including social, economic, political, cultural and environmental impacts. Globalisation has led to multi-national corporations such as Google and McDonalds, playing a massive role in the global economy. This has had a wide variety of further impacts. In many countries these MNCs have taken business from smaller companies and as these MNCs can operate using economies of scale, they can sell their goods/services for cheaper than their competitors. The MNCs have also had a huge cultural impact. The majority of these MNCs are Western, and therefore have led to a process called 'westernisation' or 'Americanisation' of cultures in non-Western countries. For example, in Japan it is now the cultural norm to have KFC at Christmas. This can lead to an erosion of culture and cultural diversity, leading to a possible homogenisation of culture.*

Socially globalisation has seen the movement of people to travel and move more freely due to the improvements and reductions in cost of transport. This has come with its own set of impacts. Cities around the world are now mixing pots of cultures, with people of all nationalities coming together. Brazil, for example, has the largest Japanese population outside of Japan. Positive impacts of this include the mixing of cultures and people, and also the ability of people to travel abroad to work purposes. However, there are also negative impacts, such as increase in racially motivated hate and also a 'brain drain' from countries that people are emigrating from.

Globalisation as a process has also led to political changes, as there has been increasing discontent with the impacts of globalisation, namely the easy movement of people around the world and the opening up of trade. For example, the Brexit vote was seen as an example of the people of the UK being discontent with aspects of globalisation and wanting to 'take back control' of their trade and borders.

Poor Candidate: A poor candidate might only focus on one element of globalisation (such as economic) and therefore miss out some of the other important elements of globalisation. Similarly, this question lends itself to case studies and therefore a poor candidate might give an example of an impact but not follow it up with much explanation or examples, which are key to this answer. It would also be a poor answer to only focus on positive or negative impacts, as it is important to show a well-rounded answer here.

Q57: If you could take a non-geographer anywhere in the world to convince them geography was important, where would you take them and what would you say?

This is the perfect opportunity to showcase any interest in geography that you have and also talk about why you think geography matters. The question is purposely very broad so allows you to decide if you want to focus on physical geography, human geography or both. Before picking your place, think about why you think geography is important, this will need underlie your answer.

When thinking about a place to pick, make sure it's somewhere that you feel you know well and that you could think of a range of geographical issues/process that occur there. This might be somewhere of physical geography significance (e.g., a glacial valley, volcanic area etc…) or somewhere with human geography significance (a big city, somewhere experiencing developmental issues etc..) or even somewhere where the two combines (e.g. San Francisco – a place of interesting urban processes alongside being on a large fault line). I would recommend using somewhere you've studied as a case study as this will mean you will have a good amount of background knowledge if you are questioned further.

In terms of thinking about convincing them why geography is important, this will depend on why you think it's important. It may be something quite practical, such as showing them the flood defences on a river bank or visiting somewhere experiencing sea level rise. On the other hand, geography might be important to you because it studies the mixing of people and cultures so you might decide to take the person to a neighbourhood in a certain city. Just remembering when you're answering this question that you can really show the interviewer why you think geography matters and also show off your knowledge about some of your favourite geographical topics.

Good candidate: *If I were to take a non-geographer anywhere in the world, to convince them geography was important, then I would take them to the rainforests of Malaysia. To me the importance of geography lies within the ability to bring different areas of academia and science together to create a better outcome for both the environment and people. The reason that I'd choose the rainforests of Malaysia is because of the conflict that is currently occurring over the use of land. Malaysia is a place of massive important to biodiversity, with amazing rainforests and a huge array of incredible, and now endangered, species. In conflict with this land use is the growing of palm oil. If a conservationist was looking at this conflict, they would say it is key for the natural rainforest to grow and for the palm oil production to be pulled back. This is because of the importance of the ecosystem and the biodiversity. An economist, on the other hand, would look at how important the palm oil industry has been for jobs and for the local economy and therefore would say that it is important for the production to continue. A geographer has the ability to approach this issue with both these arguments, and many more including the history and politics of the area, in mind. I would say to the non-geographer that only a geographer could bring together all these different fields of knowledge of this area, all of these different stakeholders and help everyone come to a conclusion that takes all of the different interests into account. And that is why geography is important.*

Poor candidate: *I would take the non-geographer to the coast. I would do this because the coast has lots of geographical features such as caves and arches that have been created through geographical processes.*

This candidate has completely missed the point of this question. It is not asking you to take the non-geographer to see something geographical, but instead is getting you to think about why geography is important and therefore where can you explain and show this importance.

Q58: It is often said that we know more about the surface of the moon than the depths of our oceans – do you think this is true, and if it is how would you fix it?

Although there is some prior knowledge that candidates could have surrounding this topic, you will not be expected to know in-depth the physics of the ocean. Therefore, this is another good chance to think out of the box and find ways to bring multiple areas of geography together. It's well known that we have seemed to have explored more of space than the ocean and it's important to think of the different reasons why.

Good candidate: If you are aware of the underlying reasons for this then definitely start off by discussing these. *The depths of our oceans have zero visibility and extremely cold temperatures, making it challenging for people or objects to explore. On top of this the biggest limit to people and machines travelling to the depths of the ocean is the huge amount of pressure, this is especially limiting when trying to send people down to explore.*

On top of the physical challenges, it is important to think of other reasons why exploring the depths of the ocean might be a challenge. *There are constant geopolitical struggles over the ownership of certain areas of water and therefore some areas might be hard for researchers from certain countries to visit and explore. Also, we are limited by technology. Although technology is constantly improving if is still a challenge to create technology that can travel to massive depths, feedback imaging and withstand huge amounts of pressure.*

The next step is looking at 'how can this be rectified', make sure that you are using some of the challenges you have already highlighted in your answer. *The toughest challenge to rectify would be the issues of pressure deep under water. The most likely way to rectify this would be through new technology. We have such incredible scientific knowledge now that we didn't have even ten years ago so we might be able to build something that can withstand the enormous pressure. In terms of the geopolitical issues, one way of remedying this would be to create a sort of cross-governmental organisation whose focus is to explore more of the ocean. In bringing in lots of different countries you reduce the chance of geopolitical tensions and you benefit all the countries involved by sharing information and technology.*

Poor candidate: A poor candidate might be limited by their lack of knowledge on this topic. They might not know the answer and stop there. Another limiting factor in an answer would be if a candidate were to answer the first part of the question correct but ignored the second part of the question. It is always important to make sure that all parts of the question are answered.

Q59: Why is there a wider range of living organisms in rainforests than there are in deserts?

This question could lead to a relatively straightforward answer from a candidate. A more impressive candidate, however, could approach this from a number of angles. The first place to start with this question would be to think about the key differences between rainforests and the Sahara Desert. Although this is obvious it's important to show you know the basics before you move on to more interesting angles. There is also always room to bring in some of your own knowledge into your answer. For example it might be worth talking about some of the threats to biodiversity that the two ecosystems face.

Good candidate: *The main reason that rainforest contain more biodiversity than the Sahara Desert is due to differences in light, humidity, water and temperature. Although both locations are hot, rainforests are far more humid than deserts and therefore lend themselves to be more biodiverse. This is because all life forms need water and only a small selection of fauna and flora can survive with the small amount of water available in the desert, whereas a much wider range can exist in a rainforest where there is plenty of water due to high humidity and constant rainfall.*

Whilst discussing these processes it would be worth mentioning examples of the type of biodiversity that exists in the two places.

This high level of biodiversity can be seen in the many types of flora and fauna that can be found within a rainforest, including exotic orchids and toucans, in comparison to the Sahara Desert which has far fewer types of fauna and flora. One of the reasons that many of the fauna exist in the rainforest is due to the flora, which exists due to the underlying conditions. All ecosystems have complex food and energy webs and networks which allow the ecosystem to continue to thrive. In the Sahara Desert these food and energy webs are much smaller due to the small number of organisms which can survive. The biodiversity of both of these ecosystems, however, is under threat. Rainforests are facing a huge threat of deforestation which will massively impact its biodiversity. For the Sahara Desert, rising temperatures due to climate change will only limit the species that can survive.

Poor candidate: *Rainforests contain lots of biodiversity because they have lots of different plants and flowers and it's a warm climate.* Not only is this answer far too short, the main issue is that it doesn't compare rainforests to the Sahara, which is the key ask of the question. Both of these ecosystems are hot and therefore it's important to mention how rainforests have far more water than the Sahara, as this is the key differing factor. When discussing ecosystems, it is also always important to talk about food and energy networks.

Q60: What geological phenomena can you think of which have had significant impacts on people?

This is a time to show your understanding of the inter-relationship between human and physical geography, which will be a key part of any geography course. Pick a geological phenomenon that you know well and have studied, you may have even studied its impact on humans. Geological phenomenon includes earthquakes, continental drift, geysers, volcanoes, weathering, glaciation and many more. Using a wide range of ways that the geological phenomenon has impacted humans, alongside examples, is a good way of showing a wide range of knowledge but also thinking outside the box a bit.

Good candidate: Using volcanoes as an example, it's not necessary to explain everything you know about volcanoes, as the question is specifically asking for its significant impact on humans. It is worth thinking of a variety of ways that volcanoes have impacted humans, rather than just thinking about the impact of eruptions. *Volcanoes have had a significant impact on humans in a number of ways. Most obviously they have massive effects on human populations whenever they erupt. The eruption of Vesuvius in Pompeii, for example, killed a large proportion of the population. Eruptions of volcanoes can also lead to geological changes which have significant impacts on humans. The islands of Hawaii were created from an underwater eruption of a volcano, and this is now a populous island. Eruptions can also lead to extremely fertile soil due to the deposits of volcanic materials which are rich in minerals. Therefore, the banks of volcanoes tend to attract farmers. Volcanoes have also had significant impacts on our ability to learn about the past. The eruption of Vesuvius led to the city of Pompeii being preserved in volcanic ash which has been key to our understanding of the Roman times. Volcanoes can also impact humans through their ability to alter our climate. As volcanoes erupt they release volcanic ash which can act as a barrier to sunlight coming in. After the eruption of Mount Tambora in the 1800s, there was a 'year without summer', which had massive impacts for agriculture.*

Poor candidate: A poor candidate might pick a geological phenomenon like volcanoes and either not go into any depth or give a very surface-level answer such as *volcanoes have had a significant impact on humans because they can kill people.* It is important to think of a variety of impacts but also to think of some case studies to give examples alongside your answer.

HISTORY

The subject interview for History can take several different formats as each college has their own way of conducting interviews. The Admissions Office for your college will let you know what format your interview will take in good time. If you have any questions about it, it's best to contact them directly.

It may be the case that you have prepared extensively for one aspect of your interview, but aren't given a chance to draw on that preparation. For example, they might not ask you about anything on your personal statement, even if you are very keen to talk about it. If this happens, try not to let it rattle you. The interview process can be unpredictable, so try to remain as calm and flexible as you can.

In a standard history interview, the interviewers will ask you a **series of questions pertaining to your subject**. Some of these will be related to topics you have studied before. Others will be related to certain areas of historical methodology.

The interviewers know what subjects and what areas of history you have studied at school from your application. For example, they will know if you have studied modern history or ancient history. They will **not** ask you for detailed knowledge about areas of your subject that you are not familiar with. However, questions on topics you've studied are fair game.

Draw on the work you have done at school to answer these questions, but be prepared that the conversation might go beyond your syllabus. Avoid saying things like 'we haven't covered this in school yet' – just try your best to answer each question.

The interviewers will also have read your personal statement (and your SAQ form, if you applied to Cambridge). They are likely to ask you questions about the academic sections of it.

For example, if you have mentioned that you furthered your understanding of historical practice by reading Richard Evans' *In Defence of History*, then they may ask you to summarise an aspect of the book or ask whether you agree with the author on a certain issue. If you have mentioned work experience in a museum, they might ask you about the work you did there.

WORKED QUESTIONS

Below are a few examples of how to start breaking down an interview question, complete with model answers.

Q1: Does the study of history serve any practical purpose?

Applicant: This question covers quite a lot of potential areas, so I will start by looking at the study of history in the context of university/higher education as that seems most relevant. Firstly, I will evaluate a few potential arguments. Studying history at university serves many practical purposes, both for the student and society as a whole. The student gains many skills such as research and formulating an argument. Society gets to benefit from these skills when they graduate. But these benefits are not unique to history alone as this description could also cover other humanities subjects such as Classics or Sociology.

The other argument is that **history teaches lessons**, without which history would simply repeat itself and humanity would go on making the same 'mistakes'. This is also not a particularly convincing view in my opinion. Though, there can be similarities between different historical events as all historical events are unique, which I believe undermines the idea that history constantly repeats itself. I think this idea is based too much on hindsight as it is easy to see similarities between events after they have happened.

Instead, I think that historical causation (what makes events happen) depends above all on the context in which those events take place. This means that we cannot necessarily learn specific practical 'lessons' from history to apply in the future because the context of the future will be completely different.

However, this does not mean that history does not serve any practical purpose. Even though I don't think one can learn concrete 'lessons' from history, being able to understand how a certain problem came about can make it easier to find a solution. This means that the **skills gained by studying history can have a positive practical impact** on policy-making. Aside from that, the study of history also serves to educate and entertain the public. Most historical works are written by historians at universities and TV documentaries are usually made with the input of historians.

Analysis: You will not be expected to answer questions as fully as this. This answer is an indication of some of the things you might be expected to talk about in response to a question like this, but the interviewer will help you along the way with additional questions and comments. The merit of the answer is that it **breaks down the question** into manageable chunks and proceeds through an answer while signposting this process to the interviewer. These are good skills for you to try to develop, but remember that the interviewer is there to help get the best out of you.

Poor applicant: A poor applicant could begin by saying "we haven't studied this in class", and make no effort to further the conversation. He or she might then, if pressed, express a vague opinion that history serves a practical purpose in that it teaches people lessons for the future. As discussed, this is not a very strong interpretation because historical events depend on a specific configuration of circumstances. It would be difficult to gain a concrete and specific 'lesson' from one historical situation that could be applied in another historical situation as no two historical situations are the same.

A **poor applicant** may also respond to this question by saying that there is no practical purpose to history at all. Unless you have a very good argument to back this up, this would be a bad answer to this question because it would overlook the practical benefits that a historical perspective can bring to various areas of public life. It would also be a bad answer because it would imply that there is no practical purpose to the career to which your interviewers have dedicated their lives, as well as the degree to which you are applying.

Q2: Is it ever possible to find out 'what really happened' in the past?

A **good applicant** will recognise the complexity of this question. Throughout school, one is encouraged to assume that every statement written in a history book is a statement of fact. But at university level, it becomes clear that sources are subjective, historical interpretations are subjective, and the idea that history is just a series of events and facts seems a little simplistic. With a question like this, a good way to break it down is to focus first on one side of the argument and then on the other before coming to a conclusion. If you do this, you might choose to say to the interviewer, "first I will look at the idea that it is not possible to find out 'what really happened' in the past", so they know your approach.

Then you might choose to discuss the fact that you can never really know whether a source is telling the truth because **historical sources are inherently subjective**. A diary entry or letter about a certain event is only written from one person's perspective and they might not have had a full understanding of events or may be recording them in hindsight, having forgotten some of what happened. Even official documents are subjective; they might have an agenda behind them or be subject to censorship. When it comes to more distant historical events, the source material is necessarily subjective because it depends on a large extent on what has survived.

So, in many ways, it may be impossible to find out 'what really happened' in the past – there are too many obstacles in the way and history is only ever an interpretation of past events, rather than an objective statement of fact.

On the other hand, however, it would be unfair to say that this means all interpretations are equally invalid. While historical sources are subjective, it is possible to come to a reasonable interpretation of past events by using a wide variety of sources that corroborate each other. If all available sources say the same thing about a certain event, we can be reasonably sure that this is correct. This is how we can determine certain facts that are beyond interpretation. For example, the French Revolution occurred in 1789. Therefore, it is possible to find out some aspects of what really happened. Even though sources and interpretations are subjective, **history is not fiction**.

Q3: Is history increasingly the study of ordinary people?

In many ways, the answer to this would be quite straightforward. Yes, history does seem to be moving away from the study of great men to that of ordinary people – whereas in the early 20ᵗʰ century, 'history' was almost synonymous with **'political history'** and focused largely on politicians and generals. History seems to have democratised in recent decades. Scholarship in recent years appears to have focused more than ever on people who had not been represented by historical studies before such as women, ethnic minorities, the working classes, etc.

A good answer may, therefore, challenge this obvious response in a few ways. While all of the above is true, it would be worth mentioning that some **parts of history still focus disproportionately on 'great men'** rather than 'ordinary people'. Political history still occupies a big part of university history curricula while 'popular history', such as TV documentaries and historical bestsellers, are more often than not focused on 'great men' (or great events or occasionally, great women such as Elizabeth I) rather than 'ordinary people'.

A good answer would also recognise the secondary question implicit in this question – **Why** *is history moving away from the study of great men to that of ordinary people?* Answers to this would perhaps include a discussion of how minority rights movements often initiate new historical interest in minorities or a discussion of the democratisation of education in recent decades (e.g. African-American civil rights or second-wave feminism).

Q4: How would a biography of a major political figure written during their lifetime differ from one written after they had died? Which would be more accurate?

This type of question is a great one to get as it gives you a lot of scope to be creative and to bring in your own knowledge. The interviewers may ask this in response to a political biography you have listed in your personal statement, which would allow you to speak about a topic you are familiar with and passionate about.

However, assuming you are asked this question hypothetically without a specific biography in mind, there are **several ways** to approach it- even if you are not familiar with any biography of a major political figure yourself.

First, it would be sensible to tackle the first part of this question in isolation and leave the additional question ("*which would be more accurate?*") for later in the discussion. A biography of a major political figure written during their lifetime would be likely to differ significantly from one written after their death.

The biographer may have had **access to meetings with the political figure** or the biography may even have been written with the input of the political figure. This may make the text richer in its detail, but may also mean that it is coloured by the politician's political agenda and desire to manage his image and reputation. A biography written after the politician's death may have access to **newly released sources** not available during the figure's lifetime. There are many possible answers to this question.

In response to the second part of the question, a **weak candidate** may have a strong opinion on this, saying something like "a biography written during their lifetime would be more accurate because the biographer would know the politician, so they would tell the truth" or alternatively, "a biography written after their lifetime would be more accurate because the biographer would have the benefit of hindsight". Both of these answers fail to take the complexity of the situation into account.

A **stronger candidate** would investigate both options more fully and would not take too dogmatic a view on what is a complicated question without a clear answer. After considering the merits and weaknesses of each type of source, a stronger candidate may conclude that one cannot deem either type of source more accurate than the other. This is because it would depend entirely on the specific biography and biographers in question, or may conclude that it would be best to draw upon both sources to get the most accurate depiction of the politician in question.

Q5: Do you think that we should be careful when examining colonial history in a postcolonial world?

Postcolonialism is the study of the legacy of colonialism, particularly the ways in which empires made an impact on colonies that still have ramifications today. You will generally only be asked questions on specific topics which you have mentioned in your personal statement or which the interviewers will expect you to have studied based on your UCAS form.

Good Applicant: Studying colonial societies is a complex task for postcolonial academics, especially those who come from a region that was a previous enforcer of colonialism. No study of colonial societies cannot acknowledge the flaws of empire, the exploitation of natives and the appropriation of their cultures. Therefore, recognising former mistakes is an uncomfortable process that postcolonial scholars have to undertake. Western perceptions of ex-colonies today are usually shaped by the legacies of Western imperialism. It is necessary not just to reverse this process, but also celebrate the individuality of ex-colonies before they were assimilated into various empires.

Poor Applicant: Postcolonialism creates a lot of problems because the history of colonialism and imperialism does not reflect well on the Western world. Most people are offended by the mistakes made during the colonial era and many choose to protest against them so that they can be remembered in a more condemning way. Colonialism is very divisive, and therefore it is a difficult thing to study in the present day.

The first applicant's answer is stronger because they display a more nuanced and sensitive understanding of the question. They note how postcolonial studies inevitably reflect badly on Western societies, but that reflection is necessary for giving them a better reputation in the modern day. They also acknowledge how there are several processes that must occur to truly reconcile with the colonial past, including a greater recognition of former indigenous cultures.

The second applicant's answer addresses the same issues but is too vague. Statements such as 'most people' and 'colonialism is very divisive' could benefit from **greater precision and clarity.**

To show even more confidence when discussing this topic in front of interviewers, candidates could make reference to some of the most influential postcolonial theorists, such as **Franz Fanon**, a strong critic of colonialism, or **Edward Said**, who introduced the term Orientalism into the colonial discourse.

Q6: Can you think of any examples of a student protest having a significant impact on the path of history?

A candidate may or may not have studied some form of student uprising before, but regardless of if they have or not, it encourages them to think openly about how people of their own age have in the past tried to influence history.

Good Applicant: I think student uprisings are hugely important because they force governments to take serious notice of the causes they are protesting for or against. Young individuals studying at universities and other institutions are the next generation to take power, and they often voice concerns that older politicians are blind to or unaffected by. For example, many campaigns in the United States in the 20th century – civil rights, women's rights', anti-Vietnam protests – became radical and violent over frustrations with the incumbent political regime. Students used their platform as a means of taking the action, provoking the US government to respond.

Poor Applicant: Student uprisings have a big role in history because governments have to listen to them. If they show too much violence against the students, they could be made villains in the media and become very unpopular.

The first applicant has though carefully about **why** students have had such an influential role in history and what makes them a particularly powerful demographic in times of protest. The example they provide, although broad, is well chosen and perhaps opens up grounds for future discussion in the interview. The poor applicant has made a valid point – that students have a certain leverage due to the sympathy they can often get from the media – but has not supported it with a specific example.

Q7: Do you think that historical eras have tangible meaning, should the 'Progressive Era' be capitalised?

Good Applicant: I think this is very important that these eras are distinguished from the widespread usage of these terms. The Progressive Era in the US, for instance, refers to a specific period of history that was marked by social activism and political reform. It was particularly concerned with the issues that were arising from industrialisation and uncontrolled immigration. Whilst the changes that the reformers were pushing for would certainly be regarded as 'progressive', the use of capitalisation helps define it as an entire era of American history rather than as a general wave of progressive reforms. Other periods of American history, such as the Civil War, Reconstruction or Great Depression, are all capitalised, so the Progressive Era should be no different.

Poor Applicant: We should use a capital letter for these eras because they refer to actual periods of history. Therefore, we must distinguish, say, the Romantic Era, from other romantic movements in history.

The first applicant has been <u>successful in making a point and then supporting it with a well-chosen example</u>. Importantly, they have shown that the Progressive Era (1896-1916) refers to an entire period of American history, and it is concerned with far more than the 'progressive' reforms that were a part of those years. **Periodisation** is incredibly important for historians, and this candidate will impress the interviewers for exploring how it can be used.

In contrast, the second applicant has not demonstrated this same level of sophistication with their example of the Romantic Era. They should have explored what exactly was 'romantic' about the Romantic Era, and therefore why it is remembered as such in historical periodisation.

Q8: Why do you want to study history?

This is a fairy common question that provides a chance for the candidate to show their passion for the subject. There really is no wrong answer since the question is aimed and what **personally** drives their interest for the subject.

Good Applicant: Personally, I enjoy history because it allows us to better understand past people and societies. I find it fascinating to learn about how previous generations around the world acted and behaved differently to how we do now, how they had different customs and values that would seem so alien to our present-day standards. I think we can learn a lot about our current world, the institutions and states that exist, by exploring some of the key turning points in our history.

Poor Applicant: I want to study history because I find learning about the past really interesting and it teaches us a lot about the present

Both applicants have given the same reason as to why they want to study history, but the first candidate has been more successful because they have provided a more nuanced answer. They have said both why the past is interesting in itself, and why it is valuable to understanding the present. A response that could have been equally successful could have given a particular example, such a piece of family or regional history that has inspired them to become more curious about the subject as a whole.

Q9: Should we exclusively teach British history in British schools?

In 2013 the then-Educational Secretary Michael Gove redrafted the history curriculum to provide a greater emphasis on world history in lieu of some traditional British topics. This process is far from complete however, and interviewees may tackle this question by addressing the gaps in Britain's current educational system.

Good Applicant: Personally, I think that British students should be learning about British history, but we are currently learning about the wrong topics. A greater emphasis should be placed on periods and themes that have a greater relevance today. For example, we should learn more about imperial Britain and its involvement in the colonies. This is important because it helps us understand Britain's role in the slave trade and how we should remember it today, while also placing British history in a more global context. Learning about monarchy and politics, as is traditionally common, is still important in understanding how our current form of government has come to be. Particularly important is how the British monarch has gone from being an absolute ruler, to a constitutional one in the 17th century, to an almost ceremonial one today. However, students should have a greater flexibility and choice over the aspects of British history that they study.

Poor Applicant: I think that British students should continue to learn British history. It is incredibly important to learn about the country to live in, and understand how present-day institutions and traditions have ended up as they were. Teachers are familiar with the topics and it would be disruptive for them to learn new things. British history does interact with many other countries as well, so students get a sense of Britain's position.

The first applicant's answer is strong because they have been explicit about *how* they would change the British historical curriculum. Both candidates have made the point that British history is important to learn as it helps us understand Britain today. However, only the first candidate has shown how there are some aspects of British history that need to be visited more thoroughly in order to get the complete picture.

The second applicant's claim that teachers should not need to learn new topics is fairly contentious, and an issue that the first applicant raises. The historical curriculum should constantly change over time so that it properly reflects on the society in which it is learnt.

Q10: Can you learn real history from films and television programmes?

Historical films and dramas often come under criticism for taking artistic license and failing to accurately represent the historical events that they showcase. However, surely it is the role of documentaries to provide the 'accurate' renditions of history on our screens? Candidates could answer this question with reference to any film or TV show that would shed light on this issue.

Good Applicant: In my opinion, historical films and TV shows have a much more important function than accurately providing the truth. Because of their cinematography, storylines and quality of acting, historical dramas attract a much wider audience than historical documentaries, and are an established part of the entertainment industry. People would go to the cinema to watch a historical film, but not a documentary. Although the truth is often distorted, historical dramas often promote interest in the watcher to then learn more about that particular part of history, through documentaries and books. 'The Crown', a TV show which has been criticised for inaccuracy, has in my opinion, had a crucial role in promoting recent interest about the history of the royal family and the major events of the 20th century through their lens. By bringing topics to a wider audience, they can encourage viewers to investigate about the past themselves.

Poor Applicant: TV shows and films about history are important because they bring history to the wider audience. Not everybody wants to read books about history, so the screen provides a more accessible format for learning. The average watcher is not concerned about the specific details that historians pick up on. They are more interested in a general idea of what was happening during the time that the film or show depicts.

Both responses argue along the lines that historical films and TV shows are the most accessible form of history for popular consumption, even if they are sometimes far from accurate. What makes the first candidates answer stronger is that they have drawn a link between the different ways in which people learn about history, and specifically the ability of mass media to inspire even casual enthusiasts to become invested in historical issues. In many ways, the very inaccuracies of some historical films and shows actively encourages watchers to do more research in order to find out the truth.

Q11: Do you think that it's possible to learn lessons from history?

This question is addressing the practical application of history and candidates could argue either for or against. They could provide circumstances when the 'lessons' of history are useful and when they are not.

Good Applicant: I think we ought to be careful about using the lessons of history. The problems we face today have arisen from radically different circumstances compared to those of the past. For example, warfare as a means of resolving political conflict is far more dangerous now than it was in the medieval era due to the increased militarisation of countries across the globe, not to mention the nuclear capacity of some nations. However, history can be useful when we remember its general patterns and lessons, rather than specific case studies of how to deal with problems. The lessons of overreaching, autocratic monarchies and states teach us to be wary of emerging dictatorships today.

Poor Applicant: I do not think we can learn 'lessons' from history as they are not applicable to the present day. In our modernised, democratic world there is no benefit from learning about the fates of flawed ideologies and institutions, such as absolute monarchy, since they already declined, and we have found better solutions to our problems.

The first applicant's answer is stronger because they provide a more **balanced** response to the question. They provide a reason why we should be cautious about using the lessons of history, before explaining how they could be useful as broad frameworks that could shed light on current situations. The poor applicant could have considered *why* our current systems and institutions have survived and others have failed, and what lessons we can draw from their success.

A great (and short) book on this topic is **Will and Ariel Durant's "The Lessons of History"**, which looks at long-term patterns and continuities from several perspectives such as race, religion, war, or government.

Q12: Currently, history is largely treated as contiguous – should we separate ancient history from modern?

Ancient History typically refers to a period from roughly 3300 BC to 600 AD. The candidate is being asked whether they think there is a clear distinction between that period and the history that follows that merits the two being studied separately, or if 'ancient' and 'modern' are simply labels denoted on a timeline.

Good Applicant: Personally, I believe that Ancient and Modern History should be viewed as one subject, and students should be able to study any period they want according to personal preference. It can be said that Modern History, due to the increased availability of evidence and presence of institutions that more closely resemble what we have today, should be studied separately because of its increased relevance. However, I think any boundary between Ancient and Modern is arbitrary. It wrong for students to not be able to study, for instance, Roman England and Anglo-Saxon England together, for the former clearly influenced the latter.

Poor Applicant: I agree that Ancient and Modern should be treated as different subjects. Both are interesting to study in their own right, but Modern History has a greater relevance today and therefore should be studied by those who want to better understand the present, whereas Ancient History should only be studied by those who are curious about the antiquity and its uniqueness.

There is no wrong answer to this question. The first candidate has created a strong argument for the amalgamation of Ancient and Modern History, but has also **acknowledged the counterargument**. This is a good way of showing to the interviewer that you are able to see both points of view. Importantly however, rather than staying on the fence, they go on to promote their own argument.

The second candidate has argued the opposite, and has made the valid point that the values, beliefs, and institutions of Modern History are perhaps a better starting point than the antiquity for those who want to understand the present. For a more sophisticated response, they could have, like the first candidate, made reference to a counterexample. What about the Renaissance, for example? Surely the revival of Greek philosophy in the 16th Century gives the Ancient World an important place in Modern History.

Q13: What would you say differentiates modern and classical sources?

This question encourages the candidate to think about how people from modern and classical societies were able to record their surroundings. Even if they have not studied classical history, this is a chance to think creatively about how sources have changed over time. The interviewer may provide a rough time scale to define what the 'classical' period was.

Good Applicant: The differences between Modern and classical sources can be explained by the development of societies in terms of literacy and education. Our classical sources are mostly limited to the writings of intellectuals and philosophers, making it difficult to unearth the oral culture of other groups in society. Modern sources feature more writings by the increasingly literate middle and lower classes. Their languages are also more familiar to us. Older languages such as Anglo-Saxon or Celtic are more separated from modernity and are therefore more up to interpretation when it comes to translation.

Poor Applicant: Since the classical era was much older, we have far fewer available sources, making it hard to understand the past. In the Modern era we have more content and developments in media have made the historian's life even easier.

The first applicant has nicely outlined two areas of difference; the societal groups who were producing sources, and the forms in which they were written. The poor applicant rightly notes the paucity of evidence from the classical era but fails to address how sources have changed in form and content, aside from a brief mention to growth of media.

The candidates could have thought more broadly about what a source actually is. The first applicant makes an interesting mention of **oral culture** and an area of discussion could be how this has been preserved in written mediums over time. Physical sources and the value of **archaeological evidence** could also be tackled in this question.

Q14: Should we ever take ancient accounts literally?

This question is testing the candidates' understanding of sources, and the problems of authenticity they often provide. Applicants could discuss the relative scarcity of classical sources available, their often poetic or rhetorical nature, and the fact that the writers were rarely present themselves at the events they describe.

Good Applicant: We must be cautious when analysing classical sources. Greek and Roman historians were more concerned about how their texts would be recited rather than read, and therefore focused more on rhetorical elements. They are full of heroic speeches by military commanders and kings that were unlikely to have happened, but nonetheless have symbolic importance and make for powerful drama. However, we should not make this generalisation about classical sources, for some Greek historians like Herodotus and Thucydides showed a greater interest in evidence-gathering, impartiality, and secular thinking; all virtues we would more commonly associate with modern sources and historical writing.

Poor Applicant: Classical sources are unreliable because they focused on drama rather than truth. Writers exaggerated battles and political events to make for vivid reading. In the modern era we have a greater availability of sources, so we can compare and contrast the alleged facts.

The first candidate's answer is strong because they have provided a **balanced argument** in which they have shown that there were two types of classical sources: the rhetorical and the 'scientific'. The second candidate has made a good comparison of what makes modern sources more reliable than classical ones, but has perhaps too easily dismissed classical sources as fictitious and therefore unreliable to the historian.

Q15: Do you think that the concept of race is useful for historians?

This question is looking at how historians approach their study of the past. Racial history has not always been a focus for scholars, but has only become more prevalent with various Civil Rights movements in the 20th century and our study of international slave trades. Interviewees could think about the role that race has played in history, especially when race was not discussed.

Good Applicant: I think race is an incredibly valuable concept for historians. We must think carefully about how humanity has gone from being ambivalent about race - evident in the monogenesis preached in the Bible - to institutionalised, scientific forms of racism during the time of the slave trade, to repudiating racial discrimination altogether in the modern day. Race is a social identity that intersects and challenges identities of kinship, nation, and religion. Countries have established deep-rooted injustices on racial grounds, such as the eugenics movement of the Nazi regime, or of Apartheid in South Africa. In no other field perhaps, have ideas and values changed so radically over time, so studying racial history is crucial to truly understanding the prejudices of the past.

Poor Applicant: Race is very important for historians. History has often focused on the role of white men and this is not representative of the past as a whole. Many past indigenous and native societies are lost in a Western-centric narrative. Race is essential to understanding events such as the Civil Rights movement in America, or the Apartheid regime in South Africa.

The first applicant has provided a complex understanding of what race is and how it can be used by historians. The **broad timeline** of racial thinking that they provide, from the Bible to the modern day, is an effective way of framing just how much assumptions surrounding race have changed, even only in the last 100 years or so. They also place race within the wider framework of social identities, and their examples are well chosen.

The second applicant has argued along the same lines, focusing on how race should be revisited by historians due to the previous suppression of non-Western cultures. Unlike the first candidate however, they have not explained *why* their examples are such important moments in racial history. To improve their answer, they could have mentioned the necessary changes in the Civil Rights movement – to mass organisation and more active forms of protest – necessary for political change.

Q16: Can you identify patterns or cycles in history?

Candidates may be familiar with some theories of historical recurrence. A very famous one, by David Hackett Fischer, proposes that European history repeats itself every 200 years. Machiavelli analysed the waves of 'order' and 'disorder' in 15th century Italy. However, candidates could equally answer this question with ideas of their own.

Good Applicant: To say that history repeats itself is too sweeping a generalisation. No events repeat themselves exactly, usually because an event results in structural change purposed to prevent that same event from happening again. However, historical events spread across large periods often bare similarities because over time the conditions for that type of event resurface, as the past is gradually forgotten. An example of this is the history of financial crises. A financial crash is usually followed by stricter economic policies, but increased deregulation over time makes the market once again susceptible to speculation and at risk of collapsing.

Poor Applicant: History cannot repeat itself because everything that happens is unique. Each event has its own causes and consequences, its own actors, and therefore should not be seen as a repeat occurrence. It is our tendency to draw similarities from events that took roughly the same form, but these are often quite forced.

The first applicant's answer is strong because they have used an example that illustrates their point very effectively. Their argument – that history is capable of repeating itself once the 'repeated event' becomes forgotten and its lessons unlearnt – is well contextualised within economic cycles of boom and bust.

The second applicant has argued that repetition in history is forced by the historians and political figures who are actively seeking to draw comparisons to their own benefit. This point could benefit from a specific case study. To use the first applicant's example, did The Great Recession of 2008 have the same causes as The Great Depression of the 1930s, or have their structural similarities been exaggerated in the interests of proving that history has repeated itself in the US?

Q17: What is the significance of medieval history in the modern world?

Good Applicant: I think that medieval history can be incredibly useful, despite the fact that many medieval ideas, values, and institutions seem so peculiar to us today. Learning about the medieval past can help us identify the transition from the medieval to the modern world, the aspects that persisted, and those that had to change in order to survive. Take England, for example. The legal system, parochial system and Exchequer all have their origins in the 11th and 12th centuries, but other elements of society, such as the absolute rule of the monarch, underwent considerable change over time.

Poor Applicant: Personally, I do not think medieval history has any relevance to us today. Unlike modern history it is too far in the past. While I can see the importance of learning about 20th century events such as World War Two and their importance in the present day, the medieval world is too far detached to have any influence on how the present-day world has been shaped.

The two candidates have taken considerably different approaches to this question, with the first applicant supporting the case for studying medieval history, and the second applicant rejecting its importance. The first candidate's answer is more successful because they have **clearly outlined** some aspects of medieval society that laid the foundations for present-day institutions, which makes his argument far more powerful. The second candidate could have made his case more persuasive by being **more precise,** showing exactly why, perhaps, we need not go that far into the past.

Another point that could have been raised is the cultural features of the medieval world. How have certain languages, religious beliefs and ritual practices survived into the 21st century? Also, a Marxist approach, using the notion of historical phases that states progress through, would work well here. Countries have had their 'medieval' phase at different times, some even fairly recently.

Q18: Define 'revolution'

Questions like this are not necessary looking for a precise definition of what a 'revolution' is, or at the very least might expect you to reach that definition after a thorough exploration of revolution as a concept. A response could discuss different types of revolution, and illustrate these with case studies, or provide a broader, conceptual definition.

Good Applicant: Revolutions take many different forms. The question of whether things like the Industrial Revolution were really just that is still being debated today. If we want to think about revolutions as a period of drastic change, or a 'Paradigm Shift', then we can say that a revolution is an instance or a set of processes in a defined set of time which result in a drastic change in one or a number of systems on a national or global level. However, for a lot of people, revolution is synonymous with revolt, often armed. Notions of technological revolutions then become more like a catchphrase that has been coined, rather than representative of the truth, and the only revolutions one can really see in history are like the French and Russian revolutions. Both approaches have advantages, but for me I think revolution is about more than a regime change, it is about a drastic shift in the way in which things are done, or the ways which people live – this definition of revolution would allow an historian to draw comparisons between political and technological revolutions, and that kind of comparative work is fascinating to me as an aspiring historian.

Poor Applicant: A revolution is when a government is overthrown by another group, usually the army or an opposition party. It typically involves violence and mass riots and protest, like in the French Revolution when the monarchy was kicked out.

The first applicant has thought creatively about the question, considering not just political revolutions (which would have been a perfectly acceptable assumption to make) but revolutions in other fields. They have also strengthened their answer by suggesting which view of a revolution is more appealing to them and why, and tied that into their own ambitions for university.

The second applicant has given a narrower, although not incorrect, definition, and has supported it with a good example. Their answer could benefit from considering if this definition applies to *all* political revolutions. Was the French Revolution unusually more bloody and violent than other revolutions? What are the differences between the French Revolution and the various 20th century coups that occurred in African nations?

Q19: Do you think that ideology exists in history?

Good Applicant: Yes, I think so. I think that ideology is an incredibly valuable concept for historians. It is the fusion of philosophical ideas with practical application. Most political movements, protests and revolutions will have an ideology behind them. For example, people in the 19th century who had a liberal philosophy believed in free markets, the extension of franchise, and constitutional limits on state power. Whilst groups and individuals can operate without an ideology and have purely practical beliefs, it is often from a philosophical base that most movements originate from.

Poor Applicant: There is definitely a concept of ideology. An ideology is a set of ideas that any person or group has, that serves to explain their actions. No one in history has acted without motivations, therefore every historical event can be explained by an underlying ideology.

Both candidates have attempted to **define** the term 'ideology', and either of their responses are acceptable approaches. However, the first applicant has supported their definition with a **specific example** that highlights both of their points; that ideologies exist as both theory and application.

The first applicant has stated that not everything can be explained by an ideology, whereas the second applicant has argued the opposite. Both of these views could have been better supported with examples. The first applicant could have continued their 19th century theme and refer to peasant and working-class movements that might not have had an ideology of their own but were influenced by a small handful of leaders. This raises a second issue that has not been addressed by the candidates; does ideology have to originate from the doctrines of philosophers and political theorists? Or can it emerge in more colloquial, folkloric forms among the illiterate classes?

Q20: How can we ever really know what people in the past thought or felt?

This is a broad and widely disputed question, with no definitive answer. However, since it is not topic specific it allows candidate to discuss whatever they are confident about. This sort of question might provide a springboard into a wider conversation or might even take the form of a mini debate between the student and interviewer.

Good Applicant: It is very difficult to understand exactly how people thought because of the limited evidence we possess of past societies. The further you go back in time, the fewer videos, audio recordings and written documents we have to reconstruct the past. Many societies had an entirely oral culture and we therefore have no official records at all. However, we can learn a great deal from interpreting interesting documents such as court cases, pamphlets, or sermons. For example, judicial records from the 17th century in England - a period I studied for my A-Level - can help us understand how people were so fearful of witchcraft at the time, a crime punishable even by death. It can be hard to relate to radical beliefs of the past due to our present-day standards, which is why it is important for the historian to try to empathise with the past.

Poor Applicant: We cannot go back in time so we will never truly understand the past. Our understanding of the past is mostly interpretations and approximations based on the limited sources we have.

The first applicant's response is strong for several reasons. Firstly, the candidate has been cautious when approaching the question; they have acknowledged the problems that historians face when trying to understand the past. Secondly, unlike the poor applicant, they have then provided a solution to the problem. It is important to always **answer the question clearly**, otherwise the interviewers will not be convinced as to whether or not the candidate understood what was being asked of them.

Thirdly they have provided a relevant example to help back up their points. This will impress the interviewer as it shows that the candidate has thought critically about their A-Level course and is able to apply their knowledge to more general, conceptual questions about history. To go further, another example could be provided, either to further support their point, or provide a counterexample of where past records and documents can be misleading.

Q21: Do you think that class is valuable as an analytical tool for historians?

Class refers to the hierarchical distinctions between individuals or groups within a society. It is typically associated with the work of Max Weber and Karl Marx. Candidates should think about the advantages and disadvantages of using class as a social category.

Good Applicant: In my opinion, class is a flawed but useful concept for historians. It divides people into groups that they may not identify with. Identities of race, language and gender exist within classes, and it is very debateable as to whether members of a class had a 'class consciousness' as Marx believed. However, it can be valuable for historians in categorising groups of people within a historical society, and trying to establish general trends. For example, in Medieval England there was no contemporary notion of class, but it is useful for historians to understand how the peasants, gentry or nobility acted as a collective group. It is also important for historians to see how class intersected with those other social identities, and in evaluating which ones created the most cohesive collective groups.

Poor Applicant: Not massively, history was written by the rich, so we only really have one class to ever look at.

The first applicant's answer is stronger for several reasons. Firstly, they have also acknowledged some the flaws of class as a social category, and have made a good reference to one of the disputable claims of Marxist history. Secondly, they have provided a useful example, since it is an era before class was a concept it highlights the way in which historians have used it retrospectively. Lastly, they have shown the relationship between class and other identities, arguing that class, like most concepts, should not be studied in isolation. The second applicant fell down because their answer was too short, limiting opportunities for the interviewer to maintain a conversation through it, and because it showed the candidate isn't particularly open minded or experienced with the diversity of sources available to historians.

To improve even further, the first applicant could have considered whether some class models are more useful or relevant than others. Marx and Weber's theories were followed by US sociologist William Lloyd Warner's six-tier hierarchy, and candidates may want to think if some class approaches are more useful than others. There are also unique hierarchies found in India, China, and Japan, providing good international comparisons.

Q22: What's the value in studying contemporary history?

There is no fixed definition for contemporary history. It generally refers to the study of past events that have a very immediate affect on the present. The contemporary past could be that of the current generation's lifetime, and so the events do not 'feel' like they should be part of history. Candidates could think about the unique problems of studying more recent history, as opposed to the more distant past.

Good Applicant: I think we should definitely study contemporary history. It has a greater relevance than any other period to our present day, especially in contextualising recent events developments. The main problem with contemporary history is that it is contentious, too close to the present and too fresh in the memories of the current generation. There is also more evidence surrounding the contemporary past than any other period. I believe that the contemporary past should be studied because it is the beginning of a long historical period. Ever since history has been written, there have been contemporary historians, who have had their opinions critiqued and revised by future generations. The study of contemporary history is therefore incredibly important.

Poor Applicant: Contemporary history, which is the history of the last 20 or so years, is important to study because it helps us understand the present, but its difficult because you can't really look at it properly, so I'm not sure if anyone teaches it. It should be studied though because we have lots of source evidence. Much of it is very reliable, and it comes in many different forms, like recorded interviews and websites as opposed to just books.

The first applicant's answer is strong because they have addressed why contemporary history matters to the present day. They have not only outlined the potential issues of contemporary history, but have suggested why it remains important in the longer-term historical process.

The second applicant, unlike the first, has **defined** the term 'contemporary history', an interview technique that can help give ones answer more clarity. However, their answer could have been improved if it were a more balanced response, considering why contemporary history has its own issues. An interviewer might challenge their argument that there is considerably more evidence for the contemporary past than from any other era. Does the accessibility of media and internet provide the opportunity for individuals, corporations, and even governments to produce fake news, or use propaganda to manipulate the truth?

Q23: Do you think historians should just tell the story of the past in the plainest terms, or should they add their own input?

Candidates should think here about the role of the historian and the ways in which they present their historical findings. Is it their job to simply tell the past as it happened? Or should they provide interpretation and analysis?

Good Applicant: I think that narration is a perfectly valid way of approaching the past, but it should be recognised as only one of the ways in which the past can be retold. Narrative history is useful because it is often chronological, and event driven. There are clear chains of cause and effect, and events are often given a focus according to their magnitude and impact. For learning simply about what happened, the narrative approach is most valuable. However, more interpretative histories also have their place, either in explaining why things happened, or by placing the narrative within a wider context. Analytical approaches can address themes and trends in non-chronological order, or approach the past from a particular angle, such as class or gender. I believe that both types of history are equally important.

Poor Applicant: I think we should narrate the past because it is the most accurate way of understanding what happened. A story-based approach is very accessible and provides the most honest recollection of what order events occurred in. We need a narrative history, with all the facts laid out, before we can even begin to think about interpreting the past.

The first applicant has successfully shown how narrative history is an effective, but not exclusive, way of interpreting the past. They have not only defined both narrative and interpretative history as two distinct categories of historical writing, but they have also explored the advantages of each.

The second applicant has, to a lesser extent, done the same. They have stated that narrative history must come before more analytical history. Their claim that narration is the most accurate form of retelling the past could be challenged, however. Adding interpretation to events can often provide greater clarity, especially if they seem contradictory or even out of place at first in the greater narrative. Both candidates could have thought about how narrative history is written. Does the historian, as a storyteller, have to sacrifice accuracy for narrative technique and literary style? This question might be picked up by interviewers in the ensuing discussion.

Q24: Do you think that religion remains important for historians of the modern world?

Religion is present in almost any society the historian studies, but modern historians tend to deal with more secular, centralised states in which the Church has lost much of its political power. Candidates should think about how religion continues to be an important social concept, and could provide examples of modern history in which religion has still been able to play an integral role.

Good Applicant: In my opinion, the study of religion remains important regardless of the period the historian is studying. National churches have become less important, particularly after the Enlightenment and rise of scientific thinking. However, especially in the lower, rural classes, religion remains an integral part of an individual's worldview. Furthermore, many modern issues are dictated more so by religion than any other factor. The Arab-Israeli conflict of the 20th century was partly caused by the growth of Zionism among Israelis and of Arab nationalism among Muslim groups. This is a reminder that opposing systems of belief can still drive wedges between people of the same nationality or ethnicity, and can escalate into political, territorial conflict.

Poor Applicant: Religion is important because a lot of what happens in the world can be blamed on religion. We need to make sure that we study it to help shed light on the damage it can cause and clarify its role in human history.

The first applicant's answer is strong because they have provided two clear reasons for the continued importance of studying religion in modern history; its ideological and political influences remain important. The second applicant has failed to interact with the 'modern' part of the question, and seems to be attaching their own value judgements to the response, which can quickly demonstrate a lack of understanding and thought.

Q25: You mentioned being fascinated by historiography in your personal statement. What does that word mean?

Historiography is perhaps most succinctly described as the 'history of history' and may have been briefly encountered by candidates whilst studying in years 12 and 13. It is an essential aspect of History at undergraduate level. Candidates can demonstrate their understanding of the term and could use examples to give a brief overview of some changes in historical thought.

Good Applicant: Historiography involves looking at how historians have, over time, changed their approach to the study of the past. This includes changes in methodology as well as the development of whole new theories. For most historical topics, regions and eras, there will be a separate historiography; historians studying the same topic will have provided different interpretations depending on which school of history they come from. For example, Marxist historians of the French Revolution viewed it a class struggle. Revisionist historians of the 20th century would take different approaches. François Furet, for instance, saw it as a liberal revolution that skidded off course. Recent feminist historians have re-evaluated the contribution of women during the Revolution. The study of historians themselves is equally important to the study of the past that they write about.

Poor Applicant: Historiography is the study of how historians have written about the past. It involves looking at how interpretations of any event or period have changed over time. Historians are grouped into schools of thought, such as Whig, Marxist, feminist, or revisionist. They have specific methods with they apply to the past, and in doing so end up with different results.

The first applicant's answer provides a more thorough examination of why historiography is important for students of history. In dealing with a broad and open-ended question like this, it is a good idea to focus on specific examples. Their brief overview of the French Revolution is an effective way of showcasing the value of understanding historiography. They could have gone further and express *why* changes in the study of the French Revolution occurred, but that might be covered anyway in the course of this particular interview as the issues have been set up nicely by the candidate.

The second applicant's answer has, like the first, provided a concise and workable definition for historiography. However, the rest of their answer lacks focus and is too vague. Their answer could be improved by stating why it is important for historians to acknowledge changing interpretations of the past, and why these interpretations have changed over time.

Q26: What do you think is the value of gender-history?

Candidates answering this question should think about why a gender-orientated approach is crucial to history, particularly in reinterpreting old assumptions about gender roles. It is important not to assume that 'gender history' means 'women's history', although undoubtedly one of the main functions of gender history is to revisit male-centric histories that have suppressed the contribution of women.

Good Applicant: Gender is an incredibly important approach to history because it tells us about the ways in which gender and gender difference have been incredibly influential in the past, and are often forgotten in political, economic, and religious narratives. Gender history involves revising deep-rooted narratives with fixed assumptions about patriarchy and masculinity. Gender as a category invites a more social approach to history, looking not just at state institutions but at household structures, the radically wide-ranging gender dynamics in different parts of the world, and changing identities. It amplifies and reinterprets the human past.

Poor Applicant: Gender history is important because it has previously been forgotten by historians. Most history is the history of men, specifically leading men. Gender history can try to undo that, but the chances of it working are slim due to the lack of material.

The first applicant has discussed gender in terms of both the roles of men and women, as well as the relationship between them. The intricate dynamics between genders is a key aspect of gender history, especially when considering how this dynamic has changed over time. Their answer could be improved by giving an example of where a gender approach to history is incredibly useful, like women in labour movements.

The second applicant has argued that gender history is important because it rebalances the exaggerated role of men in history with none of the nuance such a statement requires, and the student is pessimistic about the success of the endeavour. A better response here would have, like the first applicant, thought about the relationship between genders. A lot of 'great man' history does not necessarily think about these men in terms of their gender, rather they focus on their actions as political figures.

An article worth reading on gender history is **Joan Scott's "Gender: A Useful Category of Historical Analysis" (1986)**

Q27: Do you think written sources are less useful to historian than verbal ones?

Good Applicant: I think verbal sources have their advantages and disadvantages. On the one hand, words on a page are up to interpretation, whereas the tone of someone's voice can give a greater meaning to what the source is saying. Verbal sources might provide a more honest, visceral account of what they are describing, and provide a much more direct interaction with people who were present during the events being studied, whilst written sources are often made for a specific limiting function. However, verbal sources, as a means of understanding the past, can be less reliable if they form part of a chain of oral narratives. Stories were likely to change considerably over time, as details are added and omitted.

Poor Applicant: I think written sources are far more useful than verbal sources. Written documents are more likely to be accurate, especially for government purposes such as trial records. Before we invented recording, verbal sources had to be transferred to the written medium anyway, and in doing so probably lost a lot of meaning.

The first applicant has argued for and against the value of written sources, suggesting that their greater intimacy with the past is undermined by an element of unreliability, particularly as one goes further back into the past. Their points are well-explained and provide a good general overview of the nature of sources, although an example or two could have strengthened his answer further.

The second applicant has given a more one-sided account and could have benefitted from acknowledging the potential counterargument. Is it true to say that verbal sources were less 'accurate'? Both candidates could have made reference to an entirely oral society, (such as the Nuer, on which there is a famous anthropological study by **E.E Evans Pritchard**), from which historians have been limited exclusively to verbal sources in every rank of society.

Q28: You mentioned working on the French Revolution for your EPQ, can you compare it with a modern event of your choosing?

The French Revolution (1789-99) had many distinct phases and therefore a valid historical comparison could be made with any of them, from Bastille Day, to the Terror, to the rule of the Directorate. Stronger answers would be very clear about which aspects of the Revolution are most evident in the modern-day event that they have chosen. If you don't know anything about the french revolution at all, think about another revolution you have learned about in school or in your own work, and say something like "I've never learned about the French revolution, but I think the Russian revolution has a lot of comparisons with modern events" and go from there. The interviewers will be impressed by your flexibility and eagerness to persist. Generally, a question like this will only be asked if you have mentioned the French Revolution in your personal statement, or they know you studied it from your UCAS application, so this shouldn't be an issue most of the time.

Good Applicant: There are some similarities between the revolutionary *journées* in Paris and the riots on the US Capitol at the start of 2021. Both events highlight the potential dangers of a concentrated group of followers, provoked into action by one of their leaders. The Republican supporters that were arguably rallied by Trump behaved with the same collective mentality as the sans-culottes did under the guidance of the Jacobin leaders. The sans-culottes were convinced in the importance of rooting out royalists or anyone could be deemed 'un-revolutionary'. In both cases, the question of the agency of the crowd is an interesting issue. It is debateable as to whether or not the Jacobin crowds had an ideology of their own, or simply followed the orders of those in the National Convention.

Poor Applicant: The French Revolution can be compared to the Iranian Revolution in 1978-9 as they both involved the overthrow of a monarch. They were both led by popular protest and a discontent with the current form of rule, but whilst the French sought a secular, republican rule, in Iran a theocracy was put in place.

The first applicant has made an interesting comparison on a very recent and controversial event, discussing the role of crowd politics and the cult-like following that leaders can often obtain. Their answer is **discursive,** raising an interesting Marxist concept at the end – class or collective group consciousness – that could lead to further conversation.

The second applicant compares the French Revolution to another 20th century Revolution, but he fails to explore the similarities between them, aside from stating that they both involved a political coup d'état. They could have thought more about the ways in which the two Revolutions were quite different in their causes. The Iranian Revolution lacked many of the typical preconditions for revolution, such as a recent lost war, or a failing economy, so how did it begin?

With a question like this, it is very important to give yourself time to select a relevant and interesting example before beginning an answer. A few seconds can fill like a long time in an interview, but it is much better to give a question thought rather than immediately launching into a response.

Q29: Do you think that the events of the 11th of September, 2001 changed the way that we approach history in the West?

Good Applicant: Personally, I do not think that 9/11 has changed the way we write history, but it has encouraged certain themes to become more prevalent in historical writing. Because 9/11 was so tragic and within the lifetimes of most people today, it occupies an uncomfortable place in history, often with emotions still attached. 9/11 can be used by historians for periodisation purposes. The event marks the start of what is potentially a new era of history, in which the War on Terror and foreign policy have been two central issues. 9/11 has encouraged historians to revisit the past and learn more about the emergence of Islamist fundamentalism. It encourages us to think about the way in which religious ideologies within a denomination can change so radically over time. So, while historians continue to write in the same way, new topics have earnt a greater focus.

Poor Applicant: I think that 9/11 has made historians write more about the events that led up to it. They have become interested in developments in the Middle East and in the emergence of terrorism against the West. Without an event of that significance, this change might never have happened.

The first response is stronger than the second because it has done a better job of directly answering the question. The first applicant has clearly stated that whilst the way that history is written has not changed, 9/11 did cause some shifts in historiography. They have made an interesting reference to periodisation – the ways in which the past is divided into timeframes. Using terminology like this in an interview is likely to impress an interviewer, as it suggests the candidate has gone beyond their A- Level (or equivalent) syllabus and has thought more broadly about history as a subject.

Q30: What separates mythology from history?

Myth and history can sometimes be used interchangeably to refer to past stories, with 'myth' generally referring to narratives that are more rooted in folklore and hearsay rather than truth. Candidates could define the two terms themselves, or use examples to show their differences.

Good Applicant: I think that myths and history have many similarities. They are both narratives of the past that we use today to derive a sense of identity and community. However, myths differ in that they are less grounded in truth. They often have a historical movement as an origin, but then their emphasis is more on the social function of storytelling rather than an interpretation of events. An example of this is the 1789 Irish rebellion against British rule. The event itself would be classified as history, but the way it which it has been remembered as a revolutionary display of Irish nationalism would be considered a myth. Similar distinctions may yet be drawn by historians about the 2020 American election and the narrative of Donald Trump's fraudulent defeat in coming decades. The importance of these themes was clear during the commemorations of the bicentenary of the rebellion in 1998, when the nationalist element was downplayed in order to ensure progress during the Good Friday Agreements.

Poor Applicant: Myths are different from history because they are not concerned with factual events. They are stories used by communities to bind them together, full of symbolic stories and larger-than-life heroes and villains. They are passed down from generation to generation to preserve a sense of identity. History is more interested in interpreting the events that actually happened.

The first applicant's answer here is stronger for two reasons. Firstly, the Irish example gives their answer more clarity; it is always effective to **start generally and then move into examples to illustrate a point.** Secondly, they have explored the interrelationship between history and myth, and using their example have shown when the former becomes the latter.

The second applicant's answer makes an interesting comment on the nature of myths in comparison to history, with their greater emphasis on narrative devices to make a memorable story worth passing down generations. They could have addressed how these narratives compete with histories and whether or not the two can coexist.

Q31: How do you think people were able to justify slavery on the grounds of the economic benefits?

In modern debates about the history of slavery, it is clear that racial thinking has changed considerably since the height of European imperialism. However, the use of enslaved Africans for manual labour was also justified on economic grounds – to serve the interests of industrialising Western nations. Even if unfamiliar with the topic, applicants could think creatively about the evolution of the plantations in the colonial era.

Good Applicant: Aside from racial justification, slavery was adopted on the grounds that in was more economically profitable than its predecessor, indentured servitude. Unpaid labour and longer, more demanding working hours meant that slaves produced a greater output of resources such as sugar or tobacco, and needed less of an input themselves. In the North American and Caribbean colonies, land was abundant, but labour was dear, and therefore it made sense – in contemporary thinking – to export African slaves to the plantations in the Americas so that this land could be exploited. Goods sent home to Europe could hasten the speed of industrialisation and promote long-run economic development.

Poor Applicant: Slavery was a system that exploited Africans in a way that could not be done with white workers. Since they were not paid and could be treated worse, greater profits were made in the running of plantations. These profits could be used on other things, such as economic change back in Europe.

Both these responses outline the process by which slavery was adopted in the colonies. They are both able to identify the shift from indentured servitude to slavery and the reasons behind it.

The first applicant's answer is better because they display a more intricate understanding of the relationship between slavery and economic growth. It was not just increased 'profits' that enabled European countries to develop themselves, it was the greater quantities of raw materials than were being sent to her industrial centres that truly accelerated industrialisation.

To improve their answers, the candidates could have addressed which European powers were most successful in exploiting the advantages of slavery. Britain, for example, saw the advantages of industrialising first and monopolised on manufactured products by the 18th century.

Q32: How do you think we should commemorate the Great War?

The First World War is well commemorated annually in most of its participants. In the UK at least, the focus is on both celebrating the Allied victory, but also paying respects to those who lost their lives. Candidates could think about this question from the perspective of Britain, an ex-Axis power, or multiple nations in order to make comparisons. They could also think about the political, social, and territorial legacies of the War.

Good Applicant: I think we should remember World War One both through commemoration and reflection. We should continue, as we do in the UK, to show our gratitude every year on Remembrance Day for the fallen soldiers of all Allied nations. However, we should also think about the impact the War had on our longer-term future. Conflict abroad meant that the government was under increased scrutiny at home, enabling pressure groups to seek reforms. The War led to women enfranchisement, an extension of democracy, the regeneration of urban areas, the birth of the welfare state, and was part of the downfall of Empire. Dramatic social and political change often occur in periods of war, and the years 1914-1918 were no different

Poor Applicant: We should remember World War One because it is a significant moment of British history. It represents a major victory both militarily and of national solidarity. We should commemorate it every year to reinforce our universal identity. It should also be remembered because it led to considerable change in Germany. Arguably it laid the foundations for the birth of the Third Reich and the Second World War.

The first applicant's answer is well-constructed. It tackles the question from two different directions, namely the importance of memory and commemoration, and the long-term impacts the war had on Britain. They end their answer with the interesting observation that change is accelerated in times of war, and perhaps could have explored this further. Why exactly is this the case?

The second applicant has focused more on the commemorative aspects, but have also introduced the notion of national solidarity. The interviewer may challenge this view on the grounds that not every societal group will be able to identify with the victory of World War One. The candidate could also have more thoroughly explored the relationship between the two World Wars.

Q33: Is all history the history of great men?

This question makes a reference to the great man theory typically attributed to the Scottish philosopher, **Thomas Carlyle**. He believed that great men, due to their superior natural attributes of leadership, intelligence, and bravery, have been largely responsible for all the events of history.

Good Applicant: I think this is true to some extent. Especially before more democratic, parliamentary institutions emerged internationally, may countries had autocratic systems of leadership, whereby one person held all the executive power, the majority of the time we will find that this person is male. Historians have also been, overwhelmingly, male, and this has lead to the vast majority of historical narratives focusing on the accomplishments of particular individuals, overwhelmingly men. In England for example, the most influential individuals of the 17th century are almost universally cited as its Kings, until the Glorious Revolution of 1688 cut down their powers to the status of constitutional monarch. The other notable figure of that period, Oliver Cromwell, was also portrayed as a great man because he challenged that system, and in becoming Lord Protector he had obtained those same levels of power that enabled him to have a disproportionate influence on politics during the interregnum. It is importance that these notions are challenged, but there is an inevitable imbalance between the historical impact of great man and other groups and individuals on account of the widespread nature of patriarchy. A 'great man' approach denies importance to the societies in which these great men emerged out of. Surely Cromwell was a product of his surroundings, and therefore a history of the 17th century must include parliament, religious factions, and the combatants of the Civil War.

Poor Applicant: I disagree with this statement. One man can never be powerful or influential on his own, and he needs the support of his friends or political allies to be powerful. It discredits the role of women, of the many classes of society that have, through campaign and protest, also shaped history. It is not the great men that are powerful, but their institutions.

Both candidates provide fairly strong responses. The first applicant's two-sided approach is well illustrated by his example of 17th century England, showing both how the great men of that period were so influential, but also how they were a product of their surroundings. The second candidate is less convinced in the great man theory and takes a similar view in that great men are created by their institutions, and they also suggest that individuals cannot rule in isolation. His answer could be improved by a specific example to support his point.

Q34: What do you look at when determining how reliable a source is?

Historical books are secondary sources, based on their interpretations of a primary evidence. However, this does not mean that those primary sources are themselves entirely factual and true to events. An answer to this question could focus on either secondary or primary sources, but the responses below focus on the latter.

Good Applicant: When analysing, say, a primary written source, there are several things to be considered. Firstly, the author might have a specific agenda of their own that they are trying to express in their writing. Newspaper articles or religious pamphlets may be constructed based on the writer's alliance to a particular political party or religious faction. Secondly, the author might not have made the source of his own free will. They might have been unable to voice certain opinions that could result in their censorship or imprisonment. They might also be writing for a specific person or audience. Lastly, the source might have used exaggeration in places as a literary device, particularly evidence in the Medieval chronicles or sagas, and therefore the narrative in the source may be distorted.

Poor Applicant: When evaluating the reliability of a source, historians should think about the writer and what he is trying to achieve. Most primary sources are unreliable because their authors were not trying to write history but make a statement. It is impossible to exactly work out when and where a source was made; even if the date is included this might not be true.

The first applicant's answer is strong because it is **well-structured.** They have broken down their reasoning into three points that nicely link together, and they have thought imaginatively from the perspective of the primary source author.

The second applicant's answer also tries to achieve this and mentions that all sources are trying to make a 'statement'. To improve, they could have thought more carefully about the reasons why authors have specific agendas. To what extent are their writings shaped by their own societal context?

Both answers could have thought more widely about the types of sources available. Some, such as legal transcripts or accounting books, place a greater emphasis on veracity rather than narrative technique like the chroniclers. Does this make them more reliable sources?

Q35: Should economic history be purely quantitative?

Quantitative research involves the collection of measurable data, whereas qualitative research encompasses non-numerical information. Economic history calls for a greater use of statistics than most historical approaches. Candidates should think about whether quantitative data alone provides sufficient answers to questions in economic history.

Good Applicant: I think that economic history must be both quantitative and qualitative, in order to get the most complete picture of events. The quantitative aspect provides reliable and measurable statistics, that can be presented in tables and graphs. From these we can spot trends and identify anomalies. However, qualitative research is necessary for the historian to explain the data, especially to contextualise it within the historical period. For example, a graph might show British GDP increase over the 19th century. But the historian must have knowledge of the political decisions that enabled structural change, or of the creation of new industrial centres that stimulated economic growth. Without a historical narrative, raw quantitative data lacks meaning.

Poor Applicant: In my opinion, economic history can be studied with just quantitative methods. Economic history concerns the changes in a country's wealth and development over time. These changes are best represented with concrete data. While qualitative details can help explain any fluctuations or surprises in the data, they are not essential for the historian to make an argument.

The two candidates have argued both sides of this issue, with the first applicant suggesting that economic history cannot be purely quantitative, and the second applicant proposing that it can. The first applicant's answer succeeds in explaining the relationship between the two types of data, and argues that they are dependent on each other. One question an interviewer might ask, is whether multiple quantitative data sets could help explain each other. For example, understanding GDP growth over time could benefit from quantitative data on population growth, urbanisation, literacy rates and many other variables. The second applicant could have benefitted on making that very point, in order to defend their view that qualitative data is not 'essential' for drawing historical conclusions.

Q36: What could you learn about a past society from a pair of shoes?

This question encourages candidates to think outside the box about an unusual aspect of the past. It is unlikely that they will have studied or read about the history of shoes in any detail! Here, historical imagination and a creative use of topics covered at school are far more important than a specific knowledge of the history of shoes.

Good Applicant: Shoes can teach us a lot about the society from which they belonged. Different types of shoes may have been worn by different social groups, so we can get a sense of class hierarchies based on who had enough wealth to buy studier, more bespoke footwear. We can learn about the professions of individuals given how shoes of manual labour and agriculture take such different appearances to shoes of fashion and leisure. They can teach us about the geography of a region too, and which members of society spent more time travelling. This could be interesting in considering European migration patterns in the 19th and 20th centuries, and which lower classes were required to relocate following industrialisation, whereas larger landowners were able to stay put. Comparisons can be drawn between people for whom shoes were mostly practical and functional, and for those whom they were fashionable.

Poor Applicant: Shoes can teach us about specific individuals from the past. We can learn of their rank in society, their profession, and how rich they were. We can learn about the changes made to footwear over time and the designs that were less successful and therefore do not exist anymore.

The applicants explore some of the many things we can learn from the footwear of the past. They both mention class, wealth, and travel as things that we can infer from people's choice and availability of shoes. The first answer is stronger <u>because they engage more critically with the question</u>. Rather than simply accepting there were differences in footwear they seek to explore some of the context behind these differences, using the example of rural Europe to illustrate his point. They have set the interview up nicely for a continued discussion on the topic of migration.

Q37: What separates a terrorist and a patriot?

This question addresses a very relevant issue today, especially in the post-9/11 world. The USA PATRIOT Act (2001) expanded the definition of terrorism to include "domestic" as well as "international" instances of terrorism. The distinction between the terms 'terrorist' and 'patriot' is also brought up in debates about the IRA. Those are just two of the potential directions that candidates could take this question in.

Good Applicant: Patriots are individuals who strongly support their country and its national values. By this definition, most terrorists are also patriots. However, terroristic behaviour differs greatly from purely patriotic behaviour in my opinion. While both are prepared to participate in protests and riots, terrorists show a disregard for the civilian life around them. They are willing to use tactics of coercion, kidnapping, assassination and mass destruction in order to achieve their goals. Often, these occurrences serve to further their own interests; 9/11 for example, or the IRA bombings in Britain, were deliberately purposed to strike fear into their opponents. It is worth considering as well the extent to which terrorism can be separated from other kinds of direct conflict – if widened sufficiently, is an invading or occupying power participating in terrorism? For this to not be the case I think we would also have to argue that terrorism cannot be directly sponsored by the state, and that throws our existing understanding of terrorism into considerable doubt. Perhaps, then, the separation between a terrorist and a patriot is terror itself. If you are seeking to affect others through a climate which is intimidating or dangerous, you are a terrorist. If you do not seek these goals, but maintain the other aspects in common, you are a patriot.

Poor Applicant: The difference is just about whose side your on. In my opinion, one person's patriot is another person's terrorist and vice versa.

The first applicant's answer is stronger because they have better explored the relationship between the two terms, going as far to say that terrorism is a sub-set of patriotism. This is an interesting approach, and could have been taken further by exploring differences in ideology within the IRA. Some of its members were less convinced about the violent direction the faction was taking.

It would be worth taking a look at how the USA PATRIOT Act defines terrorism: (https://www.aclu.org/other/how-usa-patriot-act-redefines-domestic-terrorism)

Terrorism is a fairly modern concept. How can we apply it to historical examples? An interesting case to explore would be the Reign of Terror (1793-94), a period of excessive violence that caused many to become disillusioned in the ideals of the French Revolution.

Q38: If you could invite someone from the past to dinner, who would you choose and why?

This is a classic interview question that gives the candidate a great deal of freedom. It is important to **take your time** before launching into an answer, as it is likely that you will be made to explain and defend your decision in some depth.

Good Applicant: I would most want to have dinner with Martin Luther King. Firstly, I would love to hear about his experiences, how he was able to rally protesters on such a large-scale and cause such drastic change to the status of African Americans over the 20th century. Secondly, I think his skills of rhetoric, leadership and persuasion make him such a fascinating individual, and I would love to ask him about his methods and how he decided to tackle the challenges he faced. Finally, I would like to hear what he thought of other key individuals within the Civil Rights Movement, particularly those who had more radical, nationalistic views than his own.

Poor Applicant: I think Winston Churchill would be a really interesting person to have dinner with. He was such a great leader and was so important during the Second World War. He was a great speaker and as Prime Minister I think everyone had great respect for him. I am sure he would have many great stories about his career that he could share with me.

The first candidate's response is strong as they provide several reasons for why King would make such a fascinating dinner guest. They not only show an interest in *what* he did, but *how* he did it and how he perceived his own role within the Civil Rights Movement.

The second candidate has not done as effective a job of **empathising** with Churchill's position and the society he was a part of. An improved response might have included a reference to Churchill's colonial past, since that has a strong resonance in the current day and would provide a more two-sided portrayal of him. There is no historical individual who *could not* be an interesting person to have dinner with, but stronger answers will display an interest in really wanting to dig deep into the character of the person they have chosen.

Q39: What is a nation?

This is a classic historical issue that has been widely debated by historians and political theorists over the last 200 years, when many new nations were being formed across Europe. Interviewers are not looking for a short and perfect definition, but a more discursive response that begins to think about the aspects of a nation that best define it from other state entities.

Good Applicant: I believe that a nation is held together by two key features. Firstly, a clear territory with well defined borders. Secondly, a shared history or myth that all its members can identify with. Nations are not formed through all its inhabitants having a common language, race, or religion, for example, Switzerland was and still is a multi-ethnic, multi linguistic nation. A national myth is a binding tale that becomes part of a shared memory, it enables all members of the nation, regardless of their ethnicity, to identify within it. Because they have a shared past there is a common interest to further the progress of the nation in the future.

Poor Applicant: A nation is a state that binds people together, based on their common interests. They are able to operate independently of other nations, having their own government, economy, and culture. The people of a nation pursue national interests, but also cooperate internationally.

Both applicants have provided a succinct definition of the 'nation' and have expanded upon them. However, the first applicant has more persuasively supported their point of view. Their argument, that nations are multi-ethnic and are held together by a shared past, is well supported with the example of Switzerland. By making a distinction between 'history', and 'myth' – but acknowledging the significance of either – they have demonstrated to the interviewer that they have thought carefully about the question.

The second applicant successfully argued that nations are defined by other nations, and that each nation has interests that are specifically unique to them. However, they could have provided more clarity as to exactly what 'common interests' tend to bind a nation together.

Defining the 'nation' has long been a topic of interest for historians. Candidates might want to read **Ernest Renan's "What is a Nation"** (1882) as a starting point, and compare his views to those in **Benedict Anderson's "Imagined Communities" (1983)** and **Ernest Gellner's "Nations and Nationalism" (1983)**

Q40: Does nationalism have negative connotations?

Nationalism generally refers to a support for one's own nation, particularly at the expense of other nations. Nationalism can often be viewed negatively due to the actions of far-right racist parties such as the English Defence League, or due to its association with Nazism. However, candidates should think more widely about what constitutes a nationalist ideology, and if strong exclusionary policies are a necessary component of it.

Good Applicant: Personally, I believe that nationalism should not have negative connotations. Many forms of nationalism are about a passionate belief in the ideals of one's own nation, and a desire to continue to pursue those interests. Nationalism does not have to be ethnically homogenous or dangerous; this was evident during the growth of French nationalism after the Revolution. Nations can continue to embrace multiple languages and races as long as they have some form of coherent ideology based on a common past or mythology. Radical, far-right nationalisms are an exception rather than the rule, and they are more interested in excluding outsider groups rather than promoting their own national interests.

Poor Applicant: I think that nationalism deserves its negative connotations. Patriotism is largely benign, but nationalist policies look to exclude other groups and impose hierarchies. It often betrays liberal or democratic ideals that a nation is founded on. Germany was unified in 1871, but very quickly it adopted a discourse about the superiority of the Teutonic race and the inferiority of Jews.

The first applicant's response is effective because they have distinguished between different forms of nationalism. Dissecting a question like this is often a better approach than providing a catch-all answer. They have shown how most nationalisms are not ethnically exclusive and therefore should not be viewed negatively. Their distinction between patriotism and nationalism is a useful way of giving their answer further clarity.

The second applicant has argued the contrary and has provided a well-chosen example to support their view that nationalism is exclusionary and hierarchical. However, they could have benefited from confidently dismissing the counterargument, or at least acknowledging its presence. Interviewers may ask why such strong racist discourses did not emerge in newly unified Italy, or in Hungary when it achieved more independence from the Austrian Empire. A strong point of view in an interview is not a bad thing, but applicants must be prepared to defend their arguments and justify their choice of examples.

Q41: Can the study of history be scientific?

The 19th century historian Leopold von Ranke stated that "the ultimate aim of historical writing is the bringing before us the whole truth". This question is assessing whether or not history should be fully empirical, as von Ranke believed, or it should be open to subjectivity. This question has been a central part of historiographical debate for over two centuries, but candidates might prefer to voice their own opinions.

Good Applicant: I believe that history has some aspects that would be considered scientific, but it should not be considered a science. Sciences are all about systematic experimentation and a careful, methodical collection of evidence. This systematisation of results and information gathering only works because scientists have established a common methodology, the Scientific Method, to govern their approach. Historians do not have any common methodology or unifying theory, and this has lead to an incredibly diverse set of analytical and interpretive approaches, each underlined by an argument. While there is always an element of truth in history, a necessary part of the process is the historian expressing his own views. Many historians also adopt a narrative, rhetoric style in their books. Therefore, history is part science, part art.

Poor Applicant: I do not believe that history is a science because there is less of a fixed process going on. Historians do collect evidence, but they do not have to be obsessed with data and are allowed to write about their own opinions. Historians are also often writing for an audience who want to read their books, and so they have to do many of the things that authors do in order to make their work accessible and interesting.

The first applicant has considered the arguments both for and against history being a science, and they have concluded that the discipline possesses aspects of both science and art. This is a balanced and thoughtful take on the question that has resulted in a strong answer.

The second applicant has argued against history being a science, and has expressed many of the same points as the first candidate. Their point of view is fine, but would need to be well defended in the ensuing discussion. Interviewers might ask about forms of more academic history, as opposed to the popular history the candidate is referring to. Do academic historians, who propose a thesis and then test it against all the available evidence, bare many of the qualities of a scientist?

Q42: To what extent can historians ever be unbiased?

In answering this question, candidates should think about the social environments that historians write in. Some historians are not as concerned with impartiality as others; biographies are a typical example of this. They might state in their introduction that they will be arguing a specific interpretation, and are consciously ignoring other explanations. Even then, most historians will make sure their work is the product of thorough evidence and logical argument rather than personal bias.

Good Applicant: In my opinion, it is impossible for the historian to retain complete impartiality in their work. Even without trying, some of their personal views will seep into their work. Every historian has been raised in a particular society, has read certain texts, and will have met certain people. All these factors make their psychology unique and therefore their interpretation of primary sources will always be manipulated in some shape or form. Historians will always voice opinions, but they can endeavour to voice rational and thoughtful opinions. They can achieve this by addressing potential counterarguments rather than completely dismissing them, supporting their views with substantial data, and writing in a fairly neutral style that uses persuasive but non-inflammatory language.

Poor Applicant: I think that I was really impartial in my EPQ, I was able to weigh up both side of the argument and my conclusion was driven by logic and facts. If an historian can't be impartial they are a bit old fashioned I think, that said, there are some cases where impartiality is wrong, you shouldn't be impartial when you're writing about Nazism, for example.

The first applicant has successfully addressed the issues that the historian faces regarding impartiality, and have suggested several solutions to this problem. Rather than simply stating that historians cannot be impartial, they have shown how they do not have to be biased or prejudiced either.

The second applicant has argued the contrary, believing that historians can be impartial. What's more, they believe that they themselves are impartial, which suggests a lack of maturity or familiarity with academic work, and go so far as to suggest that good historians might choose to introduce bias to their work. Both answers could perhaps think about whether or not impartiality is an actual aim for historians. Some writers may actively prioritise narrative and entertainment over impartiality, in order to create history for a popular audience.

A further issue that could be raised by interviewees, is the difference between historical books and other forms of historical writing that are less concerned with impartiality, such as polemics or memoirs. Do historians looking to write more opinionated texts operate in a different genre entirely?

A good article to read on this topic is **G.M Trevelyan's *Bias in History (1947)***

Q43: When do you think the British Empire had the most power?

Good Applicant: I think that the British Empire was at its strongest in the late 19th century. After this, demands for self-government in some of the colonies was getting particularly strong, especially in India. They were seeking a similar status to that of the "Dominions" – Australia, New Zealand, and Canada. The two World Wars also shook Britain financially, which, in tandem with the moral concerns of Empire, led to its demise. However, at its peak at the end of the 19th century, it has expanded territorially as much as it ever would. There was not only unprecedented levels of trade and globalisation, but relative peace and stability in the colonies. Moral issues were, at the time, unchallenged, which meant that the colonies could continue to be subjected.

Poor Applicant: I think that the British Empire was at its most powerful just before the First World War. After this, the Empire collapsed due to post-war debt and the rise of independence movements in the colonies. The Second World War would only exacerbate these issues and lead to the end of Empire.

Both candidates have argued that Empire was strongest in the late 19th and early 20th century, and have identified good reasons as to why it began to decline. However, it is important to fully address the question that is being answered, and interviewers will expect to hear what made the Empire powerful when it was at its peak, rather than just what caused its demise. Only the first applicant has explored some of these features, and is therefore the stronger of the two responses.

Q44: At what point would you say that the English monarchy was at its height?

The monarchy in Britain today is predominantly a ceremonial role. However, it has only ended up this way through centuries of attempts to impose constitutional limits on royal power. Candidates could think about the key turning points in British history that led to monarchical power losing its executive power and state influence.

Good Applicant: I believe that the English monarchy was at is strongest at its very beginnings, after 1066, especially for the Angevin Kings of the 12th and 13th centuries. After William the Conqueror had consolidated his control over England and placed his Norman advisors in high ranking noble and ecclesiastical positions, his successors had considerable control over all state infrastructures. This period until 1215 was when the monarchy was at is strongest. The Magna Carta was the first but by no means the last attempt to constrain the powers of the crown. The barons who challenged King John were able to obtain their right to common counsel and judgement, the first loss for absolute rule.

Poor Applicant: I think that the English monarchy was most powerful during the Norman and Angevin eras. Since then, the powers of monarchs have been reduced by noble and parliamentary opposition, especially following the Glorious Revolution of 1688.

Both candidates have argued that the English monarchy was most powerful in 1066 and the two centuries that followed. They have also outlined some moments when monarchical power was reduced. However, the second applicant has not clarified *why* the monarchy was weakened during and after the Angevin period. This is not explained by the Glorious Revolution, an event that comes some 400 years later. The first applicant also mentions what aspects of monarchical power were conceded first. They therefore display a more sophisticated understanding of the question in comparison to the second applicant.

Q45: You're transported back in time with one goal – stop Hitler. How do you accomplish this?

This is a good opportunity for candidates to show their hypothetical skills, and this question is open to several interpretations. One could say how they would have ended the Second World War earlier, or how they would have prevented Hitler from rising to power at all.

Good Applicant: I believe that the best opportunity to stop Hitler would be to prevent him from consolidating his power as Chancellor in the Spring of 1933. Before then he was too inconspicuous, and afterwards too powerful. I think that the easiest way to topple him would have been through the use of the German Trade Unions. The power of the strike was evident in 1920, when the Unions almost singlehandedly prevented the Kapp Putsch coup from succeeding. Mass strikes would have forced Hitler to rely on the support of the national army, and would have undermined the capabilities of his own military force, the SA. If this happened, I do not think that Hitler would have been able to become as powerful and independent of government as he did.

Poor Applicant: I think Hitler could have been stopped if countries from across the world reacted more urgently and comprehensively to the growth of Fascism and anti-Semitism in Germany. These ideologies should have been alarming to nations and a clear threat to international stability, and military intervention could have ousted Hitler from the Chancellorship well before the war.

The first applicant's answer here is a more convincing response to the question. He provides greater **detail**, with accurate dates and facts. He uses a historical precedent (the failed Coup) to support his argument that the Trade Unions could have defeated Hitler, which makes his hypothetical approach more persuasive than the second applicant's. The second applicant's answer would benefit from similarly precise detail. They suggest that international intervention could have easily toppled Hitler, but this is very easy to say with hindsight. Was the threat of Fascism evident on a global scale in the early 1930s? This is something an interviewer might want to discuss further.

Q46: Where is the end of history?

The 'end of history' is a concept that has appeared in the writings of many political theorists and philosophers. It suggests that society will, or has, reached an endpoint in the evolution of governments and institutions. Candidates could answer this question with specific reference to some of those examples, or respond with a more personal opinion.

Good Applicant: I think any notion of there being an end to history is imperfect. Francis Fukuyama in 'The End of History and the Last Man' believed that the end of history was marked by the end of the Cold War and the defeat of Communism and Fascism over the course of the 20th century. While it may be the case in many Western societies that an endpoint of liberal democracy has been obtained, there are far too many exceptions that challenge Fukuyama's view. For example, the rise of Islamic fundamentalism, or the financial crisis of 2008. These events challenge the view that 1989 marked an 'end of history', and therefore I doubt that we will ever be able to conclude that there will be one.

Poor Applicant: When the world ends, I suppose. It's difficult to say exactly because people will always want to write about history, I think, it's really interesting. So, history will only end when there aren't people to write it.

Both candidates have argued along the same sides, but the good applicant's answer is stronger for two reasons. Firstly, their use of Fukuyama helps frame their answer, for it provides an example of a specific point in time (1989) that has been regarded as a potential 'end of history'. Secondly, they have given examples that undermine Fukuyama's thesis, strengthening their own argument.

Candidates may also have discussed how the likes of Thomas More, Friedrich Hegel and Karl Marx, all conceived of their own versions of the 'end of history', and could compare those to Fukuyama or their own views.

Q47: What are the main differences and similarities found in the French and Russian revolutions?

The French (1789-1799) and Russian (1917-23, but may also refer to the events of 1905) Revolutions were significant events at either end of the 'Long Nineteenth Century'. Candidates could draw many similarities and differences on several themes – the motivations of the insurgents, the levels of violence and bloodshed, the political ideologies involved, and the degree of short- and long-term success for the revolutionaries.

Good Applicant: The major similarity that stands out for me was how both Revolutions were led by the lower classes and challenged the authority of an absolute monarchy. The French and Russian peasants and working classes played a significant role in insurrections and protests. Both groups of revolutionaries were seeking constitutional reform, and succeeded; in Russia, the State Duma was set up after 1905, in France the monarchy had been abolished by 1792 and a Republic set up its place. The difference between the two was the French Revolution of 1789 was followed by a decade of bloodshed, and political instability, as various regimes replaced one another. After the "dress rehearsal of 1905", the Russian Revolution of 1917 saw the clearly formulated Bolshevik party rise to power and create a socialist state. The resulting French state in 1799, ruled by Napoleon as First Consul, was very similar to the former monarchy, albeit without its *ancient regime* traditions.

Poor Applicant: Both revolutions are similar because they were challenging the monarchy. The lower classes were unhappy with their conditions and therefore sought to overthrow the ruling class entirely. I think we should view the Russian Revolution as different because its initial insurrectionists succeeded in their aims and established the USSR. The bourgeoisie that led 1789 were unable to control the peasants and *sans culottes* and therefore they lost their control over the revolution.

Both responses here make strong points about the similarities and differences between the revolutions. The first candidate has thought outside the box by showing the importance of the revolution of 1905 in setting the stage for the events of 1917. Their answer also draws the important comparison between the different types of state that emerge at the end of the revolution – one an autocratic consulate, the other a communist union.

Both applicants have argued that the French Revolution was more violent and less successful in achieving its initial aims, but they perhaps could have considering the Russian Civil War as a parallel to the political unrest of the years of the French terror. It is perhaps untrue to say that the Russian Revolution saw no periods of fluctuation after 1917.

Q48: What elements were continuous between the Great War and World War II? What elements had changed?

A comparison of these two wars can be done in many different ways, especially since they were so close in time and in terms of its participants. Interviewees could explore the causes of war, the methods and tactics used during the war, or the outcomes and post-war politics that followed, just to name a few.

Good Applicant: I think one of the most interesting differences between the two wars is what they were fought over. The First World War could be interpreted as the end of an imperial era. Both sides were seeking to acquire countries, colonies, or territory so that they had more resources and more political influence on the global stage. The Second World War was also to some extent about countries seeking to expand at the expense of one another, but it was also a war of ideologies. The alliance between Communism and the Western democratic countries formed in order to oppose the growth of Fascism in Germany, Italy, and Japan. Nazi policies became so concerning that the Western powers had to take action. While some of this was territorial, and indeed the invasion of Poland kickstarted the war, there were many fears over the Nazi's belief in eugenics, and the potential consequences that might have.

Poor Applicant: I think both wars were very similar because they were predominantly about Germany seeking to expand and take control of Europe, and the Allies trying to control their aggressions. The changes were in methods of warfare. There was an evolution from trench warfare and artillery assault to more modern forms of fighting involving nuclear missiles, tanks, planes, and submarines.

Both answers address some similarities and differences between the war. The first candidate's response works nicely because it takes one issue – the nature of war – and shows how it could be interpreted differently. Were they wars of territory, or wars of ideology? They set up an interesting debate that could lead to further discussion about the extent of ideological conviction by combatants in warfare.

The second applicant's answer could have made reference to the ideological issues raised by the first applicant to show a more balanced understanding on the nature and motivations of warfare. They could also have thought about *why* warfare changed between the two wars, in such a short period of time. What were the lessons learnt from World War One, particularly in the trenches?

Q49: How might history be written by the loser?

"History is written by victors" – a quote typically attributed to Winston Churchill but has doubtless been used throughout history. This question raises several interesting issues. Who are the losers of history? Aside from military or political defeats this is not always clear cut. Secondly, is the 'losing' side of history getting greater attention today through revisionist movements?

Good Applicant: Everyone writes history, but it is the winners who get to keep interpreting it and mould the stories that get remembered by future generations. In World War One for instance, members of both sides kept diaries, memoirs, letters of correspondence and battle plans, meaning that there was plenty of source material. Yet since the Allies won, it was their sources that were shaped into sympathetic histories, whilst many documents on the Axis' side were suppressed, censored, or destroyed. However, revisionist historians who revisit the past that give the losers a greater voice. Field Marshal Haig was villainised for his carelessness in the immediate aftermath of the war, but biographers such as John Terraine or Sir John Davidson have restored his reputation as a military leader. A 'loser' was turned a 'winner' by revisionist historians.

Poor Applicant: Losers do not get to write history because their version of events is suppressed by the winners. Those in power get to influence the media, write positive histories about themselves and tell their versions of the past. The losers of history do not have the same platform to achieve this and so they become forgotten.

The first applicant has given a detailed answer crystallised around the example of World War 1, showing how both the losing side and 'losers' within the winner side can easily become condemned or lost in history. The revisionist case of Haig is well-chosen, a reminder of how history is not simply events that have happened, but events that can be constantly reinterpreted.

The second applicant has somewhat failed to answer the question. They have stated why winners often get to write history, but have not even considered how losers might find a way of writing their own narratives. A fascinating medieval example is how the Anglo-Saxon monks, although 'losers' to the invading Vikings of the 8th to 11th centuries, were the writers of history because they were the literate group. This shows that there are other factors at play when it comes to deciding who writes history.

Q50: Why did Europe not follow America's example and form a USE?

Good Applicant: I think this question is best answered if one considers why the United States of America was formed in 1776. Whilst fighting the British during the Revolutionary war, the American colonies needed to form a sense of collective identity in order to inspire purpose and unity among its members. It also provided Americans with a sense of what they were fighting for. The Declaration of Independence created a shared myth that has become the backbone of the American identity ever since. In contrast, every country of Europe has its own national myths and identities, and there is less of a need for a collective one. That is why there are confederations such as the EU, but no United States of Europe.

Poor Applicant: I think that Europe is too divided to become a United State. Europe has too long a history of internal conflict and there is little to bind all Europeans together. In contrast, the American colonies had all had a similar experience during British imperial rule and therefore were able to obtain a collective identity more easily.

Both answers have focused on the importance of a sense of collective identity in forming a United State. The first applicant's response benefits from greater precision in their reasoning. They have clearly outlined how the United States of America was formed, and in showing the specific circumstances in which it emerged, have proven why there is no European counterpart. They finish by stating that Europe only needs the EU, and this idea could be expanded further. They could think about what the EU, a mostly politcal and economic union rather than an ideological one, provides in comparison to a United State, and why those features are well suited to the needs of many European countries.

Q51: Do you think that Napoleon was a better leader than Alexander the Great?

This question allows candidates to use their skills of comparison. It is not a problem if they have not studied either of these individuals in depth, as interviewers may be prepared to give you a bit of additional knowledge before beginning a response.

Good Applicant: Both of these men were powerful leaders who were able to build large empires. Alexander the Great was the better military tactician, particularly for the way in which he established naval supremacy over the Persians. Napoleon in contrast had Europe's largest army yet made fatal mistakes during his Russian campaign. However, Napoleon was the better strategist, and therefore the better leader on whole. He played a significant role in the reorganising of Europe; he had a clear vision for France, but his splitting up of the Holy Roman Empire also paved the way for the creation of Germany. His administrative and legal changes still stand in France today. Alexander's Empire did not have this long-term vision.

Poor Applicant: I remember learning about them both at school, but they were in different years and I don't really remember. I think Alexander the Great was better because that's how history remembers him, Napoleon isn't known as Napoleon the Great.

The first applicant's response is very effective here. They have divided the issue of leadership into two components, shown how each individual performed in them, and then concluded by stating that Napoleon's capability for long-term planning outweighs Alexander's military skill. Given the considerable time difference between these two examples, a brief overview of their campaigns works better than lots of specific detail, and the candidate does a good job of this.

The second applicant has made two flaws here, they've not revised their history content from school, and when presented with a question about a resultingly complex topic, they haven't tried to work out an answer. Since they have not answered the question properly, interviewers may prompt them with some information about one leader or the other so that the applicant try to draw some comparisons. If the candidate was entirely unfamiliar with Alexander, it is better to tell the interviewers this before starting an answer and waiting for help before responding.

Q52: What can we learn from 18th century warfare which is applicable in the modern world?

The 18th century marked featured a series of conflicts between Britain and France (in the "Second Hundred Years War") and the American Revolutionary War, but there are many other examples that would be appropriate. 18th-century warfare took a very different form to the present day, in terms of technology and tactics, so candidates should think about the aspects of warfare that are less stuck in time, such as leadership.

Good Applicant: Warfare in the 18th century took a very different form to that of the present day. Battles were fought predominantly with infantry and cavalry, uniforms were bright and conspicuous, and military movements were far less regimented. However, there are many moral lessons that can be learnt about 18th century warfare. Particularly during the Wars of Independence, there was an emphasis on fighting with honour and not taking cheap shots. Shooting enemy officers from a distance was viewed as a form of assassination; the British were shocked by the shooting of Simon Fraser by American riflemen at Saratoga in 1777. The 18th century was a reminder that a good army needed the full support of its rank and file. Many 19th century reforms under Wellington, Nelson, and Cardwell were targeted towards camp conditions, the eradication of corporal punishment, and shorter army contracts.

Poor Applicant: There is little to be learnt from 18th century warfare because warfare has evolved far too much since then. Modern wars are about technology and fighting from a distance. Countries are too powerful to fight like they did in the 18th century; battles would be over in minutes after the use of modern explosives and warheads. One thing we can learn is that army uniform has had to become more camouflaged, because 18th century outfits drew too much attention to the enemy.

The first applicant's response is strong because he has shown how some aspects of warfare will always remain important. He mentions the conduct of war, which relates to moral arguments of *jus in bello,* and the behaviour of generals towards their subordinates.

The second applicant, like the first, was able to outline the ways in which 18th century warfare was radically different to the 21st century, but has focused on the practical, technological aspects of warfare. It is perfectly fine to challenge this question and firmly argue against the idea that we can learn from 18th century warfare. However, specific examples and a more thorough exploration of the differences between the two eras would have led to a stronger answer.

TEXT/SOURCE-BASED INTERVIEW

If your college decides to give you a text- or source-based interview, you will be given a piece of **academic text to look at before the interview**. You may also need to write a summary or commentary; the Admissions Office will tell you if this is the case. It is likely that the text you are given will be unfamiliar to you, on a topic or area of history you have not studied before. Do not be daunted by this – you are not expected to have any detailed factual knowledge related to the text.

The interview will then be based on the contents of the extract, and the issues surrounding it. Things to keep in mind:

- When reading the text in advance, **pay attention to the author, the date of publication, and the nature of the work**. It may be a historical source or an extract from a work of historiography by a theorist such as E.H. Carr or Richard Evans. It may be an introduction from a history book on a topic you have never encountered before.
- Try to pick up on aspects of the publication that are unusual or revealing (e.g. was it written anonymously? Is it a revision of an earlier text? Is it clearly written in response to another text or another writer's view? Who is the intended audience?)
- When reading the text, pay attention to the argument it is making. Is it a strong argument or a weak argument and why? Can you think of any counter-arguments?
- Does the text relate in any way to any other area of history and historiography that you -are familiar which can be drawn upon in the interview?

WHAT QUESTIONS MIGHT BE ASKED?

For this type of interview setting, the interviewers will ask questions about the text and the broader historical issues that the text raises. Questions about the text directly will range from content comprehension (what is the author arguing? What does the author mean by X?) to interpretation (do you agree with the author's characterization of X?) to questions of historical methodology (why has the author approached this subject in this way? Is the author's method valid?)

The thing to remember when answering these questions is not to panic! **The questions are designed to be difficult** to give you the chance to show your full intellectual potential. The interviewers will help guide you to the right idea if you provide ideas for them to guide. This is your chance to show your creativity, analytical skills, intellectual flexibility, problem-solving skills and your go-getter attitude. Don't waste it on nervousness or a fear of messing up or looking stupid.

Q53: You are given an extract from an introduction to a historical work that is based entirely on oral sources, such as Robert Fraser's 'Blood of Spain'.

Can one ever understand a historical event from oral history sources alone?

This question is asking you to evaluate a particular type of source. A good way to approach a question like this would be to look firstly at the ways in which this type of source can help to understand an event, then to look at the **weaknesses of this type of source**, and then to come to a conclusion. There are lots of aspects of a historical event that could be understood through oral history sources alone. Using the example of the Spanish Civil War, oral history allows one to understand what the war was like in terms of lived experience, as in a fairly decentralised state with low levels of literacy and high levels of censorship. Oral history can bring a perspective to the war that is lacking in other types of sources and official documents.

Furthermore, seeing as oral histories are generally collected in interviews after the event in question, this type of source allows the historian to understand not only the event itself but also its aftermath and long-term effects on those who lived through it.

However, there are several drawbacks to oral history. While it is a useful way to understand what it was like to live through an event, it only shows the perspective of those interviewed, which may not be representative of the people of Spain as a whole. It also would not take into account political, economic or international factors influencing the course of events, which can only be illuminated by other types of sources. Oral history is also fallible, in that people are interviewed about events that happened years or even decades earlier. Therefore, **recollections of events may not be entirely reliable**.

A good conclusion to this question would be that while certain aspects of historical events could be understood from oral sources alone, no one type of source is comprehensive enough to encapsulate every aspect of an event. For the best understanding of the Spanish Civil War, it would be necessary to use as wide a variety of sources as possible, including oral history.

You may be given an extract from an introduction to a history book on a very specific topic about which you know very little about, and asked to comment on the historian's proposed method. For example, it may be an extract from a work that looks at Georgian England from a woman's perspective, such as Vickery's Behind Closed Doors: At Home in Georgian England.

Q54: This work looks at Georgian England from a feminist perspective. Do you think it is acceptable to analyse a period through the lens of a concept that didn't exist during the period under study (i.e. feminism)?

This would be a difficult question to be presented with at an interview. It is important to stay calm and be open-minded, and **the interviewers will help guide you to an answer**. It would be useful to analyse both sides of such a question before coming to a conclusion. You might start by looking at the drawbacks of analysing a certain period through the lens of a concept that was not contemporary to the period you are looking at.

There are several problems with analysing Georgian England through a feminist framework (for example). Many historians argue that it is better to analyse the past through terminology that was in use in the period under discussion.

By looking at Georgian England through a feminist perspective, you may be imposing ideas onto the past that are incompatible with the period under study. You could argue that **this is not so much history as sociology**, as it is putting more of an emphasis on the modern concept (feminism) than on the period you are supposed to be studying (Georgian England).

However, there are also benefits to this type of historiography. Part of the purpose of history is to look at the past through a new perspective. Even if this perspective would not have been understood by the people who lived in the period under discussion, it may still illuminate aspects of the period that have not yet been covered by the scholarship.

You may be given an extract from a work about a certain aspect of historical theory, such as Niall Ferguson's Virtual History or Richard Evans' Altered Pasts, both of which deal with counter-factual history.

Q55: *What, if any, is the value of studying counter-factual history?*

Counter-factual history is the history of *what if?* It challenges the historian to consider what would have happened had something else occurred. A common counter-factual investigated by Ferguson is *'what if Great Britain had never entered the First World War?'*

A good answer to this question would **reflect on the merits and limitations of this type of history** and the basis of the information given in the source.

There are several merits to studying counter-factual history. It allows one to focus on crucial turning points in historical events. You may only really be able to understand the consequences of a certain event (such as Britain entering the First World War) if you have gone through the process of imagining how things might have turned out if this one event had gone differently. It may also help in thinking about causation in history. You may come to the realisation that a certain factor was a key cause in a certain event only by considering whether the event would have gone ahead without the factor. *What If?* History can also be entertaining and engaging and may be a good way of inspiring interest in history.

However, there are also problems associated with studying counter-factual history. Many counter-factual hypotheses (such as *'what if Britain had not entered the First World War?'*) can be taken too far. It's one thing to reflect on such a question in order to analyse the importance of what did happen and the consequences of Britain's entry into the war. It's another thing to imagine a complete parallel universe in which a hypothetical scenario (Britain staying out of the war) is extrapolated into a completely different historical narrative. Perhaps **counter-factual speculation** is a useful historical tool when used in moderation but can easily slide into fiction.

ESSAY-BASED INTERVIEW

Some colleges at Oxford and Cambridge will ask you to submit one or two essays with your application. The details for this will be made clear in the application process. One of your interviews may, therefore, be based in part on the contents of your essay. This is a chance for you to demonstrate your detailed factual knowledge about an area of history you are familiar with, as well as to show your passion for the subject.

The interviewer may open by asking for a summary of the piece of work, of the methodology behind it, and the conclusion reached. They may then ask some follow-up questions related to the work or the subject matter. This part of the interview will be very individual and depend on the nature and subject of the work submitted. Here are some things to keep in mind if you are submitting essays as part of your application:

- Ensure that any work you are submitting is your own. You will not be able to justify an argument you make in an interview if that argument was written by your tutor or teacher. The interviewers will be able to tell if this is the case.

- Ensure that any work you are submitting is on topics that you feel comfortable talking about in detail (e.g. something you have studied at AS-level, rather than something you have only just started studying)

- Of course, ensure that the work you submit is of a high standard that you believe reflects your academic abilities. If it is a piece of work you are proud of, you will better be able to defend it in your interview.

- Re-read the essays you have submitted before the interview so they are fresh in your mind.

- While it is good to remain flexible and open to revising your arguments, **try not to disagree with your own essay**! If the interviewer asks about a certain aspect of the essay and you respond by saying "I wrote this ages ago, I don't think it's very good", that won't come across well. On the other hand, if you have a very solid reason for revising your argument, this is something you can bring up in your interview.

EXAMPLE QUESTIONS

These questions are likely to be **tailored to the individual essay you've submitted**, so it is likely that the answers given are not relevant to the topics covered in your own essay. However, it is useful to read them anyway and think about the *types* of questions you might be asked.

The questions are likely to build on the essay you have written or they will prompt you to investigate an aspect of the topic your essay has not covered fully. A candidate who has written an essay on the topic 'Did Napoleon bring an end to the French Revolution' in which he/she has argued in the affirmative could be asked the question:

Q56: "When did Napoleon bring an end to the French Revolution?"

A good answer to a question such as this should firstly **acknowledge the complexity of the question**. In this case, this would require recognising that there are many potential answers to the question. One could argue that Napoleon ended the French Revolution in 1799 when he became First Consul, or in 1802 when he declared himself Consul for life, or in 1804 when he made himself Emperor. You may have a strong opinion in favour of one of these interpretations, but before making your case, it would be good to show that you are aware that there are many possible arguments that could be made.

If you believe that the French Revolution ended when Napoleon made himself Emperor in 1804, you would need to explain why. In this type of question, factual detail and a command of the material is crucial as the topic on which you have written an essay should be one with which you are very familiar. You may, for instance, talk about this event from a constitutional perspective and argue that this is the point at which leadership of France technically returns to the type of monarchical system the Revolution had aimed to overthrow. You may mention that the Pope takes part in Napoleon's coronation ceremony, showing that the anti-Catholic nature of the Revolution has been reversed. Whatever you decide to argue, you must show clear factual evidence to back up your interpretation.

A **poor candidate** may respond to this question in a number of ways. The most obvious mistakes to be avoided would be to reply, "I don't know" or to say "1804" and refuse to explain your answer. It would also be unwise to reverse the argument you originally made in your essay by saying "Napoleon didn't bring an end to the French Revolution" (unless you have very good reason, for example, new research to back up this revision).

Q57: A candidate who has written an essay on the Enlightenment could be asked a question such as "Why do you write 'the Enlightenment' in your essay, rather than 'enlightenment'?"

A **good answer** will recognise the complexity of the question. It is not a question about grammar and formatting at all. Instead, it highlights the issue of whether the Enlightenment (or enlightenment) can be seen as a movement that was clear and homogeneous enough to warrant being labelled with a proper noun (The Enlightenment) rather than a vaguer descriptive term (enlightenment).

A good answer would then talk this through with the interviewers, with reference to factual evidence you are familiar with. You could talk about how the Enlightenment was a very diverse movement, encompassing ideas as varied as Rousseau's *The Social Contract* to enlightened absolutism in the Habsburg monarchy. This might, be better characterised through a descriptive term rather than a proper noun as The Enlightenment makes these ideas seem more uniform than they were in reality. However, you might on balance argue that it should still be categorised as The Enlightenment because many of its thinkers referred to themselves in these terms.

A **weaker candidate** may simply say "My teacher said it was The Enlightenment" or "My textbook says The Enlightenment" and refuse to engage with the topic. A weak candidate may also say "I had never really thought about it" and leave it at that. If you have genuinely never considered an idea that you are presented with in the interview (which is very likely to happen), it is fine to say so. But then do go on to engage with the idea critically, e.g. "I had considered that but it's a very interesting point".

CLASSICS

Classics applicants will typically be asked **questions about the Classical world**, but usually not about things they have studied in detail at A-Level. This is to avoid some candidates gaining an advantage by simply having studied the topic in question since *interviews are designed to assess how you think and how you adapt to new information, not what you know.*

The interview will usually consist of a large question with many smaller sub-questions that the interviewer will ask in order to guide the applicant to an answer. The main question may seem difficult, impossible or random at first, but take a breath and start discussing with your interviewer different ideas you have for breaking down the question into manageable pieces. Don't panic. **The questions are designed to be difficult** to give you the chance to show your full intellectual potential. They will help guide you to the right idea if you provide ideas for them to guide. This is your chance to show your creativity, analytical skills, intellectual flexibility, problem-solving skills and your go-getter attitude. Don't waste it on nervousness or a fear of messing up or looking stupid.

Often questions will pick up on a theme from your written work or your personal statement and take it in an unexpected direction. For example, if you mentioned visiting the Parthenon in your personal statement, an interviewer may well ask you to talk about a particular frieze from the building and what you consider its significance to be, what its purpose might be, and who might have commissioned it. In this scenario, they would not expect you to know anything about the frieze in question, but simply to **make sensible suggestions based on the given information** and talk the interviewer through your thinking process.

The only other main section of the interview process is the language test for Cambridge candidates with Latin, Greek or both, conducted in one interview. The interviewer will allow you to study a Latin or Greek text for a few minutes and then ask you to translate it aloud, giving you assistance with vocabulary and grammar as appropriate.

This will usually be a difficult and obscure piece to ensure that no candidates are better prepared than others. Again, the emphasis is on showing a good working method for working out the meaning of a sentence, rather than knowing lots about grammar or vocabulary - remember to think aloud and ask about any vocabulary you don't know.

WORKED QUESTIONS

Below are a few examples of how to start breaking down an interview question, complete with model answers.

Q1: Why might it be more useful to study ancient texts in their original languages, as opposed to in translation?

A **good applicant** might begin by acknowledging the benefits of texts in translation, i.e. that they are more accessible and retain most of the content, but then go on to examine how translations can present difficulties. For example, discuss that some ways of thinking and figures of speech simply do not translate into English and, hence, can only be understood in the original language. A very good candidate might then broaden this into a discussion of how far it is necessary to study ancient texts in their original context and how far they can be considered to be stand-alone works, and what the merits of these different approaches might be for a scholar.

It is often useful to **break the question down into sub-parts**, which can be dealt with in turn. At this point, the interviewer can give feedback if this seems like a good start and help make any modifications necessary. In this particular case, the interviewer may well begin to ask further questions to direct the discussion once the candidate has made an initial survey of the issues. You would seldom be expected to talk about a topic unguided for a lengthy period as interviewers will always be keen to challenge your thinking and see how you react to new information.

A **poor applicant** may take a number of approaches unlikely to impress the interviewer. The first and most obvious of these is to say, "We never learned about that in school" and make no attempt to move forward with the discussion. In this event, the interviewer will likely try and prod the candidate to make an inroad by asking subsequent questions, in which case the important thing to do is make an effort to make sensible conjectures and not worry about whether you know any facts. Another typical tactic of poor applicants to avoid is the 'brain dump', where a candidate simply spouts all of the knowledge they have on the question topic without considering whether it is relevant. It is important to remember *that interviews are about giving thoughtful answers to questions which demonstrate your thinking process, not about demonstrating knowledge.*

Q2: What can we learn about Roman emperors from the depictions of them on statues and coins?

A **good applicant** will likely begin by narrowing the question to a manageable dimension. For example, talking about a specific depiction(s) or a specific emperor(s) (it is also likely that the interviewer will provide some visual stimuli to help you).

One might then explore what these items could tell us about how the emperors wanted to be seen (e.g. how widespread they are, how the emperor is depicted upon them, what the inscriptions say). It also informs us about how the emperors were seen by people in a given area (e.g. statues were often commissioned by local dignitaries in the provinces, what message did they want to send by putting up a statue of, say, Augustus?). It also tells how this might be compared with other sources, such as the written accounts of Tacitus and Suetonius. The interviewer would be likely to offer the candidate information and examples to help them test their theories, as well as asking further questions.

Outlining the concepts in this way would provide a good starting point to mention any relevant reading you have done. For example, if you have read Suetonius' biography of Claudius, you might be able to contrast his depiction in that work with his depiction in a statue or coin you have seen and suggest why that might be and what we could usefully learn from it. This type of **proactive and thoughtful approach** to the question is likely to impress the interviewer, but it is still important to listen to their directions and interjections carefully to ensure that you answer their question fully.

A **poor applicant** would be more likely to protest that they don't know anything about statues or coins, or attempt to offer a shallow and relatively pedestrian statement of the obvious. For example, they might hypothesise that such artefacts can tell us what the emperors looked like and then struggle to conjecture anything any further when asked for more suggestions by the interviewer. The worst thing to do in these situations is to seem unreceptive and attempt to derail the interviewer. Seeming interested in the topic and being seen to make an effort to consider your answers to the questions carefully is often half the battle.

Q3: What is literature? Why do we value it?

This is a very open-ended question and one to which there are no wrong answers, the key is to cut a sensible path through the material.

A **good applicant** would quickly seek to address the broadness of the question and state their angle of approach. The most useful tactic would be to try and develop a theory of literature which differentiates it from other types of written material. Such a theory might try to establish how far authorial intent goes and how far audience reception determines what literature is, as well as addressing the role of form (e.g. poetry or prose) and the question of whether anything can be said to be entirely literature or not. Other peripheral questions may be posed by the interviewer such as "Does literature have to be written down or can it be an oral culture?" - you should attempt to address these and incorporate them into your theory to provide nuance to your answer.

The good applicant might then tackle the question of why we value literature with reference to their theory of what constitutes literature, since how we define literature likely tells us about why we prize it. Such an answer is likely to make reference to a variety of ideas, possibly focusing on the allegorical and didactic powers of literature, i.e. its potential benefits to society, versus its more intrinsic goods, e.g. beauty, the human condition and so forth. The interviewer will be looking for candidates to make a **lively, intellectual, and sensible approach to the question** but will by no means expect revolutionary or fully-formed analyses of such large concepts.

A **poor candidate** is, therefore, likely to try and be dismissive of the question with a brief answer such as "books and poems" or "I don't know" and fail to engage with the scope of the topic. They may also attempt to avoid making useful analyses by simply listing things which are and aren't literature, or erring from the main point of the question by talking about their love for literature and/or its value to them. Some of these points may complement a good answer but they are highly unlikely to form the cornerstone of a good response.

Q4: Who wrote the Iliad and the Odyssey?

This question is looking to see how applicants analyse what might, superficially, seem to be a very simple question and tease out its hidden complexities and potential difficulties.

A **good applicant** would likely begin by acknowledging that these works are attributed to the poet we know as 'Homer' but in reality, the situation is more complex. An interesting avenue to start with would be what we mean by 'wrote' since we know that the works in question were an unwritten oral tradition for the first 400 or so years of their lives, which were eventually written down in Athens around the fifth century BC. Building on this, we might suggest that to posit a single author for works with a long oral tradition is inherently problematic since a work which is purely performed as an unwritten tale must be subject to constant change and reimagining by those performing it - even if the core of the works originate from 'Homer' himself.

Very well-read applicants may even be able to go further and discuss scholarly theories that the origins of the *Odyssey* are different from those of the *Iliad,* or the aspersions cast on the Homeric authenticity of some later books of the Odyssey - but this would only be the icing on the cake.

A **poor applicant** would be one who attempts to give a very short and overly factual answer to the question, which fails to be analytical. For example, to reply simply "Homer" would hardly impress the interviewer since this basic factual knowledge would be expected.

The interviewer is looking for evidence of analytical abilities in terms of how we think about texts, and, hence, would be more than likely to provide the candidate with additional information about the provenance of the works if this is not something the candidate has previously encountered. If you know very little about a topic, feel free to admit this and ask specific questions, but be sure to do so in such a way that it shows an analytical method rather than resignation to failure. A good question to ask would be something like: "*Is there any historical evidence about the origins of the works?*"

THE ULTIMATE OXBRIDGE INTERVIEW GUIDE: HUMANITIES   CLASSICS

Q5: Which of the Romans or the Greeks would you say left a greater impression on the modern West - why do you say that?

This question is another broad one and is looking for candidates to demonstrate an ability to analyse the Classical world within its wider context in a way that is less similar to the way in which they are taught at school.

A **good applicant** could take any number of successful approaches, though useful topics to cover will be language, politics, art (including literature and architecture) and possibly something more nebulous such as 'identity'. In light of this, it may also be useful to make a distinction about what you take 'culture of today' to mean: Britain? Europe? The world? Feel free to define it as you wish, but it may be prudent to restrict yourself according to your knowledge.

Linguistically, one could make a number of points about more words in English being Latin-derived than Greek, but also that Latin developed largely from Greek origins. This might tie in with a discussion of how strictly we can define Greece and Rome as civilisations, given the great deal of influence Classical Greece had on Classical Rome and the Roman rule of Hellenistic Greece.

You might also like to speculate on what effects Roman rule (until c. 400AD) had on modern Britain, from the law to roads and our sense of national identity - is the Roman past a matter of pride for Britons?

Literature is an extremely broad topic and could take any number of directions, but you could usefully begin by listing some widely read works of ancient literature and why you think they are culturally significant (or not). Perhaps with reference to the influence they may have had on more modern literature - e.g. could we have Milton without Homer or Virgil?

The key thing with this question is simply to demonstrate some sort of analytical route through the vast material which resembles an argument. The interviewer will probably question your hypotheses - responding to these with your own examples and arguments will serve you well. A **poor applicant** would be more likely to give a short answer about how we were never ruled by the Greeks and so the Romans were probably more influential. Such an answer, whilst making one useful point, demonstrates a lack of engagement with the breadth of the question and a pedestrian mode of thinking which is unlikely to impress the interviewer.

Q6: Is mythology something we can work into history?

This question is a little more specific in scope than some of the previous but still leaves substantial scope for interpretation. A **good applicant** would likely begin by defining terms that pertain to the central issue of the question, i.e. what do we mean when we say myth or history and how neatly can we divide the two concepts from one another?

The key issue to tackle in the question is how we **interpret the idea of 'compatible'** since myth and history might be of very similar significance or hardly differentiated between in the ancient world. For example, the Roman foundation myths were notionally regarded as 'historical' in ancient Rome and certainly had the cultural significance of real historical events, though they were known to be largely fictitious.

In Greece, one might argue that the question is even more vexed given that the line between myth and history is so blurred, e.g. the question of the extent to which the Trojan war is a historical fact and the extent to which it is a myth. Further, one might question whether such a distinction is relevant to the Trojan war since its significance to Greek literature and culture is unchanged in either case. Moreover, one might also discuss whether all history is a myth. For example, if 'all history is written by the victor', how far can we be sure that any 'historical' account of events is not, in fact, a biased mythologisation?

The most important thing with a question like this is to attempt to **pull the question apart** and ask to what extent its premises are valid by dissecting what we mean by the various terms and how far these terms can truly be said to be distinct from one another. This demonstrates an ability to think in a critical and original way and is likely to impress the interviewer.

A **poor applicant** would likely make some more pedestrian distinctions about history and myth being incompatible because history is about things which really happened, whereas myths are simply fairy tales and fictions, without digging much into the wider significance of the question.

Q7: What languages can you speak?

This question is an opportunity to demonstrate whether you have other language skills that may be of benefit to studying Classics, texts in translation, and understanding broader cultural influences in your reading and studying of texts. This is an opportunity to not only demonstrate that you speak modern foreign languages, but that you have a broader awareness of how languages operate, and the influences of cultural meanings in translation. Even if you don't speak other languages, this question can be used to show your understanding of the intersections between different languages and how the techniques used to analyse language in classics are also potentially applicable elsewhere.

Good Answer: I have a good level of French, having studied it at A-Level(/IB). I've actually found it particularly relevant and useful in my studies of classics so far as it has given me a broader awareness of working with texts in translation and rooting my translations in the historic and cultural contexts in which they were written. It has also improved my understanding of the way in which language is used in general, widening my perspective in terms of word choice in both speaking and translating texts. A simple example, would be the French use of 'on', third person singular pronoun, which we are taught typically to mean 'one' in English. However, when you engage more widely in French texts and spoken language, we discover that the French use 'on' far more frequently and to refer to several different people than we do in English. So 'on' can be translated as 'I', or 'we' depending on the context. I think it is these perspectives that French has brought me and that have informed my work within in Classics.

This answer is honest and based upon personal experience of working within a language. Whilst this question would seemingly be unrelated to Classics, the response has been shaped to show that you have an awareness of the complexities of operating in other languages, and how understanding broader context than simply the words themselves is so important.

A **Poor Answer** would offer a simple response stating which languages you do or do not speak, without elaborating further. This question is an excellent chance to show that you can make connections when questions that do not necessarily spoon feed you where to go with your response.

Q8: What is the value of classics degrees to the taxpayers who fund them?

This question is potentially not one that you might be expecting, but in fact it is an interesting attempt to get to the heart of why you want to study classics. This question requires you to really justify your motivations for studying classics and make you consider how classics impacts the wider world, as well as potentially your future pursuits.

Good Answer: I think it's fair to say from the outset that classics is not the only degree that I would think is subsidised by the tax payer. In terms of classics specifically, I think that it is often misunderstood what classics offers to the world. It is not just the study of dead languages, but in a way, a study of the root of western society; its languages, philosophies, and legal systems. In this way, we can still see the influence of Greek and Latin in the modern world, whether it be in our use of everyday language, medicine, or law. Classics in many ways provides the foundations for much of western civilisation as we know it, and understanding the impact that Greek and Roman societies had on subsequent societies, is fundamental to understanding those modern civilisations that we live in. I also believe that the rigours of studying classics produces graduates with a set of skills that are widely applicable in society as a whole, we have to synthesise complex information, analyse in-depth material, and formulate clear arguments. I believe that the value that classics graduates bring in the longterm more than make up for any costs to the taxpayer in the short term.

Simply put, there is no correct answer to this question. Instead, the interviewer is testing your ability to respond to a question that is not straightforward, and your ability to form a coherent and persuasive answer. Thus, this answer is structured well as it provides a short introduction, an understanding of the wider applications of classics, examples to back up your response, and ultimately an answer and synthesising conclusion to the question.

A **Poor Answer** would be hesitant in trying to understand why the interviewer may have asked this question in the first place. It would be very easy to waste time trying to understand or question why you have been asked this. Instead, you need to focus not on the reference to the taxpayer, but the justification of a classics degree, before tying it into how it relates to the taxpayer. In many ways, the question becomes easier to answer as you start generally in justifying studying classics and then specifically relating it to the taxpayer.

Q9: You mentioned a passion for Roman history – would you use Sulla as an example when explaining tyranny?

This question is asking you to make a critical assessment of the evidence around Sulla's actions. In part, this question hinges around your definition of tyrant, which is important to briefly outline. Above all, it is important to present a balanced argument and critical synthesis in order to answer the question.

Good Response: Without question, the way in which Sulla seized power, as well as the law that was enacted to maintain power, means that he was a dictator. That is, someone with absolute rule, little-checked power, and the ability to make unilateral decisions. But this does not in and of itself make Sulla a tyrant. I think that to define him as a tyrant, that is, someone who abuses their power in a cruel and oppressive manner, we must consider his actions whilst a dictator. Shortly after coming to power in 81BC, Sulla carried out hundreds, and potentially thousands of proscriptions, summarily executing all those that he accused of having acted against the interests of the republic. What is particularly interesting to note about these proscriptions, however, is that they seem often to have infrequently been politically motivated, and instead often were targeted at those whose property could be seized and sold off for profit. Indeed, Sulla undoubtedly had those who were a threat to him and his adherents killed, but the scale on which the proscriptions occurred would suggest there were ulterior motives, and would indeed support the idea that he was a tyrant.

Additionally, Sulla sought to reinforce the power of the Senate and undermine the previous intentions of the *populares* to give more power and influence to the people. This included oppressing and removing the power and influence of the Plebeian Tribune, which represented the interests of Plebeians, including removing their ability to initiate legislation and their ability to veto acts of the Senate. With all this being said, it is particularly interesting to note that once he finished his second consulship in 80BC, that he promptly resigned his dictatorship in 79BC. Despite the clear abuse of his power during his time as dictator, this final act does leave a distinct question mark of whether we should fully describe Sulla as a tyrant, for it would be logical for a 'true' tyrant to seek to retain their power for as long as they are able. Ultimately, however, I would argue that even though he rescinded his power, Sulla's actions whilst dictator, particularly his arbitrary and cruel execution of people, would lead me to conclude that Sulla was indeed a tyrant.

This is a strong answer because it begins by outlining the nature of Sulla's dictatorship, and the criterion that would be necessary to extend to him the title of tyrant. It then goes on to clearly outline some of the evidence in support of this argument. There are of course, many other 'negative' actions that Sulla took to oppress the people of Rome, such as reinforcing the power of the Senate through its expansion, but the answer sought to use the strongest evidence for him as tyrant. Finally, the answer questions whether his abdication of power is enough to pardon him as tyrant, before finally concluding that the evidence for his titling as tyrant is indeed justified.

A **Poor Answer** might fail to make the link between Sulla's behaviour and how we can define this as tyrannical behaviour. It is particularly important to relate how the evidence that you provide can relate back to the question.

Q10: What are the main similarities and differences between ancient Greece and Rome?

This is clearly a gargantuan question, and the interviewer is not asking you to compare the entirety of Greece and Rome. Instead, this is an opportunity for you to demonstrate both your knowledge of these two ancient worlds, and show the interviewer your way of thinking. To this extent, this question is a great opportunity to show your passion for the study of classics, and any reading around the subject that you may have done.

A **Good Answer**: Well, the way that ancient Greece and Rome were politically structured and governed both changed over time. Initially, both were governed by kings, who in both instances were eventually removed. At this point, Greece moved to an oligarchical system, were a few men governed from Athens, this subsequently evolved into a democratic systems where its citizens (which did not include all people, including women) were obliged to participate in governance, including making new laws and controlling all parts of the political process. In contrast, after the fall of the kings, the Romans formed a republic which combined a series of elements from democracy, oligarchy, and monarchy. In part because of the conflicting nature of these different elements, eventually Rome returned to a model of single ruler, an emperor, who was originally sanctioned and empowered constitutionally.

A particular point of contrast that interests me about Greece and Rome is the stability of the two. Whilst Rome definitely had turbulent points, it largely remained in tact until the separation of the Eastern and Western empires, whilst Greece seems to have been far more conflicted throughout its history. In part, I think that this is a result of the multiple power centres that made up Greece. In essence, its establishment was a rough organisation of otherwise quite independent city states that maintained their own interests at the expense of others, as well as the collective whole. The fact that it took Phillip II of Macedonia to invade and unify the city states for the first time is pretty indicative of the infighting that was taking place. In contrast, Rome acted as the power centre for the entirety of the Roman empire, and whilst there were significant power struggles for the control of Rome, ultimately all authority over the empire was executed from Rome.

This is a good answer because it draws clear comparisons and contrasts between Greece and Rome. In a question like this, it is really important to try to structure your answer well and not simply jump from point to point. Hence, this answer has done this well. In the first paragraph, a clear topic is chosen and then the comparisons and contrasts outlined. The second paragraph is slightly different as their are fewer points of comparison, but they are still centre around a central topic.

A **Poor Answer** could very easily fall into the trap of only providing points of comparison/similarities or only points of contrast/differences. It is important to engage with all parts of the question in order for you to fully demonstrate your knowledge of Greece and Rome.

Q11: How would you discretise the Latin and Grecian pantheons?

Initially, this question seems pretty straightforward, and it would be very easy to simply create a verbal table comparing side-by-side the differences between the Roman and Greek gods. In order to show your ability to think beyond the question and critically asses the importance of the differences between the Roman and Greek gods, you need to consider what the differences between the gods tell us about the people who worshipped and wrote about them.

Good Answer: To begin with, I don't think that are is any one single difference between the Roman and Greek gods. Moreover, we know that there are definite similarities between the gods, not least because many of the Roman gods were derived from the Greeks'. In the derivation of the Roman from the Greek, there are obvious differences in the naming of the gods. This in turn, is in fact a reflection of how the gods were perceived and described. In Greek mythology, as chronicled in the Iliad by Homer, the gods were often given human characteristics, reflecting their physical description, which in turn was often indicative of how they behaved and what they influenced in life. This latter point is particularly important as a difference, because the Greek gods were believed to play an active role in the lives of mortals, with the Greek gods' individual actions having a direct impact. In contrast, Roman gods and goddesses were described, as in the Aeneid, in gender fluid terms, and less emphasis was placed upon their physical descriptions; they were often not depicted at all, but were instead represented within the imaginations of people. The influence of the Roman gods was also considered to be less direct and less individualised. That is, the Roman gods did not play an active part in influencing the lives of mortals, but instead were seen as part of the afterlife, towards which mortals must work to reach through their actions in life. In this way, Roman gods were in general seen less as individual actors, but instead were to be honoured through mortals' actions.

This answer is strong because it gets to the heart of what in some ways the studying of Greek and Roman gods achieves; a greater understanding of those that worshipped them. After acknowledging that there are in fact similarities between the two sets of gods, the answer goes on to outline some of the key differences, and relates these to not just the descriptions of the gods, but how their role differed in society.

A **Poor Answer** might take this question very literally and attempt to simply describe the physical or behavioural differences between the gods. Whilst there is nothing inherently wrong with this, the interviewer is in many ways wanting to see what you can extrapolate from your descriptions and see how these relate to our understandings of texts and the people who worshipped them.

Q12: When did the Roman republic collapse? Why?

Whilst this question this order by asking when first and why second, in actual fact, in order to answer this question, it is best to tie your evidence of why the republic ended into arguing when it ended.

Good Answer: Most interpretations of the end of the Roman republic put the date at 27BC when Augustus was granted extraordinary powers by the senate, which in effect, gave him the power to rule as an emperor. This came off the back of the defeat of Marcus Antonius and Cleopatra in 31BC at Actium, which marked the end of the major political rivalries that had prevented such a single dominant rule up until that point. Whilst this is neat date, I think that in answering why it ended is not as simple that Augustus took the title of emperor. In many ways, by the time that Augustus took up the official mantle of Emperor, several other leaders within Rome - Marius, Sulla, and Caesar - had wielded sufficient individual power that they could unofficially be considered emperors of a kind, and we could use this to argue that the in effect the republic at least began to end in 105BC. Indeed, Augustus' position was only really afforded to him on the back of reforms and precedents set by Sulla - who entrenched the loyalty of the army to the general, rather than to the republic. In this way, the political structure of the republic was worn away over the course of 70 years, with the political power of the senate repeatedly hamstrung, and power taken more and more into the hands of an individual ruler. In this way, I argue that the end of the republic was not a single event, nor was it caused by any one single factor, but instead it was an accumulation over decades and the result of a whole series of short and long term events that ultimately led to the succession of Augustus as emperor.

This is a strong answer because it establishes the traditional doctrine of when the republic ended before going to challenge this through well-articulated evidence. This kind of critical engagement with material and evidence is exactly what your interviewers are looking for. They do not want you to blindly accept historical interpretations as fact, but instead to articulate your own opinion based upon your assessment of the evidence.

A **Poor Answer** might only focus on the evidence around when Augustus came to power without demonstrating a broader understanding of the events that led to the end of the republic. Alternatively, a failure to critically engage with the evidence would also undermine your answer.

Q13: Did Alexander the Great earn his epithet?

This question is asking you to assess the evidence that you know about Alexander the Great, and draw a conclusion based upon this in order to formulate answer.

Good Answer: In answering this, I think it is first important to establish why exactly Alexander III of Macedon was referred to as 'Great'. During his lifetime, Alexander's success revolved around his abilities as a military leader. He was the first king to defeat the Persian Empire, which had threatened Macedon and the Greek States for over a century. He achieved this in 3 years, and supposedly defeated an army of 250000 with just 50000 men, a ratio of 5:1. After this, Alexander spent 9 years conquering much of the Middle and Near East, reaching as far east as the Indus river. During this time, he founded 70 cities, including Alexandria, which he named after himself and which became the cultural capital of the region for decades . As part of his conquests, Alexander also diffused Greek culture through the region and established the Hellenistic period, which put Greek culture as a cornerstone for much of subsequent cultural development, including into the modern era. Despite these achievements, Alexander's success was not achieved in isolation, his father was the first to unite the Greek city states and was the one that ensured that Alexander received the education that he would need to go on to become king. Alexander also treated his troops brutally, sacrificing 1000s in battle, and pushing them to point of exhaustion in his 13-year campaign. There were also reports that he arbitrarily murdered thousands of ordinary citizens. Overall, I think it is fair to argue that Alexander the Great was actually great, but this should not come at simple blind acceptance of his greatness, nor should his success be considered to have occurred in a vacuum.

This answer is strong because it clearly outlines the two sides of this argument with concrete examples that support both why Alexander was and wasn't great. After providing the evidence in a logical and critical manner, the answer draws a conclusion that answers the question.

A **Poor Answer** might fail to provide a balanced account of Alexander. It would be easy to dismiss his achievements based upon many of negative things that came as a result of his campaigns, and vice versa, it would be easy to overlook his failings in favour of reinforcing the 'great' narrative. In order to answer this well, you must demonstrate that you have the ability to provide both sides of the argument.

Q14: You mentioned studying the expansion of the Roman empire outside of school time. What does the work surrounding the Numidian king Jugertha tell us about Roman foreign policy?

This question is not simply asking you to outline the relationship between Jugertha and Rome, but to consider the wider implications for Roman foreign relations based upon the events around Jugertha. For each point of history that you draw out, it is important to relate back to the question and consider what it means for Roman foreign relations.

Good Response: I think that there are two key points about Roman foreign relations from Jugertha, and they fall broadly into the influence that Rome had over foreign powers and the influence that foreign powers had over Rome. Firstly, we can clearly learn that Rome had vested interests throughout the Mediterranean, even in areas that they did not directly control. We can see this with Jugertha through the way in which Adherbal was instilled as ruler of his share of Numidia after his brother had been murdered by Jugertha, and Adherbal had fled to Rome. This immediately allows us to see that Rome's influence was extensive, for the fact that they were essential able to mediate in a foreign power's internal affairs and restore their favoured ruler. I think the second key thing that we can learn about Roman foreign relations is derived from the period after the civil war in 112BC between Jugertha and Adherbal, where Jugertha had killed Adherbal and besieged Cirta. During this siege several Roman businessmen that had aided Adherbal were also killed by Jugertha, angering Rome. The short war with Rome that followed led to a favourable peace treaty for for Jugertha, despite the supposed anger at his actions. The suggestion here therefore, is that Jugertha was able to wield significant influence in the Roman senate through bribery, which he had learned that they were favourable to during his campaigns in Hispania. Thus, this reflects the other side of the two-way-street that were Roman foreign relations. Whilst they wield remarkable influence in kingdoms throughout the Mediterranean, there was also significant influence coming in the other direction as well, even if it was eased through with bribes.

This is a strong answer because it demonstrates the multi-faceted nature of foreign relations throughout Rome. It provides two well outlined examples of both the influence that Rome had as well as the influence on Rome that foreign powers had. Importantly here, the answer has done well to continue to draw inferences from the history of Jugertha to draw conclusions about what these events actually meant in terms of Roman foreign relations.

A **Poor Answer** could easily just reiterate the events of Jugertha, without taking the analysis a step further and considering what the implications for foreign relations can be made about Roman foreign relations.

Q15: How is the study of classics useful to the modern world?

This is a question that gets to the heart of your interest in studying classics, as well as being an opportunity to show that you've thought about the impact of your degree beyond just your time at university, or that you're interested in it.

A **Good Answer:** Well, first of all I think that one of the most useful aspects of studying classics is how much of the modern world is still influenced by ancient Greece and Rome. Indeed, we have only to look at law or medicine to see just the influence of the language, and how that has affected thinking about these subjects in the previous millennia. Beyond just the language component, Roman law and Greek philosophy continue to influence thinkers in the modern world, as well as having the created the very foundations upon which many of our modern ideas are built. Hence, studying classics is an incredible opportunity to understand how some of the greatest influences of the modern Western world came to be. I also think that the practice of studying classics is incredibly rigorous, and produces graduates with skills that are useful in many facets of the modern world. For instance, almost all professions require the synthesis of complex information, the analysis of highly detailed material, and the ability to derive clear arguments from these. I think that simply by looking at the wide array of professions that classics graduates pursue and the impact that those people have is a testament to how useful studying classics can be to the modern world.

This answer is strong because it demonstrates your ability to link studying classics to different aspects of the modern world. This latter point is particularly important as it would be very easy simply to talk about how useful classics is, without specifically relating it to aspects of the modern world. This answer also shows that you are able to think about classics both for the explicit and implicit things that we learn from studying the subject i.e. both the language and cultural aspects of classics, as well as implicit skills learnt through studying it.

A **Poor Answer** might only address why you think studying classics is useful. For instance, you might argue that Classics is useful because it keeps otherwise dead languages alive. However, this misses the important part of the question asking you to think critically about the impact that classics continues to have in the modern world.

Q16: As a classicist, how do you tell fact from fiction?

This question is not straightforward, and very much hinges around how we define these concepts. What the questions is primarily asking you to do is think about the how or the ways in which we can separate fact from fiction. Here, myth and reality is given to you almost as framework within which to consider the relationship between myth and reality parallels the relationship between fact and fiction.

Good Response: First of all, I think that it is important to unpack why myth and reality are so intertwined. I think this is because our realities are in fact, constructed. They are constructed from experiences, our personal background, and our sociocultural background. On this latter point particularly, our reality is situated within oral narratives, the stories that we tell ourselves and others in order to understand and conceptualise the world around us. Given that this is the case, the task of separating fact from fiction, when the fact can be expressed and understood through fiction (or myth) is complex. Irregardless of this however, I think very little fiction is entirely fact-less. More often than not, we find through in-depth research that much fiction is derived from fact. One might even argue that fiction is simply a fact that has been embellished, or mythologised, to make it more easy to transmit as an idea. But the key point here, is that aspect of research around fiction that I mentioned. To analogise, if you were looking from one view point at a pyramid, you might believe that you were either looking at a square or a triangle, it is only through multiple points of view, or angles of research, that you are able to build up a clearer picture and derive the fact from what appears to be fiction. In examining fiction, it is therefore essential to obtain as many perspectives as possible, and where these perspectives begin to line up is where we can begin to distinguish fact from fiction.

This is an excellent response because it takes a highly logical approach, first outlining and trying to understand why myth and reality are so intertwined, before using this as a foundation to explore the possibilities for separating fact from fiction. In doing this, the answer provides a clear answer - that we must use research - and goes on to elaborate how research can be used to separate fact from fiction.

A **Poor Answer** might become fixated on the latter part of the question, without actually addressing what the question is actually asking. Equally, a poor answer might try and equate fact with reality and fiction with mythology, and draw false parallels between the two. It is important to note the question is asking you to use an understanding of the relationship between myth and reality to better understand the relationship between fact and fiction.

Q17: How would you end the siege of Troy?

This question is an opportunity to demonstrate both your knowledge and your ability to think creatively and critically about the evidence.

A **Good Answer**: We can consider various potential ways of ending the siege based upon our knowledge of other sieges from throughout history. We could consider methods such as poisoning the primary water source or using large war machines to destroy the walls, however, I think it is likely that the Greeks would not have had to technology to achieve this. Moreover, the fact that the siege of Troy supposedly lasted for 10 years, I think must be a testament to its abilities to maintain supply lines. The simple fact is, that without the ability to resupply the city with food and reinforcements, Troy would have fallen much more quickly. Based upon this, I would have taken two primary strategies. To start with, I would have identified the key points through which Troy was receiving supplies. Then, firstly I would send elite soldiers into the city in secret through these supply lines (by hijacking a convoy of supplies for instance) and ordered them upon entering the city to carry out guerrilla warfare, including setting fire to buildings, assassinations, and causing all round mayhem. Secondly, I would then cut the off the supply lines. Even if close areas into and out of the city were controlled by the Trojans, it would have been relatively straightforward to use groups of scouts to follow any supply lines and identify geographically where these supplies were coming from. I would then begin the process of cutting these off. Even if a few of the supply lines were still able to get through, over the course of a year or so, it would definitely be possible to identify more and more of these and take control of them. Once the city was starving, it is likely that it would surrender pretty quickly.

This is a good answer because it combines your ability to draw upon the evidence that we have about the siege of Troy and think logically and creatively, using this to suggest feasible ways that the siege might have been ended more quickly.

A **Poor Answer** might suggest improbable or impossible ways to end the siege (such as using gliders to drop soldiers into the city) and get carried away with the creative aspect of this question without rooting it in historically accurate contexts.

Q18: How accurate is the film '300'?

As with so many retellings of stories from history, *300* is a melting pot of historical fact and outright fiction for the sake of entertainment. Thus, this question wants you to be able to tease apart the elements of the film that are derived from history, and those that have been invented or embellished, and draw a conclusion from balancing these two sides.

Good Answer: 300 is based Herodotus' account of the battle of Thermopylae, where 300 or so Spartans held back the invasion of the Persians. However, this is really where the accuracy starts waver. Firstly, the depiction of Spartan's as extreme, militaristic, and stoic heroes is actually derived from later traditions that glorified their way of life. In reality, in Herodotus most of these are ideas are not mentioned at all. Instead their culture and way of life is described in very similar terms to those of other Greek city-states of the time. To this extent, it is unlikely that they were professional soldiers at this time, and certainly didn't go into battle bare chested. Much of the imagery in the film depicting them as a highly organised military unit forming a phalanx seems unlikely. From what I remember of the film, they also wouldn't have used entirely metal shields, and it seems likely that this was an addition for the sake of entertainment.

On the other side, much of the depiction of the Persians is completely fantastical; the 'Immortals' for instance, were not in fact immortal, nor was Xerxes 10 feet tall. Moreover, they depict the Persians as primitive oppressors seeking to take the freedom of the Spartans and other Greeks. This is wrong on two accounts. Firstly, we know that the Persians were in fact, likely more technologically and scientifically advanced than the Greeks, and secondly we know that Persians allowed the Ionians to maintain their democracies even after they were conquered in 494BC. In some ways, this reflects how the film makers wanted to create a somewhat outdated dichotomy of 'western' vs. 'eastern' civilisations and imbue it with highly questionable connotations of 'good' vs. 'bad'. Indeed, Herodotus himself offers quite a balanced account of the Persians, and demonstrates that Spartans undermined themselves through in-fighting. Thus, the core inspiration and elements 300 are historically accurate, but there has been significant embellishment for the sake of entertainment which seriously detracts from the historical accuracy of the film.

This is a good answer because it takes into account both what can be considered accurate within the film, whilst also pointing out the problematic and inaccurate areas within the film. Each point is well backed up with evidence, and the answer draws each side together in a balanced conclusion, and answers the key part of the question about the extent to which the film is historically true.

A **Poor Answer** might only focus on one of the two sides, either only pointing out inaccuracies or accuracies. This would be problematic because in order to appropriately answer the *extent* to which the film is true, you must provide evidence for and against.

Q19: What's the meaning of Stonehenge?

This is an opportunity for you to demonstrate not only your knowledge of Stonehenge, but to link it into demonstrating your broader understanding of megalithic architecture in prehistory. That is, you not only need to demonstrate your knowledge of Stonehenge, but you must also be able to draw inferences from the evidence through critical assessment. To this extent, you could consider why there have been so many interpretations of its purpose and origin, and even why discuss why it continues to capture the imaginations of professional and lay people from around the world.

Good Response: I think that one of the most significant parts Stonehenge lies in its complexity and what this complexity tells us about the people who made it. Whilst it is not the largest stone circle in the UK - that title goes to Avebury - my understanding is that it is architecturally the most complex megalithic prehistoric site. In terms of the planning and execution of the site, moving tonnes of rock and placing them into structures, some of which have lasted 1000s of years, is a testament to the knowledge and skill that the people who created Stonehenge must have had. Equally, even if we assume that they were able to create mechanical ways of transporting and moving the stones, we must consider the extent of the mobilisation of people that it must have required, as well as the significant number of hours of pre-planning, planning, and preparation it would have taken.

Beyond just considering the significance of the inferences we can make about their technological capabilities, there are now conclusions being drawn that the stones originated in Wales. Hence, not only do we have to consider how they moved these huge stones hundreds of miles, but we also have to consider how significant their knowledge of the landscape was, how far these people moved, and potentially, how much time they might have invested in this endeavour. The level of organisation, communication, and potential innovation are astounding. Finally, building upon the point about these peoples' knowledge of the landscape, we must ask why did they choose stone from Wales (and elsewhere) and decide to bring it to a specific point in Wiltshire. Why did these people feel it was necessary? This final question is one that I believe we are still trying to answer with modern methods, as well as through phenomenological human perspectives within the landscape. This in fact brings me back to my original point that overarches everything that I've outlined: I think the greatest significance of Stonehenge is what it tells us about the people that made it. It has intrigued subsequent people for thousands of years, and we are only now beginning to understand the monumentality of both the structure itself, and the achievements of the people that made it.

This is a strong answer because it achieves that key point of not just outlining the evidence, but drawing inferences about the significance of that evidence. In this way, the evidence is logically laid out and the answer is well-structure, with a neat conclusion that draws the answer back to the first point that you elaborated on throughout the question.

A **Poor Answer** might only focus on outlining what you do or don't know about Stonehenge without drawing those important inferences in order to fully answer the question of why Stonehenge is significant. Alternatively, the answer might try to argue that Stonehenge in some way isn't significant, this would, unfortunately betray your lack of understanding about Stonehenge.

Q20: Why is it important that we pay attention to changing Roman artistic style between the republic and mid empire?

It is important to note that art, especially in the context of the Romans, constitutes several different mediums including: architecture, painting, sculpture, mosaics, metal-work, gem engraving, carvings, and glasswork. Hence, whilst this question is asking broadly about the change in the artistic style, it is perfectly reasonable to outline your argument with examples from these mediums. Moreover and importantly, the question is asking you to draw inferences from the change in the artistic style to make conclusions about why this significant i.e. what its wider implications were.

Good Response: I think that the key change in artistic style between the republic and mid empire was the shift away from imitative designs - influenced by Hellenistic culture, with a focus on realism - towards the more 'Roman' originated style, which was comparatively more impressionist and grandiose in its nature. For instance, if we look at architecture in the republic, much of it was very practical, with relatively little embellishment and styles that were strongly influenced by Greek architecture. Towards the end of the Republic and throughout the beginning of the empire, there was a gradual change beginning with Julius Caesar's forum and gaining pace from there, towards more grandiose architecture. The archways which had been invented in the republic, grew in size, and along with domed ceilings, led to the construction of huge, multi-storied, elaborate buildings, both public and private.

One could argue that the pinnacle of this architectural development was the construction of the Colosseum by Vespasian, which utilised the technological advances made with concrete, along with a desire to demonstrate wealth and power through the use of marble - including statues - and gilding. I believe that these changes were significant because they represented a fundamental shift in the Roman economy, as well as in their culture and identity. Whilst the republic was characterised by regular internal and external upheaval, the empire was a comparatively stable and prosperous time, allowing the empire to flourish and invest its wealth in, among other art forms, the grandiose architecture I just mentioned. I also think its significant because it represents, I believe, a cementing of the Roman identity; they were no longer reliant upon Greek and Hellenistic influences for affirmation of their culture, and as a result the artistic styles reflected this in a clearer definition of the Roman artistic style throughout various media.

This is a strong answer because it not only illustrates the change in artistic style between the republic and mid empire, but more importantly it makes inferences about the significance of these changes and what interpretations we can draw about Roman society.

A **Poor Answer** might only focus on outlining the change in artistic style without addressing the core component and next level thinking aspect of the question in being able to make inferences about the significance of the change.

Q21: Do you think that the triumvirate was a success?

This question is asking you to weigh the evidence that you know of around Triumvirate and conclude whether it is a success. You could interpret this question one of two ways: is Triumvirate a success as political exercise, or was it specifically successful in the context of the First Triumvirate. In order to decide, it wouldn't be unreasonable to ask a follow-up question to your interviewer clarifying this, but equally if you feel confident, as always its more important to demonstrate your thinking than to necessarily reach the 'right' answer.

Good Answer: I think that as a political alliance, it is clear that there was success to be had to different extents for each of three actors in the Triumvirate. And to this extent I think that this question very much hinges on our definition of success, and who succeeded from Triumvirate. Certainly, in the short term, the Triumvirate achieved the goals of all three of its participants: Caesar received his position as consul and subsequent command of Gaul and Illyria for five years, Pompey had his acts of the settlements he had made in the Near East ratified by the Senate, and Crassus had his general political interests furthered, including the promise of future consulship. After its renewal at Lucca, the three of them then went on to control three of major Roman provinces; Gaul, Hispania, and Syria, no mean feat and definitely a success. It was only after the death of Crassus that we might begin to challenge whether the Triumvirate was a success. When Crassus died, the Triumvirate came to an end, and eventually led to civil war between Pompey and Caesar, and we know that Caesar won. Despite the way that Trimuvirate ended, this alliance did in the end last for 7 years, which in Roman political terms is no small feat. Whilst one could argue that the success for each of the three protagonists was relative, with Caesar arguably 'succeeding' the most, it is clear that each of the three achieved what they wanted out of the Triumvirate. Hence, I think that we can conclude that whilst it ended badly, Triumvirate was overall a success both as a political idea of a three-way informal alliance and in practical terms for those involved.

This is a good response because it deals with multiple perspectives on how we might define success in terms of the Triumvirate. It outlines each perspective with evidence providing points and counterpoints, and it ultimately synthesises your argument to form a conclusion to answer the question.

A **Poor Response** might only consider evidence one way or other in considering whether Triumvirate was a success. Equally, it might try and make these points with supporting evidence or critically engaging with the points that you make.

Q22: Was Alexander the Great gay? Is this unusual for the time period?

This question is an opportunity for you to demonstrate your broader understanding of Alexander the Great. In particular, it is asking you to critically engage with the evidence that you know of and draw a conclusion based upon that evidence. Importantly for this question, you must also demonstrate that you are aware that analysis of texts and historical evidence is viewed through personal and culturally constructed lenses that affect our interpretation.

Good Response: I'd actually like to answer the second part of the question first, because I think that it's difficult to use our modern sexual categories to pigeonhole cultures in the past for which there is almost no evidence of the use of these terms; I think it's anachronistic. So, in order to answer the first part of the question, I think we have to actually rephrase what we are asking, and instead consider whether Alexander was exclusively attracted to men, which in our modern concepts and terms, we would might label as "gay".

Well, there is definitely strong evidence that Alexander had male lovers - such as Hephaestion - but he also married Barsine in 333BC and had son with her called Herakles. When he defeated the Persians, he also acquired the king's harem of 365 concubines, which, it is assumed he participated with. He also then married Roxane in 327BC, with whom he had another son in 323BC. So I think that this evidence demonstrates that he wasn't just forming political marriages with women as we might expect from someone only attracted to men, but he was clearly having extended sexual relationships over the course of years with women that led to children.

So, to conclude, I don't think Alexander was gay, but neither was he heterosexual, I think he acted upon his desires, which during his time and in his culture would have meant he had relationships with both men and women, and thereby would have been completely normal during his time period. It is really only through our modern lens that we maybe even consider this a topic of discussion.

This answer is strong because it first problematises the question by pointing out how our biases affect the nature of our discussion about homosexuality in past cultures. It then goes on to reframe the question, after which it presents evidence both for and against the question. Finally, it ties everything together in a synthesising conclusion answering the question.

A **Poor Response** might only focus on the evidence for or against the idea that Alexander was gay. Even if you weren't aware of both halves of the evidence, it is important to bear in mind that absence of evidence does not necessarily mean absence of evidence; you just aren't aware of it. It would also be very easy to become bogged down trying to define labels of sexual orientation without actually getting to the question. Whilst it is useful to establish definitions, do not become hung up on semantics.

Q23: What can we learn about Roman Society from the practice of gladiatorial combat?

This is an opportunity for you to demonstrate your ability to draw inferences from the evidence that you know about gladiatorial fights. That is, not only do you need to show that you have an awareness of what was involved with gladiatorial fights and the arenas they fought in, but also that you are able to think to deeper and more critical levels to draw conclusions from the evidence. This is a really great opportunity for you to demonstrate both your knowledge and your thought process for your interviewer.

Good Response: Well, there are some obvious conclusions that we can draw about Romans watching gladiator fights, such that they must have been relatively desensitised to violence. But, we could argue that this is no different really from modern forms of violence as entertainment - such as boxing, wrestling, and martial arts. Moreover, we know from various sources of evidence that not many gladiators actually died during these contests. That is, there may not have been a particularly high death rate, despite how it is depicted in modern representations and to this extent their desire for entertainment doesn't seem to be that far from modern tastes.

I think what is more interesting are the conclusions that we can draw from beyond the nature of the entertainment. If you think about it, for Romans to have watched gladiatorial festivals potentially lasting days, they must have had a significantly stable and prosperous economy in order for everyday citizens not to have had to work all day. Moreover, descriptions of the length and extravagance of some gladiatorial festivals would lead us to conclude that there must have been enough wealth owned the state or individual benefactors to train specialised fighters, build arenas, and provide all the other accoutrements required. Finally, I think we can learn that the Romans had an incredible ability to mobilise and organise people in specialised capacities. This is evidenced not only by my aforementioned specialised training of Gladiators and the market that was arranged around buying slaves and training them, but also the construction of incredibly complex arenas with hundreds of engineers and builders involved.

This is a good response because it combines the two factors that the question is getting at; can you lay out your understanding of how gladiatorial fights worked, and what inferences can you draw from them. So the answer draws some interesting parallels between ancient and modern forms of violence for entertainment, and then considers some of the wider implications that the existence of gladiator fights show us.

A **Poor Answer** might just describe the basic level of what we can learn about Romans watching gladiator fights, like they were bloodthirsty, or enjoyed violence a lot, without providing a nuanced or critical understanding of what this actually means. It might also only focus on behavioural elements of gladiator fights without considering the organisational aspects or the extent of gladiator fights and what we can learn about these.

Q24: To what extent could you describe the Persian empire as 'civilised'?

This question is intentionally contentious. The question is not simply asking you to make a value judgement based upon your own opinion about the extent to which the Persian Empire was civilised. Indeed, this position has been used as the basis for the subjugation of peoples throughout history; for one person or group of people to believe that another is less civilised than they are. In order to tackle this question, you need to situate it within its time period and consider where the Persian Empire would have sat relative to its neighbours.

A **Good Response**: Well, I actually think we need to start by problematising this question. This is because the concept of whether a people were 'civilised' or not is a relative and loaded term. That is, especially in the colonial and post-colonial era, defining groups of people as 'uncivilised' has been used to justify their oppression and in some cases, enslavement and slaughter. The notion of whether a people are civilised or not has connotations of levels of development - that some peoples are more culturally developed than others - and this has sometimes been extended to arguing that some peoples are less biologically evolved than others.

However, I think in terms of thinking specifically about the civilisation of the Persian Empire, we can consider how relative to surrounding peoples whether the Persians had more advanced technology and knowledge. Indeed, when we compare the Persian Empire to the Greek city states, the Persians had far more advanced architecture. For instance, the Persians developed elaborate aqueducts - or *qanat* - that allowed them to move water great distances in order to provide for their cities. They also developed windmills that allowed them to grind grains and pump water. When we consider the extent of their understanding of maths, physics, and engineering required to achieve this, and then retrospectively compare this with the Greek city states, then the Persian empire was indeed more civilised.

This being said, and to reemphasise my point that 'civilised' is a relative and problematic concept, if we compare the Persian Empire with technology of today, then it would be difficult to argue that by our standards that the Persian Empire was at all "civilised".

This is a strong answer because it directly challenges and problematises the assumptions in the question. It demonstrates to the interviewer that you are able to critically assess a question and do not simply take it at face value. This being said, having formed that criticism, the answer goes on to consider how we can talk about the extent of civilisation in relative terms to their Greek neighbours, in order to actually answer the question. It concludes well by pointing out the relativity of civilisation by drawing a comparison with modern society.

A **Poor Answer** might fail to understand that this is a relativist question and attempt to answer it in absolute terms. That is, it might make a value judgement one way or other, saying that the Persian Empire was either civilised or not, without understanding that this needs to be drawn in comparison with other points of reference.

Q25: What makes a 'classic'?

This is an opportunity for you to demonstrate your critical thinking abilities to your interviewer. There is not one right answer to this, instead the interviewer wants to know how you approach and think about this kind of question, and how you use this to form a coherent argument to answer the question.

Good Response: I think that there are several aspects that make a book a classic. First of all, I think that its contents have to be worth their longevity in the public sphere. That is, there are some stories or books that remain in public discourse for years, but just because they exist there does not mean it is because of their quality. Instead, it could be because of their notoriety or controversy, such as Fifty Shades of Grey; I do not think that simple notoriety makes such stories classics. Building on that idea, I think that the story being conveyed has to have lasting relevance. If a riveting story is particularly of its time, or does not translate well into different cultural contexts or time periods, then this will inherently prevent the story from having that lasting relevance. So a classic such as the Odyssey remains relevant because the themes in story - of adventure, ingenuity, betrayal, deception, etc. - are translatable and relevant to people of all ages and across different cultures. A final aspect that I think contributes to whether a book is classic or not depends on whether it is an exemplar piece of writing in its quality and style. From my experience in biology for example, we talk about holotypes, which are examples of a species that are used to typically define that species. If we apply this same kind of thinking to examining classics, then a book that can be used to exemplify a particular genre or time period might also make it a classic.

This is a good response because it shows that you are able to consider several different ways in which we might define a classic. To this extent, there is no one particular way that makes a book a classic. Instead, your interviewer is looking to see whether you can form a coherent argument based upon your knowledge and experience.

A **Poor Answer** might focus on trying to define a classic based upon a fixed set of ideas derived from your study of Classics. That is, there are going to be classics from throughout literary time and genres, and so it is important to consider how these play into our definitions of a classic.

Q26: Based on your study of Greek, what is a neoteric?

This question is phrased in such a way to challenge both your historic understanding of Neoterics as well as what it may mean in modern terms. That is, in order to answer this question you must realise that the phrasing of the question - the use of 'is' rather than 'was' - is an important distinction and should inform the way in which you answer the question.

A **Good Response**: Well, during the 1st Century BCE, the Neoterics were a group of writers and poets that purposefully rejected the Homeric style of epic poetry, instead favouring shorter, more eloquent styles. These poets, the most famous of which we know is Catullus, dealt with topics that were not so focussed on recounting extensive stories in intense detail, but instead described the everyday, sometimes seemingly superficial ideas. Despite this seeming superficiality, reading into them, we know that there is in fact a lot of subtlety through their use of puns, innuendo, and complex allusions.

Whilst traditionally we describe this movement of poets as 'Neoterics', I think the fact that the word from Greek literally means 'new poets', that a neoteric is really any movement of poetry or group of poets that breaks with and challenges traditional styles. In this way, I think neoteric is a title that can be given to those in the next generation that are seen as avant-garde. Indeed, it is not simply a title that can be passed directly from an old to a new generation, especially if that new generation is simply a reiteration with minor changes from the old. If we think about this in modern terms, we might argue that the transition from traditional written poetry of the early to mid-20th century, to spoken-word poetry in the late 20th century, in which we can include 'poetry slams' and even hip-hop, that we would describe spoken-word poets as neoteric as they so clearly break not just from traditional styles but traditional forms and even media.

This answer is good because it lays out both your understanding of where the idea of Neoterics originated, and what a neoteric was in ancient Rome, but it also deals with that subtle phrasing of the question that wants you to consider whether the idea of a neoteric is a translatable context. To this extent, the second half of the answer really gets to the crux of this by addressing the ways in which we might consider Neoterics as a broader concept, and how we might use the term to describe modern poets.

A **Poor Answer** could easily miss what this question is really getting at and solely focus on the ancient Neoterics. Whilst this isn't technically wrong, it would show the interviewer that you are maybe unable to critically analyse the question you being asked and infer its wider implications.

Q27: Should Classicists study contemporaneous texts to Greek and Latin from other areas of the world?

This question is an opportunity for you to demonstrate your broader understanding outside of your subject, as well as how interdisciplinary studies can be beneficial in all subjects. Remember that the Greek and Roman civilisations did exist in isolation; they were constantly interacting with their neighbours, who were interacting with their neighbours, and so on and so forth.

A **Good Response**: I think that the simple answer to this question is, in the context of our modern and growing understanding of the ancient world and how interconnected it was even 2000-3000 years ago, that absolutely we should. That is, I think that we underestimate how much influence that there would have been between the Greek and Roman worlds and the rest of the world, in both directions. Particularly, in the case of the Romans with their extensive empire, it would be logical to assume that there would have influences coming from all over Asia and Africa, and that Roman influence was being felt concurrently in those places. Even if they did not have direct contact or cultural exchange with long distanced societies, an extension of World Systems Theory shows us how long-distance trade can occur in a phased manner, such that a text conceived in Rome could have theoretically ended up in ancient China.

However, as Classicists, the nature of our subject means that we focus on Greek and Latin, and reading the original texts, and so this might be a barrier to accessing the information we could find in other contemporaneous texts. This being said, I think that there is such huge value in building a wider picture of the ancient world through cross-disciplinary reading, and maybe in time building in more ancient languages in what we consider 'Classic' civilisation languages might facilitate this.

This is a really strong answer because it forms a compelling argument demonstrating that you are able to think outside box of 'classics' and consider the impact of other areas of the world on Greek and Roman societies. Using the example of the Roman empire is a particularly good angle because the Roman empire already demonstrates the diverse cultural influences of the areas of the world that they conquered, and so in some ways to consider that through trade there would have been even more cultural exchange and interaction with parts of the world they hadn't conquered is a logical argument.

A **Poor Answer** could very easily take a narrow minded approach and simply dismiss out of hand that texts other than Greek and Roman are irrelevant to the study of classics. However, particularly as knowledge of the ancient world grows from across the globe, it would detrimentally dismissive not to consider the new evidence of multiple complex societies that existed in the ancient world.

Q28: Was the Roman invasion of Britain a success?

This question is asking you to weigh your understanding of the Roman invasion of Britain, and draw a conclusion based upon your assessment of the evidence. The Roman invasion of Britain was clearly not a quick process, and their presence in Britain lasted several hundred years, so it is up to you to make these assessments and form an argument.

A **Good Response**: I think the answer to this question hinges on how we define success, and I think from the perspective that Rome invaded, conquered, and settled Britain for nearly 400 years means that we can argue that the Roman invasion of Britain was overall a success. Indeed, when we examine the lasting impact of the Roman presence in Britain in terms of art, architecture, culture, and language among other factors, then our positive answer is even more cemented. However, if we consider that Britain includes Scotland, then the existence of Hadrian's Wall and what this represents, then we have to question the total success of the invasion. Indeed, there were plenty of uprisings originating from Scotland throughout the Roman period that challenges the idea of success. Moreover, the fact that after the initial invasion, Roman troops in Britain were not particularly well reinforced might lead us to conclude that the long-term success of the Roman occupation was limited. Nevertheless, I think that the extensive time that we consider the Romans to have been in Britain, as well as the mark that they left leads us to conclude that overall, it was a success.

This answer is good because not only does it provide evidence both for and against the idea of success, but it also shows a critical understanding of how we need to engage with the idea of success in the context of different arguments. In this way, the answer is structured well by introducing this problematisation of defining 'success' before laying at the evidence and then drawing a conclusion that answers the question.

A **Poor Response** might immediately dismiss the idea that the Roman invasion of Britain could be critiqued at all. In these instances, even if you feel strongly that the invasion was a success, in order to demonstrate that you can argue for both sides, you need to somewhat play devil's advocate and suggest reasons why we might challenge the idea of success.

Q29: Should we study modern retellings of classics?

This question is asking you to consider your wider reading as well as the importance that classics still have in the modern world. In order to answer this question, it is important to remain open minded about the value that non-traditional interpretations of classic can have in our understanding and studies. It is important to use this perspective to build your argument in order to answer the question.

A **Good Answer**: I think that it's important to start by saying that modern retellings of classics will never replace the study of original texts in the original language. That being said, I would argue that modern retellings of classics are both incredibly important and offer a new take and insights on classics. Firstly, I think that their importance lies in the fact that modern retelling of classics - which I think we can include everything from Disney's *Hercules* to Stephen Fry's *Mythos* - open up the stories, and thereby the study of classics, to the general population. As classicists we know that the stories we study are compelling and intriguing, that the language is intricate, but it can sometimes be difficult to engage people with the wider importance and study of classics, and so I think that modern retellings are paramount to this. I would also argue that we cannot dismiss the fact that having input on interpretations of classics from more people can make us re-evaluate and reconsider the work that we do, because, as in so many aspects of both life and academia, diverse perspective often improve our own understanding by making us see things through a different lens. To this extent, whilst modern retellings of classics may not be true to the stories in the way that classicists are used to or may like, that studying these retellings can make us reflect on our own work and shed light on ideas that we may have never considered before.

This answer is strong because it starts by acknowledging that we are saying that we should get rid of traditional study of the classics. It then goes on to suggest the value that retellings have both for the general populace and even for us as classicists. It would be equally valid to argue that we shouldn't study modern retellings of classics, but you must still build a convincing argument for this and acknowledge the value that modern retellings have.

A **Poor Answer** might very easily dismiss modern classics in an inadvertently snobbish way without even necessarily critically engaging with the idea of their importance. No matter which way you argue the case, you need to be able to demonstrate that you are willing to weigh different sides of the argument. It is absolutely fine to have a strong opinion and come down heavily on one side or the other, but in so doing, your position will only be strengthened if you acknowledge that there are valid counter arguments.

Q30: Latin and Greek are dead languages, yet have been preserved through various means for millennia. With this in mind, how would you use this to prevent the extinction and total loss of some modern languages?

This question is an opportunity for you to really think outside the box and demonstrate both your creative and critical thinking abilities to your interviewer. In order to answer the question, you first need to consider what you know about the recording of Greek and Latin, and then think about the ways in which this might be applied to those modern languages that are going extinct.

Good Response: I think there are two key reasons why Greek and Latin have managed to be so persistent in the last 2000-3000 years. First and foremost, we have the fact that unlike many of the other languages that have existed in the past, Latin and Greek were recorded in a myriad of media, from spoken word mythology, to engravings on buildings. The choice of materials particularly in the latter instance mitigates many of the risks that are associated with recording language on organic materials, such as papyrus and parchment, and thereby making it easier for them to have survived. I think the second key factor is that Greek and Latin as spoken languages have persisted in various different forms, whether as a common tongue, or through integration with other languages. For instance, we only have to look at English to see evidence of both Greek and Latin influences.

Based upon this, I think that there are two approaches that we must take to prevent the extinction of modern languages. Firstly, we must find ways to record these languages. As many languages even in the world today still do not have a written form, I think where possible, people should be encouraged to find ways to develop their own script (to avoid the imposition of foreign written structures, as happened with ancient written Chinese with the Japanese language). If this is not possible, then in the modern age, we can make use of the variety of audio-visual technology that we have to record as much of the language as we can. Secondly, I think that we need to find ways that languages can be effectively integrated into one another. I know for example, that there are villages in sub-Saharan Africa where children are unable to speak to their grandparents because they grow up learning more widely used languages such as French or English, rather than local languages. To this extent, I think finding ways to encourage continued intergenerational transmission of languages is really important.

This is good answer because it begins by considering the ways and the reasons why Greek and Latin have been preserved, before going onto suggest ways that these essentially success stories, can be used to preserve modern languages that are dying out.

A **Poor Answer** might fail to see the potential or importance that our understanding of the preservation of ancient languages has for the preservation of modern languages. In order to demonstrate to your interviewer that you have the ability to think wider than just our subject, you must use your creative thinking abilities to fully engage with the question.

Q31: If you were offered the opportunity to learn Cuneiform, would you? And regardless of yes or no, why?

This is question is attempting to get to the heart of why you want to study ancient languages and societies. It is also an opportunity for you to argue why you would only focus on Greek and Latin, or why you would be open to the idea of exploring other ancient languages. If you are not sure what Cuneiform is, that is perfectly fine, and you are entitled to ask what exactly Cuneiform is (it is the ancient written language of Mesopotamia), before beginning your answer.

Good Answer: Well, to begin with, I can completely understand why someone might not want to learn Cuneiform, if they are already specialising in Greek or Latin. I could also understand why someone might question the relevance of studying a seemingly unrelated language that may not have an apparent bearing on their classical studies. But for me, I would welcome the opportunity to learn Cuneiform even at a basic level. I think this is because I'm a firm believer that diversifying our background and the knowledge that we have to draw upon in our studies only serves to improve our interpretations and handling of language. Moreover, Cuneiform is the earliest known written language, and I do not think that this achievement itself, nor the context in which it was achieved, are any small feat. That is, considering the proximity of the Mesopotamia to the later ancient Greek and Roman worlds, that it seems parsimonious that there must be some kind inherited relationship between the written language of ancient Mesopotamians and those of the classical world. In terms of the context as well, I think that understanding that Cuneiform was originally developed as an administrative tool is a fascinating context to consider, particularly because so much of the classics that we study are not focussed on the 'mundane' functions of language in, for example, recording the number of bags of grain a farmer produces. So to consider how a practical tool became a way to tell and relate stories and record speeches, is fascinating to consider. I honestly think that learning Cuneiform, would at the very least be an intriguing opportunity, and potentially allow me to reflect on my studies in classics further.

This is a really nice answer because it demonstrates that you are open minded to different ways of thinking about your own subject, and that you value the contributions that inter-disciplinary studies have to offer. It would of course, be completely fine to argue that you feel that Cuneiform is a language too far flung in time from Greek or Latin to make it of direct value to your studies, but it would then be important to make a strong case for this, and maybe even argue that you would be more interested in studying, for instance Old Persian, as it is more contemporaneous with Greek and Latin.

A **Poor Answer** could easily question why the interviewer was asking you about a language so seemingly unrelated to Latin or Greek without first considering the wider implications. As mentioned above, it is perfectly fine in the context of this question to argue that you wouldn't be interested, as long as you can form a coherent argument for this and not simply dismiss the idea of studying Cuneiform out of hand because you perceive it as irrelevant.

Q32: You studied Catullus at A-Level – what does his sparrow symbolise?

This question is challenging your ability to show not just your knowledge of the text, but also your ability to read into the text, explore various connotations and interpretations, including both your own and those of other critics. Therefore, in approaching this question, you can either focus on one specific interpretation (whilst acknowledging that there are others), or outline several of the different interpretations that exist.

A **Good Answer**: I think there are several levels of interpretation that we can draw from Catullus' sparrow. At a basic level, I do not think that it is unreasonable to argue that the sparrow represents a gift bestowed on Catullus' lover. Indeed, there is extensive evidence that birds were given as love gifts. Beyond this, we can question whether the sparrow is a metaphor for Catullus' himself. Indeed, the sparrow's quasi-sexual relationship with Catullus' lover could provide evidence for this. At a more explicit level, we might argue that the sparrow is not a metaphor for the whole of Catullus' being, but whether it refers to his genitals, and that in playing with the sparrow, Catullus' lover is enacting some kind of fellatio. More so, we might even argue that the sparrow refers not to Catullus' genitals, but instead to those of his lover, and that the quasi-sexual relationship that Catullus describes is in fact one of self-interaction that has been observed (or fantasised) by Catullus.

At a more abstract level, we can infer that Catullus' lover was Lesbia, whom he refers to in many of his other works, and which is believed was an alias for his illicit love affair with Clodia, wife of Roman statesmen Clodius. If this is the case, then maybe the sparrow is a metaphor for their love itself, and that its interaction between Catullus and Lesbia is fleeting and intermittent, reflecting the nature of their love affair.

Above all, regardless of which level that we make these interpretations at and whether or not it is about direct or indirect interaction, I think that Catullus' sparrow is principally about the complex sexual and loving relationship between Catullus and his lover.

This is a good answer because it offers various interpretations in order to explore the text. Not only does it demonstrate that you can consider multiple perspectives, but it also shows that you can deal with these interpretations at different levels of abstract metaphor. In this way, the answer has a coherent structure, starting with the least abstract interpretations and working to the most. In the end, it draws a conclusion that regardless of the exact interpretation, there is a potentially a core meaning behind what the sparrow is really about.

A **Poor Answer** may not give a sufficiently in-depth reading of the text. That is, it might not offer a critical assessment of the different connotations that the text has, and instead only consider that this is in some way a superficial representation of a woman interacting with a bird. It may also not show a deep enough understanding of the text by failing to read into all the different connotations that can be found in the text.

Q33: Is Classical archaeology more important than the study of Classical texts?

This question is asking you to demonstrate your understanding of the study of classics outside of simply texts. Classicists are often quick to dismiss archaeological evidence that may contradict textual evidence, but it is important to note in your answer that texts are often not written by everyday people, and the way in which citizens or slaves are described in texts may not reflect their lived realities which are often more accurately represented in archaeology. Thus to answer this question, you need to lay out evidence for both sides of the argument before drawing a conclusion.

Good Response: Well firstly, I think that the studying of Classical archaeology provides remarkable insights on the classical world that we would not otherwise have. For instance, through studying human remains, we are now able to discover information that would have been lost by only studying texts. I think that this is particularly important in understanding everyday people, as typically those who wrote Classical texts were not lay people, but people of some socioeconomic or political standing, and even where they cover topics relating to everyday people, the reality is that they are never able to fully elucidate the experiences of common Romans or Greeks. In this way, we can learn about diets, demographics, and even occupations from examining human remains. When we add this to other aspects of Classical archaeology, such as cultural artefacts and architecture, then the picture we create is far more holistic.

This being said, I don't think that this necessarily means that classical archaeology is more important that studying classical texts. This is because classical texts still give incredible insights into the lives, beliefs, sociocultural behaviours, and politics, of ancient Greek and Romans. Undeniably, there are always going to be elements from classical texts that have changed over time, that do not give us the full picture of the ancient world, but when we examine other archaeological contexts, we so often wish that we had the written words of those other peoples to give us greater insights into who they were.

I think ultimately that classical archaeology can only benefit from the study of classical texts, and vice versa. For one to ignore or dismiss the other as being in some way less relevant or important only serves to diminish our understanding of both.

This answer is particularly strong because it lays out excellent arguments and counterarguments for both sides. It demonstrates that you have a good grasp of the kinds of information that can be garnered from both archaeological evidence and texts, and how these are used to inform our understanding of ancient Greeks and Romans. In conclusion, the answer draws together both sides and convincingly answers the question based upon the evidence that you have laid out.

A **Poor Answer** might argue that classicists spend so much time studying texts and language that the archaeological elements of classics are irrelevant. This would be unfortunate for it suggest to your interviewer that you do not have a wider grasp of the various influences and sources that we can draw upon to improve our understanding of texts.

Q34: What is the difference between complex and simple societies? Do you think there are any examples of simple societies still left in the world today?

This is by no means a straightforward question, and there are some pitfalls that it would be very easy to fall into. For instance, unless you have a strong grasp of cultural evolution, it would be very easy to inadvertently discuss evolutionism (the idea that some societies are more advanced than others and therefore have a right to subjugate and dehumanise them). Thus to answer this question, you must think critically about how we might define a 'simple' or 'complex' society in order to then consider whether there are any simple societies left in the world. The way in which you define simple is particularly important as it would be easy to make value judgements about other cultures.

Good Answer: I think that the difference between complex and simple societies relates to several factors. Particularly, I think that a complex society is defined by hierarchies in both society and governance that are a result of increased population. In order to support an increased population, one of two things either has to happen, due to the upper limitations of human group sizes, as originally argued by Dunbar. One option is that populations diffuse into smaller groups so that they are able to continue to subsist by their previous methods, or they have to find a way to organise themselves so people are working at a larger scale to feed more people. In the latter case, this then requires a level of governance or organisation by a leader or group of leaders, and I think that it would also inadvertently create social hierarchies because it would be easier to hoard wealth, and thence have power and social influence over others.

So to this extent, I think that if we can argue that if there are any simple societies left in the world that they must be relatively isolated and small-scale in size. This is because with the extent of globalisation that we now have, almost every culture has been influenced by outside, potentially more complex, cultures, bringing with them cultural ideas and technologies, that often support increased populations, such as farming techniques, medicine etc.

Hence, this is a good answer because it begins by outlining what you consider are the factors that turn a simple society into a complex one, and the factors that are involved in supporting a complex society. It then goes on to use this definition to extrapolate the circumstances in which simple societies might be able to exist in the modern world. Even if you didn't know whether there were any societies that were completely isolated (which there are), you can hypothetically reason about the necessary conditions for them to exist from your definition.

A **Poor Answer** might confuse organisational complexity with behavioural complexity, and use the latter to argue that any society without the same level of technology or cultural norms, as, for example, western countries, are less developed/evolved than 'complex' societies, when in reality development is not a unilinear path, but multilinear with many different iterations of cultural evolution that are all equally valid.

Q35: Who would you reason was the most important Greek god in Greek society and why?

This question is asking you to show your wider understanding of Greek society and the role that the gods played not only in mythology, but in influencing the day-to-day lives of Greek people. To answer this question well, you need to present your evidence and understanding of one (or two) of the Greek gods and use this to develop an argument as to why they are the most important.

A **Good Answer**: For me, this question hinges around the idea of what made a god important to the ancient Greeks. I mean, the stories of the 12 Gods of Olympus are most renowned, but when I think about the importance of these gods, especially in day to day life, I feel that none of them were as important as Hestia as goddess of the hearth. For instance, I know that it was tradition that every sacrifice made to gods in a household started with Hestia, and I don't think this was a coincidence. To begin with, sacrifices to all the gods were made through burnt offerings, which would have been put on the hearth to burn, therefore without Hestia's place to burn food, the gods would have received no offerings. Moreover, in many ways, the hearth is the centre of the home, it is not only where food was cooked, but would have provided a source of warmth and light at night. Hence, as a focal point within the home, potentially seen as a giver of life in the everyday through that warmth and cooked food, I think that Hestia was the most important god in Greek society.

This answer is good because it starts by identifying what the question is really asking, and using this as a foundation to answer the question. The answer then takes a focussed approach on one god, and clearly lays out why you think Hestia was the most important god, making a convincing argument and clearly demonstrating your thought process.

A **Poor Answer** might simply argue that based upon traditional hierarchy that one of Olympian gods was simply better than others, without considering their wider implications. Alternatively, it would be easy to simply list and compare the different gods, rather than focussing on one or two and making a convincing argument.

LAW

A law applicant may be asked legal questions or questions from a related subject, including history, politics, or current affairs with a legal slant. None of the questions asked of you will assume any previous legal knowledge, as the interviewers understand that applicants will likely not have studied law before. Be prepared to explain why you want to study law and show through extra-curricular reading or activities how you've fostered this interest.

The interview will usually consist of a large question with many smaller sub-questions that the interviewer will ask in order to guide the applicant to an answer. The main question may seem difficult, impossible, or random at first, but take a breath and start discussing with your interviewer different ideas you have for breaking down the question into manageable pieces.

The questions are designed to be difficult to give you the chance to show your full intellectual potential.

For law, the questions will usually take one of a few possible forms based on highlighting the skills necessary to 'think like a lawyer'. Five main question types are:

- Observation-based questions ("tell me about...")
- Practical questions ("how would you decide if...")
- Statistical questions ("given this data...")
- Ethical questions ("are humans obligated to...")
- Questions about proximate causes (mechanism; "how does…") and ultimate causes (function; "why does…"), usually both at once.

Questions also have recurring themes which appear in many questions because they are central to jurisprudential thinking: the workings of the English legal system, problems of access to justice, the centrality of morality in legal development, the future of the legal profession, the impact of international treaties and legal institutions, looking carefully at words and drawing fine distinctions, building up an argument and applying that to examples.

WORKED QUESTIONS

Below are a few examples of how to start breaking down an interview question, complete with model answers.

Q1: In a society of angels, is the law necessary?

Applicant: Well, an angel could be defined as someone who is always inclined to do what is good, just, and moral in any situation. If I thought that the sole purpose of the law was always to achieve what is good, just, and moral, I might conclude that in a society of such creatures, law would not be necessary as angels would already be achieving this goal on their own. Why don't I continue by giving my own definition of the purpose of the law in society, taking account of the law's function as a social coordinator and as an international arbitrator? Perhaps I should also add a brief of what it means for something to be necessary and apply that definition to my discussion at hand. I may even expand this discussion further and think about what a society without any laws would look like, or indeed, if such a society would be at all possible.

This shows that **the question can be broken down into sub-parts**, which can be dealt with in turn. At this point, the interviewer can give feedback and help make any modifications necessary. In the case of the above interview, the applicant will realise that the function of the law is not just to promote what is good, just, and moral, but also to act as a method of social cohesion. The details are unimportant, but the general idea of breaking down the question into manageable parts is important. The interviewer is not looking for an expert of legal philosophy, but someone who can problem-solve in the face of new ideas.

A **poor applicant** may take a number of approaches unlikely to impress the interviewer. The first and most obvious of these is to say "I don't know anything about societies of angels" and make no attempt to move forward.

The applicants who have done this only make it worse for themselves by resisting prodding as the interviewer attempts to pull an answer from them, saying "Fine, but I'm not going to know the answer because I don't know anything about this", or equally unenthusiastic and uncooperative responses. Another approach which is unhelpful in the interview is the 'brain dump', where instead of engaging with the question, the applicant attempts to impress or distract with an assortment of related facts: "Angels would not murder each other.

Murder is a crime which can be split into two constituent parts of *mens rea* and *actus reus*, both of which are necessary for the commission of the crime. The terms *actus reus* and *mens rea* developed in English Law are derived from the principle stated by Edward Coke, namely, '*actus non facit reum nisi mens sit rea*'. This is not nearly as impressive as a more reasoned response, but the interview could be salvaged by taking feedback from the interviewer. Many of these facts could start a productive discussion which leads to the answer if the applicant listens carefully.

Q2: What are the advantages and disadvantages to a non-written constitution?

This question is looking to see if you understand something of the nature of the **British constitution** and whether you can lay down pros and cons of an argument, with a conclusion that comes down on one side or the other of the debate.

Perhaps begin by defining what is meant by a written and a non-written constitution and try to give examples of countries with each (e.g. the UK and the USA). A constitution could be defined as a legal contract which states the terms and conditions under which a society agrees to govern itself, outlining the functions, powers and duties of the various institutions of government, regulates the relationship between them, and defines the relationship between the state and the public.

Problems of a non-written or uncodified constitution – firstly, it is difficult to know what the state of the constitution actually is, and secondly, it suggests that it is easier to make changes to the UK constitution than in countries with written constitutions, because the latter have documents with a 'higher law' status against which ordinary statute law and government action can be tested. Is the problem then more with the perception of our constitution than the legal status of the constitution itself?

Are they really so different? The American constitution may be elegantly written and succinct, but it can be amended or reinterpreted or even broken as the times demand, in the same way that the UK's unwritten constitution can be. Furthermore, even a written constitution is supplemented by unwritten conventions and most countries' constitutions embody a mixture of the two. This line of argument could lead you to conclude that the issue here is really only with semantics as **there isn't any real difference in governance**.

This question could lead to a discussion of the ways the UK constitution allows for laws to be made – e.g. "should judges have a legislative role?"

A poor applicant would not attempt to address both written and non-written constitutions, instead, sticking staunchly to whatever they have read on either subject.

Q3: How would you clarify the meaning of the words intention and foresight?

The question is looking for your ability to give **accurate definitions of two principals central to criminal law**. Intention could be defined as an aim or a plan, whilst foresight could be defined as the ability to predict what will happen. Thinking about the way these subtly different definitions might be applied in a legal context, we see that one might foresee that doing X will lead to the death of B but that consequence was not necessarily intended.

This intuitive distinction is mirrored in **criminal law in the UK.** There are two different types of intention: direct intent which exists where the defendant embarks upon a course of conduct to bring about a result which in fact occurs, and oblique intent which exists where the defendant embarks on a course of conduct to bring about a desired result, knowing that the consequence of his actions will also bring about another result.

A particularly topical example of the application of this distinction in practice can be seen discussing "**the doctrine of double effect**". This doctrine is only really applied in medical cases. Consider this example – a doctor who administers a lethal dose of painkillers to their terminally ill patient in order to relieve their suffering also foresees that such a dose will kill the patient. Should this doctor be guilty of the murder of her patient? Ultimately, the doctrine says that if doing something morally good has a morally bad side-effect it's ethically OK to do it providing the bad side-effect wasn't intended. This is true even if you foresaw that the bad effect would probably happen.

A **poor applicant** would fail to distinguish the two and would fail to see how these definitions are applied in modern criminal law.

Q4: Does a computer have a conscience?

Intuitively, we want to answer this question with a resounding "no" as it seems obvious that only living things can have consciences. Computers are creations of man and therefore merely act according to our needs, having little or no agency of their own. A poor applicant would only be able to articulate this very basic intuitive response and would be incapable of digging further.

In fact, **the answer depends entirely upon which definitions you choose to give to the key terms** in the question. Conscience could be defined as a moral sense of right and wrong which is viewed as acting to a guide of one's behaviour.

A computer is an electronic device which is capable of receiving information and performing a sequence of operations in accordance with a predetermined set of variables. Given these two definitions, it could be possible to program a computer with a conscience.

You could discuss the **distinction between having a conscience and being 'sentient'**-the former being a form of moral compass, whilst the latter is merely the ability to perceive or feel external stimulus. Do you think "artificial intelligence" is possible? Is it dangerous? If a computer does have a conscience, what might this mean for data protection laws? Freedom of expression? Ownership? Would this mean that computers should have rights?

Q5: What is justice?

It might be good to begin with a succinct **definition of 'justice'** like 'behaviour or treatment which are just' with 'just' meaning 'equitable, fair and even-handed'. You might then want to expand on this initial definition. Perhaps an exploration of what justice means in the context of criminal law which might go as follows:

Firstly, custodial sentences are used for their deterrent effect. Secondly, decisions on the form and duration of the sentence focus upon the crime itself rather than looking at how the punishment will best rehabilitate the offender, appease the victim, and benefit society as a whole. This judicial inflexibility which we see in the sentencing of criminals reflects a right-wing conception of justice based on the maxim 'an eye for an eye'.

You might put forward that an alternative conception of justice might achieve fairer results - perhaps one which takes a **utilitarian approach** to punishment. This would necessitate finding the best possible outcome for the largest number of people.

However, the counter argument to this would be that this approach would not allow for the idea of **'moral forfeiture'**, the principle that in committing a crime, you give up some of your rights. This contextual approach gives us a taste of just how difficult it really is to define justice, even in such a narrow context.

We often hear the term **'social justice'** which is another context in which the term is applied. The concept in this context is very difficult to reconcile with justice as vengeance in the criminal context. Social justice too has several definitions; one might be socioeconomic equality amongst all members of any given society, whilst another might be more meritocratic and insist upon greater social mobility and fairness in general. We see that, upon examining this wider application of the idea of justice to non-criminal contexts, that the conception of justice itself is made even more difficult to define. To conclude, we have proven that our initial definition of justice was not sufficient. The concept seems to defy any coherent definition as it is so broad and subjective.

Q6: Should the aim of the law be to make people happy?

One might argue that the aim of the law is to generally make everyone's lives better. Indeed, improving the quality of citizens' lives is the explicit focus of much of the policymaking and regulatory work done by many governments around the world. If we accept this, the next question would be 'what does better really mean?' One account could be that to make someone's life "better" we should render that person more able to get what they want. Another account might be that the quality of someone's life depends on the extent to which they do well at the things that are characteristically human to do. This difficulty in defining what it might be to make any one person's life better and therefore making them happy is one difficulty with placing this as the law's overarching aim – happiness is internal – how can we accurately know what anyone is feeling, and therefore truly know how well the law is working?

Perhaps one way to combat this problem could be to develop a **method of measuring subjective happiness** – a type of well-being analysis. How might we do this? Well, we could introduce a system of weekly online surveys which would be answered by a representative portion of society on how happy they were able to make particular administrative decisions. Over time, such large masses of data would allow us to accurately pinpoint just what really makes people happier and just how the law can shape itself to better achieve this.

Q7: Which laws are broken most frequently? Are they still laws?

Millions of people who declare themselves law-abiding citizens actually commit seven crimes on average per week. The most common offences are things like speeding, texting while driving, dropping litter, downloading music illegally, or riding bicycles on the pavement. Many of these more common 'minor crimes' are committed so regularly that they have almost become legal, which might be the reason so many people aren't fazed when they do break these laws.

Are these 'minor laws' still laws? You might argue that a law is a law even if it's not followed. The definition of a law, as a law, lies in the process by which it is enacted, i.e. the legislative process. This line of argument would lead you to believe that all laws are of the same importance because they become law by the same process.

However, you might not necessarily think that is the case. For instance, most people would think that killing someone would be much worse than accidentally dropping your train ticket and therefore littering. This would suggest that there is a hierarchy of laws, and therefore, that some laws are more important or that some laws are more immoral. This would lead you to conclude that 'minor laws' are still laws, but merely a lower class of laws, perhaps because the repercussions of infringement in these cases is lesser or the infringement is seen as less immoral and therefore are less thoroughly enforced.

Q8: Define a miracle.

This question is a rather open-ended philosophical question designed to see how you define a term. This is an important skill for a law student as you would often have to define vague terms in your essays concisely and succinctly. You can impress the interviewer by giving both the surface-level and alternative definitions (with examples). This shows that you can go beyond the surface definition and demonstrate depth in your thinking and answer.

Don't worry too much if you do not know the 'right' answer or have the 'right' arguments/content which would have required a lot of research. It is better and advisable to focus on the way you **structure** and **approach** it. The interviewer is also likely to be able to help you out or guide you if you are stuck.

A **good applicant** would first give a layman definition before delving into the deeper meaning or alternative definitions to this term. A good applicant will be able to see that there are many layers to this word and be able to concisely explain this to the interviewer.

A **sample** answer is as follows: A miracle can be defined as an extraordinary event that defies natural or scientific laws. This is the most common definition and a simple example of a miracle is when the dead come back to life. Another definition would be a miracle as an interruption of the order or course of nature. This is a rather vague definition as we are unable to ascertain from this definition what is meant by the order or course of nature. Thomas Aquinas narrowed this definition by defining it as an event that exceeds the productive power of nature, where nature is construed broadly enough to include ourselves and other creatures like ourselves.

A miracle could also be defined more negatively as a violation of the laws of nature. David Hume famously adopted this definition which raised the bar higher for something to qualify as a miracle. However, I prefer the Aquinas definition to Hume's because bringing the concept of natural laws into the definition is problematic.

At this point, it is likely that the interviewer will ask you another question about this and you will engage in a discussion surrounding this.

A **poor applicant** might give a very long and irrelevant answer. It is not how much or how quickly you speak in an interview but the quality of your answer that is important. You should, as much as possible, give a concise answer that addresses the question.

Q9: After you have been to the hairdressers and had all of your hair cut off, do you still own your hair?

Intuitively, we believe that when our hair is attached to our heads, we do own it. The law supports this and if someone were to cut off your hair without your consent, you would be entitled to compensation.

However, where you have **consented to your hair being cut** off, the situation is very different and there is very little precedent to go on. You might argue that if you hadn't expressed an interest in maintaining your ownership of your hair once it had been cut off, it would be for the hairdresser to dispose of as he saw fit, in line with common practice in a hairdressers. You might think that the hairdresser's use of your hair would be of no consequence to you, but what if he sold it on eBay? What if it was used in an art exhibition to make a political point with which you disagreed? Would you then have a claim to your hair in these cases?

This question might lead on to a discussion about whether or not we own our own bodies. Surprisingly perhaps, we **have no legal right to decide what happens to us when we die** – instead, we can only express preferences and there are some things that the law will not let us do (e.g. leave your body to be used as meat for the dogs in Battersea Dogs' Home). We may contrast this with the approach the law takes to our other possessions after we die – in the case of all other property, your wishes are absolute. This contrast would suggest that we do not have the same legal relationship with our bodies as we do with our toasters, our cars, or our pocket-watches- but the really interesting question is – *should we?*

Q10: Should prisoners have the right to vote?

The **European Court of Human Rights** has ruled that Britain's blanket ban on voting for all convicted prisoners is a breach of their human rights. Allowing only some prisoners to vote would be ok, states the Court, but refusing the vote to all convicted prisoners is unacceptable.

Prison is generally considered to serve three key purposes; 1) to protect the public, 2) to serve as a deterrent, 3) to rehabilitate. Most prisoners have not committed crimes that warrant a life sentence. Most will eventually be released from prison. It's in everyone's interest that once out of prison, they do not commit any further crimes, but instead, become useful members of society. That involves reform whilst still in prison, and rehabilitating offenders to think - and act - more positively about their civic duties and responsibilities. One of the most important contributions a citizen can make to society is to take part in democracy and vote – removing a prisoner's civic duty does not, therefore, seem to accord with the aims of putting them in prison in the first place.

Alternatively, one might argue that all citizens of a country have implicitly agreed on a set of rules that gives them, and those around them, certain rights. It is the duty of every citizen to protect this framework and to respect the rights of others. If a person is in prison, it is because he/she broke the rules, and hence, in a way, forfeited his/her rights. The citizenship of prisoners can be seen as temporarily suspended along with all their rights.

Human rights do not mean that someone cannot be suitably punished or imprisoned for a crime once fairly tried and convicted. Human rights means that all humans deserve that society, and the State protects them from abuse of their basic civil rights. If the State can be allowed to abuse humans – any humans, for any reasons or excuses – then how can we justify laws against humans abusing other humans? How the State behaves must be reflective on how we want all humans to behave.

Human rights are meant to be universal, which means the rights apply to all humans without exception; to you and to me; even to criminals and foreigners, and even to those humans we do not like. Once we take basic rights away from one human, we start to erode the basic protections for all humans.

Q11: Should 'immoral' or 'evil' laws be obeyed?

Note: if candidates are unsure of what the question means, interviewers can share Victorian jurist Dicey's famous example: should Parliament legislate for all blue-eyed babies to be killed, the law would still be a valid law but citizens would be 'mad' to obey it.

This question requires candidates to take a step back and consider the purpose and basis of the law. A good candidate would be able to make some comment about **legal normativism versus legal positivism,** but this is not essential. It is more important that they can engage with concepts and ideas, not get bogged down in technical terms.

A sensible place to start would be a discussion on why people obey the law -- out of a sense of moral obligation independent of the law (e.g. if I think stealing is wrong, I will not steal regardless what the relevant statute precisely says), versus wishing to adhere to social norms (i.e. not being "looked down upon" or shunned by one's peers for being involved with illegal activities), versus actually fearing legal sanctions (e.g. avoiding recreational drugs while travelling in the Far East because I fear the death penalty being applied to me as a 'trafficker'). This should lead to strong candidates taking a step back and addressing to what extent morality should be the basis of law in a liberal society.

Candidates are free to proceed in a number of ways. It is only essential that they show that they have thought about the topic and have read some appropriate material. However, they must highlight that such 'immoral' laws would attract political criticism, and be conscious of the fact that political and legal mechanisms must work in tandem to **protect basic constitutional values and civil liberties**.

Q12: Given that juries consist of untrained people who do not have to give reasons for their decisions, are juries inherently inefficient and unreliable?

Candidates may not be aware of precisely what role juries play in the British justice system. It may be necessary to simply state that juries decide questions of fact but not law, which are used in certain more serious criminal trials, and jury members are picked at random from **all adults on the electoral role** (except for members of certain professions, such as solicitors or MPs).

Candidates must be aware of the fundamental constitutional significance of trial by jury, an institution dating back to the time of the Magna Carta: being tried in front of a body of one's peers is purported to be central to democracy as they are held to be fairer and more objective than a single judge, as the jury is drawn from members of all strata of society, and thus, better able to understand the lifestyle of the ordinary man (as opposed to the white, middle-aged, male and upper-middle-class views of most judges). Juries can also play a role in repudiating repugnant, undemocratic laws. Not having to give reasons, the jury may refuse to convict if they believe the law was enacted to be overly harsh.

Candidates should also be aware that jury trials are expensive and inefficient. A balance between these two competing factors is necessary, and being able to provide sensible reasons for their preference is all that is needed.

However, **strong candidates** should question whether unelected juries ought to have a de facto power to ignore the legislation of the elected parliament if they think the law is repugnant. They should also consider whether or not jury decisions are even reliable.

Q13: Is the British monarchy antiquated and undemocratic? What reasons are there for either keeping or abolishing this institution?

This question is general and superficially familiar to any British applicant. However, it is one which hints at the complex, **uncodified nature of the British constitution**.

Candidates should know that a large range of powers are vested in the Monarch nominally. However, the Monarch does not exercise these powers independently as a matter of convention: there is no legal requirement that the Monarch must take the advice of the Prime Minister in, for example, giving Royal Assent to any Act duty passed by the elected Parliament. However, it would be unthinkable that she would refuse such advice, and, if she were to exercise such powers arbitrarily, it is likely that legal sanctions would be enacted to severely curtail the Monarch's power or to abolish the Monarchy altogether. There must be an awareness that what is right and wrong in law is not what is right or wrong generally, and that the law is not the sole control of behaviour in society.

It would not be wrong for candidates to discuss the advantages or disadvantages of constitutional monarchy vs. republicanism in general, but they should not waste time discussing something not strictly pertinent to the question asked.

Strong candidates must frame their answer with reference to the tension between the theoretical anachronisms and empirical modernity which exist in the British constitution. A balanced approach is crucial, or, minimally, one which at least acknowledges the popularity (and therefore quasi-democratic mandate) of the Monarchy, and the importance of the Monarch as **uniting numerous Commonwealth countries** (e.g. Australia, New Zealand, Canada and the Bahamas), and how the removal of the Monarch in the UK would force citizens of many other countries to change their constitutional arrangements, possibly against their will.

Q14: Should publications like Charlie Hebdo be free to circulate uncontrolled? What kinds of restrictions on the media are compatible with freedom of speech?

If candidates are unfamiliar with the Charlie Hebdo killings, they would be told that Charlie Hebdo is an 'irreverent' French magazine which published inflammatory cartoons of the Prophet Mohammed. Outraged by these 'blasphemous' cartoons, Muslim extremists stormed the Charlie Hebdo office and killed a number of cartoonists. Many reacted with horror and immediately highlighted the importance of the freedom of speech. However, a smaller number of voices, while decrying what had happened, also highlighted the importance of responsible journalism.

Obviously, this is connected to ideas about **Freedom of Speech**. More generally, this raises fundamental questions about the nature of rights, and how rights are balanced against one another, as well as how the rights of the individual need to be balanced against the rights of the community.

A sensitive, nuanced approach would consider the overtones of Islamophobia which have tainted discourse on this episode. When the actor Benedict Cumberbatch used the word 'coloured' to refer to 'people of colour' in an interview, he was lampooned, severely criticised, and essentially compelled to apologise. In contrast, many simply speak about 'the right to offend' and the 'terror of extremism' with reference to this case.

A candidate who is able to think laterally may talk about how, in the UK, one's personal reputation is strongly protected by the **UK's vigorous defamation laws**. In contrast, offending or defaming an entire religion does not have such protection. Some consideration should be made of the role and position of religion in a secular, liberal society.

Q15: In the UK, the age of minimum criminal responsibility is 10, but the age of sexual consent is 16. A 15-year-old boy caught kissing a 14-year-old girl on the mouth could thus be convicted of various sexual offences. Is this satisfactory?

This question mixes together two anomalies in British criminal law. England has one of the youngest minimum ages of criminal responsibility in the Western world (it is 12 in Canada, Scotland, France, Germany, and Ireland), and the UN has recommended that all countries raise the age of minimum criminal responsibility to 12. Further, England has one of the highest minimum ages of consent for sex: it is typically 12 to 14 in Western Europe (but 18 in most of the US).

A **good candidate** must talk about whether or not the low age of criminal responsibility and high minimum age of sexual consent is justified. However, a strong candidate must interact with the question and be aware of the 'double whammy' effect these laws have.

One tension that must be identified is that the **law must be reasonable and realistic**. If the law were to criminalise activities which one is unlikely to be arrested for (which is inherent to the clandestine nature of underage mutually consensual sex), it may bring the law into disrepute.

Candidates must have a balanced view, however, and acknowledge how a high minimum age for sexual consent can protect the vulnerable and how a low minimum age of criminal responsibility is politically popular separately, but the interaction between the two can be problematic. It may be helpful to talk about how law is influenced by culture and the 'traditional' British attitude towards law and order and openness about sex.

Ultimately, a successful candidate must interact with the question and come to a sensible, thoroughly-considered opinion. A range of conclusions are acceptable, namely that the law should **protect the young from harmful overly-early sexualisation,** and because a 10-year-old facing a charge will not go to an adult jail (the emphasis being on rehabilitation). It could be suggested that the minimum age of criminal responsibility should be raised for the sake of compliance with international norms and the rights of the child, acknowledging their psychological immaturity and the sheer iniquity of charging children in an adult court. Also, that the age of sexual consent could be lowered so that the law should keep up with current societal norms, or some other combination of reform and consistency.

LANGUAGE INTERVIEWS

If you are applying for the French, German, Spanish, or Italian version of the course and are invited to Oxford for an interview, you should expect to be given a short oral language test as part of the interview process. Such a test is important and you must show the necessary linguistic competence. However, it is important to emphasise that the decision as to whether to offer a place on the four-year course is made first and foremost by reference to your potential as a law student, not by your performance in the oral language test.

The language test will be quite relaxed, normally with just yourself and a native speaker alone in a room. The **interview will likely be recorded**. You do not necessarily need to have a great deal of knowledge of the foreign legal system, but you should be able to articulate what it is specifically that interests you about that legal system and why you want to spend an extra year of your degree studying it. Real passion for the language, culture, and country will get you a long way too, of course!

If you are applying for the four-year Law with European Law course (to spend the year abroad in the Netherlands), you will not have this additional language interview as the course in the Netherlands is taught entirely in English.

What is the difference between Course I and Course II (Law with Legal Studies in Europe) at Oxford?

Course II incorporates all the elements of course I – you will study all of the same topics in years 1, 2 and will have the same choice of options open to you when you return from your year abroad in your 4th year. The difference between the two courses lies in the additional study of the foreign legal system.

In your **first year**, you will take weekly language classes (French, Italian, Spanish, German, or conversational Dutch). These classes will be around 2 hours per week. They are not obligatory but act as a really good way of allowing you to get to know the other students who you will be going abroad with in your 3rd year. They also help to keep up your language skills.

In your **second year**, you will take weekly introductory classes to your foreign legal system in the language of that legal system. These will be around 2 hours per week and there will rarely be additional work set. These are obligatory and provide a good basis for your studies on your year abroad.

In your **third year,** you will study abroad at one of the selected universities. You will have exams in your 3rd year but these marks will not count towards your final degree grade, instead, you must simply pass this year. You will likely be taking topics which first-year law students in that jurisdiction take, but your workload will likely be much lighter than the average law student. This year is an Erasmus year and you will be supported by grants from the Erasmus program. Furthermore, there are several Oxford-based grants which are available for students on Course II during their year abroad. You will be given the opportunity to completely immerse yourself in the local culture and custom, perfect your language, and get a real insight into how the law works in that country. You will also have much more spare time than you will have been used to in Oxford, given the significantly lighter workload. This means you'll have more time for travel and recreation. This is a fantastic year.

In your **fourth year,** you will be back in Oxford and your course of study will be exactly the same as that of someone on course I. You will not be examined on the foreign legal system in your finals.

GENERAL LAW QUESTIONS

Q16: What is the rule of law?

The solution to this question depends on whether or not you have heard of the rule of law. If you have, talk the interviewer through what you know, but don't leave it at that. Interviewers often want you to adopt an analytical approach to answering questions, so repeating knowledge you have about the rule of law without going any further (such as without discussing what you think of it) isn't a good answer.

If you haven't heard of the rule of law before, this does not put you at a disadvantage at all. Simply split the term up in your head and try to understand what it means. This is a good opportunity to show the interviewer your critical thinking skills by 'thinking out loud'. Going through your thought process shows the interviewer you are giving the question real reflection. The interviewer may tell you a bit about the rule of law as you consider what it means, and you can ask them questions, but don't ask them 'What is the rule of law?', since this shows a lack of analytical thinking.

Good answer (if you have not heard of the rule of law): I have not heard of the rule of law before, but I imagine it means a set of rules which can be applied to the law, almost like a higher-order law. For example, if the rule of law said laws cannot discriminate against people, you couldn't have a law that said something like 'blonde people aren't allowed to travel abroad'. Other beneficial characteristics of the law which the rule of law might cover are: clarity – because people cannot obey the law if they don't know what it covers, representation – because the name of the offence should reflect the conduct it covers, and consistency – because the law should be applied to everyone at all times, for it to be fair.

At this point you could offer an opinion on the rule of law, saying something like 'I think it is a good idea, because otherwise discriminatory and unfair laws could be enacted. However, it is important to have the right rules of law for it to be effective.'

Bad answer (if you have not heard of the rule of law): I don't know what the rule of law means. I haven't heard of it. *This is a bad answer because the interviewee has not attempted to understand the term 'rule of law'.*

Q17: Why should we care about the rule of law?

This question gives you a good opportunity to discuss the pros and cons of the rule of law. It is important to always give a balanced answer: never outline one side of the argument without analysing the points you have made and giving arguments contrary to. It is also important to offer more than one point in your answer. The interviewer will often challenge points you have made with a counter example, but this doesn't mean you are wrong, they simply want you to explain your answer with regard to their argument. Don't abandon your point and agree with them instantly, but equally don't stick to your point even if you realise you had the wrong idea. It's okay to say 'that makes me rethink my answer' and offer an alternative.

Good answer: a good answer would use the principles you discussed in relation to the rule of law, as noted above, and apply them to its importance. Such as: 'the rule of law is important because it governs the way laws are implemented. If we did not have a rule of law, laws that are unclear, unrepresentative and inconsistent could be enacted. This means a lot of people would not understand which conduct consists of an offence. Not only would this lead to more law breaking, but it could potentially lead to civil unrest because society would perceive these laws as unfair.

You could argue that Parliament is democratically elected so they should be able to enact any laws they like. However, I disagree with this, because the rule of law potentially stops corruption - since all laws have to abide by a certain standard. If an elected Parliament is trying to break this standard, then they should be prevented from doing so. The rule of law must consist of the correct standards in order to be effective though.

Bad answer: the rule of law is important because otherwise the government could do whatever they want and have no consequences. *This is a bad answer because the interviewee has not given any other reasons for the rule of law's importance or suggested why it could be dangerous.*

Q18: Is it fair to impose a height restriction on those wanting to become fire-fighters?

This question involves giving two sides of an argument and explaining which one you prefer. Weak answers will only explore one side of an argument, or only give one point for either side. You should include a range of reasons in your answer, including both practical and theoretical explanations. Picking apart the question is also a key skill which can be demonstrated here, for example, defining the word 'fair' is important in analysing answers.

Good answer: on one hand, you could argue it is discriminatory to impose height restrictions on those wanting to become fire-fighters. You are preventing people from having the career due to a factor which is outside of their control. If we define fair as giving equal opportunities to everyone, this is clearly not fair.

On the other hand, you could argue that it is fair to impose these restrictions. If we assume 'height restrictions' here encompass a minimum height requirement, you could argue that shorter fire-fighters may not be able to complete the job to the same standard as taller ones. For example, if a person was stuck at a height, a shorter fire-fighter may not be able to reach this. Therefore, you could argue that allowing shorter people to become fire-fighters is not fair to the public, since it potentially endangers them. However, instances such as these are unlikely to occur, especially because a taller fire-fighter could just help in this situation (though this could endanger the people they were trying to help).

I disagree with this argument, because I think it is a very slippery slope. Next somebody could say that women shouldn't be allowed to be fire-fighters, because they are typically less strong than men. Most people would agree that is this is unfair. Moreover, you could argue there should be a maximum height requirement to, because taller fire-fighters would find it harder to get through small spaces if needed. If we massively restrict the height requirements of fire-fighters, we will have far fewer of them, and this could endanger the public too. Additionally, from a practical standpoint, where would this restriction be drawn? If it was 170cm, then is there really a significant difference between people who are 169cm and people who are 171cm tall?

Bad answer: it would be fair because short fire fighters can't do their job as well as tall ones. *This is a bad answer because the interviewee has not given both sides of the argument, or thought of any counter-arguments to their own point.*

Q19: Your neighbour noticed your roof had become damaged while you were away, and fixed it, are you obligated to pay him for his work?

This question involves outlining both sides of an argument, before coming to a conclusion. Typically, with these types of questions, interviewers will give you more examples which push your argument to its limits. Don't be afraid to draw the line and admit when your argument no longer makes sense, but don't immediately abandon your point with no further explanation.

Good answer: on one hand, I should not have to pay the neighbour because I did not ask him to fix the roof. In fact, I could go further and argue he has interfered with my property without my consent, perhaps he has even trespassed on it!

On the other hand, perhaps my neighbour thought I wanted him to fix my roof. I am not sure if this would make a difference to the outcome, but it is a consideration. If he thought I wanted him to fix my roof and had reasonable belief for thinking so, I suppose you could argue that I should pay him for fixing it. Moreover, if my collapsing roof was a danger to the public or to my neighbour himself, you could argue that I had a duty to fix the roof, so a duty to pay him back for fixing it.

Despite this, if my neighbour fixed the roof with an expensive and unnecessary material, so I could have fixed the roof myself for much cheaper, I suppose there is an argument against me paying him back.

However, taking this wider, if I did not pay my neighbour back this means he would be less likely to help again. Perhaps not imposing a duty on me to pay him back actually discourages acts of public service, so for policy reasons such a duty should be implemented.

Bad answer: No because I did not ask him to do it. *This is a bad answer because the interviewee has only given one reason and not justified it very far. They should also aim to give two sides to the argument in every question.*

Q20: If I 'take' someone else's car - what do I mean?

This question involves defining key terms: such as 'take'. It is okay if you do not know the dictionary (or legal) definition of the word 'take', you are not expected to know it at all. Just go through your thought process and give examples for everything you say, and the interviewer may challenge your definition to push it to its limits. This does not mean your definition is bad, if anything it means it is good – they are interested in what you have to say in defending your answer. Don't worry about changing your mind, but also don't do this instantly and with no further explanation. If you do change your mind, it is a good idea to offer an alternative answer. Also, avoid giving 'circular' definitions, such as using the word 'take' in your definition of 'take'.

Good answer: I think taking another's car means using it without their permission, or in a way they did not consent to. For example, if my friend lent me their car and said I wasn't allowed to drive it on the motorway, and I did, then I think this would be taking the car as they did not consent to the way I used it. This also covers the typical examples like breaking into a car on the street and driving it away too.

The interviewer may say: what if your car was unlocked on the road and it was raining, so I got into it to avoid the rain and didn't touch anything, then got out again when it stopped raining?

In this case, you could say something like: well, I think that would be taking by my definition. I had not consented to you using my car as shelter from the rain. I suppose you could say you had reasonable belief that I would consent, maybe if you thought that anyone would let someone shelter in their car in the event of rain, but if I was a stranger I think that is quite a weak argument to make.

Bad answer: taking another's car means taking it away from them when they haven't told you that you can. *This is a bad answer because the interviewee's definition of take is circular, and they haven't given any examples that apply to their definition.*

Q21: If traffic wardens had the legal right to execute people caught parking in restricted areas, and as a result no one did, would this be considered a fair and effective law?

This question requires splitting up: you need to consider, in turn, if the penalty is effective, and if the penalty is just. Defining each of these terms would also be helpful here, as a standard to measure your answers against. You should consider the wider implications for this law, and any practical considerations that need to be made.

Good answer: I think this penalty would not be just, but it would be effective. Considering the former, it would not be just because the punishment of the crime does not represent the nature of the wrongdoing, or the severity of the conduct. It is important for laws and punishments to be proportionate to the offence, and this is definitely not. Parking on double yellow is a very low-level crime, and the death penalty is often associated with the most severe crimes such as murder or terrorism. Aside from representation, there is another issue of justness here. If the penalty of parking on double yellow is death, what is the penalty for murder? If this is also death, you are arguably putting murderers on par with people who commit parking offences, which is not fair at all.

However, the penalty would be effective because, as it says in the question, 'nobody did it'. One of the primary aims of law is to prevent people from breaking it, so this is fulfilled. Though the penalty acts as a deterrent, it does not allow offenders to better themselves and positively contribute to society, which is arguably another aim of law.

Bad answer: no because you are killing people for parking on double yellow lines, which doesn't make sense. *This is a bad answer because the interviewee has not justified their point further than 'which doesn't make sense'. They have also not split up the question into 'just' and 'effective'.*

Q22: If we lived without malice and ill intent, would there be any need to have the law?

This question is quite tricky because it involves you having to explore the aims of the law itself and see if they remain valid even if everyone was an angel. Better answers will give an in-depth and thoughtful analysis of the question and the aims of the law themselves. Weaker answers will give a one-sided and simplistic approach to answering the question and fall into the trap of saying 'no' and leaving it at that.

Good answer: well, I think you have to explore what the purpose of the law is and see if it is still needed if the world was full of good people to answer this question. The aims of law are potentially: to 1) maximise the freedom of individuals, 2) maintain order in society, 3) satisfy the basic needs of people and 4) to protect individual rights. If everyone was an angel, then you wouldn't need 4) because nobody's rights would be endangered. Further, not having the law at all could give everyone maximum freedom as outlined in 1), so it is not required for that either. However, I think laws could still be needed to satisfy purpose 2), because, even if everyone was good, there would still need to be basic rules so society can function beneficially and productively. This applies to 3) too, since laws often govern things like benefits which some people need. I suppose you argue that these things could be covered by conventions, things that everyone just does as a matter of common practise, but putting them into law would arguably make them clearer and therefore easier to follow.

Bad answer: No because everyone would be really good so they wouldn't need to be told to not kill anyone. *This is a bad answer because the interviewee has not justified their point and not given both sides of the argument.*

Q23: Do the girl scouts have a political agenda? Can any organisation be truly 'apolitical'?

This question is quite odd, and the answers to it can cover a very wide range of things. If you know about the girl scouts' affiliation with Trump, you could discuss that. If not, you could explore the topic and suggest some hypotheticals which would/would not mean they have a political agenda. You are not expected to know any prior information for the interview, so don't worry if something like this comes up and it feels like the question is hinting at a piece of information you do not know. The interviewer just wants to see your thought process, and I do think this is quite a hard question, so just give it a go and reason any points you make.

Good answer: I think this question is very dependent on what the girl scouts do. If the girl scouts put all of their profits back into the organisation, I don't think they do have a political agenda, unless perhaps they are funded by a political party. If the girl scouts fund a political party themselves, or a politically controversial organisation, you could argue they do have a political agenda. For example, if the girl scouts donated to an anti-abortion church organisation, you could argue that they do have a political agenda because they financially support one. Likewise, if they themselves are funded by such a company, this suggests a similar thing. However, I don't think they do have an agenda as such. Other companies could donate to political organisations too, and I think it is the buyer's prerogative to decide whether or not to buy from them.

Bad answer: I don't know. *This is a bad answer because the interviewee has not attempted to understand the question or work through their thought process out loud. The interviewee should also give examples to illustrate any points they make.*

Q24: Why do you want to study law?

There is no right answer to this question, it is very subjective and should be completely personal to you, rather than just repeating somebody else's answer! However, there are tips to make your answer stronger. For example, try and link your answer to your personal statement- this gives a sense of continuity. However, do not just repeat what you said in your statement and give no further reasons or explanation – this will just make the interviewer think you're not that bothered about studying law! Also, try and avoid cliches like 'I am passionate about law'- you may well be passionate about a certain area of law or a certain aim involved with law, but specify this – nobody is passionate about the boring bits of law like administration.

Good answer: I chose to apply for law because I am interested in learning more about the interdependence between philosophy, law and politics within our constitutional infrastructure. Appreciating the subtleties of the relationship between these entities will enable me to develop a broad knowledge of the law as a whole and how it works in practise. Once I have this knowledge, I want to use it to drive positive change in the context of human rights law, a cause I am deeply passionate about. When I was doing work experience at Latham and Watkins, I met a lawyer who was working on making FGM illegal across Africa. I would really love to use my knowledge of the law and apply it to causes such as these, representing vulnerable people. I am also interested in learning about why the law is the way it is, and how it can be reformed to enhance its aims of protecting individual rights and maximising liberty for all.

Bad answer: I want to study law because I am passionate about it and I want to be a lawyer when I'm older. I think that law is really interesting. *This is a bad answer because the interviewee is very general about law, and has not specified a specific area they are interested in. They have also not given any specific reasons as to why they want to study law.*

Q25: If someone unintentionally commits a crime, are they guilty?

This question involves an exploration of intention- whether or not someone meant to do something. You are not expected to have any prior knowledge of the law, but you may have an idea of intention and recklessness from your reading – don't worry if not, though. Weaker answers will give one side of the argument, and not justify their points. Stronger answers will explore both sides of the argument and consider wider 'policy reasons' in deciding which one they prefer.

Good answer: on one hand, you could say the person is not guilty as they do not have the intention to commit the crime. They did not set out to do it, as it says in the question, so they didn't commit the crime on purpose and therefore should not be guilty of it.

On the other hand, there is a difference between intention and recklessness. If I climbed up onto neighbour's roof and accidentally kicked the tiles off it, even if I did not intend to commit criminal damage, I still did. Most people would consider damaging the tiles reasonably likely to result from climbing up the roof, and I arguably should have thought of this before I did so. Therefore, I was being reckless so still committed the crime. However, if I was not such a reasonable person, for example I was 10, then this should be measured against my own sense of what is reasonably likely and what isn't, to avoid people being held to a standard they cannot reach for one reason or another. If most 10-year-olds would not foresee criminal damage being caused in this instance, and I didn't, then I would not be guilty of the crime as I did not have the intention and I wasn't reckless.

Bad answer: yes they are guilty because they still committed the crime. *This is a bad answer because the interviewee has not justified their point very far, and has not considered that the person may not be guilty in some instances.*

Q26: When should the state be allowed to violate your privacy?

This question involves a debate between freedom and protection, which is an important balance to strike in every area of the law. Stronger answers will give two sides to the argument and outline specific examples where the state has the right to violate privacy, and where it does not. Weaker answers will give short and unjustified points. If you don't know any specific examples of where the state can violate privacy, just think of hypotheticals where you think it would be justified.

Good answer: the state has the right to violate privacy in cases where the priority of protection outweighs the priority of freedom. For example, I don't think the state should have the right to read people's messages in most instances, to maximise their individual liberty. However, I think when reading messages are in the best interests of the public or the individual themselves (such as when an individual goes missing or in the case of a potential terrorist attack) then it is justified. It is important to strike this balance right. If there is too much unjustified state violation of privacy, then liberty is compromised, and this could lead to civil unrest. If there is too little, then individuals are potentially unprotected.

Bad answer: the state has the right to violate privacy because it is in the interests of the public that they do so. *This is a bad answer because the individual has not given any examples or other arguments to illustrate their point.*

Q27: Should anyone have the right to invade our privacy?

This question looks at an evaluative side to the previous one, which asks for when the state should have the right to violate our privacy. As noted above, the key to these questions is the debate between maximising protection and individual liberty: the autonomy v welfare debate. Stronger answers will give two sides of the argument and give examples for each of them. Weaker answers will give unjustified and one-sided points.

Good answer: the state should have the right to violate our privacy, but only in limited circumstances. Although giving the state unlimited power to violate privacy would arguably maximise protection of citizens, it compromises individual liberty and leaves the state vulnerable to corruption. Moreover, there are concerns of hacking and data protection if the state violates privacy more than it needs to. Despite this, giving the state no power to violate privacy, though upholding individual liberty, doesn't protect citizens. Therefore, there needs to be a balance respecting both principles. For example, if a person has been killed then suspects' internet history should be able to be looked at – because protection is the priority in this case. But in ordinary circumstances, things like messages and emails shouldn't be read because liberty should be the priority here.

Bad answer: the state should not have the right to violate privacy because they could potentially exploit this. *This is a good point but needs to be expanded upon. Also, giving the other side of the argument is a good idea in this case. The autonomy v welfare debate is central to this question, so any responses must address both of these principles and judge the law against them and the relationship between them. Giving situations which justify state violation of privacy and situations where it is not justified is a good idea in these sorts of question.*

Q28: Do you think that the state should be more free to operate as it chooses than the media is?

This question requires the interviewee to give a balanced argument and coming to a justified conclusion. It is similar to the ones above since, again, it balances protection and individual liberty. In law, this is called the autonomy vs welfare debate, but you are not expected to know this. The question is essentially asking you to consider real-world examples and put them into theoretical questions and weigh up different opinions on the issue before deciding which one you agree with. In law, it is really important to always give two sides of the argument. Stronger answers will also undermine arguments contrary to their point, so their conclusion appears more justified.

Good answer: On one hand, media regulation by the state would decrease the spread of 'fake news' which we have seen increase in recent years, especially with conspiracy theories surrounding the COVID vaccine and the origin of the disease. Moreover, media regulation by the state could control extremism recruitment done online and damaging posts on social media such as those promoting self-harm. Although this would undermine freedom of speech and, potentially, individual liberty, it would protect people from harmful things in the media.

On the other hand, media regulation by the state could be used to silence political opposition, any political controversies the executive wants to hide and cover up government scandal. The danger of handing more control to the state over media is that it leaves media control open to exploitation and autocracy. Therefore, a balance needs to be struck between liberty and protection. Perhaps having an independent body which can review media regulation by the state would be a way of achieving this.

Bad answer: the media should be increasingly controlled by the state because otherwise they could spread fake news. *This is a bad answer as there is only one reason for the person's point, and no counter arguments are given.*

Q29: What is the role of honesty in law?

This question suggests a knowledge of the law is needed to answer it, but it is really important to remember that no prior knowledge of the law is needed for an interview. Some people may have some knowledge, but it in no way gives them an advantage- all the interviewer wants to see is you going through your thought process out loud and give a wide range of arguments and counter-arguments to support your point: deliberation is key. This is quite a difficult question simply because it is so vague, but you can actually talk about a wide range of things, so don't worry if you would answer it differently to the answers below.

Good answer: honesty fits into law in a wide range of instances. For one, at a judgement level, a person could receive a lesser sentence if they are honest about any crimes they have committed. Also, if a person honestly believes something to be the case and this belief is reasonable, this sometimes means they do not commit the crime. For example, in rape, if you honestly believed someone was consenting to sex and you had justification to think this (i.e. the belief is reasonable) then it is not rape, even if the person did not consent. This can be quite problematic, because the idea of a reasonable and an honest belief are both very subjective ideas so they can be interpreted in multiple ways. Equally, defining reasonable and honest belief narrowly and giving little judicial discretion also means a person may be held to a standard they cannot reach: what may be reasonable for them may but be found as reasonable by the court.

Bad answer: honesty fits into law because if you reasonably believe something to be the case then sometimes it means a crime has not been committed. *This is a bad answer because, although the point is good, there are no examples or wider remarks about how having such a provision could be good or bad.*

Q30: Should the law protect people from themselves?

This question is very philosophical, so it requires a good deal of deliberation of multiple arguments and lots of points and examples given. It is a way for the interviewer to see how you think in terms of what the law is and what it should be like: rather than just the substantive aspects of it and what the law actually says. The most important thing is to give a balanced argument. Interviewers may argue with some of your points, so listen to their contention and try to reconcile it with your point or perhaps explain why you don't agree with it (respectfully). If you find yourself abandoning your point, don't be afraid to do this, but equally don't do it immediately: the interviewer wants you to try to rationalise their points. Every argument can be pushed to its limits, and this is what they're trying to demonstrate.

Good answer: you could argue that the law already does exist to protect us from ourselves, to an extent. For example, people can be detained for their own safety under the mental health act and, if someone attempts to harm or kill themselves, hospitals are under a duty to look after them until it is safe for them to go home. Another example is the law on euthanasia, which remains illegal here. I don't think the law should exist to protect us from ourselves further than these very limited examples, because otherwise it violates individual freedom. The debate key to this question is the autonomy v welfare debate, and having the law exist to protect us from ourselves means the balance shifts to welfare, infringing on autonomy. Despite this, I do agree with detention under the mental health act since an individual is not in the right state of mind to make decisions regarding harming themselves if they are in a bad place. The law on euthanasia is far blurrier, and I think it infringes on autonomy because the majority of the people who want to partake in it have chronic and long-term health conditions and have given the idea a lot of thought.

Bad answer: the law should not exist to protect us from ourselves because we know what we want to do and should be allowed to do it. *This is a bad answer because it gives no examples of where legal intervention is justified, and no counter arguments too. Also, they do not address the idea that we should be allowed to do what we like as long as we don't infringe on other people's rights, which is important to their point.*

Q31: Can a law ever be truly just if it restricts our freedom to do something?

This question is a bit similar to the one above, since the autonomy vs welfare debate is key to it. If you haven't heard of this before, don't worry, but it can be a very useful thing to know in the interview for wider, more philosophical points considering the law. Autonomy an idea of individual liberty, everyone should be able to do what they like. Welfare is a paternalistic idea, that the law should protect people and make sure their rights are upheld. Balancing these two principles is essentially one of the main things that the law aims to do, so it is a good evaluative tool to use when analysing whether or not the law is effective.

Good answer: on one hand, you could say if a law limits our freedom, then it is unjust with regard to autonomy. If we cannot do what we like because the law has placed constraints on it, then the principle of autonomy is not being upheld, and is potentially even violated, so if autonomy is the standard of justness then it is an unjust law. On the other hand, I think that in limited exceptions the law is just even if it restricts our freedom to do something. The law aims to uphold autonomy, but it also aims to uphold the welfare principle: so, in some cases one of these will need to be curtailed to respect the other. For example, the law restricts our freedom to infringe upon another's rights, like by murdering or stealing from them, which is just since it upholds the other person's welfare. Also, if we are attempting to harm ourselves then the law can intervene, to uphold our own welfare. There are arguments that the law goes to far towards the welfare principle in cases such as abortion and euthanasia, so there is definitely scope for reform and reconsideration in these.

Bad answer: the law is unjust if it restricts our autonomy because it violates individual liberty, and this should be upheld. *This is a bad answer as it doesn't consider any instances were violating autonomy may be justified or offer any further explanation of their point. You shouldn't really give one-sentence answers to these sorts of questions in the interview, but don't be afraid to take some time to think about your answer before saying it.*

Q32: Should laws ever govern what we can and cannot say?

This question involves a consideration of what the law aims to uphold and some limited examples of where freedom of speech can be limited. Avoid giving unbalanced and heavily political answers, interviewers want to see you can step away from politics and view the law from a more philosophical perspective. Of course, some political comment is good and brings your answer into the real world, but too much runs the risk of actually offending one of your interviewer's or making it look like you should be in a PPE interview instead.

Good answer: on one hand, the law should not restrict our freedom of speech. Freedom of speech is integral to individual liberty, one of the principles the law seeks to uphold. We should be able to say what we like, otherwise it is a slippery slope into a state where our non-criminal actions and more and more of what we say is restricted by the law. That is, it becomes more controlling.

On the other hand, the law should restrict our freedom of speech in some cases. For examples, it is illegal to issue death threats to people, and to defame people online. Moreover, hate speech is also illegal. The law should restrict freedom of speech in these limited instances because it arguably violates other people's rights – such as the right not to be discriminated against in the case of hate speech. The slippery slope argument is valid, but it should just promote consideration of restricting freedom of speech, rather than not doing it at all. Some countries such as France go further than us, and criminalise holocaust denial, so there is arguably need for reform and greater consideration in this area.

Bad answer: the law should not restrict our freedom of speech because otherwise it is telling us what to say, which is unjustified. *This is a bad answer because it gives no examples of where the law should not restrict our freedom of speech, and no arguments or examples of where it should.*

Q33: How would you place a value on life? Would you shoot a baby to save another person, to save a thousand people?

This question involves an interesting philosophical principle: do the means justify the ends? If you have studied RS or philosophy at GCSE or A-Level then feel free to use some of the arguments you learnt in these subjects here, and in any other question for that matter. Try not to get bogged down in the subject matter though. If not, do not worry, just consider arguments for and against the question and come to a balanced conclusion.

Good answer: this question involves a discussion of whether the means justify the ends. I would argue they do not, in this case. From a utilitarian, teleological perspective, you should shoot the baby to save x number of people, provided x is greater than 1. This is because the greatest overall happiness should be promoted, and the means justify the ends. However, from a Kantian, deontological perspective, this is not the case because the action matters more than the outcome, so the means do not justify the ends.

I would agree with the latter of these perspectives, because where is the line drawn, and what factors should be considered? In this case, the baby (and everyone else) would die if no action was taken. But what if you were on a runaway train and the track you're on has two people on it, but you can change the track to another lane, which will hit a baby? In this case, important judgements need to be considered. Would it make a difference if the track you're headed onto has 100 people on it instead of two people on it? What if these people all had three months to live, but the baby had years and years? Essentially, examples like the baby in the shopping centre can be pushed further and further to their limits and involve judgements of the worth of one life over the worth of another. I do not think we are qualified to make such judgements, so I don't agree with shooting the baby in any case.

Bad answer: yes because otherwise the baby and everyone else will die. *This is a bad answer as, although the point is good, there is no further justification for it. The individual should also consider the other side of the argument and push it a bit further to other examples.*

Q34: Do you think that euthanasia should be legal?

This question involves a consideration of euthanasia and assisted suicide. While it would be beneficial to know a bit of the current law on this, it is not essential. That said, it is helpful for interviews if you keep up with the news about things such as euthanasia, as they often come up. The current law largely prohibits euthanasia and assisted suicide in the UK. Doctors are allowed to give pain relief medication for the purpose of said pain relief, even if such medication has the consequence of shortening a person's life, but this is the only instance in which euthanasia is legal. People do travel to Dignitas to die, but if they travel with a family member to help them, then that family member can (in principle) be prosecuted, though there is a large amount of discretion in this area. If you didn't know any of this in the interview (and you don't have to), just say something like 'I'm not sure about the current law on this, but...' and you will be fine.

Good answer: I think people should have the right to die, but in very limited cases. On one hand, there are arguments for having the right to die in lots of cases. If there is a right to life, perhaps there should be a right to end that life. If a person has a very bad quality of life, they should be allowed to end it. The law promotes individual autonomy, and the right to die is arguably a necessary provision of this.

On the other hand, the law has a duty to protect people's welfare. A person may not be in their right mind when they decide to die, and as a society maybe cases of euthanasia are actually indicative of our failings to protect the vulnerable: maybe increasing funding to areas which support such people is a better option than allowing people to die. Moreover, allowing people to die means there is less funding going towards terminal illnesses, simply because there are fewer people living with those illnesses.

Despite this, I think euthanasia should be allowed in very limited cases and with provisions such as required counselling and approval for people who want to go through it. This prevents people from making rash decisions.

Bad answer: people should not have the right to die because life is sacred and given by God, so we are not allowed to take it away. *This is a bad answer because it only considers one argument (sanctity of life) and does not consider things such as if an individual is non-religious etc. Aim to give a balanced argument in all of your answers.*

Q35: Should overweight people have to pay extra on planes if they need to take two seats?

This question involves giving a balanced argument to what is quite a current debate. Try and give examples for both sides of your argument, and examples which show the limits of your points. A nuanced answer is key to questions like this, so try and draw distinctions between different situations and apply them to your argument.

Good answer: overweight people should not have to pay extra on planes if they need to take two seats. While some people are overweight because of an unhealthy lifestyle, some people are overweight because of a chronic condition or even a disability. While there are arguments for why airlines should be able to charge them for two seats- because they are taking up the same amount of seats as two people so should be charged as such, and because in some cases being overweight is a choice, I don't agree with these. What 'weight limit' would be imposed if overweight people were charged for two seats? What if they took up 1 and a quarter seats? Could the same be extended to disabled people who take up 2 seats? While you could argue being disabled is not a choice, nor is being overweight in cases of a thyroid condition, mental health conditions, economic status and things like that, and there is often a multitude of factors which contribute to someone being overweight so there is no way of effectively judging them, and to do so is quite disrespectful.

Bad answer: fat people should have to pay extra on planes because the airline is losing money by letting them on if they take up two seats. *This is a bad answer because it does not consider any arguments to the contrary. Also, they should offer alternative scenarios where this economic argument would not work, as well as scenarios which would work along these lines.*

Q36: Do you think it is legally justifiable to charge for access to a toilet in a closed environment like an aeroplane?

This question involves giving two sides of an argument, even though it appears to be relatively simple. Try and give both sides of the debate anyway and give examples to illustrate each of your points. A nuanced approach is key to this question, so try and reflect this as much as possible in your response.

Good answer: airlines should not be allowed to charge people for using the toilet on a plane. Although there are economic reasons why it would be beneficial for the airline to do this, they have a duty of care to their passengers and I think this includes giving them easy access to toilet facilities. For example, should a mother be forced to pay to use the toilet when she has to change her baby's nappy? Should a disabled person who cannot wait to use the toilet be forced to pay for it on an aeroplane? I think that enabling airlines to charge for use of toilet facilities impacts the most vulnerable people in society, and it is even potentially discriminatory in that respect. People should have a right of access to a toilet at all times. Despite this, at some train stations you have to pay to use the toilet, so I suppose implementing a similar policy on aircraft is not a far extension. However, I disagree with the policy in train stations and think toilet fares should be abolished nation-wide.

Bad answer: yes, because people choose to go on the aeroplane so they know ahead of time whether or not they have to pay to use the toilet. If people can afford a plane ticket, they are unlikely to not be able to afford a small fee for using the toilet. *This is a bad answer, though these are potentially good points, because the interviewee has only given one side of the argument and given no examples to justify their point.*

Q37: Should a jury of peers be selected based on the IQ of the defendant?

This question involves considering the justice system and potential reforms that could be made to it. Try and always give a wide range of views and examples on controversial questions like these, even if the question seems to only have one answer, attempt to understand the other side of the argument and say something along the lines of 'some people would argue that... but I disagree because...'. This gives your opinion, but shows you understand the other side too.

Good answer: on one hand, imposing a minimum IQ for jurors in a trial could be a good thing. It means jurors are potentially more intelligent, so more capable of making a reasoned and informed decision. Though it could be construed as offence, when serious offences and people's lives are on the line, it is important for the justice system to be as fair and as effective as possible, and a minimum IQ could go some way towards that.

On the other hand, I disagree with imposing a minimum IQ for jurors. Firstly, what would this IQ be? What about the people who are only just below it? Intelligence is not binary and cannot be defined by a simple IQ test, and there is evidence to suggest IQ tests are not actually very reliable anyway. Imposing such a restriction is potentially discriminatory, and the point of a jury is to give a cross-section of society, and this is inhibited if you are only allowing the 'clever' people in society to be a part of it. Deciding a person's guilt does not have much to do with intelligence, you simply listen to the evidence and both sides of the case and give an informed judgement.

Bad answer: yes it would be a good idea but it is unfair for the people who wouldn't be allowed to be jurors. *This is a good point and a somewhat balanced argument, but the person has not justified why the idea would be good. There are also no examples given here.*

Q38: What would a country without law be like?

This question is quite difficult and requires a high level of deliberation regarding a hypothetical situation. Try and give a range of different points with justification and examples for each one. For questions like these, you can also give a non-straightforward answer, as you can see below. This would take your answer to another level.

Good answer: I don't think it is possible to live in a country with no laws, or at least no rules. Even if we abandoned the law completely and people could do whatever they like, I think a body of custom would build up and essentially do the same thing as the law, but without judicial interpretation and official punishments. For example, even if there was no law governing trespassing, I don't think people would do it all the time just for reasons of custom and convention. In early civilisations, religion acted as a kind of 'law' for some people, and you weren't allowed to do things like use God's name in vain, so I think custom would act in a similar way to this. On the other hand, the only punishment for breaking these conventions would be being an outcast from society, instead of prison or fines etc, so I do think there would be more 'criminal' behaviour simply because there are fewer consequences. However, I do not think a society without laws would be total chaos because of the strength of societal convention and the fear of becoming an 'outcast' or having people take punishment into their own hands.

Bad answer: It would be dangerous to live in a country without laws because people would just do what they like with no consequences for their actions. *This is a bad answer because the interviewee only gives one point and does not give examples to illustrate it.*

Q39: In France, you are legally obligated to help a person you see in distress, for instance, if they are drowning in a river. Why do you think we don't have a law like this, should we?

This question involves a discussion of the pros and cons of omissions liability. All of the information you need to know about omissions liability is in the question, so don't worry if you don't know anything about its technicalities. It is important to consider policy reasons in these types of question: these are reasons which are essentially practicalities and consider how the law would actually work, rather than its hypothetical nature. It is a good idea to take a step back and look at the wider part of the law when you answer questions like these, especially when considering reform.

Good answer: on one hand, this should be the case in the UK. The law aims to protect people and imposing this legal obligation would lead to more people being protected and lives would be saved- this is clearly a good thing, so the obligation should be enacted. On the other hand, I don't think this should be the case in the UK. I don't know how the obligation operates in France, but there are too many questions and variables which would need defining for the law to work here. For example, would I have to save the drowning person if I myself could not swim? What if I was deathly afraid of the water? How far out would I have to swim before my 'obligation' was discharged? Would 100 people on a beach have to swim out to see if someone was drowning there and, if they did not, would all 100 people be prosecuted? These standards would have to be defined and, even if they were, there are always borderline cases in which the law is unknown. This raises issues of legal certainty because some people would not know whether or not they have discharged their obligation, or whether it applies to them in the first place. Also, there is a point about autonomy. There are issues surrounding whether or not the law can infringe upon individual liberty by forcing you to do something, rather than just inhibiting you from doing it as in most cases of criminal law. Forcing people to save people while drowning sets a precedent that the law can force people to do other things, which could be dangerous in practice.

Bad answer: yes because more lives would be saved. *This is a bad answer because the person does not give any examples or counter arguments to their point.*

Q40: Should the law be absolute, or black and white, or should it be more flexible?

This question requires a detailed consideration of the law and how it can be reformed. Strong answers consider two sides of the coin, rather than one, and give detailed and justified points. Weaker answers tend to have a lack of examples, and a largely one-sided argument. Signposting in interview answers is always a good idea and gives your answer a lot of structure, which interviewers love.

Good answer: on one hand, the law should be black and white. Firstly, this means everyone is clear on what the law is and whether or not their conduct is against it. Secondly, this makes the law easier to follow, as it is clearer. Thirdly, it means everyone is held to the same standard, which arguably means the law is fairer.

On the other hand, I think the law should look at individual cases to an extent. There are always going to be subjective questions in determining whether someone has broken the law. For example, theft requires dishonestly appropriating the property of another- so analysing whether or not someone's conduct matches this is not always going to be a black or white yes or no. Also, the point I made about everyone being held to the same standard can be undermined. Some individuals have different levels of capacity to others, so their judgement in law should reflect this. The criminal age of responsibility is 10, and an 11-year-old should not be held to the same standard as a 50-year-old- there needs to be some level of discretion, or the most vulnerable people in society (like the young and the disabled) can be impacted.

Bad answer: the law should be black and white because it makes it easier for judges to decide whether or not someone is guilty. *This is a bad answer because there is a lack of a balanced argument and there are no examples given to illustrate the person's point.*

Q41: Should the law be based on morality?

This question involves a consideration of what the law is based on and what it should be based on. As always, giving a balanced argument is key here. Try and step away from the hypothetical and think about how this would affect the real world too. After all, the law impacts everyone, it is not a purely hypothetical being.

Good answer: on one hand, the law should be based on morality. This is because it might be easier for people to understand the rationale behind the law if it is inherently moral, and therefore they may be more inclined to follow it. Also, society could be united by the law if it is grounded on a set of morals that are common to everyone, which could increase the overall happiness and productivity of civilisation.

On the other hand, I think this is very utopian and unlikely to happen in practice. If the law was based on morality, what morality would it be based on? There is never going to be an entire set of morals everyone agrees on, and why should the law impose a set of morals on someone that doesn't necessarily agree with them? If the law was based on morals, there could be civil unrest for those who don't agree with its basis. For example, some people may think it is okay (or it shouldn't be governed by law) to cheat on someone, but others may think it should be. There is no way of keeping everyone 100% happy. Also, if the law was based on morals, are there any areas which it wouldn't govern? It may be considered immoral to lie, but most people wouldn't want this governed by the law in all instances. Where would the line be drawn between moral laws and morals?

Bad answer: the law should not be based on morality as everyone disagrees on what is moral. *This is a bad answer because the interviewee only gives one point, and only one side of the argument. They do not consider why it could be beneficial having a law based on morality.*

Q42: Let's say that overnight, the Supreme Court took ownership of all judicial functions previously allocated to the House of Lords – what changes?

Although it may seem like it, this question does not require any prior knowledge of the law. It would be helpful to know that the House of Lords is linked to the Houses of Parliament, who enact law, but this can be known through reading the news etc. The question is getting at something called the separation of powers, which is the idea that the legislature (House of Commons), the judiciary (courts) and the executive (government) should be separate to prevent tyranny and to increase efficiency in proceedings. The House of Lords used to be the apex court in England and Wales (the highest court), which is what the question is addressing. This is not needed, but it is helpful to know things like this to seem really knowledgeable and well-read in the interview.

Good answer: I think this will increase public support of the House of Lords and the Supreme Court. Because the House of Lords is linked to the House of Commons, and the Lords are not elected, some people think it is unfair and illegitimate that they decided high-up cases in law. Although the judges in the Supreme Court are also not elected, they are impartial and are not linked to politics, which is not the case for the Lords. Also, the Supreme Court could scrutinise legislation of the House of Commons if it was challenged by a case, which might be hard for the House of Lords to do since it is linked to the House of Commons. It will therefore increase efficiency of proceedings also.

Bad answer: I don't know what the judicial functions of the House of Lords were, so I don't know what impact giving them to the Supreme Court would have. *This is a bad answer because the person does not attempt to rationalise the question and think it through, they just automatically get put off by the fact they don't know much about the topic and leave it at that.*

Q43: Should the legislature and executive be kept separate?

The question, like the one above, is getting at something called the separation of powers, which is the idea that the legislature (House of Commons), the judiciary (courts) and the executive (government) should be separate to prevent tyranny and to increase efficiency in proceedings. The executive executes laws, the legislature amends and enforces them and the judiciary interprets laws, developing a common law precedent. You are not expected to know this, but it would be helpful to in this question. If a question you weren't familiar with the material of came up, just go through your thought process and give reasons and examples for everything you say. The interviewer wants to see you react to unfamiliar material and think on your feet.

Good answer: on one hand, the politicians and the judges should not be kept separate because judges are not elected and politicians are, so having elected people oversee everything could increase the legitimacy of the judicial system as the public sees it. Despite this, I think it would be more beneficial to keep politicians and judges separate. If politicians enacted laws and enforced them, they have too much control and could violate people's freedom or become corrupt very easily. Having an impartial set of judges, even though they're not elected, means Parliament's laws are scrutinised, so the branches of government impose checks on each other. Also, having them separate could increase efficiency of proceedings. Moreover, politicians are elected but they belong to parties who can pressure them to act in a certain way through the use of party whips. Just because they are elected, doesn't make politicians automatically legitimate.

Bad answer: no because judges aren't elected so their actions should be overseen by politicians. *This is a bad answer because it is quite crude and doesn't offer a very nuanced approach to the question.*

Q44: Do you think that judges should be elected?

This question involves a consideration of potential reforms to the justice system. Although it can be hard to think of points for both sides of the argument for questions like this, it is very important to try and do so. Unbalanced arguments can be seen as overly simplistic and not very thought out. The separation of powers, as discussed above, is also relevant here. This is the idea that there are three branches of government (the legislature, the executive and the judiciary) and these should be kept separate to prevent tyranny and increase efficiency.

Good answer: on one hand, it would not be wrong for judges to be elected. If judges are deciding on whether people are guilty of a crime, and sentencing those people, they should be elected by the public as their job directly impacts them. Politicians are elected for similar reasons. Also, it may increase people's faith in the justice system if judges were elected, which would decrease activism and civil unrest surrounding it. On the other hand, judges should not be elected. People arguably don't know enough about the justice system to elect judges who will be effective, though this could be combatted by issuing information about the justice system. However, if judges were elected, they could end up being a party system like in Parliament, which brings politics into law and violates judicial impartiality. It may also be confusing for people to vote for politicians and judges separately. Judges are supposed to scrutinise acts of Parliament which, if elected in a way which brings politics into law, cannot really be done effectively.

Bad answer: no because judges impact people so people should have a say in who is a judge. *This is a bad answer because the interviewee has only given one side of the argument and has not justified their point very well.*

Q45: Which legal barriers prevent daily wars?

This question is quite political, but also involves international law. Try and think out loud, because it is quite difficult, so just let the interviewer know what your thought process is as you go through it. If you don't know anything, just have an educated guess and consider that it must be something to do with law, because you're in a law interview. The interviewer is looking for a range of ideas in this question, and to see how you react to subject material you are potentially unfamiliar. Moreover, they are looking for your ability to make connections between law and other areas (such as politics, like in this question).

Good answer: there are a variety of things that stop countries from invading each other on a daily basis. Firstly, there are treaties which encourage countries not to do this. Secondly, if a country did invade another country without justification, other nations could place trade sanctions on it. The perpetrating country could therefore suffer economic sanctions. Thirdly, if a country did invade another country without justification, other countries would be hesitant to collaborate with them, and their own citizens could perceive the government as illegitimate, causing potential civil unrest or even an uprising. There are also international laws which could be broken by unjustified invasion of a country, and resolutions as implemented by the UN. There is also the threat of another country taking military action against the perpetrator too.

Bad answer: I don't know, I guess countries can invade each other on a daily basis and just choose not to. *This is a bad answer because the interviewee does not analyse why countries choose not to invade each other (usually) and doesn't explain their thought process, even if they don't know much about the subject matter of the question.*

Q46: A simple case, a cyclist is hit by a car, only they were cycling in a car lane rather than the adjacent cycle lane – who is liable? Does your answer change if the cyclist had taken no measures to be visible at night?

This question requires putting the law into real-world examples, such as the one given. Try and give multiple and justified points which back up the conclusion you come to. Then consider the second example, and try to rationalise that with your conclusion, or perhaps tweak it so the ideas are reconciled. In this question, the interviewer is looking for your ability to structure answers and treat two ideas differently.

Good answer: on one hand, in the first instance, the cyclist is liable because he was not cycling in the designated lane. On the other hand, the motorist could be liable because cyclists are allowed to cycle on roads – it is not illegal – and the motorist is under a duty to drive carefully. During the day, he should have been able to clearly see and avoid the cyclist. He has therefore not done his duty of carefully driving, so I would say the motorist is liable in this case.

However, in the second case, I think the cyclist is liable. Though the motorist is under a duty to drive carefully, he could easily have been doing this and not seen the cyclist. Many cyclists wear hi-vis jackets and have lights to make themselves visible to drivers and, if the cyclist was not doing this and was driving in a car lane, an accident was foreseeable. Therefore, in the second case I think the cyclist should be liable, though it depends on whether the motorist could be construed as driving carefully.

Bad answer: in both cases the cyclist is liable because he was driving in the car lane instead of in the cycle lane. *This is a bad answer as it has not separated the examples given in the question and analysed each one individually, they have bundled them together and treated them as one.*

Q47: Which of the House of Lords and House of Commons has more power? What are the main differences between them?

While law interviews do not require any prior knowledge of the law, it would be very helpful to know some for this question. It is important to read the news and have a general knowledge of politics for law interviews, but nothing in loads of depth. In short: there are two chambers of Parliament: the House of Commons and the House of Lords. The House of Commons debates and enacts legislation, and it is elected. The House of Lords is not elected, and it scrutinises and proposes small amendments on House of Commons legislation in some areas. The members of the House of Lords largely used to be hereditary, so they inherited their membership. This was reformed in 1999, and now there are fewer hereditary peers and people tend to become members by being recommended by the Prime Minister (these are called life peers). You don't *need* to know any of this, but it is helpful for this question and any others about the House of Lords.

https://www.youtube.com/watch?v=xgMRiA9dZQs&t=238s – this video is good at explaining it, but don't just watch it and believe everything they say: the Lords aren't all bad! The House of Commons is overburdened, so the Lords provide important scrutiny of legislation.

Good answer: there are a few differences between the House of Commons and the House of Lords. The House of Commons is elected, but the House of Lords is not. Also, the House of Commons enacts law, but the House of Lords scrutinises and advises on it. I think the House of Commons has more power because they are perceived as legitimate by the public, because members of it are elected, and they have more discretion in debating and implementing legislation. The House of Lords used to have more power when it was the apex court in England and Wales, but its role is mainly scrutiny of legislation now, which is still important as the Commons is over-burdened and perhaps doesn't have as much time as is required to do this. You could argue the House of Lords has more power though, because the House of Commons' politicians often have their votes encouraged by party whips, so politicians perhaps don't have as much freedom to vote and express opinions on laws as the Lords do. As the Lords don't belong to parties, they can properly debate without having to toe the party line.

Bad answer: the House of Commons is elected and the House of Lords isn't. The House of Commons has more power because it makes law. *This is a bad answer as the individual hasn't explored the other side of the argument.*

Q48: Why do people who do some particular jobs get exemptions from jury duty.

You don't have to know which professions are exempt from Jury duty for this question, you can just give some examples of some you would think would be exempt and why you think that. Lawyers used to be exempt from jury duty, but this was lifted in 2004. It is quite a tricky question, but just go through your thought process out loud and try to give a reasoned answer. The interviewer here is looking for your ability to think on your feet and how you respond to unfamiliar subject matter. Moreover, this question gives potential for the link between law and the real world to be explored, so you could consider both theoretical and practical reasons why exemptions may be provided.

Good answer: I am not sure which professions are exempt from jury duty, but I think there is an argument against allowing lawyers, prison officers and MPs to be part of a jury. This is because there is a risk that such people will be awarded a special status by the rest of the jury, and they could influence the decision a great deal, since the profession includes a knowledge of the law. Jurors are supposed to be treated equally and are supposed to be an impartial body, so giving one person's opinion more weight than everyone else's on account of their profession is not effective. However, I think juries should be as wide a cross section of society as possible, so I disagree with barring any profession from jury duty.

Bad answer: I don't know which professions are exempt from jury duty so I can't answer that. *This is a bad answer because the interviewee has not attempted to give examples of certain professions which may be exempt and why. If you don't know something, just have a guess and tell the interviewer you're not 100% on the subject.*

Q49: When you become prime minister, what laws will you change?

This question involves a discussion of reform of laws. You can really talk about anything, it is a great opportunity to express your personal interest in a particular area of law. Stronger answers are therefore on any subject matter, just make sure your points are reasoned and give examples. Weaker answers will be blunt and overly simplistic. Explain the current law, then offer a criticism of it before proposing a change to that law you would make to improve it.

Good answer: if I was prime minister, I would change the law on abortion. Over the pandemic, at home abortions have been allowed to keep people safe from catching and spreading COVID-19. With this introduction, there has been a decreased wait time on appointments, and there have been no deaths or serious health impacts as a result of these at home abortions.

I think that the law should enable them to occur all the time, rather than just in emergency circumstances, as it stands now. This is because such a provision removes concerns of the pills taking effect while travelling home from the clinic, and it enables people to access abortions if they are unable to get to hospitals easily for whatever reason. Also, a lot of people are hesitant to get abortions due to the clinical environment in which they happen, and they may feel safer having an abortion in their own home. Moreover, having more readily accessible abortions will almost certainly decrease the number of 'back street' abortions, which are incredibly dangerous.

I would also change the law on assisted suicide. As it stands, people who help their loved ones travel to overseas clinics such as Dignitas to die can be prosecuted in principle. This has not happened for decades, so I do not see the point in leaving the law open to such a risk as it will cause many people anxiety. I actually think criminalising helping disabled people to die is even discriminatory and contradictory, because people who are not as physically disabled can just go by themselves, so the law only effects society's most vulnerable and their families.

Bad answer: if I was prime minister, I would make abortion pills legal as it gives people better access to medical care. *This is a bad answer as the individual has not explained what the current law is in any detail, or given proper justification for their opinion.*

Q50: Two people die as a result of their parachute failing due to a manufacturing flaw, would their deaths constitute murder or manslaughter?

This question involves a discussion of the differences between murder and manslaughter. For this, some previous knowledge is required, but not a lot. The difference between murder and manslaughter is the mindset of the defendant. In murder, the person must either intend the death of the victim or intend to cause them GBH (grievous bodily harm). They can also be reckless to the victim's death, if the death is a virtual certainty of the defendant's action. There are different types of manslaughter, but the standard is lower than that of murder: it tends to involve being reckless as to some harm caused to the victim, or breaching a duty to them etc. The interviewer here is looking for your ability to compare offences, and specifically to acknowledge the similarities in their conduct (i.e. death of a victim) and the differences in the intentions behind said offences. Treating the offences separately and critically comparing them will take your answer to a higher level.

Good answer: although the manufacturer has caused two people to die, I think this is manslaughter rather than murder as it was not a deliberate defect: the manufacturer did not intend for the two people to be injured or die. However, they had a duty of care towards the people, which arguably involved providing them with safe equipment. This was evidently breached, so I think they would be liable for manslaughter. Potentially, if the manufacturer was being reckless, the death of the victims could be construed as murder, but I think in this case it would be manslaughter because there doesn't appear to be any malicious conduct.

Bad answer: the manufacturer would be liable for murder as they indirectly killed two people. *This is a bad answer because the person has not considered if this killing could be manslaughter and has not treated the two crimes separately.*

Q51: If a person is convicted of a murder which did not take place, and upon release kills the original victim, can they be sentenced again?

This question considers the principles which underpin our legal system. The idea of double jeopardy is one of these, it holds a person cannot be trialled for the same crime twice. This is the principle which must be reconciled the example given here. The interviewer here is looking for your ability to pick up on potential issues with the law, and understand the principles which underpin it.

Good answer: on one hand, the convict could not be sentenced again. The principle of double jeopardy (holding that a person cannot be trialled for the same crime twice) applies here, and the convict has already been trialled for the murder of the victim once and has been punished for it. Potentially, the person served punishment enough as their initial prison sentence was for a crime they did not commit.

On the other hand, I think there should be some sort of loophole or way the convict could be trialled again for the crime. Although this would violate the principle of double jeopardy, not trialling the defendant again would violate a principle of justice which equally underpins the law – these principles must be balanced. The defendant has committed a crime and this should not go unrecognised, and he has clearly not been through 'punishment enough' as some people would argue, because he has done the very crime he was wrongfully convicted in the first place.

Bad answer: the convict can be sentenced again because he has committed a crime, which requires a sentence. *This is a bad answer because the interviewee has not picked up on the concept of double jeopardy. Even if you don't have knowledge of this, think about why the question is being asked if it seems overly simple. The interviewee here could have picked up on the issue with being sentenced twice for the same crime, even if they did not know the technical term for it.*

Q52: What does it mean when something is "beyond reasonable doubt"

This question involves analysing the actual content of the law. No previous knowledge of law is required for this question, because everything you need to know is given to you. With definition questions like these, avoid giving a circular answer, and try to ensure your answer is as reasoned as possible. The interviewer here is looking for your ability to come up with comprehensive definitions. They may give you examples of instances and ask you to see if they fit with your definition, so don't be afraid to amend it if these are inconsistent with your idea of 'beyond reasonable doubt'. When giving examples, the interviewer will push your conclusion to its logical limits. Don't be afraid to acknowledge when something is inconsistent with your answer, but equally don't abandon it instantly. If you do change your answer, make sure to give justification for doing so.

Good answer: I think 'beyond reasonable doubt' is a standard which cases have to be proved to. It requires there to be little to no uncertainty surrounding the decision, and any uncertainty is unreasonable, or irrational. The issue with such a definition is that the idea of reasonableness is very subjective. What is reasonable for me may not be reasonable for another person, so imposing such a standard in criminal cases means there will inevitably be different opinions on it. This potentially violates the principle of legal certainty, because people may be unsure of whether their conduct meets this standard. Moreover, the idea of predictability in law is not upheld by such a standard either. On the other hand, the subjective nature of the standard allows for discretion in borderline cases and for such cases to be assessed individually.

Bad answer: I think 'beyond reasonable doubt' means you have to prove a criminal case so there is no reasonable doubt of the decision. *This is a bad answer because it is circular: the interviewee has used the phrase reasonable doubt to define the phrase reasonable doubt.*

Q53: What are the legal implications of gay marriage?

This question requires you to consider the legal ramifications for a real-world issue. It would be relevant to discuss the position of gay marriage from religious perspectives here, as well as civil partnerships, which used to be the equivalent of marriage for same-sex couples. This question demonstrates the importance of keeping up with the news, because anything you know about gay marriage could be applied here, provided you make it relevant to the question. Stronger answers will consider a range of implications and justify each one. Weaker answers will give little to no justification for their points.

Good answer: there are multiple legal implications of gay marriage. Firstly, churches can currently refuse to marry same-sex couples. A legal implication of this could be that such a provision must be legally reconciled with discrimination rights which they potentially infringe upon. Secondly, civil partnership used to be the 'equivalent' of marriage for same-sex couples. Perhaps some couples in a civil partnership want to change this to marriage, so whether or not this can happen without dissolving the civil partnership must be clarified and, if not, a new provision must be added to the grounds of dissolving civil partnerships to account for this circumstance. Thirdly, any legal marriage documents should be amended to have inclusive pronouns such as they/them, instead of just having he/him and she/her, so they apply to all couples, rather than just heterosexual ones.

Bad answer: the legal implications of gay marriage are that churches can't refuse to marry gay people as this would be discrimination. *This is a bad answer as it is quite blunt, a better way of approaching this point (which is untrue: churches can refuse to marry gay people) would be to discuss potential implications of churches refusing to marry same-sex couples and how the law would have to deal with this.*

Q54: What data should our government be able to find out about us? Should foreign citizens be treated any differently?

This question involves a consideration of data privacy. With questions that ask 'to what extent' is important to give a balanced answer and justify whatever conclusion you come to. Stronger answers will consider a range of extents (high, medium and low) and decide which one they agree with. Weaker answers will only consider the extent they conclude with and won't justify their answer very well.

Good answer: there are arguments that data should be available to the government to a high extent. It would help with criminal investigations, as people's messages and internet history would be more readily available. For example, if someone is a suspected terrorist, their card purchases and social media activity could be analysed easily. This would also help with missing person's cases. Moreover, data being available to the government would mean they could prevent radicalisation and even paedophile rings on the internet, protecting people and upholding the welfare principle.

Despite this, there are also arguments that the government should not have data available to them. If there was a data leak, this could easily get into the wrong hands and end up subverting the welfare principle it tries to uphold. Also, it gives the government too much power: if they became corrupt or started using data for something the public didn't agree with, this could lead to civil unrest or mass riots. Therefore, I think data should be available in some circumstances, but not all. Considering foreign citizens, I think their country should monitor their data- unless they are potentially going to have an impact on British society, then the British government shouldn't have access to their data.

Bad answer: data should not be available to our government as they could go corrupt. *This is a bad answer as the interviewee has only considered one argument and hasn't justified their point very much.*

Q55: What is the significance of differences between American and British Law?

This question involves a comparison of US and British Law. Some knowledge of the law is required for this question, but not much. Since the differences need to be 'fundamental', try to take a step back and look at the bigger picture: there is no point talking about the gun laws in America as that isn't really a 'fundamental' difference. The biggest differences are probably that the US has a codified constitution, but the UK doesn't. Also, the US has a federal government system so each state can make its own laws to an extent, but, again, the UK doesn't. When analysing the implications of these differences, consider the relationship between the countries.

Good answer: there are two fundamental differences between the US and British Law. Firstly, the US has a codified constitution, but the UK constitution is uncodified. Secondly, the US has a federal government system, but the UK does not. The implications of these differences come to light when considering the relationship between the UK and the US. In treaties, the UK will have to clarify their position on constitutional issues as our constitution is unclear (since it is uncodified). If a new convention was formed, the UK's flexible constitution could adopt this easily, but the US would have to go through a special process of amendment to implement it into their law. Also, trade agreements between the countries depend on the state in America, as the states may have different regulations, whereas the UK (or at least England) has universal regulations on trade. These provisions will make trade agreements more complex.

Bad answer: in the US you can have a gun, but in the UK you can't. in the US, some states are trying to ban abortion, but the UK is not. *This is a bad answer because the interviewee has got bogged down in individual laws, rather than taking a step back and looking at the bigger picture.*

Q56: How would you advise a client who is refusing to attend court despite multiple summons?

This question involves a consideration of law in the real world. Stronger answers will give a lot of justification for the point, whereas weaker answers will be more simplistic. The answer is quite an easy one so, to reach a higher standard of response, try and have a very structured approach to the question here. The interviewer is assessing your knowledge of law in practical contexts, and of course in a legal career (though it is worth noting that you don't have to want to be a lawyer in order to do a law degree). Signposting is a really good idea for interview responses (using first, second and third or a, b, c and things like that) because it makes your answer far easier to understand and splits up your points so the interviewer can appreciate how reasoned your answer is. Clarity is very important in your answers, and signposting helps you achieve that.

Good answer: I would advise my client to go to court. There are three reasons I would do this. Firstly, not going to court is a crime in itself, so if my client doesn't go to court it will only add to his multiple charges. Secondly, I would tell my client he can't run away forever, at some point he will be forced to go to court, so it is better if he goes of his own accord. Thirdly, I would tell my client that not going to court will reflect badly on him in the proceedings. If he pleads not guilty to the charges, he will seem more guilty if he is not forthcoming with the judicial system. If he pleads guilty, he is less likely to get a lenient punishment.

Bad answer: I would tell him to go to court. *This is a bad answer because there is no justification for the interviewee's point, and no structure to his answer.*

Q57: A General orders a soldier to kill his squad mate. Would this be murder?

This question involves getting into depth surrounding the law on murder, and what defences apply to it. In law, there is a defence of necessity to murder, as well as others such as loss of control and diminished responsibility. It might be worth having a read up on these since they come up very often at interview. For example, the interviewer may give you some legislation outlining the requirements of loss of control, then give you examples and ask you to see if they fit with the requirements. Stronger answers to this question will consider arguments for and against this action being murder, whereas weaker answers will be one-sided. Using examples to illustrate your point and its limits would be a good idea in questions like these. The interviewer is looking for your ability to separate the conduct (like killing here) and mental (like intention or recklessness) aspects of an offence here, and analyse them according to a situation.

Good answer: on one hand, this could be construed as murder. The soldier has killed his squad mate and did intend to- the issue is whether or not the General ordering him to do it awards the soldier with any defence to murder. If the General said 'kill your squad mate or I will kill you', or pointed a gun at the soldier, then I think this would be a defence to murder because the soldier was fearing for his own life and was coerced into killing his squad mate. However, this is not the case here. The soldier may have been under some unseen pressure or fear from the General's order, but I don't think this justifies him killing someone.

Bad answer: this would be murder because the soldier killed his squad mate. *This is a bad answer because it is circular and unjustified. The interviewee also hasn't considered any circumstances where a defence would apply here.*

Q58: A doctor is asked by the wife of a patient to end the patient's suffering by killing them. Do you think this would be murder?

This question involves a consideration of the law on euthanasia and assisted suicide. Moreover, it involves patient consent and whether or not a family member can make a decision on behalf of the patient. Stronger answers will consider both of these issues in turn, giving a reasoned approach to their conclusions and analysing circumstances where their answer would be different. Weaker answers will treat the two issues as one and give a less considered approach to the question.

Good answer: firstly, I don't think the patient's family member should be able to dictate the patient's death in this instance. This raises issues of the patient being coerced or forced into dying, or even not consulted at all. Moreover, if the family member is set to inherit money from the patient's death, issues of intention must be addressed. Of course, if the patient was in a coma or unresponsive, family members would have to make decisions for them. In this case, though, I think more than one family member would have to make the decision to avoid corruption and ill-thought-out judgements.

Secondly, I don't think this situation would be murder, but it depends on the interpretation of it. If the patient was not in a lot of pain, then giving the patient pain medication to kill them would be murder, because the intention to end their life is there. However, if the doctor gave the patient pain medication to ease their severe pain (as the situation is here) then this would not be murder, because the doctor's primary intention would be to ease the pain, but this has the secondary effect of shortening the patient's lifespan. Such passive euthanasia is legal in the UK, and the doctrine of the double-effect is essentially what governs it.

Bad answer: it would be murder because the patient isn't asking to die, and the doctor can't just kill them. *This is a bad answer because the individual has not treated the two issues separately. There is also little justification of their point.*

Q59: Which law is broken most frequently?

This question involves considering law in the real world. Stronger responses will give lots of justification for their point, whereas weaker ones will not. The interviewer is looking for your ability to think on your feet, but also to explore the reasons of why someone may break the law and how these reasons can be mitigated. To take your answer to another level, discuss practical ways you could stop the law being broken, rather than just the hypothetical reasons of why it is.

Good answer: I think that driving laws such as going through a red light or parking on double yellow lines are broken most frequently. People may be confused on laws such as eating while driving (which is illegal), so may break the law unknowingly. Also, some people may not 'see the point' in these laws, or think they are lesser than other laws like theft or assault, so choose to break them knowingly. This illustrates the importance of having justified laws, but also communicating this justification to the public so they understand the rationale behind the law and are more likely to follow it as a consequence. This could be achieved by advertising statistics on car accidents considering parking on double yellow lines or eating behind the wheel: if people understand why the law is in place they are more likely to follow it.

Bad answer: I think the law on underage drinking is broken most frequently because a lot of parents and teenagers don't see the point in it. *This is a bad answer because the person has only considered one reason for why the law is broken so frequently and has not proposed a reform to the law to prevent it from being broken. It is important to consider the wider aspect of your answer when responding to the question. Moreover, they should give more reasons as to why the law is broken in their answer.*

Q60: When people are tried by their peers, why bother with a judge?

This question involves considering the state of the judicial system in the UK. No knowledge of the law is required for this question, just think out loud and give a reasoned approach to whatever you say. Try and step back and look at the bigger picture: what would happen if there weren't judges? This will help you figure out reasons for why judges are required in judicial proceedings.

Good answer: judges are required for court cases for a few reasons. Firstly, not every case has a jury, only criminal cases in the Crown court do. This means for lesser offences, judges are required to make decisions on cases. Secondly, judges are required to oversee proceedings and handle questions and challenges from lawyers. Thirdly, judges are required to direct the jury on what certain concepts in the law mean and if they apply in the current case. For example, the phrase beyond reasonable doubt, or on the balance of probability may require direction. Whether things should be construed narrowly, widely or in the ordinary sense of the word is also required to be directed by the judge. The lawyers can't do this as they're biased. Fourthly, judges sentence criminals so they are required for this aspect of the judicial process too.

Bad answer: I don't know what the point of having a judge is when decisions are made by the jury. *This is a bad answer because the interviewee has not attempted to respond to the question, had an educated guess at the answer or even gone through their thought process out loud. Always try and think of an answer, even if you take 30 seconds or so to think before you say something. It is also okay to tell the interviewer 'I am going to have a think for a second' if it feels awkward for you to just be silent.*

Q61: You take shelter from a thunderstorm in an unlocked car – have you committed the offence of allowing yourself to be carried in a conveyance without the owner's consent?

This question considers the offence of theft, and in which context it applies. Stronger answers will consider two sides of the argument and give examples which illustrate the logical limit of their conclusions. Weaker answers will be more blunt and less justified. You don't need any previous knowledge of the law for this question, since it is given to you. The standard you need to apply the example to is 'the offence of allowing yourself to be carried in a conveyance without the owner's consent'. The key to this question is the definition of 'carried', and possibly consent too.

Good answer: on one hand, this could be construed as the offence of allowing yourself to be carried in a conveyance without the owner's consent. I have not asked the owner if I can shelter in their car, so there is no consent given. If 'carried' includes remaining stationary in the car, then this is equally satisfied. On the other hand, this example could be interpreted as not fulfilling the offence. I did not ask the owner for their consent, but what if they would have consented? Whether or not this counts as consent for the offence is debatable. Also, 'carried' implies the vehicle is moving, which it does not in this instance. If I drove their car to buy an umbrella then returned it to the parking place, I would be carried in it, but whether staying still in the car as in this case counts as carried is again debatable, though I think not.

Bad answer: I am not guilty of the offence because I haven't been carried in the car. *This is a bad answer because the person has not considered the issues of consent and the definition of carried separately and has not properly justified their point.*

Q62: How would you separate the words: Mislead, Deceive, and Lie?

This question involves giving your own definitions of key legal terms and pointing out the differences between them. Stronger answers will be more nuanced in this question and possibly highlight both similarities and differences of the terms. Weaker answers will be more blunt and potentially circular (i.e. using the term to define the term). The interviewer is looking for your ability to critically compare key legal concepts and come up with comprehensive definitions for them. You do not need to know the technical or legal definitions of these terms, just try and define them in their normal sense. However, avoid giving definitions that overlap to a high extent, because the interviewer says in the question that the concepts are not the same.

Good answer: I think lying is actively concealing the truth from someone by directly telling them false things. Deceiving is more indirect than this, I think it entails concealing the truth from someone, like lying, but telling them things from which they derive false information. I think misleading is the most indirect of the three, but again entails concealing the truth from someone. In this case, this is done by withholding the truth or avoiding discussing it. The differences between misleading and deceiving are few, and I think the terms overlap in some instances.

Bad answer: lying is when you tell someone untrue things. Deceiving is when you make a person believe things that are false, and misleading is when you cause them to be misled. *This is a bad answer because the person's definitions are unjustified (and circular in the case of deceiving). They have also not directly compared the terms. Since the interviewer said in the question that the concepts are similar, pointing out the similarities of these terms would make this answer a lot better.*

Q63: Why are manslaughter and murder treated differently, what separates them?

This question involves a direct comparison of two offences. You don't need prior knowledge of the law to answer this, but it would be useful to know the differences in mens rea (guilty mind) of them. The mens rea of murder is intent to kill or cause GBH (grievous bodily harm), or foresight of virtual certainty that such harm/death will ensue from the defendant's conduct. The mens rea of manslaughter depends on the specific offence, but it is generally lower than this (or the same where a defence is used). Another thing that is relevant here is the mandatory life sentence for murder. If you are convicted of murder, you have to be sentenced to life in prison, but most people don't actually serve this long: they just have a minimum term. The life sentence means that they are monitored for the rest of their life, even when they get out.

Good answer: there are a few differences between murder and manslaughter. Firstly, murder is perceived by society as much more serious than manslaughter. If someone is convicted of murder, they are more likely to be a social outcast and struggle to rehabilitate than if they were convicted of manslaughter. Secondly, murder has a higher level of mens rea than manslaughter, which reflects its harsher labelling. Thirdly, murder has a mandatory life sentence, whereas manslaughter does not. This also reflects the offence's severity, and why there are specific defences to murder – we should be cautious to subject people to this sort of sentence. Even though a murderer may not serve life in prison, they will spend the rest of their life monitored and are much more likely to go to prison again for a less serious crime.

Bad answer: murder is killing with intent and manslaughter is killing without intent. *This is a bad answer because a) it's wrong and b) they have not defined what this 'intent' means. They have only given one point and, even if it was wrong, this would be okay if they had properly reasoned and justified it, which they have not.*

Q64: Should stalking remain legal?

This question involves a proposed reform to the law and weighing up the pros and cons of it. Stronger answers will consider both of these, whereas weaker responses will be more one-sided. Try and consider examples to justify your points where possible.

Good answer: on one hand, stalking should not be illegal. Telling someone where they can and cannot go arguably violates the principle of autonomy which the law seeks to uphold. Moreover, telling someone what they can and cannot say, and how they can and cannot interact with another person potentially does the same thing. Also, a person can get a restraining order against someone if they are being stalked, and breaching this order is illegal, so perhaps there is not a need to make stalking itself against the law. Despite this, I think stalking should be made illegal. While it potentially infringes on autonomy, not making it illegal infringes on the principle of welfare. Likewise, freedom of speech is only a right when it does not violate someone else's right, and I think people have a right not to be harassed. While restraining orders go some way to stopping stalking, there are cases which will slip through the cracks, so we need a stronger law in this area. The mental health impacts which stalking can have on someone are severe, so this should be reflected in its legal treatment. For example, a person could be stalked for years and end up with an anxiety disorder or PTSD: this is a level of harm that must be addressed by the law directly.

Bad answer: stalking should be made illegal because it can cause people harm. *While this is a good point, the interviewee here has not justified it very well or given examples which illustrate it. Also, they have not considered the other side of the argument – not making stalking illegal.*

Q65: How do civil cases differ from criminal ones?

Some knowledge of the law is evidently required for this question, but if you didn't have any in the interview, just go through your thought process out loud. The question is asking for a direct comparison of two areas of law. Stronger responses will be structured and clear, explaining each difference individually. They may touch on some similarities also. Weaker answers will give fewer differences and use more vague and complex language. Law is really about explaining hard concepts in easy terms, and you can demonstrate your ability to do that in this question: this is essentially what the interviewer is looking for. The interviewer here is also looking for an ability to consider the different types of law and how each one can be broken. Not every case is an offence of assault, or rape etc- this is what they are trying to get you to appreciate here.

Good answer: there are a few differences between civil and criminal cases. Firstly, the state prosecutes in criminal cases (via the CPS), whereas private individuals prosecute in civil cases. Secondly, criminal law relates to offences which negatively affect society as a whole and can result in prison sentences. Civil law relates to duties and rights which have been breached, and results in compensation being awarded (not prison). Fourthly, I think criminal law seeks to punish, but civil law seeks to redress. Criminal law has the ultimate aim of maintaining stability in society, but civil law deals with disputes between organisations and individuals.

Bad answer: I don't know the difference between criminal and civil law. Criminal law deals with things like rape, assault and theft, but civil law doesn't. *This is a bad answer because the interviewee has given a weak attempt at understanding the question: the question is holistic and needs looking at as a whole, rather than just discussing examples (although these could be useful to demonstrate a holistic point). The person has also not justified their answer or given it any structure.*

Q66: What would you say are the advantages and disadvantages of juries?

This question involves deliberating an aspect of the judicial system. No legal knowledge is required to give a good answer to this question, all you need to do is think of wider implications of the jury service and how they relate to the principles the law seeks to uphold (such as legal certainty, fair labelling and autonomy). Try and give a balanced argument i.e. a similar number of pros and cons. Also, try and justify your answer and give examples which illustrate it. Stronger responses will consider pros and cons within the judicial system itself, then zoom out and consider the wider ramifications of these.

Good answer: considering pros first, juries ensure citizen participation in the criminal law system. Judges are not elected so juries increase the perceived legitimacy of the justice system and the position of judges. This also may lead to more people following the law as they respect it. Moreover, juries ensure the impartiality of judges. Although judges do direct and guide juries in their decisions, the final say always comes down to them. This reduces the bias of the judge in deciding if someone is guilty.

Considering cons, you could argue that juries lack the expertise to decide on whether someone is guilty. Judges have years of experience in the field, so arguably should make the decision, instead of leaving it to 'ordinary' citizens. Moreover, there are arguments that juries are not representative of the population. A sample as small as 12 people, even though it is randomly selected, is never going to represent the different religions, ethnic groups and sexualities etc that are present within the UK population. Also, if the defendant was a member of a minority group, there is a risk of unconscious bias.

Bad answer: the pros of juries are that they prevent judges from making biased decisions. Juries also increase involvement in decisions and, because there are 12 people, mean there is greater deliberation of the decision and is being left to more people rather than just one judge. *This answer, though it contains good points, is bad since it does not outline any cons of juries. The interviewee should also work on structuring their answer and signposting (i.e. firstly, secondly).*

Q67: To what extent can you know how much you do not know?

This question is very broad, and very philosophical. You can discuss almost anything in your answers, just make sure every point you make is justified and structured. The interviewer is assessing your ability to address unfamiliar material and make connections between the law and philosophy. A lot of a Law degree considers the black and white letter of the law (i.e. what it actually says), but some of it considers why the law is the way it is and how it can be improved. The philosophical analysis that is required for such a deliberation of the law is what is being assessed here.

Good answer: I think you only know some things you didn't know before once you know them. That is, by the time you know what you don't know, you already know it! For example, I didn't know how vaccines work until I studied them in Biology, but I only became aware of my ignorance once I was no longer ignorant – because I learnt about them. Some things, however, you can know you don't know by considering whether or not you do know them. For example, I know that I don't know how to fix a toilet, simply by asking myself if I can. However, I don't think you can ever know the extent of what you don't know. I suppose how much you don't know is one of the things that you don't know. There are some experiences I will never have, so my ignorance surrounding them will never be illustrated. I can hardly think of all possible things of the world and realise I don't know them.

Bad answer: you know what you don't know by asking yourself if you do know it. *This is a bad answer because the interviewee has given no examples, which would be very helpful to clarify things in a confusing question like this. Their answer is also too short and not well-justified.*

Q68: What would you say differentiates solicitors from barristers?

This question does require a knowledge of the law or, at least, the careers that accompany it. If you don't know what the difference between a barrister and a solicitor is, have a read up on it, and read the sample 'good' answer below for some basic points. I would still recommend you read up on the difference between them though. Here is a link explaining them in some more depth:

https://www.brightknowledge.org/law/what-is-the-difference-between-a-barrister-and-solicitor

While you don't have to want to be a lawyer to do a law degree, the majority of people do and the interviewer in this question will be looking for your commitment to and interest in the course, through assessing your knowledge on a career the course leads to. The interviewer is also looking for your knowledge of how law interacts with the 'real world', taking it out of the hypothetical one.

Good answer: there are a few differences between barristers and solicitors. Firstly, barristers represent people in court, whereas solicitors mainly advise on necessary courses of legal action depending on their area of expertise. Solicitors work directly with clients, whereas barristers receive information on their client's case and work off that. Secondly, barristers tend to be self-employed and a member of Chambers or are sometimes employed by companies or solicitor firms to advise clients. Barristers provide specialist legal advice in a select area, but solicitors are more all-round, and can advise on a range of issues.

Bad answer: barristers wear wigs and gowns in courts and examine witnesses, but solicitors work a desk job and do advocacy work. *While this is true, this answer is a bit simple and doesn't go into much depth considering the differences of the work of barristers or solicitors, and the relationship between the two jobs. A consideration of the similarities of the professions would also be good, rather than just the differences.*

Q69: If you were made Queen's Counsel tomorrow, what do you think your responsibilities would be? What would you have to do to be made a Queen's Counsel?

This question does require some knowledge of the law considering what a Queen's Counsel is, but not so much considering how one becomes a member of it. With the latter, just think of the senior nature of the Queen's Counsel and what sort of qualities someone might look for in a member's application. Tell the interviewer you're not sure, but you think these things are involved in people becoming a Queen's Counsel. This shows the interviewer your thought process, and that you can think on your feet when faced with unfamiliar and unknown material- this is essentially what they're looking for here.

Good answer: A Queen's counsel is a senior barrister appointed by the monarch. Queen's Counsels take on fewer cases than regular barristers, and charge more, because these often require very in depth and specialist knowledge of the law. Queen's Counsels tend to represent each side in important legal cases, such as at the Supreme Court, because their arguments used in the judgements often set a common law precedent for lower courts to follow. I'm not sure how to become a Queen's Counsel but, given the rank's seniority, I imagine it requires a high level of knowledge of the law, perhaps a lot of experience and public speaking skills. Communication with both clients and colleagues may also be beneficial to the application process, as well as integrity of character.

Bad answer: A Queen's Counsel is like a really important barrister. I don't know how you become one though. *This is a bad answer because, although the person doesn't know how to become a Queen's Counsel, they have not attempted to figure it out. Just going through any thoughts they have would be enough, it doesn't have to be a completely comprehensive answer: the interviewer just wants to see you give it a go.*

Q70: If a parent slaps their child, are they abusing them? Does your answer change if they bruised the child?

This question involves an analysis of current law. The call to ban smacking altogether is a controversial debate at present, so it coming up in an interview question illustrates why it is so important to keep up with the news, especially surrounding legal issues. Stronger answers will treat the two examples separately, because this gives the response a great structure. Weaker answers will give unjustified points, and treat the two examples as one, or with little distinction between them.

Good answer: In the first case, I don't think slapping a child is abuse in some situations. If the child is behaving badly enough that a slap is reasonable punishment, then I don't think this is abuse. Though it is controversial, it remains legal to slap your child in this situation and some people think it is a way of teaching discipline. However, the key lies in the definition of a 'reasonable punishment'. If the child in this case had not done their chores, I don't think a slap would be reasonable punishment for this. If the child had threatened their sibling or bullied another child at school, then this could be more readily construed as a 'reasonable punishment' for their actions.

Considering the second case, I think this would be abuse. While slapping as a reasonable punishment remains legal, I don't think it is legal if such slapping amounts to actual bodily harm. The key becomes whether a bruise satisfies this requirement, but I think a bruise on a small child is worse than a bruise on an adult, so these circumstantial aspects must be considered. Moreover, if a slap causes a bruise, the punishment of slapping is less likely to be reasonable, so more likely to be disproportionate ie abuse and illegal.

Bad answer: this is abuse because the parent has assaulted the child. *This is a bad response because the interviewee has treated the two examples as one, instead of dividing them up. Their point is also not very justified, and they could give some examples to help illustrate it.*

Q71: What prevents European nations from combining into a United States of Europe?

This question considers a comparison of two types of government system. Stronger responses will give a wide range of points and discuss both practical and hypothetical reasons: a zoomed-in and a zoomed-out perspective. Weaker answers will be less justified and give fewer points. The interviewer here is looking for an ability to appreciate the relationship between law and politics, and the differences between constitutions and government systems on an international scale, rather than just within the UK. Constitutional law is interlinked with history, politics and even philosophy so appreciating such relationships will take your answer to a higher level.

Good answer: from a practical perspective, .Europe is arguably too big to be a United States system. There are many political and cultural differences between countries, let alone between individuals, and grouping all of these into a federal government system would potentially not represent them enough. Moreover, when the US was created, a strong centrality was required to unite the country and its citizens after the British invasion. Europe, on the other hand, has always been fragmented and its constitutional inter-country relations evolved, so they did not need to be clarified as in the case of the United States. A United States of Europe would also be hard to govern simply because of the distance and separation of the countries, whereas the United States of America is all one landmass. Arguably, membership of international organisations like the EU (though not for Britain) gives some of the benefits of a federal government system, so it is not needed in Europe.

Bad answer: there is no United States of Europe because it is not a federal government system. *This is a bad answer because it is circular, and it doesn't give any proper reasons considering why Europe is does not have a United States system.*

Q72: What impact did 9/11 have on western law?

No legal knowledge is required to answer this question, you just have to think of the wider implications that 9/11 may have had on law. Stronger answers will consider a range of ideas including ones very closely linked with the event but also broader ramifications which follow it. Weaker answers will think of fewer points and give little justification for them. If you do know about the legal consequences of 9/11, definitely say them, but make sure you justify each of them to make your response look original, rather than just repeating things you already know.

Good answer: I am not sure of what specific legal changes were made to Western law after 9/11, but I imagine a tightening of laws surrounding airport security is one of them. Also, I think there could have been new data collection laws introduced which authorise the government accessing suspected terrorists' messages and internet histories. Moreover, I think there would be more deradicalization laws implemented and perhaps data collection provisions in respect to these, for example stronger laws surrounding radicalisation on social media platforms and chatrooms. From a wider perspective, I think 9/11 encouraged governments to share data with each other in order to prevent such an event happening again, so maybe laws allowing that were implemented. From a labelling point of view, perhaps the standard required to convict someone as a terrorist was lowered, or the offence was given harsher punishments, to deter people from becoming an extremist and to accurately represent public opinion of terrorists at the time.

Bad answer: I don't know what the consequences were, but I think they would tighten airport security. *This is a bad answer because the interviewee has only made one point and not justified it very well. The response must be more reasoned than this.*

Q73: Who can change the law, or make a new law?

This question considers the British constitution and government. There are three branches of government in the UK: the executive (who executes law), the legislature (who passes law) and the judiciary (who interprets law). This question is essentially asking for a comparison of these three branches, and an examination of their roles. Stronger answers will consider the subjectivity of the terms in the question, and the overlapping nature of the three branches of government. Weaker answers will not be so nuanced and treat the roles of the branches of government as more discrete variables.

Good answer: while the executive executes laws, Parliament is able to amend and 'change' these laws before they are enacted. Within this, the House of Commons can make more changes than the House of Lords, who are not allowed to impose wrecking amendments to most legislation. Moreover, the public also have some weight in proposing changes to laws. Things like protests or petitions can put pressure on Parliament to amend problematic or out-of-place legislation. Courts too can set a common law precedent regarding the definition of certain concepts in the law. Though this is not a 'change' as such, it could be considered an amendment in some instances, especially when the precedent is a deviation from a previous approach to the law. Ultimately, Parliament has the most power to write and change laws, but other political and legal bodies can influence its decisions. *To improve even more, this answer could treat 'write' and 'change' separately and discuss the differences of the terms.*

Bad answer: Parliament has the power to write and change laws. The public can also influence them to change laws. *This is a bad response because the interviewee has not considered many points or many examples to illustrate the ideas they give. How could the public influence parliament to change laws? Discussing petitions or protests here would be good.*

Q74: If you could change any 3 laws, which ones would they be and what would you change about them?

This question is incredibly subjective, you can essentially discuss anything. It is a good question to demonstrate your particular interests of the law which you have a lot of background knowledge in. The interviewer will see your passion for the subjects you discuss. If you do this, which is something they look for. Just try and make your answers as reasoned and structed as possible, so the interviewer can follow what you're saying easily.

Good answer: I would change the law on abortion, the law on assisted suicide and the law on voting. Firstly, I would make at-home abortions legal. Over the pandemic, 'abortion pills' have been made accessible so people can have abortions at home without risk of catching or spreading COVID-19. There have been no deaths from such abortions and the waiting time for appointments has decreased. Moreover, this provision removes worries such as the pills taking effect on the way home from the clinic, concerns about being far away from a clinic or unable to take time off work to get to an appointment and even things like fears of being in a hospital. This will also decrease dangerous 'back-street' abortions which are what happens when proper medical abortions aren't accessible.

Secondly, I would make it legal to accompany a disabled person to Dignitas so they can die. Though this is currently illegal, nobody has been prosecuted for it in years, so the rationale behind the law is unclear, as is its effectiveness. Judicial discretion applies in the situation where it happens, but I think people have the right to know how their case will be treated, rather than having an elusive and subjective notion deciding their liability.

Thirdly, I would lower the age of voting to 16. I think if you can pay tax, get married and join the army at 16, you should be allowed to have a say in who runs the country. Though there are arguments that 16 year olds don't know enough about politics to vote, a) this could be solved by compulsory politics lessons in school and b) this introduces a slippery slope into the electoral system: what about 50 year olds who don't know anything about politics? If we base the ability to vote on knowledge of politics, where is this 'knowledge' standard made? Also, conflating age with knowledge is arguably too blunt.

Bad answer: I would change the law on abortion, assisted suicide and voting. *This is a bad answer because the interviewee has not said how they would change the law and why they would change the law, or even said what the law currently is in these areas.*

Q75: Which law do you think is broken the most often in the UK?

This question involves considering law in the real world. Stronger responses will give lots of justification for their point, whereas weaker ones will not.

Good answer: I think that driving laws such as going through a red light or parking on double yellow lines are broken every day by most people. People may be confused on laws such as eating while driving (which is illegal), so may break the law unknowingly. Also, some people may not 'see the point' in these laws, or think they are lesser than other laws like theft or assault, so choose to break them knowingly. Moreover, a lot of people drive every day, so there is a lot of opportunity to break driving laws for whatever reason. This illustrates the importance of having justified laws, but also communicating this justification to the public so they understand the rationale behind the law and are more likely to follow it as a consequence.

Bad answer: I think the law littering is broken every day by most people because there aren't enough bins in public areas. *This is a bad answer because the interviewee has not really justified their point or proposed a reform that would make the law easier to follow.*

Q76: Do you think a mandatory uniform contravenes the rights of school children?

This question is a more discursive question designed to test your argumentative skills and see your legal thought process. It would be advisable to clearly state your position at the start and outline your arguments and evidence for your position. It is likely that your interviewer will play the devil's advocate so do not be put off if they press you on certain points.

You should demonstrate your logical thought process and ability to think on your feet, as these are qualities which the interviewer will be looking for. It is usually unlikely that you will be able to prepare and predict the topic of the question that will come out in the interview so you should focus on developing skills like being able to argue for and against your position as well as presenting a clear and compelling argument.

A **good applicant** would clearly state their position and the brief arguments for their position. They should also, if they can, provide some real-life examples as evidence in support. They could also present counter- arguments to their position and how they would resolve these in favour of their position. A very good applicant would consider the different nuances in the argument and weave this into their answer. This does require to think very quickly on your feet so it would be advisable to get some practice thinking in this way and identifying the nuances quickly.

A **sample** answer is as follows: If we assume that wearing school uniforms are mandatory this could be a contravention of human rights as they violate an individual's freedom of expression. Freedom of expression is a fundamental human right which we have been given which cannot be taken away from us in a democratic society. By making school uniforms mandatory, we are not enabling children to express themselves in a way they please. In 2017, the Swedish School Inspectorate said that school uniforms were a human right violation and use of them must be voluntary.

Some may argue that school uniforms do not breach this freedom as having school uniforms does not prevent people from wearing cultural or religious symbols like the hijab or cross. This preserves the identity of the wearer. School uniforms are also thought to be useful for uniformity and ensuring that they do not distract the children during school. However, these arguments are not mutually exclusive with making school uniforms mandatory. These benefits can still arise if school uniforms are made voluntary.

A **poor applicant** might give short, non-committal answer by not assuming a clear position or changing their position the moment they are pressed on it. While it is encouraged to engage in discussion, you should not get too passionate and start see the arguments as the interviewer's personal beliefs. If you have debated before, you should not start discrediting the interviewer or adopt an aggressive manner at any point. The whole point of the exercise is to see how you argue and attempt to formulate arguments and how they will stand against resistance. They are looking for law students who think carefully and argue logically.

Q77: A man points a gun at you and says "If you don't shoot your friend or I'll kill you both". If you shoot your friend are you guilty of murder? Would you be guilty if, instead, the man had said "If you don't shoot your friend, I'll shoot you"? How about if he had said "If you don't shoot your friend, I will"?

This question has a more legal element and would likely require you to be familiar with the definition of murder and how to apply it to the facts. You are not required to know any law to answer this question, but it might be useful to understand the concepts to be able to apply them effectively in an interview. It is not advisable to cite law terms or any technical cases as this will not win you favour with the interviewer since the law faculty explicitly states that you do not need any legal knowledge. They would be more impressed if you were able to apply the underlying reasoning behind these concepts and explain how they would work in alternative situations such as this one.

The interviewer is not looking for someone who can give the answer but is looking to assess your train of thought and whether it is logical. It does not really matter whether you arrive at the "right" answer in the end if you can demonstrate that you are able to think inquisitively and logically when formulating your answer. You should ask questions, pose alternative scenarios and fully explain why you reached a certain answer.

A **sample** answer is as follows: It is important to first define what 'murder' might mean and then to consider each scenario in turn. [the interviewer might interrupt to give you a definition they want you to use or you can try to create one in layman terms]. I will assume that the definition of murder is an intentional, through an act or refusal to act, killing of another person. If I had shot in all three scenarios, under this definition I have intentionally killed my friend therefore would be guilty of murder.

However, I might try to argue that I would have a defence as I was threatened by someone else to kill my friend. Even though I shot my friend intending to kill them, I could argue that it was against my will to do so. If I had not shot, this person would have killed both of us. If I think about this in utilitarian terms, it would have been better for me to shoot my friend so that at least one of us would have lived. It could also be that my friend would have, out of care for me, pleaded for me to shoot them so that I could live.

In the second scenario, I shot my friend to save myself. Here the pressure to shoot my friend could be arguably amplified as the threat was directed at myself and I might be able to argue self-defence.

In the third scenario, I shot my friend to prevent the other person from killing them. I could argue that they might have encouraged me to kill them instead of dying at the hand of the killer. This was, similarly, against my will and I was forced to do it. However, this is harder to justify than the previous two scenarios. In the first, I killed my friend to ensure that at least one of us lived. In the second, I killed them to save myself. The third one seems a bit illogical as I kill them to ensure that they is not shot by the killer. They would die in both instances so it is harder to see the defence that might be available to me in this scenario.

A **poor applicant** might have a long, unstructured answer with assertions not backed up by logic. They might be visibly flustered and confused, leading to contradictory or inconsistent positions. The content of the answer matters less than how you attempt to solve it and go through the different alternatives and reasons you reached that conclusion.

Q78: Do we have an innate moral code, or are we taught it?

This question is a discursive question designed to get the applicant to argue and defend a position. It is likely that your interviewer will play the devil's advocate so do not be put off if they press you on certain points.

You should demonstrate your logical thought process and ability to think on your feet, as these are qualities which the interviewer will be looking for. It is usually unlikely that you will be able to prepare and predict the topic of the question that will come out in the interview so you should focus on developing skills like being able to argue for and against your position as well as presenting a clear and compelling argument.

A **good applicant** would clearly state their position and the brief arguments for their position. They should also, if they can, provide some real-life examples as evidence in support. They could also present counter- arguments to their position and how they would resolve these in their favour. A very good applicant would consider the different nuances in the argument and weave this into their answer. This does require to think very quickly on your feet so it would be advisable to get some practice thinking in this way and identifying the nuances quickly.

A **sample** answer is as follows: I think babies are born with an innate moral code and it is not learned but further developed as they grow older. Their moral code is shaped by society, their upbringing and other factors but is not created by them. Philosophers and psychologists have long believed that babies are "blank slates" and it is their upbringing and society that form their moral code. However, I believe that it is more convincing to argue that babies are endowed with a moral code form birth. A team of researchers at Yale have been studying the behaviour of babies for decades. When shown an example of good behaviour and then an example of bad behaviour, babies tend to prefer the example of good behaviour.

A **poor applicant** might give an unbalanced argument or not defend their position well. For example, they might try and adopt a 'middle' position by trying to argue that babies are born with a moral code, but they are also learnt. This is not advisable as it shows that you are unable to argue for a certain position. While you must acknowledge that there are arguments against the ones you made, you should always adopt a clear position.

Q79: What compels us to obey the law?

This question is more philosophical and relates to jurisprudence (theory of law). It is a hard question with no 'right' answer. You can impress and differentiate yourself by clearly stating your position and presenting arguments in favour of your position. You should also think about why you disagree with the arguments against your position and include these.

A **good applicant** would have done some research into common topics such as this one and be able to formulate nuanced arguments. They should clearly state their position on the question at the start and put forward their arguments in a clear manner with pertinent examples illustrating their point. The Stanford Encyclopaedia of Philosophy and Cambridge HE+ pages are good websites to start with. There are many ways to answer this question and it is a rather personal answer so do not take the sample as the only answer.

A **sample** answer is as follows: A moral obligation to obey the law should be differentiated from the moral requirement to obey the law. If it is a requirement and we decide to just follow, it does not mean we are obliged but we do so because we fear the consequences of not following. A moral obligation could be that we feel compelled to obey the law because we believe in the innate good of that law.

The interviewer is likely to interject and ask you more questions about how you defined the parameters in this answer, they might take issue with how you defined certain issues. This question opens up the applicant to some interesting line of questioning and you should just try your best to follow the guidance of the interviewer once you have given your initial position.

A **poor applicant** might give a short answer with no space for further engagement or proper explanation or make assertions without developed arguments. They might go off-tangent or give an irrelevant answer. They might show holes in their arguments or contradict themself while becoming hopelessly confused. This is not an easy topic or question, so it is best to prepare a strategy and approach with caution to avoid becoming confused.

Q80: What is the relevance of Roman Law to your course?

This question is a good opportunity to show the interviewer that you have done detailed research on the Oxbridge Law degrees. You can demonstrate that you understand the reason why Roman law is a mandatory first year module and differentiate yourself from other candidates. It helps show to the interviewer your genuine interest in the Oxbridge law degree. However, do make sure to answer the question at hand and not "why is Roman law studied at Oxford/Cambridge" which would elicit a different response. The question here is specifically asking about the relevance of Roman law to the modern study of law.

This does require a little bit of research and the Cambridge law faculty website is the best place to start for this (https://www.ba.law.cam.ac.uk/studying-law-cambridge/first-year-focus). There is a very short video by Ms Amy Goymour which I recommend you watch to understand the nature of the subject and the reasons behind its compulsory status.

A **good applicant** would have watched that video but also provide some original insight into the answer and not just paraphrased the video. It would also be good to include a brief example as it shows the logical pattern of your thoughts.

A **sample** answer is as follows: Roman law is relevant to the modern study of law because it provided solutions to many complex factual problems which also arise today. There are also many examples of traces of Roman law in English law. For example, prescription by long use was a concept which originated from the Roman system. We can see how our modern study and system of law has built on these ancient solutions and this gives us a better and deeper understanding of our modern laws.

A **more detailed** answer could also include an example: One example would be where A owns a chariot, but this was stolen by thief who then sold it to an innocent party B. A finds the chariot and wants it back but B alleges that it is his since he purchased it in good faith and paid money for it. The Romans position on this issue influenced and is very similar to the English position which is that the law generally allows the original owner to retrieve their item except in certain exceptional circumstances.

A **poor applicant** might go off tangent and start talking about why Roman law is a mandatory subject at Oxbridge without really addressing the focus of the question which is the relevance. They might also try and dispute this question and say that Roman law is not relevant which is again, not what the question is asking for. The question did not ask you to debate or discuss the relevance but rather wants you to address how learning Roman law can be useful when learning the modern systems of law.

Q81: What would you say was the most ignored law?

This question is designed to see whether an applicant can put forward a law and explain logically why they think it is broken most frequently. The laws you propose must be backed up a good reason and you must explain how you reached this conclusion. It is likely that your interviewer will play the devil's advocate so do not be put off if they press you on certain points.

You should demonstrate your logical thought process and ability to think on your feet, as these are qualities which the interviewer will be looking for. It is usually unlikely that you will be able to prepare and predict the topic of the question that will come out in the interview so you should focus on developing skills like being able to argue for and against your position as well as presenting a clear and compelling position.

A good applicant would clearly state the law they think is broken most frequently and the brief reasons for their position. They should also, if they can, provide some real-life examples as evidence in support. They could also present counter- arguments that might arise to their proposal and how they would resolve these in favour of their position.

A **sample** answer is as follows: I think that littering is a law broken most frequently. We are all guilty of having littered at least once in our life and if this was multiplied by even 90% of the population this would be the law that was broken most frequently. While laws like underage drinking and speeding might also be other laws broken frequently, there are sections of the population such as people of drinking age and people without cars whom the offence would not apply to. Littering applies to a wider range of people.

A **poor applicant** might not be able to explain why they decided a certain law was most frequently broken or not go into enough detail. They might say something generic like "I think speeding is a law broken the most because many people speed" and fail to explain why. Whilst speeding is a perfectly acceptable answer to this question, it is important to be able to explain your reasons. You could say that speeding is frequent because a lot of people on the earth own a car and be able to contrast it to another similar offence like jaywalking and why speeding is more frequently broken.

It is important that the interviewer is able to see your thought process or where you derived your ideas from, so they are able to engage with you in conversation and further develop their impression of you.

Q82: Do you think that the state should pass laws governing what we can eat? What laws would you introduce to combat obesity?

This question is designed to see whether an applicant can formulate convincing and practical laws. The laws you propose must be backed up with good reasons and you must be able to explain why you decided to propose such laws. It is likely that your interviewer will play the devil's advocate so do not be put off if they press you on certain points.

You should demonstrate your logical thought process and ability to think on your feet, as these are qualities which the interviewer will be looking for. It is usually unlikely that you will be able to prepare and predict the topic of the question that will come out in the interview so you should focus on developing skills like being able to argue for and against your position as well as presenting a clear and compelling argument.

A **good applicant** would clearly state their proposed law and the brief reasons for their position. They should also, if they can, provide some real-life examples as evidence in support. They could also present counter- arguments that might arise to their proposal and how they would resolve these in favour of their position.

A **sample** answer is as follows: I would introduce a law to regulate advertising, food and presentation. Research has shown that individual food choices are associated with cultural and socio-economic circumstances and can be manipulated through advertising and presentation. As food choice is one of the main factors contributing to obesity, law can help curb obesity if it can redirect consumers to eat more healthy food. This might be in requiring certain food categorised "unhealthy" to have plain packaging or limit their ability to advertise in certain spaces.

A **poor applicant** might not explain why they decided to introduce a certain law or not go into enough detail. They might say something generic like "I would introduce a law requiring more people to exercise" with no actionable steps or clear reasons. It is important that the interviewer can see your thought process or where you derived your ideas from so that they are able to engage with you in conversation and further develop their impression of you.

Q83: What does law have to do with the environment?

This question is an opinion-based question designed to see whether an applicant can formulate convincing arguments in favour of a certain position. It is likely that your interviewer will play the devil's advocate so do not be put off if they press you on certain points.

You should demonstrate your logical thought process and ability to think on your feet, as these are qualities which the interviewer will be looking for. It is usually unlikely that you will be able to prepare and predict the topic of the question that will come out in the interview so you should focus on developing skills like being able to argue for and against your position as well as presenting a clear and compelling argument.

A **good applicant** would clearly state their opinion/position and the brief arguments for their position. They should also, if they can, provide some real-life examples as evidence in support. They could also present counter- arguments to their position and how they would resolve these in favour of their position.

A **sample** answer is as follows: I think there are several reasons why we bother with environmental protection. The main reason is for human health and all the other reasons can be linked to this. The state of the environment largely impacts our current and future quality of life. It is in our bests interests that we help maintain a healthy and functional ecosystem. As the climate change is quickly becoming a problem for our generation, it is imperative that we take serious steps to protect the environment if we want to live comfortable lives in the future and for future generations.

We also bother with environmental protection to protect the earth we live on. We currently are currently not able to live on any other planet. This is imperative to ensure that we do not go extinct as a race. We also bother because we might want to preserve the natural beauty of the earth for us to continue enjoying.

At this point it is likely that the interviewer will interject and ask you more questions about what you said.

A **poor applicant** might give an unbalanced argument or not defend their position well. For example, they might misinterpret the question and argue for or against environmental protection without addressing the part of the question that asks for your opinion on the issue. The question specifically asks why we bother – you must tell the interviewer why you think people bother with it not just generic arguments for and against environmental protection.

Q84: What is a country?

This question is a rather open-ended question designed to see how you define a term. This seemingly easy question is rather complex! It is an important skill for a law student as you would often have to define vague terms in your essays concisely and succinctly. You can impress the interviewer by giving both the surface-level and alternative definitions (with examples). This shows that you can go beyond the surface definition and demonstrate depth in your thinking and answer.

Don't worry too much if you do not know the 'right' answer or have the 'right' arguments/content which would have required a lot of research. It is better and advisable to focus on the way you **structure** and **approach** it. The interviewer is also likely to be able to help you out or guide you if you are stuck.

A **good applicant** would first give a layman definition before delving into the deeper meaning or alternative definitions/grey areas to this term. A good applicant will be able to see that there are many layers to this word and be able to concisely explain this to the interviewer.

A **sample** answer is as follows: There is no universally agreed definition to 'country' and the definition varies depending on various factors. For political reasons, there are examples of countries which do not recognise other 'countries' as such. For example, Taiwan claims to be a country, but China does not recognise it as such and sees Taiwan as another part of China. As a result, other countries who do not want to maintain good relationships with China might choose to also not recognise Taiwan as a country.

A common definition of country is one with a population, a defined territory, a government and capacity to enter in relations with other states. But there are many people who oppose to this definition and prefer the definition that if enough countries recognise you as a country, you are one despite not having control over territory or your population. Another common way may be that if a place is a member of the UN, it's a country. But this definition is problematic as Vatican City is considered a country but is not a member of the UN.

A **poor applicant** might give a long and simplistic answer. It is not how much or how quickly you speak in an interview but the quality of your answer that is important. You should, as much as possible, give a concise answer that addresses the question.

MEDIEVAL AND MODERN LANGUAGES

At the start of a subject interview for Modern Languages, an applicant may be asked to discuss a short text in the target language which will have been presented to them shortly before the interview.

During the preparation time, you will have been expected to read through the text thoroughly and to **ready yourself for a short discussion** of its main ideas and features.

When reading through the text and preparing for discussion:

- If you don't understand every word in the passage you've been given, then don't panic. It is probably supposed to be difficult and applicants are not expected to have already achieved fluency in the language they wish to study.

- Apply the knowledge you have acquired at A-Level and from wider reading to unfamiliar scenarios. You may not recognise the text you have been asked to read, but that is probably deliberate.

- Think about the style of the text. You may not be told its source, so you will have to engage critically to decide what sort of text it might be. Does the style reflect that or an article or an extract from a novel? Does the type of language tell you anything about what time period the text might be from?

- Pick out parts of the text that you find interesting. The interviewers will be keen to see evidence of your personal response to the text. Is there an idiomatic phrase which you particularly like? Does a certain line remind you of another text you have already read? What effect does the passage and its use of language have on you as a reader?

- The interviewer will want to see that you've tried to read and comprehend the text as best you can, and also to have engaged critically with it.

- If there is a word or concept you don't understand, talk these harder texts through carefully and the interviewer will help you reach an answer. Be prepared to accept some help and assistance from the interviewer - that is no bad thing.

- Remember, making mistakes is normal. If you have misinterpreted a word or an idea, the important point is that you address the mistake head on and attempt to revise the statement, with the assistance of the tutors where necessary.

- Following a short discussion of the text, subsequent questions will reflect the various different elements of the Modern Languages course.

This interview will require you to demonstrate passion and a genuine desire to study your chosen subject, so be prepared to voice your personal interests beyond those mentioned in your personal statement. Material mentioned on your personal statement can be used as a starting point for the conversation.

The tutors know what topics you have studied at A-Level within your chosen subjects. *They will **not** ask you for detailed knowledge about areas of your subject that you are unfamiliar with.* Nobody knows every aspect of their subject.

An applicant will most likely be asked about their reading/engagement with cultural material in their chosen language areas. It is worth emphasising that the Modern Languages courses at Oxbridge privilege the study of literature and applicants will be expected to have pursued their personal interests beyond the remit of their A Level/IB/Pre-U syllabus, even if they have not had the opportunity yet to study literature at school.

Learning a New Language

At both Oxford and Cambridge, there is the option to learn a new language *ab initio*. If one of the languages you have applied for is one which you have not previously studied, then you will be expected to demonstrate your curiosity and enthusiasm for learning it. You will not be expected to have developed knowledge of the language, but **you will be expected to have made a decent attempt at learning some of the basics** and engaging with the culture of its speakers.

What Questions Might Be Asked?

Most of the questions asked in the interview will be broad, allowing the candidate to use them as a springboard for discussing their personal interests.

Smaller sub-questions may be used by the interviewer to prompt and guide the candidate into an active discussion.

The main question may seem difficult, impossible or random at first, but take a breath and start discussing with your interviewer different ideas you have for breaking down the question into manageable pieces. Don't panic. **The questions are designed to be difficult** to give you the chance to show your full intellectual potential. They will help guide you to the right idea if you provide ideas for them to guide. This is your chance to show your creativity, analytical skills, intellectual flexibility, problem-solving skills and your go-getter attitude. Don't waste it on nervousness or a fear of messing up or looking stupid.

As well as specific questions about a book, the course or a topical issue in the language-speaking country, applicants may be asked questions of a more philosophical nature. These questions will not have one specific answer, rather they will serve as an opportunity for the applicant to consider an idea.

The interviewers will be looking for inquisitive minds that can engage creatively with new problems. Don't be afraid to present your trains of thought out loud- the interviewer will be just as interested in seeing *how* you tackle the question as to the response you give. Often, the interview is most concerned with **how** you think and how you tackle difficult and challenging problems.

WORKED QUESTIONS

Below are a few examples of how to start breaking down an interview question, complete with model answers.

Q1: Is silence something we can hear?

With a more abstract question such as this, it is best to try and talk through your thought process, engaging with the question and applying logic as best as you can to work through your ideas. If you are thrown by a question, start by linking it back to your subject. Think about the question in relation to the study of languages.

It's a good idea to start by thinking about the subject of the question. A solid piece of advice for any humanities student- start by questioning the question:

What is silence? How do we define silence? How do we experience silence? What is the opposite of silence? Is silence a sound? Is silence a state independent of a listener? Does silence depend on an ear?

Asking these types of things out loud will demonstrate your active engagement with the original question.

Q2: How would you define language?

With broad questions such as these, it can be useful to **draw upon specific examples** to back up your argument. Try to analyse the role of language in day to day speech and how that compares, for example, to the *language* as seen in a poem/text you have recently read. What are the common defining features of language? What are the differences seen in its usage according to context?

Think about what constitutes a language, the uses and limitations of language, and the role and nature of communication structures.

Follow up questions may include: "Do you need more than one speaker for a language to exist?" And, "Is a language only a language if it is spoken?"

Q3: What does a nation's literature tell us?

This question provides an opportunity to demonstrate a real enthusiasm for critically engaging with literature - this is important as literature features heavily on the Oxbridge Modern Languages Courses.

With a question as broad as this, a strong response would **use a framework** in order to engage more incisively with the key issues at stake (the role of literature, the place of literature in the society, the relationship of literature to a given society). For example:

Nation and narration are inextricably linked. Literature creates a narrative for a society and its people. It can provide an aperture into new worlds: their cultural specificities, mindset, and histories.

From my initial engagements with literature from Latin America -namely readings of poems by Neruda- I have been struck by the ability of the writer to cast an eye onto the parallel worlds of his nation. In his verse, we find commentary on Chilean politics, embedded within a lyric which references the heritage of past civilisations.

I have read sections from the first and final parts of *Alturas de Machu Pichu* (1945). Here, in entering into a dialogue with his nation's ancestry, Neruda both celebrates the achievement of Machu Picchu and condemns the exploitative slavery that made it possible. Furthermore, In *Canto XII of his Canto General* - considered one of the greatest political poems of the last century- Neruda calls upon the dead to be born again and to speak through him. In doing so, he references the power of literature to connect us not only to the present but to a nation's past.

Q4: How would you discretise language from linguistics?

This question encourages a **technical response**, demonstrating the candidate's understanding of the broad theoretical terminology that underpins their subject.

A well-structured answer may begin by defining language and linguistics. The candidate will then draw the two definitions into dialogue in order to address the original question of 'difference'. The best responses may also reference eminent theorists of language.

Language is a system of signs which serves to enable the communication between beings. According to Noam Chomsky, language is a "set of sentences, each finite in length, and constructed out of a finite set of elements." And Aronoff states that "it is impossible to separate language from literature, or politics, or most of our everyday human interactions." (2007)

Linguistics is the scientific study of language. The difference is that as a discipline of study, it applies itself to language. It is to explain language; it references and analyses the working mechanisms of these systems of signs. According to Aitchison, linguistics "has a twofold aim: to uncover general principles underlying human language, and to provide reliable descriptions of individual languages." (1992)

Q5: Will automatic translation software make human translators redundant?

This question will allow a good candidate the opportunity to engage critically with pertinent questions in the current climate of language learning. It encourages the candidate to also consider its underlying question- what is the need for learning languages today?

Thanks to the internet, we live in an increasingly interconnected world. Technology has been said to 'shrink' the world, bringing us closer together through instant means of communication. What's more, technology has been employed for the purposes of **transcending linguistic barriers** to communication, through innovations in computerised translation.

The availability of devices such as Google Translate and other translation apps force us to consider whether machines will ever be able to fully replace human translators. However, because languages are complex and nuanced, **words are often defined and understood according to a given context**. It seems unlikely that a machine alone could ever replicate the job of the human translator.

Through an article I read on Foreign Tongues, The Market Research Translation Agency, I was introduced to a program called Unbabel, which is a combination of technology and crowd-sourced human translation.

Unbabel first uses computers to translate a customer's inquiry and then splits it into micro-tasks for its human translators to refine and check for errors. Unbabel then puts the text together and sends it back. Customers can send and receive their text through email, online or through Unbabel's API.

So, when it comes to documents demanding accurate translation to the level of a native speaker, it seems unlikely that software as rudimentary as Google Translate will ever be able to replace the human translator. Another way to engage with this question would be to implicate literature and the poetic voice.

Our use of language in accordance with aesthetic parameters (forms, rhyme, allegory, metaphor, simile, idiom) render literary language resistant to the face-value translations of the machine.

Q6: What do you think are the main differences between Latin American Spanish and European Spanish.

This question encourages both a **historical contextualization** and **technical understanding** of the Spanish language.

A good candidate will be able to demonstrate their understanding of this linguistic colonial legacy and its relation to the development of Latin American Spanish. They will also be able to cite some specific examples of the difference between Latin American and European Spanish:

When Spanish colonisers travelled the world, they brought with them a language that was in the process of changing back at home. A linguist called Marckwardt came up with the term "colonial lag" to describe a situation where the language spoken in colonies does not keep up with innovations in the language in its country of origin. An example in English would be the use of 'fall' in the USA and 'autumn' in Britain; when British colonisers went to America, 'fall' was more common than the Latin version in British English. The older, Germanic word 'fall' later became obsolete in Britain but has remained in common use in the USA. This process happens with vocabulary but also with grammar. Later on, immigrant groups from different parts of Europe brought linguistic traditions with them to Latin America. In turn, these groups met different local linguistic traditions, creating variations in local dialects.

One of the clearest examples of that process is the **use of 'vos'**, primarily in Argentina, Paraguay and Uruguay. Originally, a second-person plural, vos came to be used as a more polite second-person singular pronoun among one's familiar friends. It was commonly used in Spanish when the language reached the southern cone of the Americas. It fell out of use in Spain but stayed in Rioplatense Spanish. Nowadays, just like 150 years ago, at a bustling Buenos Aires café, you are much more likely to be asked "de donde sos?" than "de donde eres?"

Then, there is the question of pronunciation: in many parts of Central America, 's' isn't always pronounced and in Argentina, the 'double-l' that is usually pronounced like the 'y' in yellow is pronounced like the 's' in measure.

Q7: What have you been doing on your A Level course?

This is another example of a question that may be used to put you at ease. Good responses to these questions will not simply list the various tasks and materials engaged with on the course. Rather, they might draw upon one or possibly two areas which have been of particular interest and talk about these in more detail.

"This term we have studied a piece of literature for the first time. We are looking at Sartre's *Huis Clos*. I have particularly enjoyed engaging with the fundamentals of existentialist philosophy through the medium of theatre.

"In fact, during the half-term break, I went to see a production of the play in London in order to help conceive the text more fully as a dramatic piece. I was interested to see in the performance the use of space and shape formations between the three characters to demonstrate the relational power-shifts within the trio.

"I was also intrigued by the Valet, a character 'without-eyelids'. As the only character to move in and out of the closed room, entering with each of the characters, I thought we might read his unbreakable stare as a reflection of the unbreakable gaze within, of Estelle offering herself as a mirror and of the definition of self in relation to the other."

The interviewer may then pose further questions about the play, the eyelids, existentialism etc.

Q8: How would you say that your travel has affected relationship with language?

Questions about travel are frequently asked in modern languages interviews- which is not to say that extensive travel is by any means expected of a candidate. Evidently, those who have partaken in excursions, school trips, exchanges or gap year travels will be able to reference these experiences. However, an absence of these opportunities will not put a candidate at a disadvantage.

A question such as this, above all, seeks to engage with the motivations for learning another language. When drawing from travel experience - or thinking ahead to future travel aspirations- what the candidate should consider is:

- What does it *mean* to communicate - in its broadest sense?
- What does it mean to communicate with speakers of a different language?
- How much of a nation's culture manifests itself in language?
- Does language provide an access point to that culture? How?

Q9: How would you define language?

Here, the greatest challenge lies in the **broadness of the question**. This is a subject which has been central to philosophical interrogation.

The important thing to keep in mind here is that sometimes the applicant's first response serves only as a discussion starter. There is no need to include everything you would want to talk about, the interviewers only want to hear a few points they can start from. They will then drive the discussion in the direction they want to.

It is perfectly reasonable for the application to ask for a minute to consider the question and organise their thoughts.

Candidates should try to move beyond the '**system of communication**' answer, perhaps by showing their awareness of theoretical problematizations of language:

- Estimates of the number of languages in the world: 5,000-7,000
- What constitutes a language? They can be spoken, signed, encoded.

Depending on their interests, the candidate may wish to reference the philosophy of languages, drawing upon the works of key thinkers of the 20th century: Wittgenstein, who argued that philosophy itself is really the study of language; or with regards linguistics, they could reference Saussure's distinction between sign and symbol or the work of Chomsky.

Q10: Can you tell me three reasons that reading could be considered dangerous?

Antagonistic questions such as this are often unexpected and as such, unprepared for. This is part of the exercise- to see how candidates respond and process a completely new stimulus. The interviewer will primarily be interested in the thought processes behind your response. With a question such as this, a stimulating response may manifest as a working through the various possible ways of interpreting the question:

"Of course, we could on one level, consider this question in terms of pure practicality: we don't know how badly it can affect our **eyesight**…although I'm quite certain that's more to do with **Vitamin D and sunlight exposure**… so perhaps reading is at its most dangerous when done inside. Then there is the **environment**, and **increasing paper shortages**.

"But it's not just the act of reading, it's also a question of the material being read. Propaganda is certainly dangerous. The disseminated written word, when imbued with malice or political agency, can become a potent form of contagion."

Q11: What was it about this book (mentioned in Personal Statement) that particularly caught your attention?

Questions framed in this manner are designed to elicit personal responses to cultural material. The interviewer will be interested to hear specifically about your reaction to the text in question. Giving opinions and backing them up with reference to parts of the text will be expected. The level of detail into which a candidate is able to go will demonstrate their level of preparation.

"Cien Años de Soledad" was unlike any other book I have ever read. Through it, I have been introduced to magical realism and its distinctive form of narrative. To me, it felt a bit like lucid dreaming.

"Despite having difficulty initially with keeping a firm grasp on the plot as it unfolded, due to the number of similarly-named characters, I learnt to stop resisting such confusions, but rather embrace them as a crucial and intentional part of García Márquez's cyclical narrative.

"For me, it was striking to encounter a textual narrative which allowed for forms of linear progression and other treatments of time, which perhaps can be seen to allegorise the metaphor of history as a circular phenomenon, seen through the recurrent characteristics in the six generations of José Arcadio and Aureliano.

"On a further note, Macondo's turn in the final chapter from a city of mirrors to a city of mirages can perhaps be read as a reflexive comment on the nature of literature itself."

It is likely that the interviewer will interrupt the candidate during this response, **commenting in reaction to the points** raised: "In what way did this compare to lucid dreaming?" or "What do you consider to be the effects of this cyclical narrative?" or "What do you mean by the nature of literature, how so?

FURTHER QUESTION AREAS

If the applicant has mentioned linguistics as an area of interest, questions to do with the nature of language itself may also be posed. It may be worth looking at recent controversies/new schools of emergent thought in this field.

It has also become common for interviewers to ask about the changing status of language in the modern world and the position/role/importance of multilingualism in an age of increasing globalisation. Consider crucial turning points in this narrative- the internet as a space for global communication etc. Think about why you still value the importance of learning new languages. What does it mean to study languages today?

Q12: Why do you think we see such variation in the number of tenses between different languages?

In this question, the interviewers are gauging your ability to identify some of the differences in the grammatical complexity of the languages you are applying for, and, in turn, between those languages and English. This is a particularly good opportunity if you are applying to study languages from different language families, as this will enable you to draw some really interesting points of comparison, say between German and Italian, or French and Arabic. Even if you are applying for an *ab initio* language, and you have not yet studied the tenses or grammar of that language, it would prove beneficial to demonstrate that you have undertaken at least a preliminary survey of language, so that you can show that you know what you will be facing as a beginner. Does your *ab initio* language rely on verb inflections, or word markers to indicate tense?

Furthermore, the question allows you to demonstrate curiosity about languages beyond the few that you have studied so far. For example, it would be impressive to show that you have read about Mandarin and how it employs time markers rather than verb tenses in order to indicate differences between the Past, Present and Future, even if you do not intend to study that language. It would be equally impressive to question whether or not a language *needs* to have many tenses and a complex grammar in order to be an 'effective' language. Is Japanese necessarily a more 'effective' language than Esperanto, an artificial language designed with simplicity in mind?

A **good answer** would start by explaining the purpose of a tense — to distinguish between time periods, such as Present, Past and Future. It would then explain that many Indo-European languages have complex verb conjugations, with many different tenses communicating subtle temporal shifts. For instance, French has seven different past tenses, many of which have fallen into disuse. A good answer would then contrast this with another language; even just English. It might then be remarked that it is curious how, despite the supposed universality of how humans experience time, it can often be very difficult to translate tenses from one language into another.

It would then be beneficial to hypothesise why this has occurred. An **awareness of the cultural and historical backdrop to your particular languages** is key here. Even a comparison between close languages can prove fruitful. For instance, it would be useful to show an awareness that the use of the *passé simple* in French has been almost completely relegated to literature and very formal situations, whereas the equivalent in Spanish, the *pretérito*, is an intrinsic part of even the most colloquial speech. Could differing perceptions of formality be a cause of this divergence? Could standards of education be better? Is it true that languages with more complex grammars, such as standard Italian, are often derived from complex literary traditions accessible to only a few elites? Is it possible that languages with less complex grammars have richer oral literatures, where vocabulary, context, sound and imagery are more important than fine grammatical nuance?

A **poor answer** would lack awareness of how tenses are conveyed in different languages, and make it appear as though it is the first time the candidate has tried to compare their languages. It would show an assumption that languages are more or less grammatically similar, and a lack of sensitivity to the cultural contexts of the languages which they intend to study. Above all, it would betray a lack of curiosity about the question. It is essential to appear enthusiastic about the questions posed and the issues they raise.

Q13: Will the total number of languages in the world change over the next 100 years?

For this question, interviewers are looking to draw out your knowledge of the wider social/political/historical context which languages exist in, and examine what leads to language death, and, conversely, language creation. Although there is no single correct answer, it would be much more reasonable to argue that the number of languages will decrease.

A **good answer** will indicate an awareness of the languages you study in what is an increasingly interconnected world where English has become a global lingua franca for international communication, with a few other languages such as Mandarin, Spanish, French, and Arabic occupying dominant positions too. As such, anecdotes of lexical borrowings from English into your chosen languages would be good evidence to show the prevalence of English. However, there is a huge difference between simple lexical borrowing and language death. Indeed, many people are brought up bilingual, speaking a minority language at home and learning another to facilitate interactions with the wider world. Take, for instance, Aboriginal communities in Australia. This does not always lead to the death of the minority language over time, although the United States is a case in point for how minority languages usually die out over the generations.

A **good answer** would look at emigration, cultural assimilation, prestige, accessibility and political upheaval, among other factors, to explain why so many minority languages have dwindling native speakers. To take the example of political upheaval, it would be good to explain how the concept of nations is actually a European political phenomenon, and how the need to create a national identity has often entailed the enforcement of one single language, or just a few languages, to aid the assimilation of myriad different ethnic group. For instance, Castilian Spanish is now commonly accepted as the single language of the nation of Spain, and several of its minority languages are dwindling: Aragonese and Galician for instance. However, a good answer would also note that it is not all one-sided, and that some language revival initiatives have been successful. Catalan for example, once suppressed under Franco's regime, is now thriving in north-east Spain. This is still nevertheless an exception to the trend. A good answer might also touch on creole languages, or even draw historical comparisons to empires such as Rome and the spread of Vulgar Latin.

A **poor answer** would reflect little thought of the place the languages you wish to study occupy in the world. It would show little knowledge of the factors dictating language use and not treat the question as an interesting one. It may show a lack of awareness of the pressures which languages face, and what increasing globalisation means for them, or assume that language use does not change over time.

Q14: What can you learn from an accent?

This question is an excellent one to show off your knowledge of the cultural sensitivities in English and the languages you wish to study. Care must be taken not to give the impression that the assumptions we make of somebody based on their accent are necessarily always correct.

A good answer would start by explaining how what we infer from someone's accent depends just as much on our own prejudices and subjective experiences as it does on any fact. That said, accent can give use many clues to an individual's identity, occupation and geographical origin, but also their social aspirations.

For instance, many individuals in the UK attempt to use a 'standard' English accent in business contexts to give an aura of professionalism, or when dealing with non-native English speakers. A good answer would question why we place great value on authenticity and why fake accents can provoke such different reactions — from laughter when a comedian attempts a Welsh accent, to scorn when a Scot attempts to sound 'posh'. It would also indicate that these assumptions can often be unjustified, and arguably what we infer is a hindrance more than a help.

A good answer would then explain how we are stripped of the clues which accents in our native language give us when we learn a new language. This is because we have to learn these cultural stereotypes and biases from scratch. If, say, you were applying for ab initio Italian, you would be blind to the assumptions conveyed in a rural farm worker's accent, and likely not able to distinguish the accent from that of a bourgeois politician. You would then question whether it is right for you as a non-native speaker to let these acquired stereotypes colour your own judgment of people. Has it changed the accent you adopt in your chosen languages?

A poor answer would assume that the same stereotypes and accents in our mother tongue can be found in other languages. For instance, it would assume that Mandarin, French and Icelandic all have an equivalent of 'posh', and that the baggage that that a 'posh' accent in English can be readily translated. It would also suggest that somebody's accent is necessarily a reliable indicator of that individual's personality and qualities. A poor answer would not convey how accents can carry lots of different connotations and can also be a major source of identity.

Q15: How would you simplify English?

This question allows you to show the interviewers how well you are able to reflect on your knowledge of English, of its peculiarities, in addition to giving you the opportunity to compare it to the other languages of which you have a solid grasp.

It would be **good to start this answer** by quickly addressing the question of whether or not English needs to be simplified at all. One possible argument for simplification is that it would become simpler to learn, especially for foreign students, and one possible argument against simplification is that it could have the adverse effect of needlessly eliminating the many nuances of English and the traces of its historical development. Once this preliminary issue has been addressed, a good answer would continue by picking out any particular features of the English language which jump out as unusual, or unnecessary. It would be particularly useful to pull out some examples from any translation work you may have done. For instance, you may have noticed that English spelling is somewhat irregular, that it often has multiple adjectives meaning the same thing, or its phrasal verbs are notoriously challenging for non-native speakers. A comparison can then be established with any languages you have studied. For example, Spanish spelling is much more uniform, but verbs in French have many possible conjugations, and there are three noun genders in German. Perhaps this comparison could lead to you reflect on the development of Modern English from Old English. Modern English is in many ways already much simplified — it has lost grammatical gender, and most of its inflectional forms already.

A **poor answer** would indicate to the interviewers that your study of foreign languages has never led you to reflect on your own mother tongue. In this way, a poor answer would not have many solid examples to draw from and would not be able to establish a comparison with English and another language. It would also fail to reflect on the purpose of simplification, since this can lead to an interesting discussion in its own right.

Q16: What's so complex about translating something like the Bible?

In this question, the interviewers are looking for you to highlight some of the major factors which translators must take into consideration when translating. This is an excellent opportunity for you to demonstrate knowledge of some of the difficulties which translators face when they have to find a compromise between meaning, style and context. It is also an excellent opportunity for you to demonstrate your knowledge of what makes texts like the Bible so challenging to translate — the fact that it has multiple authors, was composed over different centuries and its passages, at least in its modern versions, have been translated from other languages already. There is no original, singular 'Bible'.

A **good answer** would state that texts like the Bible have so many different forms, so many different authors and have been translated from so many different languages that they are in effect a huge intertextual document. Indeed, it would be very difficult to identify a single source text from which to translate! A good answer would also highlight the fact that a translator must consider his target audience. Is the objective to make the Bible's teachings more accessible to a larger audience, in the vein of Martin Luther? Would this be at the expense of losing many of its nuances and historical details? Would this stray too far from the text, and be considered an alteration on the original? Or is the objective to render such documents as faithfully as possible, at the risk of sacrificing intelligibility and of shutting out the layman? Indeed, for religious texts like the Bible which have so many disparate interpretations, the act of translation could add layers of meaning which were not intended in the first place, or, conversely, miss out important nuances in the original, which would in effect butcher the text. How would you translate idioms from the original? How do you make the text culturally intelligible to a modern readership, without straying too far? It would be beneficial to make reference to other texts 'like the Bible': say other religious texts, or any other text which has a long and complex history spanning many cultures.

A **poor answer** would fail to articulate any of the major facets of a text which a translator should pay particular attention to besides meaning, such as tone, imagery, sound, formality and accessibility. It would also not examine what makes texts like the Bible particularly difficult, such as its many versions, that fact that the source text may have already been translated multiple times, its multiple authors, and its myriad different interpretations.

Q17: What are the differences and similarities between Spanish and Portuguese.

Spanish and Portuguese are well known for being very similar lexically, even more so than other Romance languages such as French or Italian. In this question, interviewers will of course be interested in hearing about their similarities, but they will be particularly keen to see what differences you are able to find between the two.

A **good answer** would state at the outset that, on the written page, the two languages look very similar. They have very high lexical similarity, and arguably a Spanish speaker would be able to understand the gist of a Portuguese written text with some perseverance, and vice versa, without having studied Portuguese. Indeed, verb inflections are very comparable too. However, one major disparity is in tense usage. Although present, imperfect and preterite tenses are broadly similar in usage, standard Portuguese uses more tenses than Spanish. Standard Portuguese employs the Future Subjunctive, which is more or less obsolete in Spanish save for a few idioms. Another example would be the Personal Infinitive, which is very common in Portuguese, and has no equivalent in Spanish. Besides verbs, the word order of Portuguese pronouns is more complex than it is in Spanish and have many inflectional forms.

A **good answer** would also remark on how divergent standard spoken Portuguese is from standard spoken Spanish. Portuguese is notably more nasal, and not as stress-timed as standard spoken Spanish is. Both languages have a very wide range of spoken dialects, such as Brazilian and Angolan Portuguese, or Cuban and Chilean Spanish. Brazilian Portuguese has significant vocabulary differences and idiomatic grammatical choices from standard Portuguese, whereas Spanish dialects tend not to have split to such a significant degree. An exception would be Argentinian Spanish, which uses 'vos', has significant Italian vocabulary influence and a particularly divergent accent (the pronunciation of 'll' for instance).

A **less impressive answer** would struggle to locate areas of difference, implying that the use of tenses and grammar is broadly similar (which is not the case). It would lack an awareness of the languages as they are used globally, outside the Iberian peninsula. Furthermore, it would stick to generalisations without making any specific insights, neglecting to home in on particular words or usage differences.

Q18: What do you think makes one language easier to learn than others?

In this question, interviewers are testing your ability to draw out the various aspects of language learning which are necessary to form a full grasp of the language being studied. It is a good opportunity to highlight areas of the languages you wish to study at Cambridge which you have found easier, and, conversely, more challenging. An honest answer is best here — it will not impress anybody to say that you find every aspect of the language easy!

A **strong answer** would start by referencing some of the aspects which make one language easier than another. An obvious example is languages which share common vocabulary, common grammar, or similar sounds. For instance, Dutch will likely be easier on all of these fronts than Japanese. There are many cognates in English and Dutch, a related grammar and many similar sounds. Japanese, aside from anglicisms, will have no common vocabulary, a completely new grammar and many new sounds to learn how to pronounce. A good answer would build on this by saying that cultural fluency is an equally important factor in how easy a language to learn. Many European cultures share core fundamental values and a shared history which poses less of a cultural barrier, whereas if you were learning a regional South American language or an Aboriginal Australian language you would likely have make significant cultural adjustments to know how to correctly use the language. You may be able to draw on your own experiences from a cultural perspective.

A **poor answer** would try to pretend that you have never faced any challenges with language learning or would stick to the obvious factor (vocabulary similarity) without exploring some of the more interesting aspects, such as cultural distance, phonetic challenges (such as tone systems) or grammatical novelty (new moods or structures for formality). It would also lack specific examples from your own language learning or lack suggestions for how you tackle the more challenging aspects (such as spaced repetition or immersion).

Q19: What is the big deal about fluency? Isn't being able to be understood enough?

In this question, the interviewers will be able to ascertain your reasons for studying languages at university level and assess whether or not your aspirations are realistic! This question will allow you to explore some of the opportunities that a more fluent grasp of a language will grant you — such as access to literature, history or general culture.

A **good answer** would explain that basic communication is not the sole benefit of learning a language. Granted, communication is the most fundamental aspect of a language, and a basic command of a language will allow you to navigate through a new country or order something at a restaurant. However, it would be a good idea to explain that a deeper knowledge of a language allows you to communicate on a more personal, authentic level with a native speaker, and gain a much more insightful view of a particular culture. In this way, you are much better able to attempt to integrate when we are able to understand shades of meaning in a foreign language — from humour to particular nuances of speech which would be missed by a beginner. This takes us beyond the level of simply getting by, to potentially thriving. The ability to get to grips with literature, politics, or simply relate on a personal level to a native speaker leads to a much more enriching and authentic experience. Having said this, it would be a good idea to stress that you know that native-level fluency is very hard to acquire, and that you will perhaps always be learning new vocabulary or cultural knowledge after your formal study has come to an end. Examiners will appreciate this dose of realism, and the acknowledgment that simple fluency is a commendable goal in itself.

A **less strong answer** would not make reference to the various elements which an advanced grasp of a language offers to a student — from film, literature, politics to philosophy. These cultural aspects are the major focus of Modern Languages degrees, and a lack of interest in them would not put you in a good light. A weaker answer would also display a certain naivety to language learning, perhaps not expressing the idea that language learning is a lifelong process, and not explaining the difference between fluency and native-level fluency.

Q20: How does the German language shape people's mindsets in different ways to the Russian language?

This question is a test of your ability to identify some of the national stereotypes associated with Germany and Russia and examine them for any truth! You should be wary of making broad generalisations, and it will be necessary to deconstruct what 'German' and 'Russian' mean exactly.

A **strong answer** would begin by outlining some (potentially offensive!) stereotypes of the mindsets of Germans and Russians. Say, for instance, that Germans have a very practical mindset, whereas Russians are notoriously sullen. It would quickly point out that stereotypes, despite often having a grain of truth, do not account for the individual and can be more of a hindrance than a help. It would problematise the idea that there could be a single national mindset — Germany, for instance, is still a relatively young nation, and Russia is the world's largest nation made up of many distinct regional identities. In this way, it is deeply problematic to assume that every German thinks like Kant, or that every Russian thinks like Trotsky. Indeed, this is an excellent opportunity to highlight that individuals have many different identities, beyond their superficial nationality. For instance, a Catholic sheep farmer from Bavaria, or a Muslim Chechen from Grozny. Is nationality a good lens through which to judge a mindset? It is also a good opportunity to muse on the impact of language on mindset. Does an Austrian or Swiss-German speaker share a similar worldview to a *Hochdeutsch* speaker in Hamburg? Does an ethnic Russian living in Latvia have a share the mindset of a Latvian taught Russian at school? However, it would be useful to acknowledge that there are sometimes truths in characterisations of national mindsets.

A **weak answer** would make broad generalisations about Germans and Russians, or conversely, simply assume that all stereotypes are completely inaccurate. After all, many modules at university do choose to look at material through the lens of nationality. A poor answer would also fail to account for regional differences and fail to remark on the huge differences between national identity in Germany and Russian, even if both are ostensibly single nations. It would also fail to remark on the interesting question of how language may influence one's outlook.

Q21: What was the most recent film you saw?

This question is designed to catch you unawares and will assess how well you are able to talk about something which you may not have not formally studied, or be expecting to analyse in an interview! Unless the film is a particularly unsuitable choice, any film which you have seen recently and which you would be able to talk about in sufficient detail would be a good choice. Even if you believe the film is not 'high-brow' or 'too Hollywood', I would stress that it will still be a good choice because this can lead to interesting discussions on what is 'low' Art and 'high' Art, and if these are problematic categories. Interviewers will be just as interested in a Netflix film just as an Art film. What they are looking to see is your ability to analyse how films are constructed and how they can be 'read'.

A **good answer** would give a brief overview of plot, explaining succinctly the important events which occurred, so that the interviewers have their bearings in case they have not seen the film. It would then proceed to analyse various aspects of the film text which stand out to you as particularly engaging. Was there an unusual use of sound? Tone? Imagery? Silence? Shapes? Was the editing very slick, or draw attention to itself? Was its pace exciting, or boring? Did you identify with the protagonists, or was it full of clichés? Was it too self-conscious, or carbon-copy? Overall, what underlying message or tropes was it playing to, and was it successful in doing this? It would be particularly beneficial if you were able to link style to content or find areas of criticism where you think the film fell short. Perhaps the narrative or stock characters lack nuance. This is a question where you are likely to be in discussion with the interviewers, so be prepared to react spontaneously and defend your points of view.

A **poor answer** would be hazy on the details of the film, perhaps picking a film which you think would impress examiners, rather than one you are able to talk engagingly about. In this way, you would not be able to highlight particular scenes or sequences of interest. It would stick to a superficial analysis, focusing mainly on plot, without venturing into discussion on how the film is structured, edited and styled. It would also lack the ability to link up various elements of production — say sound and imagery — to identify the narrative which the director is trying to push. Above all, it would fail to react insightfully to the interviewers' interjections, sticking to safe territory rather than following the direction in which interviewers are trying to steer you.

Q22: What was it about this book in your statement which particularly caught your attention?

As this is a book which you have mentioned on your Personal Statement, the interviewers will assume that you are able to talk about it in quite a lot of depth. They will be looking at your ability to analyse a book beyond mere plot/character, and to be able to discuss elements of its style and themes in an engaging way. However, it is important not to sound like you are reciting a pre-rehearsed answer. Granted, you will have prepared aspects to discuss in advance, but it is important to keep the discussion natural, and be happy with the discussion going in a direction which you had not anticipated. The interviewers will be most interested in how you cope with discussion you have not prepared in advance.

A **good answer** would highlight a particular area of a text which you would most like to discuss — this is your main opportunity to steer the discussion in a way which suits you. Rather than focussing on a minute detail, it is best to start more broadly, homing in on the author's use of imagery, style, genre, or perhaps how he subverts particular expectations. The interviewers may pick up on the way you described the text in your Personal Statement, so be prepared to defend your point of view. It is better to have an opinion than to sit on the fence, although if you find yourself defending an indefensible point of view, it is better to concede! It is important to appear enthusiastic about the text, as a lack enthusiasm will not reflect well on your motivations for studying literature at a high level. You may find that the examiners try to push you into a corner or suggest points of view which you had not previously considered, so it is essential to not resist this and to be able to work with the information they volunteer to you.

A **poor answer** will stick to a pre-rehearsed response and fail to pick up on the points which the interviewers try to hint at. It will not work with the perspectives proposed by interviewers, lacking the ability to examine points of view which have not been prepared in advance. It will also lack confidence with textual details, for instance forgetting major events, or missing out key parts of any analysis, such as genre, or historical context. It is essential to be familiar enough with any text you mention on your Personal Statement so that you can discuss it confidently, pick out specific details, and defend your point of view. On the other side of the spectrum, it is best to not appear overly confident, or totally inflexible in your views.

Q23: What is 'language'?

This question is an open-ended one which is deigned to provoke open reflection, rather than have a defined answer. As an answer could cover many different topic areas, the interviewers will be looking at your ability to choose a few select areas and explain them in a coherent manner. As such, this is an assessment of your ability to create a clear, intelligent response from an unusual or very broad question, which is the case for many essay titles.

A **good answer** would be as honest as possible, rather than reeling off statements which you think are impressive but instead appear rather shallow. You may start from the premise that language is our instinctive means of self-expression and communication, but you could also state that we are able to self-express and communicate without language (say through art, or even with gesture/non-language sound). You may at this point broaden the scope of 'language' to include any medium which communicates: one can speak of filmic language, textual language, non-verbal language, even coding languages. Do languages have to communicate between beings? How does explain the fact that we talk to ourselves? Is human language an efficient means of communication, or can language actually impede communication? Perhaps you could conclude that language is an expression of power, and as such it can mislead just as well as it can inform.

A **poor answer** would stick to a very narrow definition of language, without interrogating the concept of language as a whole. It would struggle for inspiration, and not be able to give a personal response, instead sticking to rather superficial general points and lacking interesting content. The ability to define and expand on terms is key in answering any essay question. A poor answer would also come across as monotonous, seeing the question as a barrier rather than an opportunity to explore interesting ideas.

Q24: Has travelling changed the way you feel about language?

This question is potentially quite thorny if you have not been lucky enough to have travelled much, or to have travelled to a country where your chosen languages are spoken. As such, it is a good idea to think about the idea of travel more broadly, say even just in the U.K between cities or regions.

A **good answer** would pick out a couple of experiences and explain how they have made you think about the nature of language. Perhaps travelling has opened your eyes to the power of language (say how English is spoken in territories as far apart as New Zealand and Alaska) and how it can close borders, or conversely it has made you reflect on how vulnerable languages can be to external influences (say how English is now spoken more commonly than Welsh in most of Wales' regions). You might therefore think about how language has been used as a medium of cultural violence. How was it that Romance languages came to be spoken over such a wide area? How come French is spoken in many regions of West Africa? How come Mandarin Chinese is starting to take precedence over many regional languages in China? On the other side of the coin, travel may have inspired you to learn more languages because you realise how key language is so accessing a culture, or travel may have put you off a certain language because you did not enjoy your travel experience! It may have made you reflect on how certain languages are more useful than others when travelling, or you may have tried to make your English more neutral in order to communicate with somebody who is not a native speaker. Do you speak more slowly, or use simpler vocabulary? Do you find that travelling affects your command of your mother tongue?

A **less strong answer** would stick to some fairly cliché remarks — perhaps you have become aware of how many different languages there are, how key knowledge of multiple languages is to enable communication across borders, or simply how language facilitates travel. These are all perfectly acceptable observations, but they do not necessarily show any particular insight, or draw from personal examples.

Q25: What would you say were the principal components of a language?

This question assesses what you identify as the underlying characteristics and purpose of a language. As it is a broad question with no single answer, the interviewers will be looking at your ability to communicate a credible argument without getting muddled up in too many details or losing your thread. The key is to pick out a few key characteristics and critique them so as to establish whether or not a language necessarily has to have that particular characteristic to be considered a language.

A **good answer** would analyse the features that underpin our concept of language in common parlance. Does it have to be written? Does it have to be spoken? You may argue that a language has to follow a set of rules, else it would be gibberish, but this might not account for the fact that almost all human languages have exceptions to these "rules". Perhaps language goes beyond mere communication to self-expression, not necessarily needing to be understood by anyone else but yourself. Perhaps it is a conduit for emotions, or a manner or exerting influence on others. You may choose to broaden the term 'language' to include computer languages, which are not used in the same way as human languages and are ruthlessly logical — so much so that they may even be counterintuitive. You might conclude that a language usually has to communicate information from one entity to another.

A **poor answer** would be stumped by the question and not able to identify some of the features which make a language, language. It would lack the ability to think about language in a broader context, say non-verbal language, coding language, or even "language" in other animals. If the candidate is struggling to find a response, interviewers might suggest some avenues to follow, and this can be a positive, as it allows the candidate to demonstrate that they can think on their feet and work with a supervisor. If, however, a candidate fails to pick up on the hints, it would not be well received by the interviewers.

Q26: Would you agree with me that translation is reproduction?

This question is deliberately provocative, and interviewers are looking for you to be able to sustain an argument and defend it, albeit not to a ridiculous degree. As the objective of translation is commonly held to be the faithful reproduction of the original text into another language, it is necessary to state that translation is rarely as easy as that. Interviewers wish to assess how you approach translation.

A **good answer** would indicate that it is an unrealistic goal to be able to perfectly reproduce a text in another language. A translator will frequently have to find the best compromise between competing interests such as meaning, tone, style and historical context. A translator is not necessarily able to reproduce the historical or contextual ambiance of a text particular to a certain region into another. How, for instance, could you reproduce a Regency novel into Cantonese? Indeed, despite the cliché, some words are frequently seen as untranslatable: 'hygge' in Danish, *awkward* in English or 'dépaysement' in French. This poses an interesting question: does translation recreate a text, instead of merely reproducing it? What is the point of translation? Can a translated text actually improve on the original? You may choose to expand the scope of the word 'translation' to include shifting between media: how well does a novel translate to being portrayed in a TV series?

A **poor answer** would not rise to the challenge of creating an argument and would fail to tackle the loaded meaning behind 'reproduction'. Is a carbon-copy reproduction of a text necessarily what a translator should be aiming to achieve? In this sort of question, it is necessary to unpack the terms. A less strong answer would not be able to pick out some specific examples of where words cannot be translated into another language, or where an ambiance cannot be recreated in the translation. Have you come across any translations which you thought were particularly impressive/underwhelming? Are film adaptations always a faithful reproduction of the novel they use as source text?

Q27: What's the point of learning a language at all these days?

This is another deliberately provocative question. You could of course argue that there is no point in learning any other language since English is so dominant, but this would not necessarily reflect well on your application! Therefore, interviewers will be looking at your motives for studying foreign languages at a high level, and assessing your knowledge of globalisation.

A **good answer** would stress that there are myriad advantages and disadvantages to globalisation: for instance, it leads to increased inter-connectivity and, theoretically, a more cosmopolitan mindset, but it also leads to issues of hegemony, cultural erasure and vulnerability to external shocks. It would be a sensible idea to explain the position that a select few languages, such as English, French, Spanish and Arabic, have come to occupy in the world. If you have applied for one of these languages, be prepared to explain why you have not chosen a less global language, such as Croatian or Persian. If you can get by in basic English in locations as diverse as Portugal, Canada, Zambia and Pakistan, then what is the point of learning another language? Strong arguments would be that knowledge of another language enables you to engage more closely with particular cultures, access their literature and thought, or even form different perspectives on your own language and nation. Perhaps, more simply, you could make the point that English and other such global languages may be used on a superficial level to facilitate communication between two strangers, but that is the limit of their role. A native Urdu speaker would speak Urdu at home and a Brazilian Portuguese, even though it is likely they would both attempt to communicate in English. You may argue that the increasing interconnectivity of the world means that there is little excuse.

A **poor answer** would not offer compelling reasons for why languages still need to be studied despite the dominance of a select few. It would therefore appear that the candidate's choice of degree has not been informed by much reflection. You should appear motivated but the study of a language's culture, even if its language is not as dominant as some others. A less strong answer would not be able to pick out any particular contexts where certain languages are used/not used, or it would assume that globalisation is inevitable, and that language use does not change over time.

Q28: What's the relationship between the spoken and written word?

This question assesses how sensitive you are to differences between spoken and written forms of the same language. Key to your discussion here will be discussions of register. The interviewers will be looking at how aware you are of the differences in the languages which you intend to study, so you will need to pick out some examples from them.

A **good answer** would begin with one of the candidate's proposed languages. Say it were French, it would be beneficial to point out that there is quite a large difference between spoken and written forms of French. Standard written French is not usually an exact replica of speech: it is notably more formal and retains certain elements which are considered arcane or simply old-fashioned in speech. For instance, it is common to abbreviate 'tu as' to 't'as' in spoken language, whereas this sort of abbreviation would be very much frowned upon, or perhaps even misunderstood, in the written language, except in very informal messaging. It would be a good idea to explain that written French has not changed anywhere near as quickly as spoken language, making reference to certain novel features such as *verlan* or the use of anglicisms, and it would be worth referencing how the *Académie française* is seen as an increasingly irrelevant authority. It would be worth comparing this to any other languages you may have studied, or even English. How divergent are spoken forms of English from standard written English? How does that compare to Spanish/Italian/German? You could perhaps come to a conclusion, arguing that standard written forms of the language fail to capture the variety of spoken language, and that rules should be relaxed.

A **less strong answer** would struggle to identify areas of discrepancy between written and spoken forms of the languages the candidate wishes to study. This would suggest a lack of familiarity. It would also lack insight into how the written form of the language has developed: how recent has the language been standardised? Is there a standard spoken variant? How well do speech and writing reflect one another? It would also fail to establish a comparison between various languages.

Q29: What draws you to other cultures?

In this question, the interviewers are trying to gauge your interest in the cultures of the languages you wish to study, beyond obvious clichés such as the weather or food. The connection may be a personal one, or you may have never been to a country where the language is spoken, but this question is a good opportunity to discuss the various aspects of the culture which you have engaged with — say film, poetry or history.

A **good answer** would pick an area of the culture which they have already explored and which they would be willing to discuss. Perhaps you were attracted to an aspect which is very different from England, say the importance given to Philosophy in intellectual culture in France, or the huge diversity in dialects in Italy.

There may be areas of similarity, say between Scottish nationalism and Catalonian nationalism, or areas of divergence, say the status of minority languages in England and France. Is there a novel/poem/film/historical period which you have studied which relates to this and particularly interested you? If Spain's rapid progress from civil war and dictatorship to regional power has caught your attention, perhaps you could explain how this has been explored in modern literature, say Laforet's *Nada*, or in film, such as Erice's *El espíritu de la colmena*. Of course, there is no set answer here, so the interviewers will want to see how you have personally engaged with the cultures. Equally, there may be aspects which do not appeal so much to you — say a reputation for homogeneity, or a frustrating political situation/public debate which misses the bigger picture. You are not expected to like everything about the culture in France/Spain/Italy!

A **poor answer** would not be able to demonstrate engagement in the culture of the target language. For instance, a candidate may not have read any literature in the language, or their choice of literature/film may sound read like a teacher's list rather than one the candidate has chosen to explore personally. It is important in this question to appear engaged by the topics you choose to raise, as the interviewers are trying to ascertain your interest in the course. What is it which *you*, personally, like about the cultures? It is also important to go beyond the realm of clichés — what do France/Spain/Italy offer besides good weather and food?

Q30: You mentioned being fascinated by Latin American culture in your personal statement, but didn't elaborate on why - what would you say interests you the most about it?

In this question, examiners will be looking to see how you have explored the 'Latin American' culture which you have mentioned on your Personal Statement. Latin America is a hugely diverse area, so it will be necessary to break down this statement and show awareness that, just as, say, the United States is not culturally homogenous, nor is Latin America. It would be best to pick out a few texts (from art, film, poetry, novels or history) which you are familiar enough to discuss at interview.

A **good answer** would show the examiners that you have tried to engage with a variety of texts which come under the term of 'Latin American'. You may have studied poetry from Peru, a film from Colombia, or art in Bolivia, and it would be good to attempt to draw thematic parallels between them, if possible. Is there a focus on revolution? The magical? Memory? Indigenous issues? Exile? This would allow you to gesture at what attracts you to the region as a whole. A knowledge of historical context and contemporary issues would be excellent to draw on here. If, say, you chose to focus on Venezuela, you could explore Bolívar's legacy through to the quasi-dictatorship of Maduro. Or, if you have an interest in Mexico, you could discuss how Mexico's relationship with the United States is reflected in its culture. Perhaps you may have knowledge of Portuguese and Brazil too, which would allow you to add another perspective. It is important to stay away from stereotypes, such as a 'relaxed attitudes' or 'friendly people'. It may be beneficial to contrast the examples you use to those of other postcolonial territories which you are familiar with, such as the United States.

A **poor answer** would not problematise the term 'Latin American' and imply that the candidate assumes that 'Latin American' suffices as a term to explain the work of any Argentinian, Honduran or Mexican alike. It would fail to pick examples from a candidate's own studies to explain what they mean by Latin American, and it would lack comparisons/contrasts to other works of literature/film/art. For instance, it would fail to understand regional differences, or be unable to place an example in its historical context.

Q31: What role does language play in our identity?

This is a particularly thorny question, as it could provoke any manner of response, or become very abstract without any specific examples. As it is a very broad one, the interviewers will be looking at your ability to choose a select few points and to stick with them, giving a few examples to back up your claims. This way, the interviewers will be able to see how you structure an argument and avoid getting muddled up between different thoughts. Interviewers will be expecting you to question whether language does actually define our identity, or if indeed it is our identity which colours our language. Is our identity limited by our language?

A **good answer** would start with one particularly interesting facet of the relationship between language and identity, such as in cases where the use of a language which is endangered. Are there movements to increase use of the language? Say, with Welsh or Breton, does language serve to reinforce one's identity as Welsh/Breton even when a region has subsumed into a wider nation? Is someone less Welsh/Breton if they have spent all of their life in that territory, but only speak English/French? Perhaps you may conclude that the use of endangered languages can serve as a reaffirmation of identity, or that when a language dies out so does that cultural identity. How does that apply to second-generation immigrants, however? Should a monolingual American whose parents are Chinese not consider themselves as having any Chinese identity? How does this apply to cultures where multiple languages are spoken, but in different contexts? Say, for instance, an Ivorian businessman who speaks English when dealing internationally, French when dealing on a national level, and a regional language when in a domestic environment? Or, conversely, you could argue that the identity we strive for changes out use of language. You may change your accent in an effort to appear as though you are from a different socio-economic background, or you may be learning French in order to become more cultured, or to 'feel' more European, for instance. You might conclude that language use both defines, and is defined, by our identity. They are not static.

A **poor answer** would not problematise the question or seek to explore the tensions between language and identity. They are not discrete concepts, but a weaker candidate might assume that they in fact are completely separate. They might also not look at ways in which languages have been used as a tool to force an identity onto a people, or to erase an identity. A weaker answer may also not show awareness of the dwindling number of languages spoken, or how this question fits into the wider globalisation vs. regional identity debate. Equally, a weaker candidate might assume that someone cannot have multiple identities at the same time.

Q32: Tell me about the differences between French poetry and English poetry.

If you have mentioned that you have read French poetry in your Personal Statement, you should be prepared to know a couple of poems in sufficient depth to be comfortable discussing them at interview. In these questions, interviewers will be keen to see how you have reacted to the poems and analysed them for stylistic features, such as meter/rhyme/imagery.

A **good answer** would suggest a few poems the candidate is most comfortable discussing, say a couple from Baudelaire's *Les Fleurs du Mal*. The interviewer would then ask some specific questions based on the poem, such as asking the candidate if there were any particularly striking features. Although it may be tempting, this is not the place to attempt to impress the interviewers with your knowledge of literary terms — they are not so much interested in whether you know the technical term for the device, but whether you can actually identify the device in the first place. For instance, the poem you have selected may have an unconventional structure, odd vocabulary choice, or it might be completely conventional. The key is to identify how it has been constructed by the poet. Does the poem belong to a particular movement? What does the liberal use of vowel sounds indicate? Or the heavy use of the letter 's'? Is the poem designed to subvert or meet our expectations? Is there a perceptible agenda in the poet's work? The interviewers will likely try to draw you out of your comfort zone, so it is a good idea to work with whatever information they give you and appear enthusiastic when discussing new ideas.

A **weaker answer** would either attempt to impress the interviewers by name-dropping poets and poems without actually being able to follow up with a deep knowledge of the poems in question or would not be able to show an understanding of the poem beyond content/plot. As such, it would appear that the candidate is not familiar with the poems and has not spent time trying to deconstruct them and put them into their context. A less strong candidate would not be able to work with new information and ideas presented by the interviewers and prefer to stick to pre-prepared material.

Q33: Do you think that poetry is a different language to that used in prose?

This question allows you to demonstrate your knowledge of any novels, short stories or poems which you have read in any of your target languages and compare them to see if language works in the same way across both poetry and prose. The interviewers will be looking in particular to see how you analyse the way in which language is manipulated and understood in poetry, as opposed to less lyrical forms. Is there anything additional which poetry does with language? Should we read poetic language in the same way as we read prose?

A good answer would be able to articulate ways in which poetic language achieves a different effect to prose. For instance, a good candidate would be able to identify a particular poem (even just in English) where language has been manipulated to achieve this desired effect. Does the rhythm add a musical quality? Is there a play on dissonance? Does the presence of rhyme give the poem an incantatory feel? This would be a good place to point out the fact that we often have to learn to read poetry differently to prose: such as specific rhyming schemes so that we know where to put the emphasis.

The fact that poetry is usually intended to be read out loud might suggest that it has different qualities to a novel, which is not usually read out loud. However, more modern poetry often does away with any set structures, so what still makes it poetry and not just prose? It would also be a good idea to problematise the question's assumption that novels and short stories employ language in the same way: perhaps you may identify features of short stories which distinguish them. Have you read any short stories which had a poetic feel? Or where individual words are used to greater effect than they are in a long novel? Can a novel never be poetic?

A poor answer would struggle to identify features where poetry differs from prose and would fail to pick up on elements of style/sound/rhythm/structure which make hearing a poem different from simply reading it. It would also lack specific examples of texts where you think language is used differently, say between a Maupassant short story and a Goethe poem. A key part of the course is a close analysis of how language is manipulated by writers to achieve a desired effect.

Q34: Would you say that the words we are exchanging now are in the same language as a work of great literature?

This question offers a good opportunity to show the interviewers your analysis of the ways in which literature has a different effect on the reader than speech, and the ways in which speech can convey meanings which literature cannot. Interviewers will be assessing your ability to pay attention to the unique features of literary style and discourse which make them both effective in their own right.

A **good answer** would pick out a couple of examples from literary works which a candidate has studied in order to argue that literature can often convey certain qualities of which speech is not capable. Has a particular novel struck you as particularly evocative of a certain era or historical moment which a simple History lecture would not be able to convey? Does the fact that literature is highly stylised, and can be re-edited ad infinitum by an author, give it a certain artistic quality which spontaneous speech lacks? Does the fact that literature often uses phrases which would sound clunky or archaic in speech achieve a different effect? Or is literature hampered somewhat because it cannot convey all the intricacies of speech, such as accent, intonation and tone, which can make certain speeches so effective? Speech, after all, is the origin of language and often demands an immediate response of the interlocutor, whereas literature is usually read internally and does not demand a verbal response from the reader. Indeed, could you not argue that many pre-planned speeches by orators resemble literature more than they resemble ordinary speech?

A **poor answer** would struggle to identify the ways in which novels, plays and poetry must be read differently to simple speech. The fact that they are highly stylised and refined would surely indicate that they have higher expectations of their readers than ordinary speech does. A less strong candidate would also be unable to identify the aspects of speech which literature cannot communicate, such as immediacy, context, tone, and visual cues which add to the overall picture and can add more nuanced layers of meaning, even if speech can often be grammatically incorrect.

Q35: How do you feel about ambiguity?

This question is designed to throw the candidate, and as such interviewers will be hoping to see how you cope with such an open-ended and vague question. Key here will be to ground your answer with some examples, such as where particular words have been used ambiguously, whether or not that is an issue, and how we commonly deal with ambiguity. Perhaps ambiguity is a key theme of a novel you have mentioned in your Personal Statement, or you may choose to direct the discussion into a more abstract territory, such as arguing that some degree of ambiguity is inevitable.

A **good answer** would begin by defining what ambiguity means; namely a statement or enunciation which is not sufficiently precise so as to offer multiple credible interpretations. You may select an example of a text where the theme of ambiguity has been explored, or if you are not able to do this, you could explore how you deal with ambiguity in your everyday life. Is it always a good idea to ask for clarification? What do you do when you have to act on the ambiguous statement, but are unable to get clarification? Or have you ever been deliberately ambiguous, perhaps because you were not sure of the statement yourself. Your interviewer may then attempt to move these general points back to literature or art and ask you whether or not ambiguity is sometimes necessary. You may argue that there is not always a single correct interpretation, or that ambiguity can actually make us question the facts and come to even more fruitful interpretations. After all, if there were no ambiguity, then there would be no questions, and the study of literature at university is nothing but questions! Perhaps ambiguity can be used as a device to manipulate language and to influence others. Or you may conclude that too much ambiguity is counter-intuitive, and that, taking the example of certain works of Modernist art, leaving too much room for interpretation can achieve nothing at all, or just leave you frustrated.

A **poor answer** would fail to define ambiguity and would be reluctant to work with the interviewers and discuss concepts or areas which are completely new to the candidate. As this is such a broad question, interviewers will be looking for interesting, original, enthusiastic responses, and as such a poor answer would not tackle some of the interesting questions which ambiguity poses. It is likely that interviewers will try to build on this question to try to challenge you and see if they can reach a point where you have to ask for assistance, so do not be afraid to stand your ground and hold your own! If they do offer assistance, be sure to work with the information they give you. Asking for assistance can sometimes be a good idea after you have attempted the question yourself, especially if it is with a particularly gnarly question, since it demonstrates an ability to discuss and engage with the interviewers. This is a central part of the supervision/tutorial structure.

Q36: What is your favourite word?

This question is designed to catch you off guard because there is obviously no correct answer. There is also no pressure to choose a word simply because you think it would impress the examiners, it would be much more advisable to choose one which you actually like. If you cannot think of one off the top of your head, then take a few moments to find a word which is particularly interesting to you — is it onomatopoeic? Does its sound interest you? Perhaps it has an unusual etymology, or it may even be a word you struggle to translate into another language. The word does not need to be one in your target languages, it could just as well be an English word as a Swahili one.

A **good answer** would have a few reasons for why the word is your favourite. You might refer to the contexts where the word is used, its origins or simply its sound. It could be something as simple as the word 'really', since it can have many different meanings depending on your tone or the stress you place on it in the sentence. Or it could be a word in your local dialect, such as 'yem' or 'spelk', perhaps because it has origins in another language or because it has a special significance to you which its mainstream English equivalent does not have.

A **poor answer** would not have a reason for why it is the candidate's favourite word. Instead of just saying that it sounds nice, you could try to explore why it sounds nice. Does it have many vowel sounds? Does it relate to the action it describes? A poor answer would also appear thrown by the question, or not sure of how to answer. Given that this is a question which does not require much knowledge or argumentation, the interviewers will be looking for enthusiasm.

Q37: Make up a word for me – what does it mean?

This is another curveball question which might require you to take a moment to reflect and think of a response. Rather than blurting out a jumble of sounds, interviewers would be more impressed with you identifying a vocabulary gap in English or your target languages, where you think a word is 'missing'. You can, of course, choose any word you like, but it is best to try to avoid anything too comical because it risks not working.

A **good answer** would use the languages you know to help you arrive at a word. Have you struggled to translate '*awkward*' into Italian? Does English lack a word which can translate 'flâner' from French adequately? Or perhaps you cannot find a way of translating 'mutterseelenallein' from German. You may wish to explain why you think there is not a good equivalent in the language for that word, perhaps giving a few possible translations and explaining why they are not a good fit. It might be a word used a lot in that language, which suggests that it ought to be a common enough experience to feature in the language in which it is missing. It might even be an invented word which you use informally with family or friends which you think should become a word in its own right.

A **poor answer** would not be able to give a convincing reason for why the candidate has selected that word. The answer might also appear to have been selected at random, or in a rush, so it is best to pause to think for a good response. Interviewers will of course allow you time to think, and there is absolutely nothing wrong with asking them for this. A considered response is usually better than a completely spontaneous one. A poor answer might also seem unusually concerned with giving a good answer — as this is a less serious question, the interviewers would prefer a more light-hearted response, without openly fretting about 'why' that word should be chosen or changing the word halfway through.

Q38: What is the practical difference between Chinese whispers and translation?

This question assesses how you approach translation and whether or not you recognise certain aspects of translation which are often inevitable, such as uncertainty, mistranslation and contextual issues. The interviewers will be looking to see if you can draw some parallels between Chinese whispers and translation, but the main focus of your answer should be on the differences.

A **good answer** would begin by briefly explaining what it is you understand by Chinese whispers and by translation; namely the game where one person whispers a message in the ear of another player and so on, and the act of translating a literary text into another. You may wish to establish a distinction between translation and interpreting here, since, strictly speaking, translation is more commonly associated with the written word than spoken language. One of the main differences is the fact that when translating, you often, though not always, have time to think about the word on the page, so you are often able to try a few translations in your head before settling on one. In Chinese whispers, you only have one shot at hearing the correct sentence. Secondly, there is almost no interpretation involved in Chinese whispers — you are not meant to think about the response, simply repeat what you believe you heard. In translation, however, you very much have to think about the sentence in its context. In this way, translation requires reflection and skill in judging the right compromise between meaning, tone and image. Having said this, there are some parallels too. For instance, in both you may not have enough contextual information to make the best response and be forced to make your best guess. Furthermore, just as there are usually inaccuracies in the game, it is almost impossible to find a perfect translation for any given text, and as such it is perhaps inevitable that some nuances will be lost in translation.

A **poor response** would focus on similarities rather than differences, or it would struggle to find differences. The inability to identify differences would suggest little familiarity with the 'art' of translation and the various skills it requires. As translation is a substantial part of the language modules at university, this would not reflect well on the candidate. It would also not reflect well if the candidate did not know what Chinese whispers was and decided to fudge a response regardless — it is a much better idea to ask for clarification, if it is really needed, before embarking on a response!

Q39: How would you describe a cucumber to an alien whose translator can only understand Spanish?

Another curveball question, the interviewers will be trying to assess how well you think on your feet, and also how well you can explain something potentially quite complex to somebody not familiar with the topic. This is a common feature of both essay writing and supervision presentations. The second part of the question is designed to get you using your target language in a novel way, so the challenge for you will be to not make it too complex so as to be unable to communicate it in Spanish.

Without taking the question too far, it may be worth asking if the said alien can communicate in human language. The interviewers would likely say yes, as the only other options which would remain are gesticulating or illustrating! A **good candidate** would realise that this is a test of how to explain something clearly to a layperson, so it would be a good idea to break down a cucumber into its basic facts or parts which are recognisable to the alien: it is eaten like a vegetable (presumably the alien sustains itself somehow, and would recognise the consumption of resources), it is green (a colour associated with the new and the fresh; perhaps the alien is colour-blind but could still have a way of identifying things which are new and fresh in its own home planet), it is cool and refreshing since it contains a lot of water, the most important resource for us (presumably the alien has at least one staple resource of its own even if water is an unknown concept), and is relatively turgid (presumably the alien is familiar with objects of differing textures, such as rock versus sand). The interviewers will appreciate the fact that you are trying to relativise and break down unfamiliar concepts into familiar ones.

The challenge would then be to translate this into Spanish. You may not know all the vocabulary in Spanish, so you will need to be able to use some synonyms. For instance, if you did not know how to say 'turgid' in Spanish, you could use an approximation such as 'duro' or 'rígido'.

A **poor answer** would not rise to the challenge and attempt to break down the concept of a cucumber into more familiar, general ones. It would not empathise with the alien, insofar as making an effort to keep your description as clear and simple as possible. Such an answer might also get distracted by the fact it is an 'alien', rather than realising that the question is more about asking whether or not the candidate can explain a complex topic to a layperson. A poor answer in Spanish would get caught up in the detail, and not keep the communication simple. You are allowed time for reflection, so do not be afraid to ask for a few moments to gather your thoughts and think of a few key words.

Q40: Would you describe human thoughts as malleable?

This question is potentially quite challenging insofar as it requires the candidate to construct an argument on an area that is quite abstract, so it will be necessary to ground the answer with some examples. It will also be a good idea to give examples of both when our opinions are open to change and external influence, but also when our opinions are hold steadfast, regardless of pressure from others or lived experience. The interviewers are looking for a response which is well balanced and sufficiently broad.

A **strong candidate** would begin by explaining the disparity in the categories of belief and thoughts that we hold. For instance, many of our opinions fluctuate based on the views of others, or simply from lived experience. An example would be our thoughts on what is fashionable. Bombarded by advertising, television and what we see and hear online and in the street, our thoughts on what is fashionable and what is not is changing all the time. This can be applied to clothing, vocabulary choice, or even what is considered to be *politically correct*. You could compare mainstream political views from today to those in 1970, and remark on how wide the gap is in some areas. Indeed, it could be a source of concern that our thoughts on such subjects could be subject to such wild fluctuations. Nevertheless, a good candidate would also cite examples of where our thoughts and beliefs seem invariable to change. For some this could be strongly held religious convictions, deep-rooted political affiliations, or even how we think of ourselves as individuals. A good candidate may elaborate on this category of thoughts and posit that these thoughts are often seen as key to our identities, and that we cling to them because we need a strong, stable sense of identity in order to thrive. This is also potentially a cause of concern, because these sorts of beliefs often fly in the face of logic and remain impermeable to contrary evidence, even if they do give us a sense of independence. Overall, perhaps we should monitor out beliefs so that they are neither too fickle, nor too resistant to change.

A **poor answer** would fail to distinguish between categories of thought and belief, and instead try to give a black-or-white answer. Such a candidate might not acknowledge how our thoughts are often susceptible to external influences, whether or not we know it, or may argue that our thoughts and beliefs are always changing. A less strong candidate would also struggle to find examples or make a hesitant response which demonstrates a lack of comfort when dealing with unfamiliar or unusual questions to which there may be no correct answer.

Q41: Have electronic translators rendered linguists obsolete?

This is a deliberately provocative question, and although it would obviously not be a good idea to say that studying languages is not pointless, it would not be a good idea to say that modern electronic translator will not change the study of languages at all, because that is definitely not the case. In this question, the interviewers will be trying to assess whether or not you know the course you are applying for well enough, and know what the study of languages entails beyond school.

A **good answer** would acknowledge that electronic translators are an exciting development, and that online resources such as *Wordreference* and *Reverso* offer excellent alternatives to the more traditional physical dictionary. A strong candidate, however, would emphasise the point that electronic translators will serve to increase the quality of the *tools* which a linguist has at their disposal, rather than do away with the need for human linguists entirely! After all, you would always need a real thinking human for all the cultural knowledge and idiomatic nuance that an electronic translator cannot offer. Besides, the study of languages at a higher level is more than just vocabulary lists and grammar. Translation is not the major focus of language courses: at university, the focus will be on literature, intellectual culture and potentially linguistics. Being able to copy and paste a text into a translator will not teach you the knowledge and context needed to become a good linguist and Humanities student. Electronic translators will therefore assist linguists with research, but they will not do the research for you.

A **poor answer** may try to impress the interviewers by saying that electronic translators will not change the work of a linguist at all, because this simply not the case and would actually be counter-intuitive since electronic translators can be an excellent tool if used correctly. A weaker answer would also focus on translation, rather than explain that the study of languages entails so much more than just translation work. It may also suggest that translators are infallible, given that translators usually have no context and are not able to detect nuance or tone. Therefore, a linguist's job is to always make sure that the translation proposed by an electronic translator makes perfect sense.

Q42: Newsflash! We are at war with Europe. The ministry of defence has asked for your advice on which languages their personnel should be taught, how do you answer?

This is a question which is designed to test how you think on your feet and come up with a logical answer on the spot. It is important not to get too carried away with the situation in the question, so you should focus on the key idea, namely what degree of fluency is needed to get by/understand/infiltrate, how to be efficient, and whether or not native level fluency should be the end goal for any linguist. Some originality in the response would also be a bonus.

A **good candidate** would indicate that it is unrealistic for people to acquire a high level of fluency in a short period of time, so it would be unrealistic to suddenly train language novices at the MoD to the level of fluency. Instead, they should be trained to a basic standard, so they have some familiarity, especially in vocabulary related to their job. Instead, resources should be focussed on training those who already have advanced skills so that they are able to tackle most of the language work in order to increase efficiency. It is equally unrealistic to assume that most individuals can get to a level of fluency such that they appear as a native. Therefore, those with the best language skills should be prioritised for frontline reconnaissance work. Fluency is likely not needed for most roles, as most personnel will only need to understand and follow commands rather than interpret and act the evidence in a foreign language for themselves. A good candidate might argue that the focus should be on recruiting as many bilingual/trilingual speakers as possible (i.e. those who have been brought up with the target language) to avoid having to train non-native level speakers, or that more-than-basic language knowledge is only relevant for those actually deployed in the country/intercepting communications, rather than all roles.

A **poor answer** would be hesitant with a response or start answering without having taken time to quickly reflect. Any answer would involve some form of thinking out loud, so do not be afraid to share your thoughts with the interviewers because they may help to steer you in a new direction, or help you explore these same ideas from a different perspective. A weaker answer might also risk being totally unrealistic (even if the question is!), and not consider resource allocation/the fact that different roles require differing levels of fluency, and some may not require any fluency at all.

Q43: What is the driving force behind the evolution of language – do you think this could be halted?

This is a very complicated question which a candidate could not possible be expected to cover in sufficient depth at interview. Therefore, the priority for the candidate should be to consider a few salient factors which influence language evolution, and to draw out some real-world examples of where languages have been codified, or possibly where the use of a language has remained largely the same for a long period of time. The interviewers are looking for a response which is logical but is also grounded.

A **strong candidate** would summarise two or three major factors contributing towards language evolution. For instance, they may point to contact with external languages. To take the English language as an example, the various historical influences of the Celts, Normans and Vikings, and more recently the British Empire, have significantly influenced the direction which the English language has taken, particularly in terms of vocabulary, but also in terms of grammar too. The words 'forbidden' and 'restriction', for example, are of Viking and French origin, respectively. A second factor would be political motives, one of which may be artificial formalisation. For example, Modern French has been heavily influenced by the Académie Française, which was created in the 17th Century and was designed to enforce a standard French language. However, attempts to prevent a language from changing have almost never been successful. Modern spoken French is not the same as it was at the creation of the Académie Française, even if it may contain significant similarities. Languages change with the people who speak them, and language use cannot realistically be policed.

A **poor answer** would not be able to identify some of the various factors which influence a language's evolution. It is expected that you would have a rough knowledge of the history surrounding the languages you wish to study. A weaker answer would be unable to explain how attempts to codify a language may have some success but will likely never be able to prevent at least some small changes in the language. Languages are, above all, spoken, and save in the case of forced language abandonment, which is a different topic, how a language is spoken will change with its speakers.

Q44: Where do accents come from?

This question can lead to an interesting discussion of the meaning of the terms 'accent', 'dialect' and 'language', and of the various factors which may affect the development of an accent (politics, immigration, cultural shifts, perception). The interviewers will be looking for an understanding of the 'language situation' in the principal countries where your target languages are spoken. Is French as varied in terms of dialects and accent as English, Spanish or German? How are accents viewed there?

A **good candidate** would explain that an accent refers to how people pronounce the same words in a different manner, or with a different cadence. It is often interchangeable with the term 'dialect', but the latter usually includes broader differences, such as in grammar or in vocabulary which differ from the 'standard' version of a language. It would be a good idea to compare some examples from one of your target languages if you can. For instance, in standard Castilian Spanish, the word 'césped' would maintain the 'th' sound at the start and the end, whereas in many dialects, such as Andalusian Spanish or in many Latin American varieties, the 'th' sound is lost at both the start and the end, with the combination 'cé' pronounced more like an 's'. It would then be a good point to explain how they arise. Factors vary from immigration, such as the influence of Viking settlers in Orkney, or the huge number of Irish immigrants in Liverpool, to associated prestige, for instance the high cultural capital of Received Pronunciation in England in radio and TV. Another factor would be political, such as standardised language at school, as in French lycées.

A **poor answer** would not be able to explain how an accent relates to other similar terms, such as dialect, or remark that the distinction between 'dialect' and 'language' is often arbitrary. It would also not be able to draw on examples of accents or accent change in the candidate's target language, given that interviewers will hope that the candidate has a general familiarity with issues surrounding language use in the principal country where the target languages are spoken.

Q45: Can culture shape vocabulary?

This question could lead to an interesting discussion on whether or not language and culture are two separate things, or, rather, if language and culture both influence one another and ought not to be considered separately. Interviewers will be assessing you on how aware you are of the some of the differences in vocabulary choice between English and your target languages, and in expression more broadly. Can these differences be explained by culture, or is it only one part of the picture?

A **strong candidate** would be able to articulate how culture can impact vocabulary choice in some areas. You should arrive at these areas by comparing with your target languages — is the stereotype that the British are reserved in character reflected in the often-subtle use of vocabulary and tone in the Britain, compared to, for instance, stereotypes of Italian flair and passion? Or perhaps the comparative lack of culinary terms in English than in French can be explained by the latter's cultural emphasis on cuisine. However, a good candidate would express that vocabulary choice is often not easily related to a country's culture, and that, in the case where a language has been forced on a people or a nation, that the new language can influence that nation's prior culture to some limited degree, among many other factors.

A **less strong candidate** would treat culture and vocabulary usage as exclusive concepts that can easily be explained away, or that the influence only goes in one direction. Alternatively, such a candidate might not make the interviewers aware that cultural stereotypes ought to be treated with caution, and that there are many other factors influencing vocabulary choice. In many cases, vocabulary choice is determined by context and the limits of vocabulary in the language itself. A weaker candidate would also not be able to cite specific examples from any cultures they are familiar with.

Q46: How do babies learn language?

A question difficult to prepare in advance, the interviewers will not necessarily expect you to know 'the ins and outs' of infant language acquisition, but they would expect you to be broadly familiar with the differences between learning a language 'informally', so to speak, and, alternatively, in a formal context, such as at school. It would be a good idea to highlight some occasions when it is easy to spot a native speaker from somebody who has learned a language formally (accent/vocabulary choice/non-verbal language)

A **good candidate** would explain that the primary difference between how babies learn languages and how we learn them later in life is the fact that a baby is primed to acquire language at a rate much quicker, and, ultimately, more successfully than later learners are. They acquire the bases of spoken fluency without so much as needing to study the language at all. Extremely attentive to how parental figures communicate; they learn by osmosis and observation rather than through a textbook. Indeed, unlike later learners, they do not learn a language through another language. In fact, the instincts acquired through one's own native language often act to prevent a later learner from acquiring native level fluency in a new language (false friends, tense usage, cultural cues). However, those who have studied it formally often have a better grasp of formal language than those who have simply spoken a language at home and not formally studied it, because in many languages there is a large gap between spoken and written registers.

A **weaker candidate** would not make it clear that babies learn languages by osmosis, and not through another language, unlike later learners. In this sense, it would be more accurate to say that they acquire a language rather than learning it formally. As they are primed to learn how to communicate, and extremely attentive to parental figures, they learn languages much more efficiently than later learners, who must usually formally learn it. A weaker candidate might not also remark that it is usually relatively easy to spot a later learner because they will usually have hangovers from their mother tongue.

Q47: You have a very short space of time to learn a new language, what is your strategy?

This question is a good way to show off your approach to language learning and to show how you have gone above and beyond simple classroom-based learning. Interviewers will be looking for evidence that you have tailored your learning style to your own personal strengths, and how you tackle your weaker areas. What works best for you? At the same time, interviewers will be looking for a little bit of humility — you still need to give the impression that you are open to new styles of learning and constructive criticism.

A **good candidate** would reflect on their own language learning process and provide examples. They may show evidence of research, and how they have applied this to their own learning. For instance, has the candidate started using flash cards because they have realised that they are a visual learner? Or perhaps the candidate learns best through context, so they learn best passively, via target language media. Indeed, the interviewers will probably expect you to show evidence of reading/wider engagement in your target language than is offered at your school. Have you found that your grammar and vocabulary have improved after reading a text in the target language? Have you gone out of your way to immerse yourself via radio or film? This will show the examiners that you take an active approach to learning, rather than expecting that learning vocabulary lists will do the task for you. You might conclude that there is no quick way to learn a language to a very high standard, because at some point you will need to acquire cultural knowledge to improve your fluency, and this usually takes a lot of time and dedicated immersion.

A **weaker candidate** will not demonstrate evidence of how they have adapted their learning style to their own interests and strengths. As university study is mainly independent, the interviewers will be looking for a high degree of self-motivation, and a degree of self-awareness regarding what works for you. A weaker candidate might also give the impression that they have not explored language-learning beyond the classroom environment. Most of the language learning at Oxford and Cambridge is not formal, and you are expected to be pro-active in addressing the gaps in your knowledge independently.

Q48: Do you think there's a limit on how many languages someone could learn, what do you think that limit might be?

There is obviously no fixed answer to this question, but interviewers will be assessing the candidate on how realistic their goals are, and whether or not they are aware that fluency wanes over time and must be worked at frequently to maintain a steady level. The interviewers would also be looking to see what the motivations for your language study are — would there be any point in you learning a thousand languages if you only planned on visiting countries where just ten of those languages are spoken?

A **good candidate** would explain that it is possible to have a superficial knowledge of many languages, but that a solid grasp of many is much harder to acquire. Therefore, the answer to the question depends on how you define 'learn', given that somebody could get to a basic level in many Romance languages relatively quickly, but to become fluent would take a lot more effort. The question also depends on how similar the languages are, because it is likely that fluency in Japanese, Swahili and Khoisan would take longer than achieving fluency in Norwegian, Danish and Swedish.

It would also be beneficial to add that fluency comes and goes over time, and as such it might take some time to get back to the level you had once achieved in a language which you have not used for a while. As such, you might have learnt five languages in total, but at any moment in time you may only be able to use three of them comfortably, because it is unlikely that your lifestyle would enable you to have contact with more than three or so languages on a daily basis. Besides, what are your motivations for studying languages? Do you think a good level of fluency in three languages is better than a rough level in ten? What is your end goal?

A **weaker candidate** would not differentiate between different levels of fluency and would not examine some of the reasons behind learning a language. Are you wishing to learn your target languages in depth because you will be able to engage with their culture better? If you give the impression that you are purely interested in acquiring languages and not so bothered about their literature/art/history, then interviewers may find fault with this. Furthermore, candidates who are not realistic about language-learning goals may give the impression of being idealistic. For instance, you may wish to be fluent in every European language, but it is necessary to show that this goal is highly unrealistic.

Q49: What are the issues when studying multiple languages simultaneously?

This question is a particularly good one if you are already studying more than one language, because you will be able to draw on your own experiences. Interviewers will be looking to see if you are able to handle the advanced study of two languages at the same time, so it would be a good idea to show techniques you use to make sure that you give them both equal attention and maintain them at a roughly equal level. If you are planning on studying an *ab initio* language, you will need to demonstrate that you will not neglect your existing language!

A **good candidate** will explain that it can be both a help and a hindrance to study languages which stem from a similar root, such as Spanish and Italian, simultaneously. For instance, both Spanish and Italian have a broadly similar grammar and vocabulary, so knowledge of the one will help you to fill in the gaps of the other. However, once you have gained a basic level in both, there are several factors which can prove more of a hindrance. There are many false friends, grammar is not identical so you may find yourself inventing phrases and structures which do not exist, and the proximity may mean that you are not able to differentiate them in your head so that they exist as two entirely separate languages. For example, in French, 'black and white' is 'noir et blanc', whereas in Italian it is 'bianco e nero'. Similarity can lead to a lack of depth of knowledge in each. Nevertheless, although there is much less similarity between Italian and German, say, it is still important to monitor your learning of both so that they proceed at roughly the same pace. If you find one easier than the other, then this should mean that you focus more on the harder one to bring it up to the right level.

A **poor answer** would not recognise some of difficulties which arise when studying similar language, or, equally, give the impression that language similarity is always a problem. A weaker candidate would not be able to explain that learning two languages at the same time requires you to be consistent in your approach to both and not neglect one over the other. Especially if the second language to be studied is *ab initio*, the interviewers will be looking for candidates who show strong motivation to bring the new language up to scratch in a short amount of time, but without neglecting study of the other.

Q50: What is used to convey the gender of a noun in German?

This is not a particularly tricky question, as you will appreciate that there are some useful patterns which help with determining the gender of nouns in German, but it is not always possible to tell the gender of a noun just from the word itself. The interviewers will be looking to see how you approach vocabulary learning and whether or not you are aware of the various helpful patterns which make vocabulary learning significantly easier.

A **good answer** would explain that there are some very helpful patterns which can help you determine whether or not a word is masculine, feminine of neutral. For example, nouns ending in *-ig* tend to be masculine, the nouns describing most plants, shrubs and trees are usually feminine, and nouns ending in *-lein, -sel, -ment* or *-ma* are usually neuter. However, it is not always as easy as this. A prime example would be *Mädchen*, which, despite meaning *girl*, is neuter. As such, it is best to always learn a noun alongside its gender. It would be beneficial to mention some ways you can use the rest of the sentence to determine a noun's gender if you have forgotten it. For instance, you will be able to tell the noun's gender by the article it is used with, or perhaps from its plural form and the adjectives used to describe it.

A **weaker answer** would not make the interviewers aware of the various patterns which can help you determine a noun's gender and would not show the interviewers that you are also usually able to deduce a noun's gender from the various articles and adjectives used in the sentence. Indeed, interviewers will expect you to be familiar with most of these patterns because without them your language learning and accuracy will be much poorer. A weaker candidate might also suggest that a noun's gender is not important, when in fact it dictates how a lot of the surrounding sentence should be constructed.

Q51: Do people from different parts of the world have different difficulties learning English? How would a German's experience of English differ from someone from Asia?

This is potentially a tricky question is you have had limited exposure to foreign English speakers from a variety of areas. If you are not familiar with their characteristic difficulties, you would be advised to think of areas which were difficult for you in the European/Asian languages with which you are familiar, as it might be expected that these same areas would be challenging the other way around. If you are already familiar with the difficulties, then all the better, but it is necessary to define your terms clearly. How are you defining Europeans? How are you defining Asians? Particularly in the case of Asians, you need to make it clear if you are speaking about Indians, Chinese, Japanese, Korean or any other nationality.

A **good candidate** may be alert to some of the particular difficulties Romance language speakers have with English. English has many more vowel and consonant sounds than, say, Spanish or Italian, and therefore these speakers are often unable to make the correct sound in English. They may also struggle with the closed vowels in English. A broader factor which most Europeans struggle with is the complicated use of emphasis in English. Stress on certain words can completely change the sentence, and this is especially challenging in languages which have stricter grammatical structures, or are unfamiliar with the varying use of stress and tone in English. Another area is phrasal verbs, which do not exist in Romance languages and do not always follow a logical pattern. Most European languages do not have a present perfect tense unlike English, so they may struggle in determining where to use '*I did*' and '*I have done*'. In comparison, depending on how you have defined 'Asians', you may remark that the Chinese are often unable to pronounce '*l*' and '*r*' properly, and are unaware of where to put the stress in English, so questions, for instance, often sound like statements. They usually have a harder task than Europeans because Asian languages are completely unrelated and cannot rely on cognates. In particular, Asians often have more difficulty with cultural cues due to the significant cultural gap.

A **weaker candidate** would not be able to figure out some of the difficulties which are particular to European and Asian speakers, even if they have limited experience with them. For instance, they may assume that the difficulties are broadly the same, which is not usually the case. They may also fail to define their terms, and as such may put Indians and Japanese natives in the same category, which is obviously not very useful. They would also not be aware of the features unique to their target languages or be able to explain some of the factors present in English which their target languages 'lack', and vice versa. Besides simple grammatical, vocabulary and pronunciation difficulties, cultural familiarity is a huge factor which should not be ignored.

Q52: What steps would you take to make Google Translate a better service?

This is a question which allows you to show the examiners what factors can turn a translation from clunky or barely adequate, to one which is nuanced and context specific. Although Google Translate does have a reputation for offering less-than-impressive translations, it is a good idea to refrain from criticising online translators too much in an effort to impress the interviewers — they are an increasingly useful tool for linguists, even if they are by no means perfect. The interviewers will be looking for you to identify how you can make your own translations better.

A **good candidate** would explain what goes wrong with some Google Translate translations. Perhaps you have found that it works better for single word translations, or that it is better for full sentences. Has it ever given you the completely wrong word for something? Has it not understood the tone, or do you feel that it needed to take context into account? How can a translator take context into account? At this point you might want to point out other online translators which have a more sophisticated approach. *Linguee* and *Reverso* are good examples of this, since they provide several alternative translations within a wider sentence. This allows you to compare and contrast to select the best translation. Nevertheless, their offerings are not perfect either — sometimes it can be difficult to ascertain if the texts are written by authentic native speakers, or already translations. You may want to explain that digital translators are likely never going to be a perfect tool, but they are increasingly useful if you a translating under pressure and would like to sound your own translations against their own suggestions.

A **weaker candidate** might give the impression that Google Translate is a tool they frequently use for their language work. There are currently much better options out there, such as those mentioned above, or indeed *Wordreference*. They would also struggle to specify exactly what it is that makes Google Translate suggestions poor in some cases — it is necessary identify what it is about them that makes them poor translations. A weaker candidate might also suggest that online translators can be used without reflection on the part of the human translator — they should be treated as a tool, and only part of the process of coming up with the best solution.

Q53: Do you have a favourite author? What is it you like about their work?

This is a question which gives you a lot of scope for manoeuvre and for you to direct the discussion onto a topic which you are comfortable with, so make sure you make the most of the opportunity. It is a good idea to be as honest as you can — it will not impress the examiners if it comes across that you have only selected the author because you think it sounds more intelligent. There is equally no pressure to identify a reader in one of your target languages, because it is unlikely that you would have read sufficiently widely in French/Portuguese/Italian to have found a *favourite* author. If you cannot identify one single author, it is a good strategy to pick one who has written several texts you know, since this will give you more to discuss.

A **strong candidate** would be able to talk about their selected author with enthusiasm — as this is your 'favourite' author, and you are applying to study a course which has a significant emphasis on literature, the interviewers will be expecting to see some passion. It is also important to be able to discuss why you enjoyed their works, beyond simply plot lines. What is it about their style which intrigues you? What themes do they deal with? Are these continued throughout their work, or are some of their texts better than others? Would you be able to explain why you have chosen this author over the other authors you have read from? A good candidate might also indicate that it is not always useful to analyse texts through the prism of their author — should we necessarily be mindful of the author's identity when reading a novel or a poem?

A **weaker candidate** would not appear particularly enthused by the author they have chosen. Granted, over-enthusiasm is to be avoided, but some evidence of motivation and passion goes a long way. In the same vein, a weaker candidate would appear hesitant when discussing the author, as though they do not feel confident discussing the material, or as though they do not have much to say. Furthermore, a weaker candidate would not seek to discuss the author and their texts on a deeper level than mere plot and character. Granted, these are important, but not the most interesting aspect of literary study.

Q54: Is any language actually 'dead'?

In this question, interviewers will be assessing you based on your knowledge of contemporary language use issues, and on whether or not you are able to home in on specific words to explore the avenues they open. The key word in this question is 'truly', so it will be necessary to describe what you mean by 'die'.

A **good candidate** would be able to cite examples of languages which have, for all intents and purposes, died out. A good definition of 'died out' is a language which has no native language speakers left and has stopped being used in a community setting. However, Latin is an example which is potentially an exception to this definition, given that it is still used in academic discourse and in liturgy. Examples could be drawn from many communities where the process of cultural assimilation has led to monolingual Spanish, English or French speakers. Nevertheless, it is necessary to examine whether or not a language has 'truly' died out. Indeed, most languages spoken on Earth today are descendants of languages which have formally died out, but which live on in some limited way, either through vocabulary or grammatical structure. An example would be Proto-Indo-European, whose descendants have billions of speakers. Of course, many languages have well and truly died out, leaving little to no trace in any other living language. There are many examples, such as certain pidgin or creole languages, as well as languages which have historically been very isolated or spoken in small communities, for instance in South America.

A **weaker candidate** would not be able to explain what is meant by 'actually' or be able to explain that some 'dead' languages have many spoken descendants, such that they continue to live on in other languages. Alternatively, a select few languages are no longer spoken but remain used in certain formal contexts and remain understood. Examples include Sanskrit or Coptic. Understanding the hints and nuance of a question are key elements of success at Oxford and Cambridge.

Q55: Could a language exist using nothing but numbers, and without grammar?

This is potentially a tricky question as it can become complex very quickly, so it is wise to keep to a general structure, which helps you to avoid getting mixed up in the details or avoid contradicting yourself. Interviewers will be looking for you to examine what makes a language a language, and what we mean exactly by language. Can numbers on their own communicate? Do we need a common structure in order to communicate?

A **good candidate** would explain that letters, characters and numbers are arbitrary unless we give them meaning. In this way, we learn to associate certain values with them. The letter *m* does not intrinsically communicate the sound or value we associate with it. As such, most people agree that some sort of structure is needed in order to be able to identify meaning and to communicate information, else we would not be able to interpret these arbitrary symbols correctly. If a 'grammar' is reduced to the idea of a structure, then it would be very difficult to communicate anything that is not incredibly basic without some acquired structure. How would we be able to indicate the relationships between concepts or letter combinations without some sort of structure? Even programming languages follow a rigid structure, regardless of whether or not we call this a grammar. Indeed, it could be argued that numbers are a language of sorts — we learn to associate them with a value, and the structure of Mathematics is ruthlessly logical. In this sense, logic acts a grammar for Mathematics. Mathematics is a 'language' understood by people across the globe, even if they do not speak the same languages. However, numbers in the way we use them are relatively limited, as their quantitative quality is not applicable to most aspects of our life. How could you indicate that you would like sugar with your coffee with numbers?

A **weaker candidate** would not show enthusiasm to tackle what is a difficult question. Even if you do not have a definite answer, it is a good idea to walk the interviewers through your thought process. A poor response would not seek to analyse what makes a language comprehensible, and whether or not numbers and Mathematics can therefore be understood as a language. Languages do not necessarily need to communicate the same ideas (Tagalog and C++ are both 'languages', though used in completely different ways and contexts, and cannot be translated into each other). A weaker candidate would also not act on hints given by interviewers, as this shows an inability to assimilate and use new information.

Q56: What separates a modern language from a medieval one?

This is a question which is designed to get you to think about the contemporary use of the languages which you intend to study, but also to examine the various sub-meanings which the term 'modern' implies. The interviewers are looking for candidates who are sensitive to terminology and willing to expose the implications of any words used. It is a good idea to propose a definition of 'modern' at the start of your response.

A **strong candidate** would define 'modern' succinctly; perhaps as describing something which has a contemporary value, current, or even have novel value. Or it might be defined in opposition to an antonym, such as 'medieval', which is commonly thought of as describing something which has long since occurred, something which is well and truly confined to the past. In this way, it goes without saying that English, French and Spanish are languages which are 'modern' because they have millions of native speakers and are the sites of cultural innovation, but they could also be said to have non-modern elements too. All three such languages have literatures stretching to the Medieval period, and much of the vocabulary in these languages is no longer in modern use, even if still listed in the dictionary. Some languages, such as ancient Egyptian and Sanskrit, are more easily classified, given that they are no longer spoken or developing; they remain a source language of academic interest rather than innovation. They are no longer developing in any sense of the word. Perhaps, therefore, what makes languages 'modern' is their capacity for change and evolution.

A **weaker candidate** would not be able to dig deeper into the term 'modern' to explore the various meanings which the term connotes. It is a heavily loaded term, and as such candidates should be able to recognise this. A less strong candidate would, in any case, have trouble defining at least some of the characteristics commonly associated with 'modern', and would be reluctant to walk the interviewers through their thought process. If you are struggling to formulate an answer, it is much better to pause for a few moments and then think aloud, rather than sit in silence or immediately ask for help. The interviewers are very much there to help you along.

READING LISTS

The obvious way to prepare for any Oxbridge interview is to **read widely**. This is important so that you can mention books and interests in your personal statement. It is also important because it means that you will be able to draw upon a greater number and variety of ideas for your interview.

- **Make a record** of the book, who wrote it, when they wrote it, and summarise the argument. This means that you have some details about your research in the days before the interview.

- Reading is a passive exercise. To make it genuinely meaningful, you should **engage with the text**. Summarise the argument. Ask yourself questions like how is the writer arguing? Is it a compelling viewpoint?

- **Quality over quantity**. This is not a race as to how many books you can read in a short period of time. It is instead a test of your ability to critically analyse and synthesise information from a text – something you'll be doing on a daily basis at university.

LAW

- Glanville Williams: *Learning the Law*
- Richard Susskind Tomorrow's Lawyers: *An Introduction to Your Future*
- Tom Bingham: *The Rule of Law*
- Anthony King: *The British Constitution*
- Nicolas J McBride: *Letters to a Law Student: A Guide to Studying Law at University*
- Helena Kennedy: *Just Law*

MML

French:

- Margaret Jubb and Annie Rouxeville: *French Grammar in Context*
- Glanville Price: *A Comprehensive French Grammar* (Blackwell)
- Roger Hawkins and Richard Towell: *French Grammar and Usage*

Spanish:

- Pilar Muñoz & Mike Thacker (London: Arnold, latest edition): *A Spanish Learning Grammar*
- Grammar Practice: *Uso de la gramática española - nivel elemental, Francisca Castro* (Edelsa, Spain, latest edition).

German:

- *German Grammar in Context*
- S. Fagan: *Using German Vocabulary*, (2004)

CLASSICS

Texts in Translation:

- Homer: *The Iliad*
- Homer: *The Odyssey*
- Virgil: *The Aeneid*

Secondary Works:

- The Oxford Classical Dictionary, Oxford University Press
- Beard/Henderson, Oxford University Press: *Classics: A Very Short Introduction*
- Any scholarly works that take your interest, especially if relevant to texts you have read. E.g. Those interested in Roman History should consider reading Andrew Wallace-Hadrill.

GEOGRAPHY

- Sassen. S: *The Global City: New York, London, Tokyo*
- Fanon. F: *The Wretched of the Earth*
- Brockington, Duffy and Igoe: *Nature unbound: conservation, capitalism and the future of protected areas*
- Gray, L.C. and Moseley, W.G.: *A geographical perspective on poverty-environment interactions. The Geographical Journal*

EARTH SCIENCES

- Davidson, J et al: Exploring Earth: *Introduction to Physical Geology*
- MacDougall, JD: *A Short History of Planet Earth: Mountains, Mammals, Fire and Ice (Wiley Popular Science)*
- Nield, T: Supercontinent: *Ten Billion Years in the Life of Our Planet*
- Zalasiewicz, J.A. & Williams, M.: *The Goldilocks planet: The Four Billion Year Story of Earth's Climate*

HISTORY

- E.H. Carr: *What is History?*
- Richard J. Evans: *In Defence of History*
- Marc Bloch: *The Historians Craft*
- Josh Tosh: *The Pursuit of History*
- Geoffrey Elton: *The Practice of History*
- Marc Bloch: *The Historians Craft*
- Josh Tosh: *The Pursuit of History*
- Geoffrey Elton: *The Practice of History*
- Richard J. Evans: *In defence of History*
- Andrew Marr: *A History of Modern Britain*

ECONOMICS:

- The Economist / The Financial Times
- Steven Levitt: *Freakonomics*
- Partha Dasgupta Economics: *A Very Short Introduction*
- Paul Krugman: *End this Depression Now!*
- Robert L Heilbroner: *The Worldly Philosophers*
- Dan Ariely: *Predictably Irrational*

PPE:

- J.S. Mill: *On Liberty*
- Jeremy Bentham: *Defence of Usury*
- Niall Ferguson: *The Ascent of Money*

ENGLISH

Think about how your other subjects might illuminate your study of English. For instance, perhaps you study Psychology and can use this framework to criticise Freud's theory of the Oedipus Complex in relation to Hamlet. You might study History and find this invaluable when analysing Shakespeare's history plays, informing your arguments about the importance of myths and legends, the theme of nationality, or tropes of traditional kingship, and so on. Even more interestingly, you might have studied Physics, Music, or Maths: did these otherwise distinct subjects enhance your study of English in a more oblique way?

There are infinite guides out there for English reading, but the main thing is to follow your interests like a cultural sniffer-dog. A few useful guidelines are given below for general reading around the subject.

There are many anthologies which can give you an excellent overview of chronological literary periods and 'traditions'. **Margaret Drabble's *Oxford Companion to English Literature*** will provide a wide-ranging scope, while **Andrew Sanders' *Short Oxford History of English Literature*** is very useful too. For poetry, in particular, *The Norton Anthology of Poetry*, ed. by **Ferguson, Salter and Stallworthy** is good, while **Christopher Ricks' *Oxford Book of English Verse*** is a detailed spectrum of styles of poetry, with a fantastic introduction that he expands upon in his *The Force of Poetry* or *Essays in Appreciation*. Pair this with oft-studied essayistic collections like **T.S.Eliot's *Selected Prose of T.S. Eliot***, or **William Empson's *Seven Types of Ambiguity***, which will make you think deeper about the art of studying poetry and the difficulties of being a good critic.

It is worth investing in a meaty critical anthology like **Bennett and Royle's *An Introduction to Literature, Criticism, and Theory*** which will give you a rough but valuable guide to a chronological overview of critical history that you can dip in and out of easily for reference. **The *Norton Anthology of Theory and Criticism*** is another valuable guide. However, use these as rough outlines, and broaden your thinking with **Terry Eagleton's *Literary Theory*,** which will provocatively debate many of these terms and ideas. A more readable guide is **James Wood's *How Fiction Works*,** which is a broad but detailed examination of the novel as a genre.

It can also be useful to have a dictionary like **Chris Baldick's** *The Oxford Dictionary of Literary Terms*, which will have bite-size snippets of information in the form of comprehensive definitions.

Pair this with **Raymond Williams' Keywords**, which is in effect a radical literary dictionary designed to make you question and expand these straight-forward definitions. Brush up on your practical criticism and close reading skills with **John Lennard's *The Poetry Handbook: A Guide to Reading Poetry for Pleasure and Practical Criticism*** – a true classic, and very readable. Pair this with giving yourself exercises in close reading, setting yourself extracts, and thinking about what you might discuss or point out.

If you read any classics, read **Homer's *Iliad*** and ***Odyssey*, Ovid's *Metamorphoses*** and **Virgil's *Aeneid*** in any reputable translation if you have the time, preferably in the Penguin or Oxford World Classics editions: these are foundational, and will prove incredibly useful in deciphering allusions. The same applies to the **Bible** or at least a selection of the most pivotal sections: Genesis, Exodus, The Song of Songs, the gospels of Matthew, Mark, Luke, and John, Revelation, the Book of Job, the Song of Solomon, etc. If you find this theological approach interesting, go on to read **John Milton's *Paradise Lost***, which is surprisingly absorbing in its poetic dramatization of Adam and Eve; Alastair Fowler has edited an excellent critical edition.

It may sound obvious, but read or watch as many of **Shakespeare's** plays and poems as you can; they really are foundational and will stand you in good stead throughout your course. A guide like ***Reading Shakespeare's Dramatic Language: A Guide* by Hunter, Magnusson, and Adamson** will provide a readable introduction to the specifics of Shakespearean verse. Think more about the practical aspects of staging plays and theatrical history, from stage building to props, aspects which are often neglected at A-Level: **Tiffany Stern and Farah Karim-Cooper's *Shakespeare's Theatre and the Effects of Performance*** is fantastic, as is **Stern's *Making Shakespeare: From Stage to Page*** and **Andrew Gurr's *The Shakespearean Stage***. In general, Cambridge and Oxford/Blackwell Companions are always very good and provide strong leads for further reading, such as **Hodgdon and Worthen's *A Companion to Shakespeare and Performance***, but feel free to use modern dramatic criticism like **Peter Brook's *The Empty Space*** to deepen your ideas.

ARCHAEOLOGY

- Timothy Darvill. 2010. *Prehistoric Britain.* 2nd Edition. London: Routledge.
- Clive GAMBLE. 2000. *Archaeology: The Basics.* London: Routledge.
- Ian Hodder. 2012. *Archaeological Theory Today.* 2nd Edition. Cambridge: Polity.
- Barry Kemp. 2005. *Ancient Egypt: Anatomy of a Civilization.* 2nd Edition. London: Routledge.
- Colin Renfrew and Paul Bahn. 2012. *Archaeology: Theory, Methods, and Practice.* 6th Edition. London: Thames & Hudson.
- Chris Scarre. 1998. *Exploring Prehistoric Europe.* Oxford: Oxford University Press.
- Chris Scarre. 2009. *The Human Past: World Prehistory and Development of Human Society.* 2nd Edition. London: Thames & Hudson.

BIOLOGICAL ANTHROPOLOGY

- Robert Boyd and Joan Silk. 2012. *How Humans Evolved*. New York: Norton.
- Robert Foley & Roger Lewin. 2003. *The Principles of Human Evolution*. 2nd Edition. Oxford: Wiley-Blackwell.
- Peter Gluckman and Mark Hanson. 2004. *The Fetal Matrix*. Cambridge: Cambridge University Press.
- Matt Ridley. 2004. *Nature via Nurture*. New York: Harper Collins.
- Chris Stringer. 2012. *The Origin of our Species*. London: Penguin.
- Jared Diamond: *Guns, Germs and Steel*

POLITICS

- Benedict Anderson. 1983. *Imagined Communities: Reflections on the origins and Spread of Nationalism*. London: Macmillan.
- Headley Bull. 1977. *The Anarchical Society*. London: Macmillan.
- John Dunn. 2005. *Setting the People Free: The Story of Democracy*. London: Atlantic.
- Niccolo Machiavelli. 2003 (1532). *The Prince*. London: Penguin.
- James Mayall. 2000. *World Politics: Progress and its Limits*. Cambridge: Polity.
- David Runciman. 2006. *Politics of Good Intentions: History, Fear, and Hypocrisy in the New World Order*. Princeton: Princeton University Press.
- James C Scott. 1998. *Seeing Like a State: How Certain Schemes to Improve the Human Condition Have Failed*. New Haven: Yale University Press.
- Adam Watson. 1992. *The Evolution of International Society*. London: Routledge.

SOCIAL ANTHROPOLOGY

- Lila Abu-Lughod. 1986. *Veiled Sentiments: Honor and Poetry in a Bedouin Society*. Berkeley: University of California Press.
- Adam Ashforth. 2005. *Madumo: A Man Bewitched*. Chicago: University of Chicago Press.
- Rita Astuti, Jonathan Parry, and Charles Stafford. 2007. *Questions of Anthropology*. Berg: Oxford.
- Thomas Boellstorff. 2008. *Coming of Age in Second Life*. Princeton: Princeton University Press.
- John R. Bowen. 2007. *Why the French Don't Like Headscarves: Islam, the State, and Public Space*. Princeton: Princeton University Press.
- Michael Carrithers. 1993. *Why Humans Have Cultures*. Oxford: Oxford University Press.
- Sharon E. Hutchinson. 1996. *Nuer Dilemmas: Coping with Money, War, and the State*. Berkeley: University of California Press.
- Jean La Fontaine. *Speak of the Devil: Tales of Satanic Abuse in Contemporary England*. Cambridge: Cambridge University Press.
- Joel Robbins. 2004. *Becoming Sinners: Christianity and Moral Torment in a Papua New Guinea Society*.
- Michael Stewart. 1997. *The Time of the Gypsies*. Colorado
- Yunxiang Yan. 2009. *The Individualization of Chinese Society*.

SOCIOLOGY

- Nicholas Abercrombie. 2004. *Sociology*. Cambridge: Polity.
- Anthony Giddens. 2006. *Sociology (5th edition)*. Cambridge: Polity.
- Anthony Giddens. 1973. *Capitalism and Modern Social Theory*. Cambridge: Cambridge University Press.
- J.A. Hughes. 2003. *Understanding Classical Sociology*. London: Sage.
- K.J. Neubeck and D.S. Glasberg. 2005. *Sociology: Diversity, Conflict, and Change*. Boston: McGraw Hill.
- W. Outhwaite (ed). 2003. *The Blackwell Dictionary of Modern Social Thought*.
- Richard Sennett. 2006. *The New Culture of Capitalism*

HSPS

- Karl Marx: Communist Manifesto
- Hogg & Vaughn: *Social Psychology*
- Schaffer: *Introducing Child Psychology*
- Durkin Blackwell: *Introducing Child Psychology*
- Schaffer: *Making Decisions About Children*
- Manfred Steger Globalisation: *A Very Short Introduction*
- Jan Art Scholte Globalization: *A Critical Introduction*
- Colin Hay: *Why we Hate Politics*
- Andrew Gamble: *Politics and Fate*
- Bernard Crick Democracy: *A Very Short Introduction*
- Joy Hendry: *An Introduction to Social Anthropology*
- Chris Browne & Kirsten Ainley *Understanding International Relations*
- Nicholas Abercrombie: Sociology: *A Short Introduction*

FINAL ADVICE

BEFORE YOUR INTERVIEW

- Make sure you understand your curriculum; your interview will most likely use material from your school courses as a starting point.

- Remind yourself of the selection criteria for your subject.

- Read around your subject in scientific articles and books, visit museums, watch documentaries, anything which broadens your knowledge of your favourite topics while demonstrating your passion for your subject. They may ask you at the interview which articles you've read recently to check you are engaged with the subject. Scientists should try New Scientist's online articles to start you off; TED talks are also a great way to be quickly briefed on cutting-edge research, and it's more likely you will remember the name of the researcher, etc.

- Practice common questions or sample questions – this is better done with a teacher or someone you are less familiar with or who is an experienced interviewer.

- Make up your own questions throughout your day: Why is that flower shaped like that? Why is that bird red-breasted? Why does my dog like to fetch sticks? What did I mean when I said that man wasn't 'normal', and is this the criteria everyone uses? How do I know I see the same colours as others?

- Re-read your personal statement and any coursework you are providing. Anticipate questions that may arise from these and prepare them in advance.

- Read and do anything you've said you've done in your application – they may ask you about it at the interview!

- Check your interview specifications – what type of interviews you will have for which subjects, how many there will be, where, when, and with whom they will be so there are no surprises.

ON THE DAY OF YOUR INTERVIEW

- Get a good night's sleep before the big day.

- If you are travelling from far away, try to arrive the night before so that you're fresh in the morning. Getting up early in the morning and travelling far could tire you out and you might be less focused whilst being interviewed. Many colleges will provide you accommodation if you're travelling from a certain distance away.

- Take a shower in the morning and dress to your comfort, though you don't want to give a sloppy first impression – most opt for smart/casual

- Get there early so you aren't late or stressed out before it even starts.

- Smile at everyone and be polite.

- Don't worry about other candidates; be nice of course, but you are there for you, and their impressions of how their interviews went have nothing to do with what the interviewers thought or how yours will go.

- It's OK to be nervous – they know you're nervous and understand, but try to move past it and be in the moment to get the most out of the experience.

- Don't be discouraged if it feels like one interview didn't go well – you may have shown the interviewers exactly what they wanted to see, even if it wasn't what you wanted to see.

- Have a cuppa and relax, there's nothing you can do now but be yourself.

THE MOST IMPORTANT ADVICE...

- ❖ Explain your thought processes as much as possible – it doesn't matter if you're wrong. *It really is the journey; not the destination that matters.*
- ❖ Interviewers aren't interested in *what you know*. Instead, they are more interested in *what you can do* with what you already know.

✗ **DON'T** be quiet – even if you can't answer a question. How you approach the question could show the interviewer what they want to see.

✗ **DON'T** rely on the interviewer to guide you every step of the way.

✗ **DON'T** ever, ever, ever give up.

✗ **DON'T** be arrogant or rigid –you are bound to get things wrong, just accept them and move on.

✗ **DON'T** expect to know all the answers; this is different than school, you aren't expected to know the answer to everything – you are using your knowledge as a foundation for original thoughts and applications under the guidance of your interviewer.

✗ **DON'T** think you will remember everything you did/wrote without revising.

✗ **DON'T** be afraid to point out flaws in your own ideas – scientists need to be self-critical, and the interviewer has already noticed your mistakes!

✗ **DON'T** be defensive, especially if the interviewer is hinting that your idea may be on the wrong path – the interviewer is the expert!

✗ **DON'T** get hung up on a question for too long.

✗ **DON'T** rehearse scripted answers to be regurgitated.

✗ **DON'T** answer the question you wanted them to ask.

✗ **DON'T** lie about things you have read/done (and if you already lied in your personal statement, then read/do them before the interview!).

✓ **DO** speak freely about what you are thinking and ask for clarifications.
✓ **DO** take suggestions and listen for pointers from your interviewer.
✓ **DO** try your best to get to the answer.
✓ **DO** have confidence in yourself and the abilities that got you this far
✓ **DO** be prepared to discuss the ideas and problems in your work.
✓ **DO** make many suggestions and have many ideas.
✓ **DO** show intellectual flexibility by taking suggestions from the interviewer.
✓ **DO** take your time in answering to ensure your words come out right.
✓ **DO** research your interviewers so that you know their basic research interests. Then ensure you understand the basics of their work (no need to go into detail with this).
✓ **DO** prepare your answers to common questions.
✓ **DO** answer the question that the interviewer has asked – not the one you want them to!
✓ **DO** practice interviews with family or teachers – even easy questions may be harder to articulate out loud and on the spot to a stranger.
✓ **DO** think about strengths/experiences you may wish to highlight.
✓ **DO** visit www.uniadmissions.co.uk/example-interviews to see mock interviews in your subject. This will allow you to understand the differences between good and bad candidates.

AFTERWORD

Remember that the route to success is your approach and practice. Don't fall into the trap that *"you can't prepare for Oxbridge interviews"*– this could not be further from the truth. With targeted preparation and focused reading, you can dramatically boost your chances of getting that dream offer.

Work hard, never give up, and do yourself justice.

Good luck!
This book is dedicated to my grandparents – thank you for your wisdom, kindness, and endless amounts of love.

ACKNOWLEDGEMENTS

I would like to express my gratitude to the many people who helped make this book possible. I would like to thank *Dr. Ranjna Garg* for suggesting that I take on this mammoth task and providing invaluable feedback. I am also grateful for the 30 Oxbridge tutors for their specialist input and advice. Last, but by no means least; I am thankful to *David Salt* for his practical advice and willingness to discuss my ideas- regardless of whether it was 4 AM or PM.

ABOUT US

We currently publish over 100 titles across a range of subject areas – covering specialised admissions tests, examination techniques, personal statement guides, plus everything else you need to improve your chances of getting on to competitive courses such as medicine and law, as well as into universities such as Oxford and Cambridge.

Outside of publishing we also operate a highly successful tuition division, called UniAdmissions. This company was founded in 2013 by Dr Rohan Agarwal and Dr David Salt, both Cambridge Medical graduates with several years of tutoring experience. Since then, every year, hundreds of applicants and schools work with us on our programmes. Through the programmes we offer, we deliver expert tuition, exclusive course places, online courses, best-selling textbooks and much more.

With a team of over 1,000 Oxbridge tutors and a proven track record, UniAdmissions have quickly become the UK's number one admissions company.

Visit and engage with us at:

Website (UniAdmissions): www.uniadmissions.co.uk
Facebook: www.facebook.com/uniadmissionsuk

Printed in Great Britain
by Amazon

85846162R00312